MONDO ENDURO

MONDO ENDURO

by

Louis R Bloom, Mark Friend, Clive R Greenhough, Bill
Penty, Charles Penty, Nicholas A Stubley, Austin E Vince &
Gerald H Vince

edited by Austin Vince

Published in 2006 by Ripping Yarns.com, an imprint of
Rockbuy Limited, Findon, Aberdeenshire, Scotland
Website: www.RippingYarns.com

First Edition 2006

British Library Cataloguing in Publication Data
Data Available

ISBN 1-904466-28-1

Printed by
Bell & Bain Ltd, Glasgow

Distributed by Cordee, 3a de Montfort St, Leicester, England

Front cover: Travelling through Ethiopia
Back cover: The Mondo Enduro team at Irkutsk

CONTENTS

Foreword

by Chris Scott

editor of
The Adventure Motorcycling Handbook

Authentic and doggedly independent; that's what struck me about *Mondo Enduro*, the globe-spanning ride that by chance (then reputation) became the cult TV show and now, ten years down the line, is the group's collected *Diaries*.

At the outset they concocted some extraneous challenge about the longest route in the shortest time, but to me at least, that was uncharacteristic pandering to the media-led chest-beating we expect these days. It was the gusto, humour and, it has to be said, satisfyingly British unpretentiousness with which the team took on the year-long ride which really set them apart. Traversing the not insubstantial width of Russia, the near-polar length of the Americas and the span of Africa, the fact that they managed to shoot an original, gritty and irreverent film on the way was all the more amazing.

These days many aspirant round-the-worlders tie themselves into knots over equipment choices and route options, or assume their adventure deserves the approbation of sponsorship. "Sod that," thought Mondo "let's leave now and pay later". They rode machines most of them happened to own anyway and adopted a refreshingly low-tech approach that harks back to the well-known journeys described by Ted Simon, Danny Liska and Robert Fulton Jnr.

"Adventure motorcycling" (as overland travel on two wheels has come to be known) is said to be the fastest-growing arm of motorcycling. The first-timer can now be better informed and better equipped than ever and it's easy to forget it's primarily about the raw adventure of autonomous travel on a motorcycle, a perilous activity that cannot be tamed. Mondo remind us it is possible to just get out there and do it, how ingenious and eventually blasé you can become in the face of daily trials – and how futile it is to pretend a poncho is a tent!

Chris Scott, October 2005

The Team

Gerald Vince (38) – Bike N1

Austin's big brother, elder statesman of the group and in many respects the man at whose seasoned distance-biking teat the rest of the group suckles. Gerald had many jobs as a youngster including being the barman at the Star and Garter Putney when it was used in the film "Sweeney II". However, at 19 he went onto the railways and staffed numerous booking offices including Harrow & Wealdstone, Watford Junction and South Kenton. Gerald is suspected of having an IQ of more than 150.

Austin Vince (29) – Bike B2

At 23 years old Austin found himself recently graduated in Civil Engineering. Within a few weeks he was at the Royal Military Academy Sandhurst and struggling to conceal from the Army that he had become a pacifist whilst being sponsored through university. Two years and £6000 later he had bought himself out and had become a maths teacher at Mill Hill School. His claim to fame is that he once shook Lee Marvin's hand.

Mark Friend (29) – Bike D3

A childhood friend of the Penty brothers, Mark was a wheeler and dealer in the City. He feels he needs a break and has joined the line-up. Interestingly, his brother is a founder member of crusty band 'The Levellers' a crime that Austin is hard pushed to forgive. Mark plays the French horn and is the least experienced rider in the team. He has gamely crashed several times while he explores his limits. He claims he would rather be on a bicycle.

Bill Penty (29) – Bike K4

Bill is Chas' fraternal twin. They were raised in Uttoxeter, Staffs. He is a French teacher and hockey maestro. He spent most of his twenties in Japan and consequently now speaks and teaches Japanese. He is certainly the most sensible person on Mondo Enduro but shares Austin's love of mid-sixties garage punk. His favourite film is *Yojimbo*.

Charles Penty (29) – Bike K5

Born in Nottingham Chas came late to motorcycling, passing his test and buying his first bike – a Yamaha XJ 650 – 25 years later. Trips to Spain and the Netherlands with future Mondo colleagues including Gerald, Austin, Mark and Bill (his twin brother) fired a passion for long distance travel on two-wheels.

After graduating in history from Cambridge University, he trained as a journalist and worked as a reporter for the Stoke-on-Trent Evening Sentinel and Yorkshire Post (Hull office). Chas brings "all-rounder" skills to the Mondo venture: he speaks some Spanish, has been taking Russian lessons and writes Teeline shorthand and 110 words per minute.

Nick Stubley (28) – Bike A7

"Have been working in the Aerospace industry since leaving Bristol University in 1987 where I met most of the co-riders. Why did I want to join the team? Whilst still in my twenties, no family yet, I could trip out the usual clichés. Two ways to sum up the expedition; first FREEDOM - just seven guys seven machines across thousands of miles. Second, well to convey the feeling close your eyes and listen to Baba O'Reily by the Who at a sensibly loud volume. Sands of youth running out, independence and camaraderie. Hope to come back a different person, stronger in many ways, a couple of Welsh words spring to mind; Hyder and Hiraeth. I guess that means a spirit of confidence and a longing for what you leave behind. Time will tell if I was right."

Clive Greenhough (25) – Bike H6

Clive was born in 1969 in Hampstead, London, to former members of a dare-devil motorcycle stunt troupe called the '*motor psychos*'.

Like Austin he attended Mill Hill School in North West London and then went to university in Bristol, where he studied Business and Finance and where he continued to play rugby. After university, he began training as an accountant.

However, Clive ditched accountancy and hitch-hiked from London to Cape Town. Clive is the youngest and by coincidence, most suave member of the team.

MONDO ENDURO

PART 1

LONDON TO MAGADAN

MONDO ENDURO

Mill Hill School, April 5th, 1995

At 11.30 p.m. all is quiet in our Mill Hill base, except for the sound of banging and the occasional curse. Gerald's attempts to affix his long-range fuel tank are not going well. The rest of us sit down to try to remember how Mondo Enduro came into being and how we got to this exciting point in our lives.

The reminiscences start to flow amid frequent interruptions, oaths (and corrections) from Gerald who is probing his tank mountings with a pen torch and screwdriver. We all agree that Mondo "began" in the early winter of 1992 when we all met up in a pub in Nottingham. Austin, Gerald and Andy Bell, our doctor friend, had summoned us to discuss another long-range bike trip. What was the bond that joined this diverse group, including Gerald, a British Rail ticket clerk, Austin, a maths teacher, and Clive Greenhough, a dispatch rider, to the East Midlands on a foggy night in November? All were friends or brothers of Austin, Bill, Nick and Andy, colleagues from Bristol University.

We were all inspired by a trip Austin, Gerald and Andy had made to former Soviet Bloc countries in Eastern Europe in 1990. Travelers' tales from behind a newly-rolled-up Iron Curtain had inspired us all. Two schools of thought emerged from our Nottingham pub night with Gerald proposing a journey across Russia and Andy backing a trans-Africa route. Gerald argued that the tentative opening of borders in the former Soviet Central Asian republics presented an opportunity too good to miss. A scenario began to develop in which we'd ride all the way to Vladivostok on the Russian Pacific and then board a ship for Japan.

It was left to Austin to sketch out the more ambitious scheme of riding all around the world, an option that also would neatly resolve the Russia versus Africa dilemma. He reasoned that if we rode to Japan it would take us three months anyway, long enough to force most of us to give up our jobs. The evening ended on a non-committal note but with a preference for the Siberian option and a commitment to make direct debit payments into a shared bank account at the Abbey National.

At this stage of course, we were still in the grip of an escapist fantasy that so easily could have been dashed by a Monday morning at work. Here we are, though, 4 days away from departure and with ferry tickets purchased one-way to Le Havre. Gerald has ditched a 17 year career on the railways, Austin has negotiated a four-term teaching sabbatical and Chas and Mark are "freelancing" and at liberty to spoil their careers if they want to. All of us are in some way "between jobs," unmarried or otherwise freed by circumstances to embark upon this journey.

Undoubtedly Gerald kept the momentum going by immediately immersing himself in the quest to identify the bike best-suited to our needs. "Jupiter's Travels", the classic book by Ted Simon describing his four-year journey around the world on a Triumph Bonneville had been a big inspiration to all of us and we started by weighing up the qualities of modern bikes of a similar size. We checked out the BMW GS series of flat twins before working our way down to Yamaha XTS, the 650 cc Kawasaki KLR and the Honda XL600.

In the end, though, the Vinces, the most mechanically adept among us, surprised us with the proposal that we all buy identical Suzuki DR350s, a small-engined off-road bike. Gerald noted that the DRs could get 300 miles from a custom-built 5 gallon tank. By riding identical machines we could interchange parts and carry fewer spares. He also sold his terraced house in Bournemouth to help fund the trip. Here was a clear statement of resolve on his part on one to make us all focus on the task in hand.

The next raft of thoughts concerned luggage. Austin forged ahead and designed an interchangeable clip together modular system made entirely from plywood. After endless sketches and fruitless demonstrations to the rest of the team he saw sense and the wooden saddlebags have been consigned to the back-burner where they, like most of his improvisations, will eventually catch fire. Gerald picked up the torch and has equipped most of us with a set of tough plastic panniers made by an Italian firm called *Givi*. They clip on to a neat sub-frame and are interchangeable between bikes. They are basically waterproof and of course secure. We have got hold of most of them second-hand saving a small fortune. Austin remained unconvinced and spent a week making his own saddlebags from thick leather. Clive has the quickest solution with two old rucksacks tied together and thrown over the seat. Time will tell which 'system', if any, is the best.

The rest of us got on with the task of thinking about kit, trying to line up sponsorship and also better understand the route ahead. In the England of 1995, it's still hard to dig out hard facts on countries like Georgia and Turkmenistan, unavoidable obstacles in our path. We know for instance that one possible route through northern Siberia will take us within 100 miles of Oynyakon, the place where, in the winter of 1944, the temperature gauge plunged to −72°C. With the Soviet Republics road atlas bought in Zwemmer's bookshop, Charing Cross, we think we've charted a route to take us to the Russian Far East. It's open now in front of us on page 63 and there is NO ROAD between the Siberian settlement of Chernyshevsk and a town called Never. What lies in this strange hiatus or lacuna in Russia's road network that we've nicknamed the "Zilov Gap" we have no idea, though mud and mosquitoes probably feature in some capacity. Mark says he's got a mate who knows of some French people that bicycled this route in reverse last year.

Apparently they just pushed their bikes alongside the railway until the road started up again.

In the meantime, we can ponder our Russian visas, printed on what looks like blue cigarette paper and listing these "compulsory" destinations on the road to Vladivostok: Barnaul, Vlovokuznetsk, Abakan, Irkutsk, Ulan-Ude, Chita, Skovorodino, Blagoveshkensk and Khabarovsk. Ten words. Five thousand miles! Of course, we're concerned about Siberia but there's a long way ahead of us before reaching Irkutsk.

The country we fear most, the one that most makes us tremble in our boots, is Georgia in the Caucasus. Making difficult choices on routes, perhaps with life-or-death circumstances, has become our stock in recent months. In a recent U.S. State Department advisory on Georgia, we'd read that "Police authority in many cities has collapsed" and foreigners "have become targets." The BBC congealed our fears even more by running a documentary on brutalized life in a former Soviet Caucasus at the mercy of mafia thugs and bandits. We called the reporter, someone called Gordon Brewer, who said we "wouldn't last five minutes" after crossing the Turkish border at Batumi. A more upbeat analysis came from the waiters at a Georgian restaurant in Stoke Newington who spoke highly of the generous temperament of their countrymen, beauty of their womenfolk and wine from South Ossetia. Read on in this log to see who's right!

At this moment, Bill is laying out our cooking gear and cleaning it a last time before departure. Our pride and joy is a ceramic water filter supplied by a well-wishing camping supplies company (it can purge radioactive contamination, apparently.) Actually, we've done a decent job getting sponsorship for items like the filters and stoves and we paid "trade prices" for others such as the sleeping bags and air mats. Thanks to all our benefactors!

They do not include Suzuki who've resisted repeated requests for all the chains, sprockets and brake pads they could muster (and perhaps the odd DR 350, or seven?) Here's the reply from Suzuki to Austin's last letter requesting sponsorship: "Motorcycling says something about you. It says you like the exhilaration. The freedom. The performance. The way of life. Whether it's race-replica, sports tourer, custom, trail or Lightweight, you'll find Suzuki has one of the most comprehensive ranges available today. Experience the thrills and excitement of genuine motorcycling with Suzuki. Contact your nearest dealer now:

REX JUDD Ltd 415 Burnt Oak Broadway Edgware Middlesex HA8 5AH DO IT NOW WITH SUZUKI! Yours Sincerely etc Colin Pattison, Suzuki marketing man.

There are no hard feelings though because these bikes are great and we're sure they'll get us round. We're in good health and spirits and ready to have fun and an adventure. The idea of this daily "Mondo Log" is to record our experiences in a detailed way so we can look back on impressions and experiences many years from now. LET'S GO, MONDO ENDURO!

PS: Some readers may be wondering how much all this costing. We estimate 7,000 pounds, including the cost of the bikes, which are second-hand.

England

Day 0
9 April 95 6pm
Mondo Miles today: 0
Mondo Mileage: 0

In a way, they were like the country they came from – slightly depressed but given to extravagant fantasies, and so the Mondo Enduro expedition was born...

The time for our departure in a clatter of churning pistons came and went. We were supposed to leave today at 1pm but were not ready. About a hundred friends and family were expecting to see us off then and were gathered for that very purpose.

So duly we posed for the World's media in a stage-managed 'official' departure from Mill Hill School, resplendent in our matching T-shirts and with gasoline literally pouring from the leaking balance pipes on our custom made petrol tanks.

The first leg of Mondo Enduro, from the school portico to Mill Hill Broadway, was captured by the cameras of Channel One television. The Edgware and Mill Hill Times and the Harrow Observer sent special correspondents to record our fifteen minutes of fame in spite of remonstrations from Chas who said it wasn't a story. The ranks of well-wishers applauded enthusiastically as we drove off across North London and then hid in the Burger King at Apex Corner. We waited an hour for the crowds to disperse and then stole back to Mill Hill School for our last 24 hours of frantic packing and moving Austin out of his flat.

P&O were called and our 9pm ferry passage to Le Havre postponed until the same time tomorrow. Amazing to think that with seven of us to share the tasks between and with 30 months of preparation, we were unable to leave on time.

England

Day 1
10 April 1995
Mondo Miles today: 90
Mondo Mileage: 90

Over the last week of pre-departure 'build up' we have taken to treating ourselves to morale boosting breakfasts at the local greasy spoon. We have a friendly rapport with the owner so there were scenes of desolation this morning at the Circle Café as we said goodbye to Peter and his culinary artists fortified by scrambled eggs (twice), bacon, fried slice, black pudding and extra onions. We vowed to fast until our return in 18 months time. Unfortunately our best intentions lay in ruins when Gemma Greenhough (Clive's mum) arrived, bearing burgers, chips, spare ribs and milk shakes. It would have been rude to refuse.

The 6pm departure time came and went in an orgy of confusion. The awesome task of clearing out Austin's flat took us well past the time when, by rights, rubber should have been burning. When finally the time did come to depart we bade our farewells in perfunctory fashion, anxious to reach Portsmouth and the rest of the world.

It was disconcerting to realise that we had never packed to 'leave' before. We didn't know where to put anything and it seemed our kit was a collection of singularly awkward and unhelpful shapes. At least the camera kit was all neatly stowed in the colossal wooden chest Austin had tailor made for it. He was convinced that the 'con' of the inappropriate size of this mighty crate was easily offset by the 'pro' that it carried *all* the video, super 8 and stills equipment including the tripod. Austin had affixed special D-ring eyelets to the outer walls of the box. These allowed it to be tied down onto his saddle with 'Arno' straps in such a way that the lid of the box could still be opened, hence giving Austin the quick camera reactions of a CNN news team. However, with only minutes till the off, the nylon straps were tensioned and the eyelets ripped from their mountings as if affixed with Blu Tak.

We left with the box tied down but with lid restrained so that no camera could be removed without at least 20 minutes notice. We need to sort this out.

We faffed around trying to get gas at the A41 Esso station. We are meant to have a communal 'Mondo' wallet that makes for a swift group payment but as certain people reholstered their pumps the dials kept re-setting. We need to sort this out.

We were guided by ex-couriers, Clive and Austin, and by the time we reached Hammersmith we had been separated three times. The convoy skills were very poor and somewhere between Castlenau and Roehampton the team once more disintegrated. We need to sort this out.

After two hours we had conquered the A3 and at last Mondo Enduro, after two years of talking, was actually underway. At the P & O ferry port we were greeted by a friendly official who recognised our Mondo petroltank transfers as the same which had adorned our letterheaded paper upon which we had made the optimistic request, weeks ago, that we somehow deserved free passage across the Channel. The P&O group must, of course, receive fifty letters a day from people trying to get them to subsidise their holidays so we were flattered *in extremis* that they afforded us a 15% discount. By way of recompense for this generosity may we exhort any reader to travel with P&O and *only* P&O.

The seal was set on our new status of manly bikers as we tucked into the tea and marmite and peanut butter sandwiches proffered by Phyllis and Geoffrey Vince (Austin and Gerald's mum and dad) from the hatch-back of their camper van. They and Bill's sweetheart Claire waved us on our way onto the ferry and our journey into the dark blue yonder. Crumbs, we won't be home for a year and a half.

France

Day 2
11 April 95
Mondo Miles today: 198
Mondo Mileage: 288

Le Havre was shrouded in mist when the 'Pride of Portsmouth' docked in the ferry port. An attempt to film our traversal of the stupendous Pont de Tanqueville was aborted due to low battery power and a container lorry which filled the viewfinder. The incident only served to highlight the difficulties of making a travel documentary with no money, knowledge or equipment.

Unperturbed we found our way to a roadside rest stop patronised almost exclusively by truckers and made a bulk *café au lait* order. The hot caffeine injection garnished with croissants revived our spirits after a brief dash through freezing fog; fog which condensed on our visors and spectacles and refrigerated vital body organs.

The first major Mondo mishap occurred when Clive discovered his money wallet containing several hundred dollars appeared to have been stolen on the ferry. Frantic phone calls to P&O and a trip to the local gendarmerie were of no immediate avail so we consoled him with generous portions of steak and frites.

The remainder of the day was uneventful as we ploughed an almost horizontal furrow through the featureless plain of Northern France. The journey was enlivened by Austin's attempts to test-drive his bike along a seldom used stretch of railway line. Why? Because 10,000 miles hence is a section in Siberia where the railway continues but the road stops. Austin has regularly mooted the idea of traversing this gap by simply riding along in between the rails. He dropped the bike repeatedly and ultimately had to be helped out from between the rails by Gerald. This process took about 3 minutes of huffing and puffing, not the deft 'bunny hop' that would actually be required with a sixty wagon Magnitogorsk-bound bauxite train bearing down on you. This rehearsal does not bode well for the Russian Oriental stage of our journey or indeed Austin's 'alternative' approach to problem-solving.

A brief separation with Nick was ended when we went the wrong way round a roundabout in Orleans and headed for Ferte St Aubin. Reconvened we checked into a municipal campsite, erected the tents and Nick created a vegetarian cordon bleu stew of egg plants, mushrooms and tomatoes with a flick of his wok slice and we retired gratefully to our sleeping bags with one minor conundrum teasing our minds. Was that the freight trains rumbling past or the sonorous rhythms of Gerald's snoring diaphragm?

France

Day 3
12 April 95
Mondo Miles today: 190
Mondo Mileage: 478

After a sound sleep- despite the incessant cargo trains hurtling past throughout the night – the Mondo Enduro team were woken by yet another train and a cup of coffee made by Clive. Such a selfless act infused us all with a terrific sense of camaraderie and Clive was cheered as if he had just single handedly brought peace to the Balkans.

We are dashing across France heading for a small town on the Côte d'Azur called Golfe Juan. There is going to be a wedding there on Saturday (today is Thursday) and Austin and Bill are to be the joint best man. The groom is their chum Phil. Schooled in Catford but with a French mum; so here he is returning to his roots for this special day. Because of the cloying inflexibility of trying to tie in the start of Mondo Enduro with the narrow window that is the Siberian summer, Phil generously scheduled his wedding reception to fit in with *us* and not vice versa, very understanding of him. Nevertheless, in a quiet aside Phil's betrothed made it clear that we had better not miss the wedding or there'd be fireworks.... So here we are, on a mission within a mission.

A late start but good progress was made thanks to the straight roads from Ferte St Aubin to Issoudun. We are surprised at how boring this riding is and we feel slightly guilty. It is going to take ages to get to Istanbul (2000ish miles away) and even reaching Japan seems beyond comprehension. Lunch in Culan on a wooden pallet and time spent supporting Bill's bike, which has a tendency to leak petrol everywhere at the same time, the balance pipe problem far from solved.

A cheer of delight as Nick turned up out of the blue in Culan at 3'ish as we had been separated all day! Next Nick ran totally out of petrol – due to caning it at 80+mph doing recces and Gerald carried on into the sunset oblivious to all this. With his lightweight 'rack' and luggage Gerald's mpg was excellent – so we ended up having to do multi fill ups – more time wasted! We had decided to rough it tonight – so we could make an early start and save money. However, another municipal campsite appeared before our very eyes and we succumbed to its temptation and moreover daylight was rapidly sliding away!

Another stupendous effort from Nick and his culinary delights for supper – we certainly won't die from malnutrition or boredom on this trip.

France

Day 4
13 April 95
Mondo Miles today: 388
Mondo Mileage: 866

"Thought for the Day" – France is Big!!!

Dawn broke over the tired travellers in a cool, quiet campsite. After a quick look on the Autoroute we headed back to Vic-le-Comte for a twisty climb up and over to Ambert. Scenery has changed from flat/rolling to semi-alpine in appearance. A burst of 88 miles was had by the first tea break at 11.00am. With another 300 miles to go to Golfe it was a quick slurp 'n' nosh before heading on to Le Puy. This was to prove our last humble repast before arriving chez Phil. For the Mondo members, day 3 gave them each a different flavour of Provence as we each made our own separate ways to le Midi. Austin and Nick Stubley headed down the old N7 and onto the coast road to make up lost time trying to figure out Gerald's route plan. Fortunately Nick's confusion helped him re-unite with Austin as he found him heading the wrong way up the N7 from Orange. As we amended our route plan, the scent of pine resin and burnt wood gave us our clearest hint that we were close to the Mediterranean. The coast road was a real twister with a close shave between the Mondo riders and a tour bus on one particularly nasty hairpin. A quick swerve and we were on our way once again.

From a personal point of view, the weight on the bikes gradually pales into insignificance and after a few days speeds of 80+ mph and full cornering is achieved (scraping of side stand is now regular). To save cash (but not time) we brewed up on the side of the road. After we arrived at the Gare Golfe Juan we spent a good hour looking at the trains waiting for the others to rendezvous. Whilst phoning the UK, Gerald arrived and led us up the short drive to La Grandmere Philippe. After a quick intro to the folks it was off down to the Pizzeria and disco bar for Phil's belated stag night. We crept back to our beds after a long hard day with a mental list of maintenance to perform. Austin's 2nd toe-nail had fallen off adding another item to the list of broken bits. The ardour of the 388 miles achieved today has precipitated a few nervous glances if this is all the next year promises. Wearily I write the log after the hardest day so far and with heavy eyelids I take to my bed with the sobering thought that we have covered about 1/70th of the total journey – 882 miles from Mill Hill.

France

Day 5
Friday 14 April 95
Mondo Miles today: 0
Mondo Mileage: 882

We awoke to a beautiful day in Golfe Juan. There will be a fair amount of bike maintenance to do today. Laundry will also be done. Mondo Enduro are paying for a barbecue tonight for the host families. Rain in the afternoon forced the cancellation of the barbecue, so everyone is going for a pizza instead. I went out to look for a campsite for Mum and Dad but no luck, so they have been booked into the same hotel as other guests. Bike maintenance has been slow but sure. This is all basic stuff that should have been done before we left.

When we arrived last night, P & O had telephoned to say that Clive's wallet had been found in the ferry cabin so we only have to figure out how to get the money to him. I have at last found a pair of plastic sandals. Everybody staying here went for a meal at the same pizza restaurant as last night, about 20 persons in all. A jolly pleasant evening was had by all. There has been a lot of expenditure by Mondo Enduro in France so we are all hoping that when we leave here on Monday things will become cheaper as there will not be any family and friends but just seven Mondurites, save Mr and Mrs Vince in the short wheelbase Ford Transit camper van temporary support vehicle.

France

Day 6
Saturday 15 April 95
Mondo Miles today: 0
Mondo Mileage: 882

Today is Phil and Tania's wedding day so the whole Mondo team is really quite excited. Even Plymouth (Austin's teddy bear) has chipped in his few supportive comments on this most happy of occasions.

After the horrible thunderstorm yesterday we were greeted at dawn with clear skies and a stunning view over the Golfe Juan harbour as the sun reflected off the water and dazzled us. Clive went for a run and a swim in the sea so respect is due since the rest of the team lay snuggled up in Rab land. Austin's toe-nail has stabilised and the pus that was leaking from behind the nail so enthusiastically in the Pizzeria last night, has thankfully congealed into a manageable yellow crust. More good news in that all the Hi-8 video batteries are fully charged and Austin nervously shot the first interviews since leaving the UK.

Around 11.00am Mark, Chas, Gerald, Austin and Bill swang into usher and best man mode. Clive and Stubley came down to the Plage Hotel for the rendezvous with the coach that was carrying us all to St Raphael (25 miles away). Mr and Mrs Vince had rolled into town the night before and were pivotal in today's proceedings by providing the suits that all of us wore.

The service in St John of the Evangelist was very fitting and it was lovely to see the affection that the happy couple were clearly feeling for each other. Tania was 35 minutes late in fact, which was quite exciting!

The coach bore us all back to a new beach restaurant at Golfe-Juan called 'Vallauris Plage'. The atmosphere on the beach, with the superb weather, sun and sand, was like a picture postcard. After this initial champagne reception, Nick and Clive had to repair to the house since sadly they could not be accommodated in the exceedingly cramped restaurant. It's worth pointing out that Nick looked like an eastern European security operative who was on some kind of familiarisation visit to the capitalist West, whilst Clive was as silver tongued as ever as within minutes, Phil's friends became his friends. Bill and Austin made speeches and after an hour's dancing the revellers were turfed out into the rain. Sheltered by an awning, we all slept on the patio under a full moon serenaded by croaking of what seemed like 500 frogs (amphibians that is, not the locals).

France

Day 7
Sunday 16April 95
Mondo Miles today: 0
Mondo Mileage: 882

The full extent of the hospitality that has been heaped on us during our sojourn on the Cote d'Azur was evidenced this morning by a close inspection of the toilet. French cuisine has had nearly a week to wreak havoc on our digestive systems and the white ceramic bore the scars. Given that the number of people staying in and around the house reached double figures last night we dread to think of the tales that the bountiful bowl could relate.

Today has been a day for some gentle maintenance and plenty of bumbling. Chas and Mark met many of the wedding guests nursing hangovers over a cafe-au-lait. Chas discovered that one of the young ladies was in fact gainfully employed as a writer for the Paul Raymond empire on such titles as Club and Mayfair. She says it's true that most of the letters are made up (only because the real ones are too twisted) and that readers' favourite features are 'girl on girl'.

Back at the ranch Austin had got the camera set up in preparation for tomorrow's filming. His massive wooden camera chest has been voted off the trip. As an example of his inability to get things right it has no match. Italy looks mighty big and there's some long days driving ahead of us if we're to make the Thursday night ferry. There's talk of pushing back the ferry departure to Friday night if we can swing it. Apparently this can be done over the phone. Why are we always so slow?

Phil and Tania went off on honeymoon; Bill and Austin escorted them to their ferry in Nice on the bikes. They rode as an advance guard, stopping all the cars at roundabouts and waving on the happy couple's taxi. On the way back they paraded down the Promenade des Anglais, waving at the ferry as it steamed on to Corsica.

After today we'll be tightening our belts in readiness for some exciting times over the next few months. Destination Istanbul, no more weddings for a while now...

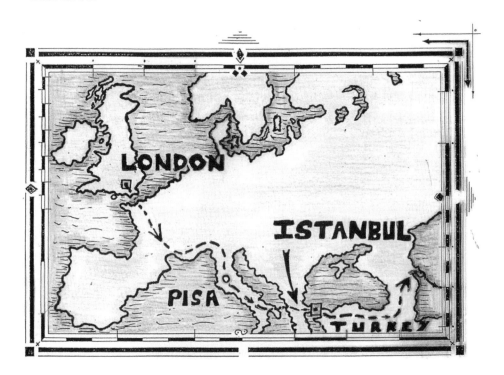

France

Day 8
Monday 17 April 95
Mondo Miles today: 180
Mondo Mileage: 1062

"MONDO CARLO"

And so to Italy... bedecked with pink roses, tokens of Phil's Mum's apparently inexhaustible goodwill, the engines were finally fired up at 9.45am. Hearts were heavier than our laden bikes when we rode off down to Chevin de la Migionette, 3 lovely and generous people waving to us in our mirrors (la Famille Alexander, minus one nouveau – Marie). Let it be recorded in this log how much we enjoyed our stay in Golfe-Juan, a magical time for so many reasons – and a superb start to the entire venture.

It is 600 miles to Bari and a boat to Greece. Bill led the caravan to the Autoroute, a Nice-avoidance policy in force due to the two best-men's experience of dense traffic on the Promenade des Anglais yesterday. We came off it above Monaco, and headed down town towards the casino. Mondo Enduro was always meant to be a big gamble but alas, the nearest we got to the roulette table was a run down towards the casino with Mr Vince filming us on the video camera....Naturally, it was great fun to take the Loews Hairpin on our humble 350cc bikes. Great footage was however caught for posterity, putting us in the mood for a lunch prepared by the inimitable Mrs Vince and served from the hatch-back of their camper van. Time limitations forced us onto the autoroute to try and consume some kilometerage. Mr Vince was again showing his cinematographic flair as the final filming of the day harbinged some hard, bottom-aching riding, as we were transformed from Autoroutiers to Autostradists, crossing into Italy through tunnel after tunnel and over viaduct after viaduct of beautiful road. We completed our 1000th mile from home, then all paid a £10 toll to get caught in a tailback of traffic, but which afforded us the perfect stage on which to show off the agile filtering capabilities of our little bikes.

We pushed on through Genoa, having agreed to RV (rendezvous) on the slip road down to Rapallo, and finally met up (Gerald and Nick, supposedly behind the others, were already there, having gone through a time hole). Thanks to some expert scouting by the camp team (double-entendre fully intended and justified) we were camped near Chiavari. Arrival spelt relief – a superb supper of pasta, potato and another Stubley sauce rounded-off a very tiring but satisfying day – the first to witness us riding well as a seven and arguably the first to see Mondo Enduro in all its absurd glory. We are faced with a long ride through Italy and it is proving difficult to conceptualise the huge distances coming up across Russia, but bikes and bottoms permitting, the seven (mental) dwarves will hi-ho their way South, leaving great memories, a brace of Vince parents and Roman civilization behind. We had better make it on our own, that's what this is all about really.

Italy

Day 9
Tuesday 18 April 95
Mondo Miles today: 91
Mondo Mileage: 1151

When we awoke it was like a wet weekend in Wales except in a few significant respects. For one thing it was Italy; for another it was Tuesday. One similarity, though, was the dreadnought grey of the Ligurian skies which anointed us with a brief shower.

The dismal setting was however entirely appropriate for the sense of sorrow we felt at bidding farewell to Phyllis and Geoffrey Vince. They have been an enormous help to us on the administrative front and a miraculous force for culinary food.

Today they sent us on our way with a breakfast of scrambled egg and bacon followed by bread rolls and marmalade. When will we again savour the sweet taste of home? We wish them well on their homeward journey via Venice and hope they will toast us with a bottle of fine wine bought with our spare French change.

In Chiavari our first task was to find a 45 litre Givi panier to replace Austin's expertly-made but overly cumbersome Mill Hill camera coffin. Gerald and Austin completed the mission while Bill, Chas, Mark and Clive sashayed into Moneglia to admire its curious and ingenious tunnel system. Someone with more dynamite than sense obviously thought it a good idea to blast a succession of tunnels through the living rock to link this charming but irrelevant village with the outside world.   The exquisite irony, the contemplation of which must trouble his departed spirit, is that the road is a dead end and leads to nowhere except a rather seedy hotel.   This is Italy, after all, and even in the land of Leonardo and Galileo we must expect some idiosyncrasies in the civil engineering department.

The tunnel system did however provide ample opportunities for some totally 'spontaneous' filming. We also made the most of a "falling rocks" road sign to perform a cameo which will provide the centrepiece for the forthcoming Mondo movie. While Mark kept watch for roving carabinieri, Bill, Chas, Nick and Gerald hurled stones onto the road from a rocky promontory while Clive negotiated the unlikely hazard.   A local teen, resplendent in a pink shell suit, watched us for a while before driving off in the opposite direction. Austin reported that the sequence, once reviewed in the view finder was rather unfunny and he apologised for wasting our time.

We then set off bound for La Spezia through the beautiful Ligurian hills. Perhaps in wonderment at the awesome scenery, we got split up briefly before meeting at a closed remote roadside Pizzeria patronised by two lasses with a taste for rave toons. As they pumped 500 lire coins into an outdoor juke box, we performed an impromptu dance routine for Austin's camera. The juke box was clearly tricked out with an after-market amplifier which was pumping up the volume to deafening levels of euro-disco madness. The pitiless smashing of the Tuscan idyll by this awful noise could well be today's most unusual experience.

From thereon it was a 50mph crawl through La Spezia and the largely featureless suburbia of Northern Tuscany. The boredom was briefly alleviated when Chas, Clive and Austin accidentally took the autostrada to Massa while the others, who took the 'slow' road, arrived about two minutes later. We pitched tents at Viareggio, an uninspirational town redeemed by its well-appointed campsite. Quite how we intend to motorcycle around the world doing only 91 miles a day is vaguely troubling. While Bill and Mark concocted the first full Mondo meal (complete with a side salad anti-pasti) of vegetables braised in chilli, the rest of the group rejoiced in Clive's latest cut-price camping deal 55,000 lire down from 69,000 lire. Mindful that the "Toiletti Vomine" was but a brief waddle away, we prepared for a lengthy drinking session. And so, as the poet said, to bed, perchance to dream...

Italy

Day 10
Wednesday 19April 95
Mondo Miles today: 196
Mondo Mileage: 1347

As the seven men slowly aroused to the sporadic splattering of rain on their canvas and nylon flysheets... they were reassuringly reminded they were no longer on a wet rainy cadet camp in Leek... but on their final leg of the Italian Riviera.

Captain Cadets Clive and Austin had set up and packed their poncho quicker than it took for our Mondo pot to boil... leaving the others struggling with their tent poles and pegs.

Spirits were soon livened a few kilometres out of town, when we came across two scantily clad ladies of disrepute just standing on the side of the tree lined road to Pisa. This was our first experience of the roadside prostitute but we wondered what their *modus operandii* would have been.

Onwards through bland suburbia and we finally reach the world famous Leaning Tower of Pisa. Bill managed to disperse most of the crowds not seeing the "No vehicles whatsoever" sign. Clive wrote a postcard home and we relished being normal tourists for an hour. When finally altogether again we filmed some of the bellissimo young ladies around the tower and headed off for Siena.

We had a rest in front of the railway station and imagined that as a monument to Mussolini's dream of modernist fascist architecture it must have no equal. Having filled up with both gas and food we ventured South-ish on the SS2 to Bolsenna near a huge lake. The scenery was beautiful –the rolling hills and little roman towns were a stark contrast to Siena's grim industrial outskirts...

It was still fairly early so we decided to make a dash through the next major town Vertibo and up into the mountains. This ride was breathtaking and icy cold at the same time- there was snow dotted here and there. We were amazed that snow could be found this far south in Italy.

As we edged over the top of the mountains we could now see the serene Lago Di Vico, a truly superb mountainous setting. Austin and Clive went off to do the recce for the camp site, whilst Chas and Nick waited for Mark, Gerald and Bill who were close behind.

We entered the site one-by-one, so as not to compromise our location. Once settled we set about the norm (tents and food) but unfortunately the MSR stoves failed for the first time. Austin stepped in proudly demonstrating his Venture Scout fire-lighting badge and "Hey Presto we were cooking!" However, whilst Austin was lighting this fire – his Irish blood and inquisitive mind led him to start dousing the fire with petrol and yep, you got it – the fire backtracked and he was bomb handed, flames licking out of the neck of the petrol flask. A mild panic set around the camp but our firelighting expert (being a bit mental) decided to continue holding the flaming bomb and screw the lid back on. Oxygen denied, it was made safe in an instant.

A few beers and a couple of bottles of wine to end this fine adventure were certainly in order. Our first night of proper rough camping, at last...

Italy

Day 11
20 April 95
Mondo Miles today: 151
Mondo Mileage: 1521

After our first night of rough camping, we awoke to the dawn chorus and the roar of the MSR all fuel stove as Bill and Austin readied breakfast. Today's plan is to bypass Rome and lunch at Monte Cassino. Lunch was a half-kilo of Parma Ham and cheese with fresh bread bought by Chas. We were surrounded by snow-capped peaks, and could just make out the tourist buses as they headed up to Monte Cassino. The re-built monastery was in tip-top condition. Inside, the courtyards were in pristine marble, a huge amount of work had been done leaving no trace of the wartime destruction. Today tourists mix with the monks as if nothing untoward had ever happened. All the stonework was immaculate as though freshly quarried. The view from the courtyard was splendid, with the town of Cassino, the Polish war cemetery and distant Apennines on the horizon. Time flew by and we reported to the local campground, and so to bed in Cassino with its looming Monte.

Italy

Day 12
Friday 21 April 95
Mondo Miles today: 185
Mondo Mileage: 1706

We awoke to a cloudless sky. It soon became very hot. We discovered the completed but unopened Cassino bypass which once intruded upon, we had to ourselves for some helmetless filming and goonery. We made good progress and at 14.00hrs after 80 miles we stopped for lunch by a small river. Bill and Nick went shopping for lunch to a 'one donkey town'. While they were away Gerald unloaded his bike and successfully forded the river, only to find the far bank was not the picnic Shangri La we had hoped for. Lunch is the usual bread, cheese and ham. Clive has gone ahead to Trani to recce a campsite; we will meet him as soon as we can.

Southern Italy has become much poorer the further south we go. All the half finished buildings have reminded us of Morocco, the miserable towns and empty villages are reminiscent of Romania and its getting cooler now we are nearer the sea. Butchers selling horsemeat proliferate, although today's lunch was with some of the nicest bread purchased so far.

After meeting Clive at Trani, who had nothing to report, we decided to rough camp. While Austin and Chas recce'd the rest of us went to a bowling alley nearby. As Chas returned and led us to the chosen spot we were seen by a few people. We realised that we had chosen the local 'lovers' lane'-cum-'Needle Park'. There were syringes everywhere. Oh well, at least we are by the sea. As Chas was turning around, his front wheel plunged into a ditch hidden by undergrowth. He rode along the ditch to get out at the end but his rear wheel became tangled in some thick wire. We had to wait until Nick arrived with the hacksaw before he could be freed. When it came to cooking supper Austin realised that he had not bought any veg. So it was potatoes and pasta. As it was such a pleasant evening the tents were not erected. Sleeping under the stars certainly has its benefits.

It's our last day in Italy tomorrow.

Italy

Day 13
Saturday 22 April 95
Mondo Miles today: 113
Mondo Mileage: 1819

While we slept *al fresco* the last night was dreamy as the stars looked down on us, the cool sea breeze turned to a film of unwelcome condensation which effortlessly permeated our up until then indefatigable RAB sleeping bags. At about 0545 a rich purple sunrise melted over the tips of the reeds which flanked one side of our campsite; we almost filmed it but rapture rather than poor lighting got the better of this particular shot.

We all awoke uncannily concurrently at about 0700 and although last night our location seemed pleasant, the crispness of the adjacent shore raised our mood further. Clive got the customary brews going and with these to hand Mondo Enduro moseyed down to the beach for our first official group photo since our departure from Mill Hill. On a few huge boulders the group posed in front of a gorgeous backdrop of crashing waves and crystal clear blue sky. Nick set up the single-8 Fuji and filmed a short burst of the team doing a sea shanty. Austin continued his attempts to become the Roger Vadim of Mondo Enduro with a silhouette shot that strangely lent more towards "Help!" than "Barbarella".

After this session Austin gave a quasi military lecturette on parts and use of the remarkable Fujica single-8 camera.[1] Chas then elected to become the cameraman for this format for the foreseeable future.

We rationalised the bulging first-aid/medical chest and discovered that we had loads of Canulae and hypodermics surplus. These were creamed off and plans made to use them as a form of currency hereafter.

Time was very much on our side as it was only about 1100hrs, we had struck camp and with only 100 miles to go to our 2100hrs ferry deadline at Brindisi. Hence, with an air of casual abandon, affected somewhat by the knowledge that very little of interest lay between Trani and our destination, we holed up at a bar that was connected to an Esso station on the outskirts of town. The full heat of the day helped to contribute to Austin's redness and Gerald having to keep his sparsely planted pate out of the sun.

We saddled up at about 1400hrs and drove down a strangely straight 100 miles of surgically perfect tarmac to Brindisi.

En route we found petrol stations that accepted our plastic less frequently but eventually our thirsts for "Accessible" petrol was slaked. At the Esso station Austin noticed a prime example of what we have discovered is a frighteningly popular Italian male stereotype: quite good looking, long styled hair (possible a Steven Segal ponytail), mirrored shades and a cocky swagger that is more Sid the Sexist than Don Juan. These guys look ridiculous in the extreme. I write this with Gerald padding around us wearing white plastic sandals, ankle high leathers and woolly hat.

Our arrival at Brindisi reminded some of us evermore of frontier towns like Ceuta and Mellila in Morocco. Everything is tatty, closed, broken and dusty. You don't need to read the Economist to see how Northern Italy and secondarily the EEC, is keeping this part of Europe afloat. Even the infamously impoverished Andalusian parts of Spain seem wealthier than this.

The quayside at Brindisi, like all points of international departure, is quite exciting and all of us have looked in awe at the Iranian 'Artics' that line

---

[1] Technical Footnote: The 'Single-8' format is in fact the name given by Fujica to their super-8 cameras. The industry standard is for all super-8 cameras to accept the film cartridge developed by Kodak in the 50s. In the 1960s Fujica broke ranks and designed a new slimline film cartridge into which they loaded super-8 film. This seemingly unhelpful step allowed the Japanese need to miniaturise to be applied to Super-8 camera design. The new, smaller, Fujica cartridge, now christened single-8, had a range of truly tiny film cameras designed around it. A few years ago an old storeroom had been discovered in the Osaka plant. It contained hundreds of these groovy, petite 1960s film cameras; brand new, boxed and in mint-condition. It was one of these that Austin had bought for only £29 from Lee's Cameras in Camden. The Fujica stock has to be sent back to Japan for processing (it takes 7 weeks!) but the degree of colour saturation is awesome, certainly outclassing Kodachrome 40.

the parking bays.   There are two English vehicles parked up but the occupants eye us up and send us a message something like "back off".

Gerald highlighted our route through Italy in preparation for sending our Michelin map back to Mr and Mrs Vince for the archive.   Clive plans the route through Greece. loading the ferries seems to take forever as lorries enter and then leave the same vessel in an attempt to get the most from a given volume. Gerald counted the slices of cheese in his roll while Mark discovered (by phone) that he has been sent a letter from Georgia.

Hopes were raised for subsequent phases of the trip when independently, Clive and Austin/Gerald got chatting to the Iranian truckers who, like us, were waiting at the quayside for permission to embark.   They were well informed and had a surprising command of English.   They were adamant that all of Iran's land borders are not only open, but that road traffic flows freely across them. We are not clear how we are going to get to Kazakhstan. No one seems to know exactly what the state of play is with all these newly independent former Soviet republics. Meanwhile, there is a town in northern Iran called Mashad from which a road leads over the frontier into Turkmenistan and it was about this route in particular that they were rigorously quizzed.   They quoted a petrol price of a tank bulging 40 litres for US$1!!

The boat was loaded up at 2130hrs with our bikes unhelpfully hemmed in with pallets of olive oil.   One of the deck-hands was a Ukrainian who had cheek bones you could bend sheet metal around.

Up on deck we came across some heavily 'cool' Californians who were skateboarding their way across Europe. Austin interviewed them on the Hi8 and was harangued by an American girl who demanded to be interviewed too. Sadly, she turned out to be rather uninspiring.

Our position at the fore of the ship meant that all our kit was almost blown away once the ship was moving.   Hence we relocated to one of the calmer decks but we lost on the setting since we had strong halogen bulbs searing into us all night.   Austin had an encounter with a heavily drunk American 20-year-old girl – but he did the decent thing and passed her on to a Californian.   As a group we failed to make much of an impact on a gang of six Americane girls, pretty and outgoing too.   Oh well, off to our well-lit vibrating beds and the new day brings us to Greece, our third country.

Greece

Day 14
Sunday 23 April 95
Mondo Miles today: 100
Mondo Mileage: 1919

Welcome to Helas, Zeus's passage of milk and honey on the Mondo route to Istanbul. We woke to blue skies, yet again, and the pine-clad hills of Igoumenitsa harbour. The full extent of the car-deck staff's unhelpful parking was revealed this morning as they attempted to usher us off in extra quick time, only to discover that motorbikes can't be driven in reverse. Fortunately this presented us with the chance to witness the extreme patience that Italians and Greeks are so renowned for.

A dozen miles or so out of Igoumenitsa we stopped at the side of the E90 for a brew and breakfast. We were joined by three Germans (who were eating sausage to keep their figures intact) stopped next to their transit van which was pumping out some obnoxious modern music (post '71). Whether they had any direct influence over our conversation is questionable, but it veered from tales of foreign legion valour to an explanation from Gerald about the New Zealand film "Smash Palace" (he'd forgotten the ending) to the relative merits of sidewinder missiles and their role in winning the Falklands War. Another dozen miles or so down the road we stopped at some spectacular viewpoint for a comprehensive photocall. Bill as MC had us all posing and preening ourselves and Austin inspired us to more helmet less Hi8 action as we rounded a mountain bend at 'the end of the zoom'.

The roads are excellent, the views wild and beautiful and our mood wild and effervescent. After 90 miles or so of riding we were hungry and Metsovo represented the stop we all needed.

Clive had got lost in Ioannina but was not far behind us getting to Metsovo. We parted ways to recce a suitable picnic spot and Nick came up trumps with the best one of the trip to date. A meadow full of buttercups, daisies and the flowers surrounded by snow-capped mountains was to be the scene for our afternoon's entertainment. Nick stir-fried lunch, during which time some Greek dirt-bikers on Yamaha 200's came up to pass the time of day. They put on an exhibition of off-road riding which Austin filmed. Their actions accompanied by applause from a Mondo team thoroughly impressed by their close control and ability to storm up the steep slope opposite. Undaunted, our intrepid off-road pioneers Clive, Austin and Gerald set about discovering the true use of a Suzuki DR350, skilled as it is at carrying a bunch of naïve young men on a trip to foreign parts, it's true talents lie not on tarmac.

Clive proved the point by storming up the slope, his body thrown over the handlebars to prevent a double backward flip – it was pretty clear that the Mondo team had caught the bug, and it had nothing to do with the red and black mites lurking in the long grass. We all had a run around the locality and then Austin set up a course for some trialling. The first water hazard proved to be a major sticking point for Mark, Gerald and Bill. Clive sailed over for a time of 2 minutes dead, closely followed by Nick. Chas nipped in between them with a time 2m11s. There then followed a head to head between Austin and Clive with the lead swinging backwards and forwards between the two determined Mondurites. Clive recorded a very impressive 1m20s to beat Austin's 1m23s. No further attempts by Austin could break the magic 1'20s barrier. Screams of delight could be heard from the various ditches lining the course as Austin rearranged his front rack from muddy crashes in ever more desperate attempts to beat Clive. Gerald had succeeded in trashing N1's clutch lever screw and in fact all the bikes looked the full-on bollocks (apart from K4 which kept its virginity intact). This impromptu Greek mountain meadow trial was exactly why we had packed in our jobs, borrowed £10,000 and set aside a year for motorbike gooning. It was indeed a Mondo moment.

Once everyone had inspected their injuries and packed their gear we headed off to look for a campsite whilst Gerald and Mark recce'd the town of Metsovo (2 miles hence). There was no decent campsite but we did notice a couple of discos and a load of bars throbbing with locals. We went back to the barn we had spotted earlier in the day and erected our sleeping quarters. A quick bowl of soup from Austin and we were ready to hit the Gstaad. Clive, Bill and Austin ferried the rest down on the back of their bikes (Austin with Gerald *and* Chas on the back). Metsovo was a happening little place and although the cashpoints would not entertain the thought of supplying us with Drachma, we managed to scrape enough together for our evening's entertainment.

First stop was an empty bar in the main square while Mark and Bill went off in a futile attempt to get cash and phone loved ones. Nick returned with the good news that his contact in Istanbul (Sally Campbell) had arranged accommodation for us with students from the University who are keen to improve their grasp of English. Comments ranged from general murmurs of approval to Austin's "will there be any ....." We should reach Istanbul in about 4 days time. We moved on to Bar/Disco "La Noz" which was rocking.

We occupied a central position and watched while the locals took up positions around the edges of the room to avoid getting too close to us. We drank ourselves into the start of a stupor and things start to liven up. The DJ played "Under my Thumb" followed by "Ticket to Ride" followed by an obscure Housemartin's number. Austin and Clive made a move on four girls on the next table and Chas was soon helping them along.

The group has so far shown a wide variety of mating habits. Austin and Clive favour a direct approach. Chas is somewhat more reserved but does not waste much time, Gerald was put forward as a classic Englishmen (how can anyone say that about one who wears a suicidal-tendencies scarf), Bill adopts a cool and hard look, Nick relied on his Greco features and "come to tent" eyes to attract the locals, whilst Mark almost blundered into a bizarre homosexual threesome with Guy and Alexandre from Lanessa. Mark did manage a bit of dancing with local girls and guys to some of the bazooki music they are so keen on around here. The DJ lurched back to some Western classics (Jumping Jack Flash) towards the end. Around 2 o'clock, we spontaneously sobered up and rode back to our Hellenic alpine barn.

And so to bed. The Mondo bank had distributed all its assets (along with most of Gerald's), but its backers agreed that it was money well spent and that further attempts to understand the local culture would be made in the future. Nick's new tent has revolutionised the comfort factor at night, and it looked the business after being erected for the first time. Clive and Austin snuggled down in the barn and we all slept like drunken pigs. If we had to go home *now*, this would already have been the trip of a lifetime.

It is worth recording that this is a stunning campsite. A meadow full of wild flowers with rolling hills covered in trees, undergrowth seemingly transplanted from the New Forest and snow-capped mountains all around us.

"The best day of the trip so far".........Mondo Team.

Greece

Day 15
Monday 24 April 95
Mondo Miles today: 235
Mondo Mileage: 2194

We awoke having slept like this book in the clear mountain air. Julie Andrews is expected any minute to remind us that the hills are alive with the sound of, well, farting... and indeed, we broke camp (and wind) as reluctantly we prepared to leave our secluded, mountain idyll above Metsovo, scene of such revelry and sad masculine vain glorious hope the night before. We set off up the Katara Pass (1705m), through more snow than we'd seen in the UK all year, in search of the emergency "fuel dump", the by now familiar routine of stopping for petrol and voiding our overworked bowels at the same time. Not many petrol stations were found at altitude, and none that took plastic, and certainly none with the complimentary toilet, usual in England, into which to empty that brown substance which the precipitous drops on both sides of the Katara Pass road had brought so uncomfortably close to the exit of even the most experienced rider's anus.

The precious fuel on plastic was eventually found in Kalambaka, set below some remarkable rocks/cliffs; very impressive, but not as breathtaking as Mark's fuel consumption figures – an incredible 78mpg! Gerald's fuel economy league of shame was calculated to an accuracy of 2 decimal places which Bill suggested was unnecessary. Clive came last, a statistic which he was sure to improve upon as we rolled on along a road so straight we would have died of boredom had not lunch beckoned, enjoyed by a river in the foothills of Mount Olympus. Mark left early in search of somewhere to relieve his straining bowels and the rest followed at a more sedate pace, Bill peeling off to follow Mark's example.

Bill pulled into a dusty, wind-blown garage to be ushered quite unexpectedly into a palatial bog. He later emerged breathless, but relieved from these Elysian fields, only to find the garage owner and his extended family posing for shots by K4. Delayed with this unexpected moment of glory, he was late for the RV at Elassona, whence the group, intact once more, headed North and pointed front racks along the road skirting Zeus's pad, Mount Olympus – a majestic peak, yet sufficiently unimposing to ensure that Gerald missed it completely. Another great road for motorcycling, and as Clive proved in dramatic style, a great road for crashing too, as the corner just proved too tight to handle.

His composure and bike restored, Clive joined Bill and Austin's attempt to catch Mark in the fuel consumption stakes by free-wheeling the rest of the way down the mountainside, before the group opened their throttles onto the Thessalonika expressway. Austin took the lead, adopting his casual 'easy rider' position, before he was forced into a pit-stop with his boot ablaze having rested it too long on the exhaust pipe. Old hot foot had a further come-uppance further down the road, where he shelled out 200 drachmas at the toll-through which the others had blended through so effortlessly without paying (down the police-only emergency slip-road) only minutes earlier. Thessalonika reached, Bill and Austin headed into town while the others went off in search of a place to kip on the far side of the city. The former team met with success, tracking down the Turkish Consulate, cutting spare Givi keys and obtaining cash from the most advanced cash machine either of them had ever seen. Their success was compounded when the cutest babe in Europe chose to cross the road just as they passed by, causing Austin to swerve in front of Bill who in turn nearly piled into an Interflora display. Shaken, they headed out of town to make the 9pm rendezvous with the second group, who had conversely met with no success and were found completely demoralised by the roadside. No campsite, rough or official, had been decided upon, and time was marching inexorably on. Finally, the team cut their losses with pizza and a beer before creeping into the grounds (broken-glass strewn – look out thermarests!) of a ruined building. It is a strange thing being in a different place every night, what a year of this will do to us we cannot tell. It's all so exciting but many of us are missing home already! Oh well, we've got each other.

Greece

Day 16
Tuesday 25 April 95
Mondo Miles today: 80
Mondo Mileage: 2274

We had made our bed, and we had to lie in it – so how come it smelt of excrement, and urine and was sprinkled with hypodermic syringes? The desperate straits of the night before had forced us to repose in a stench-ridden sewer of someone else's making. Road camping tip: Don't look for a 'rough' campsite when it's dark, you can't see what you're getting. Only the soft light of a grey dawn revealed the full and awesome squalor of the gutter in which we had slumbered.

There is, however, a phrase in the English vernacular which equates happiness with pigs in muck. So we slept on, content in the knowledge that our new found Mondo freedom allows us to live like swine if we want to. Any fool can have a down-filled duvet and hot running water after all.

We awoke to overcast skies which made us all feel a little homesick. They also provided a welcome respite from the wall-to-wall sunshine we have enjoyed almost every day since leaving Albion's shores. Austin made the most of the moment by high-tailing it in Thessalonika in search of assorted hardware items and Turkish consular approval for our drug-rich medical kit. In the time-honoured tradition of official idiocy, however, the flunky in question would not so much as allow Austin into his seedy Ottoman parlour, preferring instead to parley with him outdoors. Mondo Enduro would do well to put this episode down to experience, for even more Byzantine bureaucracy surely awaits us in more Eastern climes.

Mark, Chas and Bill meanwhile nipped into town for a quick café-au-lait while Perea roused itself to face a new day. The waiter appeared to take pity on the leather clad waifs and gave them a plate of stale bread Free of Charge to chew on while they slurped their caffeine. As Wild West music blazed from the speakers, the aforementioned trio met Nick and Gerald in the town square. It was a scene straight out of the OK Corral and the ensuing stand-off could have proved nasty if Greece did not have such tight firearms controls.

Time had hastened on in the meantime to nearly 11 o'clock and Clive was still lounging in the mire of our previous night's accommodation. Mark and Chas made the most of the hiatus in the day's events to nip down to Thessalonika airport where their leathers allowed them to mingle anonymously with the throng of international business types. Chas chatted briefly to two Aeroflot stewards who, on hearing of our itinerary, said they were from Moscow and grinned knowingly as if sharing a private joke.

Today was officially maintenance day and we finally left in search of an impromptu garage about 2.30pm. Our hunt took us down to Sithonia the second of three fingers of land which project downwards into the Aegean like a Masonic handshake. We think this is the area where the mountain-top monasteries perch as featured in 'For Your Eyes Only' but we are not really sure.

It quickly became apparent that we were about a month too early to meet the hordes of Scandinavian go-go dancers and Teutonic sun-seekers who undoubtedly populate this romantic coastline in the summer months. We did however find a makeshift service area next to what appeared to be a water pumping station on top of a steep hill. While Mark and Bill recce'd a possible campsite, and later prepared a mouth-watering veggie curry, the others completed the first Mondo 2000 mile oil change.

The exercise was sadly not without mishap. Gerald's overladen bike crashed to the ground, bending a Givi panier strut. When Austin heaved on it to straighten it, the fatally weakened alloy metal shattered, completely leaving all the hard-luggage wallahs to contemplate an unpleasant Doomsday scenario. A trip to the nearest Givi bazaar in Istanbul will be an early priority. Meanwhile, Austin's cherished leather panniers have had their first cone uppance. They are starting to deform and sag like slow melting wax. And speaking of melting, they rest against the exhaust side panel and become extremely hot. So much so that Austin's prized 'wash-kit' Tupperware box completely melted as did the shampoo bottles etc. He has taken to jamming twigs and pebbles between the pannier and the exhaust so as to create a protective buffer of insulating air. We shall see...

The camp ground found by Bill – Rea International Camping – was one of the best thus far encountered by Mondo Enduro and will surely earn a special commendation in our soon-to-be published almanac. The showers were spotless, the water hot and the patron's teenage daughter had enough upper lip hair to attract a small EC agricultural subsidy. This latter fact proved perversely comforting in a country where all the girls seem to possess a rare classical beauty, highly tormenting to motorcycling enthusiasts whose sexual frustrations increase at the same rate as the decline in their personal hygiene.

We all look forward to the fleshpots of Istanbul and her wealth of charms. Greece, however, has been a revelation and will certainly get an honourable mention when Mondo Publications issues its definitive guide to the world.

Greece

Day 17
Wednesday 26 April 95
Mondo Miles today: 0
Mondo Mileage: 2274

A wonderful sense of well being was shared amongst our team as we slowly arose to a truly superb day. The campsite was second to none with the beach only a stone's throw away. Clive was up first with an early morning dip in the Agean and was back in time to set off the standard Mondo Alarm Call – the MSR stove's throaty roar. It is indeed a substantial morale booster to be awoken by the sound of a fellow rider selflessly preparing seven coffees.

Gerald was up next for his power meal of the day; a ciggie followed by a coffee and within minutes he was ploughing the 70 miles back to the big city of Thessalonika to hunt for a replacement Givi pannier bracket.

Today was another official maintenance day – a hub of activity at a leisurely pace – boots a polishing, leather waxing, oil changing, suspension hardening and side stand straightening, touching up paintwork – all in the glorious sunshine. Hoorah for the hols!

The group is set to split for only officially its second time; Gerald and Clive to stay and hunt for the Givi rack whilst the remainder act as an advance party in Istanbul.

8pm and still no Gerald and mild concern around the camp – but we then remembered siestas can go on till 6pm. Whilst waiting for dinner Austin reminisces on a movie he saw at the cinema called "The Pissing, Shitting, Eating and Drinking Film" and the bizarre camera angles that were achieved... this somehow stemmed from a conversation about a girl he once met who modelled her hands for a living. In a chance conversation on classics of 1960s cinema Clive revealed that his uncle Tim was an extra in no less than: Where Eagles Dare (Bierkeller arrest scene), Billion Dollar Brain (he was the one who put a chloroform pad over Michael Caine's face in the frozen house of Dr. Karnak) and Chitty Chitty Bang Bang (role unknown).

Gerald had done well – after finding the shop where he could order the part was closed... he persistently scouted around and eventually got a complete result – someone in the middle of Greece managed to have the right bracket in a pile of their scrap metal. So now we didn't have to split, we'll arrive in Istanbul as the gods of the road intended, as a seven.

Greece

Day 18
Thursday 27 April 95
Mondo Miles today: 191
Mondo Mileage: 2498

Gerald writes:

We awoke once again at Camping Rea to a calm yet idyllic panorama of the Aegean sea. Austin had substituted the alarm services by howling in pain as he de-pressurised the cooker in a cloud of steam at 0730hrs. As Gerald had been wearing out the road surface between Rea and Thessalonika, we still had the new Givi and suspension jacking to perform on his bike. Chas, meanwhile, has purchased some porridge oats and was busily making breakfast to the clanging of the suspension being raised. After some filming along a wooded windy, windy road consisting of Clive burning down a logging road to undertake the others, we sped along the coast with an RV at Kavala at 114 miles hence. Gerald and Mark had just witnessed some motorists settling their differences over some wild punching. Meanwhile Austin and Chas were gooning around on the seafront somewhere along the way. The first coffee break of the day was after about 50 miles, where the Roman God Tantalus had left some beach balls for us to play with, but unfortunately, just like the famous grapes and water, once they appeared to be in our group, they mysteriously moved away again! How strange!

So on to Xanthi and across a delta/marsh area with bird reserves and fertile arable land. To the North loomed the Anatolik: Rodopi mountains of Northern Thrace, marking the border with Southern Bulgaria. Following the E90 the next RV was to be Roditis or Rod-it-is! Unfortunately Stubley hung a right and made a 60K detour back to where he had started! One hour later he arrived outside the Grand Supermarket to find the other 6 members of the team laden with western consumables, sirens (emitting a wailing squeal befitting a 'clown' police car), illuminating dash-board hearts and all the usual Mondo essentials.

A quick recce had been done and a meal site chosen. The meal of squid and chilli sauce with pasta was a triumph of catering in the field and Chef Mark was toasted and cheered!! After washing up in a nearby stream, we adjourned to a half-built house on the hill that was to be our humble abode for the night. Nick and Clive, despite Austin's needlessly detailed briefing, drove straight past the dirt track turn off leading up to the house. After a quick U-turn and lights off we rode up the rutted track out of sight of the passing E90 traffic. We bedded down in the concrete box on the first floor that we imagined is intended to be the master bedroom and exchanged stories late into the night. A bottle of gin appeared which helped today's 191 miles seem ten times that and as it coursed through our veins we nobodies felt like somebodies...

Greece

Day 19
Friday 28 April 95
Mondo Miles today: 88
Mondo Mileage: 2587

Gerald writes:

As usual by now the sky was cloudless when we arose. Sitting here outside the roadside chapel waiting for the water to boil I'm wondering how long it will be before clouds appear. I can't wait to fit my siren. In fact, will stop logging...

Siren mounted but not yet wired up.

Almost midday and we have not moved from the outdoor church where we had supper last night. We have all been to the supermarket to use their toilet facilities. Austin and Nick taped a spoof cowboy dishwashing scene; others wrote postcards and sunned themselves. Bill is reading the Turkish guidebook and we are deciding whether to make a detour to Gallipoli. After a brief ride sans helmet I am convinced that an open faced helmet is not for me.

66 miles to the border. I have passed the 3000 mile mark since leaving Bournemouth. As expected the sky has become overcast and we have just missed a rain shower, but, as I write the sun is reappearing. We have passed quite a few army vehicles today. Is there an exercise or is it because we are so close to the sensitive border?

Everyone except Austin arrived at the border promptly and partook of the usual lunch, but unusually, no cheese today. Whilst waiting for Austin to arrive a game of cricket started with Chas, Mark and Clive. Nick joined later to become wicketkeeper. Austin has at last arrived and explained his tardiness with a tale of yet more Tupperware purchased, as well as having had a lead custom-made for the microphone in the last town we went through. The border crossing took longer than expected due to *another* Austin bungle. In the rush to pack back in England he had grabbed his V5 ownership document but only now has he discovered that it is for his van not the bike he is riding. Naturally, he hasn't even looked at it until today because we've been in the EEC. Anyway, after much to-ing and fro-ing he got stamped into Turkey but heaven knows how he'll get stamped out without the single document that customs men worldwide are patiently waiting to inspect.

We found a municipal campsite and as we sat down to eat the owners came over with seven glasses with which to drink our wine out of. Later a plate of salad appeared and later still a plate of apples and strawberries. And then a jug of Raki, a Turkish aniseed based liquor. I'm not a great lover of pastis but we all made a show of enjoying it. Despite only doing eighty eight miles today almost everyone is tired and wants to be in bed soon (before 22.00hrs). Mark stayed up with the owner to play a few games of backgammon. We are all looking forward to Istanbul tomorrow. The end of Europe for us until we come back this way a year from now with hopefully, Russia, the Americas and Africa behind us.

Turkey

Day 20
Saturday 29 April 95
Mondo Miles today: 150
Mondo Mileage: 2737

The tent rich Mondo Enduro team had a sound night's sleep punctuated only by the insane barking of the campsite dogs. Amazingly they only piped up once during the small hours. The site here is curiously free of mosquitoes, flies, midges or other creatures which cause us to question the wisdom of the diversity of creation. This absence of pests seems strange since at the foot of the gardens where we are camped there is a huge man-made lake. The water is obviously still and this has allowed the locals to develop their particular brand of floating chemical and oil bottle collage. This particular example is all the more striking as the bright blues and yellows of Esso and Shell corporate packaging, contrast neatly with the deep blackness of the water on which they float. The feast for the senses doesn't end there as the nose is treated to a pungency that reminds you that you are no longer in England.

Clive and Austin filmed some big toads jumping into the swamp of effluent in their bid to escape the supposed threat of the humans. It seems incredible that they can survive even <u>one</u> immersion in the stagnant pool that they use as their sanctuary.

This is our first morning in Turkey and everyone is filled with an air of anticipation as we approach Istanbul, a city which is fast being regarded by the team as a last chance to hook into the sundry Western technological and financial services that we expect to see little of between here and Tokyo.

As these lines are written in the courtyard of our ultra generous host's property – Turkish folk music blares out through this straining cone of a duplicate Japanese boogie box. If it were a soundtrack it would set the scene perfectly, but in reality the distortion on every range, from Bass to Treble, makes it disturb the peace rather than enrich the local colour – oops! He's just turned it down – so now it does sound *very* atmospheric.

Chas kindly played with the campsite owner's young son. We were shown enormous kindness yet the strangeness of seeing the women's tasks so clearly allocated into the menial domestic sphere is uncomfortable. We watched some men put the boot into a little dog for almost no reason and then turn and warmly offer us coffee. Our minority pressure groups would have a field day out here – and this is Western Turkey coveting EU membership!

Saddled up we opened up the engines for their 125 mile push into Istanbul. The road was poorly surfaced and plied by slow trucks which belched a rich black exhaust, a sort of gaseous version of the fluid we'd seen in the lake.

The action hotted up as we hit the suburbs of Istanbul. The road's characteristics were: 4 lanes wide, no road markings, non-stop weaving (no indications) and of course, even more exhaust and a burning mid-day heat and just loads and loads of traffic.

Gerald guided us down to the area of the Dolmanbache Palace where we parked up, filmed, watered and Gerald and Nick Stubley recce'd Sally Campbell's flat. Sally is an acquaintance of Kathryn (Stubley's sweetheart) from their time at St Giles's College in Highgate.

Sally accepted us into her lovely flat as if we were old friends, despite the fact that she has never met any of us before. Within no time she had arranged a venue for tonight's ho-down and sundry female company!! Her flat gives onto the balcony of a minaret of a tiny mosque opposite. We heard the call to prayer loud and clear.

Barbaros, Sally's Turkish friend, had military contacts that allowed us to be booked into an Air Force club on the other side of the Bosphorus. We walked down to the quay, took a ferry over to Asia, met Zana and Miio (US and Japanese friends of Sally) and after Gerald was made to shave by the concierge we were afforded entry to this Turkish Air Force venue. It was packed, and we were virtually the last to take our seats. The courses, French style, were almost 50 mins between being served.

A five piece folk band set up then struck up – it was a fantastic sound which the locals, i.e. absolutely everybody else, totally loved. There was much clapping of hands and singing along by our fellow diners. It was great to see middle aged men, leaping, unembarrassed, to their feet and doing a little dance that looked unusually similar to 'Zorba's dance'. What has happened to folk music in England? This scene would be impossible back home.

Next stop, a cab ride back on the European side over to a 'Hard Rock' club called 'Mr No'. Here we encountered a head banging rock group called Knucklehead who, with huge slash-like hair do's entertained us with note perfect and gutsy rock anthems that would have brought any AOR fan tears of joy. The rum and cokes flowed and in no time all seven of Mondo Enduro were rocking all over the world. Back home at 0500hrs, no blending as feared, but easily the best night of Mondo Enduro.

Turkey

Day 21
Sunday 30 April 95
Mondo Miles today: 0
Mondo Mileage: 2737

Austin clearly had something of a mental blank about last night's antics. No mention of his reaction to the belly dancer, of stripping off on the dance floor of 'Mr No', impressing the locals with his display of modern jazz dancing, falling asleep in the corner and relieving himself over a candle.

Most of the team got up at 11am and were taken by Sally to a nearby restaurant in a park for breakfast. Here, they witnessed a sight that will live with them for the rest of their lives. It was clearly a dog (and dog-walkers) heaven in the park café with pampered pooches being dragged in while their owners enjoyed a Nescafe and Kahvalti. One pooch was clearly on heat and earlier in the afternoon we had watched her enjoying the close attentions of a lusty admirer. An hour later she was clearly in raptures as a new lover's love bonio exploded into action. Both mutts had almost human expressions – she looked soft and dreamy, he looked keen to get it over with before she changed her mind. As they reached the high point they found themselves locked together – an unfortunate muscle spasm had left him trapped inside her and they were locked back to back yelping in agony. After ¼ hour of watching the spectacle one of the owners dragged them off to the side and got her date to separate them. As they licked their wounds, it was clear that he had come off worse – his engorged member was touching the ground and was bright red, like some funked up frankfurter.

The whole team went on an excursion to the local hammam where we revealed our milky white flesh to the glowering masseurs. Chas was first on the slab as he was scrubbed, soaped and washed down and then slapped around a bit. Clean and refreshed we Mondoed around doing TH Lawrence impressions with the giant tea towels – Gerald was officially renamed "Plug of Arabia" following an afternoon of hoovering and unplugged one-liners.

Austin got busy on his Brown Bottle impression in the evening as Sally introduced us to yet more of her friends. More interpretative dance to the strains of Acid Servis in yet another grungy rock bar soon had the place rocking. On to Kenarche where we all went mad to the strains of a Turkish punk band covering The Specials, UK Subs and Cramps– slam dancing is set to be the next big craze in Istanbul. Most of Sally's female friends were scared off by our exuberant display and so it was left to Clive, yet again, to try to persuade an American couple to indulge in a threesome. As the best looking of us, he carries a heavy load...

Turkey

Day 22
Monday 1 May
Mondo Miles today: Misc miles around Istanbul
Mondo Mileage: 2737

We awoke around 11am. Nick and our silently-suffering hostess having left at 8am for a rendezvous with some Mongolian babes at Sally's Turkish class. Nick returned to find us emerging bleary-eyed from the addictive comfort of our Rab-Thermarest combies, as we relived yet another rockingly cool night out in some of Istanbul's grungier music clubs.

Today was a day for Achievement, and tasks were shared out accordingly. Bill and Nick packed the now biologically active dirty laundry into a hermetically sealed bag and set off in search of an unsuspecting and hitherto unsuffering launderette. Down the road they met with incongruity in its most extreme form: in a typically Turkish street bustling with hawkers, shoeshine boys and kebab parlours, they stumbled quite by chance on the launderette of the future; gleamingly new and heaving with state-of-the-art German technology – our two intrepid launderers manfully tried to come to terms with computerised Kleiderwashen, but in vain, and they were usurped by Mrs Efficient who couldn't bear to see her beauties being so abused by two such bumbling idiots. She therefore relieved them of the laundry bag, blissfully unaware of the horrors which awaited her inside, and they gratefully beat a retreat to a café for lunch. The proprietor, when asked by Nick in his most fluent tourist English, "You have kebab, yes?" grinned and nodded, and returned with 2 beers. They finally managed to get a chilli salad and a delicious meat dish, which was consumed slowly, neither wishing to confront the fury of Mrs Efficient once she'd been attacked by Austin's smalls. They found her, greyer and strangely subdued, and recovered the clothing, now miraculously clean.

Austin and Clive have met with semi-success: their attempt at Amex to get Clive's dollars was completely bogus, and has meant that they will probably have to spend more time in Istanbul. This setback was further compounded by the 280,000 lire (each) fine imposed by an over-zealous

Trafik-Polisi for not wearing helmets. No cloud is without the lining of silver, however, and their trip into town bore ripe and juicy fruit in the form of a stamp, fashioned in the darkest recesses of an Istanbul back alley, designed to give authenticity and credibility to Austin's dodgy Transit van log book, iffy-replacement for the absent Suzuki V5 document. His hand-written alterations to his van V5 so as to audaciously transform it into his bike V5 needed to be 'validated' so he has had a rubber stamp made especially. It simply states: *Authorised by DVLC Swansea SA99 1AR.* It is with blushing pride that its first stamping is hereby made on Clive's V5 registration document. GET A LOAD OF THIS:

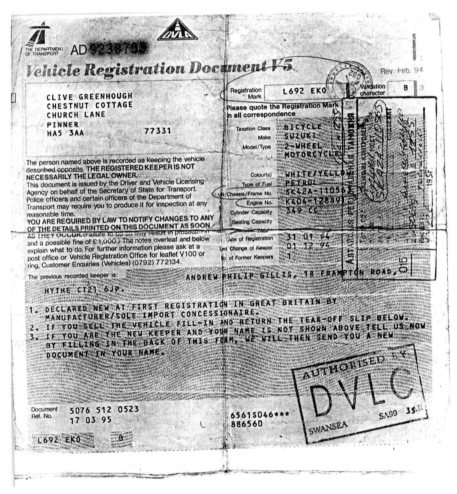

Trouble-free border crossings, here we come!

Mark and Chas were last to materialise, having waylaid a Russian Diplomat outside their consulate as he was making a dash for home in his 2.1 BMW, he was Mundoed before he knew what hit him and proved helpful and informative, suggesting that our visas could become multiple entry ones at one stroke of a stamp (hopefully a bit more convincing than that appearing above). It will mean waiting a couple more days in Istanbul but hey! Who's complaining? When we all finally got together, it was decided to go and meet Sally at her class and then go on for a meal. We arrived there early at her request and blended with her students for 15 minutes chatting and letting them see some real-life "normal" Englishmen. We met up with her mate Gordon, and then went out for a monster kebab blow out, which so drained us that we returned bloated and belching to what, by recent standards, was an early night. So ended another full day – a day of haircuts, visa hunting, stamp skullduggery and the 60⁰ mixed fabrics version of 'vorsprung durch technik'.

Turkey

Day 23
Tuesday 2 May
Mondo Miles today: 230
Mondo Mileage: 2967

The streets around Sally Campbell's flat were flooded with our metaphorical tears since the time had come for us to leave Istanbul behind and forge ahead into the Asian heartlands.

We all awoke refreshed after a long and deep sleep punctuated only by the occasional warbles fermented by last night's kebab feast. Even the Mullah, who bears a startling resemblance to the television comedian Rab C Nesbitt, could not disturb our repose with his 5am alarm call.

The day's tasks began with a trip to the Iranian Consulate by Austin in the forlorn hope of securing our passage into Turkmenistan or Azerbaijan. The mission was fruitless as anticipated but still worth a try as the official in question did not dismiss our request out of hand. Instead he asked for a 1.5m Turkish Lira deposit non-redeemable in the event of our application being turned down. It would take 10 days to 'judge' any application. Aggro delayness. Mondo tip: Get every visa before you leave home.

Chas and Bill went to the bank to exchange dollars while the rest of the gang got on with the not inconsiderable task of removing any trace of our presence in Sally's flat. Just so she doesn't forget us (an unlikely event given the high jinx of the previous three days) we presented her with a group photo portrait of ourselves posing outrageously by the Italian seaside. One day it will be worth millions we assured her, although not with complete conviction.

Much to the relief of the Mullah, who was clearly a traffic warden before taking religious orders, we packed up the bikes outside Sally's flat and bought food from the local supermarket. A local leatherworker treated Chas to Chai while he fixed his troublesome leathers belt buckle free of charge and then offered to throw in a pair of women's flip-flops "gratis". The offer was graciously refused.

We left Istanbul sometime after 12 noon bound for the Toll road to Ankara some 350 miles away. As we crossed the Bosphorus Bridge into Asia our brains worked overtime thinking generous thoughts about the City of Constantine and her rocking fleshpots.

The Bosphorus Bridge toll was 10000 TL each – or an inflation busting 15 pence.

Chas could not help thinking smug thoughts about the Humber Bridge which costs a whopping £1.40 to cross on two wheels and leads only to the Lincolnshire frontier town known as Barton-on-Humber.

By contrast, we were crossing the borderline of an entire continent as we sashayed serenely into Asia Minor. Our first stop after a throttle-hand numbing 50 mile stretch of pristine motorway was a Mobil garage. There we were made welcome by a friendly petrol pump attendant who showed us a photo of his English girlfriend – a sultry lass from Ilkley, West Yorks, who was a student at Oxford, apparently. It's a funny old world, was the thought which collectively crossed the Mondo brain.

The garage's plastic table and chairs ensemble was charming in every way and made the perfect setting for our homely repast of bread, cheese, biscuits and chocolate washed down with warming draughts of Nescafe. It had not escaped our notice that the weather had become unseasonably chilly and several of the party broke out their waterproofs for the first time since Mondo Enduro began all those many years ago now.

A long, uneventful and it has to be said utterly boring journey ensued for nearly 200 miles. The ennui was relieved by an utterly mental drive on a 'normal' stretch of road when the motorway ran out and was replaced with rutted dirt track. The truck-dodging experience was stressful indeed and seemed like a dusty hybrid of 'Rollerball' and 'Jeux Sans Frontieres'.

The motorway after Bolu was characterised by its almost complete lack of cars, lorries, or exits. We saw several interesting trucks, however, including one stacked with wheelbarrows and another loaded entirely with foam. We finally reached the turning for Camildero where in the Mondo spirit of thrift and parsimony we crashed the toll barrier before the disbelieving eyes of the dozing official.

We rough-camped in a dramatic lunar landscape festooned with rocks and some kind of torso-like shrub. Mark and Bill cooked the familiar but delicious "Legumes a Mondo" while the lads gathered up the sparse supplies of kindling to make a roaring fire. We are in Asia Minor and it's exciting.

Turkey

Day 24
Wednesday 3 May
Mondo Miles today: 77
Mondo Mileage: 3044

"Priority Admin" was the sense of order for the day so after a slow start we headed up to Ankara railway station to get our bearings. Our missions were the tourist Information point, town maps, embassy, DHL and Amex addresses. The romance of the world road trip is rudely interrupted every few days by such tasks. The idea that you just jump on yer' hog and get goin' is a myth.

Lots to do but so little time after various mis-directions into town.

Mark and Chas went off in a cab to hunt the Russian Embassy down. When they finally got there, they were told to return on Wednesday, unlucky. When they told Comrade Stubliniski it *was* actually Wednesday, he decided to make it Friday – all extremely suspect.

Ankara has certainly a lot less traffic than Istanbul but with equivalent noise pollution levels, the incessant hooting drives you insane. The weather has taken a turn for the worse to a cold and cloudy day followed by continuous rain.

Gerald, Mark, Chas, Bill and Nick went off to recce the campsite whilst Austin and Clive went to the British Embassy and Council, Amex office and DHL office.

We found out it was bad news on the Armenian and Georgian front (borders are definitely closed) so it seems that as a last resort we will have to go to Trabzon, then boat across the Black Sea to Sochi in Russia.

Result at Amex where we got £300 in Sterling on Austin's card with no problems. Despite having our air filters bulging with cash we seem to always be short of it. The thought is that once we get to the former USSR there will be no cash-point machines.

We cannot seem to get going having constantly to visit this web of embassies and consulates. Why on earth did we not sort this all out before we left the UK?

Incidentally, while waiting in the station during the course of the day many army vehicles frequented the car park – loading and unloading crates of missiles labelled as being made by a company in Tucson Arizona.

Turkey

Day 25
Thursday 4 May
Mondo Miles today: 0
Mondo Mileage: 3098

And the rains came to pass: enough to re-float the Ark from Mount Ararat. The Mondo campers woke up to a soggy scene, as all night the pitter-patter of tiny raindrops accompanied their slumbers.

With chores a plenty the gang split up with various missions...

Nick, Clive and Bill went to DHL to collect the Deet and mosquito nets from London. Before we left we bought a litre of Deet, a vicious oily substance that aggressively attacks many plastics. However, it is the most potent and aggressive anti-mosquito repellent synthesised by man. We deftly managed to leave it behind and so Austin's dad had sent it over. Suzuki spares were investigated via our British Council Contact Arilla Kore who says he rides a DR800. Chas and Mark went to the Russian Consulate to try and extend the visas for our Sochi option. Austin and Gerald set to work on B2 for siren fitting and brake pad replacement. Chas and Mark found the Russian Embassy closed, but had better luck at the Georgian Embassy, whose consulate had nothing but praise for the situation out there. Today's filming consisted of map pointing, with the whole group as well as some pyrotechnics with the pressure cooker and a giant banger Austin had bought on a school trip to Boulogne. Later Bill recounted his close shave on the way back from the station last night when he dropped the bike to avoid hitting a Turkish motorist. News from London is that DHL will deliver by Monday although the Ankara woman suggested Saturday morning as a possibility. Delivery will consist of a chain for A7 and a new number plate for Austin's B2. This isn't because there's anything wrong with his licence plate; Because of the van V5 documentation bungle his dad has got a licence plate made up with the *van's* number and this will be fitted to his bike so he can use the van V5 (complete with authentication stamps!) from now on.

Other maintenance consisted of concealing dollars onto and into the bikes. Weather is cool but at least the rain had stopped. The campsite is deserted and makes an ideal base with its wooded surrounds, shower block and covered eating area as well as regular visits from the security/maintenance/manager Turk who's glass-tipped Lada sits at the gatehouse all day. Tonight we can look forward to another game of Monopoly in a relatively comfortable covered seating area after one of Austin's special pasta suppers.

After more discussions on routing we decided to split with an advance party going to Kars in the East. Chas and Mark decided to sample the nightlife of downtown Ankara. Unfortunately Mark met a large pothole – Unlucky! – so some late night puncture repairs were needed. So it was back to camp to call out the rescue party.

Turkey

Day 26
Friday 5 May
Mondo Miles today: 0
Mondo Mileage: 3098

Everyone up early to get to the various embassies when they opened in Ankara. The reader should know that we want to get to Soviet Central Asia (Uzbekistan et al) but the possible routes there all cross the newly independent republics of the former USSR, these seem to be drifting in and out of civil war, enclosed by borders which we are fairly sure we lack the visas to cross. Most irritatingly, there are neither guidebooks nor London embassies for these fledgling states so before leaving the UK it was impossible to sort this all out. So here we are in Ankara, trying to resolve which country we are going to next: Iran, Armenia, Georgia, Russia or the Ukraine (the latter two by boat across the mysterious Black Sea).

Nick and Gerald stayed at the campsite to clear up and get everyone's personal kit ready for a hopefully rapid departure on a return from town.

Austin and Clive were first back having spoken to every relevant embassy and deduced almost nothing. Nobody seems able to give us a straight answer. Gerald mended the puncture on Mark's bike. The weather improved greatly with a good break in the clouds. Two French campers pulled in, so we have had to vacant the ablution block which had become our second home and workshop. The remainder of the city party returned, plans were made and we eventually departed at 1600hrs leaving Gerald and Nick to await the arrival of the chain and van number plate from England.

The group of five were off to Trabzon and Kars in a bid to ascertain the possibility of the border crossing into Armenia and hence the whole Caucasus issue. In fact, no subject has caused such a large amount of discussion and variance of feeling within the Mondo Endurists. Georgia is the touchiest area since, after a recent BBC 'Newsnight' special it was apparent that all was not well in this particular republic. Stories of frequent roadblocks, unrestricted ownership of guns, and dilapidated infrastructure weighed heavy on everyone's minds. It sounds anarchic but not in a fun way.

Anyway, when it rains it pours; after last night's drenched tyre changes in the suburbs of Ankara, we had gone but 6 miles from the campsite when Mark's repaired tyre flaked out. We pulled up, jacked up the bike on a boulder, fitted a brand new inner tube and continued. Only 66 miles out we found it to be already 7pm and we found a fab campsite in a quasi French poplar forest.

Turkey

Saturday 6 May
Miles today:
Mondo miles:

Editorial note; There was a mistake heading up the pages subsequent to this in the actual diary. As a consequence this entry has no mileage or day number. This wasn't discovered until our return and so all the subsequent day numbers are one less than they should be. We beseech the reader to forgive our misplaced jubilation on Mondo Milestones such as day 100 which in reality was day 101. The 'incorrect' day numbers and Mondo Mileages hereafter have not been altered so as to preserve the authenticity of the diaries.

Up and at 'em, driving across the Turkish plains by 0900hrs. The weather had closed in but apart from a slight chill we kept a tight formation and rode well as a five-man team. Mark and Chas kept at the front in case of any further air escapement unhappiness.

Right on cue, and exactly 30 miles into the day's motoring Mark's back tyre was flat. We pulled off the main drag onto a mud track and began the strip down.

Since it was a new inner tube last night, we correctly pre-assessed that the impact Mark had sustained two nights ago must have damaged the wheel/tyre such that one of them was impinging on the virgin tube, if you'll pardon the expression. Sure enough a 1½" nick on the inner wall of the tyre had 'nibbled' a hole in the tube. None of us have ever known of this phenomenon before. We pared it down with the scalpel (purchased at Buck and Ryan), packed it out with silicone gel to negate the nibbling effect due to tyre flexure, patched the cut and heavily powdered the whole tyre and inner tube prior to re-assembly.

During this operation music to our collective ears was heard. Gerald's Greek disco siren!! We looked up and in the distance Gerald and Nick Stubley appeared. This clearly indicated that the chain and false number plate dispatched by Dave Greenhough (Clive's younger brother) on Thursday had arrived early this morning in Ankara. Hence, with new chain fitted to Nick's bike the team was hopelessly behind its self-imposed schedule but reunited once more. It's worth recording that (after less than a 24hr separation) we still felt morale visibly and tangibly soar to Stanley and Livingstone proportions just because we were seven Mondo men again. Almost instantaneously a decision was made to scrap the recce to Trabazon and all steam ahead to Kars. With a destination and a goal we kicked buttocks.

Forty miles later we rolled into Yozgat. This relatively large town is worth describing as it is typical of what we have since become used to in central Turkey: the buildings are all apparently half-finished, red-tiled and surrounded by mud, rubbish and children. The main road through town, despite being asphalt, appears to have been sprayed with a veneer of mud as well. Although the sky was heavy with cumulus-nimbus the whole place was so lifeless and doom laden that it may as well have been deserted.

We pulled over for petrol at a gas station which miraculously accepted Mastercard and Chas revealed his puncture. Same cause precisely as Mark's. Luckily we were adjacent to an Oto Elastiki tyre vendor who helped us out rather than see us do the dance of the three Italian levers. We cooked up supper simultaneously on a huge monolith of old tiles. We filmed single 8 of Chas being mobbed by a squad of beaming children. They were all charmed and entranced by his tyre removal and as he moved around the forecourt they followed him like a little line of ducklings.

We finished the day at a rough campsite down on a meander in the river valley – we talked and drunk Raki on the spit. Our conversations revealed that pre-Mondo not one of us had ever mended a puncture on a motorcycle. That's all changed now.

Turkey

Day 27
Sunday 7 May
Mondo Miles today: 182
Mondo Mileage: 3280

The Mondo Enduro team set an all-time record for striking camp this morning. As usual, we all ignored Austin's urges to get de-rabbed and yet another 11am start beckoned. The situation turned around when a 4 x 4 Sherpa truck rolled up containing two irate Turks (or were they Albanians?) who pointed at the bikes and mouthed off wildly. Unfortunately for them their windows were shut but they had got their point across. Within ten minutes of their departure the Mondo team had packed Rabs, Thermarests and tents and were on their way to a nearby café where we treated ourselves to a slap up breakfast.

And so began a journey so cold and bitter, that Austin was forced to don overgloves, Clive started dancing on his bike and Mark and Chas tried to initiate false stops by looking for punctures and complaining about handling. Gerald had misread the scale on our tyre pressure gauge at the *Oto Elastiki* and Chas's tyre was bursting with 65psi of air in it causing an obligatory stop for emergency deflation.

140 miles from the start of the day we pulled into a Shell Garage for a Nescafe and ended up eating a 3 course lunch of soup, broth and lamb meat with a mound of bread. Austin burst in about an hour later with a classic tale of filming "cock-ups" and high jinks. Having stopped to film a train riding on a single track line he set the camera up between the two rails pointing west. All of a sudden a train sneaked up from the opposite direction leading Austin to make a dive for the microphone which was lying by the tracks and report live as the locomotive rattled past. Epic footage? Unfortunately not, as the camera had failed to record for some reason. A few minutes later the target train rolled in from the west and Austin recorded his piece as all 5 drivers waved and hooted. But alas, the Hi8 had failed to record again. The jury is still out on whether it was human or mechanical error. By some strange coincidence he met up with the same loco at the only place where the road met the track. Much waving and a-hootin' ensued.

30 miles on to a re-fuelling stop at Zara and then over the mountains and a 2190m pass to a welcome cup of Chai at a desolate, smoke-filled roadside café. One hundred miles done and a puncture-free day? Alas no. Mark's back inner tube blew out big time after overtaking a couple of trucks. Somehow he held it together (Chas and Bill following were witness to the carnage that so nearly ensued). We ended up fitting a new back tyre (Gerald is carrying four). Meanwhile, Bill and Nick, on their way ahead stopped to

photograph themselves against a back group of sheep-tending nomads. As Bill set up the shot and Nick posed, a squad of soldiers screeched to a halt and pointed their guns at our man. Realising that he needed a close shave even more than they did, they all became best friends. Bill's camera was then for posterity linked arm-in-arm with the gun-toting Turkish militia.

Once at the campsite, a spoof session for who was to wake us all up in the morning was lost by Gerald after Bill saw through his double-bluff.

Turkey

Day 28
Monday 8 May
Mondo Miles today: 176
Mondo Mileage: 3456

Gerald did us proud with an effective wake-up call but the tyre dilemma was still smouldering, too, and it was finally decided to try and repair Chas and Mark's, which was achieved at the local Oto-Elastiki at the neighbouring Petrol Ofisi station while Austin and Bill headed into Erzincan to ferret out spare inner tubes and food respectively.

Erzincan is pot-hole city, good training ground no doubt for roads to come, and its bypass was just a feint to lure us into pot-hole hell, designed to bring on punctures in not 2 but 7 bikes. Chas, Mark and Bill headed off early to test the new tyre set-up, leaving Austin and others gleefully filming the fitting of the new number plate to his bike. Their next rendezvous was the city limits of Erzerum, where they met late afternoon; Austin had successfully filmed a train at the sign of the Beheaded Sheep, apt symbol of the desolate surroundings, situated opposite the notorious Plain of Erzerum, described in the Cadogan Guide as follows:

"You may have seen the Dakotas or Saskatchewan, Yakutsk or the endless Gobi; you may have travelled the world over in search of the bleakest and emptiest landscapes, but you can't say you've seen it all until you've been on the lonesome Plain of Erzerum."

Here we are in a town whose average temperature equals that of the most northerly town in Norway, and this fact amongst others (7 frozen motorcyclists, flagging morale, puncture-drunk) led to the "Find Hotel" decision. We holed up in a taxi-rank, whence Austin, Mark and Bill dispersed to recce hotels. They returned to find Gerald enjoying that 15 minutes of fame to which we are all entitled at least once in our lives, as Dogu TV interviewed him live, to be broadcast to an unsuspecting nation as part of their Comedy '95 season. Austin had negotiated for us to put our bikes in the foyer of a hotel, but the price couldn't rival Mark's find, which was made even more attractive when Nick found a lock-up garage for the night. We moved in, and headed gratefully for the shower. We emerged pink-bodied and gleaming, and headed out in search of food: supper was found across the road, amongst chandeliers and rubber plants, and gratefully eaten. Over the meal a sweepstake was convened where we all guessed what the official Mondo Mileage would be once we reached Alma Ata in Kazakhstan.

Inevitably, we were all too tired to explore Erzerum, exotic city of the East whose streetscapes have not changed for centuries, but chose the irresistible temptation of a bed and clean sheets: bliss... a good night's sleep is called for, before we head for Kars (the word itself means "snow" in Turkish) and more finger-tip punishing motorcycling, en route for the Armenian border and adventure, entering lands that none of us has yet visited – to go where no Mundoist has gone before.

Turkey

Day 29
Tuesday 9 May
Miles today: 178
Mondo Mileage: 3877

Today was the day Mondo Enduro fought the law and the law won. But the law was so gracious and generous in victory that we will forever be in the debt of the Turkish judiciary.

The day for all of us began tucked up in a warm hotel bed in the eastern metropolis of Erzerum. We were thrilled that last night we had been mistaken for celebrities and had been interviewed for the local TV channel. Our vast expenditure on food and accommodation – about £6 each – had proved excellent value in terms of the collective boost to morale after exactly a month's hard travelling.

We left Erzerum in two groups after an excellent Turkish breakfast of olives, cheese, bread and a curious jam and honey confection. We also got chatting to an American traveller on the road from Rome to China. The book he was reading 'The Seal of the Soul' implied that his journey was more spiritual than mechanical and he seemed somewhat bemused by our visceral disdain of Giles Whittell.

The 170 mile ride to Aliyatia on the Armenian border was not without incident. The first group, consisting of Clive, Austin and Gerald travelled as far as Kars before misfortune struck in the form of a broken chain. The team repaired to a nearby garage, run by the fattest family in Turkey, who kindly offered the use of their angle grinder.

The second group, meanwhile, pressed ahead through some beautiful scenery, not dissimilar to the Glens of Scotland. They stopped briefly in

Horouun for kebabs, a delicious rice and nutmeg pudding and fuel freedom in the form of four 10-litre plastic jerry cans, which by virtue of their plasticness are arguably not really cans.

Nothing so far, not the huge Turkish slogans etched into the mountainside, the florescence of Turkish facial hair, the balloons on the head of the sheep condemned to die in tomorrow's Kurban festival – could prepare us for the humour, farce and adventure of the evening's events.

Both teams of outriders met up briefly in Aliyatia before pressing ahead up the dirt track which we took to be the highway to unfettered motorcycling in Armenia. The rolling pasture was as much Brecon Beacons as gateway to the Caucasus and on the minor summits that the track encountered we espied, far away across the prairie, the amorphous grey jumble of Leninakan, capital of Armenia. The road had downgraded itself to a hard baked clay track and we suspected all was not as clear as the crisp sunny afternoon sky would suggest. The error of our ways was soon impressed upon us when we rolled over a small brow and arrived at the border having ignored an inoffensive notice informing us that we were entering a grade one military zone. There was a sense that this was by no means the bustling international crossroads we had hoped for and Chas filmed Clive saying as much.

Hence, it was with a mixture of concern and amusement that we watched a group of soldiers swarming from their barracks and into all sorts of slit-trenches and other defensive positions. A young second lieutenant lined us up in a row while his eager warriors fingered their assault rifles nervously. Austin's tongue-in-cheek suggestion that we should make a run for it was met with the uncompromising riposte "You can die". What could have been an uneasy stand-off quickly became more relaxed while the bemused subaltern came to terms with the extent of our idiocy. After a brief exchange with an NCO a runner was sent back to the command post, literally running. In a few moments he returned, walking as fast as he dare whilst bearing an ornamental copper tray bedecked with seven steaming glasses of chai. With his buzz cut army hair-do and almost-sloshing beverages he looked like the latest confused fancy dress entrant in one of those speed walking events. Our trip to the Caucasus was off for the time being and we gazed across the rolling plains towards Armenia and what might have been.

Talking to the young officer – a charming bloke by the name of Mehmet Toprak – it emerged that frontier incursions such as the one perpetrated by Mondo Enduro were not part of the daily routine of the Turkish border battalion stationed on the Leninakan border. The last foreigner to attempt a crossing was a solitary Frenchman sometime last year and no-one was quite sure what had happened to him. One wag remarked that the fact that there were seven of us meant that English people were more stupid by a factor of seven. Second Lieut. Toprak confined his response to a nervous smile.

Meanwhile, we had been ushered away from the checkpoint, which despite being stunningly appointed was cold enough to transform our testicles into a chilly gonad gazpacho. Instead we were taken inside the small barracks where we were treated to more chai and a kind of Topic-style chocolate bar.

When the captain arrived from the local army barracks, we tried vainly to impress him by standing ramrod-like to attention. The ruse appeared to work as he smiled benignly and told us to follow him in a 20mph convoy to the nearby army headquarters. He kept our passports.

On arrival at the Divisional HQ we were immediately ushered into the office of the CO – a beaming Major who seemed more amused than concerned by the inept insurgency perpetrated by Mondo. Through a decidedly twitchy monoglot interpreter lance corporal he informed us of the gravity of our infraction in the following terms:

Major: "You must realise this is an important crime for us."

Gerald (who, as the oldest, we are now regularly appointing as the 'chief' in situations like this):   "We are sorry."

Major: "You have entered a restricted military zone"

Gerald: "We were waved through by many previous checkpoints and thought it was ok."

Major: "You could face a jail sentence of five to ten years."

Gerald: "Sorry sir."

Major: "Would you like tea or coffee?"

The non-sequitur hit us with a comic force equal to the complete works of Tony Hancock and we could not restrain a collective giggle. Unmoved, the gallant Major passed round more chocolate bars and cigarettes and ordered another round of chai.

Reluctant to miss out on the biggest foreign presence in Aliyatia since the Mongol invasions, the Brigadier rang up to find out exactly what was going on. "I don't think you have been very clever" was the best he could do by way of a reprimand.

By this stage, however, all thoughts of Midnight Express-style retributions for our trans-caucasian *faux-pas* had been put behind us. Mehmet assured us of his belief that we were not PGG (Kurdish separatist 'terrorists') but 'sympatic' Englishmen who had unexpectedly livened up another night of boredom on one of Europe's most beautiful but coldest frontiers.

By way of assuring us of our new-found status, we were escorted to the soldiers' canteen where we were treated to mutton broth, pillau, apples and a delicious Turkish pastry. After dining we were encouraged en masse to the

Barracks Haman for collective ablutions and a pore-bustin' steam bath. Our nervous conscript escort waited outside denying himself the chance to enjoy our collective punyness. After a towel down and putting our dirty leathers back on we were soon taking coffee with the Major in the officers' mess.

The ante-room itself was a curious environment where kitsch and political incorrectness fought a constant battle for décor supremacy. In the corner was a lonely goldfish, who despite his solitude must have counted his blessings whenever he looked at the stuffed birds and furry animals which seemed to have been stapled to the wall above the TV set. The Major told us about his Cyprus service – an obvious reference point for Austin – and conducted the by now familiar football chit-chat.

It was then announced that we would spend the night at the Turkish government's expense in the local Jandarma (military police) base. Our arrival there was greeted with near mass hysteria by the militia lads who ushered us into a small room and served us yet more chai. The base commandant, called Inysut seemed at first utterly bemused by our presence and gently beckoned Gerald upstairs for a chat in his office while the rest of Mondo waited slightly anxiously. As we drank endless draughts of chai and Coca-Cola, we mused idly about the kinds of agonies being suffered by Gerald at the hands of his Turkish torturers.

We need not have worried. His conversation consisted of a discussion as to the relative merits of Elvis and Elton John. As an act of friendship, Chas handed over his Elvis Presley driving licence (purchased at Graceland) to our grateful host.

Our sleeping quarters was the floor of a cramped room in an adjoining barracks building which served our purposes admirably. A great team building opportunity. As we drifted off into a peaceful slumber we thought what great blokes Mehmet and the Major were and indeed the entire Turkish nation.

We also resolved to break the law more often as a means of securing free drink and victual.

Turkey

Day 30
Wednesday 10 May
Miles today: 109
Mondo Mileage: 3986

The festival of "Kurban" had arrived and we emerged from our deep much needed sleep to yet more hospitality – Turkish TV AM with rose jam, olives, cheese and bread followed by stunning babe TV presenters doing their bit to confuse us as to where exactly this country stands on the issue of women as sex objects.

All 'good times' have to come to an end and to an abrupt one this certainly did. We moved to our bikes for our final departure, which were in front of the barracks surrounded by a perimeter wall and guarded by an armed soldier throughout the night. Couldn't be safer we crassly hoped... but to our dismay we found our bikes' loads had been lightened by our military hosts.

The roll call of missing items consisted of Chas' Pentax camera, Clive's Oakley sunglasses, Gerald's watch, Mark's toy bear, a tin of Quaker's porridge oats and a couple of mouthfuls of tango to wash down the culprit's guilt.

We were shell shocked by this discovery and decided it was best to inform our host, captain Inysut, of the night's activities. He was as alarmed as us and totally embarrassed. He beseeched us to be certain this had happened in *his* barracks and not at the border or back at the Divisional HQ. We *said* we were not sure – but under our breaths we were convinced it had happened here.

There was a lot of activity to follow as orders rang out from the Commander to his NCO's. The entire base was summoned and the young conscripts fell in at the double. The sgt major character bellowed some obviously irate threats and then he called the squad to attention. They fell out and the great search began. It only took a few minutes for the porridge to turn up. Obviously the least desired and least disguised of the booty.

We returned to the Commander's office for more chai and began to explain that we had insurance and needed a statement from him in order to claim back for our mislaid goods; this was very difficult but we persisted. He was into his second paragraph, 1½ hours after the event when the camera surfaced from a dirty plastic bag. It had been found partially buried near the assault course.

Everyone was a lot happier now: Clive's glasses and Gerald's watch would no doubt appear on some squaddie when he finished his national Service.Another setback, Chas's tyre was flat; so we set about repairing whilst Gokca, the captain's daughter, a sweet little 6 yr old, played around us.

Next, the slaughtering of the sheep Sweeney Todd style and followed by the skinning and de-gutting, all which was captured on film. Clive was bloodied along with Gokca by the Turkish barber himself, then the roastings, and we all sat down in the forecourt to dine with the Commander, whilst the last remaining live sheep, spotting our huge appetites, made a dash for the gate. Once again the armed guard failed to notice anything untoward happening for the second time in 12 hours. Thusly, the sheep escaped out into the street.

After lunch we bid farewell to Captain Inysut and took a bearing of true North to attempt the Georgian border. It was not long before we ran into the long arm of the law after our burning up off-road style around a beautiful lake. He asked us to follow him to the station or was it to stay put? Neither was adhered to after our Grade 1 military encounter – we are high on a heady brew of unstoppablity and cheap 75 octane gasoline.

So we rode on, oblivious to the obvious fact that Turkish police have two way radios and were stopped at the next checkpoint with the fuzz asking why we didn't stop at the last checkpoint. Once again our feeble excuses prevailed "the police car just drove off" we claimed and eventually they got bored and let us carry on.

We climbed the next mountain pass but this supposed "A" road coloured red on the map was more like a stage in the Turkish Lombard Rally than a major trunk road. The snow drifts, admittedly bathed in sunshine, were so deep that our spokes became clogged with snow and ice as we powered through them as fast as we dare.

Our off-road skills are non-existent but we scrambled our way through the snow, slush, and potholed mud over to the easier green run on the other side. Austin exploited the fabulous light and captured everything on super 8 rather than the video. We had seen similar woodland settings in Austria and Bavaria; the views were truly magnificent.

It wasn't long before the inevitable happened: another puncture was afoot. Stubley's this time at 5.30pm (our 13th!!!!). So Clive and Mark went on a recce for a campsite whilst the others mended the puncture and Gerald headed for Georgia. This is officially the most beautiful mountain glade so far. Veggie Curry with standard pasta was on the menu in a picturesque setting. We camped on the slopes of this wooded mountain and sat around a roaring fire, this is the life. Lights out around 9.30pm, Georgia tomorrow!

Turkey

Day 31
Thursday 11 May
Miles today: 116
Mondo Mileage: 4102

After a clear night, the campers awoke to very mild drizzle. Stubley and Chas had lingering punctures to fix from the day before. Our objective today is to get into Georgia and out of Turkey. As Mark made the coffee the dawn cloud began to clear to reveal a stunning Alpine view. We imagine that the Alps looked like this about 50 years ago with unmade roads and no tourists. An oxen-drawn wagon appeared and creaked up the rough trail towards us. It was jockeyed by the oldest man we had ever seen. We waved him good morning and in a thrice Clive had given him a fistful of the red Marlboros that he keeps handy for such hearts and minds opportunities.

Bill and Mark went off to recce the frontier post at Sarp. The easy run down to Hopa via Artuih seemed well within our grasp as the bikes wended their way down some steep-sided gorges of mind-blowing scenery. A fast torrent of melt water accompanied us down towards the Black Sea. This enjoyment of arcadia was to be interrupted by a wheel sliding blow-out from Chas. A big spill but he's merely shaken. Removal of the tube showed a flakey patch. Damn that cheap Indian glue. Austin went to meet up with Mark and Bill at Sarp. The weather had picked up with a hot dry breeze blowing up the valley. After a trip to the local *Oto Elastiki* (roadside tyre repair shack) and faffing about, we finally got away as the dusk gathered. We rode up the final pass before Hopa and at the top we came upon the Black Sea with a stunning view of a sunset. And so, onto the frontier at Sarp.

Bill and Mark had spoken to some lorry drivers at the border with encouraging news about trans-Georgian expectations. And so to bed at the

Turkish-Georgian border with a 5am start to get ahead of the Mafia. Tomorrow will test the mettle of the Expedition Mondo Enduro; we aim to punch across Georgia in one day. We were keen to visit Georgia but every where we turn for advice we are met with shaking heads and tutting. It surely cannot be that dangerous? There are *seven* of us and we shouldn't be anxious. Nevertheless, this is not 'our' world, it is the Caucasus, and if the law of the jungle was to apply anywhere in Europe it would be here.What will we meet tomorrow? Hi-jack, armed bandits or none of the above, time will tell...

Turkey

Day 32
Friday 12 May
Mondo Miles today: 135
Mondo Mileage: 4237

(This entry is written by Gerald)

Last night we slept under a lean to, adjacent a hybrid beach café and truckstop. 0500hrs came and I was the first up, as usual. The sky was clear and it remained so for the rest of the day. To the Georgian border, only 800 metres away!! The police, who had to stamp our passports initially, were still asleep. A different set of police told us to wake them up for the first of much stamping and signing. Bill woke the chocolate kiosk man to spend the last of his Turkish Lira; and so to the head of the queue at the Georgian 'entry' gate which did not open until 0700hrs.

At last Mark and Clive were ushered through, the once electrified gates being closed behind them. After what seemed like hours to the rest of us they were informed that our Russian visa is **not** valid as a transit visa for any former Soviet republic. Back in London we had been told it would be. However, the Leonard Rossiter look-a-like they spoke to said we can go back to Trabzon to get a transit visa, apparently the Georgians have had the presence of mind to set up a consulate there. Result, this means at least we don't have to drive 500 miles back to the Georgian embassy in Ankara.

So, we about turned and had to re-enter Turkey.   Aggro.   This required getting all the Turkish stamps and signatures unstamped and un-signed.   A brief discussion took place and it was decided that a longer discussion was needed.   Along to a small beach where all the options were aired and it was decided to *all* go to Trabzon for two reasons; to be in a position to get the visa's *and* check on boat departures to Sochi in Russia, thus by-passing Georgia altogether.

It was estimated that Trabzon was about 160 miles so we were all pleasantly surprised to find that it was only 120 miles. A brief rendezvous at the outskirts and the tasks were divided up.   I went to the Georgian Consulate with Mark. He stayed with the bikes and I went off. The clipping from the Lonely Planet Update Newsletter was deadly accurate in its directions and information. A few minutes wait saw the Consul stamping up the passports at $15 a time. No queues, no 'letter of introduction', no aggro. Half way through Nick burst in, "Stop, Stop, there's a boat to Sochi tonight" "Gulp"!! We approached the Consul to explain that we may not need the visas at all, but stamp went another $15 visa into another passport. They closed at 17:00, which was in two hours time. We left the passports with him.   The others were at a pleasant square with tables, chairs and sunshades. Trabzon is like a Turkish Cannes.

I collected Mark and yet another discussion ensued. This time there were two choices. Georgian Visa-ed back to the border or boat to Russia tonight. The deadline was set at 1600hrs. Also at the café we encountered two Belgians and a German but they didn't know each other. The Belgians were *walking* around the world and so was the German, quite coincidentally. The options were presented and discussed. It was a very pleasant location for such an important decision. The round the world walkers clearly had a more leisurely tempo than us and were perturbed by the anxious and urgent tone of our 'getting out of Turkey' conference. They don't realise how we are in a cul-de-sac and any chance to move the itinerary eastwards is to be embraced.

After a few hours it was decided that the Georgian route was the one to go for. The one proviso was that tomorrow should be a rest and maintenance day. Clive and Bill went to scout a rough campsite nearby and the remainder would follow shortly. After collecting the visas I walked past a few tool shops and soon found what I was looking for. The mother of all foot pumps for only £7. It looks very 1950s and is the tall barrel plunger type. I expect the air raid warden guy in Dad's Army would have owned one. Our bicycle size hand-pump needs two billion 'pumps' to inflate a tyre and if the repair is flawed then you're pumping fruitlessly for ages before you can safely say that it's not taking the air. On the way to the campsite we met Bill and Clive coming the other way. Their choice of slot was not as nice as we had been led to believe. An alternative quick recce saw us crashing out in the ground floor of a block of flats still under construction. Mark had bought some chicken and rice (from a roadside stall) so the only cooking done was coffee. After a can of Tuborg (for a change) it was to bed, knowing that there was nothing to get up for tomorrow.

Turkey

Day 33
Saturday 13 May
Mondo Miles today: 0
Mondo Mileage: 4237

Every time we wake up it seems strange as we never really acquaint ourselves with our campsites properly the night before. Last night's partially completed multi-storey complex was true to this rule of Mondo thumb and our group arrangement (Austin on a plinth of planks, Chas, Nick and Bill on a mat of lumber, Gerald with head catching the morning rays, Mark tucked away near the lift shaft) was as bizarre as we could remember.

Our surreal rough camping experience was not over as the trickle of Turkish labourers arriving on site turned to a stream; however, not one suggestion of a harsh word and there was no suggestion that we were trespassing. Instead, handshakes, beaming smiles and a clearly perceptible joy that of all the building sites available, we chose theirs.

As we planned to unwind with a lie in, a few feathers were ruffled as our Turkish worker ants went about their chores and hence accelerated our departure.

Out on the verge, Mark practised the harmonica, and then bemused some roof-top Turks with homage to "The Jerk" as they jigged and "yeee-hahed" hopelessly out of time.

A forward recce had been sent off in an attempt to secure a 'private' Black Sea beach which we would make our base for a day's R & R and EMM (Essential Mondo Maintenance).

The ten mile threshold from the campsite yielded nothing. However, we noticed an old section of road (by now overgrown with grass) that rounded a spur and had been blocked off from the new carriageway by a huge mound of earth and rubble. The setting was idyllic albeit visible from the road. This obstruction was defeated by an improvised trials section but everyone made it over. Mondo Enduro de-packed after an admirable 10 mile haul!

Oil and bread were purchased, the weather seeing the lads stripped down to shorts and the heat-sink black leathers were gladly discarded. Sunburn beckoned, and Clive didn't need much coaxing! As has become the form on rest/maintenance days, time slipped by so quickly that we couldn't believe that by dusk all we had done was change the oil and write a few postcards.

Nick suggested we spend the night here seeing as all our kit was by now spread over a huge area. This was met with varying degrees of acclaim. Tomorrow is planned to be huge mileage, but more significantly, the psychological push across Georgia. Our present location is 90 miles from the Turkish: Georgian frontier so staying here would mean a 4.45am start and a long drive before breakfast. We mulled as only Mondo can and eventually it seemed that we'd stay put and attempt what would probably be a 400 miler tomorrow.

To get fuel problems to one side, Austin purchased three more ten litre containers which basically turn the range of each bike up to around 450 miles.

Another staggering sunset, a meeting with the local landowner (quite charming and in no way aggrieved at our trespass) and an attempt to clean out the larder (finally solved by doing the washing up in it); local children gleefully ran back to their house to fill our empty Pepsi 'water' bottles.

A full moon looked down on us as we snuggled down unfeasibly early. Everyone is nervous about Georgia but if we had known what the morrow would bring on the *Turkish* side of the border we would have slept less than fitfully.

Turkey/Georgia

Day 34
Sunday 14 May
Mondo Miles today: 106
Mondo Mileage: 4343

Written by Mark at 12.10pm (Turkish time):

We rose at 4.30am, surprisingly refreshed, ready to face all that the Caucasus could throw at us. Riding in formation (Chas, Clive, Austin, Mark, Nick, Bill, Gerald) we ate up the 90 miles to Sarp. The idea was to practice riding as a tight knit blob and at speed. We surmised that this would make us less susceptible to the ambitions of the heavily armed highwaymen that we have been lead to believe have all but taken control of Georgia's trunk roads. At 6.45am disaster struck...

A few km beyond Findikli, on a long, straight stretch of road, an old crone was tottering about on the other side of the road. Chas hooted repeatedly and started to slow down. She saw him at the last minute and stopped her crossing (in the middle of the road) as Chas and Clive went past. All of a sudden she appeared to panic and made a dash so as to cross in front of Austin. I was riding right behind him. He swerved to the right, to the left, back to the right, but she mirrored his every swerve, and the last one brought them into violent contact. She seemed to jump in front of the bike. He couldn't have missed her. They both went down and I piled straight into the flailing jumble of Austin's bike, skin, bone and shawl. Bill and Gerald, riding behind, tell me it was the most spectacular crash they have ever seen. My whole bike did a somersault and landed further down the road. As I picked myself up I heard Austin's "Oh my God" and saw the old woman lying in a motionless heap by the side of the road.

Austin, Clive and I picked her up. Incredibly, she was conscious. We were all running on adrenalin but the force and speed of the impact was horrendous, Austin was easily doing 45mph when she had tottered out into our swarm of bikes. Austin was the group's unofficial doctor and was checking for her ABC vital signs when a car came around the corner. Incredible, it was a taxi! Nick flagged it down, mimed the word 'accident' and we heaved her whimpering frame into the taxi. The combined effect of hefting her skinniness and blood smeared face and headscarf was pretty chilling. She felt like a set of golf clubs in a leathery bag. Austin jumped in the cab, Clive and Chas followed on their bikes. First stop, the local doctor – his verdict – Mrs Brady was tired! He stuck a drip in her for good measure and sent her off to Rize hospital. She pulled the drip out indignantly and complained all the way to Rize – a good sign.

All this news was courtesy of Chas, who also informed us that Austin and Clive were on their way to Findikli police station to give statements. We settled down for a long wait, fearing the worst.

14.40 (Turkish time) There has been lots of comings and goings in the past couple of hours. Bill and Chas rode down to Findikli police station. They returned within half-an-hour. Police came along to look at the scene of the accident and Nick pointed out the patch of rapidly congealing blood on the asphalt that neatly marked the touchdown spot.

They had pieces of paper (in Turkish) signed by Austin and bearing his thumbprint. They were very calm and kept saying "no problem". The relatives (we think) arrived to collect the old woman's shoes and look for something else (not found). They were full of "no problem" as well. I know that most of us *would* have a problem if we were knocked down on our way to town (by seven Turks), even if it were our fault. As usual, lots of Turks stop simply to gawp at our heavenly machines.

No sign of Austin and Clive by 1500hrs.

What happened to Austin (in his words):

At the time I regarded it as an act of Satan that this senseless old woman had chosen *my* bike with which to make her suicide pact, yet also an act of God that the first car on the scene should be a local taxi that was swift to drive 'Mrs Brady' to the local Health Centre!

I, like the rest of Mondo Enduro, have no third party insurance for the bike. I was convinced that Mrs Brady was about to die through shock if nothing else. Let the reader be informed though, that she had received a *full on* 45mph impact from my bike – glancing blow it was not. I couldn't believe she was still alive when we first dashed over to her limp stick-like body. I reckon she was about eighty years old. Anyway, my head was filled with selfish thoughts of self-preservation (shame on me) and evading a nationwide manhunt.

The taxi took us the 20 miles down to Rize hospital where she was treated. It was by now clear to me that she would be fine. Amazing Mondo moment – nobody knew where I had gone so I was certain that it would be many hours before I again laid eyes on a Mondo man. Incredibly, as we pulled into a back street of Rize, the cab/ambulance passed Clive and Chas who were parked up, but pulled out to follow us as we passed them. However, this was a fluke, they had no idea I was in that particular vehicle and were only alerted to this when I opened the door and shouted back to them! They followed the cab up to the A&E dept. Reunited, what luck!

Meantime, at the hospital, I was interviewed by the in-house detective. He carried a cool shoulder holster and as the adventure unfolded it became clear he was an amenable chap. With Clive hanging around as moral support and with the help of the ubiquitous local 'translator' I acted out the story of how I had come to hit Mrs Brady.

My audience had by now swollen to include most of the porters, the traditional quota of middle aged men just hanging around and sundry nurses and policemen. I envisaged this was going to be my only chance to make my case and so I redefined melodramatic and with the aid of diagrams had the Police Tec on my side even before I'd got to the part when I ploughed into the hapless old woman!

I was relieved when the policeman said that Mrs Brady's injuries were not consistent with an impact speed of 50km/h, as I had claimed, instead he promptly changed his report to read that I had been riding at a modest 20km/h.

Clive further sweetened the locals by producing Camels at opportune moments. It was interesting to see that I was breathalysed (0930 Sunday) and that Mrs Brady's statement was not signed but instead bore her thumbprint.

An unexpected development occurred when an unknown Turk began to play the Devil's advocate, most passionately, and was clearly not happy with my claim that the old woman had literally <u>run</u> into the path of these seven (unlucky for some) infidel motorcycles. He was soon enjoined by an older but clearly junior policeman/security guard character. It was obvious that the latter was losing face by *not* being part of the interrogation team and he was not going to make it easy for this youngster with whom he had to work in this sleepy Hippocratic crime non-career waste ground. Disaster, the main policeman emerged having gently interviewed the old woman in the ward. He wore a serious expression and stated that her version was different to mine; she had been standing on the verge, waiting to cross the road, when suddenly we had driven into her. O reader, I promise you, this isn't true but it didn't bode well for the quick release Clive and I had in mind.

After much negotiation the A&E detective made a call and a Jandarma Land Rover turned up to take me away. Fortunately it was just back to their barracks, a few miles from the scene of the accident. More questions, sketches and the inevitable mindless discourse on Manchester United. More phonecalls to their HQ and after a $6 fine and a signature I was free. I cannot believe it.

Back to Mark's story:

15.10hrs Clive turned up telling us that the British Embassy was now involved and Austin was going to be held in Rize until next week! We'd all be stuck in Turkey for another month. Suddenly, Austin appeared from the side of the road, so it was all a huge wind-up. We tried to bundle Clive over the side but he was too quick for us (as always). Austin's version of events fails to say what a relief it was to have him with us and in one piece. We had fully envisaged a month or so of court grief. Instead Austin had been let off with a small fine and we were back on the plot. Up into the mountains above Hopa to a campsite found courtesy of Nick. A wonderful place with snow-capped mountains and full moon rising. Nick and Gerald cooked while Chas went on a mercy mission to Rize and returned with hard liquor. The landowner turned up after dark (with a mate dressed in a Megadeth T-shirt) and shared our booze. We settled down to a quiet night under the star. Maybe we'll get into Georgia tomorrow.

Georgia

Day 35
Monday 15 May
Mondo Miles today: 265
Mondo Mileage: 4616

A fitful sleep (showers and a full moon keeping even Gerald awake) was scanty preparation for our 5am wake up made even ruder by the fact that Clive and Chas's Thermarests had joined the Puncture Club. Nonetheless we arose briskly; keen to tackle the Georgian border as early as possible. Our paranoia that we will be flagged down at a bandit road block, robbed then murdered: has spawned a strategy of literally not stopping once over the border. We have enough gas to get us the 340 miles to the Azerbaijani frontier and are up this early so we can make it there in one day, such is the fear of rough camping in Georgia.

We rode down from our mountain hideout and stopped for fuel before hitting for a second time the dust road to Sarp and freedom from Turkey. The by-now familiar customs formalities were speedily gone through and we found ourselves on Georgian soil before we knew it. The border post is a ramshackle affair perimetered with wonky fences festooned with a barbed wire that somehow seems more menacing than normal. The muddy compound is mostly staffed by teenagers in raggedy mustard colour Red Army fatigues. Upon encountering us they seemed both nervous and cocky but we reminded ourselves that only a few years ago this would have been where the southern limit of the Soviet Union met the decadent West, small wonder it looks like a set from 'Funeral In Berlin'. Clive and Bill were the first through and were met with incredulous laughter when they rolled up at Customs – the language barrier was overcome when a blonde babe was wheeled out before our eyes (on springs) to interrogate us ("Do you carry more than $50?" – Gulp!).

Customs formalities lasted about 30 seconds (a conservative estimate), as Bill reassured our gorgeous questioner that dollars were few in our luggage and we were impecunious adventurers – as the frontier we had most feared proved to be the easiest to cross to date, and we were waived through with backslaps and smiles. Austin fitted his van number plate whilst hiding between two lorries in no-man's land. His van V5 ownership document, with all the engine numbers etc altered with biro and validated with his home-made stamp, satisfied the Georgian customs officials. We are incredulous.

We hit the road North along the Black Sea coast to Poti – super-twisty and like a British C-Road, with enough hairpins to hold even Rapunzel's hair in a Beehive – before turning east on the M27 (not quite the Portsmouth

Road) towards Tiblisi. This was peppered with Police road blocks, not a single one bothering to stop Mondo Enduro as it blazed its inexorable trail towards Central Asia. It's fair to say that few heads remained unturned as 7 bikes purred past the cattle, disused factories/army bases/factories/sex-madam which bordered the road. We had all been led to believe that this is a country almost in a state of anarchy, and that at least 2 of us would exit with bullet wounds, but today's ride proved the doom merchants wrong;

Andy Daventry – British Consulate in Istanbul: "Under no circumstances go to Georgia" –

Gordon Brewer – BBC Newsnight journalist: "I only got through the checkpoints because I'm BBC"

Andy Bell's mate: "You won't get 100 metres before you get everything nicked".

Apart from the extremities of weather, Georgia has so far been without any problems, we only hope that tomorrow's entry will tell a similar story. Moral: don't believe the moaning minnies, just get amongst it.

Georgia itself is in a state of decay, looking as though it had been emptied or lying fallow for 2 years before anyone was allowed to return. Everything is rusty, and yet some things remain impressive such as Workers Monuments, bus shelters, War memorials and the almost universal availability of petrol. Also remarkable is the fact that everything seems to have been designed by a Central Design Agency, with an undeniably individualistic attitude and vision. The number of luxury western cars is also very evident, the only indication so far of the corruption which is supposedly so widespread here yet which to us has remained hidden. Let us hope that Chas' entry will not make Bill eat his optimistic words.

We called a halt after 100 miles in Georgia and enjoyed a light lunch and rest stop (Bill's balance pipe sprung a leak again) before hitting the road again (literally in Mark's case, as he misjudged a particularly nasty corner and found his bike upside down for the second time in 24 hours). Another stop beckoned at the 200 mile point, and tea was enjoyed as it started to pour down: just as Mark announced that his rear tyre was once again punctured. We slung a poncho between two bikes and got to work sheltered from the relentless Georgian rain. We then headed towards the capital Tiblisi and the Azerbaijani border, but a ferocious storm set in to foil our ambition and the miles remained uneaten in the rain. We were stopped by the Police who advised us that under no circumstances were we to stop as it was too dangerous, so needless to say, we stopped a few km down the road, pissed off with the rain and unwilling to go any further. We spotted a burned out abandoned factory and not fancying to camp, headed towards it – we blended down a track but it veered away from the concrete ruin we had in our sights and instead lead towards a brick bungalow in a glade. We beseeched the Georgian gentleman we encountered (Lee van Cleef lookalike) with the most ridiculous mime explaining our miserable sodden state and he was perfectly willing to give us his (unoccupied) house as shelter for the night! Hurrah for Georgia!!

Once settled, he produced his homebrew Vodka which was at least 150% proof (and which accounts for the inadequate and poorly written log entry for today) and we warmed up internally if not externally. We fraternised with our by-now perfected mime routine, the net (proof) result being another bottle of intestine stripper to encourage sleepiness, but not before Chas, Clive and Gerald had fed our grumbling bellies. Our host and his father (war-hero with more gold in his teeth than the Georgian Maritime Bank, Stalin-lover, 90 years old but all marbles intact) retired. We are not sure where they live. That was our cue to turn in, vodka and a long day of excitement ensuring a deep and satisfying slumber.

Azerbaijan

Day 36
Tuesday 16 May
Mondo Miles today: 200
Mondo Mileage: 4816

When the official history of Mondo is written (though on reflection, this *is* it), our journey through Georgia will surely be one of its most glorious, if uneventful, chapters.

We awoke to a beautiful morning with the sun streaming through the cracked windows of our impromptu "dacha". Soon, its life-giving rays were micro-waving an assortment of steaming socks, boots and grundies left sodden in last night's inundations.

We left our slightly bemused but utterly charming hosts to contemplate their strange Mondo encounter and what looked like a complex clutch problem on the family Lada. Father Abraham – he of the gold gnashers and distinguished Great Patriotic War record – was interviewed for our film archive. Stubley brandished the microphone at him and said, in English; "Can you tell us about all your medals from the war?" Grandpa could not understand him yet on cue delivered a perfectly lucid response in a language (either Georgian or Russian) that none of us can understand. It will be many months from now before we are able to find out what he just said!

It was 9.30am when we finally hit the road after much flesh-pressing and pledges of eternal amity. We took the opportunity to photograph the surreal shell of an abandoned petrol station at the bottom of the road. Its outside walls were decorated with a highly appropriate mural depicting the custom cars that apparently formed the Soviet version of Whacky Races. The entire work (on all four walls) was a mosaic, thousands of pieces each the size of a postage stamp creating a catalogue of truly imaginative auto design that we marvelled was only ever to exist in the imagination of a local artist clearly dreaming more of the Indianapolis 500 than bumper wheat harvests. It would be great to track down the team that actually created this fabulous work. Back in the UK this would be a listed structure but here, smashed up and forgotten; it was a melancholy commentary on a socialist dream as shattered as the rusting petrol pumps nearby.

On we rolled through more grotesquely potholed roads, occasionally rousing the traffic police from their ennui. The Tiblisi by-pass presented an eerie vista over a hideous cityscape of crumbling apartment blocks and empty roads. The bus depot looked like it had been the recent victim of an artillery bombardment and was littered with the hulls of trolley-buses. The road was deteriorating badly now and was scarred by deep potholes filled with water from last night's rains. In places the entire surface seemed to be falling in on itself as if dismantled by an unseen hand. A bit like Georgia itself, really.

Of the much-feared Mafia there remained no sign. This was strictly motocross country and no place for your flash western automobile. Ladas and clapped out buses weaving a path through the shattered highway made a tragicomic sight. So Georgia, which had been on our minds for so long and for so many reasons, presented Mondo with no more problems than a heavy rainstorm and, after one particularly venomous pothole, erratic handling.

On we rolled towards Azerbaijan's border, along roads flanked by outbursts of scarlet poppies, through countryside sometimes resembling North Derbyshire and past towns like Rostov which despite having huge welcome signs in three scripts (Georgian, Cyrillic and Latin) still looked singularly uninviting.

We came across the border almost by surprise when we were stopped at a ramshackle concrete cube purporting to be Georgian Customs. After initially requesting a $70 bribe and eyeing up Bill's sunglasses lasciviously, they sent us on our way.

The Azerbaijani frontier sported a mad flying saucer shaped control post but presented us with few problems apart from one irksome soldier who nearly blinded himself whilst examining Clive's mace spray. Bill and Clive exercised some of that by now famous charm to secure the cherished visa stamp which showed a small crescent moon and star symbol. Any doubts that we were once again in Turkish territory was dismissed by a Customs Official who informed us that everyone from Azerbaijan to the Altai mountains was a 'Turkey brother'. We would probably have guessed as much anyway by the cars with their absurd multi-toot horns.

After buying food and Fanta from some handsome women at a roadside stall, we ate lunch and more miles to the town of Kazakh. There we met with a less than welcoming reception from some flakey looking solders, one of whom was the image of the Butcher of Baghdad himself. Was this to be the moment of roadside robbery that the doom merchants had foretold? There was a palpable mood amongst both us *and* the soldiers that in the next two minutes, it could all kick off. After confiscating our passports, they took us to the police station (phew) where a large crowd gathered before a short but portly Superintendent came out to shake each of our hands and apologise for our trouble.

By way of recompense for the heavy handling we had received from the army checkpointeers, he then ordered us to be escorted to the city limits. There didn't seem to be a police car available so a lime green Lada was commandeered, a 12V blue flashing light clipped to the battery and held onto the roof by the passenger. The farce culminated with the Lada rallying across town in the style of The French Connection despite there being no other vehicles on the road. We could barely keep up.

By now Clive was on reserve and we faced our first petrol drama in the former Soviet block. We found another abandoned gas station and were just about to drive off when out came an old man from the seemingly defunct 'booth'. Result, he would accept U.S. bucks. Actually, it all went rather swimmingly with 150 litres purchased for a cool $45. We are talking 90p a gallon here, lads.

After a brief break to fix another puncture on Mark's long-suffering tyre (replaced by the Trabzon spare) we put another 80 odd miles behind us before Gerald's chain snapped again. While Austin and he affected roadside repairs, aided by Clive, the rest of the gang made for a scrubland campsite recce'd by Stubley.

Unfortunately, a small stream with treacherously muddy banks proved too much for Chas, Mark and Gerald who all tipped their bikes in dramatic fashion. Supper followed, prepared by Mark and Bill and featuring Azerbaijani apples and rice by way of variation from our usual fayre, and then bed. Our only disturbance being discovered by a gushingly friendly Azerbaijani, fired by Georgian vodka, who was determined (out here in the semi-desert) to procure us women.

As a full moon rose, we contemplated the long straight 200 mile drive to Baku and the hope of a boat to Turkmenistan.

Azerbaijan

Day 37
Wednesday 17 May
Mondo Miles today: 207
Mondo Mileage: 5023

Baku here we come!!

6am and the first phase of the Mondo Enduro Squadron rose to take flight by 7.15. We left our campsite unscathed after all successfully traversing the water hurdle and went on to complete our first 95 miles like a breeze.

The scenery was taking a turn from scrubland to lunar landscape when we stopped at the half way mark to Baku for a pot of chai and a loosening of bowels.

A 40 min repose but once rolling again we were engulfed in a vicious sandstorm that scoured our flesh and consumables. This eventually subsided to reveal the emerald green Caspian Sea. We felt like a small group of motorcycling Israelites fleeing the sandy stranglehold of The Pharaoh. This was a refreshing sight and we hoped it would be taking us on to new and pleasant lands.

This Western side of Baku was similar to that of an early Dallas except their derricks were not wooden but steel. It was an endless forest of 'nodding donkeys' but they were totally static, not nodding – it was more like a ghost town than an oil producing city. The eerie decay of this latest scene of post Soviet industrial petrification may make the drive into Baku one of the defining Mondo Moments. Such is our ineptitude as 'chroniclers of our times' this striking scene was committed to neither video, single 8 nor 35mm stills.

We moved directly to the British Embassy where Clive and Austin met Tom Young (British Ambassador) and his assistant Clive. We had hoped to blend some accommodation and food. Instead we were greeted by a bit of a stiff and his sidekick who grinned at us all the time.

We gave them our good news on Georgia and in return found out most of the information we required. Tom Young's wife, however, was a sweetheart and was delighted to meet us. She immediately offered to send back any letters to the UK for us. Upon reflection we wished the Ambassador was not there and that his wife had greeted us instead; we would have loved to stay a night in Baku to be pampered by her.

Lochin, the Ambassador's guide and driver, was real cool Baku smoothie. Sporting his Wayfarer Raybans he showed us to the best petrol station with the highest octane levels. This was needed for the official embassy white Land Rover Discovery, easily the flashest motor in town.

We were then directed to obtain our transit visas – as apparently we would not get out of Azerbaijan without them. Quite why we were so breezily waved into this country from Georgia, *without* transit visas is of course a mystery. Anyway, Lochin was tasked by his embassy overseers to take Mark and all our passports to an obscure fifth floor office somewhere downtown. Lochin brokered the whole process and in fact seemed to be on first name terms with the bored official who stamped and stamped. For this sole nugget of assistance to us DBNs (Distressed British Nationals) we all agreed that a lifetime of paying income tax to fund the Foreign and Commonwealth Office was very little to ask. They were $20 each (no photo required).

Back to the RV at British Embassy where we met Robin Forrest in charge of Expats for Baku – he worked for the DTI and reported to Michael Heseltine himself. There is an incredibly strong sensation here that this is a country where anything is possible. Oil rich, newly independent and keen to emerge from under the Russian shadow and use those petro-dollars to go it alone.

Robin Forrest was a Scot who lived in Derbyshire and was chuffed to meet the Mondo Men and knew friends of the Friends (*Friend* is Mark's surname).

We found the latest news on our boat out of Baku; there is a service every four days and the next one was tonight! Visas were no problem, ferry to Krasnodovsk (Turkmenistan) going 6-7pm (Baku-Krasnodovsk is the Dover-

Calais of the Caspian Sea). Price is a whopping $95 which got talked up to $135 after negotiation!!!!– unlucky Mondo Enduro! This was caused by a language barrier of mountainous proportions. All of us were in Baku and we were set to go. Lochin had already alluded to the idea that no visit to Baku was complete without a visit to Disco-Bar 'Magnums'. This will have to wait for another time as Mondo Enduro didn't wait for the dust to settle... we were all set to advance ever eastwards.

Down to the port to RV and Chas had run out of petrol.We were all bemused by this as none of us (including him) had even gone onto reserve, so he ended up almost pushing his bike out of Azerbaijan. Passports and V5's were produced for Customs and Border Officials and Austin's false number plate and doctored ownership document makes its third successful border crossing (although first inspection). Forgery rules!!!

After many bribe attempts we boarded the ship, a stark contrast to the P & O and Greek ships we had taken. Total mayhem and confusion reigned as all the vehicles were parked to the rear of the ship. We parked the bikes ourselves and took any valuable items we cherished off the bikes as all and sundry were wandering around down there.

Another result – we secured two cabins which wasn't so bad for $135 – we didn't have to worry about accommodation and we would cover 300 miles without a single rev from the bikes, all whilst we slept. This was the ropiest boat any of us had ever seen.

In the restaurant we were served some nice soup followed by a grim burger and noodles (typical commie grub). We met two other tourists! A friendly couple composed of a Kiwi lawyer (65ish) and his Austrian wife: (they had just spent 12 days in Georgia and were taking a similar route to ourselves. They seemed to have made it their quest to holiday well and truly off the beaten track and they gave us some good news; Alaska airways have expanded west into the old USSR and have started up flights from a place called Magadan (far NE of Siberia) to Alaska and Seattle. It looked as if an alternative route from Vladivostok was plausible but naturally, they had no idea if it would be possible to put seven trail bikes on the plane.

Extra news: Chas got offered sex for $2 in a toilet by a female attendant but settled for just the loo for a $1... meanwhile, Mark got his hair washed by a toilet attendant. So there we have it, Vladivostok has been usurped as our destination by Magadan. The reason is simply that going there will allow us to drive for even further in Russia. Result.

Caspian Sea

Day 38
Thursday 18 May
Mondo Miles today: 148
Mondo Mileage: 5171

Our first real bed in a long time, and with an ETA at Krasnodovsk of 11.00am we slept in too. The night's passage had been smooth as we lay in our roach infested bunks. Austin, Gerald and Nick in one cabin and Mark, Bill, Chas and Clive in the other. Peering out of the porthole we could see Turkmenistan in the distance across a beautiful lime green Caspian Sea. Although the Caucasus was a new experience for us the impending hybrid of desert and USSR has us all itching with excitement. It is a part of the world about which no information exists but we know of a chap from Bristol called Sean Hawker who came through here about 6 years ago pre-glasnost. In fact we all went to see him (in Bristol) after reading about his Central Asian odyssey in British Bike Magazine. He did it on an old 1950s side valve BSA which being of a WWII design effortlessly digested the truly crap Soviet gasoline. Back then you couldn't travel freely without a government approved guide escorting you throughout the country! We can barely comprehend this level of government control. He reminisced that the guide turned up driving, wait for it, a beat up old Lada and incurred so many punctures that they exhausted *his* tyre repair kit!

Meanwhile, back down in the seedy restaurant, shell suited Turkmen smoked their first cigarettes of the day. The laundry women came back for $2 more and was politely refused. The half full ferry seems to be in rapid decline as no-one can afford to travel any more, who knows how long this service will continue. It's hard to see what bouncing Azerbaijan needs from its poor neighbours apart from unskilled labour.

With the Caucasus behind us, it now feels like real uncharted territory, with the Central Asian towns now on our horizon. It will be interesting to see how religion has coped under and since the Soviet Union. In Georgia and Azerbaijan, there was little evidence of mass religion.

After exchanging greetings with some entrepreneurial Azeri, Chas came back with a bag half full of garlic. The people concerned were on the garlic run to Almaty. Each had built a cocoon out of old cardboard around the driving seat of their Lada, rather like a bus driver's. This allowed the passenger seats (front and rear) to be filled to the brim up to the roof with loose bulbs of garlic (boot already full). These two chaps are planning to drive their two garlic-mobiles the 1700 miles to Almaty in Kazakhstan.

Engines started and the fery hold filled with diesel fumes as the vehicles jostled onto the gangway. There they waited and waited in the boiling midday sun for the Turkmen to start the formalities. The 3-day transit visa and motorcycle permit was a hefty $70 each. Some of the officials had vaguely oriental features, yet more evidence of our progress. This is where the Turkish/Caucasian features are giving over to the Mongol/Chinese look. The converted hotel is now Customs with its intelligent Customs officer who, on seeing *William* in Bill's passport said: "Do you know William Shakespeare". "My favourite play is Macbeth!" As the $50 sign on the wall announced, the price was official so we had to bite the bullet. A shed load of dollar bills were handed over and the anti-counterfeit squad got into operation. The reader should know that seeing as these new republics of the former USSR do not have embassies in London it was quite impossible to learn what Visa requirements there are. We have arrived here with no 'paperwork' save a Russian visa so the fact that they let us enter at all, without having secured a visa in advance, is cause for considerable celebration.

One Turkman soldier sat on the bench in the shade preening himself using a mirror and cleaning his fingernails. And so we wended our way out of Krasnodovsk (in process of being renamed Turkmenbashy) at about 4.30pm. Five hours to clear customs but we're in! Result!

Mondo Enduro meets its first camel. The main Ashkabad road was of high quality. Desert scrub surrounded the riders as we headed first southeast and then east. Road signs gave warning of the camels and indeed we saw loads grazing by the roadside. There's not much to eat out here so they must be very easy to please. What would happen if you put a camel in a lush Devon pasture? Would it mind?

We rode on until it was nearly dark and the landscape turned to a sandy desert with long straight roads flanked by the telegraph poles. As the sun went down Austin filmed a super eight shot of all the bikes traversing an embankment with the clean golden desert sun setting behind us. He said it was the best shot filmed thus far. We have to send the Super 8 to Japan to get processed so we will not see what he means till we get back to England in a year's time. This was the Kara Kum desert and was our host for the night. On the endless sand flats that surround us, finding a place to set up camp was effortless. Gerald found a waterhole for the washing up but it turned out to be heavily saline and wouldn't make lather. The temperature waned and the stars came out. We decided to rise early tomorrow to beat the heat of the day, quietly ecstatic that we are on The Silk Road!

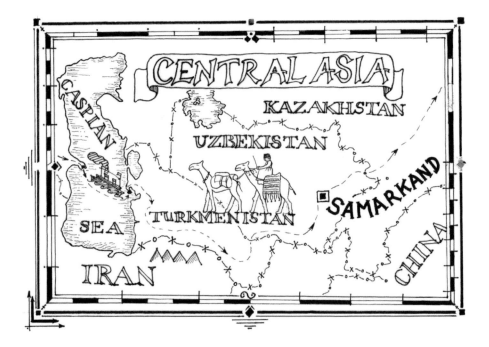

Turkmenistan

Day 39
Friday 19 May
Mondo Miles today: 274
Mondo Mileage: 5145

Awoke to a cold and windy flat desert. We departed camp at 06.50hrs deciding not to have any food or drink until 100 miles were done. In the event 85 miles were the limit for Gerald's knee, so we stopped in a bus shelter, partially out of the wind. We finally consumed the porridge unstolen in the Turkish Barracks whilst Bill brewed up seven coffees. Mark had an electrical fire when his cigarette lighter got stuck in the on position and got too hot. Gerald was unable to undo the cheap combination lock in time to release the fire extinguisher, so precious drinking water was used to tame the inferno. A Ural sidecar outfit spluttered up to our bikes and drew to a lazy halt. It was a husband and wife coupling and he was curious about our machines. We chatted in Chas and Mark's broken Russian but it took a few minutes to notice that he only had one arm (and no prosthetic).

We pressed on until 1300hrs and while we had a quick break a gentleman pulled over who was clearly the worse for drink. He must have been of note since he had a driver who was clearly at his bidding. He was fascinated by the bikes and quickly offered us bread, cheese and vodka to cement this new Anglo-Turkmenistani entente. The quick break turned into a long break until he was finally driven off by his chauffeur, extremely tired and emotional. On to Aschabad and a haggle over the price of fuel. 180 litres for $30, all in the burning heat. This is the capital city and Stubley informed us that British troops had been rushed here from Persia (Iran) in 1920 in a futile bid to stem the tide of Bolshevism seeping down from the north. History lesson over, we sourced fuel, food and water to ensure the continued momentum of the Mondo Expeditionary Farce.

Five of us went to the new airport whilst Clive and Austin went shopping. The airport building had just been completed and there was a heavy police presence because the new President was flying off to Moscow this afternoon. Stubley explained that a recent Radio 4 special on this chap had not painted a picture of a man who was specifically enamoured with democracy or indeed *anything* that did not increase the personal fortune of him or his immediate family.

We parked right by several police who we assumed would keep an eye on the bikes. Imagine our delight when we entered the building to find it air conditioned. We pitied our two team members shopping out in the afternoon inferno.

The airport is greatly under-used at the moment. There were no flights to anywhere outside the former USSR. To the snack bar for a cold coke and to compose a fax back to HQ for some replacement bike parts ($18) phew!! The washroom facilities were used and abused by all of us and despite our Pepsi bottles not fitting under the tap we filled up with water as best we could. We encountered the General Manager of the airport and he spoke excellent English. He revealed that the last international arrival had been a freight 'special' from Newcastle upon Tyne! Apparently this is home to the printing works of security document giants De La Rue and the plane was packed with a fresh consignment of newly minted Turkmeni passports. We chatted for a while but he was a busy man and eventually had to leave us. By now it was 19.30 and so only an hour later we were 50 miles away and camped a few hundred yards off the road. We are on a dusty prairie but only two miles to the south are some rugged peaks and over them, Iran.

Turkmenistan

Day 40
Saturday 20 May
Mondo Miles today: 265
Mondo Mileage: 5729

Last night we were goosed. It was 11 o'clock before we turned in and everybody slept absolutely soundly. Hence it was no surprise to wake and find the sun relatively high in the morning sky and everybody still totally knackered. Despite this, Gerald was working like a Trojan employing the centre stand he had so assiduously carried all the way from Bournemouth.

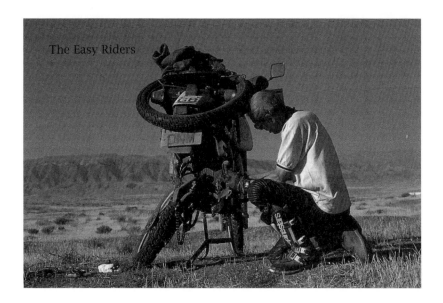

The Easy Riders

We had planned to make today a huge 300 miler so that tomorrow we'd be within shouting distance of the Uzbek border. Although the ancient city of Mary lies *en route*, we'll speed past it and nail it out as far as we can.

The road stretched out as it has done for the last 600 miles as the proverbial ribbon of tarmac. Straight as a die but instead of the almost reassuring audacity of the Georgian potholes and craters, these Turkmen roads exhibit a lumpy nature that just fades in and out of the normal carriageway. These asperities are hard to perceive and invariably come in clusters as if on a formally designed suspension-testing-surface at the TRRL.

This is our first proper desert since London so of course we are all gushing with a new infusion of expedition-euphoria. Back in England, Mark had showed us a 1970s TimeLife publication curiously titled; '*Soviet Deserts and Mountains*' and the majesty of this undeniable scenery, which hardly any Englishman had seen, encouraged us to get to Siberia on *this* route through Central Asia rather than via Poland, Ukraine, Moscow etc. Although boiling hot there is a palpable Arabian Nights mystique that has us all deeply enchanted with this mysterious sea of sand.

A new game developed today (on the straight sections) whereby at a minimum of 55mph you drive along with your eyes shut and merely see how long you dare sustain this for. The best so far attained is 10 seconds.

We pushed 130 miles before lunch and then pulled into the traditionally ramshackle roadside hut to enquire if he had any water. We ended up staying for a bottle of weakly carbonated peach soda and two shish kebabs each (charcoal BBQ'd on site). We have discovered that these are called *Shashlik*.

The heat of the day is awful. We sweat profusely in our leathers. If we need to pull over and it's not shady, then if you sit on the bike, the heat of the engine roasts you from beneath. The old physics O-Level fact that black absorbs heat better than white is superbly illustrated on our trousers and sleeping roll stuff-sacs which almost burn. However, once on the move it is rarely too hot to be uncomfortable. So we continued on and after another 50 miles pulled in for a cup of chai and the oft repeated request for water. The search for relatively clean drinking water goes on.

After chai, Austin went to use the Katadyne filter on the local river water. It was only the second time it has been used since we left the UK and takes 10 minutes to pump through (with difficulty) 1½ litres. Its use is so infuriating that we suspect we are doing something wrong. Nick got a thorn through the front tyre. He and Gerald stayed to repair it while the remainder hit the bright lights of Mary to do an advance search for the elusive 93 grade petrol. Stubley pointed out that Mary is called Marv in some cultures so it's nothing to do with the Blessed Virgin etc

Mary is massive and seems well maintained compared to the little villages we pass. It is fairly depressing though: crumbling phosphate factories, poorly built workers' apartment blocks and almost nowhere to buy Petrol. We eventually filled up for a staggering 14p a gallon and moved on. We are struck by the profusion of beautiful slender Russian beauties that remain so immaculately groomed amongst the dust and post-Soviet chaos. Their impact is all the more evident since the small villages out in the desert we've transited are 100% indigenous Turkmen, not a blonde hair in sight.

We passed a lonely T-junction with another battered sign splashed with impenetrable backwards Cyrillic. Chas and Mark (who have had a few lessons in the lingo) pulled over to study it and it revealed that turning right would lead us to Afghanistan, less than a hundred miles away. We pondered that this turning probably saw a fair bit of traffic back in the eighties. However, the Uzbek border beckons and we managed a further 46 miles before pulling onto the patch of scrub that for the next ten hours would be home. It was already home to huge beetles with polka dot backs and wasps the size of sugar cubes. Everyone is dirty again but we'll reach Bukhara tomorrow hopefully.

Turkmenistan

Day 41
Sunday 21 May
Mondo Miles today: 185
Mondo Mileage: 5914

We broke camp around 8am (urged on by Austin). After 30 miles or so we came across two dazed Turkmen who'd just come off their Planeta 5 motorbike (two stroke 350cc) and were rather badly cut up. They seemed to be wearing dressing gowns, had no helmets and of course, both looked like Lee Van Cleef. Bill, Clive and Austin saw to their wounds and then Chas drove them home (three up). It is worth noting what had caused their crash; they had no front inner tube and with staggering simplicity had improvised their own 'mousse'. This consisted of *another* front tyre which had been crammed into the actual tyre. Whilst rumbling along this lonely road the inner mousse tyre had somehow erupted free, caught in the front forks and was substantial enough to have locked the front wheel solid sending them both flying. We imagine that as they tell the story of today's bad luck they will ponder as to the good fortune that the very next vehicles to happen upon them were a septet of motorcycle Samaritans with a medical chest literally bursting with dressings and ointments.

Nick, Bill and Mark pushed on to a chai stop a further 20 miles – chai and chicken all round. Local truckers gave us salt and candy, not sure if this constitutes some kind of curse. Then we filled up with petrol and rocked to the border. Unfortunately, Gerald rocked quicker than the rest of us and went the wrong way out of Carjew, keeping us waiting on the border for a couple of hours. Some Iranian truckers tipped us off that Customs were going to try and fleece us for a fistful of dollars. Sure enough they took uppance at the video camera and their noses were twitching at the thought of some easy dengue coming their way. Unlucky: we palmed them off with a few glib assurances and talk of the BBC. The Uzbek 'officials' were real sleazeballs, but we managed to get through on $20 and a packet of fags, Chas and Mark testing their Russian ability to the full.

On to Bukhara. People in Uzbekistan seem a lot more surprised to see us than people in Turkmenistan. Everyone stops and gawps or waves. Despite an offer of someone's house for $10 we opted for the $15 a head Hotel Varakhsha. They allowed us to put all seven bikes inside, under the stairs! All of us, except Austin (re-setting tappets) ended up eating and drinking in the Hotel Bukhara (12th floor café). This is where the Bukhara 'monde' comes to be seen. Naff disco lights, western music, expensive beers but the chicken and shashlik were excellent.

Uzbekistan

Day 42
Monday 22 May
Mondo Miles today: 0
Mondo Mileage: 5964

We awoke earlier than we had hoped when Jackson arrived to inform us that our bikes were to be removed from the foyer due to a leaking petrol problem – fair enough – we were soon dressed and ready to stroll into Old Bukhara, which Chas had already recc'ed for us on a 7am sortie. Bukhara is a blend of ancient mud and Soviet concrete. It's hard to believe that the Muslim caliphs, who for centuries had ruled this part of the world, were only usurped by the Russians 100 years ago. There is mystery in the air as we contemplate the rich but sandy history of this ultra remote Silk Road metropolis. There must be a word for the effect upon a municipal psyche caused by being so far from the open sea but none of us know what it is.

Nick, Gerald and Bill were first to the liab-I-Khauz, ancient watering and washing pool and one of the two remaining after the Russians had drained them (and thereby removed the ever present threat of plague and 'guinea worm' which had bedevilled Bukhara for centuries). There we met for an excellent breakfast of 'plov', boiled eggs and pancakey-type thingies, before Gerald, Austin and Clive bid the remainder adieu and set-off for Samarkand. The ultimate destination is Alma Ata and its second ever motor show. We are booked into this event next week as a 'novelty attraction' by an old school friend of Austin's who is co-ordinating it. There is a suggestion that in return for our noveltyness the organisers will put us up for all the time we are there. Result.

Nick, Chas, Mark and Bill, fortified by countless cups of chai, were ready to explore Bukhara, starting with the Kaylan Minaret, or Tower of Death, the only part of pre-1220 Bukhara spared by Genghis Khan and from which countless miscreants were thrown (death by 'jaculation') until as late as 1920.

They then took in the Mir-I-Arab Madrasa, the only working Islamic seminary during Soviet times. While Nick and Bill were attempting to cajole a few songs out of the gatekeeper for the video, they were joined by a small group of students with their teacher from Tashkent's University of World Languages and their local guide, a Tajik teacher of history. We were invited to join them, and so began an exhaustive and exhausting day of sightseeing a la Uzbek, being carted from sight to sight in a bumpety truck-like bus while being regaled with the eager and excellent English of the professor and her protégés. We took in the following:

Keylan Mosque – huge in scale with a capacity of 10,000 people
Uleg Bek Madrasa (opposite above and oldest in Central Asia)
Abdulaziz Khan Madrasa (interesting but made tacky by little stalls selling goods to tourists at inflated prices).
The Zindan (local jail, with the infamous 'Bug Pit' – where notably two British Officers shared their last days with rats, scorpions etc before being beheaded in front of the 'Ark' at the height of the Great Game's diplomatic shenanigans).
The Ark – Citadel and Palace of the Khans

We were then bundled back into the 'bus' for another bone shaking ride – this time back to Laura's Bukhara Auntie's place for dinner, in a worker's estate apartment block: apricots, cherries, stuffed cabbage, salad and great banter. We returned to our hotel to freshen up before a couple of beers on the roof of the Hotel Bukhara. Hard to believe that only a century ago the number of British people that had ever been to this city would barely reach double figures and yes, we were secretly thrilled that the number of Brits that had ridden here from London would be even less.

An early night beckons, for we must depart early in the morning. The Pakistani PM, Benhazir Bhutto is to drive by around 10am tomorrow, and the concierge warned us that if we emerge on our balconies, we are likely to be shot as potential snipers.

Uzbekistan

Day 43
Tuesday 23 May
Mondo Miles today: 175
Mondo Mileage: 6039

Mondo Log, stardate May 23 finds the team full of enterprise. We remain in two groups, separated by miles but not ambition as we blend ever onwards towards Alma-Ata and her depraved charms.

After a refreshing breakfast of pasties, boiled eggs and chai at the Lyanb-I-L-Lazz pool, we made urgent efforts to check out before being enveloped by the combined security and culture operation. Uzbek dancing girls mingled with the cops as we ferried our suspicious-looking Givis and petrol cans to the waiting bikes.

A comparatively short journey, by Mondo standards, of 170 miles to Samarkand ensued. It was punctuated with frequent stops by the police and a lunch break. In one particularly irksome encounter, a young Bow Street runner, clearly star cadet in the Uzbek Police Academy class of '94, entered all our vehicle registration details in a voluminous black ledger. It was clear from the billions of previous entries that this was one of the ways of keeping tabs on the population that the cops just couldn't bear to relinquish.

At lunch in a shady roadside café, we bumped into the same group of middle-aged Swiss women whom we had met in the Bukhara Museum of Numismatics. The fact that they were all middle-aged, of some means, and driving in a white Red Crescent minibus led us to believe they were nurses or doctors. As saucy thoughts scampered through our brains, Nick confessed to thinking constantly of Kathryn, not the Russian Tsarina but his bilingual Welsh sweetheart. We admonished him, pointing out that Jesus had spent 40 nights in the desert. Not four, for heavens sake. Another highlight was Nick's toilet stop in a field – watched by a group of cheering Uzbek women.

We blended not entirely effortlessly into Samarkand where we met Clive posted outside the Intourist Hotel sporting a stylish set of shades purchased for $4 from the bazaar. He, Austin, and Gerald were rough-camping in a rubbish tip about 3 kilometres out of town.

The others, meanwhile, blended to the Hotel Zarafshan, a sprawling fleapit suffering from a bad case of faded grandeur. The rooms were clean and cheap at $10 each and there was secure parking for our motorbikes. As the rest of the group moved from their RV with Clive, Chas got chatting to a portly local and his utterly stunning Tajik girlfriend who invited him to the restaurant for tea. Soon, cheese, yoghurt, salami and bread was being served along with the inevitable vodka. As Uzbek-Anglo relations reached ever greater depths of warmth we all got up for a quick shuffle with the golden-toothed belly dancer. The talk soon turned to cars and it transpired that our friend had a Merc which he had ordered directly from the German factory. As the end of the evening approached we offered him $10 to pay for the meal, upon which he produced a huge wad of 100s of bills from his pocket. His girlfriend, meanwhile, continued to enchant us all and we cursed that immutable law of capitalism which says cash is such an effective babe magnet.

As the others retired to their less than salubrious quarters, Mark traded heavy metal riffs with the house band guitarist who had 'Rainbow' and 'Deep Purple' tattooed on his fingers. Very rock n'roll.

Uzbekistan

Day 44
Wednesday 24 May
Mondo Miles today: 50
Mondo Mileage: 6089

It was with a dry mouth that we awoke, remembering our meeting with the Mafia man and his medical student girlfriend. The pre-arranged RV with our other half at the Hotel Samarkand spurred us to leave the restaurant at the rear of the Hotel Zarafshan; and so we set off to see the crossroads of the Silk Road that is Samarkand. After postcard writing and coffee at the Intourist Hotel, we RV'd with Clive and Austin. They were heading off to Tashkent today. A guide from Kyrgyzskan highlighted to us the areas of the Tien Shan mountains that were worth seeing. This would mean a visa stop in Tashkent in order to visit some of these places.

And so down the Registan to the most impressive set of madrasas this side of Bradford.

Thanks to Lenin's decree in 1917 to preserve and restore ancient monuments, we saw immaculate glazed tiling with gold leaf interiors. Video handed, Nick shot away. The blue of the domes along with the patterns was quite breathtaking. These were the most impressive sights of Samarkand. But even these great charms could not impart the same feeling as Bukhara, that of a timelessness with its pools and tea houses. Samarkand is too sterile and busy. Too industrialised to make you feel relaxed. Bukhara for the genuine Central Asian ambience, Samarkand for pure architectural superlatives. We went on to the cultural museum which had a limited showing of Soviet war propaganda posters. Mark and Chas went on to the bazaar and to the Mausoleum of Tamerlane. The friendly policeman let them down into the crypt where the ruler's body lies. We intend to re-visit the tomb tomorrow and to see the huge jade slab which covers the tomb. The guidebook said that on the jade was an inscription threatening that if his body was disturbed then all of the earth would tremble. In 1940, the archaeological dig that first revealed this tomb was coupled with the invasion of Russia by the Germans. His re-interment was coupled with Paulus' surrender at Stalingrad...

After an RV at the hotel, we went on for a late supper at the Samarkand Hotel. Bill was refusing to have any more shaslik so soup it was, then kebabs were devoured between the other three. On the way back to the hotel, Bill was caught short in the park boulevard.

Uzbekistan

Day 45
Thursday 25 May
Mondo Miles today: 175
Mondo Mileage: 6264

There was a good road towards Tashkent but a few stops by the Police slowed us down, as did 2 chai stops in the first 100 miles. The second stop led to us attempting to eat some disgusting, fatty soup. We failed. There is an Uzbek phenomenon of people selling vegetables by the roadside. We imagine it is grown by them though it's usually children or OAPs who are actually minding the stall. This is a result for us since while (self-catering) on the road we have lapsed into an exclusively vegetarian diet even though none of us are veg. We have no stomach complaints as a result. Result!

Ten miles outside Tashkent we spotted Austin and Gerald by the side of the road. In a desperate attempt to match Mark and Chas's puncture count, Austin had managed three within 24 hours. They gave us the good news that Clive had blended us in for a night at the British Embassy. He'd managed to get the *American* Embassy to give him a driver who drove him all over town and bought him lunch. It has to be said that Clive looked like something out of *Chips* and his abilities for charming assistance from diplomatic staff are taking on near mythical status.

First impression as we ride into Tashkent is of complete dumbstruck awe. This is a truly ancient metropolis, but of the 7th century Samanid oasis citadel there is no trace, instead, we gaped and winced at what must be the ugliest capital city in the world. Why? Because on April 25th 1966 a vicious earthquake (7.5 Richter) ripped through here and destroyed literally everything. What we were now cruising through was the 'new' city, redesigned, reborn and rebuilt at incredible speed by thousands of Soviet 'volunteers' over the Summer of Love. The end result is literally a concrete jungle. Every building is in the optimistic ultra-modern (but Sovietised) sixties Gerry Anderson style rather like Centre Point but realised in a manner where the overall effect is shabby and tatty. There is no parallel in our collective experience for such well intentioned town planning going wrong. Prince Charles has clearly never been here to pass judgement but if he did we suspect he would go a bit easier on The Bull Ring, South Bank Centre etc.

Anyway, Gerald led us all over town looking for the British Embassy ("It's OK lads, I've got the map") but we only found it by spotting Clive. This fledgling outpost of our home-country has only been open a few months and has a staff of three. We are possibly the first Brits to have driven here since it opened which may explain our vague novelty value. We actually got to meet the Ambassador, Barbara Hay, who instead of dismissing us, gave us an escort to Sean Melbourne's pad (vice-consul) and gently suggested that he would like to host all seven of us. Result.

His detached dacha is a fine example of late Czarist architecture and seems to have been spared by the earthquake. He was a gracious host to us and he kindly plied us with Heineken and beef stroganoff before picking up his Tartar girlfriend, Ella. We were happily watching Mondo footage through his TV until he suggested a VHS of 'The Wrong Trousers' (funny), followed by Billy Connolly live (not funny).

We slept in the Summer House, leaving Sean and Ella to further Anglo-Uzbeki relations.

Uzbekistan

Day 46
Friday 26 May
Mondo Miles today: 0
Mondo Mileage: 6264

Brief entry from the ambassador; Barbara Hay:

"Well, my Vice-Consul Sean Melbourn, told me yesterday that "a biker" had been in to The Embassy and was on a mad trip around the world: What's more, he had two mates. Actually... he was a wee bit shocked when several more materialised!! Anyway, now that we've got used to the idea, we're rather enjoying the unique adventure and wishing you all the best for the rest of your trip. You've certainly started my tour of duty as HMA, Tashkent with style; I can't imagine that many interludes will be such fun – or certainly as original! Natasha, the cook, hasn't seen food disappear quite as quickly before; and my guards' jaws will never drop so far again as they did when one after another of you pulled into the yard to park under the awning of diplomatic bags. They'll be talking about it for ages!!! Kypuyzytola (that's Uzbek!) Barbara."

Friday was an admin and maintenance day in Tashkent. Bill, Nick and Mark went off to do some sightseeing, check the *post restante* address and make a few calls to the UK. Austin and Clive went to ITE (people organising the motor-show who have an office here in Tashkent) and The Embassy. Chas went to see a motorcycle mechanic and Gerald stayed home at Sean's house to repair Austin's puncture.

It was a pleasant day spoilt by rain in the afternoon: soon after lunch Austin and Clive returned with the unbelievable news that tonight we will be wined and dined at the home of the Ambassador! What's more, she insists we stay the night! The ITE meeting went very well and it looks like they will blend us in. Nick, Bill and Mark also returned with some footage of the only metro in Central Asia and one letter from home. Bill's girlfriend Claire is trying to find out about this supposed air route between Magadan and Anchorage. Chas was the last one back having bought a jerrican from the ex-champion motocrosser of Uzbekistan. So now, with Austin having bought 7, we had 8. One will become a water can.

A procession of bikes behind the ambassadorial Land Rover to Barbara's house, and a flag-waving arrival for the video record. Local champagne flowed followed by Uzbek soup and main course. As repayment Nick and Mark got the TV system working. Shortly before midnight we retired to the guest house welcomed by a beaming signed photo of John Major. We cannot believe our good fortune.

Uzbekistan

Day 47
Saturday 27 May
Mondo Miles today: 97
Mondo Mileage: 6384

"When will it end? – "today"

The quotation above came as a question from Austin and a brotherly answer from Gerald. The reason for the query was Austin articulating what we were all thinking; Barbara the Ambassador was treating us so incredibly well that we thought we would surely plode, her im-, and us ex-. The weather that greeted us as we arose around eight was crystal clear blue skies to the chink-chinkle sound of taxpayer's crockery being set out on the patio; underneath the awning made from old diplomatic bags sewn together.

Our breakfast of muesli, coffee, jam and bread was not particularly noteworthy at face value save the amazing fact that it was all *British* food. Even the milk, although not actually from Eden Vale, was reconstituted Marvel.

The previous night we had bandied around a men-of-action ER time (engines running) of 0900. This H-hour came and went as did every hour on the hour until about 1200. Instead of a cuckoo clock for us to keep time by, the call of "perhaps there's time for another cuppa" became our beverage inspired chronometry.

After collecting all the unspent zum (Uzbek currency) and re-checking the map, Mondo Enduro pulled out of the British Embassy driveway en route for Alma-Ata (some 500 miles away). As a group we knew that our own nearest and dearest couldn't have spoiled us as Barbara Hay had. It could only go down hill from here.

In fact, it went neither up nor down as Clive led us through the heart, soul, suburbs and housing estates of Tashkent in his route to the frontier. The scene as we wove our way in between the eight storey workers' housing blocks, baffling all the tenants, was hilarious and like much of the trip so far, quite surreal. It was almost destiny, that after leaving an Ambassador behind, top lip quivering, eyes reddening and tear ducts dilating, we were almost immediately at <u>another</u> International border, into a new era and leaving the past, whether we liked it or not, quite definitely behind.

Rumour control had fanned the embers of speculation that the Uzbek/Kazakh border was weirdly easy to slide over. However, Mondo

Enduro, always trying to be one wheelbase ahead, was keen to anticipate an irksome and tortuous crossing that would leave us all sweating in the afternoon sun as Uzbek Customs tore holes in our proposed tissue of fiction concerning why we had so few currency exchange receipts and between us had little evidence of time spent asleep in 'approved' Intourist Hotels.

We parked up just short of the constriction in the road that indicated the border and shuddered when we saw the queue of Iranian and Turkish artics waiting their turn.

Gerald went ahead for a recee and came back with the news that you could just "drive through!". We started to become more confident as we fingered our ITE letter of invitation hoping that it would give us the ace up our leathery sleeves. Austin and Chas changed our Uzbek zum into Kazakh tengi with a street side money dealer, who was clearly Michael Palin's missing Kazakh twin brother. Strangely, his neatly folded and sorted wadlets of Kazakh Tengi were in no apparent order. He produced bundles of notes that totalled 170, 300, 410 Tengi etc. Baffling and unhelpful in keeping a check on his deft fingerwork as he counted and re-counted the notes for our transaction. He was photographed helping Chas decipher the Russian Road Atlas.

We bought some recession biscuits which were neatly boxed up and labelled as the produce of the Shining Crescent Biscuit Co, Tehran. It felt strange to buy biscuits that Iranians exported thousands of miles overland only to find out that basically they were really horrible and you wouldn't even give them to people you were trying to offend.

Onward into Kazakhstan and a huge change in scenery. Flowing, rolling plains with a perfect dual carriageway plastered across it. There are roadside tanker lorries selling petrol everywhere and so far our 350 singles are coping with the low octane fuel without a murmur of discontent. This seems to be a country of herdsmen and we lost count of the horse-mounted teen shepherds corralling their flocks of cows and sheep.

We camped on the crest of a superb dry valley, and celebrated the Penty twins' (Bill and Chas) birthday with a miracle tin of Tetley's Ale (brought from England for this purpose) and a superb meal cooked on a fire.

Kazakhstan

Day 48
Sunday 28 May
Mondo Miles today: 120
Mondo Mileage: 6481

"Off Road, Heaven here we come"

After coffee on our rekindled fire, we followed Gerald's trail down into the valley next to the campsite. A perfect U-shape and bone dry, the meandering valley was a dirt bike playground of the first order. Even if it wasn't, arriving in this vast country last night, camping, dropping our luggage then dirt biking for an hour was exactly why we had come on this trip. Although not one of us can do so much as a wheelie we were intoxicated on a heady brew of freedom and Uzbek onions – the bikes, reminiscing from Metsovo (day 15), eagerly raced along the valley floor whilst Mark filmed our fun. Up the steep sided valleys went Austin, Clive then Nick all leaning forward and gunning it up the slope so as not to wheelie, loose balance and wipe out... If ever we needed reassuring about rejecting the Yamaha XT600 or Honda Transalp and choosing these little 350 trail bikes then this hour of gooning was it!

After more coffee and recession biccies ... quite tasty, one should add – we broke camp (12ish). The Vince family were particularly unlucky with 1 puncture and 1 sore head.

Back on the plot and low and behold – puncture – Austin's tyre went flat for the second time today. A new inner tube sidestepped our inferior repair kit and we were rocking once again. We can now see the Western peaks of the Tien Shan capped with snow to our right as we head for Almaty and the International Motor Show.

Around 6pm and after 100 miles Clive's chain (split pin) snapped leaving Bill's bike the only one problem free. Supper was prepared by Mark and Bill whilst Gerald and Austin assisted Clive in chain repairing. After supper Nick and Mark recce'd a light wood as our camp site whilst the rest of Mondo Enduro packed up and cleared up.

Nick returned around 8pm to lead us to our new dwelling via a "Candy Stop". Beer and coffee around a fire and it was lights out for the boys but as we fell asleep there was a murmured yearning for Barbara Hay and her homely comforts ... what an angel and motherly figure for the Mondo boys.

Kazakhstan

Day 49
Monday 29 May
Mondo Miles today: 144
Mondo Mileage: 6625

Nick's pessimism of the previous night paid off, as he awoke to the pouring rain safe in the knowledge that his flysheet was up and that his lot was a drier one than that of the others. They were scrambling for ponchos and fly sheets as the first rain for a while established itself. The morning was written off as a fire was lit under a suspended poncho. Once the rain got a hold we were too befuddled to get going, content to wait it out. An impromptu and uninspiring quiz was all our sodden minds could come up with to fill the time as we waited for the rain to abate, which eventually it did, giving way to sunshine which was quickly used to dry all the kit out. Unfortunately, Chas' Thermarest was not tended with sufficient vigilance and as a result the fire's heat caused the air inside it to expand, rupturing its delicate foamy interior. Hence, when he blows it up a huge air blister appears.

Mark and Clive started to cook and Austin went off in search of bread and pasta. Food was eaten, camp was struck and the team headed East (at 4.45pm!) towards Bishkek, following the beginnings of the Tien Shan Mountains on our right. Once over these lofty peaks you're in the foothills of the Himalayas. 144 miles were done, uncharacteristically without a problem, along easy roads with fine mountain scenery on the right all the way. The most striking element was the emergence of the yurt for the first time in quantity (even a Yurt bus stop), as well as the numerous horse-riding shepherds. The combination of mountain, yurts and fur-hatted horsemen gave a truly authentic feel to our Kazhak experience. At 8pm, we stopped to set up camp. A fire was lit, the billy-can went on, a brew was made, and sleep crept up to and claimed us before we knew he was really there.

Kazakhstan

Day 50
Tuesday 30 May
Mondo Miles today: 187
Mondo Mileage: 6812

The thick smog which hangs over Almaty and other Soviet cities in winter has nothing on the smug expression defiling Bill's features today. The mileage sweepstake arranged in that distant Erzurum dining room has been won by the aforementioned who has blended himself a $35 tote after foretelling our mileage thus far at 6800. Just 12 miles out – how he was able to predict this is almost unsettling...

Thirty days hath September, April, June and November. So also 30 May and it was to be one of pleasure, pain and above all profitable blending.

The morning broke earlier than usual for some in the Mondo team awakened by a deafening chorus of dogs a'barking, cocks a'crowing, Lada Niva's a' pinking and Jacksons a'rriving. The said vehicle rumbled up the track to our campsite about 5.10 *a.m.* (!!!!) disgorging a posse of Kazakh herdsmen and three – it has to be said, given the usual caveats regarding a cowboy's simmering libido after 50 days in the saddle, - quite tasty birds. Complex negotiations ensued regarding the travesty which was this year's collective farm of the year competition and the proliferation of Kyrgyzstan's nuclear arsenal before our new friends blended back into the gloaming.

Meanwhile, Austin, Clive, Gerald and Mark prepared for an early assault on our next destination – Almaty 'City of the Apples' and we dared to hope, other tastier fruits. Their journey will not feature further in this annal as it was entirely without incident or mishap.

Not so for the other party consisting of Bill, Nick and Chas who conducted further negotiations with our aforementioned Kazakh colleagues. As usual they were keen to learn full details of our employment status, salary levels and Inland Revenue tax bracket etc. When Chas returned the compliment by asking what one of them did for a living, he replied that he was a *'Tractorist'*.

And so the journey continued against a stunning backdrop of scenery which could have adorned Britain's more picturesque national parks. Always on our southern flank, or in our rear-view mirrors was the precipice and wall of rock and ice which marked the Kazakh border, the southern edge of the desert steppe and the start of the Tien Shan mountain range.

After about 65 miles, Nick pulled over having suffered a front tyre puncture. A disgruntled sense of *déjà vu* soon turned to one of mild alarm as we realised that Mark had left with the reserve repair tools but fortunately a roadside Shashlik vendor not 500 metres away offered his services and a repair was affected using superglue, a crowbar and assorted items of kitchen cutlery as levers. (Philosophical note; one such spoon began life on a British Home Stores shelf before being purchased for use in the Penty's Uttoxeter household – it's eventual service, not an implement for feeding soups and puddings into hungry mouths in rural Staffordshire, but as an impromptu motorcycle tool on the steppes of Kyrgyzstan surely demonstrates the strange machinations of the wheel of fortune). Nick Stubley blended him $5 by way of saying "*spassiba*".

On the subject of utterly unprovoked acts of kindness by Jacksons, a burley Russian driving a Vauxhall Astra gave us 60 Tenge for no apparent reason and also a bottle of curious Fanta coloured liquid which turned out to be a highly effective fuel additive. Unlucky 70 grade Benzine! A tea break in a 'Little Yurt' also saw us blended free chai by three generations of female Kazakhs while we posed for photos by an ancient single cylinder 140cc motorcycle of indeterminate Soviet identity. It's owner, a fair-haired Russian, wore Army moleskin trousers, jacket and padded flying helmet which drew envious glances from Mondo Enduro. We are realising that here in the former USSR there is no use of artificial fibres giving everyone's wardrobe a truly vintage feel.

We were blending into Almaty behind a Moscovitch saloon when Chas suffered a spectacular tank-slapper caused by locking his front wheel into a tram-line. A kindly Russian called Alexander, driving a black Merc, risked the ire of a Kazakh *babooshka* to help move the battered vehicle from the road. She was apparently accusing him of preparing to steal the bike plus luggage, but instead he guided us to the Hotel Otra where Nick and Gerald were waiting.

The early birds had, in the meantime, done some serious blending even by the lofty standards set by Clive in Tashkent. Negotiations with ITE had secured the use of a two-bedroomed flat (gratis) for the duration of the Motor Show at which Mondo Enduro was to become not exactly the star attraction but at least a minor asteroid. Our stand in the Conference Centre was near the door and slightly overshadowed by Hyundai but the important thing was that we were THERE and only yards from Shell Oil. The Mondo members will have to be at their most charmingly unctuous to secure free supplies of this liquid gold.

Chas meanwhile had survived intact from his close examination of Kazakhstan's road and rail infrastructure. Natasha, our next-door-neighbour and another of the lovely ITE admin girls Rita, took Chas to Almaty Central City Hospital for a precautionary x-ray. The doctors there all wore little white chef's hats and grey moccasins and one was the spitting image of Alan Whicker. The x-ray itself was an ancient machine which left Chas feeling thoroughly irradiated and no doubt further moulinexed the Penty gene pool causing yet more grotesque mutations. Whilst in the hospital Chas discovered that the Russian word for 'X-ray' is *Roentgen* whilst 'pencil' is *carandache*.

As we left, the surgeon shook Bill's hand, tickling his palm as he did so. All very dodgy and the sense of menace pervaded further as we climbed into the homeward taxi with Natasha. The plinky piano riff of the Russian love-song on the radio, the driver's scarred neck and the teak dashboard of his Volga saloon combined to create a sinister Cold War atmosphere.

An utterly delicious meal of recession pasta and vegetables prepared by Nick set the seal on a day which in every way had been eventful if not always comfortable. The flat has hot and cold running water, a tape player and soft beds, not to mention wallpaper comprised of a collage of soft porn and old rouble banknotes. In our neighbours Natasha and Rita we have the most charming hosts and nursemaids and what is more we are in Almaty and in one piece. Somehow, the train keeps a rollin'.

Kazakhstan

Day 51
Wednesday 31 May
Mondo Miles today: 0
Mondo Mileage: 6812

Once again blending was afoot. After a rush collection of kit to display at the Motor Show, we headed on our 4 mile commute from our flat to the AIMS '95 second Almaty Motor Show with our new found guide/hostess Rita.

We had forgotten the route to the rear of the Exhibition (suppliers' service entrance), so we went in through the main entrance (pedestrian entrance) up the steps past the stewards (who carry AK47s) and straight into the Exhibition Hall. Our stand, more like corner of the hall, was opposite Hyundai and right next to the main entrance – so most people would see us as soon as they walked in – which was most certainly to our advantage.

Our set up consisted of bikes standing back to back with the Union Flag draped and centred against the back wall. The poncho was set up with Plymouth (Austin's teddy bear) in his sleeping bag and on a Thermarest with head torch fitted too – ready for his bedtime story which never came! Kit, stove, water filter, tools, first aid as well as various other bits of kit were put impressively and improvisingly on show for the world to see.

The opening of the exhibition was at 10am and Mondo Enduro was talked about on KAZAKH TV for approximately a minute – '7 English Sportsmien' as we are known here. All 7 of us (correction 6, Chas was busy lapping up hospitality with Natasha) were on the stand to start – we were introduced to the Minister of Transport, Vice Prime Minister and some other Kazakh top knobs, in addition to hoards of businessmen and beautiful girls. It was a grand morning and we were visited by larger crowds than some of the 'real' stands.

Gerald used his years of experience in the booking office to create a comprehensive rosta so that our stand was staffed for the rest of the week and this afternoon saw Nick and Mark on duty whilst everyone else went to do various bits of admin. Back at the flat and Chas was feeling a lot better after being pampered by Natasha most of the day.

We left the flat around 8pm and went out for a most interesting evening. We were in fact invited to the motorshow opening night dinner type thing at the 'Almaty' hotel – when we arrived the banquet was in full swing and most people had finished eating.

Our table was laden with bevies: Vodka, Champagne, Wine, Beers and Fantas. The food was cold meats and fairly grim canapés. There were also diced mushroom ones which Austin ate about 3 of in 3 seconds and which he would later regret.

Once the bevs had been flowing Mondo Enduro was on the dance floor. Clive blending with Rita, Nick with Helen, Chas with a 17 year old model from the GM stand, Mark and Austin with Natasha. When the music stopped it was next door into the Casino for Clive, Bill and Mark – the rest of the gang headed back to the flat with Rita and Natasha for coffee. Austin's head went into spin mode when he laid down to sleep and then began to throw up his diced mushrooms.

Meanwhile, back at the Casino, Ed Strachan (the Old Harrovian ITE fixer out here) had turned up and proceeded to get more and more goosed with the Mondomen. Clive changed all the money he had on him ($70US) and $10 each from Mark and Bill's to feed his gambling needs. A bit of blackjack and then into the roulette. Bill and Mark headed off as they had seen Clive lose all his money and Clive blended some cash off them before they left in return for showing them the way home (they got lost and took about an hour – alcohol being the problem, not Clive's directions).

Clive went back into the Casino and spent the last of Mark's Tengi and Dollars. He was then penniless. Fortunately, there was no credit card or cashing facility otherwise he would have lost all that too.

Desperate to try and win his money back – he then remembered the bogus Tag Heur watch purchased for $20 from Istanbul in his pocket. So then his stories began, the fact that he had paid $800US for the Tag and that the winder had broken off in a crash. The potential buyer (local man he was gambling with) noticed the "9" on the watch had fallen off – his explanation for this was "it must have come off in the crash too".

The management were not interested in buying it – but the co-gambler ended up buying it for $150!!!! (But Clive couldn't remember the amount in Tengi – being completely pissed and then gambling more). It was time to duck and Clive having some more money wanted to find a friend. A cabbie took him through the streets of Almaty in search of pleasure but to no avail. He turned up at home at 7.45am after an hour or two in a cab paid for in return for an ITE VIP pass to the motorshow.

Kazakhstan

Day 52
Thursday 1 June
Mondo Miles today: 0
Mondo Mileage: 6812

Austin's prophetic statement, "Hey! These mushrooms are pre-diced for easy vomiting" came horribly true"...

Mark and Bill headed off at 9.30am for the Motor Show duty. Austin, Nick, Gerald and Chas divvied up the remaining chores whilst Clive remained completely comatose. Gerald and Nick went to get supplies and to check out the US Embassy. Chas went to DHL and the Reuters office. As Chas entered the office, the English correspondent was quizzing his secretary about the local newspaper's account of the English Motorcyclists who had arrived for the show. The translation describing the feat of driving the 10000km was "childish" (sic). Nick's report had been reproduced on Page 3 as well as his name in Cyrillic. The trip to the Embassy was mediocre with no hard facts. Austin found the Aeroflot office and quizzed them on whether there was an Aeroflot service from Magadan to Anchorage and a full answer awaits for tomorrow. It is the answering of this type of simple question that seems utterly impossible here in the former USSR.

Whilst Gerald and Nick were walking down to the Embassy, they saw two women hanging off the back of a trolley bus whilst the vehicle free wheeled around the corner to the next set of electric lines. As the two women swung on the pantagraph like bell ringers, another trolley bus crept up behind and started tooting to get by. More swinging on the wires brought the trolley bus back to life and it trundled away.

Chas returned with chains, letters and food packed into the parcel. A full invoice was inside from Geoff Vince, each item being fully detailed including a 1kg jar of Marmite. Result.

Kazakhstan

Day 53
Friday 2 June
Mondo Miles today: 0
Mondo Mileage: 6812

Another clement day. Nick and Clive went off with Rita to do the morning session at the show. Austin, who had made contact with an interpreter, has got a long list of things to do which will be easier with a native speaker. Mark and Bill have gone to the mountains which are 20km away and Chas is off to the US Embassy to meet a contact. The German Embassy is just around the corner from here and there is always a large queue of ethnic Germans, deported here by Stalin, applying for visas. Chas may write an article for the Yorkshire Post about it - worth about £100. Gerald (me) is all alone in the flat at the moment getting ready for his shift at the Motor Show and painstakingly transferring sugar cubes one by one from a flimsy Kazakh cardboard box into one of our nineteen Tupperware boxes.

(Editorial note: Chas has agreed to complete Gerald's log entry in return for completing his chain replacement).

Austin, meanwhile, made contact with Svetlana, the interpreter, and they completed a range of chores requiring the local information. Rita insists that she is a prostitute and that Austin beware her offers of 'translating'. The rest of the gang had also been using their time wisely building strength for another big night. The highlight of the early evening's entertainment for Chas at least, was the pillion ride he gave to Oxana, the babe from the Hyundai stand. As he flogged his flailing chain just one more time, she clinched his leathers tightly screaming "faster, faster". Truly, a Mondo moment.

In the meantime, we were all preparing ourselves mentally and spiritually for a night in Almaty's fleshpots. Fortified by Spag Bol and salad cooked by the saintly Natasha, we meditated to the sounds of a live Julio Iglesias concert as we contemplated the ordeal in store.

Our rendezvous was Shaggis (sic), a grotesque burger restaurant in the grounds of the Hotel Kazakhstan where we met Jean-Francois, the Norman valve salesman, and his charming assistant Medina (more later).

This encounter between such varied human genetic materials was the ideal opportunity for us to split the dire fast food joint as we divided into two groups. Nick, Bill, Mark and the gals blended seamlessly into a building which once served as a finishing school for Almaty's most equal communists. Now it was a nightclub run by some grungy Yanks with goatee beards, not unlike Lenin's, and we all absorbed the historical irony.

Austin, Chas, Gerald, John, Clive, Medina had meanwhile blended to the 'International Business Club'. There, Svetlana the translator had arrived with a gaggle of top babes including one wearing a backless beige silk dress. Incidentally, she is still 'translating' for free and has offered no 'extras' to any member of Mondo Enduro.

Chas, with Medina on pillion, followed to a nearby nightclub which was utterly dead. So morbid was it in fact that the babes who had accompanied Austin had chipped while he returned to collect the rest of the party and he returned, alas, to his bed alone. There was a strong vibe when we first arrived in Almaty that some of us might get a result but it is increasingly looking like the best we'll manage is some 'translating'...

In the nightclub meantime, Oxana the Hyundai babe and Alexandra were indulging in simulated lesbian sex on the dance floor while the lads looked on approvingly.

A veil has been drawn discreetly over the rest of the evening's events except to say that Medina's opening chat-up line was "I hope you don't mind getting my microbes". It was only after a minute's bafflement that Chas realised she was referring to the possibility of sharing coke from the same can.

The clubbers sitting in the gallery were meanwhile treated to the sight of the gang cavorting wildly to 'Dancing Queen' (a favourite of Bill's) and 'London Calling' dedicated by the DJ to Mondo Enduro.

We retired to our beds after a night in which we had kept our honour intact – as well as our promises to preserve that of various other Motor Show employees of the female gender. On the morrow we shall all toast Clive's gambling prowess and the end of our involvement with Kazakhstan's flourishing automobile service industry. And so to sleep, perchance to dream of long nights in the Siberian wilderness with only a 4lb club hammer for company.

Kazakhstan

Day 54
Saturday 3 June
Mondo Miles today: 0
Mondo Mileage: 6812

The gang poured into the flat and still awestruck by the chance to rest in a real building, slipped off to sleep for five hours before an 8.30 start. Chas is the hero of the hour, not for romantic achievement the previous night but for an event that turns and twists the collective Mondo Enduro stomach with an envy so intense that a new hue has been coined known simply as "Mondo Green"!

The story is this: Kazakhstan's top model (aged 17) Oxana is booked to glamourise the General Motors' stand: something she does so phenomenally that she gives a new meaning to the idea of 'this year's model'. Hence, she attended the ITE sponsored banquet the evening of the first day of the Motor Show and way, hay, hay – she's sat at the table adjacent to ours and in no time had relocated to *our* table wedged in twixt Austin and Chas. Sadly she speaks no English so Austin resigned himself to Chas (who has learned some Russian) building this particular international bridge. Throughout the rest of the evening they were inseparable, and although Chas made excellent progress on the strength of his looks alone, the trickle that he had initiated in this blue eyed sweetheart, irresistibly turned to a flood once Chas played his trump card – his "cheeky" dancing.

Cut forward to the next day and Clive makes a foray to shed 7 where the GM stand is located. He scans the stand and in no time he is clocked by our gorgeous model friend who glides towards him. Clive, confident, tanned and muscular, starts to build a house of cards each one a heart, as she comes closer and closer, fixing her gaze on his and her mouth breaking into a chain-loosening smile. Sadly, Clive's structure of love collapses as she breezes up close to him and almost in a whisper breathes: "Chas?" As if this weren't enough for Clive to bear, she follows it up with "Chas?...Chas...? It was truly a Mondo Moment if nothing else, we remaining six know when to doff our helmets, be they open or full-face, at this great display of male attraction, be it fatal or just a flesh wound....

So today, Saturday, is the last day of the second international Kazakhstan Motor Show. Austin and Bill took the first shift and went through the by now familiar routine of explaining in simple English who we were and what we were doing. It has been amusing to observe the surprise that the locals' exhibit when they realise you are not trying to <u>sell</u> these dirty old motorcycles. They can hardly imagine how far away England is, the 10,000km thus far helps to quantify it but it's the 6,000km yet to go that actually impresses them. It is clear that the very mention of the word 'Magadan' causes much rolling of the eyes and alarm, almost as if it was accursed. We do not understand. Sometimes we lapse into a false sense of achievement when Kazakh and Russian well-wishers urge us on for a successful trip. With such a minority ridden to date, Magadan doesn't bear thinking about, yet alone Alaska to Argentina followed by South Africa back to London.

We chatted to a German spectator who, it transpired, worked as a consultant for a major German Bank who advised the Kazakh Ministry of Finance. He had been working out here since 1991 and his high level observations were fascinating.

'Independence' and 'Freedom' gained virtually overnight were more of a hindrance than a help

As in Rumania, the top jobs were all still filled by the old guard who did the same things as before but whizzed around in Mercs now instead of Skodas.

Industrialisation had only hit this part of the world in the 1930's ie two generations ago. Up until then, this vast area had been populated by herdsmen who lived a hand-to-mouth existence but who did not take very easily to being turned into an urban proletariat.

Hence, even after throwing off the old Soviet system, the Kazakhs, instead of being filled with a wide-eyed euphoria about what shapes they could mould from the slab of national clay that had fallen into their laps, instead were quite happy to let foreign business consultants sow their seeds and just lie back and casually see what came to fruition.

The ministers were fully "sovietised" in that they wanted to see foreign banks put up huge finance (many billions) for lumbering, prestigious, gargantuan industrial schemes. Economically, the idea that small is beautiful has not really found many fans here.

There is no middle class at present, and crucially, the last four years has been wasted in that nobody was moving in this direction even now.

Finally, too many top Kazakh officials have been told that the nation's immeasurable oil reserves were going to be their 'get out of jail free card'. They wouldn't have to diversify and graft since it would all come out in the very oily wash – to put it crudely.

Anyway, the German went, more visitors came and the most frequently used lie became our claim that we had hand built our bikes from exclusively British components around a Japanese block. Only one sussed up local queried this and asked "Aren't those Suzuki DR 350s?"

In the afternoon Mark set about videoing the stand and then moved with Chas and Clive over to the sirens at the GM stand and had a hilarious time filming them with Oxana the queen of them all. The video will reveal all but it was very surreal and an interesting indictment of these very, very, beautiful girls. NB: Clive is pursued by the heavily scarred Kazakh that he had sold his bogus Tag Heur watch to for 3000T three nights earlier. Clive eluded him....

Come 1700hrs we dismantled our display and could feel that we had done ITE proud with our tow rope turning into a perimeter wire exemplifying how we had improvised a quite interesting stand from basically nothing.

We drifted back to the flat and floundered in the by now expected confusion that is the unwelcome pre-requisite to us going out in the evening as a unit of seven. It must be like a scene from ACAS as we reconcile the irreconcilable, compromise the uncompromising and settle the unsettling in our attempt to weave together food, the sundry offers from disparate groups of girls, our own various states of financial distress and physical exhaustion.

Across the hallway, Natasha, Rita's mother and ever increasingly *ours*, had cooked up a humungous feast of soup and plov (a risotto-esque dish) and all of us dug in with the Russian overdubbed version of "Dead men Don't wear Plaid" murmuring in the background. Somebody's fork stood upright in their bowl and it was commented that "the plov thickens". This along with Lee Van Cleef's "Thanks, half soldier..." caused more amusement than was warranted.

Come half ten we all managed to drift away from Natasha's dinner table. This is a difficult task as she constantly plies us with "just one more liqueur/coffee/sandwich. Much hormonal upsurge was detected when Oxana, the model described earlier, turned up at the flat. She was accompanied by her photographer svengali-Arturo. He looks just like Simon from Vibrasonic and was really into The Animals and early Stones. We really couldn't believe that she was sitting next to us. Arturo showed us some of her portfolio that he always carries – it was really unbearable – Oxana is <u>so</u> beautiful, luckily her being so vacuous really helps to offset this.

Off then to the Keema disco at the Students' Union. It only had about 120 people there but the music was a respectable blend of grunge, disco, 60's beat, punk et al. Austin was threatened by a Swede who warned: "Just because you're English you don't have to dance so crazy..."

We all fell back to the apartment except Chas and his spherical headed, toothy-grinned cohort Medina. We all wondered where on earth they were. They hadn't even got to the Disco.

Kazakhstan

Day 55
Sunday 4 June
Mondo Miles today: 0
Mondo Mileage: 6812

Chas's story from last night:

Medina is recovering from hepatitis which causes her to require the toilet at regular intervals. As they cruised towards the cinema Oman in search of a funky, flashing light experience she found herself facing a pressing need. Chas pulled over and she forced her way into the middle of some suitable looking foliage. In mid-bush she came face-to-face with an officer from the military police station across the way, who was happily relieving his bowels. He marched her back to the road, pulled out his baton and threatened both Medina and the waiting Chas. They were apparently trespassing within the grounds of the presidential palace and faced arrest and death by Jacksoning. Chas eventually talked his way out, on condition that he return with his papers, and he and Medina struggled back to Chez Svetta. He had witnessed 2 Kazakh girls being slapped around in the police station and the stakes were high. It took him 4 hours to talk his way out, and then he only succeeded when they realised that he was writing a novel that would include them and their baton wielding techniques....

Kazakhstan

Day 56
Monday 5 June
Mondo Miles today: 0
Mondo Mileage: 6812

A day in the mountains for most of us and a chance to visit the insane 'Medeo'. This is a colossal Olympic sized ice rink, surrounded by towering grandstands and jammed into a dramatic V shaped valley. It was the premier ice rink in the old USSR but is already showing signs of neglect now that Kazakhstan has gone it alone. It looks like it was built in the 50s and has the predictable Stalinist humungous iron frieze of two 10m tall speed skaters riveted to a cracked and blistered concrete panel. As an optimistic and truly forward thrusting *objet d'art* that suggests that in this socialist garden of Eden anything is possible, it takes some beating.

Spent the evening at the high class pick up joint that is The International Business Club. We met the guy who is the Pepsi rep out here and is cultivating this particular emerging market. We quizzed him about the Coke vs Pepsi turf wars and he said that was all crap. Apparently, they sit down over a map and divvy up the world in advance, hence we assume that Kazakhstan is a Pepsi protectorate, whilst Colombia, for example, is controlled by Coke.

Kazakhstan

Day 57
Tuesday 6 June
Mondo Miles today: 0
Mondo Mileage: 6812

The rays of sunshine streaming through the window caught Mondo Enduro at apparently their most innocent, sleeping like babes in their little sleeping bags.

Appearances, as we all know, can deceive. Dark secrets would surface of last night's disco exploits, not least from Gerald who has a breakfast and luncheon appointment with Svetla. We all look forward to the outcome with interest.

The morning was consumed in a frenzy of minor and mostly irrelevant tasks. Gerald, who had given his love interest a lift to work, returned with the film package from DHL, thereby depriving us of any further excuse for tarrying in this generous city.

In the morning Austin tracked down some engine oil and also silver spray paint with which to touch up Chas's battered fuel tank. Gerald, meanwhile, fresh from washing Svetla's hair at a breakfast date, promptly fell asleep with the excitement of it all in a downtown pub and was awakened by a waitress.

Chas meanwhile, blended with Arturo and the lovely Oxana down to the German Cultural Centre for his excruciatingly boring article on the plight of the Kazakh Deutsch. Not even the sight of her bra-less form in a skimpy tee-shirt would raise the pace of his prose but it did have a hydraulic affect on other moving body parts.

Nick changed his front tyre – having purchased a new one from Bill whose own transport will carry him across the Soviet Orient. In the afternoon, Austin and Clive took the Hi-8 camera downtown for a spot of filming. The idea is that we have a montage of top babes for the Mondo Movie and they were greatly assisted in their aim by the unexpected appearance of Oxana.

From Rita, twenty year old ITE employee and friend of Mondo Enduro:

My dear boys

It's so wonderful to see you here every day. I'm so grateful to ITE for this amazing meeting. I could never expect that it would be such a great time, such a great fun with you. I have so many feelings overwhelming my heart now that I can't express them in words clearly enough, but I hope you understand. You brought a lot of sun in our lives, you're great people from all possible sides. It's so romantic to ride around the world on the motorcycles on these super friends of yours. I hope they never break. I'll have a little chat with them for being so devoted to you so that you are able to complete your journey successfully.

It was a great feeling for me to ride with you. I felt myself like bird flying in the clear blue sky over the snowy mountains, I felt fresh air blowing into my face and you all so strong, handsome, romantic, so different, each one is so special, so COOL! Each one the best. You're the best!!! I wish you to meet no troubles on your way, not a single one! To meet many kind, generous, beautiful people. I'm so happy I've met you now. I have seven more friends, and I really hope to see you in America or if not anywhere on this Earth, but definitely I must meet you again. I will write you and hope you'll also do. Thank you for coming and you're welcome here anytime. You have true friends here now. Have a nice time in your lifetime. Be happy and lucky.

I love you very, very, very much!

Kisses Rita. Mondo Enduro – I love you!

Yes, she really did write that.

Kazakhstan

Day 58
Wednesday 7 June
Mondo Miles today: 0
Mondo Mileage: 6812

"Goodbye Almaty we'll miss you"

The inevitable time to leave had arrived. Once again we find ourselves in a city of the highest hospitality. We believed we would never see kindness to surpass that of the British Embassy in Tashkent. Only 550 miles later we are in Alma Ata where we have been received home from home.

A prompt departure was on the cards, but when we awoke 9-10am – everyone without exception was reluctant to move. Why? On account of us staying opposite an angelic mother and daughter (Natasha and Rita) who couldn't offer us enough of their love and attention. They want us to stay longer and this temptation is immense.

As Clive writes the log (4pm) there is no sign of Mondo Enduro looking set to leave. There must be some powerful enchantment preventing us from doing so. So the Mondo Enduro team tie up their final laces of admin as they set to stay just one more day. Our world record attempt may indeed be jeopardised but them's the breaks. It made sense as we were not ready to leave. There was no shopping, no-one had petrol and group kit was not fully divided, personal kit wasn't fully packed and Svetlana's flat was still a tip. Tasks were allocated: Chas and Clive went to check for final faxes and letters at Hotel Otrar, buy flowers for our hosts and send some cards and letters.

Bill and Austin went to get 4 day's supplies of food. Result: tonnes of food, letter for Bill, stunning roses for our hosts which they well and truly loved – as Chas and Clive were showered with kisses.

Back at the flat – filming was afoot. Nick, Mark and Gerald were standing to attention whilst Austin interviewed them about the enormous line of produce displayed before them. Nick was superb at doing his Sergeant major role. Plenty of footage has been shot here in Almaty and it has been probably the best so far… as we have put a lot more thought in to this area… It would appear we now have enough shots to make a Mondo Enduro trailer!

So once again after a few international calls were received for a few of the crew, we were once more taken in to Natasha and Rita's flat for what could be our final supper in Almaty. A bowl of bucked wheat augmented by Tommy K, lubricated with black tea.

Back to packing and we were just about finished by midnight… The weary men snuggled up in their beds for their last time. We'll be on the road and in the field for at least the next 1200 miles until we get to Novosibirsk, in Russia.

Kazakhstan

Day 59
Thursday 8 June
Mondo Miles today: 177
Mondo Mileage: 6812

And so, farewell to Almaty, where the Mondo riders had enjoyed a week of wine, women and, yes, plov. A quick clear out of Svetla's flat, and yet more food and tea from Rita and Natasha, saw us ready to leave by about 10.30am. Stubley had been nominated to lead the party out of Almaty. So with a few final photos for old time's sake we headed down past the Hotel Otrar and over on the 4-lane A351 towards Chilik. After a week off the bikes, and a whacking 4-day load of provisions plus oil and petrol, the bikes creaked and groaned their way along the well metalled tarmac. The sun blazed down with the Alatai mountains appearing huge, but hazy, to our right. All seemed to be going swimmingly when a mad police Lada almost ran Clive off the road. Clive responded in good old West End dispatch fashion, which didn't seem to go down to well with the old Bill. A photo of Mark at our stand at the motorshow is on the cover of today's 'Caravan' newspaper, and we have a copy. Fortunately a quick flash of this Kazakh tabloid seemed to calm the coppers down and they let us go with just a snarl.

So we sped on with a brew after 100 miles. Highlight of the day was finding the flat arrow-straight road suddenly widen to 'four lane' but with no central reservation. Some chunkster letters were painted on the ground then we realised; the road had become a landing strip! Sure enough, a mile later it narrowed back to normal. We took advantage of this extra width and Austin filmed what will surely be the only shot of us riding six abreast. Result.

As 4 bikes needed an oil change, we decided to ditch the old oil and use up the 2 gallons we had bought in Almaty. A7, K4, K5 and D3 were hot blocked and ready to go. Iranian Pars Jam oil (an oil for all seasons) was decanted carefully into the thirsty DRs. With 200 miles on the horizon, everything seemed OK, when the town of Chundzha was sighted. We were heading for the Kazakh version of the Grand Canyon for some amazing scenery but as we were so close to the Chinese border (we had seen Chinese trucks) the Kazakhs had seen fit to declare the area a military zone so access denied! About we turned at the improvised sandbag roadblock, gassed up in Kokpek and returned to the oil change site for the night. It had its babbling brook, and was well off the beaten track.

Bill and Clive cooked whilst Chas dropped his bike. And so to bed under the stars of a balmy June evening in deepest Kazakhstan but with er... China only 20 miles away.

Kazakhstan

Day 60
Friday 9 June
Mondo Miles today: 256
Mondo Mileage: 7045

We were all sad to leave Almaty. Some more than others. Gerald commented on the fact that he slept much better inside than out under the stars. It is a combination of being plagued by insects and the restrictions of the sleeping bag and the hard ground. At least he can smoke all night. Svetlana asked us why there were no ladies on the trip, this morning, and every morning that we are in the field the answer was obvious. A windy and chilly first 100 miles. Then a stop for coffee. We turned off the main road to by-pass Almaty and it was the first time that we were not riding on an "A" class road since we were in France. Another 60 miles and the threatened rain started, forcing a mass stop for waterproofs.

During the rainstorm a service area hove into view. Up until now the weather had always permitted alfresco dining but today we dined on shashlik in a yurt. It was a modern one with trellis and canvas walls, unlike a traditional one which was next door made of branches and felt. Whilst eating, the rain stopped so we decided to start looking for a campsite as it was beyond 1800hrs.

The road reached out to the east and just when we decided to eat it began to rain. Luckily the route went over a river so once the bikes had scrambled down the embankment we were sheltered under the bridge to at least eat but maybe to sleep as well. Whilst the rest of the team began cooking Mark and Gerald went to look for a better rough campsite. They came upon a deserted village, although the gardens were still tended. They returned back to tell the others that they could have a house *each* only to find that they were reluctant to move on. Oh Well. Nick and Chas did the usual excellent job with the evening meal. Mark did the decent thing and shopped for alcohol. Beer and Vodka arrived soon from a roadside booth. The damp clothing was hung off protruding steelwork in an attempt to dry it. Those who had bagged the hooks nearest the fire had a better chance. By 21.15hrs the sleeping kit was laid out and Nick Stubley was in bed straight away. Nearly forgot. Whilst eating in the yurt, a man came up holding a copy of yesterday's 'Caravan' newspaper which had mentioned, amongst other things, that Natasha was the 'Queen of Plov'. As far as we could gather he claimed he was the "King of Plov" and that we must go to his house and eat plov until our back teeth were awash with the stuff. Unfortunately he lived 300km away, but we have his address so we may yet call in. Mark was also recognised from the article while buying the beer. Chas's Thermarest bubble was the cause of much amusement this evening as 5 of us are sleeping all in a row on the ponchos. As always when camping our worst nightmare is being Jacksoned. This time was different. Two lads, slightly the worse for drink stumbled under the bridge at 2300hrs. We thought they had come to chat with us but in fact they were looking for pigeons. They were armed with a torch and a catapult. After a fruitless 30 minutes of shooting stones up into the beams they left. They were only a few yards from us yet seemed to notice neither us nor the seven motorcycles.

The next disturbance was far more incredible but first, some background info; the petrol stations out here have a different system for dispensing gas than we're used to. You have to know what volume of gas you want in advance, report this to the cashier in the booth, who actuates the pump from therein. In truth, this isn't too onerous unless you have over estimated your requirement. The problem then, is that the trigger on the pump nozzle thingy is often deactivated so the fuel just *keeps* on coming, backing up past the filler cap, all over the tank until you are hosing the forecourt with grade 75! There is a petrol station up above us on the road before the bridge and it's rather 'open plan'. Not normally an issue apart from the fact that they have set up a Public Address system so that the cashier can bark orders at the customers. Result, the normal semaphore hand signals between the client and the cabin are no longer necessary. However, all night and into the small hours the tranquil idyll of the eastern Kazakh steppe was punctuated by incredibly loud, fuzz-drenched and distorted Dalek-like shouts of "*Skolka Liter?*" (how many litres?). Aaaah, the perils of the rough campsite with even vaguely urban characteristics...

Kazakhstan

Day 61
Saturday 10 June
Mondo Miles today: 199
Mondo Mileage: 7244

We are as close to China as ever.

The Kazakh steppe rolls on – ceaselessly unchanging but always beautiful or striking enough not to be monotonous.

Last night's intrusion by the locals was extraordinary as they appeared to want nothing from us, nor did they even pay us any attention. The complete opposite of our usual experiences during the day. Anyway, we all slept well and started the day with Bill's kindly brewed coffee and Clive's sad news that his heroic dawn excursion to film our impromptu concrete canopy was a total failure. In classic Mondo Enduro style it took us till noon to get up, strike camp and get some gasoline at the screaming tannoy petrol station.

The weather had cleared up pretty much after last night's awful unending rain. We finally set off and save a few small mishaps made the first 100 miles in 2½ hours. An event on this leg was us passing the combined civil and military aerodromes at Taldy-Kurgan. What was strange was to see literally tens of fighters and Suzis fighter/bombers draped in tarpaulins and "mothballed" outside their poorly constructed bomb-proof hangars. Alongside these victims of the warming up of the Cold War were about ten civilian planes and some bi-planes which were clearly the Russian copy of the Junkers 33.

Onwards past the town of Sarakand, where candy and cola were freely available but bread requests met with a shake of the head. Onto our 100 mile tea break as has become standard.

NB: Mark's already damaged luggage "system" begat further trauma when it sagged to the extent that it began to abrade on his back wheel. Goodbye waterproofs and Clive's tent and Bill's canoe bag. OOPS!!

All the team save Nick and Mark were installed in a grassy nook and so that the latter did not miss our picnic location as they drove past, Austin placed his white crash helmet on the verge with the peak 'pointing' down a track and hence acting as a lunchtime beacon. Unlucky Austin! A passing Kazakh car-full pulled over and helped themselves to this clearly discarded decorated western head protection. Unlucky Nick and Mark, with 'signpost' removed they missed the turning, burned past the others and earned themselves a bonus prize of 20 extra miles by the time Chas had zipped out to apprehend them and bring them back to the fold and now Austin has no helmet.

The pm riding session yielded some more upland areas and a twisty road that was a little more interesting. There is definitely no shortage of Kazakh cowboys and they are totally impressive as they herd their flocks of sheep and cows. They invariably give us a wave as if they sensed a certain affinity with us on our Japanese iron horses.

The big, big sky that the steppe offers gave us a lovely blue puffed with totally picturesque cumulous clouds of purest white. With miles still to do we reached our n'th Police check point but unusually seemed to be getting a little more attention than we would like. Austin pretended to about turn and roar back to Alma-Ata much to the confusion and consternation of our temporary captors: even more to Austin's confusion and consternation was the loss of drive and crunching of metal that can only mean your chain has snapped!!

In fact Austin's front sprocket was badly damaged but thankfully still serviceable. He and Gerald put in a new soft split link while Clive filmed, Chas interviewed whilst Mark and Bill prepared an excellent roadside feast. Throughout this whole episode we were studied intently by a Kazakh wearing a superb pork pie hat. Austin offered to buy it but was politely rebuffed. Gerald found a superb campsite within 1km and we toasted ourselves with Tolstoi Vodka mixed with an orange flavoured dust called 'Yupi'.

Kazakhstan

Day 62
Sunday 11 June
Mondo Miles today: 248
Mondo Mileage: 7492

Last night's campsite looked great this morning, complete with silty river and yurt 200 yards away. 86 miles of steppe saw Austin, Mark and Clive meeting up with Chas, who had a flat next to a stunning purple patch of flowers. Gerald (who had the repair kit) had stormed ahead with Bill and we had to wait half-an-hour for Nick to bring them back. A painless repair to the inner tube allowed us to have a welcome cuppa and the remainder of the recession biscuits. Bill, in his role as general fruit inspector, declared the bananas ready to eat after they had spent 3 days nuzzling up against his exhaust.

No roads have we seen straighter than those which cut across the Kazakh steppe. Today's ride sailed past as we chased each from one horizon to the next. The ground, clouds and sky all seem to glow. The fact that the glow increases each day is clear evidence that we are approaching Semipalatinsk. Some of the filming should come out well – notably the train chase sequence. Clive knocked over Austin's coffee at the next stop and it had to be left to Chas to adjudicate as to who was at fault.

Tonight's campsite defies belief – Austin and Gerald went off to a disused-looking air base and found it completely deserted and strewn with empty nuclear fallout bunkers. Gerald went off the recce further afield and on this treeless landing strip found firewood and a well. He also discovered a jet engine lying on the runway (fun and games for Nick tomorrow). It looks as though everything has been smashed up by Jacksons and everything of value removed. Soldiers have scratched their names, home towns and dates of service on grafittable areas (Jackson Jacksonville, 1977-79). Over dinner we discussed the fun and games to be had on the morning and the route to be taken from hereon in. Sweet dreams Chas and Gerald, let's hope you wake up intact...

Kazakhstan

Day 63
Monday 12 June
Mondo Miles today: 157
Mondo Mileage: 7649

We were scrambled at 0830 by Comrade Austin with a brew. This abandoned airbase will surely be the strangest place we ever sleep. We imagine its exact coordinates are logged into some NATO computer somewhere but we mused that we could be amongst the first westerners to have the run of the place. So it was chocks away by 0915 as our combat-ready MIG 350's were wheeled out of their hangar for yet another off-road, low-flying combat mission. We aimed to establish an improvised moto-cross circuit on the grassy domed coverings of the hangar-bunkers. Austin and Gerald headed off on patrol, while Clive followed on a photo-recon mission: the others were left to guard the base, and not in vain, as multiple bogies came low out of the sun on a strafing run, to finally give us a Steward's after a whole night of rest-easy, uninterrupted rough camping. The first wave was the expendables, locals easily shot up by your well-rehearsed excuses, but the second wave was of decidedly heavier bombers – military police with an apparent allergy to smiling. Chas told them that we'd be gone in 1 hour, but was sternly corrected and told that we would be gone in 5 minutes, or else... Gerald, Austin and Clive returned to find the base occupied by the enemy, having judiciously hidden the video camera, thus keeping intact our strenuous assertion that "Oh no, no... no pictures, officer... there's nothing really worth photographing..." This was sneakily retrieved, and once again, Mondo Enduro found itself on the road fleeing from officialdom – this time smug in the knowledge that they had got away with an adventure for which, 5 years previously, there was no precedent.

A group decision chose Semipalatinsk over Ust-Kamenogorsk en route into Siberia, so we headed towards this former site of Soviet Nuclear Testing. Sixty miles on and an alluring riverside spot tempted us into stopping for a brew forty miles short of the by now habitual 100 mile stop. Thoughts of residual radiation poisoning had us pessimistically scrambling for the Katadyn filters, as both were pumped in anger for the first time on the trip. Secure in the knowledge that pure Swiss Alpine water was passing our lips, we did not stop at the tea, but gorged ourselves on Yupi and soup too. Clive helpfully offered to wash up the tea billie with petrol and then tried to rectify this by washing the petrol out with used oil. At least our joints will be moving well, if not our brains.

We broke camp with approximately 15 litres of Katadyn-ed water and headed for Semipalatinsk, which hove into view as a mass of chimneys and smokestacks. Belching smoke gave an accurate introduction to the town, which proved ugly and entirely uninspiring. It failed as a victualling centre, too, as the abundance of fruit 'n' veg in more southerly climes had evidently been left behind us. Onions we found, but little else, although recession biscuits, doughnuts and pasta supplies were easily replenished, as was the flow of 'Yupi', usurped in style by 'Invite', one sachet making 2 litres in a much wider range of flavours, our favourite being 'grape'. A second shop-stop produced condensed milk, more biscuits and some admirable vino collapso with which to celebrate leaving Central Asia (we are fast approaching the border with Russia). It also produced thieves a plenty, one of which made a try at Gerald's camera, happily in vain. Conversely, another local was offering us free import beer to welcome us to his city. As we pulled out of town, a huge steel Soviet star 'sculpture' came into view – symbol of the defunct Soviet system. It was decided to stop for a group photograph as it symbolised "what Mondo Enduro is really all about". As we clambered eagerly over this astral monstrosity, police arrived to inform us that photography was a no-go, before wandering down to the bus stop to wait for a bus... we therefore spent a couple of minutes whistling innocently and kicking pebbles until their bus arrived, and then proceeded to complete our posing for the camera.

We finally hit the open road to Barnaul and the border; skirting a forest which offered us too many juicy rough camp opportunities to resist. We finally pulled into a wooded glade where the brothers Vince prepared a monster meal (plus emergency ration served in a *bucket!*). The Vino Collapso-filled plastic cups were raised in honour to Central Asia, a beautiful, varied and fascinating region, populated by lovely people, which we will be extremely sad to leave behind. However, we look forward to Siberia tomorrow, harbinged perhaps by the tracts of pure forest we have come across, and more ominously by the giant mosquitoes which seem to lurk in them.

The Kazakh steppe is gone and this area, with its graceful Scots Pines reminded us of Wells-next-the-sea in Norfolk. Bursting with over consumption we reminisced around the fire on this, our last night in Kazakhstan. We retired, Bill and Austin to their Poncho/Mozzie net combie, the others to tents, laughing at the vainglorious attempts of our insect enemy to pierce our tanned skins and drink our vino-filled blood. War is declared;

will Deet and headnets prevail, or will it turn into an orgy of proboscis plunging and bite scratching? We will get to Russia tomorrow.

Russia

Day 64
Tuesday 13 June
Mondo Miles today: 188
Mondo Mileage: 7837

Life's rich pageant was none the poorer today following Mondo Enduro's effortless incursion into Great Mother Russia, if you get my meaning.

We awoke at about 08:00hrs to the sound of Gerald being a busy bee and the very hive of industry around the billy can. Brews soon followed and we slurped contentedly as we listened to pilgrim's tales from the long road behind us. The story of Austin's tripartite vomiting three years ago in Tatler's flat caused especial merriment and we hit the road scandalously late at about 10.30am.

It is worthy of note that the first clash of proboscis between Mondo Enduro and Siberia's mosquito population ended with honours divided evenly. The combo of mossie net and Deet repellent, plus smoke from the camp fire and Gerald's 'Laser' fags, all coalesced to keep the little blighters at bay but toilet excursions by various Mondo members had left them caught with their pants down both literally and figuratively, and several left the wooded glade nursing bites to their private parts.

Moving swiftly on, the road to the Russian border passed swiftly and uneventfully beneath our 18 and 21" wheels. We stopped after about 30 miles to spend our few last remaining Tenge at a roadside store and came across an intriguing new Israeli powdered drink sachet called 'Cheer Up'. Our strenuous attempts to purchase it were foiled by the shopkeeper but she did sell us two packs of 'Risk' cigarettes which we donated to Gerald.

On to the border and we realised that there were *no* Kazakh formalities, they literally didn't have a border post. Our entry to this mighty country was the same; we were stamped *out* of Uzbekistan but were never stamped *into* Kazakhstan. Hence, there is no official record that we were ever here!!

Before we knew it, the Russian border was upon us marked by a watchtower painted in the cream, pink and blue colours of the Confederation of Independent States. Our arrival was met with the usual fevered interest by Custom officials and truckers of assorted nationalities who clustered round making the by now customary "*skolka*"? Inquiry (how big is your engine?). Bill and Mark sashayed through the Customs hall into the den of the bureaucrats who processed our visa formalities with a no quibble efficiency which was quite unexpected.

In the meantime, the border mandarins had taken a lunch break and we brewed up behind the sheet metal Customs Hall. As we did so, we raised a collective beaker in a toast to Central Asia which lies behind us, and the Siberian Wetlands in front. Clive, meanwhile, had blended a loaf of bread from a custom's man, who perhaps took pity on our plight. By way of a token of gratitude, Chas knocked over a vase of flowers, spilling water onto a thick volume of vehicle details. Soon we were back on the road, spilling through scenery which switched between typical Russian (ruddy peasant faces, corpulent Babushkas, empty shops, etc) and quintessential East Anglian (hedgerows, flat fields, wetlands). We are now on a similar latitude to England and the landscape looks very familiar. The giant conundrum remains with all this deeply fertile black Russian soil, why aren't there any fresh vegetables for sale at the roadside? With 5,000 miles to go to Magadan, Mondo Enduro awaits the answer with interest.

Our campsite was an idyllic but mosquito-strewn meadow near a railway track which thundered to the sound of freight trains. Bill and Nick Stubley concocted a meal worthy of the great Fanny Craddock consisting of onions, garlic and no less than three larder ingredients – curry powder, chilli and herbs. After dinner, the lads played 20 guesses and a strange logic game while we completed this journal awaiting the morrow with barely suppressed excitement. All that Soviet iconography. So many acres of ripening wheat...

During the night and just before morning hath broken, Bill's bowels hath spoken and according to him we could solve our water shortage problem with a little bit of help from our Katadyn filter.

Russia

Day 65
Wednesday 14 June
Mondo Miles today: 130
Mondo Mileage: 7967

Mondo Enduro 7: Mosquitoes 0!

The mozzies didn't stand a chance this time, even though Mondo Enduro was heavily outnumbered. Our defence system of bodies heavily clad in leather and drenched in Deet, mozzie nets, a roaring fire and smoke kept them at bay throughout the night until dawn.

A tad after dawn and Clive and Austin were up to rekindle the fire and brew up (hardly a mozzie in sight they had crawled back with their stings between their legs).

We broke camp around 9.30am and left our campsite to start a big riding day to Novosibirsk – the setting was idyllic: beautiful blue skies, a couple of whispy clouds, glorious sunshine and countryside akin to that of back home. Stubley has pointed out that Novosibirsk sort of means 'New Siberia' because as the Russians expanded eastwards from Moscow it was the end of the railroad and the start of the 'unknown'. Gerald suggests that we think of it as a Russian version of St Louis (Missouri).

70 miles of wonderful countryside and we arrived in Barnaul, where we supposedly had to register with Customs and officialdom. These were the vague instructions given to some of us by passport Control on entering Russia.

So Mark, Chas and Nick went to investigate the 'registering'. Bill and Austin went to change money and stock up with supplies whilst Chas and Gerald recce'd the way to Novosibirsk and guarded the bikes from Jacksons.

An hour later Mark, Chas and Nick returned having had no joy at all – they proceeded back to *another* Customs House for better directions. They did in fact find it in the end and came face to face with that salubrious bureaucracy reserved for Russia, a *five-hour* wait until they were seen. All this aggro is purely because we're riding bikes (worth only ⊡1500) and they have to be 'registered' to stop us selling them. Why the goons at the border couldn't have done this is of course a mystery. Next time someone bemoans the borderless EU we'll quickly put 'em straight. Meanwhile, Bill and Austin returned with a load of food including those luxury items of coffee, Top Twister and frankfurter rolls. No shops to speak of, everything being bought from kerbside kiosks or improvised greengrocers operating from the boot of a car. We have to eat whatever we can get.

As per usual, when Mondo Enduro pulls up in a town, the bikes attract a crowd. It wasn't long before we had to deal with a gaggle of about fifteen onlookers.

Vickor, a Siberian bike enthusiast presented himself to us along with his two sons and was totally intrigued by our steeds. He was most surprised that our 350s were all second hand and unmodified and marvelled that we were paying for this trip ourselves and were not supported by Suzuki. He himself had a Jawa 350 and stayed with us for most of the afternoon totally fascinated by our DR's. He went home for a bit then returned with an 80s Soviet 'Sportbike' magazine. Said publication featured an article about him and three others riding off-road to the Arctic Circle and indeed a piece about how to make your own sprockets!!

Around 5pm we had Sergei, an excellent English speaking ruffian, acquaint himself with us. He was keen to take us on a tour of the town and urgently gushed facts about Barnaul's prestigious past as a copper and silver smeltopolis. This city was well established by 1750 yet seems to have that Tashkent tinge of all having been built in an awful hurry within only the last thirty years. Gerald suggests that we think of it as a Russian version of Coalbrookdale.

Things progressed and after an hour we had a photo-journalist and an hour later a TV news crew turned up out of the blue to film us for a bulletin on this evening's '*Barnaul Today*'– all of which was caught on our camera by Clive as well as a magnitude of various titbits of footage in and around Barnaul. We saw a civilian driving an armoured personnel carrier down the road and it looked like it was his only form of transport (two goats on the roof!).

We headed for Novosibirsk at 7.40pm and 50 miles later encountered the giant popart sign that heralded the town of Iskitim.

We espied a campsite in a tangle of silver birch and rode into the wood with 2ft high grass everywhere and the highest mosquito count yet endured on Mondo Enduro – not only that, we had come across the biggest Red Army ants seen and they were a carpet of movement beneath our feet. Clive and Austin set about making a fire on their infested ground with lashings of petrol. Unlucky ants as they went up in flames. Five minutes later and the area was crawling with them again – unlucky Mondo Enduro. Dinner was prepared with some caution and mosquito headnets were worn by most; even by Gerald, the semi-dead one, who doesn't get bitten. It must be conditions like this that explain why some people just *don't* go camping.

Russia

Day 66
Thursday 15 June
Mondo Miles today: 95
Mondo Mileage: 8062

To gain shelter from the night's rain, an army of mosquitoes had ensconced themselves in the porches of each tent. This meant that first up had to run the gauntlet to the Deet before the day's chores could begin. Rain in the night meant that a brief drying out period was required, but we still got away by 1.30pm. The road was of concrete construction with long straight stretches. At regular intervals there were large socialist signposts with one either being repaired or dismantled (one suspects the former).

As we approached Novosibirsk, huge chimneys reached up from the horizon each one urgently belching smoke. British smoke would be whitish but this Russian stuff seems to be more orange and gooey than we suspect we're used to. The traffic intensified and we holed up at the city limits. The roadside candy-Kiosks were full of Snickers, bananas and liquor. Whilst waiting, a middle aged chap introduced himself to us as Vladimir. He spoke excellent English, revealed that in 1988 he had cycled from New York to Los Angeles, was now a 'businessman' and insisted that if we needed assistance in his city then we should consider him to be at our service! We wonder if a group of Russians at the Cooper Dean roundabout on the outskirts of Bournemouth would be approached in this manner.

The rendezvous was the Hotel Siberia, with a fully modern suite of services. We rode into town, past the main square, with its full complement of Soviet statues. At $100 per night, the Siberia was out of reach. The Novosibirsk at $159 for 7 was a reasonable choice. With one bath between 7, queuing was made with Gerald first in the tub. Naturally, the 60s hotel seemed to have been designed by somebody who was deeply impressed by Marineville out of Stingray.

After a quick beer in the bar, it was out on the town to the main square (Lenin Square?). Here we saw a full dress rehearsal for a parade of goose stepping soldiers, Ladas with blue lights, fire engines and armoured personnel carriers. Later, a team demonstrating hand-to-hand combat went through their motions. We tried to imagine the equivalent scene in the centre of Bournemouth.

Meanwhile the Mondo diners went first into a strip joint on the square. A leggy Russian woman proceeded to remove all her clothes just after Nick and Gerald had left. So it was on to the Hotel Centro (which is also the DHL office) for steak and chips. All except Austin and Bill that is. They went back to the strip joint and had a hot dog and made calls to the UK. Austin had a stewards' from his dad about lack of letters etc, but Ambassadress Barbara

Hay had sent a favourable school report (addressed to Austin and Gerald's *dad*) from Tashkent to Bournemouth, so this made amends.

Naturally, Austin, Stubley, Mark and Clive have decided to grow mustachios á la Mexicana Yosemite Sam style. By the time we split from Magadan we should have a full set of handle-bar moustaches. And so to bed in a dry, warm mossie free environment.

Russia

Day 67
Friday 16 June
Mondo Miles today: 0
Mondo Mileage: 8062

As I write this at 1900hrs sitting on two tyres in a car yard I am looking at a babe sitting on Clive's bike. More of which later.

Everyone was up fairly early. Austin to the Hotel Sibir to hook up with Vladimir who is helping him find a new front sprocket. Nick and Gerald went to the train station and promptly got separated. Chas was out and about early looking around town. Bill and Mark stayed indoors.

At the Hotel Sibir Austin discovered that Vladimir was one of many entrepreneurs who had rented a room indefinitely and made it his office. He had a secretary and crucially, a juicy fax machine into which Austin swiftly fed an update of our current situation, destination Mondo Mission control in Dorset. Vladimir was extremely charming and utterly empathised with our predicament of being on the road in a strange land, four thousand miles still to go and not being too good with the lingo. He reminisced about the 'old days' under communism. He made it very clear that the Soviets most certainly didn't see themselves as labouring under the yoke of a police state. They were happy, he explained; you knew what would happen in your life, you could "make a plan" (his very words). Russians didn't suffer from slumps or recession. He made it sound like the workers' paradise that we had always been lead to believe it wasn't. As an example that Brezhnev's era in the 60s and 70s really *was* the Golden Age of the USSR he cooed that you could go into a shop and buy....oranges! His faith in this epoch, a time so clearly unconcerned with the mire of excessive consumption in which *we* currently wallow, was inspirational indeed. Furthermore, at a stroke, Vladimir had painted a picture of workaday Russia which was of course no more an 'Evil Empire' than the Poole and Sandbanks Rotary Club.

Vladimir had done a ring round and presently in came one of his comrades, a second hand car dealer called, you guessed it, Vladimir. He was clearly the man since he owned a Honda VFR400R which, parked outside, was the first *non-Soviet* bike we had seen since entering Georgia 32 days ago.

He was full of beaming energy and in a thrice Vlad 1 was bade farewell and Vlad 2 had whisked Austin to a bike breakers but unfortunately no-one there seemed to be interested in helping them find a front sprocket. Determined to come through for us he offered all of us a free night's bed and also arranged a TV interview! We all decided to take up this kind but needlessly generous offer.

At 12.30hrs Clive, Austin and Gerald went to the yard owned by Vladimir 2 where Andrei, his chief mechanic took the old sprocket off to get a new one made. Austin and Gerald went to lunch with Vlad 2 and his colleagues. It had become clear that Vlad 2 had zero English but this was compensated for with endless Russian largesse, including a banya (sauna) convened for 10pm! Meanwhile, Mark had dropped a jar of jam in the hotel foyer and it took a while to clean up. After lunch the TV crew arrived and interviewed us. They also had a look at some of our own footage and taped some of it to use in the broadcast which would be shown on next Tuesday. Vlad 1 turned up with a lengthy fax from Mr Vince in UK.

Andrei the mechanic returned and Austin kissed his feet. The splined centre of the worn front sprocket had been cut out with an acetylene torch and a fifteen tooth sprocket (with *its* centre cut out) had been welded on to it. Hey presto! A new sprocket. Notwithstanding the Turkmeni tyre 'mousse' (day 41) none of us have ever seen such an audacious nugget of improvisation. Meanwhile back at The Sibir, Bill and Nick had met a British lorry driver who worked for Motorola and after a chat said that he could arrange to fly their bikes from here to Khabarovsk (big city over near Vladivostok) for *free*. They are going back to The Sibir to negotiate with him again.

It was a fast 40km drive to the banya in 2 cars with a stop on the way for drinks. The location was in the countryside next to a lake. A civilised setting but we had to wait half-an-hour for the sauna to be vacated. The time was passed by walking down to the beach and playing a game of hide and seek. At last the sauna was ready. There was anticipation at this point by some members of the team since Olga, Vlad 2's girlfriend, turned up and there was talk of further women arriving, leading to interesting times. In the event it turned out to be all above board. Everyone undressed and towelled up and entered the sauna. The heat was OK until Vlad 2 put some more water onto the hot rocks. Those sitting on the top bench became uncomfortably hot and Austin had to move down a step. Out of the sauna and into the swimming pool. Fantastic, even Gerald who is not normally a keen swimmer enjoyed it. The whole process was repeated twice over. Olga even got naked in the pool with us but everything remained limp. Mondo Enduro won the aquatic singing competition with a rendition of "Jerusalem" which echoed around the room. The Russians couldn't match it. Then we all sang a Beatles tune.

The call went out that the food was ready. The table was laid with sausages, tinned meats, smashed potatoes, bread and gherkins and of course

Vodka. Many toasts ensued. These Russians certainly don't need much excuse to party but more seriously, their kindness has made us think about how we might try to emulate them when we get home. Rather than mountains, mosques and sunsets, the stand out feature of this trip is the way people will help us and host us even though we are strangers.

At 0100hrs everyone changed and left to drive back to the yard expecting to sleep on the workshop floor. Vlad 2 would have none of it and insisted he treat us to a room at the Hotel Ob. Austin was missing though, Vlad explained that he was staying with Andrei, the mechanic who had made the new sprocket. We finally checked in at 0200hrs looking forward to a good night's sleep after one of the most eventful days so far, also wondering what mischief Austin was getting up to.

Russia

Day 68
Saturday 17 June
Mondo Miles today: 0
Mondo Mileage: 8062

Mondo Enduro went to bed last night after a superb day of kindness, assistance, hospitality and most importantly, generosity. Hence, we knew our time in Novosibirsk was coming to a close and that today, Saturday, we would have to make a move in an easterly direction but not as a seven, as a two and a five; Nick and Bill have arranged for their girlfriends to come out and meet us in Anchorage several weeks hence but there is a fear that we will not get there in time (still 4,000 road miles to go), of more concern is the section after Ulan Ude where there is *no* road marked on the map and the last 1000 miles to Magadan which is just a dotted line in our Russian Road Atlas. Given how terrible many of the 'motorways' have been we are not sure if it will be possible to drive all the way to Magadan. As far as we know, nobody has ever done this. Hence, Nick and Bill are entertaining going ahead to Alaska by plane and we'll see them when we get there.

Anyway, Austin had nothing more exotic to report from last night at Andrei the mechanic's than condensed milk excess. Poor old Andrei lived in a three roomed flat in a tumbledown block on a rough and ready housing estate on the West side of the river. Like almost everything Soviet we have seen, the whole place had the appearance of being a partially completed but well intentioned slum. However, Andrei's hosting could not be faulted and a trip through his archive of national Service (Black Sea navy 81-84) photos was fascinating. Better was yet to come when he ordered Svetlana (USSR omni title) his wife, to leaf through his back catalogue and unearth any pictures with a motorcycle pedigree. About ten came to light, all black and white and grainy. They were totally phenomenal shots of his days as a works URAL side-car champion and no more a macho display of understated cool was ever seen.

NB: one of the apprentice mechanics at the yard is a ringer for Michael York save the advanced state of decay that his teeth have acquired.

Some oil was blended in a staggering Mondo moment whence $78 worth of 10W/40 (from Bury, Lancs!!) was donated to our slush/lube fund, totally gratis! By feeble way of recompense, Mondo Enduro's elder statesman, Chief Gerald, went into a meeting (plus interpreter) with the Don, Vlad 2, for a meeting about the market for second hand car parts in the UK. Gerald emerged an hour later and reported that once the interpreter was available it became clear that Vlad 2 only handled stolen cars. His meetings with Gerald had been to try to establish a British outlet for them. Perhaps it is better that we are leaving in a few minutes.

Chas and Bill meanwhile made their way to the GPO to make a couple of calls and send off some single 8 films – these weighty items proved too much for the Russian postal system to handle, so they will be sent on later. They returned to the car yard base to find the others ready to leave, with Vlad 2 eagerly over-revving his Honda in anticipation of leading five shagged British trail bikes out of town. Nick 'n' Bill were therefore sad witnesses to the first splitting up of Mondo Enduro, as the ongoing 5 pulled out of the yard, bikes sagging under the weight of extra kit discarded by the two stay behinds, Nick and Bill made their way to The Hotel Sibir to meet up with Motorola and hopefully some free plane seats to Khabarovsk. As expected, no firm information was available, so they returned to the Ob, Nick to bed and Bill into Andrei's Mercedes for his second sauna trip in as many days. A few km of dark back streets led to some huge security gates embossed with red stars, which swung back to admit us into a heavily guarded Military Base where Andrei (inevitably) had a couple of contacts. The others (Georgi, Andrei, Igor, Olga) were already there and invited Bill for a pre-sauna play on the anti-aircraft guns and missile launchers before leading him inside for more sweat-letting and birch-branch slapping. The plunge pool was the size of a swimming pool and was a luxurious place to cool off before business talk (in towels) was broached, again about second hand imports to Novosibirsk. Bill, expert in this field, managed to keep the discussion going till 2am, when he was finally chauffeured back by Andrei, gliding silently through the dark back streets of Russia's third largest city with a violin lament playing atmospherically over the car stereo, and so to bed, to join Nick Stubley in his TV induced slumber.

Russia (Irkutsk)

Day 69
Sunday 18 June
Mondo Miles today: 208
Mondo Mileage: 8373

Our first morning as a fivesome. The heavens were mourning the loss of comrades Bill Penty and Nick Stubley. Snug in our RABS we lay and listened to nature's tears tapping on the flysheets. Would they blend a free flight to Khabarovsk with Motorola? Would we see them again in North America? Will Tintin find the answer to the riddle of the crab with the golden claws? Find out in future editions of the Mondo log. No answers to these questions will be revealed on this page of the Mondo Log.

The rain put paid to our plans for an early getaway. An attack of idleness overwhelmed us with the result that we didn't leave until 1pm. Today's ride was wet. Siberia appears to be gripped in the clutches of a massive rain front which did what it does best on us for the whole day. It is on days like this that little things give us a disproportionate amount of pleasure as shortly after leaving the campsite we saw a sign for Irkutsk saying 694km. Chas double checked and our spirits soared. Of course it should have read 1694km, but for a few minutes we simple souls were well pleased. After 70 miles we stopped in Kedrova to find petrol and discovered instead a bakery serving delicious pizzas and coffee. Some police took Chas away to the only petrol station open on a Sunday. It was hidden away in the middle of some allotments. Little did we expect to find, in the midst of freshly sown cabbages and sundry root vegetables, the best petrol station in Russia. Not only did the petrol pump work, not only was the owner straight but the armed guard resisted the temptation to bring Mondo Enduro to a sudden, lead-pumped halt. It is impossible to convey how welcome the bakery cum coffee shop was to five cold, wet riders. The dyed blonde was less than impressed but did have the courtesy to serve us our pizzas and coffee (twice).

There followed a wet 138 miles of riding through the Taiga, broken only by a leg-stretch. We resolved to find cover in a building for the night as the rain showed no sign of stopping. We found a barn that was dry and full of hay so we settled in. It's great to have it all to ourselves and reminds us of the saucy climax of 'The Go-Between' but without Julie Christie (or Alan Bates for that matter). We made do with soup and bread as we were too tired to do a proper meal. Tomorrow will probably deliver 300 miles of drenching driving, so it's time for an early night. Gerald has found his eyrie, Clive is happily passing wind inside his RAB and Austin and Chas are quietly talking each other to sleep.

Russia (Irkutsk)

Day 70
Monday 19 June
Mondo Miles today: 252
Mondo Mileage: 8625

On opening the sheet metal doors of our night's refuge we saw a sky as tortured as the soul of a Russian writer. Big black clouds and little white ones merged into a welter of impending inundation. If this is the middle of June (which it is) heaven help those that find themselves here in January.

For the first 50 miles, the heavens were merciful to us – after a fashion. Although the rain held off, the temperature plunged to new depths of chilliness, leaving us shivering on our acrylic fur seats. Fortunately help was at hand in a tiny railway and logging settlement called Vogatol which was at first slow to reveal its charms. The streets sloshed with the mud and debris of a seemingly eternal winter while a queue of residents waited for an apparently non-existent bus.

Fortunately the attention magnet which is Austin's motorcycle soon drew admiring glances from workers at what appeared to be a wood mill. An innocently absurd inquiry as to the whereabouts of the nearest restaurant immediately solicited an invitation to dine at the staff canteen. We gorged ourselves on soup, then potato and meat stew and a lukewarm apple compote before departing amidst pledges of lasting international amity. The moment featuring a line up of archetypal Siberian faces plus Austin, Gerald, Mark and Clive, was captured on camera by Chas.

The endless stream of mud and diesel which passes for roads in these parts flowed onwards past a small and uninspiring industrial town. On the outskirts, opposite a spooky cemetery, we turned off the highway with the intention of drying our clothes round a warm fire. The mere act of gathering kindling sticks was taken as a prompt by the rain god to drench us with intermittent downpours. Vaguely dejected and with the endless rain starting to spoil our mood we set up a poncho to shelter beneath. A break in the drizzle gave us a chance to finally get a fire going, brew up and warm our sodden feet.

The next 50 miles told their own story of moisture and misery as we ploughed onwards through an iron curtain of mud and rainwater. As the clouds finally parted, Tulun came into view revealing its sordid corsetry of heaving industry. Just as we braced ourselves for a final 100 mile surge through the by now not inclement weather, a link in Gerald's chain broke; necessitating lengthy repairs in a less than charming picnic spot, much strewn with old engine parts and at least one dead dog. Gerald got tool-handed while Mark, Austin and Chas did an oil change, Clive, in the meantime, lit a fire and made coffee for one and all.

A day which was developing a certain film noir intensity in its overlapping shoots of good and bad, still had one or more surprises in store. However, by now, the weather had opened again bathing us once again in its muddy urine which, bespattered on goggles and visors, made navigation ever more difficult in the fading light.

After another 50 miles or so we turned left into a small town characterised by an abundance of large wooden houses with roomy garages which, we dared to hope, might serve as our night's shelter.

In our aspiration we were not to be disappointed. Cutting our engines so as not to appear menacing (although by now the entire populace seemed aware of our presence) we assembled near what in England would be called the village green but which in Siberia is often a muddy cesspool, and decided that Chas and Clive should attempt the first full-on face-to-face Mondo blend since Georgia.

There in the gloaming, the two sportsmen espied their victim like pumas eyeing up their next meal of gazelle or elk. Decidedly friendly-looking, with an open, innocent face, Oleg looked a likely quarry, his two fiercesome hounds notwithstanding.

Our kindergarten Russian ("It is raining"... "Tents your garden"..."Sleep in shed") at first drew bewildered glances from our goatee-bearded friend who retreated indoors to consult his wife.

The full extent of our success was only revealed when instead of sharing a berth with a pig, cow or other domestic animal, we were ushered into the kitchen by Oleg's gibbering wife and served English breakfast tea with milk fresh from the udder that morning.

Soon she and someone we took to be Oleg's sister were slaving away at a three-ringed Baby Belling type appliance preparing us a succulent meal of stir-fried potatoes, assorted vegetables and bread, part of which appeared to have been soaked in petrol. Acutely embarrassed at this tidal wave of unnecessary hospitality we tried to take over the cooking and Mark appeared at the kitchen door gesticulating with our onions and carrots that we could provide for ourselves. The two ladies shooed us away with a workers' fish slice whilst Oleg shrugged his shoulders and encouraged us to relax, leave the hosting to the Russians and join him in some boozing. A Vodka toast was raised to Anglo-Russian friendship while Oleg puffed contentedly on a packet of camels donated by Mondo Enduro. That, several badges and a Union Jack flag seemed a miniscule price to pay for the extravagant hospitality we were receiving from complete strangers.

By now Mrs Oleg and Aunty Oleg were heaving bedding into the lounge (where a large soft porn image of a blonde bathing in a mountain pool appeared to have been posted for our singular benefit) and we prepared for bed safe in the knowledge that our bikes were secure, chained outside to the Siberian Hound of the Baskervilles who would keep an all-night vigil.

But as in all good horror stories, the most chilling moment came when it seemed our heroes were safe. As Gerald pulled off his tee-shirt he emitted a shriek of terror when he saw what at first seemed like a weeping wound to his abdomen.

Closer examination revealed a small insect which had burrowed into Gerald's skin leaving only his legs protruding. Austin, our chief medical officer applied a tot of Vodka to the beast who merely waved its legs enthusiastically in the air.

At a loss as to how to coax the little blighter out, we consulted Oleg who immediately applied cheap ladies perfume and then kerosene to what we now knew to be the ornithodoros tick, encephalitis bearer and typhus carrier.

Mrs Oleg had by now been called into action and soon obliged by plucking the creature from Gerald's tummy. Presumably by way of an insurance policy, she made the sign of the cross over the angry wound while Gerald winced in pain. We rebuked her gently, reminding her that he was in no need of the last rites as he was already half-dead, a bit like a zombie really. The rest of the team examined their private parts, armpits and the recesses behind their earlobes nervously. We snuggled up, toasting this life we are lucky enough to lead and hoping that Gerald has not just been infused with the deadly virus encephalitis B.

Russia (Irkutsk)

Day 71
Tuesday 20 June
Mondo Miles today: 262
Mondo Mileage: 8877

So after what seemed a short rest and by no means a good night's sleep, it was our wake up call for breakfast.

Our hosts' kindness stretching further than beyond our imagination for when we entered the kitchen we found to our joy more English tea, fried eggs and wonderful milky mashed potato. Furthermore, Gerald's recently departed host had not sent him into a fever for the 7 to 12 hours that it was supposed to if he was to get an infection from the burrowing tic.

We proposed to leave and failed dismally to leave Oleg with a 50,000 rouble note for his family's kind hospitality. They did on the other hand have four momentos of Mondo Enduro including Mark's Kardoramas so it was not that bad after all.

On the road and it was a pleasant and fine overcast day (waterproofs were on as a precaution though). On account of the time being another hour forward without our notice we left later than anticipated but were still going to strive for 300 miles plus.

The weather improved and the scenery just got better and better too. Alpine and European it may have been but it was a welcome sight for the Mondo men.

The first fifty flew by and the second fifty even quicker. We drove into Kransk for a shopping stop and a café hunt and to our joy we found another canteen – not a mud factory or a wood mill this time but what appeared to be a bus depot. The choice was first class for Russia; the lads were straight in for a soup followed by a meat stew with mash and pasta filled with mash as a side order, all sloshed down with some chai and at excellent value too!

Onwards we ground and the first to the 150 mark were Clive and Gerald, whilst the others went shopping for onions but to no avail. A short rest and Mark headed off first and said he would see us at the 200 point. Unfortunately, the others saw him sooner at 180, back wheel puncture, "Uh, oh, here we go again!" Gerald assisted Mark with the puncture whilst Chas lit a fire and brewed up. The others soon came and we took this opportunity to film these bad, bad roads, which were so much fun.

So it seemed the end had come for Black Top and only occasionally did it rear its smoothness only to lead you into a false sense of security for short moments.

We pulled over at 250 miles for a snack stop right by a graveyard. It was opposite a huge wood mill where remarkably there were thousands and thousand of logs strewn around. Gerald at this point began to reminisce about Vancouver and how someone would be a "look out" whilst on Neil's boat looking for that wandering log!

Off went Mark again "see you in 50 lads", and once again we found him sooner – this time with police, a lorry, motor bike and side car and a handful of Jacksons! To even up his misfortune he had acquired a front wheel puncture – but it was quite a meaty rock that had overcome the unsuspecting inner tube.

Mark had gone to overtake one lorry to find another one just in front, also billowing up even more dust, so he did in fact end up riding blind over the dodgiest terrain so far on Mondo Enduro. To his dismay he encountered front wheel blow out on rough terrain. Outcome; this mere Mondo man came out with just a bruised ankle, extremely fortunate considering there were huge trucks trundling around him.

So campsite recce'ing time and conveniently we were adjacent to huge amounts of silver birch forest. A site was found and Chas and Austin set about preparing supper, whilst Gerald inspected and repaired Mark's front wheel. The brand new inner tube wouldn't inflate even after the heftiest pumps from Gerald's lean frame. After examination of the inner tube Gerald found 5 punctures dotted around it (a curse had set in for Mondo Enduro). These had to have arisen whilst putting the tube in and somehow it was pinched and punctured by the levers. Repairs to the two splits in the original inner tube were to no avail either and the daylight was rapidly running away.

So tools up and on to the campsite which was superbly located in a clearing just 100 yards in to the thick forest. The food was ready and was delicious, despite the limited ingredients available to Austin, the chef for the night.

So as we sipped our evening brew, we pondered over the fact that the weather and scenery had become more delightful and the roads challenging but excellent fun. More fun and hard riding awaited us though: Apparently the road stays like this most of the way to Irkutsk.

Russia (Irkutsk)

Day 72
Wednesday 21 June
Mondo Miles today: 0
Mondo Mileage: 8877

Today is the longest day of the year. The weather changed for the better, in fact it was glorious. Because of Mark's accident and his injury it was decided to spend the whole day here convalescing, repairing and maintaining the bikes. Austin and Clive fetched water, Chas and Gerald fetched wood. Mark rested. We started to discuss what all of us would be doing on Day 100. America and Canada were at the front of our minds. Gerald told us about the pleasures that his old school friend, Neil, would have in store for us in Vancouver. It was enough to focus our minds on moving on. We decided that Clive and Gerald should push ahead to Irkutsk to recce the potential blends and for Gerald to be given his dose of encephalitis vaccine. Mark's leg was still a-mending so he, Austin and Chas stayed put for an extra night.

Austin filmed Gerald and Clive pelting down the firebreak before they headed off, Clive screaming out "Mondo Enduro". Austin took Mark's bike for a spin to check the front wheel repair and then went out again to film some monster trucks in the clouds of dust they throw up from the road. Unfortunately they wouldn't come out to play so he returned empty handed. In the meantime Chas and Mark survived near Jacksoning as some suspected forest ranger types drove their landrover to within 10 feet of the campsite but didn't spot us. Struck down by lethargy it took the boys about 3 hours to pack. A cold dinner of bread and spreads gave us ample satisfaction.

Footnote: As Gerald left, he was asked whether he wanted some of the puncture kit. His reply was "No hombre, I've never had a puncture of any type".

Russia (Irkutsk)

Day 73
Thursday 22 June
Mondo Miles today: 402
Mondo Mileage: 9279

The group started today in a record <u>three</u> sub units. Squad 1 – 'Advance Party', Gerald and Clive having left last night and aiming to arrive at Irkutsk as soon as possible. Squad 2 – 'Stay behind group' nursing Mark's injured foot and seeing that camp was properly struck leaving no trace of our visit, save a patch of flattened grass and a pile of broken glass and plastic bags. Finally, Squad 3 Bill and Nick; they are the party catching up with us from Novosibirsk.

The reveille of 04.30hrs came and went and the three sleepy sausages that were Austin, Chas and Mark waited for the suspected 'rain' to clear.

Mark's riding ability was still suspect so he left 20 minutes ahead of the others so that he wasn't rushed on this latest stretch of dirt, aggregate and boulders that is known in this area as the M53. The Russian Road Atlas quotes the 'M' class as the highest category of Soviet highway and it is denoted by a chunky and flamboyant yellow stripe with two red edges. Rather like a stretched out Spanish flag. The idea that the *only* road traversing a former superpower is a dirt track for hundreds of miles is baffling. We take our hats off to the propaganda ministry because whilst the west was practising hiding under tables in fear of the red menace it was still not possible to drive from one side of the evil empire to the other.

The rubbly road lasted another suspension testing 20 miles and then, as if we were the subjects of a virtual reality experiment, we were treated to some of the finest tarmac we have ridden on since Europe. With this lace of black silk underneath our grateful gripsters we initially teased the throttle and then moments later, wrenched it back to deliver a trouser filling 60mph. With morale and speed this high it was with a "chink-chink" of metaphorical champagne glasses being toasted that Chas and Austin were re-united with Mark, 50 miles from the campsite but all effervescing as if they'd covered 500.

These three late-starters made waves and rocked the boat during a misunderstanding over the delivery of some bought and paid for 93-grade benzin. The messy and embarrassing finale to this crossed wire was Austin spraying the forecourt with pungent petrol and the Madame of the pumps emerging to rift him, baffled at these two star simpletons.

Onwards and upwards this tenacious mile-hungry trio devoured a further 4km before pulling into a blandly exteriored restaurant that belied the bland decor waiting inside.

A smouldering waitress raised the collective pulse and as she swayed her way back to the kitchen, napkins were reached for and brows were dabbed.

The little town that housed this eatery straddled a river of hugeness. Alongside the existing M53 road bridge there was the old timber trestle structure which clearly had been partially washed away (a common feature in Georgia we had noted).

So at 09.00 and envittled, Mark, Austin and Chas pulled away (noticing a very saucy smile from another of the restaurant staff as they left) and knuckled down for some serious riding.

Two hours later, as they rounded a bend in the forest section of road they had to swerve to avoid a section of corrugated asbestos sheeting that had been propped upright on the edge of the carriageway. Scrawled onto it, here in the middle of nowhere was the familiar to us couplet "**MONDO ENDURO→**".

We followed as directed, 200m down a track to a disused and deserted power generating plant. Another piece of informative graffiti told us "LEFT AT 10.30". This was clearly Gerald and Clive's campsite last night and with echoes of Tuco pursuing "Blondie" in The Good, the Bad and the Ugly; we found their still smouldering fire, revved up pointlessly and set off after them.

The road really sparkled up and long beautifully graded sections of tarmac allowed us to gobble up mile after mile in quick time. On a rough section of road we perceived a beggar in the distance. As we approached it transpired that it was Gerald, hunched over back wheel with Clive alongside, coping and brewing up. Gerald's steel mug the lone cooking vessel as it was used to warm up a pint of "bogue" water.

Gerald's puncture mended, he and Clive sped off again, still intent on being an advance party at Irkutsk.

One hundred miles later the rearguard 'slow movers' caught up with Clive once more. He informed us that Gerald's chain had snapped (again!) and that they had been separated while in pursuit of petrol. We weren't sure if Gerald was in front of or behind us, so Clive found a pebble and used it to scratch a message in the tarmac. Gerald's 'GHV' initials were oversized to catch his attention as he sped along.

We all continued as a four, suspecting that Gerald was ahead of us. With 350 miles under our belts and on the home straight into Irkutsk we came across not the welcome sight of the 'city limits' sign but Gerald crouched, as nature intended him, at the rear of his bike, his chain had broken for the second time today!

We cheerfully set about de-linking and re-assembling using the punch, club hammer (4lb) and a mysterious steel pipe emerging from the embankment alongside us, as an anvil. Clive filmed Chas and Austin interviewing Mark (ankle drama) and Gerald (chain/tyres etc). The mood was ebullient and a carnival atmosphere prevailed as we all reflected on the large distance covered this day and wallowing in the knowledge that we would be cruising into Irkutsk within five minutes. To make up time Chas and Mark set off in advance of Austin, Clive and Gerald. A rough rendezvous. At the Intourist hotel was set for 21.00 with all of us wondering how we would occupy our spare time prior to the meet-up once we'd arrived.

The answer was provided for the stay behind chain detail when, 25 minutes after leaving, Chas returned with the news that Mark had suffered a front wheel puncture 5 miles down the road. Groans all round; Austin had the repair kit so he accompanied Chas forward to the location. Instead of arriving at a melancholy scene with Mark at his wits end, Austin and Chas discovered the unlucky friend being wined and dined in the central reservation (no booking required?) by a flock of workers from a Tarmac black top train that was surfacing nearby. The sunset was settling in for a huge sky full of heart melting reds and purples and no more a romantic backdrop for tyre removal could ever be asked for. Clive filmed Gerald doing a piece to camera describing the scene. It was 9.30pm.

Austin was duly given the free food and chai treatment as were Gerald and Clive when they turned up chain handed. All was smooth except for the job in hand on Mark's front end ...

The rubber solution acquired in Novosibirsk proved utterly useless. After 3 attempts we couldn't get the patches to stick. Some burly beefcake Tarmackers came over and helped out, stripping down the rubber to scratch and taking a lot of care in their work. These chaps turned out to be Moldavian and proud of it. They were ideal film material but by now it was 23.00 and it was just Gerald and Austin at work, all the others having moved into town (Mark rode in on B2, Austin's bike). These happy helpers had hands like mole grips, permanently sweating, they screamed and laughed without interval. To say they stank of Vodka would be an understatement and it wasn't clear why their foreman was allowing them time away from their regular tasks to help us.

The repair was a success but they continued to surprise us with their tips from the East by insisting that we inflate the mended tyre not with air but with water! They achieved this hydraulic infusion by dismantling our hardcore Turkish stirrup pump and pouring cups of water in until the barrel was full. The cap was screwed back on and then they gleefully pushed down on the almost impossible-to-depress plunger. Reluctantly the water was forced through the tyre valve and duly they stripped the pump down again and repeated the whole operation a further four times! Gerald and Austin were convinced that a process this unfeasible just had to be genius and they naturally concurred with the Moldavian open-palmed flicking gesture towards Irkutsk which they took to mean that this was a "go faster" secret that would clearly have us running smoother than ever before.

Tyre inflated and seated (using Mark's Travel Wash liquid soap as a lubricant) there only remained to slide in the axle and fit it to the front forks. As this was being done the whole tyre seemed to rumble then explode with sweetly perfumed suds oozing under pressure from behind the bead. It was midnight and we were very definitely back at square one.

The youngish James MacArthur lookalike Tarmac operative who had offered us the food then approached our sorry site at the roadside. He appreciated that we had wasted the last 2½ hours and volunteered his canteen wagon to put Mark's bike into and drive it to a "vulcanizer" in Irkutsk. His offer was the elixir required and negated the need for Gerald and Austin to sleep out here on the verge with a view to further lastic attempts on the morrow.

But how was this heavily laden bike to be loaded into the high rise rear of the mobile kitchen, even the Herculean Moldavians would not be enough help for this lift. The answer came in a crane. With an Uzbek operator darting like an ant from strop to bike to controls, D3 was raised hydraulically from this cursed spot and laid to rest at 45 degrees behind the cab of the crane truck.

Austin rode shotgun, Gerald followed behind and by 01.00 the convoy had arrived at the almost secret forest HQ of the road plant fleet. While the bike was tenderly lowered onto the mud-baked deck of the compound the Moldavians appeared out of the shadows and casually woke up a wiry Steven Berkoff/Wilfrid Brambell duplicate called Viktor. Viktor was the gaffer of the workshop here and with wheel removed for the nth time (where n is a large integer) the squad of five (Gerald, Austin, Moldavians x 2 and Viktor) soon swelled to ten as sundry highway and plant operators leaked into the workshop.

The remaining 1½ hours saw four different punctures being repaired by the Moldavians. After the first one they insisted Austin drink a slug of Stalyanka Vodka to celebrate. By the end of the repairs it was the lightweight be Vodka'd Mondo Enduroist who needed patching up. Throughout this episode Viktor went through a series of rages and depressions, violently kicking the drawers and cabinets of the workshop. A man sleeping on a bench in the corner woke up after about 45 minutes and stumbled stuttered to Austin that we were invited to sleep somewhere 18km away. Somehow the Vince brothers escaped at 02.40 leaving the Moldavians roaring and still sweating. They camped in a glade roughly 1 mile away. 402 miles (our record) – what a Mondo Day!

Russia (Irkutsk)

Day 74
Friday 23 June
Mondo Miles today: 0
Mondo Mileage: 9279

Clive, Chas and Mark woke up in Room 402 of the Hotel Angara in time for the rendezvous with Austin and Gerald at the Hotel Intourist. The two saviours of D3's front end turned up at the Angara and recounted the previous night's events to the amusement of the rest of the team. We wandered off to find Miva's Bakery which was reputed to have the best coffee in Russia. It was all lies – the coffee machine existed but the guy refused to operate it for us. We blended to a nearby café where the security guard initially refused us entrance because of our unseemly appearance. The blonde manageress rebuked him and ushered us in, simultaneously turning away a Russian bloke who was infinitely smarter than us.

Everybody was exhausted and made their way back to the Angara to sleep. Chas found a foreign language college and buttered up the middle-aged English tutor, persuading her to help with our long list of administrative tasks. Bill and Nick turned up in the afternoon. Their Motorola blend in Novosibirsk had fallen through and they had ridden hard and fast to catch us up. Gruesome tales of eating no more than a banana and half a Marathon a day didn't ring true given Nick's legendary appetite. The explanation was simple. Bogus bacteria had infected his stomach, stopping his appetite and emptying his bowels.

A budget meal in the Angara sufficed to fill us up before Bill, Chas, Gerald, Clive and Austin (briefly) wandered down to the Hotel Intourist to get their kicks, Mark and Nick staying home to tend their wounds. Austin chipped back fairly quickly and the remainder were left to strut their stuff. Chas and Clive were repeatedly asked to dance and Clive looked as though he might get an away result with a Russian blonde (Chas was being chatted up by the blonde's mum). Witnesses say that the Mondo boys acted with decency and discretion and that the populace of Irkutsk will always remember us for the sterling example we set in gentlemanly behaviour.

Russia (Irkutsk)

Day 75
Saturday 24 June
Mondo Miles today: 0
Mondo Mileage: 9279

Admin day today, seeing Chas and Gerald go off with their Russian student translator friend in search of sprocket makers, Austin to Aeroflot and Nick and Bill to the station – all with varying degrees of success. Chas and Gerald came up trumps with Tool Shop 17, one of the mechanics promising sprocket happiness for Monday. We trust that the reader is as startled as we are that on a Saturday afternoon one can find somebody that will take a worn rear sprocket from you, measure it and have three copies machined by Monday. This type of old school engineering savvy is clearly normal here in the USSR, and we love it.

Austin meanwhile found Aeroflot closed, but sought solace in his floor lady and her impressive, but hardly cheap, laundering capabilities. The Railway Children found the International Ticket office, and with the admirable English of Alexander, the literature professor turned private security guard, mugged up on train prices to Khabarovsk. Mark meanwhile stayed back at the Angara nursing his ankle.

Later, we all convened for coffee and eggs on Floor 4 (there is a café on each floor!) Clive trying to get potatoes by miming a digging action to the bewildered lady, who eventually allowed him back into the kitchen to visually locate what he wanted. Evening fell, and so did Austin, into his bed, while the others headed for the Hotel Intourist and a rendezvous with the Motorola roadies at the Bar Genghis Khan, where we sat for a couple of hours in eager anticipation of the rugby World Cup Final on Satellite but got 2 hours of Star Trek memorabilia instead. This drove us downstairs into the Disco Restaurant, where we danced and talked the night away, in the company of the 2 British girl backpackers whom we'd met earlier at the station. Bill and Nick, lightweights both, were first to bed followed by Gerald, while Clive, Chas and Mark returned to the Angara Casino for a bout of drinks and money losing before finally crashing at somewhere around the 6am mark.

Russia (Irkutsk)

Day 76
Sunday 25 June
Mondo Miles today: 0
Mondo Mileage: 9279

After yet another night in the Intourist Hotel, we awoke with the main task of the day being to buy rail tickets for Khabarovsk. Bill, Nick and Mark are committed to meeting their sweethearts in Alaska in three weeks and at this rate they don't think they are going to make it. So we are suddenly in our last days as a seven; all still heading east then north for Magadan but with three on the train and four on the road.

However, as Mark and Clive had not returned until 6am, a heavy lie in was required and hence a slow start. And so to the Railway Station. On yesterday's visit Bill and Nick had waded through the thronging crowds of conscripts to the sumptuous luxury of the international ticket office. On today's visit we again met Alexander the ticket office security guard. He had halting but refined English which seemed out of place with his side-handled baton, hand-cuffs and Rambo length facial scars. It turned out that he had been a guide on Baikal, a student and teacher of English literature. He helped us buy the tickets and explain our tickets to the ticket saleswoman. We spent our 1.6m roubles for train No 2 and would need to blend the bikes into the luggage car. It turned out that the security guards along the whole of the rail system are Cossacks, noted for their epaulettes and striped trousers as well as moustaches. These colourful guards are known as puppets by the locals. Chas enquired about the KGB grave as well as the road to Magadan. Alexander was most helpful in his responses. After a quick recce of the platforms by Nick and Bill we headed back to the Angara.

Russia (Irkutsk)

Day 77
Monday 26 June
Mondo Miles today: 0
Mondo Mileage: 9279

The gentle clarion of the Room 402 phone awoke Clive, Chas and Mark from their deep slumber. It was Clive's mum Gemma, ever a comforting voice from home, conjuring visions of junk food and exquisite cuisine served to musical accompaniment by Elvis Presley.

The morning was spent in a slow frenzy of administrative tasks. Gerald and Chas were joined by their guide Julie for a sortie to workshop 17 of the machine tool co-operative, where they were greeted with warmth by the industrial comrades. The walk from the factory gates to the tool-room was a journey back in time to the days of the Stalin era. The groan of sixty-year-old plant filled our ears and we walked along a railway line heaving under the weight of a working goods train. Gerald managed to control his ecstasy and instead drafted Russian railway tales with which to regale his co-workers in the booking office at Bournemouth station. After Mondo we suspect he'll be the toast of Network South-East.

We reached the workshop where we were greeted with polite bewilderment and enormous warmth by middle management. The various parts displayed in glass cases in the Deputy Manager's office revealed the true purpose of his and his workforce's existence – to produce heavy duty and metallic components for gold-digging machinery. The notion of manifesting two rear and one front sprockets for a Suzuki motorbike was clearly beyond their immediate remit but Igor, the Stanley Matthews look-alike deputy, said they would try to. We await the results of their industry with anticipation.

Walking back through the factory, we rolled back the cumbersome millstone of Soviet industry. An aluminium statue of Lenin exhorted the

Siberian workforce, while the exiting gatepost bore a plaque proclaiming "*Thank you comrades for your labour*".

Most surreal of all, bearing in mind the hopelessly neglected and almost satanic atmosphere of the factory was a notice bearing the following legend: "*Esteemed workers! Please remember that keeping your workplace clean and brightly painted can cut electricity costs by 26 per cent!*" (all of these translated for us by Julia).

The trio also collected the vulcanised (repaired) inner tubes from the demonic forges while Clive and Austin checked out Aeroflot arrangements (we still don't know if we can put our bikes on the plane from Magadan to Alaska). We then went shopping at the Central Market; an attempt to buy a humble jotting pad was a failure. There is still a huge culture that you can only get what the shops sell and that's not much. Hence something as nondescript as a notepad is an unavailable western luxury whilst a handmade sprocket is a reasonable request. Victuals and fresh vegetables for the road cost a cool $110. Summertime and the livin' is easy, cheap it ain't.

A giant shadow was cast across the day when it emerged most of Austin's $500 had apparently been stolen overnight from Room 335. Bill, Mark and Nick meanwhile made ready for the train purchasing vast quantities of dehydrated products and Nescafe for the Samovar.

Earlier, Chas and Julia had courted the Lois Lane of Irkutsk journalism, Tatiana, to come and do a feature for Irkutsk alternative television. Her inquiry about the pulchritude of Russian girls was answered effusively in the affirmative. A feature for the Irkutsk 'Number One' thrice weekly news rag was also in the offing thanks to Oleg, their denim suited reporter and his portly female interpreter who professed an ambition to cycle from Lands End to John O'Groats. Also most afternoons Mondo Enduro attracted more media frenzy from an unidentified news organ; the infinitely tidy brunette reporter drew admiring glances from Austin, Clive and Gerald.

Julia our shy but charming translator has presented Chas and Gerald with an image of Black Coat, the Buddhist protector deity. A metaphysical duel between him and Aunty Joe's St Christopher for the right to watch over Mondo Enduro will no doubt soon ensue.

Dinner was a feast of fried eggs, sausages and mash on the 6th floor buffet. Thereafter we sashayed in full leathers to the Theatre Bar to hang out with Irkutsk's small troupe of so-called hippies to drown the pain of Mondo Enduro's imminent disbandment, albeit temporary. Bill, Mark and Nick test the railroad tomorrow morning at 5.30am while the others make their way to Magadan – an awesome 3000 miles hence. The melancholy but grating strains of 'Communiqué' by Dire Straits seemed somehow apposite to our mood. Bedtime saw Chas, Gerald, Clive and Austin, blending past the formidable beehive-haired Devooshka into a double room while Mark did likewise with Nick and Bill. We toasted the road ahead with a final ale in the Second Floor Bar "*A va de ces jours*". Hopefully we will be safely reunited in Anchorage.

Russia (Irkutsk)

Day 78
Tuesday 27 June
Mondo Miles today: 100
Mondo Mileage: 9379

Well the sad time arrived; 4.30am as Mondo Enduro set to split once again for its longest time so far, with an rendezvous in Anchorage on or around 22 July 95.

Clive, Chas and Gerald were in semi-slumber and so were too tired to get emotional, just a couple of grunts and groans for their farewell to the 'Train Gang' Nick, Bill and Mark. Austin escorted them down to the station, in case the bikes couldn't get on the same train. They arrived around 5am and soon discovered bikes and Mondo men could not go together ... unlucky Train Gang! This desperate situation called for desperate measures. Mark with his accentuated limp entered with his sob story that their expedition had ground to a halt because of his injury and that is why they had been forced to take the train. Gullibly the station master took all this in and after two to three hours of slight panic for the Train Gang – they ended up blending. It had turned out that they could post their bikes to Khabarovsk on the postal train for a mere $30 each. The Magadan men were still in the dark about this at the time though.

Meanwhile, the Magadan detail was preserving their energies by lying in until nearly 11am. First call for the hardcore riders was a well deserved breakfast of omelette, fried eggs and coffee. Austin went off to cash some money on his Visa card after he had $500 go walkabout on him, whilst Gerald, Chas and Clive finished off packing.

Chas had his rendezvous with Julia and they went off to see if the men in workshop No. 17 had come up with the goods (fabrication of a 1 front and 2 rear sprockets from 2 shagged ones - a mammoth task by any country's means).

Whilst Clive and Gerald were making their final adjustments to the DRs outside the hotel Angara – shock, horror the 'Train Boys' returned claiming they had been blown out totally – we showed no consolation and soon realised it was just a wind up. They were 'posting' the bikes tonight and catching the train tomorrow morning; arriving in Khabarovsk on Friday night, the bikes set to arrive on Saturday morning. We took a team photo, the last time we'd be together as a seven for a while:

Austin, Chas, Gerald, Bill, Mark, Clive, Nick Stubley

Mondo Enduro

So we all proceeded to wob out in the sun waiting for the impossible to be done. Whilst we were waiting the obnoxious glue sniffing Street Kids, all as high as a kite, came over for their daily sermon of gibberish comments in a slow motion hallucinatory manner. These kids of 10 or 11, who incidentally, all smoked, were shabbily dressed and led by a sadder individual of about 14. They carry old plastic one litre soda bottles in the bottom of which is a slosh of gasoline. They stagger around gulping in the vapours and wiping their permanently runny noses on snot encrusted sleeves. These are the casualties in new Russia, and they made us feel awkward.

Austin returned having success after multiple attempts at cashing money.

He also had news from Aeroflot they *do* take bikes from Khabarovsk at $5 a kilo and all in for around $1300. A significant rise from the $650 we were quoted in Almaty. We do not have enough cash for this; will they take credit cards at Magadan airstrip? We fear not.

Julia, our English speaking angel returned triumphantly with a pleased as punch Chas "U" Like. Were they about to announce an Anglo Russian engagement or did they have some pressing good news for the Magadan foursome. To the Vince brothers' joy it was brand new sprockets done by the friendly workers in the dimly lit factory No. 17. The price? Gratis!

Cameras were out to record this historic moment and it was a wrap on the second take. Later Julia when being praised by the Mondo men for her angelic services revealed to us "I am not an angel – Chas paid me" – she was so sweet and could do no harm to anything or anyone, except maybe to Chas' heart.

In the meantime more preparation was being done but this time on the hair front to go with the Mexicana Moustaches. Clive, Austin and Chas returned as the 3 bald eagles looking more suited to a night out at the elusive "Blue Oyster" bikers' bar than making an attempt at the 'Road of Bones' to Magadan.

After a group photo of the Magadan four we bid farewell to Nick, Bill and Mark for the second time that day and headed towards Lake Baikal along a dusty mountainous road. After 70 miles we could see the 'Blue Eye' of Siberia stretched out before us. A bit of filming and we were on our way. At 102 miles we found a campsite, not one of our best but a lakeside wooded meadow and right next door to the only polluting plant on the lake. Unlucky lads – but a huge fire and the chunky meal that followed more than made up for it and we crashed at around 12pm.

Russia (Siberia)

Day 79
Wednesday 28 June
Mondo Miles today: 225
Mondo Mileage: 9604

It was a dull and dreary day alongside Lake Baikal until Clive noticed his rear wheel was acting strangely. Further inspection revealed that one of the bearings had gone. Never have we seen a bearing replaced so quickly, not by us, but 4 local lads. Austin and Clive pulled up at a bus stop to work in the dry, but cows had been using it. As usual they were soon surrounded by people offering help and advice. Once the problem had been revealed one chap went off with Clive and they returned with a new bearing, another with a massive flaming blow torch. The old bearing was heated up and eventually knocked out. The local police arrived bearing a grease gun. The new part went in and everything else followed in the usual manner. The whole process took less than one hour.

The by now customary offer of food and drink was made and taken up by us. At that time we did not know that these men were Vodka Monsters... so back to Sergei's house where he had a violent argument with his wife. We suspect that blows were exchanged. She left, taking the children with her looking very much as if she had been slapped. This made us very uneasy but we were already too deep into the vortex of hospitality to extricate ourselves. Once she was despatched to a safe house our host, Sergei Kalashnikov, shipped in his mates and the 'party' began. A freshly killed salmon was produced (from Lake Baikal), the blood filling the bowl that it was in. Sign language and our phrase books were our only help that evening. Clive went to get more Vodka, arm-wrestling and videoing (priceless footage is shot) then Chas went for even more Vodka. No other food was offered and so we were all very drunk very quickly. The few English phrases that they knew included 'English Wanker' so we were all 'English Wankers' and they were all 'Russki Wankers'. Our hosts then wailed Russian songs from (we presume) their time in the navy. Then came 'Scartime' where everyone displayed their scars. Clive has a superbly messy knee injury with a wiggly scar akin to a racetrack. Gerald boasted his seventies appendix removal slash, a scar so undeniable even the Siberians were impressed. Almost as an afterthought Gerald produced his right shin. A living honours board of motorcycle accidents spanning three decades, one-fifth anaemic flesh, four-fifths scar. Clive became arm-wrestling champion. During all this Sergei's wife came back, grabbed him by the shirt front and dragged him outside along with their eldest son who up until then had remained with us. Sergei returned after a few minutes. We arranged to sleep in the childrens' room. Austin and Clive went to bed but Chas and Gerald were marched off across the road to someone else's house. Chas and Gerald walked into a huge argument between their host and his wife but they were so drunk and tired the outcome will remain unknown. These poor Siberian women...

Russia (Siberia)

Day 80
Thursday 29 June
Mondo Miles today: 296
Mondo Mileage: 9900

So the day began in the not unfamiliar way of the group being separated after a knees-up the night before. Clive and Austin were head to tail in a single bed in Sergei's house with Gerald and Chas on the floor of their host's. The latter were charged for their stay so they weren't particularly chuffed. It was well past 11.00 hrs before all the bikes were out on the mud road in front of the house.

The atmosphere was still quite tense as a result of the various domestic rifts that our arrival had caused and needless to say it was an all male party that waved us off. Austin was already quite drunk once we left since he foolishly had got sucked into the vortex of early morning Siberian drinking. One of our new found drinking and ball-bearing pals turned up with a plate of roast potatoes dug from his back yard only an hour before. We witnessed local child-care dietary tips from Gerald's host who took his little 2 year old daughter, plonked her in a high chair and served her up a breakfast of bread and a bowl of sugar.

As we took our farewell photos and re-run highlights of last night's arm wrestling champions' tips, it was a good time to reflect on the latent toughness of the Siberians. As well as their undeniable physical strength they live a lifestyle that is crude and basic in the extreme. The village was on the main road across the country, it rains all the time yet these people have no running water or sanitation disposal. Long live the revolution! There seems to be no hint of a complaint about their lot.

We pulled out under an overcast sky, confident of a repetition of yesterday's huge rains. We pulled over after 50 miles for a brew and some head clearing. The Vodka had taken its toll and drunk again, none of us really felt like riding or doing anything at all.

The weather began to clear at about the same rate as our Mondo hangover. The biggest surprise of the day came with the advent at 1pm of a totally gorgeous sunny afternoon. Huge rolling clouds lumbered across the sky but never seemed to block out the sun. The road too noticeably improved and long straight stretches of fine black top gave us an average of 58mph.

The scenery could have been the best since we left London, the difference being the scale. The views along river valleys were often up to ten miles distant. Another feature is the distinct lack of human furniture and trappings. Apart from the occasional powerline there were hardly any fences or farmhouses. Streams and rivers meandered casually across rich green meadows and pastures. There was no evidence of any grazing apart from close to the villages. We maintained our routine of stopping every 50 or 60 miles and were hence rarely exhausted by a ride and could keep it up all day. Pine tree covered hills and mountains constantly beckoned us onward and we all relished the sunshine and the awesome ranges of green that Mother Nature had provided for us.

Around 8pm we attempted a filming session with us riding off into the distance. We set up the camera carefully, gunned up the bikes and roared off across this huge unspoilt meadow. The grassy quilt beneath our tyres remained constant, but the earth did not. We all ploughed at full pelt into a marsh. Gerald and Chas were buried up to their axles and once entombed by mud, we were plagued by squadrons of mosquitoes who virtually laughed in our faces as we sweated and toiled to extricate the bikes. Gerald hogged a group can of Pepsi once finally free, after much over-revving and splattering of faces we moved on with the sun setting on what was by now a clear evening sky.

Note: Little kids play in the streams in shorts or trunks – seemingly unaffected by mosquitoes, what is their secret?

Pleased with nudging 300 miles we cruised off the steppe and back into an area slightly more undulating and forested. We found a campsite with ease and all the usual tasks set into motion. After a few minutes it hit us – a powerful smell of decomposing flesh which after a search revealed the fetid corpses of sundry sheep. By now we had unpacked most of the gear – it was 10pm and in our tiredness we resigned ourselves to a smelly night in this paradise. Taken along with our lakeside spot adjacent the humungous pulp-processing plant on Lake Baikal, we haven't chosen too successfully over the last couple of days.

The site was infested by grasshoppers of every shape, size and colour. They totally covered Gerald who had to set up the net to protect himself. Some *still* secured ingress in the night so they chatted and made friends.

Russia (Siberia)

Day 81
Friday 30 June
Mondo Miles today: 114
Mondo Mileage: 10014

We awoke from a long slumber having been disturbed by strange dreams and dark portents. Gerald's repose was disrupted by the frenzied sport of sundry critters while Austin had four "full on, epic" dreams which he could not remember in the morning. Clive has a premonition about four-wheel driving on the road to Skovorodino while Chas conjured up visions of Oxana and her black baby – fathered by her Jamaican bobsleigh runner boyfriend. And so it was that the first hour of the day had a somewhat surreal element as we slowly struck camp. The stench of our night's repose in the sheep charnel house, and three days on the road, had left us feeling scruffy in the extreme. It was with some relief that after 14 miles on the road, we chanced upon a perfect campsite situated next to a gushing stream.

Soon the Billy can was singing cheerily on a roaring fire while the salami sausage was surrendering itself to the cruel knife. Austin, Chas and Clive plunged in the icy torrent for an all-over body wash while Gerald spruced up with a 'no soap' shave.

As we cleared away our victuals, a Russian lorry pulled in and the driver came over for a chat. The map shows a 400 mile break in the road after Chernyshevsk and we are desperate for details of the way ahead. We pumped him for info using our Russian road atlas to clarify our ambitions. As a rusty cleaver hung lazily from his left hand he assured us that there *was* a road to Magocha and it was asphalted. We listened with great glee, but some suspicion. Nobody out here gives you the same advice and truth be told it's looking like further east some of the roads marked may well not exist. The proof of the pudding will come with the eating.

The road to Chita was almost entirely without incident and dark storm clouds circled threateningly but ineffectively around the fringes of a great valley. In England, the field of vision is so frequently trespassed by the agency of humans. Not so Siberia with its vast vistas of gently rolling hills and flooded wetlands, devoid of the activity of man.

Chita revealed itself after about 150 kilometres in a haze of humid smog. The three chimney stacks of a power station were raised like some kind of enormous obscene gesture, exhorting us to get stuffed. Notwithstanding this unfriendly signal we piled into town along a tortuous route intertwined by a brutal spaghetti of above-ground duct pipes and tubing. Every Russian town is girdled with this ugliness; they are the pipes that carry hot water from a colossal central municipal boiler and distribute it in abundance to every crumbling apartment block. We've heard rumours that when things go wrong your cold tap runs dry while its neighbour gushes endless gallons of unmetered scalding *voda.*

Onwards into the main square and its impressive monument to the Great Patriotic War 1941-45 (which is what they call WWII). Gerald pointed out that Chita was the western limit of the advance of British soldiers sent inland from Hong Kong in 1920. Like their compatriots at Aschcabad they were unsuccessful in halting the Bolshevik maelstrom but with more than 2500 miles of land ahead of us we were impressed at the level of their incursion. This city is a big deal place for out here but is noticeably tattier than anywhere else so far. We suspect that as we penetrate Siberia further this trend will continue.

After parking up by a crossroad, Gerald and Chas undertook a shopping sortie, securing Picnic bars, bananas, Russian chocolate and a fetching plastic bag. Further negotiations would secure fresh stocks of those brown nuggets of solid gold otherwise known as the elusive Russian onion.

Gerald and Austin were on a mission to telephone the UK, so out here that means one thing, the post office. Chita's population are graced with a telecom system that does not handle the notion of an inter-city trunk call very easily. An international call *cannot* be dialled from home and must therefore, be booked at the exchange and there they all were, about 30 citizens in a gloomy dark wood panelled hall, slouched on benches and patiently waiting to be told that their call had been connected. With zero Russian between them Gerald and Austin were struggling. The whole exchange was run solely by middle aged women whose interaction with their public was from behind a large concrete wall with tiny hatches cut in it (much like the petrol stations). The intense white heat of Siberian hospitality was in here, cooled to an icy stare and the phone ladies became very irritated very quickly that the brothers Vince could not understand them. The impersonal hatch all but snuffed out the flickering chance of mime, that medium which normally facilitates any translation impasse so it took literally 15 minutes and the intercession of a waiting physics student for the call to be booked. Naturally it was pre-paid and only 4 minutes could be afforded.

Exhausted by the exchange they took their seats on the bench and waited. The modus operandi saw your number dialled by the ladies behind the screens, if someone 'picked up' they would tell them to hold on (in Russian!) and then patch an announcement through the tannoy instructing the person who placed the call to go to one of the twenty numbered booths that walled the waiting area. Once inside you would pick up, report to the operator you were there and off you go. It was immediately clear as the crackling orders came over the PA that Austin and Gerald would have no idea when they were being summoned. After 45 minutes of patient British waiting they flipped a coin to decide who would approach the hatch to follow up the call. Austin lost and received a torrent of barking and perfume through the hatch. It was impossible to be sure but he reported back to Gerald that he feared they had already been connected and summoned without realising. The phone woman wanted more money if a second call was to be booked so it was back to Chas for a fistful of Roubles. It was 1 hr 45 mins after initially entering the telephone exchange that they were finally speaking to Mondo Mission Control in Bournemouth.

Clive meanwhile was fraternising ferociously with a beaming lad by the name of Vladimir who offered to show us the way out of town. Austin and Gerald's lengthy but unsuccessful trip to the telegraph office, plus the fact that we had unwillingly entered another time zone meant that time was moving on apace.

Vladimir ended our deliberations by offering us the use of his country 'Dacha' for the evening and we followed him and his beautiful cream-dress wearing girlfriend – as they rumbled along the dirt road in their $2000 white right-hand drive ex-Jap Nissan saloon. We eschewed their offer of a "Russian Banya" in favour of a Mondo fry-up accompanied by healthy portions of radish and chives and potatoes from their well stocked garden. In comfy beds with full tummies and under a dry roof we congratulated ourselves on achieving our ten thousandth mile today and marvelled at how we found ourselves yet again, the overnight guest of somebody we'd just met in the street.

Russia (Siberia)

Day 82
Saturday 31 June
Mondo Miles today: 239
Mondo Mileage: 10253

We awoke after a poor sleep in Vladimir's country residence. His house in the forest was unfortunately adjacent to a dozen other country residences only 18kms from the city centre. After a hearty breakfast that is standard on Mondo Enduro, a coffee and a banana, we set off on a cloudy miserable day to Senechinsk. We were guided by Vladimir who had insisted on showing us on the new road to Chernyshevsk. A few light showers and the sun was blazing through again. Mondo miles were being crunched at ten to the dozen. Tarmac finished back to dirt road.

It is true that every cloud has a silver lining and at the end of that one we discovered a huge dirty white converted Land Rover Defender with Australian plates. The Kincaid family resided in this fine example of robust British engineering. We couldn't believe our ears they were heading the same way as us and even had the same maps as us. What was even more bizarre was the fact that they had been travelling with two Swiss motorcyclists on Africa Twins doing practically the same trip as us.

We were not surprised to hear they were struggling with the immense weight of these machines off-road and they were totally unable to pick them up when dropped without sheer strength and effort. Hurrah for the little 350!!

The Australians told us of their proposed RV at 7pm with the Swiss at the city limits of Chernyshevsk. So we raced ahead on the dirt road that had recently started – it seemed the tarmac had finished for the next 2000 miles to Magocha.

Diana Kincaid writes a short note followed by her daughter:

Amazing to be here on a Siberian hillside with the overland travellers. I hope you make the trip to Skovorodino and of course to Magocha. It will be great if you succeed. Best Wishes for a terrific journey.

Diana Kincaid	*Mother*
Peter Kincaid	*Father*
Hilary Kincaid	*Daughter*
John Kincaid	*Son*

Dear Mondo Enduro
Fantastic to meet someone who speaks English in itself but great to meet you all from North London to Siberia. Best of luck in reaching your objectives – let us know how it all goes. You'll love South America.

Bon Voyage
Vaya con Dios
Hilary Kincaid

So for the next couple of hours the Mondo Enduro team overtook the Aussies and vice versa several times on the way to the RV. A few clicks before the RV, Clive came across a Toyota recently overturned with children and adults splattered in blood wandering aimlessly around. They were attempting to turn the car back over. Gerald didn't take a blind bit of notice and just carried on, the Aussies did the same too, but Clive was good enough to stop and make sure everyone was OK. After helping the drunken Siberians heave the car back onto its wheels, he then administered first aid to a young lad whose head was quite badly lacerated at the rear of his skull.

He then tried to film the mini-disaster but was soon stopped instantly by the Russian wives. Clive secretly filmed them anyway!

A few kilometres down the road and we met one of the Swiss guys with Gerald and the Aussies. We proceeded to the campsite Adrian and Martin (the Swiss guys) had recce'd up on a hill 1km away. The Aussies have one of these new fangled GPS things and confidently state our location as follows:

N.52degrees 28' 30"
E. 116 degrees 58'51"
ALT. 651m

The Aussies went off to get some beers and met us on the hill about an hour later. We set about exchanging info with the Swiss certain that they would be better informed than us. Their information had led them to believe the road to Magocha was impossible in the summer. So they were getting on the train with the Aussies until the road started again going east to Khabarovsk. Apparently, the permafrost melts in the summer moistening the Tundra which makes it impassable for any vehicle.

Austin got a fire going and offered to watch over the saucepans placed on it from all three national groups. This gave everyone else a little more free time to relax and enjoy this unusual international meeting. His attention was poor and the stick holding up the Australian billy can burned through and it toppled over spilling its four little pork chops into the glowing embers. Austin made an executive decision to conceal this mishap from the Kincaid family, dusted off the meat and put it all back in the pot to continue cooking. If they ever read these words he offers a full and formal apology for his bungling. So we ate our respective suppers, supped on beers, munched on chocolate and exchanged travellers' tales and tips. It seemed the Aussies and us had the most to say, whilst the Swiss listened in. Everyone seemed enthralled by Austin's account of his near manslaughter of an old Turkish lady at the Georgian border (day 34) and how he got off so lightly and quickly.

Russia (Siberia)

Day 83
Sunday 2 July
Mondo Miles today: 55
Mondo Mileage: 10308

We slept last night on a grassy knoll overlooking the ramshackle village of Chernyshevsk. We were suddenly adjuncts to a weird collective of international travellers: two Swiss Germans on giant Africa Twin 750s and an Australian family of four in a lumbering homemade long wheel base Land Rover mobile home type thing (painted in 'U.N.' white). How, after months alone crossing Central Asia and Russia, we should chance upon these two quite unconnected couplings, separately and at the watershed where our road east runs out, we shall only wonder for years to come. They, like us, were all heading for the far eastern prison outpost of Magadan and they, like us, had almost no idea of what was happening or more tellingly, what kinds of roads (if any), lay ahead.

For us four, Chernyshevsk was expected to be literally the end of the line, or more accurately, the beginning of it. Because down there ahead of us, in the mild valley of the Nitoshka river wound the one sliver of civilisation that this lonely part of the world has to hang on to: the Trans-Siberian Railway. Typically, our new travelling friends had a strategy whereas we, did not. Swiss Cheese, Aussies and Brits alike, *all* had procured a copy of the single approved Soviet Auto Federation Road Atlas (Chas had got ours from one of those funny book shops in the alleys that connect Charing Cross Rd with St Martin's Lane) and this crucial tome, a beguiling blend of helpful facts and propaganda fuelled disinformation, shows that the trans Siberian *Highway* terminates right here, at Chernyshevsk.

The road atlas showed the purple line of the road picks up again at a place called Skovorodino about 400 miles east from here. Hence, the TransAlps and the Land Rover had (yesterday afternoon), secured a passage on a flat bed railway wagon and were getting to Skovorodino by train. Quite a fluke out here in the wild east one might imagine but not so. Chernyshevsk is clearly a 'Motorail' depot of some standing. We know that because we can see it from here. Whilst the green carriages of the Moscow to Vladivostock 'expresses' clatter past, a gaggle of cars, vans and trucks jostle to be loaded onto the waiting flat wagons. They are like piglets fighting for a teat, honking and shoving but gradually filtering up a loading ramp at the end of the siding and bumping their way onto the train. We can't help but notice how the Russian way of doing things seem so distinctly military yet chaotic at the same time. The scene in the marshalling yard is half Jabberwocky, half Von Ryan's Express.

We would go down there and join them were it not for the fact that we could clearly see, wending away from the bustle of the railhead and across the rolling plains, a sandy track that most obviously follows the railway east. It urges us on and a mini-meeting saw four votes for having a go and none for putting the bikes on the train. We bade our farewells and 'good lucks' to our new friends and set off. The decision to press on is motivated by an inherent mistrust of the 'official' version of which roads actually do and do not exist in this part of Siberia and the gradual realisation that the locals out here are full of a pioneering can-do attitude. The idea that they somehow have, without official approval, driven their own route across the hills and through the forests, seems utterly plausible.

The track was sound and we made good progress. The sun shone hard and by 11am we had 45 miles under our belts. As we got away from the town, the rolling hills were less pasture and became more peppered with bushes and light forest. At this rate we would be in Skovorodino in two or three days. A small hamlet approached and we topped up every tank and jerry can from an old baboushka selling 75 octane from her front garden. Our range is easily 300 miles per bike now.

The way soon deteriorated and became a lumpy sand/clay amalgam but we were still following a recognisable route and that's what counted. About half an hour later we had our first wake up call, the track just stopped at a dead end. We suddenly realised that the road was still being built, and this is how far they've got.

Sure enough, across the scrubby and birch bristled taiga there was a neat barren slash, rather like the tell tale streak that gives away the course of an abandoned railway. However, this scar clearly marked the course that this road is intended to follow as it slowly advances eastwards. Clive got a fire going and brewed up whilst Austin went ahead to see if this faint 'way' was rideable. There was even a hope that there might be another road progressing towards us, in the same way that they dig tunnels from each end. He returned 20 mins later, perspiring from his recce and reported that there was not.

Minutes later several dumper trucks arrived laden with hardcore to extend the road a few metres at a time. They are tipping an embankment and we were standing at the end of it looking out at where one day, the road will be. This really was Land's End, but the scene ahead, rather than the inspiring Atlantic, was a sea of unconquered scrubby taiga. The road gang told us that there was nothing ahead, but if we turn off and ride across the adjacent field to the railway line, there was a track that connected to a proper road two miles away. Hurrah for the Russian road gang! They pointed to the north and sure enough, about a mile away, we could make out the distinctive line of the railway embankment bristling with the wonky concrete posts that held up the sizzling Soviet catenary. A sketch map was drawn in the sand and the foreman type guy demonstrated that there was a bridge under the railway down there that we should head for. We strained our eyes to see but were confounded by that least expected of Siberian problems, heat haze!!!! Anyway, in the distance we could make out a discontinuity in the line of the embankment and we took that to be the bridge to which he alluded.

The bulldozer was ordered to be started up and a ramp was graded to get us back down to 'ground level'. Gerald recce'd the first several metres. It seemed do-able, so off we went. It was not do-able. Gerald fell over and trapped his leg in a very painful position between his bike and the edge of a deep rut he was negotiating. He had to wait for Clive to rescue him. We cast a glance the 60yds back to the road team and sure enough they were transfixed by our crashing cavalcade. Soon we were all stuck in the mossy bog. What made it worse was the giant Kamas lorry 6 x 6 wheel tracks which were up to one foot deep and virtually impossible to cross. What these lorry tracks were doing here was a mystery, maybe they had been driven here by previous cohorts of road workers. After 30 mins and bikes strewn over a 100m stretch of tundra the road crew were sufficiently bored to stop their gazing and return to work. It soon became obvious that we were going to be here for the rest of the day. It took the next two hours but we finally managed to get Austin's fully-laden bike down to the railway bridge. Clive, Chas and Gerald proceeded to slowly move their bikes down-hill.

Austin eventually returned with news of what lay ahead. It was not good. There was *no* road or track beyond the bridge. Due to the heat we were all exhausted. Also, as we toiled with the massively over-loaded bikes, sweat streaming off us, we were set upon by squadrons of a breed of vicious horsefly that we had never encountered before. Their bite was a sharp sting and they were not shooed away with a sweep of the hand, instead they had to be swatted. With our hands 'full' coaxing the bikes across the rutted taiga it was clearly our lot to be bitten wholesale. It was decided to get down to the shade of the bridge with the Katadyn water filter and powdered Israeli water flavourings. Chas and Gerald were too tired so left their bikes embalmed in the mud and we all stumbled forward to the bridge. Clive got his bike to the bridge this time though.

We filtered 6 litres of water from a muddy pool and it soon went. Two hrs later we were still gathering our strength but we were all feeling better for the rehydration. At least the scorching sun had now been obscured behind what looked like a continent wide blanket of cumulus greyness. Austin and Clive unloaded their entire luggage and went on their bikes to check out the way ahead. Chas and Gerald walked back up to their bikes to collect all the kit needed to stay here overnight but with the intention of leaving the bikes where they were. It has become impossible to ride them and they can only be moved with three or four of us heaving them across the bumpy rutted land. Hence, they will stay where they are until the whole team can get their hands around them for the old heave-ho. It was now 5pm and it had taken 4 hrs to do the last mile.

Next to the track was a hut made from old sleepers. Railwayman Gerald informed us that it provided a refuge for the men working on the actual rails and ballast, the so called 'permanent way'. He said that on British railways they could be found every mile or so. As Gerald and Chas settled in, it started raining.

The hut had a stove (which Gerald stated would be standard) and when it had been swept out and the leaking roof mended it was warm and cosy. Clive and Austin returned after two hours of scouting, wet through and through but with relatively good news. The boggy track was possibly passable and lasted 800 yds. From there on it was dirt road to a large town 10km away called Arsenio-Zilov (it's not on our map). However, that was in the dry. If subjected to much rainfall the going would obviously be tougher and slower, we are riding on virtually bald road tyres and it is still raining hard.

We ate and dried out what we could and slept soundly but not before discussing the day's morale-sapping events. It was impossible for us not to notice that if this afternoon was a template for what was to come then it would take about a year to get to Skovorodino. Trains sprang to mind but we decided to press on tomorrow, hoping the rain would have stopped by then.

Russia (Zilov Gap)

Day 84
Monday 3 July
Mondo Miles today: 800 metres
Mondo Mileage: 10308

We awoke in our tiny log cabin like four peas in the proverbial pod. Clive was predictably decent and slipped out to get a fire going under the railway bridge adjacent to the cabin. After a hearty coffee we set to, getting bikes N1 and K5 down from the hill 300m distance from the railway. The weather conditions, as crucial to us as they were to Eisenhower on 5 June 1944, were poor, so under a heavy sky flicking us with rain we pushed back up the hill to rescue the bikes.

The dew on the long tussocky grass and the rain meant that we were soaked in no time. Sweating hard and with all our boots full of water we sherpa'd the gear from K5 down the hill. Painstakingly we cleared individual routelets for the bike which Clive and Austin took turns in riding. Like Stalingrad, gains were measured in clumps of meters. It took 2 hours to get just Chas' bike back and by our return (only 100m covered) we were all shattered and hungry.

The fire had been loaded up with old planks and logs and was by now literally roaring. Keeping up the WWII references Chas asked exactly what was meant by a 'firestorm'. We all stripped down to *unterpanten* and rigged up a huge 40mm steel reinforcing bar as a makeshift drying rail. As the day proceeded we realised that much of our sodden kit was merely being incinerated such was the ferocity of the fire. With more caution, gear was spared but the soup was placed one foot away from the fire yet still boiled rigorously!

The tiny hut was evacuated and we formally set up camp under the bridge, plenty of space and sheltered from the rain. Like so many of our campsites on Mondo Enduro, the scene under the bridge gradually became more untidy and chaotic as panniers were opened, washing up remained undone and tools seemed to end up on every flat surface.

As the rain came, went and came again, we realised that the bridge wasn't actually 'watertight'. It's designers had endowed it with a network of drainage tubes and conduits that took the rainfall landing on the railway above and encouraged it to trickle down unwelcomingly onto our new home. We became increasingly skilful at dodging these vertical nasties and eventually we adjusted our piles of equipment so that they weren't being soaked. This, only after the lesson was learned by Gerald's painstakingly dried out waterproofs being erroneously laid in the path of a water dribbling which swiftly re-soaked them.

After a salty soup lunch we set off again up the hill, this time to rescue Gerald's steed N1. We returned just over an hour later, Chas flushed with confidence of riding the bike back across the tussocky tundra which so readily had ripped the front forks from Clive and Austin's hands, sending them keeling to one side.

With both bikes rescued and therefore all the machines and our effects safely under the bridge, that was the day's work completed (since we have resolved not to try and get out of here whilst it's raining). So all we did was hang around (hoping the rains would somehow be prepared to arbitrate with our representatives) and making incessant cups of coffee. A minor Mondo mishap was logged when the former jam jar holding the condensed milk was smashed. The reader should know that the Russian sweetened condensed milk (moloko) constitutes a daily morale boost to the team. Also, the 1960s pale and navy blue packaging has a strangely pop-art feel that when gazed upon, always brings good cheer. Only the desperate men of this motorcycle trip would carefully extract the slivers of intestinal threatening glass rather than suffer the horror of having to drink black coffee.

Austin changed his sprocket (but slashed his knuckle open pretty badly on one of the teeth – still bleeding 2 days later) and put on a new Russian inner tube (more like linoleum than rubber) and his new tread-rich Dunlop rear tyre. This sees the end of full-time service for what was Bill's rear tyre. Surely the lastik equivalent of a long service medal should go to this particular ring of road holding tenacity – still going strong and changed only because of the Tundra. His is the only new tyre on the team but as Gerald somberly observed, it is a fully road legal touring tyre and should, under no circumstances, be ascribed 'off-road' capabilities.

The sheer mass and volume of the clobber we are carrying has of course now hit us squarely between the eyes. Amongst the unnecessary items which we have been heaving across our own personal Siberian Krypton Factor are; a guidebook to Japan, a 4lb club hammer, *five* ten litre jerrycans, a joke latex 'Mr Spock' ear, two harmonicas and of course, Austin's teddy bear: Plymouth.

Clive knocked up a superb meal which Gerald took a long time to eat. This was noteworthy since it was a portent of a mild flu that he had acquired during the day. (come bedtime at 22.30 he was shivering violently and was very weakened, is this encephalitis B?). Clive brewed up a Beecham's and we all donated him an extra layer of clothes. Eventually we were all asleep back in our little cabin, like 4 peas in the proverbial pod. No booze. Hopefully it won't rain tomorrow.

Russia (Zilov Gap)

Day 85
Tuesday 4 July
Mondo Miles today: 18
Mondo Mileage: 10326

The 'rump' of Mondo Enduro was chastised this morning by the urgent tones of Clive, lighting the fire, serving coffee and enthusing about the new day. A bright sun was quickly melting a blanket of white mist which signalled the start of a Siberian heatwave in miniature.

In the bright sunshine, our assault on Zilov did not at first seem daunting, especially when fortified by mushroom soup with stale bread croutons also prepared by our aforementioned and soon-to-be-deified chef. But any false bravado was quickly stifled by our realisation that our route, so easily negotiated by Clive/Austin on a clear evening two days ago has become a loamy morass of mud and water in the heavy rains. Coupled with the poor 'road' conditions was the perilous state of Gerald's health. His mild chill of yesterday, which had made him so strangely reluctant to complete the mechanical tasks which normally bring him so much joy, appeared to have developed into a full-on viral infection, leaving him useless and utterly exhausted. He needs rest so we are going to move ourselves and the bikes forward in short legs of 500m at a time. Gerald is too weakened to ride across the field and so he will walk whilst the rest of the team take turns shuttling his bike forward.

Austin, Clive and Chas were soon hard at work, ferrying luggage items to our first staging post by a bubbling stream some three-quarters-of-a-mile distant. It was with some, but not much regret, that we left the bridge and plate-layer's hut combo which had served as a refuge in the storm. Our departure was watched by a group of recently dropped off railway workers, clearly amused by our daft endeavour. The sun shone brightly.

The next section, up a muddy and rutted track was if anything even more treacherous. Clive's bike was soon followed by Chas in being nearly up to the rear wheel each in a muddy puddle. Only massive muscular effort and much 'portage' – the posh word for the human hauling heavy luggage items across muddy fields – enabled us to complete this gruelling stage of Mondo Enduro.

The subsequent part of what by now, was no longer the Krypton Factor but had evolved into our own personal variation on the Ho Chi Minh Trail, was an assault on the sodden causeway which we had been led to believe was the route to the village. Clive drove Gerald's bike down a dirt track to a well-disguised swamp which soon claimed it in its muddy embrace. Chas's attempts to negotiate a similar trail was only successful thanks to a shove from Austin and a heave-ho from two jovial bulldozer drivers enjoying the perpetual lunch-break which renders real labour impossible in this erstwhile workers' paradise.

The incessant stress of the 'Road to Never' (Never is a small town just east of Skovorodino, hopefully we will get there) had now wrought its damage and Clive's bike which had developed an electrical fault. As he and Austin pummelled leads and massaged termini, Gerald and Chas negotiated an unforeseen obstacle in our path – a shack containing two vodka-wielding Siberians.

As deftly as The Man with No Name, Anatoly drew the bottle from a holster of flab beneath his shirt. Staring down the barrel of yet another Vodka binge, Chas faint-heartedly accepted the first deadly slug.

Fortunately our Siberian friend and his hopelessly inebriated nephew proved amenable to our request for Chai. Gerald staunchly defended Chas from further Vodka volleys with the well-justified plea that he was officially off-games. To keep our hosts happy we stuffed ourselves with bread and chopped chives from their poorly-stocked table.

The final section to Zilov was tackled more or less without difficulty. As we rolled along the sandy road to the village store we counted the cost of the day's endeavours – Austin's badly gashed knuckle, Chas's and Clive's smashed wing mirrors and all of our creaking clutch cables. The shop itself contained the usual miscellaneous stock of cheap Chinese tracksuits, antique tools and inedible foodstuffs. We settled for three bags of 'recession' pasta, jars of Moldavian tomatoes, tinned Moloko and Hi-NRG peanuts and raisins. For Mondo readers we bought some more South Occotion Vino.

As we emerged onto the veranda of the humble wooden store we froze. Directly ahead of us was the ubiquitous Trans Siberian Railway, another train creaking past at about 15mph. Nothing strange there, but suddenly the Australian white Land Rover appeared. We couldn't see the actual wagons it was resting on so it looked as if it was serenely floating through the town. Next to it were the Swiss bikes, gliding along too. How could it have taken them so long to get this far?? We shouted and waved but they were about 100yds away so would never have heard us above the din of their railway heaven. It was all over in about 7 secs, they slid out of view behind some silver birch and their train was gone. Austin got a bit sad and with us barely a quarter of our way around the world the railway travellers seemed to have the right idea. We all tried not to dwell upon thoughts of anything along the lines of us giving up.

A callow youth astride a grumbling Minsk 350cc motorcycle was happy to answer our plea to show us the road out of town. He proceeded to lead us through a labyrinth of railway track and sandy trails to a handsome trail leading eastwards. One particularly loathsome pool, which we had tried vainly to avoid, left us all spattered with an oily film of black brine.

After about 10 miles of relatively problem-free motoring, past lonesome pines and bustling locomotives, the little Minsk tootles to a halt. Here, our guide informed us, the good road ran out to be replaced with 60 miles of dirt track. At the time of writing Mondo Enduro is at a loss as to what to do. So many variables come into play: Gerald's health, Austin's rear sprocket and all our aforementioned clutches. Above all, we fear the weather which can change so whimsically in these parts from fly-blown heat to freezing downpours which dissolve riding surfaces like so much concentrated hydrochloric acid.

Our campsite was a rubble-strewn and midge-populated glade next to the Trans-Siberian railway. The day of many trials and much tribulation ended on a note of mild discord with Austin and Clive disagreeing over what attracted ants the most, snot or spittle?

As if seeking a metaphor for our mood, Clive torched an anthill with petrol. But we retired to our tent and poncho filled up with 'Great Wall' Chinese tinned beef and a tot of Georgian brandy. Life, we reflected, is not all bad, unless you happen to live in Zilov all the time.

Russia (Zilov Gap)

Day 86
Wednesday 6 July
Mondo Miles today: 45
Mondo Mileage: 10371

So we awoke early (7am) and as usual on Mondo Enduro, we allowed ourselves a couple of hours to pack and have several brews before we hit the road.

Chas and Clive set off first to scout ahead, whilst Austin waited for Gerald to get dressed. We allowed him to have a lie in, in order to bring himself back to health: he had literally sweated the virus out – a quick sleeping bag change in the morning (his is now saturated with sweat so he got Austin's) and he was as right as rain. A barometer of Gerald being back in good health came when he emerged from his second sweat drenched sleeping bag and produced from his luggage his spare pair of underpants. They were clean white y-fronts and had been stored 'rolled up' like a cigar. Gerald deftly held one edge and flicked them open so they unrolled with an almost jubilant spring. At this very instant he made a 'boing' sound affect that perfectly accompanied this moment of rebirth. Whatever had smothered his normal good spirits these last 36hrs, it was certainly gone now. We had our leader back.

Chas and Clive had reached the point of no return after 6 miles when the pleasant sandy road turned into huge 6 x 6 mud tracks baked hard in the sun, with the occasional soft spot to keep you on your guard.

We had one eye on the road and the other on the weather; we knew we had roughly 60 miles of this and if it started raining we could well be stranded in the middle of nowhere with our limited supply of food, waiting for the inevitable perpetual rain to cease. Moreover, we were in the knowledge that the Siberian weather had a mind of its own after being held up under that bridge for 2 days.

So the duo riding at point carefully made their way over this treacherous terrain for several miles when they came across one of the 6 x 6 Kamas trucks by the Trans-Siberian. Surprisingly enough the railway workmen were having a break at the time. This is rapidly becoming a common feature in this land renowned for its hardworkers. Clive and Chas got chatting to confirm their worried thoughts on how long this death road could possibly go on for. As per usual, the reply was a few kilometres down the line and it is "*horosho*" (good) all the way to Mogocha. Mogocha is the next substantial town; it represents the halfway point from Chernyshevsk to Skovorodino.

As we trundle and struggle along this railside trail, it is becoming clear that in no way is it meant to be the 400 mile lifeline that spans what Austin has started calling 'The Zilov Gap'. These tracks are completely ad hoc and our desperate wish that suddenly it will all sort itself out and become rideable is clearly unrealistic. There is no traffic on the trail, even a 4x4 would struggle. All the little villages and towns we have encountered are *on* the railway. If you want to move around out here, you do it on the local one carriage 'sprinter' service that we have observed, not by car. The one exception to this rule are these ginormous Russian Kamas lorries that seem to be used to insert railway workers into position. Unfortunately for us, their 'off-road' capability is so superb that they do not need anything like the molly coddling that we do. However, we keep encountering stretches of track that are about 5 miles long where the going is super easy and our spirits soar. The depressing thing is realising that this will never be the norm. We just don't know what's in store around the next corner. Nevertheless, we keep asking everyone we meet what's coming up next.

The Vince brothers turned up soon after Chas and Clive and we told them our news. However, *their* news that Austin's front sprocket was shagged set panic in the hearts of the Mondo Enduro team. Fortunately, Austin had kept Gerald's old front sprocket which was only *semi*-shagged.

As Austin changed sprockets there was a 'ping' and the circlip holding the front sprocket onto the driveshaft sprang away into the grass. Austin assembled the team and we crept forward on hands and knees combing the undergrowth for this vital retaining doo-dah. Their tea break over and vaguely curious, the rail workers drifted over and looked as well. Austin drew them the piece on a scrap of paper but they shrugged their shoulders. Gerald then had a brainwave and grabbed something from the floor; it was a piece of the thick copper wire used in the railway's overhead electrics. He carefully wound it around the shaft and tightened it into place with his leatherman pliers. Amazing, it looked delicate but better than nothing. Heaven knows if this sprocket will last though, the teeth are massively hooked and deformed and two of the fourteen have snapped off completely

A quick chai stop in the back of the 6x6 and we were back on the twisted track. The road improved slowly and before long we were on the sandy road again. Hurrah!! We were on a high note now, this had to be the road that went all the way, surely?

Gerald discovered for us, after a front wheel skid, that the road suddenly disappeared under water.

This was only a temporary set back, as we scrambled up the edge of a bank supporting a railway bridge. We proceeded a further 30 yds to find another river flowing straight across our path. A quick recce and we were over in no time – a film opportunity was taken, great shot! Onwards we went once again making great progress until we encountered a village with no name – well, not listed on the map nor any welcoming signs. We befriended a local who guided us out of town and on the road to Never.

The sandy track was there again and it was not long out of this town with no name that the road split in two – we followed the nice track for a few miles but it was unused and went in the wrong direction. About turn and back to the fork. Well, Plan B was afoot, the 'Bogus Route' in the right direction and through the first of what was to be huge puddle ridden

tracks. Most of these were filmed with both Gerald and Chas caught with their engines stalled in the middle of them, 1-2ft deep water filled trenches. Gerald and Chas frantically and hopelessly trying to kick start the bikes there. How we craved electric start.

This wicked terrain went on endlessly until something had to give way and it was Chas's sprocket this time: finally failing after going through the Mother of all puddles. Close inspection revealed rounded off sprocket teeth – the chain had started to jump! Hereafter Chas rode bravely and most carefully knowing the team was miles from any help and were more likely many miles from somewhere that could fabricate a sprocket. The bikes were finally giving way – the weight was proving too much for their meagre 350 working bodies.

Meanwhile, Clive had stripped his bike down (ditched the luggage) and cut ahead to see what he could find. It was truly a superb Enduro circuit and unladen, a total joy to the bike, however, 3.7 miles later the track once again disappeared into a river – this one 50m wide but fortunately no more than 1-2ft deep – nothing our trail bikes couldn't handle.

Meanwhile, Austin had ditched half of *his* luggage and he followed in Clive's tyre marks in an attempt to make a little progress. Whilst negotiating a small lake he lost control and the whole bike was submerged in the silty soup. He was beside himself with fear and remorse, since we do not have any experience in the re-starting of water-logged bikes. Incredibly, it fired up second kick and he was able to catch up with Clive. They hooked up as Clive was on his return journey and Clive mooted the idea that they all get to the bridge he'd found, hole up there tonight and ride *back* tomorrow to collect the remainder of the luggage.

Back to the lads and they had made little progress, with Gerald's Givi hard luggage bracket bending in a crash and now catching in the back wheel. The sun is roasting us to a crisp and the biting flies love our pale flesh. Ironically, the byword for our overloadedness, the 4lb club hammer, proved most useful to Gerald, hunched at the rear of N1, straightening the Givi bracket!! Chas's sprocket ailment is getting worse and now any attempt to even accelerate out of 'trouble' sees his chain being dragged over the stumps of his back sprocket. The resulting harsh clattering and grinding sound is unbearable and cuts through us like a banshee wail of mechanical despair.

Wearily, the Mondo men soldiered on saturated with wet mud, slipping and sliding their way through this tricky Enduro circuit with obstacle after obstacle looming around each bend. Even more of the kit was left behind to preserve Chas's sprocket and make the journey to the bridge a little bit more bearable.

The light was finally fading via a stunning Siberian sunset (at 10pm) when the huge girder bridge finally came into sight on the last stretch of track down to the water's edge. A sight to raise the sodden spirits of the physically and mentally shattered Mondo Enduro team. The campsite was on the sandy beach of the river's edge – a comfortable and convenient spot but there were only 2 lots of bedding between 4 men. We had left the rest back on the trail.

An emergency meal was the order of the day, after this marathon riding effort. A fire was soon started and bedding was improvised to cater for four. The team was too tired to have even their favourite drink of coffee, everyone sleeping in their leathers, soon fast asleep. We are about 100 miles in, 300 to go and only managed 18 today. Can we keep this up?

Russia (Zilov Gap)

Day 87
Thursday 6 July
Mondo Miles today: 0
Mondo Mileage: 10371

Despite the lack of sleeping kit we all slept well and only the patter of rain made us get up and repair to the nearest lineside cabin. No sooner had we settled in then the legitimate users arrived, having been dropped off by the works train. The rain came down in its usual Siberian style that is all or nothing. We just hung about. After lunch with the rail workers, Austin, Clive and Chas returned to the site where the remainder of the gear was left. They walked via the railway line which turned out to be a much shorter route (2 miles). Although it was raining and they had a lot to carry back it only took them 3½ hours. They had left some gear for Gerald ensuring that we all did one trip. Gerald set off when the rain had stopped, walking in the sun admiring the very pleasant scenery which we were unable to enjoy yesterday. When he arrived at the site there was nothing there. It had all been stolen. Every cloud has a silver lining: at least Gerald didn't have to carry anything back.

List of stolen gear:

Arai Giga helmet
Gloves, puncture repair kit
Sleeping bag and thermarest
Nut and bolt box
Tank bag (inc contents)
Givi kitchen pannier
MSR Stove
Various cooking bits and pieces.

It will lighten the luggage from here since Chas's sprocket will not take much load.

Russia (Zilov Gap)

Day 89
Friday 7 July
Mondo Miles today: 9
Mondo Mileage: 10380

As we all snuggled together in the railway hut and unconsciously thought that every train that passed was about to stop, the dawn arrived and Austin got up first to get the fire afoot. Today was to be another day of off-road reckoning. We had heard several irritatingly conflicting reports about the length of and quality of the track that lay before use. Before we could contemplate tackling the 15km run into Sbega we had sundry other dramas to be squared away: Chas's front sprocket had by now been worn to a rippled disc. Amazingly it can still hook the chain on the horizontal but steep hills and/or heavy luggage quickly negate this miraculous reprieve. Gerald's stolen gear included the puncture repair kit and vitally, our only spare front 21" inner tube. These tubes are quite specifically unavailable out here unlike our 18" rear wheel which is prolific on local machines. Austin's front sprocket is history and Gerald's old front sprocket is struggling. Clive's H6 seems to be holding out but a mysterious electrical starting virus afflicts him in the worst possible way ie intermittently! Ugh!! The deep mud/water splashes have done little to preserve the integrity of the delicate circuitry. Finally – today starts with the crossing of the Chernyeva river. Two options presented themselves – fording the river or using the service footpath on the huge single span pratt trussed girder bridge that carries the westbound line of the Trans-Siberian. A flip-flop recce last night proved the river to be just a little deeper than we would like, whilst a look at the bridge and approaches showed this to be feasible if only a little more risky because of the limited clearance between m/c and train, were one to come along once we were crossing the bridge.

Austin attempted the bridge crossing first. It was selected because basically it meant not having to get our feet soaked so early in the day – and besides – it seemed a little more fun than yet another fording.

Up onto the embankment, weaving around abutments and railside furniture, the crossing proved trivial to the ultra-nimble trail bike. Once off the far embankment Austin just kept going; he adjusted the bike and made four miles down a sound sandy track in the direction of Sbega. He came across a local, driving at full pelt towards him on a Jawa 350. A farcical mimed and 4 word vocabulary conversation revealed (we think) that the road to Sbega was OK and the deep rutted nightmares that have plagued us in getting this far were to torture us no more. Bearing this gleeful news Austin returned to the railside hut and the endless activity associated with us striking camp ground into motion. It was in fact another <u>four</u> hours before we finally had the last bike over the bridge and loaded up on the far side. By now it was a baking hot Siberian July afternoon. We have now started to become accustomed to the fickleness of the weather out here. The range of temperature experienced during any one day is only matched by the speed with which the climate transforms from pleasant to intolerable.

Our local guide's information was 100% correct and we were euphoric as we lapped up 4 trouble free miles. It had taken us five hours to do the same distance the day before yesterday! Our hearts sank as we rounded the last bend near a village and there the track led straight into the river again. Heroic as ever, Clive was already immersed up to his knees scanning the undulating river bed for what in his opinion (quickly becoming *the* river crossing opinion) would be the easiest route. Everyone was wet up to the knees but in 20 mins we were all across. The track almost instantly deteriorated into a heavily rutted mess. Deep muddy water filled trenches gave us the blues and basically scared us away. Austin attempted a by-passing manoeuvre through the adjacent silver birch forest and after initial success waved the others through. His advice was bogus and within five minutes the team were lost in the undergrowth, shouting to each other and unable to move the machines.

After extricating ourselves from this forestry fiasco we called it a day and headed up to the village – collecting supplies from the lone shop that was blended into the railway station. What a surprise to find 'Jawa Man' from the track this morning, sitting inside, his wife was the proprietor. Chas gave his daughter a Mondo badge and she threw it away. This event noted in the log since it represents an atypical reaction to Chas-u-like.

We think constantly what it must be like to live in one of these little railway villages. All the structures are log cabins and of course there is no evidence of any civic infrastructure, pavements, street lighting etc. Our trials in even reaching these places reinforces our impression of the island mentality that they must have, the only way in or out is by train. Throw in a six month winter that's the most brutal on this planet and it seems to make perfect sense when at two in the afternoon you find men staggering the streets, utterly shitfaced.

We were told by Jawa Man that Spega, the next sizeable collection of sheds, logs and mud that passes for a village was only 20 mins drive away and that the track was not going to cause any quivering of the top lip. We hammered on, lost Gerald, re-found him headed out of town and hit another huge ford. We crossed this, went two miles then crossed another. Austin gamely but foolishly went first, without unloading his bike. Eventually he made it 80% of the way across then predictably lost control and dropped the bike over into about a foot of water not only soaking all of the airbox and carburettor but trapping himself under his bike. All the while the river water effortlessly flowed into his giant leather pannier, inevitably soaking everything inside. Clive was next to the river and waded in to right the bike and release Austin.

Austin pushed the bike a few yards further through the channel but caught a rock at an awkward angle dropping the bike under the chilly Siberian flow once more. However, this time it was on the other side which until then was still dry. Now everything he has is soaked, including two rolls of 35 mm stills film which were in no way waterproofed or protected. What a genius. Eventually we were all across – naturally, B2 (Austin's bike) wouldn't start.

We set about the evening meal and were soon discovered by a tractor driving Vodka monster. He taunted and irritated us and showed off in his beast. It was frightening and pathetic. He performed lavish handbrake turns in the tractor swinging his huge steel plough attachment behind him. He was clearly trying to intimidate and possibly injure us with some terrifying near misses. This went on for 10 mins and it was only a matter of time before he either injured one of us or smashed a bike to pieces. We couldn't leave; all of Austin's possessions were spread all over the ground drying. We were scared, this was *his* world and we'd all seen 'Deliverance'. The mace pepper sprays were twitched...eventually he got bored of taunting us and snaked off across the fields. Austin revealed that he had contemplated murdering him and had worked out what to do with the body but couldn't think how to dispose of the tractor.

We moved to sleep 400m away in a small depression where Gerald had set up a poncho and we eventually relaxed. If the vodka tractor man returns, he will hopefully not find us in this sleepy hollow.

Only nine miles today and we have a complete set of wet kit, an engine full of water and only three sleeping bags between four of us. Result.

Russia (Zilov Gap)

Day 90
Saturday 8 July
Mondo Miles today: 34
Mondo Mileage: 10414

The cloudy pool which is the collective consciousness of Mondo Enduro at any time before 8am was rippled today by Gerald exhorting us to rise and shine. The sun was streaming from a clear sky upon a new day chastening us with fresh challenges.

The first of which was the urgent need to start Austin's bike which had been so badly drenched in last night's tip into the river. The morbid response from his first attempted kick start pointed to a heavy morning's maintenance which then ensued.

The slow striptease of B2 was something akin to a Haynes Manual line workshop as first the spark plug was inspected and cleaned. Bit-by-bit the motorcycle's ignition system came apart in Austin's greasy hands – the air filter, air pipe and carburettor. As each component was slowly inspected it became clear that his bike was suffering from self-treated water contamination, evident by the cylinder which appeared to be full of mud and liquid.

As usual Austin opted for the violently dramatic option in terms of motorcycle maintenance. A syringe was broken from the medical kit and used to spray petrol in through the spark plug hole to achieve maximum cylinder dryness. As Gerald gingerly ignited Austin's engine with a blowtorch, Clive attempted vainly to capture the moment on camera.

Just before our lunch of beef soup and stale bread croutons, the person we least wanted to see in the entire Asian landmass put in another surprise appearance. It was the Siberian tractor driver of last night's acquaintance and a moustached accomplice, both thankfully sober and apparently *compos mentis* after a morning's threshing in the field adjacent to our campsite. Happily there were no agricultural machinery antics today. They came, sat around a bit, picked up various engine parts and asked a series of incomprehensible questions before departing bored across the meadow. We are not hardy types but we think it reasonable that tractor man was lucky not to have been viciously beaten up by us.

As thunder clouds gathered ominously, Austin finally managed to start his motorcycle before the heavens opened, forcing us to shelter briefly under a poncho. By about 2pm we were on the road and fording our first river of the day – a shallow but fast flowing stream which somehow seemed strangely familiar. The road, by the constricted standard of The Magocha County Council's Highway's Department, had by now turned into a veritable Autobahn of sand and rubble which skirted the river and stretched into a forested distance. Soon we chanced upon our last and most testing obstacle – the same river which we had already crossed four times. Oh how we cursed the phenomenon of 'meandering'. This time it was a barrier of truly Rubicon proportions with an 80m wide tricky fast channel which would test Mondo's crossing skills to the full.

Finally, and watched by a delinquent audience of Siberian children on the far side, the team was over and supping on Snickers and Yupi (Russian water flavouring crystals) purchased by Gerald in one of his many moments of brilliance.

And so we gazed on Sbega, which repaid us poorly for the considerable effort we had expended in securing our bridgehead. It was an original one ironhorse town almost completely ignored by the Trans-Sib which sailed past imperiously with the exception of three passenger-only trains a day. This neglect was evidenced by the high proportion of scrap metal littering the streets and by-ways of this scattered community. As we foraged for confectionery amongst the flotsam of heavy industrial plant, we asked ourselves, not for the first time, how we ever ended up on the Road to Never...

Casual enquiries in the signal office, bedecked with fruits of the forest and populated by three bemused but helpful workers, revealed the impossibility of freighting our bikes by train to the East. Chas's bike was by now complaining angrily under the burden of stretching a shagged chain across the decayed teeth of his front sprocket. The other motorcycles were straining under the load of most of *his* luggage and nursing a workshop manual's worth of ills – creaking clutches, dodgy electrics, flaky sprockets and clattering chains.

The gold-toothed signalman indicated that we might care to wait until morning and blagg our way onto the next Mogocha Sprinter – but neither he, nor we, expressed full confidence. There seemed nothing for it but to flog our bikes another 40km to Kysen-Yevka, another railroad town which it appears takes freight and harbours somewhat more of the cultural life associated with large conurbations.

We turned off the road at about 8pm and made our way along a short firebreak. Supper, briefly delayed by a rainstorm, consisted of tinned Irish beef, assorted soups and chopped salami. By way of variation, we ate salami slices on bread as hors d'oeuvres.

Austin and Gerald endured the Ooloo one more time, nipping off to the nearby river to collect water. We could all *clearly* hear its poetic babbling refrain as it danced past the rocky river bed. However, out here in Siberia the soundscape is beguiling and it transpired that the river was easily a mile away. Boulders fallen trees, forest and endless coarse long grass meant that the Vince brothers' water run took an incredible two hours!

Coffees all round ensued before we adjourned to bed – Austin to his poncho, Clive to his RAB sleeping bag and Chas and Gerald to the singular team building delights of the shared unzipped Ajungilak.

Russia (Zilov Gap)

Day 91
Sunday 9 July
Mondo Miles today: 0
Mondo Mileage: 10414

There was no joy from Spega, as far as trains were concerned, so Clive and Chas descended upon Kysen-yevka upon that Sunday morn to see what this larger array of wooden huts had to offer. Gerald and Austin were left in the fire break campsite tasked with writing letters home on the back of old maps that we no longer required. On the train saga, the mystery got larger, and no bikes on the train here despite our reports from Spega and the towns before that advice: try the next town Kisley-Kluch, they will take your bikes for certain – where had we heard that before?

On a blending trip Clive and Chas went around the town until they could track down a sprocket or someone in the know about sprockets. An hour later after Chas had jumped in a 6x6 Kamas – we had an Ural sprocket in our hands. Back to the train station where there was chai, soup, salad and sweets awaiting for Clive and Chas to keep their spirits high. The two Dorris's who worked there had fallen for the two dirty Englishmen. They called around frantically to their friends and colleagues but unfortunately to no avail.

Whilst shopping around the corner, Clive got chatting to Vlad, a security guard at the nearby 'Gold Mine Depot'. Vlad spoke reasonable English which he had perfected serving with the UN force in Yugoslavia. He informed us that his boss could help. So Chas went off with him to the station to explain to Doris and Doris what was happening, whilst Clive was spoilt with chai, tinned pork and candy by a beautiful, dodgy hair dyed Siberian lass. Meanwhile, Gerald and Austin were patiently waiting for Clive and Chas to return from their train timetable recce not anticipating the epic blend that their co-riders were currently brokering.

Our next move was to get the 6am train to Kisnekluch tomorrow to the Gold Digging Factory and our problems would be solved. However, that wasn't enough for Clive and Chas. They soon got bored of Sacha, the 72 year old Marxist vet in the dormitory above the station and took to going for some Champers and chocolate in the park at 10.30 in the evening with the two red haired girls instead. Little did they know these two ladies were sisters and both worked in the Gold Factory. After a few bevvies it was off to the director's house to blag a lift to the factory. No point in waiting for the train that went at 6am the next day was there?

The director was on the phone so we were led to the firm's HQ 2kms away where we were vodka'd and dined before being shown to a company room with *ensuite* lounge and bathroom.

An angel has watched over us and has out here in Siberia provided us with champers which we gleefully accepted. So now Chas and Clive are snuggled in a 'company bedroom' whilst poor Gerald and Austin were drinking bogue water and being pestered by merchants in a fire break.

Russia (Zilov Gap)

Day 92
Monday 10 July
Mondo Miles today: 00
Mondo Mileage: 10414

It is our anniversary today. Three months away from home and still 200 miles to Magocha and the lure of the bright lights of Anchorage. How we wish it was closer. Gerald woke up during the night for a smoke and *another* tick got its teeth into him. Austin went to get his head torch and pulled it out with some pliers before it gorged itself on his watery blood. Lethargy has taken a vice-like grip on the two Mondoites who remain here whilst Chas and Clive are away getting new sprockets made (hopefully). Austin and Gerald have taken to writing letters on the back of the redundant maps. They make very good writing paper. The lens in the Mondo camera had got water into it after Austin's latest river submersion so we undid every screw we could find. It is now drying in the sun and we can only hope that we can re-assemble it correctly. Larder and kitchen boxes are the next thing to be cleaned. Chas returned with 2 men in a lorry to take his bike away to get the new sprockets fitted. We were invited but decided to stay at the campsite. He went off, hopefully we will see him tomorrow with the new parts. As soon as he left Jackson and Son appeared on a Jawa 350 and we had a chat. All was going well until he saw the camera lens in pieces. He proceeded to dismantle the lens even further and took an age to get it back together all in the wrong order. We do not believe it will take another photo until it is professionally repaired. Austin went to the river to wash and collect water. Upon his return we dined on pasta and plov. A substantial argument developed about the time that the pasta sauce should be cooked for, Gerald favouring a longer 'reduction' while Austin encourages a quick 'sear-then-serve' approach. This was followed by a pudding of tea. More letter writing and some leather repairs. The mystery bottle turned out to be red wine, so we drank it. Just as we were about to retire for the night Camera Jackson returned. So Austin offered him a ride on B2 – off he went. Gerald went to bed and had fallen asleep before he came back with a pretty girl 25yrs old and a bottle of red sparkling wine. The usual toasts were made and when the wine was finished they left.

Russia (Zilov Gap)

Day 93
Tuesday 11 July
Mondo Miles today: 28
Mondo Mileage: 10442

The team was split for another day, Gerald and Austin tucked away on the gas pipeline firebreak – Chas and Clive bunked down in the guest quarters of the gold mine maintenance depot. Gerald and Austin were starting to show signs of what over the next few days would soon develop into a startling bout of Mondo Enduro lethargy. They arose around 10am, staggered the 6 yards to the fireplace and by using gasoline kicked a brew into life and exhausted themselves by drinking it. It was noon before they were able to get up and walk over to Austin's panniers to get a piece of paper and a pen for more letter writing. It was a real scorcher by now and so the letters waited while friendly Jackson (Anatole) did not. He made his first of many appearances that day and through our usual sign language we compared bikes and he oooed and aaahed at the DR. After a humble (too lazy to cook) noodle lunch Gerald and Austin erected a poncho for shade and mossie net for protection. The latter being far the more useful as we were now up against the most hated 'Oakley Sunglasses' wearing fly/waspoids. These bastards have the tenacity of spiders, the sting of a bee and the proliferation of the Chinese. Huge black ants still punctured the net at ground level and feasted on the exposed zones of the snoozing Vince Brothers.

Meanwhile, Chas and Clive had been busy blending and at 7pm Clive turned up in a truck with 3 shouting, drinking Russians. The leader (he that shouted loudest) made cucumber jokes while we toasted, then left. The trio struck camp, burned Austin's old boots that he'd been issued with when he first joined the Army and headed the 28 miles north to Kisly Kluch and Chas. Re-united, Mondo Enduro bathed and beat themselves (with leaves) in the banya and ate in the workers' canteen, sleep in a REAL bed!!!

NB: Clive's journey south with these three Russian bears was peppered by quasi-formalised vodka stops and on arrival at the campsite, he was not well.

Russia (Zilov Gap)

Day 94
Wednesday 12 July
Mondo Miles today: 0
Mondo Mileage: 10442

The lads, re-united after their brief separation, awoke in the comparative comfort of the Goldmining Collective Guest Hostel to a day full of sunshine and promise. Their good cheer was the result of grand hospitality and expert workmanship at the hands of their Siberian hosts, but in spite of a restless night's sleep Austin had been troubled by mosquitoes whilst Chas had severe genito-urinary problems caused by overdosing on Georgian Black Tea. The label on the packet went like this: "*All Union Scientific – Industrial Amalgamation of tea and subtropical crops, Ozurgeti.*"

The day saw Nicolay, Alexander and other members of the lathe gang turn out the *five* sprockets which hopefully will mean untrammelled motorcycling for Mondo Enduro.

After a breakfast (double helpings) of sugared milk and spaghetti, served by the flirtatious and feisty kitchen maid Tenya, the lads repaired to the workshop for a bout of bolt tightening and filter cleaning which we took to be the order of the day. Yura, the ageing Estonian son of the workshop mafia, found Gerald a hand-drill so that he could repair his rickety Givi bracket with a brand new bolt. It was at this juncture that Alla, our saviour of two nights previously, made a surprise appearance. It transpires that she and Sasha, the cool-as-permafrost jeep driver, were going to Magocha on business. Would one of us like to come and make some inquiries about platform facilities to Skovoradino?

Chas volunteered for what promised to be a pleasurable task and set off along the bumpy road to this minor jewel in the tawdry crown of the Chitastaya Oblast. After several trips to the workers banks and various social calls, they made their way to the Collective Locomotive Union for a spot of sprocket tempering. Unfortunately Alla had not realised that the teeth of the component were as yet unsharpened and so it was something of a wasted journey. It was made more pleasant, however, by a visit to the Stolovaya (works canteen) where they supped on fried fish, vegetable broth and tins of Danish "Faxo" export beer.

Their next task was to discover the price of railway transportation to Skovorodino – the last port of call on the Road to Never. At the State Transport Offices were various Leninist slogans applauding the honour of Labour ("An individual's effort is the State's Reward"/"Work is the Path to Honour" etc) while everybody sat around apparently doing nothing. Alla returned from the inquiry desk in a state of anger and promptly tore up the piece of paper which said it would cost us 2 million roubles (400$) each for the 12 hour journey.

The homeward journey took in a trip to a training shoe factory before arriving sometime after 6pm. The rest of the lads had spent the day doing maintenance tasks, socialising and sleeping. Austin had filmed what promises to be priceless footage of our hard-bitten but kind hosts with hearts as golden as the plentiful mineral deposits in the Uryun River.

Supper was a predictably bogus recipe of pasta and pork fat with half a cucumber thrown in for nutritional reasons. Afterwards we repaired to the dormitory to discuss our next move and count our cash, only to be called upon by Yuri and various other workers who were vastly amused by the 'Karavan' press cutting from Almaty. Even Yuri, the flinty Estonian gagger, asked for a signed photo from our Metsovo collection. While Doris, the well-proportioned kitchen lady also paid a call to our dormitory.

Russia (Zilov Gap)

Day 95
Thursday 13 July
Mondo Miles today: 0
Mondo Mileage: 10442

Another lazy day on the horizon, as Chas went off with Alla for money changing and train checking. Austin, Clive and Gerald slept most of the day away. The routine was fairly set by now. Get up, stuff yourself with food and chai from the canteen and return to our quarters for a few hours sleep. This professional resting and time wasting was carried out 3 times per day.

On the admin front Austin wrote a letter to our Chief *inspirateur* Chris Scott and Clive duplicated it to Sean Hawker. Gerald had the mammoth task for day to change over a Givi clip for Chas. It was all too good to be true.

Chas returned around 5pm to bring us the news that the train was even more expensive at 2.6m roubles and if we didn't get it tomorrow it would be 4m roubles. He did also have pleasing news, that the 5 sprockets were heat treated (tempered) for the measly cost of 20,000 roubles. What a complete result! Chas had done well!

Alla, our fly-by-night hostess, had a far more important and interesting job than Mondo Enduro originally realised. She was power-dressed today in a beige linen suit with substantial epaulettes. Chas witnessed her wheeling and dealing in Magocha whilst he was unknowingly standing in as her angliski toyboy mascot. All the clients were impressed as she finished the day with a crate of beer, 2 bottles of champers and a host of other goodies which little did we know were soon to be guzzled down by us.

So after a bottle of champers and a beer each with Alla and Sacha in a gravel pit near the Union River, we were persuaded to blend back to Alla's new home in Kesyn-Yevka for her housewarming and our last night in these island towns.

We spent an hour or so at Zena's house resting watching Russian TV and her kids playing video games, whilst Alla prepared our supper. It was worth the wait for there was a classic Russian feast prepared consisting of fried pork and liver, potatoes, cucumber, cottage like cheese with cream, gherkins, bread, fresh tomatoes, apples, oranges and jam all washed down with beer, Champanski, raspberry liquor and Vodka. The only slight downer was the incessantly loud techno music being played for the whole evening. It was a fabulous evening with a few pictures taken on Alla's advice. We slept in pairs in the same room – Clive with Gerald – Austin with Chas.

Russia (Zilov Gap)

Day 96
Friday 14 July
Mondo Miles today: 46
Mondo Mileage: 10488

Despite Alla's promises we did not leave her house until 0900hrs. A lift back to the camp in an omnibus all to ourselves got us back there by 10.00hrs. We packed and said our thank-you's and goodbyes and left at

11.30am. Austin crashed after a few miles when he went straight into a huge hole whilst waving to a lorry driver. All of us except Chas had misfiring trouble on the road to Magocha. The decision has been made to do the rest of The Zilov Gap by train. We are dejected and crestfallen since we all know that if there is any kudos for its conquering; it will not be ours but some later team that passes this way. Even more irritating, the 30 miles before the Gold mine depot (ridden a few days ago) was excellent sandy track and the 25 miles we rode into Mogocha was equally unchallenging. We collectively squirm at the possibility that the second half of this roadless section might all be like this, that the worst is behind us and that we don't need the train at all! It is the ignorance about the way ahead that is most exasperating.

We were told the train left at 14.00hrs. We arrived at 13.30hrs to be told it was leaving between 18.00-20.00hrs. Chas did his bit and bought the tickets then to the bank, food and petrol. Back to the train yard we loaded the bikes onto our very own wagon. A diesel shunter came and collected us and took us down to the station area where we joined up with the main body of the freight train. We were all very excited by the fact that we could never have done anything like this in Europe. Doors open, chugging along; our euphoria was short lived as we settled down for a long wait for the electric locomotive that would take us to Skovorodino. 20.30hrs and we're still at a standstill. Everyone had a good laugh at Gerald's 20 year old passport photo. The sun is going down and I'ts getting colder. It may be a cold night. The later we leave, the hour of our arrival becomes more civilised. At 23.00hrs we closed the doors and went to bed. At 01.00hrs we were woken by the most almighty noise as we finally started our journey. But not for long. After an hour or so we stopped for quite a long time. There were people shouting and milling about, torches were shone onto our wagon and eventually we began crawling eastwards again.

Russia (Zilov Gap)

Day 97
Saturday 15 July
Mondo Miles today: 0
Mondo Mileage: 10442

The deafening noise inside the goods wagon continued all night and we slept fitfully. There was much sweating reported from under the sleeping bags as the full temperature range out here made itself felt. Austin was dreaming of being served in a top restaurant when Clive kicked him and the remainder awoke at 07's with the news that we were approaching Skovorodino. Sadly he was wrong but the scene for a few minutes as we scurried about our eight wheeled home trying to pack was quite ridiculous. Gerald, super-cool assured us from within his sleeping bag that we were here too soon and hence this couldn't be Skovorodino. He was of course right, and it transpired that we had only completed a fraction of the journey from Magocha. We all went back to sleep quite quickly. At <u>that</u> time none of us would have conceived that Skovorodino though less than 100 miles by rail was still more than 24hrs away.

Soon settled down to what we thought would be a few more hours in the wagon before we arrived at Skovorodino. We immediately mused as to how long it would have taken the Swiss and the Aussies on their far longer journey. They had been quoted 36hours – pah!!! They are probably <u>still</u> travelling by flat bed. We dangled our legs out of the permanently open doors, urinated into both embankments and cuttings and tried to spot the kilometre post by the railside so as to accurately predict our arrival at Skovorodino.

Eventually a town loomed up (it was noon by now) but its distinctive shape and lack of towers/radio beacons in appropriate places told us, via the ONC map, that this was Uskuska, <u>not</u> Skovorodino. We must surely have been caught in a space: time continuum as we still had 60 miles to go but surely we had rattled further than 40 miles all morning?

Things calmed down from the racy-pacy clickety-clack of the Trans-Siberian as we were shunted into the becalmed parallel world of the Uskuska marshalling yard. The hot afternoon sun baked us as the minutes turned to hours and our locomotives were uncoupled from our train and sent off to haul the doubtless more urgent loads of freight that waited alongside us. We all became timetable enthusiasts as we duly noted that lumber moves slower than crude oil which moves slower than local passengers which moves slower than express passengers. Mixed freight, us, moves not at all.

Eight hours later, with a gorgeous Siberian sunset to the north, we creaked out of the siding. We were at the rear of the train now (whoa!! Special treatment) and watched it snake ahead of us over guarded bridges and alongside an annoyingly well made dirt track. We could hardly bear to look. We pulled into Skovorodino at midnight. Chas was heroic and levelled the mountain of paperwork generated by our arrival– despite doing absolutely nothing we all were tired again – the Mondo curse that afflicts us all.

Russia (Yakutia)

Day 98
Sunday 16 July
Mondo Miles today: 329
Mondo Mileage: 11027

The Mondo day started with warm sunshine streaming into the goods wagon which had served as our shelter for the second night. Upon arrival at Skovorodino station, we had been shunted to a siding in the early hours. Whilst our automobile-driving colleagues made good their escape in double-quick time, Mondo Enduro retired to sleeping bags for much needed shut-eye.

The drawing of the wagon doors certainly caught our good-natured security guard and colleagues by surprise. They proffered the first of what will no doubt be plentiful and hopelessly contradictory intelligence about the Road from Never: bad as far as Tynda, then bad before getting good on the approach to Yakutsk. The road from Yakutsk to Magadan is passable by motorbike, apparently.

After a steady drive of no more than half-a-mile, Austin pulled over to a candy booth where Zuko, the much loved powdered fruit crystals, were bought in a batch of 10 sachets. Onto the railway station where we met our first self-important official since we entered the blissfully unpoliced Urgum River Valley. A copper, obviously keen to establish his gendarme credentials, ordered us not to drive on the station forecourt. As Clive kept vigil over the bikes, the others patronised the station buffet where they were served large almond biscuits and sugared tea. This humble repast would set us up for a long day's drive in what promises to be a further extension of this mini-Siberian heatwave.

On out of town, past the peeling Lenin posters and the dilapidated Palace of the People (above) and on to Never. As the name suggests it was an anonymous little town totally undeserving of all the mental tribulation centred upon it since Chita. Already we have sight of the M56 signs which we followed gleefully with the exception of Chas who was pulled over by the

GAI (police) for not wearing his helmet. Their initial inquiry "are you a rocker?" revealed that they had seen our clip on Irkutsk television.

The 'motorway' surface, although conspicuously devoid of asphalt, nevertheless made for fairly easy motorcycling. A pattern quickly emerged in which we would follow the blue kilometre markers on the right hand side of the road for intervals of 100km. Chas, with his goosed air filter and lack of nerve, kept up the rear. The dust is quite debilitating and encourages us to spread out, an inevitable recipe for separation problems.

After about 160kms, we were surprised by a stretch of, by Russian standards, superb tarmac which led the 10kms or so into Tynda. We drew quizzical and admiring glances as we filed through this surprisingly happening town before pulling into a service station for gas. There we were very much the centre of attention, even attracting free cartons of L-Orean free juice from one admiring Toyota driver and friend. He also invited us to a café for lunch, but we declined, mindful of the black cloud which was forming like an angry thought over to the North.

Out of Tynda we were stopped by the GAI at the airbase. A nervous moment for us that is visa related: months ago, when we had booked our Russian visas we had been required to list the cities that we intended to visit and in what order. This list is typed (in Cyrillic) onto our visas. Back then, none of us knew that it was possible to fly from Magadan to Alaska and so had assumed that we were heading for Vladivostock, ferry to Japan and then onto the USA. When we alighted from the train this morning we swung north, leaving the main drag that heads east to Vladivostock and our 'official' itinerary. It must seem overly paranoid to the reader but we won't be surprised if a jobsworth plod tells us to about turn and get back to our schedule as published. In fact, our real fear is if this scenario unfolds at the instant we report to passport control at Magadan airport 1500 miles from here. A shrug of the shoulders and a curt "You are required to leave from Vladivostock, you must go there" doesn't seem too pessimistic a forecast. Luckily, the policeman paid only passing attention to the absence of Yakutsk or Magadan on our visas. Instead he seemed happy with our explanation that we were going to Yakutsk before driving back to Vladivostok.

The asphalt continued for a further 60kms or so before petering out into the eminently navigable sand and gravel surface which had been our lot prior to Tynda. Suddenly the Angry Thought expressed itself in an explosion of freezing hail which crashed down on our helmetless ears like so many ball-bearings. Fortunately, this particular storm lasted only about a minute – but did not bode well for the Yakutian weather systems which lie ahead.

Onwards through surprisingly empty roads which occasionally, and usually briefly, gave over to stretch of asphalt. The last section was quite gruelling, studded with potholes and jarring every hinge and bracket on our long suffering motorcycles. Chas's fuel tank is now obviously loose, whilst Gerald's front rack is dangerously rickety. Our brave intent to complete 600kms for the day was frustrated by fatigue and the fact that a tempting track afforded us the opportunity of an early night after a mere 500kms. Supper was cooked by Austin. Consisting of onions, garlic, Bulgarian tinned tomatoes and cabbage, it was a return to our healthy eating habits of old after our recent candy binges and the literally gruelling diet of the Goldmine Maintenance gang.

For the record, Yakutia looks everything that Siberia should be, gently rolling hills swathed with huge Scots pine forests disguising the existence of new and as yet unscientifically described species of biting insects. Not to mention bears and wolves. Unlucky Gerald under the poncho.

Russia (Yakutia)

Day 99
Monday 17 July
Mondo Miles today: 225
Mondo Mileage: 11252

Gerald woke us up at 6am then again at 7am to a glorious sunny day, blue skies. An early start so as to go for the big 400 miles or thereabouts to get us within shouting distance of Yakutsk. It was all going so well when unlucky for some, Gerald had a double puncture only 13 miles from base camp. Clive had ridden on to the 600km post and slept for an hour or so, also partaking in his first paperless dump on Mondo Enduro – in the trees and with leaves – Oh so naturel!!

Chas and Austin had also ridden on oblivious to Gerald's misdemeanours to a town 40 miles from base camp – too small to have a name in the road atlas but they managed to blend some oil and Chas was photographed making a purchase of sweets and vodka at the only guaranteed oases out here, the candy booth.

The consumer desolation of this part of the world is completely turned upside down at these precious little cabins. They are stocked with an excellent range of Cadbury's products, loads of booze and a full range of fags. The distribution network that keeps the shelves full is clearly not available to the purveyors of any 'normal' food. The shops are basically empty.

Back on the trail, Chas and Austin realised Gerald was up to something – as he was not being his speedy self. Chas stayed behind to get Jacksoned whilst Austin went to rescue his big brother but rescuing he did not need. Whilst waiting for Austin to return to assist him in his hour of need – a jeep full of detectives on its way from Yakutsk saw Gerald's International thumbs down distress signal and pulled over. They helped him repair his puncture, gave him a full repair kit, 5 boxes of '*Vache qui Rit*' cheese and breakfasted him with cheese and veggie dumplings. After the work Gerald was soon reminded that he was no longer in Siberia but in Yakutia, when he was offered Vodka. A nice change to have it *after* work rather than before, during and after as in Siberia.

Suddenly out came the plain clothes detective's service revolver and it was time for an international shoot out of the now empty Vodka bottle. The copper went first followed by his mates but to no avail – stand back and Lee Van Gerald twirled the copper's piece and cleanly shot the Voddie bottle into smitherines.

Addresses were exchanged and off went the friendly bunch in their Jeep – minutes later Austin arrived to find his gun toting delirious brother pissed from his recent encounter – he recounted his adventure and was soon back on the plot – well, after another 20 miles the back tube went down and it had to be changed for the 1 remaining Ruskie inner tube of the 7 purchased earlier in Irkutsk. The rest had been pinched by a 6x6 driver in the Zilov Gap as well as a lot of other useful kit – unlucky Mondo Enduro.

Back to the Skovorodino-Yakutsk rally as the Mondo Enduroists battled it out with themselves and the giant 6 wheeled lorries on the unlevelled M56

Sub-base – one crash and many near misses as the Magadan men hurtled at 52mph over this dusty unstable surface towards their uncertain goal.

While taking our first break two trucks pulled over and we were soon in deep conversation with the drivers. They revealed there was *no* road from Yakutsk to Magadan for the first 200km and that even the 6x6 Kamas trucks couldn't entertain the route! Well that was pretty disappointing but then again, on closer questioning it transpired that none of them had ever driven to Magadan.

Our next break found our problems answered, as we encountered our first cyclists on Mondo Enduro – two Siberians who just happened to have cycled from Magadan on their way home to Baikal – 4000kms an impressive feat for sure. They were both well built and darkened by the sun's rays. They had been 60 days on the road and enlightened us on the route we should take. For certain not the road we were going to take but by barge from Yakutsk: North then East for about 400ks to where the track/road started to Magadan at an inland port on the Aldan River called Khandygar. We filmed them and they took a few snaps of us – we wished each other good luck and parted company on our separate missions. They were completely hardcore.

Shock, horror – Clive's back tyre has a thin bit of wire spiked in it which hissed at his when he tried to pull it out – it was left to rest – but after almost 12,000 miles without a puncture Clive realised even his tyres were vulnerable! At Kilometre post 857 we stopped to cook and camp. A useful but stony site. A handsome feast was prepared by Chas and washed down with sweet tea. Spirits are high after the recent news from the Magadan cyclists as we put our heads down only 170 miles from Yakutsk.

Russia (Yakutia)

Day 100
Tuesday 18 July
Mondo Miles today: 197
Mondo Mileage: 11449

Our century today but rather a dull one until our arrival in the Northern Siberian city of Yakutsk. Despite meeting the cyclists the confusion surrounding the way ahead infuriates us all. A short ferry ride took us across the Lena river and on to tarmac for the last 100km into town. Our simple town plan torn from the Lonely Plant Guide was not enough to get us to the main hotel, The Lena, to use as our base. Whilst still a few km from the ubiquitously named Prospect Lenina we pulled over to ask directions of a good looking girl. Valentina was her name and by chance, and our good fortune, she spoke excellent English. After the directions were given we agreed to meet her later as we feared she maybe the only English speaker in town. At the hotel Lena, Chas and Gerald went to reception only to be turned away because of our dusty appearance. The hotel next door was 55$ so that was out of the question. When they came out two Canadians were chatting to Austin and Clive. They had been here 6 weeks and were learning Russian until September. Next came the TV interviewer and a trio of passing female reporters from the local newspaper. Clive went with the TV lady to another hotel in the hope that it would be reasonably priced, only to find it was 150$. Chas and Austin went off to collect Valentina armed with a big list of things to do. The TV lady then offered to accommodate us in her flat at no charge. We gratefully accepted. Gerald went to the hotel to phone Bournemouth and report that we were ok (last checked in 19 days ago) and to get the flight information that the others had faxed to him from Alaska. It was all good news from the train trio. They had arrived in Alaska on the 3 July. 84$ worth of telephone conversation later he put the phone down.

Clive went to the flat with Sveta (the TV correspondent), for that was her name. Austin came back with no real information to report. Gerald went to the flat to shower and eat and then back to the Hotel Lena to RV with Austin who had been driven off by Boris, yet *another* good Samaritan (our third in this city within an hour!) to find out more barge information. The news was mixed: with Austin and Boris was the master of a barge who was going to Khandygar where *we* wanted to go. Also on the barge was a small bus with two guys who were going to drive it to Magadan. If they know they can do it in a minibus then we can do it too. Result. It was midnight by now, the bad news was that the barge master and Trevor Eve lookalike (Valodya) wanted us to put the bikes on board immediately. A quick discussion in the courtyard ascertained that we would have time to get food for the voyage in the morning, prior to casting off. We said our goodbyes to our hostess Sveta, grateful for the offer of a room for the night but needing to strike while the iron was hot. We loaded up and followed Boris and Valodya to the dockside. We do not know how much this ferry will cost us, Valodya said not to worry about the price. Departure is another unknown quantity. It is clear that we are being blended into a rather ad hoc situation and that our ship's captain Valodya is merely inhaling his first whiffs of the perfume of entrepreneurial spontaneity.

The deck of the barge was flat and empty except for the minibus and two containers. It was also about 12ft below where we stood on the quay. The bikes were unloaded and lowered down using ropes and Russian muscle power. The occasional scrape being the only damage. Because of the time of year and latitude that we are at, all of this was happening at 01.20hrs in almost full daylight! Since the sun rises at 02.30hrs it means that everyone was up and about as if it was the middle of the day and not the middle of the night. Once everything was on board out came the Vodka and food. Valodya's wife (Marina) supplied the food. The crew from the next barge, who had helped load us, were also present. Three teenagers arrived bearing five bottles of Vodka. We knew we were in for a long session. The teenagers were sent packing after the first bottle and the other four soon followed the first. Eventually at 05.00hrs, totally shitfaced, we retired for a few hours sleep, although Clive decided to go and phone home. Austin and Chas got a cabin, Gerald slept in the minibus and Clive slept on deck upon his return. Another massive Mondo day with the incredible and never expected consequence that we really are on our way to Magadan.

Russia (Ferry)

Day 101
Wednesday 19 July
Mondo Miles today: 0
Mondo Mileage: 11449

Seeing as Mondo Enduro was still up and rocking at 05.00hrs on its 101st day we were chuffed to have had such a full and exciting centenary. Gerald noted from former log entries that we had supposed that we'd be wining and dining in Vancouver by day 100. In fact, since the notion of being barge boys was only 30hrs old now, it was still a great novelty to be aboard this unusual vessel with, as usual, novelty characters each with their story to tell.

So, it was ever the selfless Clive who woke the hungover Austin and Chas at 10.00hrs with the news that he had already been back into town, called home and collected two rucksacks full of provisions for our estimated week afloat (mostly bread).

His stores lordmanship was praised as he had everything that Mondo Enduro craved, save Candy. Sadly the Magasin he had perchanced sold only the internationally rejected shameful bogus unacceptable Russian chocolate. It may not interest the reader to know that the two British confectionery giants of Cadbury's and Mars seem to have an equal market share out here. One thing's for sure, they offer the most superior products in the candy/fags/canned food booths and are only laughably competed with by obscure Australian and American sweetmeat nobodys who tout chocolate covered irrelevancy such as "Hawaiian Sun" or "100 Grand" that fails to challenge the Herculean caramel might of Twix or Picnic.

By noon the Autobus duo, Sacha and Sacha, had brewed up a casserolesque bowl of Kartoshki (spuds), onions and canned 'beef in own juice' (a tinned meat widely available out here and labelled as coming from a factory in Co Roscommon, Eire). We were keen not to appear parasitic and scoff what would probably be half of the meal so we went for about two-thirds of it and left the remainder to the burly chefs. Bread appeared as if by slight of hand and was sliced Russian style. This does not mean that it was left to rot until inedible, <u>then</u> distributed to the workers, rather, down the centre and then into demi-slicelets of bitesize doughy filling. Yumski!!!

The similarity with our day on railway bogies to our home here on the barge was utterly clear. We clearly had plenty of time and plenty of small tasks and repairs to perform around our existence. Hence, with the experience and judgement that comes with 100 days spent on the road, we did absolutely nothing all day.

We lazed and loafed in the sun until plagued by flies, we pressed "erect" and slung up the mosquito net for sanctuary. This move reminded us of London since all we achieved was the incarceration of a family of flies <u>inside</u> the net and we mused that the bird hangar at London Zoo must have been conceived similarly. Such was the inactivity that Austin, after merely writing a short letter, came and boasted about his achievement to the others. The stagnation that had set in was probably more to do with our maritime limbo rather than sheer British Disease. Sadly, our barge was hooked up to the tractor tug at 21.00hrs, pushed away from the quay, causing the predictable ripple of "we're on our way to Magadan" comments. It was not to be... These tricksters at Yakutsk port control had successfully delayed, nay, arrested our progress by ordering our Captain to drop anchor 2 miles north up the Lena River. The view back to the Yakutsk skyline is shown on the next page.

The tug disconnected in a miserable post-orgasmic cloud of non-achievement and left us marooned, empty and wondering if our rashness in the alcoholic haze of last night had all been a little too_hasty. Keen to contribute to the slowly coalescing sense of community that was developing between the three sub-units on board (Valodya, Marina & son; Sacha and Sacha; and Mondo Enduro) we approached Marina and requested that we be allowed to provide and prepare the evening meal. The only kit we needed was the Agar oven that lay in the kitchen (dormant at 1700). Valodya got the fire going with some recently Brit-chopped wood. Chas and Austin stocked up for the meal, seeing as we were cooking for nine. Even the pasta was double rinsed and it could be said that we really pushed the boat out for this one. With accursed bad luck the bogus Russian pasta congealed like a crystal but remained just edible. Chas and Austin became genuine below-deck workers as the oven imperceptibly grew hotter and hotter, turning Marina's homely kitchen into an unbearable sweat box that flashed our dripping brows with recollections of Turkmenistan.

A stunning, nay, awesome sunset and rainbow double whammy accompanied our post-meal deck sweeping session on stationary barge number M-27. Bed at midnight and it isn't even vaguely dark.

Russia (Ferry)

Day 102
Thursday 20 July
Mondo Miles today: 0
Mondo Mileage: 11449

Life on board the good ship M27 continues amidst an atmosphere of impeccable international relations and in glorious sunshine. Today is by far the hottest day of what has been an unanticipated heatwave for the last fortnight or so. A breakfast of bread and nutella, and coffee brewed on the Autobus duo's petrol primus, was served on the fore container deck. The day stretched out before us like an elongated bungie and we despaired a little at how we could fill the long sunsoaked hours. Fortunately for us, Valodya, the ship's skipper, had organised a Siberian sport triathlon to keep us amused and guard against the onset of physical and moral decay. The three disciplines were log-sawing (small-bore), log-sawing (large-bore) and log-cutting, and we toiled manfully, if not particularly effectually, under the scornful gaze of our companions. Sasha taunted us with the observation that Englishmen probably splice their pines with effeminate electric saws. If we spoke Russian we would probably have retorted with self-satisfied remarks about central heating and coal delivered direct to the door but we let the matter rest, we were, after all, confronted not for the first time with the unmanly ease of western life-styles which must seem soft in the extreme to the hardy Siberians. As if to rub it in, one of the Sachas impressed us all with a virtuoso display of the tree-feller's art, coaxing a log up from the floor with a flick of the hatchet and then performing a violent execution with a graceful arc of his right arm...

In the meantime, Marina, Valodya's wife, had been slaving at the rusty stove on deck outside the living quarters to produce a hearty meal of buckwheat and fried onions washed down with chai or coffee. We filled the empty void of a seething afternoon by laundering some of the clothes worn through the mud-soaked Zilov Gap. The results, it has to be said, were somewhat mixed and Austin lost his little brown nail-brush overboard in a frenzy of mostly ineffectual scrubbing. Despite all this effort, the M-27 had moved not one league since yesterday when we hove to in the shipping roads of the River Lena. From a distance of about two miles, the container cranes of Yakutsk taunted us with scornful gestures about our lack of progress. At about 9pm the Autobus lads produced a very palatable, if somewhat half-measured, meal of spaghetti Bolognese. As our digestive systems churned slowly into overdrive, Valodya asked whether we fancied a trip to the beach.

And so it was for the first time since Camping Rea in Greece that Mondo Enduro had a proper trip to the seaside. Actually we are probably 1000 miles from the Arctic Ocean and the same distance from the Sea of Okhotsk but the width of the river, the softness of the sand and the splendour of the evening sunshine made for effortless self-delusion.

Valodya started his small speedboat and ferried us out to a pine covered island in two journeys. We frolicked awhile in the sands, Alyosha (Vladimir's 10-year old son) chatting up two similarly aged girls, while the rest (except Gerald) swam and Austin made a helter-skelter out of sand. Apparently such feats of civil engineering were a regular feature of Vince family holidays but it still seemed strange to see the self-same construction skills learned on the beaches of Southern England at work in the river systems of Northern Siberia.

Meanwhile, Chas, Clive and the Siberian-with-no-name-as-yet were playing catch with Alyosha's tennis ball. Our fragile sense of English pride was massaged somewhat with the observation that while Siberians might have well-developed huntin', shootin' and fishin' skills, their hand-to-eye co-ordination is apparently poor. Compulsory cricket nets would be an easy and cheap remedy for this massive shortcoming in their sporting prowess. It was while the helter skelter was getting its first test-drive that Valodya suddenly became animated. The tug-boat which would act as our tractor unit for the next four-to-five days, had moved into view. Bob Hope and Bing Crosby never made a film about the Road to Magadan but if they had, this might have served as the opening sequence.

And so we sped back to the M-27 which had temporarily been invaded by orange life-jacket wearing naval cadets. Our collective spirits rose as the barge started to move surprisingly quickly along the downstream current of the River Lena. As it in celebration, Marina produced plate after plate loaded with a delicious variety of potato fritters. We gorged ourselves raising coffee cup toasts for this wild and wonderful land...

** Mondo Log City Page Stop Press: Valodya, our esteemed skipper with a heart as golden as his top set of gnashers, took Chas aside to name his price for the journey to Khandygar. The fee came to 1 million roubles or approximately 200$. Something of a steal we all thought for a five-day cruise complete with free food, sport and sunshine.

Russia (Ferry)

Day 103
Friday 21 July
Mondo Miles today: 0
Mondo Mileage: 11449

Another superb day was on the horizon as we awoke to the M-27 slowly chugging East now along the Aldan River having hooked a starboard during the night. It has been extremely reassuring that we are constantly moving even while we sleep. However, on the Aldan the current is against us and we move at a little over walking speed which is slightly frustrating, as it will certainly take us at least 4 days to sail to Khandygar. Well there were certainly no complaints on this snail like procession from the Mondo Enduro team as they installed themselves into their ship routine – it was all Mondo Enduro could ask for in terms of R & R except there was no English candy. We did however have bogus Ruskie "confetti" and Berlin Nussa hazelnut spread as alternatives to our Western sugar cravings.

Today was a maintenance day and it was carried out in teamwork fashion: Clive on the 8 & 10mm, Chas on handle bar and gear lever tightening, Austin on 6mm Allen key and 12mm spanner and Gerald on 13 & 14mm sockets. This frenzy of work should have inspired and excited us as we hummed in a bee like fashion around the bikes but our minds and hearts were shattered when we discovered N1's frame cracked in two and B2's backbone semi-fractured. How they wished they had let sleeping dogs lie as the odd bolt sheared just to add insult to injury. Well better here than out on the trail, that was for sure. It was now imperative we find a welder in Khandygar.

The rest of the afternoon was that of leisure. Clive crammed himself in a 2ft long x 1ft deep galvanised steel tub using an unscrewed wing mirror to shave. This was shortly followed by a spot of 'plunge washing' – soiled items tied to a section of rope lashed to the sides of the barge and then hurled into the river and left to ski shotgun to the M-27 for a period of approximately 10-30 minutes depending on the degree of soiling. Other activities included letter writing and sleeping. Supper consisted of meat and potato broth which was exquisite – Marina had certainly excelled herself on this meal.

As the sun dipped down to set around 10.30pm into a serene fire glow setting, there were swift exchanging of words between the bridge captain and Vladimir. It turned out that Vladimir had persuaded the captain to hold up the non-stop 4 dayer to Khandygar for a wee bit of fishing.

Sacha, Chas and Clive were thrilled at the news of midnight fishing and set about winching the speedboat down, deeting up and collecting bait (Clive's concentration camp of a dozen or so Oakley wasps were being prepared for their final torture: being skewered through their thoracic region by a fishhook and finally nibbled and swallowed whole by the ravenous Yakutian pike. One would have thought it a high price to pay for their innocent instinctive biting of the Mondo Enduro team? – "No way Jose, no mercy for merchants" we cried!).

The ship dropped anchor and Vlad, Sacha, Chas and Clive sped a kilometre up stream to recce a fishing site, it was on a slight bend of the river where a 200m dead end section had formed and hopefully was the hanging out place for the unsuspecting "Riba"!

We set up a net across the dead end and perched ourselves on the bank and began the inevitable waiting bit that drives the average non-fishing person around the bend. It soon became dark and fishing became futile as the "Riba" wouldn't be able to see the bait and were probably having a quick nap. So Vlad lit a fire and disappeared into the bush with Sasha. A little while later they returned with wild spring onions and elder berries and a bunch of flowers for Marina – nope, there was no 7-11 around the corner – we were in the wilderness here and were heavily outnumbered by mozzies at about 1000:1. We waited for dawn and consumed some confetti and chai to pass the time.

Meanwhile, a crew from the tug had turned up, set up their 30m net and carried on further upstream to find a fishing spot too! Dawn arrived and the thick soup-like river began to boil. Vlad and Sasha began hooking in the fish at ten to the dozen. Clive managed to catch two fish (his first time fishing) but Chas miserably had nothing to report! Clive and Chas both scratched their heads wondering how these large fish literally threw themselves on to the Russian hooks and not on to their own ... favouritism they guessed. Around 4am it was back to the boat for the descaling and gutting and pity was shown for those who work in the docks and fish markets around the world; what a grim and arduous task. A cup of coffee and a few raising of glasses to the bridge. To bed at 6.30am after a long day on the river, what a blissful journey this is turning out to be!

Russia (Ferry)

Day 104
Saturday 22 July
Mondo Miles today: 0
Mondo Mileage: 11449

The riverbank on both sides has remained exactly the same since we set off from Yakutsk. On reflection, the scenery has changed little over these last 4000 Russian miles. The fish caught last night were served for lunch. Later Mondo Enduro cut up one of the logs, during which Chas and Clive won the log-sawing competition. 1st place time 1m 13s; 2nd place time 1m 23s. After the exertion Austin felt queasy and lay down, it did no good, he vomited. More fish soup for supper, but not for Austin, followed by pancakes and a filling of condensed milk and sugar. The rain clouds have held at bay all day, but we have a feeling that sooner rather than later we are going to get soaked. No rain.

Russia (Ferry)

Day 105
Sunday 23 July
Mondo Miles today: 0
Mondo Mileage: 11449

The night was as dark as we have seen in this part of the world, but that was as much to do with the gloomy clouds that recently have arrived, poised to disgorge their cargo of rain simultaneously to Valodya disgorging *his* cargo of British motorcyclists.

Austin was indeed most violently sick and reported that the half litre of cherry flavoured squash that he had carefully sipped at bed-time was dramatically and swiftly added to the Aldan river along with everything else, solid or liquid that his body was so inexplicably rejecting.

The morning came and went and saw no sign of any of the occupants making a move. Austin's numerous visits to the on-board shower/toilet combo rather embarrassingly found him encountering Vlad and Marina quietly reading in the kitchen well past 4am. This insomnia of theirs may explain why they were asleep during the traditional morning hours. They both read books that we have seen for sale at many pavement stalls; large(ish) print hard backs with full-colour covers. Vladimir's was a trashy detective thriller that left nothing to the imagination with a cover illustration featuring a recently undressed blonde with a colt-45 pressed to her temple. Marina seemed to have more sedate choice than the corrupting pulp favoured by her gold-toothed spouse.

Austin had slept alone in the cabin and was first up. He joined (at Clive's invitation) the other three under the billowing double poncho mosquito net harem (minus girls) that had been our home for the last four days. Gerald surprised the team by smoking several cigarettes. It transpired that his habit aided his contemplative powers when it comes to writing this journal.

Whilst on board Neil Diamond continues to be the 'most hummed' artist with 'Solitary Man' and fittingly 'The Boat That I Row' coming in as his two most popular choices for the Mondo Enduro Accapella choir. Clive keeps the Neil Diamond embers fanned by constantly singing tiny 2 or 3 word segments from "I'm A Believer" though we are not sure if he appreciates who authored this song.

In a moment of international brotherhood our captain Valodya grasped this log and herein scribed his address. Impressively he wrote it twice; in both Cyrillic and in perfectly formed Roman lettering. The latter is reprinted here:

Pocclir Ropoa Campapa
Yn Cophyze Gum 97/99
Kbaptupa 12
Rymkhhy Bnagumuph
Russia

The afternoon was passed with all of us predictably exhausted after getting up at 11am and having done nothing since. As has become quite common in situations like this, an impromptu Mondo Enduro Quiz sprang forth. We assembled under the shade of the poncho and sharpened our wits. We started with the "twenty questions to guess who I am" game. Clive went first and chose Ken Reed. If the reader furrows an eyebrow at this unusual anonymous selection then that would be forgivable. This is because Ken Reed runs the Anchorage Suzuki franchise and none of us playing the game had ever met him or seen his photo. Austin had spoken to him briefly on the phone though. Clive's inability to answer yes or no to the simplest of questions about his 'choice' of person soon led the contestants to realise that Clive had chosen someone he didn't know. Austin went next with Ted Simon, Chas sponsored Jools Holland (which took the others 200 questions to decipher) and Gerald went local with Valentina, the girl we had met in Yakutsk who had so superbly guided and translated for us.

We followed this excellent recreation with an 'Around Britain' Quiz. This saw us starting at Cornwall and, taking a county in turn, posing a question germane to that county to the others. These ranged from: "Where was my bike bought?" (Clive-Kent) to "Which part of North Lincs was subsumed into South Humberside as a result of the 1974 boundaries changes?" (Chas-Lincs). Quizzed out – exhausted, the game eventually became "What am I thinking of" which only lasted about 90 secs but was hilarious as we out-obscured each other in our boredom drenched haze.

After an attempt to pack our kit ready to hand over to the Sashas on the Autobus it was soon time for supper.

This was to be our last sit down meal together with our Russian friends and so like any good touring party it was time for speeches and presentations. A Mondo badge each to the Sashas. We had been the victims of Valodya and Marina's generosity "in extremis" whereby Alyosha, their skinhead son had come bearing gifts from within their tiny cabin. The conveyor belt ran as follows: To Chas: a crank powered torch (metaphor for Russia; lots of effort that makes you physically strong but the dim glow of an end result was poor reward"). Austin: A plastic comb, ship's mate's hat and a wallet of 1970's colour postcards of Leningrad's canals and rivers. Clive: Plastic goggles and a bi-metallic strip thermometer (range + 40⁰ to - 40⁰C) but quivering at 27⁰C in the night's coldness). Gerald: a very sharp penknife with moulded plastic stock depicting a forest scene.

In return the Brits videoed the scene and donated our ONC map of Yakutsk, Harmonica, chicken shocker, flag of the union and a whistle to Marina.

We bedded down at midnight ready to dock at approximately 0300hrs. Then, it started to rain...

Russia (Kolimar)

Day 106
Monday 24 July
Mondo Miles today: 43
Mondo Mileage: 11492

And rain it did... they beat a rhythmic tattoo on the double poncho combo while Clive, Gerald and Austin struggled vainly to achieve prolonged sleep.

Chas meanwhile was being treated to an impromptu concert by Junior Bargee Alyosha on his newly acquired Blues Harp. A peek in the kitchen at about 2.20am saw him listening to Clive's walkman, playing Game Boy Tetris with one hand and the harmonica with the other. Clearly a Techno-junkie in pupa form.

The four travellers, wearied after their prolonged sabbatical at sea during which they have done almost nothing, were awoken by a frantic Valodya at 7am. After five days on the ocean waves, it was time to put into port and salve our by now quite serious cabin fever.

After a pancake breakfast served by the angelic Marina, the Rosa Mota of maritime cuisine, we prepared for imminent disembarkation. As is so often the way in terms of Russia's transport infrastructure, a 10-hour wait at anchor off Khandygar was in the offing.

We amused ourselves with minor packing tasks while Valodya paced somewhat tensely around deck and Marina, not for the first time, busied herself at the stove. To fill some more of the time vacuum which is Siberian barge travel, we set up a makeshift trials course on the aft container deck.

To add to the spice of international competition to the event, Sasha (dark-haired) was summoned from his Autobus siesta to take part. Despite not having ridden a motorcycle for 10 years, he distinguished himself with a highly respectable time. Austin, keen to smash the course record, actually came close to knee capping a watching Yakutsk sea cadet at the end of a particularly rapid circuit.

By this stage, the vodka-bingeing crane operators in Khandygar port had completed what looked to the untrained eye like the simple task of unloading a timber barge. In fact it had taken them almost six hours and by the time the M27 hove to at the makeshift wharf; it was time for another break whilst the *Militsic* got document-handed.

At first Dimitry, the casually-dressed port fuzz, cut a menacing figure as he wafted his ID card and demanded our decidedly disordered paperwork (forged vehicle docs, non-Yakuti visas etc), he even launched a low-level steward's inquiry into exactly how much we had paid for our voyage (Nothing, Officer) and what we had been charged for food (we cooked our own, honestly). Events took an apparently sinister turn when Dimitry refused permission to offload the motorbikes until an interpreter had arrived. The said flunky, a portly Yakutian English teacher wearing an overly-revealing pink dress, arrived with her gap-toothed husband in tow.

Instead of leading us further up the blind alleys of post-soviet bureaucracy Traterina (for what was her name) offered a guiding hand to Mondo Enduro. It transpired that she had won a language scholarship a few years ago and had been sent to study English at a language school on the Lansdowne Road in Bournemouth. After all that we have experienced over the last 100 days and 11,000 miles this encounter, in the most remote place any of us have ever been, stands alone for sheer idiosyncrasy. She had been summoned merely to help us in any way and was at the disposal of the Khandygar port Authority.

In the meantime a strange vision was manifesting itself on the foreshore and we watched transfixed as if in a religious ecstasy. Rumbling slowly along the rubble-strewn strand were two what at first looked like Africa Twins but were in fact BMW Funduro 650s.

Astride their heavily-customised bikes(upside down forks, 1100km fuel capacity) were two Bearded (sic) Norwegians on the way back home via Central Asia after a trip through America via New York and Anchorage. They brought glad tidings about the Road of Bones which cuts through beautiful mountain scenery and crosses 20 fords apparently. This was their Second journey along this highway which they first navigated in 1993. So much for Frith Maier and her "no foreigners to my knowledge" Trans-Magadandstraga Oblast Baloney.

Austin filled them in on the delights in store on the Zilov Gap section, drawing detailed maps of the nightmare sections on the reverse of their ONC map. The slight disappointment that we feel about our great adventure not being wholly unique is outweighed by the enormous pleasure felt at meeting Trans-Mondo bikers. We wished John and Oleg luck on board their, (to our eyes) massively-laden motorcycles.

Meanwhile Dimitry had cast off his thin disguise as a bothersome copper and had metamorphosised into an all-round good bloke. By this time he had marshalled the drunken crane gang into some semblance of order and they emerged bearing welding gear to repair Gerald's cracked frame (motorcycle, that is). He even donned the gloves and masks himself, to give a virtuoso display of the metallurgical arts.

Chas and Clive meanwhile have been summoned into the crane operator's living quarters where they partook of sugared chai and an utterly delicious strawberry loaf. The workers were by now all gone after precariously but professionally winching the bikes off the M27 and noisily insisted that we should take a shower, drink Vodka and spend the night.

What on another occasion might have been an intriguing ascent through the hellish circles of Russian alcoholism was passed over this time in favour of an early (9.30pm) getaway on the Magadan highway.

Dimitry and the two Sashas took us to get grade 93 petrol (!) and we were ready for the off, reluctant to say our goodbyes to Valodya, Marina and Alyosha. The little mite was clearly moved by our departure and especially sorry to see Austin go.

So it was time to say farewell to our gentle hosts, our Norwegian SAS aircraft engineer friends and our various benefactors in Khandygar. After five days on the high seas we were all itching to get back on the open road.

A first there seemed nothing skeletal about the Road of Bones which began as a well-pressed stretch of white aggregate. More chilling by far was the weather which had turned an icy cold leaving us all with frozen Gulags. After about 43 miles, Clive did the decent thing and suffered a rear puncture forcing us to pull off the road into an impromptu campsite. The two Sashas, whom, it transpires, are going to follow us to Magadan carrying most of our luggage, were quick to inform us of their view of Russian pasta which is vastly inferior to the unsurpassable potato apparently.

And so to bed, Austin and Clive sharing the Ajungilak and Chas and Gerald in Rabs. It seems strange but the end of the Boulevard of Nightmares, which is the Russian highway network, could really be in sight. Through high-powered binoculars which can see across nine hundred miles of unasphalted roads, that is....

Russia (Kolimar)

Day 107
Tuesday 25 July
Mondo Miles today: 312
Mondo Mileage: 11804

After what seemed a millisecond after we had shut our eyes, dawn had arrived and we were being toasted in our maggots by the scorching morning sun. Coupled with this the Mondo Enduro team were easy prey for those morning, noon and night any place, any time, any where 'merchants' – yes you guessed it – we were breakfast for the Road of Bones mosquitoes; the most wretched and ravenous of them all but still those Mondo men did not flinch. It was the wails of Sasha and Sasha that made us wake almost instantly, as they had now become our support team and for that we were totally in debt to them. However, when we woke up Clive's back tyre was flat. Clive pumped up the back wheel and headed off with Chas and the bus off to the nearest town in search of a *vulcanizars* whilst the Vince brothers broke camp.

The *vulcanizar* was a similar set up to the Goldmine Maintenance Yard in Kisley-Kluch. A large factory yard area with a whole warehouse dedicated to vehicle maintenance. The workers here however were all sitting outside the factory chatting the day away. Needless to say as soon as we arrived and explained our predicament, one of the hundred set about vulcanizing. Once again Mondo Enduro were on the receiving end of a blend. Meanwhile, back at the bus the lads were brewing up and purchased 20 cakelike patties which were scrumptious.

By 10.30 we were fed and watered and our 2 inner tubes were vulcanised.

Away from the dusty roads onto a sub-base of a road like back home. The scenery was breathtaking as we made our way up into the Kolimar Mountain range. The trees were now a perfect example of the Christmas trees at home all seen many times before, but seemed much more magnificent in this wild part of the world. As we made our way along and around the wooded valleys we crossed the tributaries of the Kolimar river. The waters looked very similar to that of the Peak District, amazingly clear with a blue/green tinge, flowing fast along the valley floors and under the many rickety bridges on the highway.

Most of the bridges were substantial enough for our motorbikes but the Kamas trucks more often than not would have to drive across the river bed, which they took in their stride and certainly would hardly even slow down for them . The bridges are exclusively of a timber trestle construction. Obviously there's plenty to go around but then again, there's plenty of stone too. With the numbers of slave workers available over the last sixty years it is amazing that the Soviets couldn't even construct a proper road from Magadan to Irkutsk. Maybe that's the downside of forced labour, but it didn't seem to be a problem for the Japanese building the Bridge Over The River Kwai. Oh well...

Adjacent to the bridges we crossed over were the remains of the bridges actually built by the prisoners from all over the Soviet Union.

As you ride across these bridges and along this "Road of Bones" your mind wanders and you begin to imagine how fierce and harrowing the conditions must have been for these prisoners working on these bridges and on the highway. The area is so remote with towns literally a hundred or so miles apart with absolutely nothing in between. It is now quite apparent why these camps would strike fear into even the hardest men of Russia. The most frightening fact about the Gulag administration is that you could be sent to the prison camps for the most trivial of 'crimes'.

We passed a prison type camp thing and it was as terrifying an institution as we've ever seen. It looked abandoned and tumbledown (as is the way in Russia) but the lone conscripts in the watch towers attested to its vigour. Rusty tangles of awkwardly twisted barbed wire adorned the wonky shoddily built perimeter walls. Heaven knows what cruelties have come to pass just a few yards from where we now breezily motorcycle? The gates hung at every angle in the book except 90⁰ and everything was festooned with a jumble of criss-crossed telephone wires. If this was a penitentiary adjacent the 'main' road, what were the camps like far away from prying eyes? All across the Soviet Union our stated destination of 'Magadan' had always elicited much eyeball rolling and tut-tutting. The hushed and almost reverential fear in which the Russians hold this place is now starting to make perfect sense.

We stopped for lunch around 4pm in an abandoned railway carriage by the side of the road. How it got here we did not know and could not imagine as the nearest railway was about a thousand miles away. Anyway, there was a small stove inside and we soon had a fire going with all the scrapwood littered all over the floor. The Sashas arrived about half an hour later and we had lunch consisting of bread, *Vache Qui Rit*, cucumber and the remaining pasties purchased earlier. 'Oscar' as Austin is now known to our Russian comrades tried to display his strengths, by attempting to lift up a monster tyre but failed miserably.

Back on the road and along a huge plateau that was truly magnificent. Chas, Gerald and Austin were ahead when Clive's back tyre went down again. It was in fact a *new* puncture and not a bogus repair from the Vulcanizer.

Clive pumped up the back wheel and caught up with chaps at the thirty miler. Meanwhile, Chas had found some goodies in the Yakutian village nearby. The lads arrived (Sashas) and had to wait whilst we changed Clive's inner tube.

Tomtar was the next town and we stopped for some filming. We got going again and Chas and Gerald raced off ahead failing to see the petrol station at the edge of the town, also failing to realise that we were actually in Tomtar and there was no petrol for another 350 kilometres.

Clive and Oscar stopped with the bus and after an initial 'steward's inquiry' and a wait of around 20 mins they opened the petrol station especially for us. There were then a series of river crossings which were extremely easy. There was no sign of Gerald and Chas at the next 30 miler and the daylight was rapidly disappearing.

Clive and Austin wondered if they had taken a wrong turning or perhaps Chas and Gerald had. We were reassured when we saw their tyre tracks in some wet sand. Shortly after, we found them as Gerald was preparing to ride back and find us. They were still hoping to find Tomtar, so we explained to them that they had ridden straight through it. It was by now almost dark and freezing cold – so we found a perfect little campsite next to the road and got a huge fire going. The bus arrived and the Sashas were not happy with the site because they feared getting a puncture on the tree roots and stumps scattered around so we prepared to move on in the dark a further 12 miles and arrived at a river crossing where we parked up and got another huge fire going. We prepared a magnificent feast after this long day's ride of over 300 miles. It was a fine meal which consisted of potato and beef soup, pasta, beef curry emergency meal, tomatoes, onions, garlic and peppers. Vodka and cucumber for an aperitif. A perfect end to a long hard day. We snuggled up next to the fire and slept al fresco.

Russia (Kolimar)

Day 108
Wednesday 26 July
Mondo Miles today: 234
Mondo Mileage: 12038

Awoke early to a glorious sky, Clive rode across the river effortlessly which is more than can be said for Austin. For some reason he decided to take an unproven route and lost it big time. The bike and rider plunged into a deep section and promptly fell over, the entire machine becoming submerged. After yesterday's late start I could see the two Sasha's groan at the prospect of another Mondo Enduro day. Gerald navigated successfully and so did Chas (except for stalling in the last few yards). Thinking that it would take all day to re-start B2 we were fully prepared to say goodbye to the bus crew. We reckoned without Russian mechanical tricks of the trade. The spark plug was removed and B2 was towed by H6 then slammed into gear. The engine was forcibly turned over thus expelling the river water in the cylinder far more quickly than any other method. After re-assembly it started after a few kicks. If only we had known of this (admittedly obvious) technique back on day 89.

Off we sped fully un-laden it was a joy to ride out that morning. Everything was in our favour. Stunning mountain scenery and a road which was far beyond anything that we had been led to believe, mostly we suspect, from people who had never been anywhere near this road. When we awoke this morning the scene was of a biker pushing his bike across the river.

Further questioning revealed that he was a Kazakh from Almaty who had ridden to Magadan for his holidays.

Without doubt, all of us feel that this part of Mondo Enduro has been the most spectacular and well worth the time and effort in getting here. Today's road has not been as easy as yesterdays but not difficult either, more care had to be taken. It must have been very difficult for the bus as there were numerous potholes and large trenches. We stopped on the outskirts of a town. Austin and Gerald went in to buy some provisions only to find it was one of the most grim and pathetic places that we have ever passed through. The bus caught us up and said it would soon be time for petrol and tea. As always the petrol stop was a kerfuffle, this time with a difference. In all our fuel stops since Barnaul we had never come across a gas station that would not accept our money. This one would only accept special coupons. Help! Fortunately Sasha bought some coupons from another driver and filled the jerry cans. Straight after the fuel stop we happened upon the worst section of road, since, well we could not remember. Somehow only the road was wet, it had not been raining. It must have been sprayed with water to keep down the awful dust of the previous few miles. The result due to the heavy traffic on this section was mud, glorious mud. There was no grip for our tyres and steering became almost impossible. It was a miracle that no-one fell off. Before we reached the end we turned right over a mountain range down into the Kolimar valley. Yet more stunning scenery and a very well surfaced dirt road. At the summit we stopped for tea and biscuits. An idyllic spot with superb views to the front and rear but also a sober reminder that roads like this can be dangerous. There was a memorial shrine to a victim of a fatal road traffic accident (made from a lorry tyre) complete with offerings of cigarettes and sweets.

The next RV was arranged with the bus and off we sped. After 30 miles there was an drama when Gerald discovered that he had a front wheel puncture. Fortunately re-inflation would last 5-7 miles. It was getting dark as well. Clive and Gerald made slow progress to the overnight stop at a road workers' cabin on the river side next to a long bridge. As this was to be our last night (sic) on the road we had a large meal using the last emergency meal and "boom" pasta. That is Chas and Gerald did. Austin, as always, was tired and he and Clive went straight to bed. Sasha indicated that tomorrow we would be starting at 0800hrs sharp and that they would brook no timekeeping tardiness. What they neglected to tell the only one of us with a watch was that we had crossed another two time zones. We wondered why we were being woken at 05.30hrs by Sasha who was getting agitated when I just lay in bed when they were leaving in 30 mins. But they reckoned without Mondo Enduro's tyre repair rigmarole. But that's for Austin to relate.

Russia (Kolimar)

Day 109
Thursday 27 July
Mondo Miles today: 209
Mondo Mileage: 12247

Mondo Enduro slept superbly in the Bridge workers' cabin. It was beautifully snug, all the more so because it was raining substantially all night. The ponchos and tent would have been a serious pain in the bottom for such a brief stay at this site.

It was recycled veg. curry that Chas kindly rustled up for breakfast and even the kilometre thirsty Sashas would not dream of departing without a portion.

Fog, drizzle and the usual potholded greasy road awaited us. Gerald's rate of front tyre deflation was reaching irritating levels and his first 3 miles were all he could manage before alighting to depress the Turkish plunger. The reader should be reminded that our spare inner tube was stolen in the Zilov Gap amongst Gerald's unlucky luggage. We were in another dilemma, with the Sashas hot on our heels and keen to not be delayed by puncture ridden Angliski, we reckoned we needed the skills of a *vulcanizar* since we had lost faith in our own lastik repair skills and we had certainly lost faith in the highly bogus Russian rubber cement (probably cement rubber). Unfortunately the local motorcyclist who was equipped with the mobile vulcanising kit was drunk, thus while the heating process was going on to repair one hole the heat was creating another hole. After three attempts it was refitted and we left, only for it to last eight miles. When Gerald was forced to stop he noticed that his entire luggage had fallen off, including the clamping device given to us by drunken Jackson. Clive retraced the route and managed to find everything except the large screwdriver which was being used as a tyre lever since the Zilov Gap theft. Using just the crappy factory tool kit the inner tube was removed and patched up but it refused to inflate. Several attempts later and we were out of solution and patches. We tried vulcanising but that also failed. Helping us with all this was the shopowner outside whose premises we had carried out the first repair. Eventually he threw down the inner tube in disgust saying, in Russian, it was crap. He indicated that he would return as soon as he could with a permanent solution to our dilemma. He left us a tin of frankfurters, we poncho'ed up and after much petrol got a fire going to heat them. A passing Kamas driver donated a tin of Beef In Own Juice which we had just started to eat when the "Brian Denehey" look-a-like retailer returned. Out of his car he pulled a 19" inner tube (the wheel is 21") and a thick rubber pipe of the same diameter as the tyre. Take your pick he said. Bearing in mind we had seen the effect firsthand, in Turkmenistan of running a tyre with no air we opted for the smaller inner tube. It went on with a lot less trouble than we anticipated and we were soon on our way. We left our temporary campsite at 19.15hrs having been there since midday, knowing that Chas and Austin were 100 miles away

Clive and Gerald made good progress and caught Austin just as he was about to leave the 100 mile RV after waiting half the day. A few more miles of greasy dirt road then disaster. The sub-frame of Austin's bike fractured and his whole rear mudguard, number plate etc just collapsed onto his back wheel. The abrasion was total, making the bike unrideable. Brainwave! Austin sat on the saddle and we jury rigged two straps to go from the back mudguard, up and over his shoulders and down to the handlebars. It worked perfectly but to develop sufficient tension to support the rear end weight Austin's shoulders were virtually crushed, the handling ruined and of course, he could not alight from the machine until his co-riders had released him. Luckily he had obtained some bread and cheese from the bus. What a morale booster. A quick snack saw us on our way with the virtually impossible task of riding 150 miles in the fading light. We stopped after 30miles for a warm up and Gerald warned that the riding conditions were leading up to the highly likely "accident waiting to happen" stage. At least the 19" inner tube successfully held air and there was no further trouble.

It was decided to try to blend at the next house we came to since we had no sleeping bags on us. In the event it was not a house but a road workers' hut similar to last night's, only with electricity. We espied the faint glow from about a mile away and our spirits tentatively hovered. We gently knocked on the door in a way that we hoped sounded polite and it was wrenched open to reveal yet more incredibly rugged and weatherbeaten Siberians. The four occupants were Yura, Anatoly and Sergei and they were building a bridge here. They would appear to be the only humans involved in any kind of highway maintenance for 500 miles in any direction. The fourth member was already in bed and stayed there until after we left the next morning. Naturally, they were not expecting company, yet alone the first Englishmen any of them had ever met but they smiled warmly, sprung to their feet and fussed over us like long lost brothers. Tea and Vodka were, as always, immediately forthcoming, followed shortly by a large pan of eggs, beef and onions. They hosted us with the kindly smiles and largesse normally reserved for old friends. They sheltered us without hesitation and after these long dusty/muddy days they were doing more to foster Anglo-Russian friendship than they could ever know. We were cold and tired so it was a really big deal. The last 109 days and the trials encountered since we went down to a four piece were all worth it for just this deeply special evening alone. The conversation flowed and it transpired that Yura was celebrating his 33rd birthday at this location. He was clearly depressed at the idea. And so to bed. Austin and Clive share, Yura magnanimously surrendering his bunk and exiling himself to the cab of a lorry, Gerald solo and Chas somewhere ahead, hopefully having made it to the end of this lonely highway.

Crumbs, this is almost certainly our last night on the road in Russia for tomorrow we should make Magadan.

Russia (Magadan)

Day 110
Friday 28 July
Mondo Miles today: 80
Mondo Mileage: 12322

As the sheet metal doors of the Magadan bus depot opened, the sunlight streaked in, announcing the dawn of a day of blue sky and abundant promise. Chas had followed the two Sashas into Magadan last night along the asphalt road from Palatha. Soaked by a teeming downpour and fatigued by a hard day's travel, his cry of victory at reaching the city limits sign had been choked to a barely-audible whimper. And so it was that he gazed on the conquered city from the fortress of the bus depot where he had spent the previous night fortified by fried fish, bliny and chai. As he cast his eye across the sea of Okhotsk his brain was troubled by a nagging query – how had England fared in the recent test match series back home against the West Indies?

A less pressing concern was the whereabouts of the hombres still out on the open road. After a quick reconnaissance of the local hotel facilities, he headed out to the city limits to make the 11am rendezvous with Austin and, hopefully the other weary travellers.

And so it was with great joy that he cast eyes on Gerald arriving almost simultaneously from a northerly direction. The other guapos were not far behind and we congratulated ourselves on a not insignificant achievement – navigating the world's largest landmass by motorcycle (well, almost).

Onwards into town, firstly to the Otean Hotel where we fraternised with the female staff before heading to the nearest university. There, on the fourth floor, the statuesque secretary of the faculty of foreign languages overcame her alarm at Chas's unsightly facial hair and general state of deshabille to ring a student called Dima who offered his translation services.

The earlier reconnaissance now identified the Hotel Y6V (*ooh-veh-deh*) as our most likely base for the next few days. Centrally situated, close to a *stolovaya* (workers' canteen) with abundant supplies of bliny, and run by a middle-aged *debooshka* who honoured our request for personal loo-roll and kettle, it seemed like the ideal setting for some much-needed repose. We checked in, blissfully unaware that our fellow guests were all policemen and other Interior Ministry flunkies. Our next task was to go to the depot and reclaim our luggage from the Autobus. There we found the two Sashas anxious to help us transport it by van to the hotel and delighted to accept our invitation to join them for dinner – although not at The Hotel Otean which is run by the Mafia, apparently.

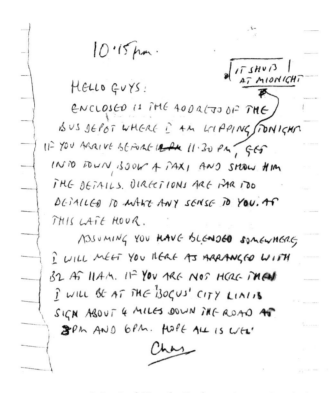

10.15pm.

IT SHUD AT MIDNIGHT

HELLO GUYS:

ENCLOSED IS THE ADDRESS OF THE BUS DEPOT WHERE I AM KIPPING TONIGHT. IF YOU ARRIVE BEFORE 11.30 PM, GET INTO TOWN, BOOK A TAXI, AND SHOW HIM THE DETAILS. DIRECTIONS ARE FAR TOO DETAILED TO MAKE ANY SENSE TO YOU. AT THIS LATE HOUR.

ASSUMING YOU HAVE BLENDED SOMEWHERE I WILL MEET YOU HERE AS ARRANGED WITH BZ AT 11AM. IF YOU ARE NOT HERE THEN I WILL BE AT THE 'BOGUS' CITY LIMITS SIGN ABOUT 4 MILES DOWN THE ROAD AT 3PM AND 6PM. HOPE ALL IS WELL.

Chas

A typical Mondo Enduro signpost note.[1]

After a frenzy of ablutions and facial hair surgery (Chas removed his rather attractive beard along with the utterly offensive tash much to the other hombres' horror).

It was time for some much needed shuteye in advance of the evening's festivities.

We met Dima, as arranged, at The Otean at 8pm and soon caught up with the two Sashas, the smaller of whom had brought along his wife Natasha, it soon became clear that Dima's mastery of our Mother tongue was

---

[1] As the team would ebb and flow a practice evolved of leaving notes for each other affixed to the rear of the signs displaying the names of towns as you approached them. This was highly effective.
This note was left by Chas for Clive, Austin and Gerald at Magadan 'city limits'. It was written on the back of an old paper bag. This seemed an appropriately raggedy format as we finally reached this, the last town of this leg and a destination that has taken on near mythical status in our collective psyche.

such that he would revolutionise our contacts with our Autobus benefactors who, as the mists of linguistic incomprehension started to clear, began to become focussed as real people. It soon became apparent that the Otean Restaurant, with its spicy food and reasonably priced menu, had shut at the late hour of 7pm – forcing us to look elsewhere for victuals and alcohol. We searched no further than the Imperial Nightclub on Proletarian Street with its pricey bill-of-fayre and live band of almost infinitely questionable talent. Sasha, meanwhile nipped across the road to a booth where he bought a two litre Jeroboam of Vodka and some Champanski, which the Stephen Fry look-a-like *maitre D* chose to ignore.

And so the alcohol flowed at a roughly equable rate to the conversation as we discussed various aspects of our journey along the Road of Bones. There was almost a minute of respectful silence as our thoughts turned to M-27 Marina's Bliny and caramelised moloko topping after one of the evening's most enthusiastic toasts.

By this stage we were getting to know the two Sashas a little better. Big Sasha, true-to-form was a man of few words but a dazzling smile who is clearly Magadan's very own Clint Eastwood. Small Sasha is more garrulous with a slightly suspect infatuation for the western lifestyle. No doubt we will come to know them better as he and Natasha have invited themselves to come to England as guests of Mondo Enduro.

After a stretch of hard road, every cowboy has to loosen his bullets a little, and the weary motorcyclists were no exception to this most immutable of nature's laws. We all sashayed onto the dance floor attempting to ingratiate ourselves with the array of female talent dressed as per normal in the clashing shades of acrylic and crimplene which we find so alluring. Clive in particular cast his hungry gaze in the direction of a well proportioned and dramatically made up blonde who rewarded his advances with a smoochie dance.

And the band played on. Led by their singer, whose voice was as strong as her dancing was hackneyed, they wielded the butcher's knife over a succession of hits including the 'Yacky-Da' song and 'Yesterday' which was sung in our honour. In the meantime, while Austin fought off the attentions of a platinum blonde, we soberly contemplated the $300 cost of the night's entertainment. We stumbled back to the hotel with no regrets. Everybody deserves a bit of easy road…

Russia (Magadan)

Day 111
Saturday 29 July
Mondo Miles today: 0
Mondo Mileage: 12322

A well deserved rest for the English chaps was in order as they had achieved their first major destination on the globe: Magadan; the mark of a third of the way around the globe. As far as we know we are the first European motorcycle expedition to do this journey overland all the way from London. This tremendous effort has now left us lying in our hotel beds with 6 days of well earned rest ahead of us before we move onto Anchorage for the second landmass down to Buenos Aries. Magadan is vaguely depressing but weirdly, is a *proper* big town. It sports all the trappings of a Soviet Workers' Metropolis; brown buildings, huge central square (for endless parades) and no evidence of any shops. It is only gradually dawning on us after the lonely thousands of miles getting here overland that everyone and everything arrives here by air or by sea (there is *no* railway). It is essentially an island. It seems clear that it hasn't been 'forgotten' by the ministry of transport back in Moscow and this isolation is intentional. The whole rationale of this capital of the Gulag district is that once you've arrived here, it is very, very difficult to leave.

We went on to the 4th floor of what is allegedly the most sophisticated hotel in Magadan and its coffee lounge which was inconveniently shut in the middle of the afternoon. Dima had a few words with one of the staff and she opened the door to the lounge to reveal an office with a cabinet full of western goodies and a kettle on the side but we were going to pay for this service. We drank coffee and ate cookies for about an hour whilst Dima told us the mournful history of Magadan and the prison camps.

After these interesting accounts from Dima, we overhead some American accents. We investigated further, Austin getting out first. The voice overheard was someone calling out to Jim in a broad American accent. We discovered that to certain Americans, Dima was known as 'Jim'. It was a religious squad from the Alaskan Church of Christ, that well known sect. They were here attempting to convert some of the Magadan population, little did we realise that Dima was well known – for they greeted him like he was their long lost brother (which in the broader Christian sense he surely was). He was certainly the man to have as an interpreter and we would have been completely emasculated without him. The lay preachers had also hoped to employ him since he had apparently served them well the last time they were in town (another brick in his mansion in heaven). We bade them farewell and they wished us luck, invited us to one of their sessions and to their home in Fairbanks, Alaska too. Unfortunately that is not on our way so we won't be heading to see them. These poor old Russians, within a few years of 'freedom' arriving, their country is hijacked by organised crime and over-run with foreign missionaries.

We crashed out reasonably early as we had had a huge night out the day before.

Russia (Magadan)

Day 112
Sunday 30 July
Mondo Miles today: 0
Mondo Mileage: 12322

We had a ride out to the 'Welcome to Magadan' sign at the city limits and filmed ourselves proudly displaying our Union Flag for this edge-of-the-world milestone on our journey across Russia. Tonight's meal was to be at Sasha and Natasha's. We tried to tidy up and Austin started to pack for his departure tomorrow. He also had to strip down the rear end of the bike ready for the welding at the bus yard. Sasha arrived at 20.30hrs; we thought it was a bit late, frankly. A 20 minute walk to his flat where Natasha had prepared a mountain of bliny along with the all important condensed milk filling as well as our newly discovered cream/yoghurt filling. Gerald took his life in his hands and tried the battered fish which tasted fine and there was no reaction. Bogus taped music, which Sasha insisted on playing too loud for the tiny kitchen almost made conversation impossible. Most of their possessions have already been containered to their new home on the Black Sea. They are clearly relieved to be getting out of this most depressing of far eastern Russian outposts. For a change Cognac (but Russian not French) was used as the toasting alcohol. As we were leaving soon we presented the Russian/English dictionary to them, complete with addresses inside and Austin's weighty Abus 'Granit Plus' D-shackle padlock (complete with two keys). Sasha presented Austin with a pocket watch, complete with a box and guarantee, although it was new and had never been used; the guarantee was already out of date. The bogus cognac was finished off by which time it was 01.00hrs. We walked home along unlit streets, replete, after one of the biggest pancake feasts of all time.

Tomorrow Austin would be leaving on Alaska Airlines to Anchorage to try and get things moving a bit faster. Hopefully when the rest of us arrive we will not be wasting any time and keep our stay in Anchorage to a minimum: cities always find us spending far too much money and lethargy sets in at an alarming speed if we are sleeping indoors.

Russia (Magadan)

Day 113
Monday 31 July
Mondo Miles today: 0
Mondo Mileage: 12322

The morning after the night before began early for Mondo Enduro as Austin responded to his 7am alarm call with unusual alacrity. Time waits for no man, especially when there is sub-frame welding to be done, and he busied himself with packing tasks while the others abused him soundly from the comfort of their beds.

Austin had high-tailed it up to the Autobus depot by about 8.45am and while the welder worked his metallurgical magic, the others looked fear and lethargy in the eye and started tidying up.

Dima, our 19 year old translator on whom we have come so much to rely, put in an appearance at about 10am. Physically shocked by the state of our room, we revived him with coffee whilst discarding our rubbish, which included the spare rear tyre and Gerald's jack. It was stacked in the corner as neatly and unostentatiously as their considerable bulk would allow.

Meanwhile Austin and Clive, who had joined him earlier, were back from the Autobus depot with a further tale of Russian mechanical mastery to report. For the price of a bottle of 'Rossija' Vodka, the fractures had been expertly sealed by the welder's alchemy.

While the three lads drove to the airport Chas busied himself with a few administrative tasks. The first was a call on the local newspaper, the Magadanskya Pravda where he was welcomed by the economic columnist Sergei. It made a pleasant change not to be treated as the earthworm of the journalistic world and Chas was asked his opinion on the great issues of the day including Russian politics and the chances of a lasting peace in the former Soviet Union.

The "MP" is currently locked in a circulation battle with its deadly rival "Territoria" and has recently become a twice-weekly rather than daily newspaper. It was because of this financial stringency that the editor-in-chief could not invite Chas for dinner but instead suggested that he take him for lunch on the morrow. This suggestion was acceded to with enthusiasm, despite its inherent cheekiness.

Chas and Dima then took a look around the local recreation ground which, unlike its English equivalent's collection of swings and seesaws, boasted an array of former Red Army weaponry including MIG-21 fighters, a helicopter, a tank, an armoured car, amphibious landing vehicle and missile launchers. The sight of old missiles, stacked like logs against the side of a lock-up garage, was surreal. Unlike British "reckies", the former Soviet version also included 3 potentially deadly gyroscopes dangerous enough to delight even the most lacklustre official of the Health and Safety Executive.

By 5pm Dima had been released from his Mondo chores into the embrace of the Alaskan evangelists and it was time to meet Gerald and Clive back at the Ooh Veh Deh. They reported total success at the airport where Austin had boarded his Alaskan airlines plane without even the hint of a steward's inquiry from customs officials or passport control despite the currency and visa irregularities which are so much a feature of our journey.

His bike, meanwhile, has been safely stowed in a transit area while Clive and Gerald got busy on the customs area electronic scales. It seems that our luggage items will not remotely reach the 40kg threshold and so unhindered customs control is a genuine possibility.

Unfortunately there was no sign of Sasha (small) at the hotel when we made our 5pm rendezvous there. The sympathetic administration was happy to let us leave our luggage there but as minutes turned to hours it became clear that if our would-be benefactor was going to put in an appearance at all it would be at an unconscionably late hour.

After feasting on a double snickers and topic supper, the guys summoned enough mental energy to make an executive decision. The $4-a-night airport looked the best option given the impossibility of contacting Dima, who had offered us some accommodation through some friends (he was at the Mission) as Sasha was nowhere to be seen. We moved up there with haste through freezing mist and into perhaps the most perfect sunset we have seen in Russia.

At the airport hotel we were somewhat shocked to discover that the 20,000 rouble-a-night per person room tariff had mysteriously nearly doubled since Gerald and Clive's inquiries earlier in the day. Further investigation revealed that the price went up in August – but Mondo Enduro pointed out with some justification that it was still only 11pm on the 31 July.

As we pressed our case, we won several locals, including a charming semi-English speaking Aeroflot pilot called Valodga and a pissed Caucasian, to our cause. Finally confronted with the overwhelming weight of public opinion, the *devooshka* relented – even providing us with hot water for our bedtime hot toddy of coffee and red Spanish wine.

We went to sleep thinking of Austin feasting on his first burger and fries in the home of universally available candy. And Grade 95 petrol. And milk shakes. Not to mention English speaking GIRLS .....

Russia (Magadan)

Day 115
Wednesday 2 August
Mondo Miles today: 0
Mondo Mileage: 12322

Clive and Gerald slept in until midday. Then, spurred on by the lunchtime closure of the freight and customs offices, sprung into action.

Tania, the freight babe, took us over to have the bikes weighed. We tried to tell her that 120kg was correct but somehow we don't think she or her colleagues believed us. As the scales were above ground level they decided to weigh only one bike. Clive and Gerald set about H6 removing everything we could in the few minutes available but to no avail. We heaved the DR onto the scales only to see the weight rocket skyward and come to rest at 150kg. Imagine our horror as we estimated the cost per bike (the rate is calculated per kg). Off we went with Tania to the custom's warehouse where the bikes would be stored until tomorrow's flight. The paperwork was to be finalised here. Clive struck gold. He had somehow persuaded Tania to reduce the weight of each bike to 120kg (the original dry weight). A group saving of 120kg. In other words, one free bike. We could not believe it. Better news came next. We were not to be charged any warehouse rent. Another saving of $25 and Aeroflot costed the passenger tickets at an extremely favourable rate of 4465R=$1 thus $420 per passenger instead of the original $439 we had calculated. So, a combined cost of **$840** for one bike and rider. As we had expected to pay the same high price of $1300 that the Train Trio were charged we were elated. There was one slight fly in the ointment. Chas was told when he telephoned that morning that he must return from the city by 14.00hrs to check his bike in personally.

At 17.00hrs he rang to say that he and Dima had been trying to start his bike since 14.00hrs. There was no choice but to pay a charge of what eventually became $50 to a lorry driver. He and Dima arrived at 20.00hrs. Clive had already started cooking, so more pasta was piled on. Another bottle of wine purchased and our last night in Russia came to a close with all of us talking after lights out, except Chas who was so tired after a long day that he never even got his clothes off before sleep overtook him.

And so to Thursday 3 August, our last day in Russia. Chas was up at 09.00hrs to check in his bike. No paperwork to do but it still took 2 hours. It took 2 trips each to convey our luggage to the departure lounge, where we took it in turns to guard the bags. Dima and Gerald caught the delicious Tania returning to her office and she promptly invited us to coffee and cake. Much waiting about and trips to candy booths to spend our last roubles. At last, check in, no trouble for Clive and Gerald but unlucky Chas. On to the plane but not before Radio Babe interviewed Gerald in the privacy of the customs office.

Gerald's Impressions of Russia: It is the first country on the trip that I have been sorry to leave. Beautiful girls, wonderful people and spanning ten time zones. How long will it last.

Clive's Impressions of Russia: Truly a huge and amazing country that I am also sad about leaving. The trip really started for me after we left Inkutsk the scenery became wilder and more breathtaking whilst the people became friendlier and friendlier. I sincerely hope we will come across people from other countries on the rest of our trip that will be able to match the friendliness and generosity to total strangers that the Russian folk have shown. The Russians certainly are a tough act to follow.... So prepare yourself America and Africa: Mondo Enduro is coming your way!!

Chas': A big sky and a larger heart – a place to lose yourself in and we did just that on more than one occasion. The home of bodged sprocketry, alluring girls, a sad history and endless miles of lovely scenery. I am totally gutted to leave and America has a lot to live up to in terms of generosity, beauty and atmosphere. Mondo Enduro over and out from Magadan...

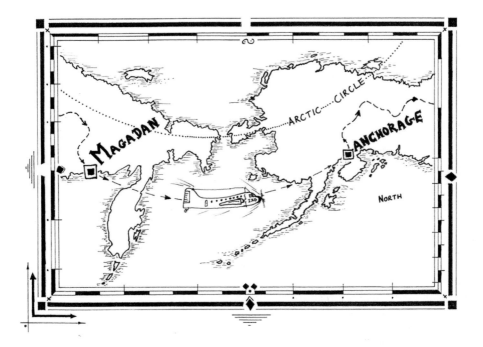

MONDO ENDURO

PART 2

ALASKA TO CHILE

Alaska (Anchorage)

Day 116–126
1-11 August
Mondo Miles: 0
Mondo Mileage: 12322

My God, it's like we've been in prison.

The madness of Russia in general and the former USSR in particular, has only hit us since we got here, civilisation. The irony being that the Yanks clearly regard up here as the back of beyond yet for Mondo Enduro it's a paradise without compare. Phones work, shops sell things, and if you want something, you go and buy it. We are at the same latitude as Magadan yet we are not assailed with excuses from the natives about how the brutal winter blocks normality, the cold wrecks the roads, the concrete gets cracked etc etc. We are not specifically Americophilic but it seems that while the Soviets used their northern reaches to foster the biggest culture of incarceration the world has ever seen, Uncle Sam set out to make something of it. True, the Siberians are rock hard but within only a few hours of arriving in Anchorage it's clear that while the Russians endure this world, the Americans have tamed it.

A cheer of delight as Nick turned up out of the blue in Culan at 3'ish as we had been separated all day! Next Nick ran totally out of petrol – due to caning it at 80+mph doing recces and Gerald carried on into the sunset oblivious to all this. With his lightweight 'rack' and luggage Gerald's mpg was excellent – so we ended up having to do multi fill ups – more time wasted! We had decided to rough it tonight – so we could make an early start and save money. However, another municipal campsite appeared before our very eyes and we succumbed to its temptation and moreover daylight was rapidly sliding away!

Another stupendous effort from Nick and his culinary delights for supper – we certainly won't die from malnutrition or boredom on this trip.

With every hour that passed after touchdown the incredible experience of having ridden to Magadan is coming into ever increasingly sharp focus. We had begun to forget what the rest of the world might be like; everything was inconvenience, hardship and unpredictability. No-one could ever describe the road ahead; no-one ever knew if the way was open, if the ferry was running etc; whilst here, we are bombarded by choice, information and certainty. Guidebooks burst with the best Alaskan trails, almanacs of diners and welcoming log cabins. The days of sheltering with a road gang in a place that no tourist had ever been to were over. With its 270,000 motels the USA was going to be easy street and, for a month or two at least, Mondo would be hard pushed to do anything but enjoy themselves.

Within about two hours of clearing customs we were being tuned in. The rubric of long distance travel, with all the chances to broaden the mind, is thrown into disarray; as we finally realise that the sweet warm glow of being hosted by strangers is in fact the paramount rush that we have experienced over the last four months.

"I met them at the gas station...." These were the immortal (to us) words uttered by Anchorage resident Roger Wilson as he explained to the NBC TV news crew how it was that he was hosting four Englishmen in his home. Convinced that we were looking at hundreds of dollars of Motel 6 bills it was a blessed miracle worthy of St. Francis that saw us rescued from the real world and plucked from the forecourt by this saintly Alaskan truck driver. He had moved up here recently, was making a go of it and enjoying the tax free life that the federal govt promotes. Shrewdly, Washington has realised that if you want your citizens to endure a winter (whilst toiling on the Fairbanks avgas pipleine) that is beyond description then it's worth giving a little back in return. Essentially, every registered Alaskan resident gets a cash bonus from Capitol Hill to encourage them to stay here, make a life and do what its takes to stop Anchorage turning into Magadan.

The hospitality trickle turned to a torrent and Roger conscripted his buddy Craig to host the extended Mondo family of Bill, Nick Stubley and their respective girlfriends. Mark had already left town and was heading south for a rendezvous with his sweetheart in Vancouver. So that was another milestone, Mondo Enduro would never be together as a lucky seven ever again. We always had a hazy vision of reunification but we would never have guessed that our six month round the world adventure team would have fractured as early as day 66, the last time we rode together as a seven. From here on it was to be all the more uncertain with only Clive and Austin committed to getting to Buenos Aires. Chas was hesitating and had decided to visit some relatives in the North West Territories whilst he pondered his next 6 months. Gerald had run out of cash so was heading for Vancouver and a job at Ralph's Autos, a breakers yard owned by his old school buddy Neil James. Nick Stubley and Bill were only available for another few weeks, each having jobs that called them back to England. So there it was, a rather disparate group of British motorcyclists at the top of the world, only one road out of town but all riding it at different times...

Meanwhile, we were on the front page of the Anchorage Times and after being on the news were recognised constantly around town. Sadly, our visits to premier strip joint The Alaska Bush Company didn't result in any blending but we had cheeseburgers bought for us by an elderly couple we met on the highway heading to Canada. Result!

Adding to the group of fly-over well-wishers were Clive's dad and younger brother, Ray and Dave Greenhough. They have jetted into Vancouver (2200 miles away), hired a car and are presently tooling up the Alcan Highway to meet Gerald, Clive and Austin heading south. Clive and Austin, lacking

Gerald's iron man constitution left the night before, expecting Gerald to catch them up on the way south, somewhere just over the frontier into Canada. He never did and the reason why follows shortly. Slightly concerned they hadn't been caught up by him, Clive and Austin pushed south and on the banks of the crystal blue Lake Kluane espied a car parked in a scenic lay by. Nothing unusual there but as they approached it became clear that the maroon saloon was caked in AlCan grit and grime and in the dust, along the length of the car, two words had been etched by a finger: *mondo enduro.* Dave and Ray Greenhough were crouched behind the car and hence didn't see the two bikes approaching until they pulled up alongside. It was quite a reunion for all concerned and a festive night was had amongst the pine trees of a nearby firebreak. Interestingly Gerald had not been seen but how could he still be behind us?

The next day the car party about-turned and we rode south in a mini convoy. The powerful hire car got ahead as the 350s trundled along at their steady 54mph. It was a time of breathtaking Canadian scenery. Everything the travel brochures had promised; beautiful weather and with credit cards widely accepted, a 2000 mile stretch of genuinely easy road.

So when Clive and Austin crested a hillock and discovered the Mondo car upside down in the roadside ditch and Dave staggering across the gravel it spoiled the mood. The car had suffered a blow out, careered out of control and flipped as Ray battled with the steering. Dave's arm had been lazily dangling out the window and in the ensuing spinnery had been mercilessly dragged along the gravel; bone and gristle sandwiched between steel and gravel. The wound was so horrendous it looked like his arm had been folded and his elbow jammed down into a blender.

What a hoo-hah, the road trip was over, Dave was whisked off the 30 miles to Whitehorse where indeed after massive grit removal he flew back to Vancouver and within three days he was on the slab at Northwick Park hospital in Harrow enjoying a skin graft. With the hire car officially written off this left father Ray high and dry. He'd been looking forward to this Yukon hook up with his eldest son and so a scheme was hatched: Austin ceded his bike to Ray so the father and son duo could at least do 1800 miles together whilst Austin would hitch-hike to Vancouver. The Greenhoughs had a cousin in Vancouver and thusly that's where a rendezvous was proposed.

Austin's hitch was trouble free with only two lifts getting him all the way in 60 hours. The first was an old dude in a beat up pick up who used to be a full on trapper. On discovering that Austin was planning on sleeping rough he tutored him with his very own Grizzly Adams top-tips for keeping warm in the wilderness. Every night, when he was out in the forests he'd stoke up a mighty fire around four or five hefty boulders. Then he'd dig a shallow grave, rake the baked boulders in and cover them with ferns and moss. He joyfully exclaimed that this hot rock practice gave him guaranteed snugness at a time (1950s) when the phrase 'four season' sleeping bag was yet to be coined.

The next lift came from Brad, a chunky Californian from the substantial but not well known metropolis of Bakersfield. He'd flown up to Alaska, had bought a Toyota Supra and was driving it back to SoCal. Not the most amazing story but he had entered himself into his own personal Cannonball Run and was clearly determined to establish some kind of overland speed record for the journey. He was basically a remorseless driving machine and if ever a hitch-hiker felt he had been abstracted from the hard shoulder to keep someone company then this was it. He puked out lengthy verbal plot summaries of the latest Hollywood blockbusters so that Austin felt he was essentially tuned into a radio play! Brad was good value though and as the hours passed he opened up to Austin with stories from his delinquent past as a teen gang member high on a deadly cocktail of Cocaine and multiple gun ownership. Whilst drilling down the Alcan at 80mph he exhibited his huge gallery of gunshot wounds and stabbing scars. It seemed that Brad's entire midriff was a cover version of Gerald's beleaguered shins. Brad was proud that he'd left those days behind him and verily, his life path now saw him being employed as a councillor to Chicano teens and youth offenders. Brad was grateful that unlike so many of his adolescent buddies from the 'hood he was still alive and trying to stop kids going astray as he had done seemed the right thing to do. Hurrah for Brad, he was an inspiration!

Meanwhile, what of Gerald....

Editorial note: Gerald was bringing up the rear and was carrying the Mondo diary. Expecting to catch up with Austin and Clive he dutifully kept up the log. However, events conspired to scotch this reunion and Gerald ultimately ploughed on all the way to Vancouver solo. Hence, these entries are the only part of the five volumes of Mondo diaries that were written entirely by one member. Gerald was the founding father of the venture and as such it is fitting that for a few brief days the official version of it was recorded solely by him. Also, as an achievement in endurance riding on a pretty knackered 350 we think it's impressive. In our relatively wide circle of 'small trail bike owners', Gerald still holds the unofficial distance record of 600 miles in one day.

Anchorage to Vancouver, by Gerald Vince

Day 126
Friday 11 August
Mondo Miles today: 442
Mondo Mileage: 12764

Chas was abandoned in Anchorage today as I left him alone at Craig's house. Left the Wilson nest at midday and made good time despite the bike weighing 460lbs. The weighbridge clerk was very helpful and chatty. It took a few miles to get used to the laden bike again. It was last ridden like this when we arrived in Yakutsk (18.7.95). Filled up just before the Canadian border to find I'm getting 70mpg. There is a 20 mile no man's land between US and Canadian customs. It was on this stretch of road that my front sprocket finally gave up. Luckily Austin and Clive left the last remaining Siberian goldmine sprocket behind. It was fitted in minutes and off I went again. Such was the condition of my chain the new sprocket lasted ten miles before it gave up at Beaver Creek. By this time it was 22.30hrs so I got out my new sleeping bag and mat and went to bed.

Day 127
Saturday 12 August
Mondo Miles today: 0
Mondo Mileage: 12764

Arose at 06.00hrs to inspect the damage. It didn't seem so bad. The custom's post was one mile down the road. Entry for 3 months was granted. A further two miles and I stopped for breakfast and to warm up, as well as to decide what to do as the sprocket would last no further. A hearty breakfast and lots of coffee were consumed. The friendly waitress informed me that next door was where stricken bikers usually went for help. Walt of Far West Services said I could leave the bike in his workshop. I had decided to hitchhike to Whitehorse, buy new parts and return to Beaver Creek with them. To the edge of town to start thumbing.

Beaver Creek seemed to be some sort of black hole for road traffic. Almost all the cars that I could see coming down the long straight main street were turning off. Only one or two ever re-appeared. After two hours a large minibus stopped, Murray the driver was going to Whitehorse. Also on board were 2 other hitchhikers Dwayne and Molly and their dog. Murray drove fast and we soon were overtaking all the cars that didn't stop for me earlier, what a pleasant sensation that was. Stunning scenery and a running commentary from Murray, who was a tour guide, made the ride enjoyable. Two catnaps during the trip and we arrived in Whitehorse at 16.00hrs. Murray got to the

Suzuki dealer just in time. They only had a front sprocket. As that was the most important part I was quite happy. Unfortunately I will have to wait here until Monday to get a chain from one of the other dealers. I checked into the Regina Hotel (I think it's a chain) and had a wash to wake me up.

Before leaving Anchorage Austin called to say that Dave and Ray had had an accident in the hire car. We had arranged an RV at the Kopper King Diner for 10.00hrs Sunday. I rang them and also later took a taxi there to see if there were any messages but there was not. A quick walk around town to get my bearings and back to the hotel for a nap. Went out and had a few beers and finally retired at 01.30hrs.

Day 128
Sunday 13 August
Mondo Miles today: 0
Mondo Mileage: 12764

Overslept this morning so I missed the RV. I doubt it they were there anyway. Checked into the hotel for another night. Had breakfast and did some shopping. My pre-paid telephone card doesn't appear to work in Canada. Had a bath and a snooze then went to see "Die Hard 3". Then back to the hotel for an early night. Whitehorse is a town of 22,000 people and very clean and tidy. The town centre is compact and easy to get around. Hopefully, I can get out of here tomorrow morning with all my bits and pieces needed to affect a repair.

Day 129
Monday 14 August
Mondo Miles today: 113
Mondo Mileage: 12877

Off to the Honda dealer as soon as they opened. The only suitable chain they had was a 530 non `O' ring. But it was only $50. A long walk out of town got me sweating profusely; four minutes after I first put my thumb out a car stopped and dropped me off at the major junction. 40 mins later I was back on the road with Jim, who was driving form Arkansas to Anchorage in his new pick-up and towing a trailer with 4 quads in the back. At Haines Junction we picked up a girl, she had to sit in the back of the pick-up until I got out. Arrived at Beaver Creek at 18.00hrs and was on the road again at 19.00hrs. The new chain and sprocket make a huge difference. Got as far as Burwash, the sign said free camping, and it was. Had a coffee to warm me up and a few beers and to bed at 00.50hrs.

Day 130
Tuesday 15 August
Mondo Miles today: 600
Mondo Mileage: 13477

With an 08.30 start and confidence in the bike at an all time high the Mondo and personal distance records were bound to be broken today. Despite having to stop in Whitehorse again for currency exchange and to collect my luggage, I had soon done 300 miles. Fuel consumption was *90mpg* at a steady 60mph. Numerous roadworks held me up otherwise 700 miles would have been covered. Turned off the ALCAN onto the CASSIER highway. The first 50 miles were excellent, beautiful road and stunning scenery. Unfortunately, just as it was getting dark, ploughed into some low lying clouds and the tarmac ended. I almost turned around. There is always light at the end of the tunnel though. At 22.00hrs Dease Lake Shell hove into view. Two coffees later and I was told that I could sleep in an abandoned station-wagon out back. Some of the windows were open and could not be shut. But it was better than being outside on such a nasty night.

Day 131
Wednesday 16 August
Mondo Miles today: 424
Mondo Mileage: 13901

15,000 miles since leaving Bournemouth were passed today on my odometer. There was a road closure for two hours today. As I did not want to get caught by it, it meant having to ride 250 miles before I could stop. After a late breakfast I met a guy on a DR650. We had coffee together and it transpired that he was having chain trouble as well. It may be the weight of the bike. As we were about to pull away he pointed out to me a patch of canvas showing through on my rear tyre. It did not give me confidence to know that at any moment all could be lost at the back end. Passing through Houston I noticed a Harley dealer with a rack of tyres in the window. I pulled in and was surprised to find it still open at 2200hrs. Only one 18 inch rear available. A Cheng Shin 4½". Too big but beggars can't be choosers. $100 and it was mine. I checked into the motel next door and slept soundly.

Day 132
Thursday 17 August
Mondo Miles today: 274
Mondo Mileage: 14175

As you can see 14,000 official Mondo Enduro miles. Which means the Mondo mileage is wrong or somehow I've ridden 1000 extra miles. Because the tyre was too wide for the rim it would not seat at all, but it does not seem to affect handling. I pulled a nail out of the old tyre. A stitch in time etc. Did not leave until 13.00hrs. The rain getting the better of me. The usual problem of water collecting, then leaking into the groin area, so I called it a day at 19.00hrs and booked into the Valhalla Motel on the outskirts of Quesnet. I was hoping to get to Neil's tomorrow but it means riding 400 miles by a reasonable hour as I do not want to arrive too late. We shall see what the weather has in store.

Day 133
Friday 18 August
Mondo Miles today: 442
Mondo Mileage: 14617

At last I met up with Swiss motorcyclists Adrian and Martin on the road today. We swapped stories and I was happy to hear that they and the Kincaids decided to go to Magadan. We rode together via Whistler to Vancouver through heavy rain. Arrived at Neil James's at 20.30hrs. That's the end of Mondo Enduro for me.

Vancouver

Day 134 to 149
19 Aug to 3 Sept
Mondo Miles: 0
Mondo Mileage: 15837

Gerald has finally run out of money. Despite selling his house to finance Mondo Enduro he was always under-funded and so here in Vancouver he's got himself a job in a car breakers. As the founding father and elder statesman of our trip it seems quite unfair, after all we went through in Siberia, for us to leave him here like this. It's the worst news for Mondo Enduro so far.

He's going to be working for Neil James, his old Canadian school chum from Quantock School where they co-attended in the mid seventies. Neil inherited his father's wrecking yards which go by the name of 'Ralph's' (we think that's his Dad's name).

He now is reputed to be the largest volumetric car breaker type guy in the whole of British Columbia, and maybe even the whole of Canada. There seems to be a new wind of change blowing fiercely into this particular industry and it is a wind which is predominantly eco-friendly. It was incredible to see that the places where the cars are physically stripped down have vast, tennis court sized drip trays on the floor. Every last drop of engine fluid, coolant, brake oil etc is painstakingly collected and carefully disposed of.

But it wasn't the end for Clive and Austin. Chas was still on his way south from the Yukon and was no closer to confirming whether he would or would not be 'going all the way'. So Mondo is down to two. Mark is in San Francisco but there is a suggestion that a Phoenix will rise from the ashes if we (Austin and Clive) can hook up with Chas and Mark down in SF and push on into South America as a four-piece.

Much of the time in Vancouver was spent doing a rebore on Austin's bike and we enjoyed our first night in a disco where English was widely spoken. Enormous efforts were made to meet girls but all were failures. We had been having coffee in a diner and this dishy beatnik girl came over and said: "You guys look pretty interesting, mind if I join you?" Amazing, nothing like this had ever happened to us in our lives before. This is what it must be like to be a celebrity. However, even this liaison came to naught when she of course discovered that we weren't that interesting.

Time to give up and hit the road, Buenos Aires was still 15,000 miles away.

Leaving Vancouver

Day 150
Monday 4th September
Miles today: 64
Mondo Mileage: 15901

It took forever but we eventually broke free from city life. We were euphoric to be back on the road. The Canadian/USA frontier was of course utterly civilised and naturally we were flattered that this great nation lets us Brits just roll in without all the aggro of visas etc. By nightfall we'd only reached Bellingham so we retired gracefully to a roadside tavern called 'Billy McHales'. We hoped to meet two hot American beauties and impress them with our stories as told in velvety English accents that have them squealing in delight. An hour later we were bedding down under a poncho on some waste ground at the back of the bar, alone.

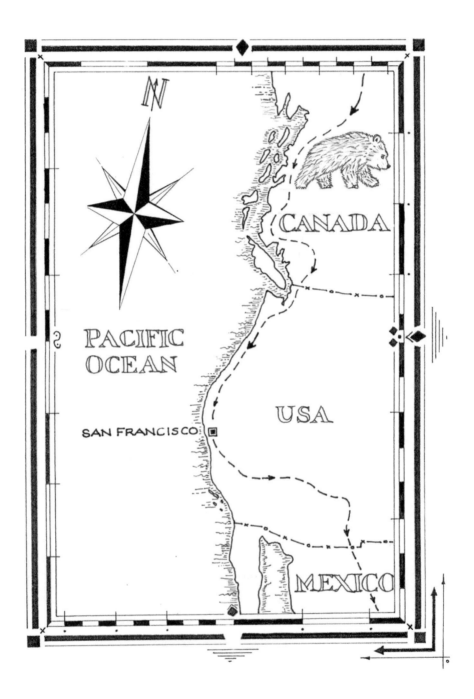

USA

Day 151
Tuesday 5 September
Mondo Miles today: 158
Mondo Mileage: 15995

Austin and Clive awoke from underneath the dew soaked poncho to the realisation that here in land of the free they had chosen a rough campsite that could only be described as bogus. This damnation was endorsed as Clive's painfully bald back tyre failed to make the grade in the apparently straightforward task of riding out from the depression that he and Austin had slept in. After several pushes and shoves H6 finally made it up the bank and a lesson was learned that even within sight of a mall there can be two wheeled drama.

Our destination was Seattle, most notably the factory and offices of Cascade Designs, makers of Seal-line stuff sacs and the widely acclaimed Therm-a-Rest inflatable camping mattress. We rang ahead and spoke to Tom Myers – their head of marketing. We arranged a 3pm RV and emerged from the State Visitor Information Centre where we had called from and consulted the town plan. As we walked out we were approached by 6'2½" of Steve. He was a local DR rider who'd clocked the bikes and was curious about the Mondo Enduro story. Clive and Austin made small talk for about 10 mins. And then Steve got to the nub of the matter by inviting us both back to his house for lunch. Here we met his strangely beautiful children and cooed over his seemingly immaculate DR350.

Onwards and Southwards down Interstate 5 and off into the amazing warren of under-passes and flyovers that literally pass underneath downtown Seattle. Although no strangers to motorway/congested driving (cf Ankara) Austin and Clive agreed that whizzing along this system was as exciting as anything they'd done so far. Time was killed at a quayside café and the bikes, humbly parked were inspected by loads of passers-by. We weren't really prepared for this as we thought that the curiosity thing had been left behind in Magadan. We had our picture taken by a few locals who interestingly were more impressed with where we were going rather than where we had been. It has come clear over the last few weeks that Canadians and Americans all view a trip down to Mexico or over to the East Coast as an unparalleled Odyssey. The experience in the Yukon, where a road worker asked us: "*where in the hell is Argentina??*" has also prepared us for the notion that some North Americans are bound not to really understand where we're headin'.

It was with childish (but not unseen) before on Mondo Enduro, optimism, that Clive and Austin parked up outside the surprisingly huge Cascade Designs factory and meekly reported to reception. They immediately realised they were out of their depth and hence wasting not only their own, but Tom Myers' time also. They passed literally tens of 'thank you' letters and endorsements on the staircase walls, all from clearly high-end civilian and military adventurous training expeditions. For all its amateurish bravado, Mondo Enduro was neither famous nor was it prestigious as Cascade's previous legions of satisfied customers definitely *had* been. Tom Myers had made it clear on the phone that he had precious little time this afternoon and so Austin and Clive were basically ready to make their apologies and leave as their opening sentence. Imagine their surprise, when they departed the factory more than 2 hours later bearing literally hundreds of dollars worth of free camping equipment grabbed willy nilly from the warehouse. It just goes to show how wrong you can be. We saluted Tom Myers and his astute hunch that one day our visit would be written up and published in the diary of the trip. Indeed, if you are planning a camping trip, burn all of your equipment and replace it exclusively with products manufactured by Cascade Designs and its subsidiaries. If you don't, you are a loser.

Two miles later a 2" self tapping screw tapped its way into Clive's back tyre and so it was life on the hard shoulder once more. Austin went in search of new tube, levers and pump leaving Clive to his own devices. These devices included Clive tracking down a lorry tyre and wheel centre!! Austin did what he thought was really well by tracking down two British Bike shops that were unusually both still trading at 6pm. He bought a part worn 18" road tyre for a paltry $10 and was rightly thrilled to bits. AEV returned to the hard shoulder to find Clive with rear wheel removed and a message carved in the sand that Clive could be found "Down the road apiece". Sure enough Austin arrived at the tyre depot to find Clive re-seating and inflating the wheel in record time. Phenomenal luck and now we had full spare tyre kit etc.

Just as we finished re-fitting the rear wheel a bloke pulled over and checked out if we were OK. The beautiful aspect of <u>this</u> was that he'd passed us by 10 mins earlier, took the next exit (3 miles on), doubled back and gave us a 2nd pass. Ahh...America!

Onto the "Haven Tavern": (In Parkland, Nr Tacoma); coffee, phone-calls and a gorgeous bar-lady. A notice in Haven Tavern: "If it has tits or wheels you'll have trouble with it eventually..."

Bedtime in a firebreak between a small group of houses. No poncho.

USA

Day 152
Wednesday 6 September
Mondo Miles today: 300
Mondo Mileage: 16295

An early rise for Mondo Enduro as they awoke in a small section of common land that backed on to around five houses. The common problem of moving into a campsite after dark – it is virtually impossible to know how the land lies. We did the best we could under the circumstances and once again got away with it.

We headed straight for Mount St Helens - a nice ride up until it started raining. Breakfast was pricey in a railway carriage dining-car café in Elbe at the foot of Mount St Helen's. Ten miles later in Randle, Austin got chatting to 3 firemen (Jay, Jeff and Fool) – we can't remember his real name, so his nickname will have to suffice. They were a decent bunch of blokes and offered to buy us breakfast which we gleefully accepted, even though we were still uncomfortably full from our first breakfast ¾ hour earlier.

At breakfast we shared stories of motocross events, Evil Kneivel, firemen's pastimes and awkward, hilarious call outs... It was a great moment for male bonding. We left them our address in England and we left with one of their Union Cards and a $20 cash handout to help us on our way. God Bless America! The generosity is flowing thick and fast after our box full of goodies from Tom at Cascade Designs, free coffee on the road and now breakfasts being bought for us; back to blending we guess.

We reached the summit of the largest volcano in North America but couldn't see a lot due to the foul weather. However, we could see clearly how all the trees had blown over and were totally singed to death. We also saw the edge of the blast zone where it suddenly changed from dead trees to green trees. Since 18 May 1980 when the volcano erupted the State has implemented a massive ecological development programme and the results are clearly visible today... we know what the Russians would have done if they had this same disaster... zilch.

By 5pm we entered Portland where the rain stopped for the first time that day. A quick visit to Burger King for a coffee, phone calls and chatting to the locals. We had an RV of 9.30pm in the Garibaldi Pub in Garibaldi and it was 80 miles away, so it was soon time to hit the road again.

Lo and behold it began raining again as we ventured down Route 6 to the Oregon Coast. It was a total mission; rain and darkness. Our vision was useless with bogus shades and even a pair of swimming goggles – we ended up riding with no eye protection so our eyes were soon sore from the driving rain, but we rode on as we knew a warm tavern was waiting for us with our new host Fred at the end of our journey. Austin had been sat next to Fred on his flight from Magadan (day 114) and they had made friends. Fred was an Oregon shrimp baron and had been acting as a consultant (sponsored by the U.S. dept of trade) to a collective of Magadan shrimpers. They were throwing off the shackles of state-owned shrimping and Fred was sent in to help set up their minnow capitalist operation.

Arriving at 9.20pm we were early for our rendezvous. After coffee and fries to warm us up we were back on form. We met two of Fred's friends and shortly followed by Fred himself and Vicky. A few memoirs of Russia were discussed including Fred's revelation that his shrimping apostles paid substantial kickbacks to the local mafia to avoid having their operation shut down. Eventually back to Fred's for a steak and finally to sleep after a few beers. More American hospitality. Result.

USA

Day 153
Thursday 7 September
Mondo Miles today: 0
Mondo Mileage: 16295

Morning time, and hence daylight, revealed just how beautiful the ocean view from Fred's balcony was. We laid out the still sodden kit from last night and the welcome sunshine dried out the contents of Austin's sports bag which, it transpired, was considerably less waterproof than he had anticipated. Vicky, (Fred's young girlfriend) percolated coffee, was sent shopping and rustled up a hearty porky stroganoff breakfast. Fred was keen to go for a ride on his motorsickle (Harley) so we leathered up and picked up Doug Strobel (another friend on the rebound and living in an Airstream) on his 1978 Ducati 900 SS. We only covered 10 miles and wound up at a municipal picnic area up inland. Fred and Vicky had just bought new leather suits from Portland's world famous Langlitz leathers. They were stoked because they were measured up for them 18 months ago but such is the over demand it takes that long to get them made. In fact Clive purchased a 23 year old pair of Langlitz leather jeans for $100 from John Hannah, the grizzly Adams look-alike who is masterminding the building of Fred's extension. He is ably assisted by Becky, his recently paroled girlfriend. Becky was a ringer for Janis Joplin c.1969 and reeked of that can-do pioneering spirit that America was built on. There must be 15 years between her and old man Hannah but she can see his inner decency a mile away and sticks by him. Together they talk, shout and rap literally non-stop. Becky's retorts were often funny. As an aside she complained to John "You promised me money but you never said anything about working!" and whilst marking up a plank for sawing lamented: "What happened to the life of adventure you promised me?" We couldn't see why she had been sent to prison when she seemed so lovely.

After a visit to the relatively extensive Smith's Pacific Shrimp Company we witnessed first hand Fred's wealth base. We also saw the recently sewed on finger tip of one of the employees who had caught his index finger in the canning machine. It was quite gruesome.

Evening time and Fred had convened a substantial BBQ with about 25 guests. Fred's preparation of slabs of tuna with honey and bacon was extraordinary. Many of our host's Harley biker buddies showed up and they were truly excellent company. Big Al, bike workshop guru, Big Bill – Charlton Heston look-a-like and Korean Naval veteran and the Moose; the Moose had shaved his beard off as part of his Amway soap powder sales sacrifice. This particular pyramid selling scheme had ruffled many biker feathers in otherwise sleepy Garibaldi.

Fred was an excellent host and everyone had full plates and glasses all evening. Here we are surrounded by Harley-riding stereotypes. Huge bandana-wrapped white men with bellies, beards and at least two items of Harley endorsed merchandise per person. They guffaw and backslap all evening as they ridicule the whole notion of Japanese engineering and their motorcycles in particular. Stories are burped out of 'rice-burners' being set on fire at Harley meets as the Budweisered crowd cheers on approvingly. We feel sheepish about our workhorse Suzukis. Clive begins a strand of dissent suggesting that a Fat Boy Knucklehead wouldn't have been much use in the Zilov Gap but is quickly put in his place by Fred with the suggestion that cruising route 66 is real motorcycling whereas being up to your knees in sludge is not. He, of course, has a point.

The guests eventually dispersed and Clive and Austin retired to the bedroom. Austin heard Fred lamenting our early bedtime and cast aspersions as to the suitability of these two Limeys for a trip round the world. Austin was awake and distressed at these comments, but too tired to get up and do anything about it.

USA

Day 154
Friday 8 September
Mondo Miles today: 80
Mondo Mileage: 16375

We awoke to a glorious blue sunshiney day in Fred's place with swollen tummies from last night's meat binge. Whilst slowly trundling around the flat, Doug appeared with his pick-up loaded with his Ducati and ready to go to Portland, in order to attend a biker meet called the 7th Annual 'Pig Roast' tomorrow. We bid farewell to Vicky and Fred around 2pm and headed to Tillamook to pick up Austin's jacket which was having a new zip sewn in at Bob "Crafts" leather emporium for thirty bucks.

Back on the road but strange that Doug is driving his bike to the Pig Roast in his pickup, why doesn't he ride it? We arrived at Steve Nagy's house (friend of Doug) around 6'ish. There then unfolded two days of being the batons in our very own hospitality relay race. We were greeted and spoiled by so many different people, all of it without any preparation, and we remembered again that this was what made our journeys so invigorating an affirmation of the innate decency of our species...

Steve had a red 1973 Moto Guzzi Le Mans in pristine condition. A few beers, birthday cake and more biker friends turned up with more classic bikes Eric Sowle and Paul Nagy (Steve's brother). There then followed three hours of these guys holding forth on the superiority of European motorcycles. After the all-American Harley mob from last night this was quite a revelation. Steve Nagy lectured us endlessly on the Ducatis of the mid 70s, an epoch of motorcycle design that, in his opinion, will never be surpassed. He insisted that a 1974 750 Super Sport with factory race kit high pipes, Imola cams and Imola tank was better than anything out. But that his 1973 750 Sport was almost as good. He added that the '74 didn't mean shit unless the owner was riding it on a daily basis. We are the only chaps here with Japanese machines but Austin was at pains to point out that he only sold his 1969 TR6R Triumph Trophy to buy the Jap 350 trail bike because that was the rule; we all had to have the same machine. Engines kicked over and as a ten bike convoy we then proceeded to the Strip bar (Docs) which was brilliant. We returned to Steve's via Eric's about 1-2am a little worse for wear. Crumbs, we are hanging out with bikers.

USA

Day 155
Saturday 9 September
Mondo Miles today: 70
Mondo Mileage: 16445

After such a late night it was no fun being woken by the sound of Steve vomiting into the toilet bowl adjacent to Clive and Austin's room. Doug soon appeared followed by Matt followed by Steve playing Pearl Jam *very* loudly.

In no time we were all saddled up and on our way to Tom King's Portland motorcycle shop. Outside the shop were gazillions of bikes and bikers young and old. We all registered and paid our $12 fee for the legendary Pig Roast. We got a chance to introduce ourselves to boss man Tom King who was very friendly and supportive of Mondo Enduro. He had motorcycled extensively in

Mexico and was quick to warn us to be on our guard once we had crossed the Rio Grande.

There was a 200 mile trip to the venue which most people took but not us. We rolled out of town and managed to stop every 10 miles with B2's gear lever falling off, motorcycle exchanges and Taco stops. Clive got a free Burrito in 'Taco Time' when a large piece of plastic appeared in his Pepsi.

Matt was 'packing' and he was photographed holding Mondo Enduro hostage in front of a sign proclaiming: "firearms prohibited!"

As our little convoy wound its way up the Clackamas River Valley the scenery became progressively more beautiful. The route was peppered with a host of state campsites that were all really gorgeous. The Oregonian Euro-bikers were amazed at how slowly we rode and we in turn were deeply impressed by their high speed cornering and sheer knee-down skill.

Around 3pm we reached the camp ground where the Pig Roast was being held and most people had arrived by then. The weather was superb all day and in no time Austin was asleep while Clive set to changing his rear tyre and repairing his inner tube. This task seemed to fascinate the locals and in fact he spent most of his time explaining to other motorcyclists who we were and how we got here.

Night-time saw Eric Sowle, Paul Nagy (Steve's Brother) and the Triumph Speed Triple riding Jeff all arrive. Eric in particular was good company and amazed us with stories of the home-made movies his former room-mate had created in the basement of their house.

These guys that we've met through Doug are all excellent value. They have already invited us to Steamboat in Colorado for a weekend of non-stop classic and vintage motorcycle racing around the streets of the town. This sounds superb and their company alone would be reason enough to go 1800 miles out of our way. Bedtime was unusually pre-midnight and we lent Jeff and Eric our surplus Therma-rests.

Old man Doug refused to retire until he'd attempted to chat up every woman on the site...

USA

Day 156
Sunday 10 September
Mondo Miles today: 217
Mondo Mileage: 16662

We left the biker gathering shortly after eating and were now heading for the "Harley Drag Races" roughly seventy miles away – more bike entertainment and camaraderie. This time there were seven of us and it was brilliant to be riding in convoy as we reminisced of times on Mondo Enduro when we all rode as a septet. We arrived in Woodburn where the Drag races were happening and discovered it was $20 – far too pricey to watch a loada Hogs riding up and down. So we headed for the nearest pub to sink a couple of ales to drown our sorrows and quench that thirst from the roasting hot sunshine. We had a group photo shot outside the pub. Then to top it all Steve came out of the tavern with the beautiful brunette barmaid called Angel. She was wearing a white T-shirt branded with the slogan "*Do it to me*" – Clive and Austin posed with this delightful young lady whilst Steve took control of the camera and directed the saucy shots. Steve is the most brusque and confident of this crowd which may come in part from his likeness to adult film star Ron Jeremy.

We parted company with our Oregonian buddies and headed South Westerly towards Route 101 and then ever Southward along the coast.

Austin called Mark (in San Francisco), Chas had not been in contact and Mark wanted to head South, he was apparently short of cash. Decisions, decisions have to be made... Austin and Clive ended up in Newport on the Pacific coast, did a recce on a near roadside campsite and then headed for RIPTIDE a local tavern/club for a Stolichnaya vodka session. Amazingly, only a year ago Austin was teetotal, not any more.

USA

Day 157
Monday 11 September
Mondo Miles today: 210
Mondo Mileage: 16872

More strangeness as Mondo Enduro wakes up in another unusual location. The alcoholic nightcap from last night was still wearing off and as a result of its longevity it was realised that more Vodka had been drunk than was anticipated, intended or remembered.

The road (highway 101) beckoned southwards and so off we went. Superb tarmac, ace hairpins but most importantly, what was definitely the most gorgeous scenery so far. This Oregon coast line is beyond description and certainly more impressive than route 1 in the Big Sur area of California. This is the most staggering place we have ever been.

The driving style employed on this day was a cocktail of reckless and erratic. Several RV drivers are probably shaking their wrinkly-skin covered fists at the uncertain number plates that passed them. It is becoming more of a regular occurrence that we scream out from behind a truck, narrowly miss the oncoming traffic, weave around on the double solid yellow lines and then catch a glimpse of a sign warning: "DO NOT PASS". The nimble 350s are excellent on these twisty roads and we are like hornets, or is it bees?

After 100 miles of fun and games we pulled over in advance of the huge multi-span steel lattice arched bridge over the estuary at North Bend. The lay-by was lovely, lawned and the edge of the grass went all the way up to the water's edge whence there was a vertical 10ft drop to the water. Austin stepped forward to this edge for a welcome emptying of the bladder and a cleansing from last night's alcohol. While pretending to strafe the German troop trains lying below he spotted what was clearly a bulging Filofax. Sensing another adventure, he climbed down to investigate. Sure enough, Mondo Enduro has discovered a large amount of paperwork, letters and admin. It all belongs to a certain Michele de Sando, 29 years old and post graduate student at the UCSB Department of Anthropology. First lecture was this morning. We assumed this young lady had been robbed and her effects dumped here. The foolish thief should have been more thorough as he had left her Blockbuster video membership card!! We found her telephone number on a UCSB sheet and left a message in Santa Barbara saying what we'd found then we took a picture of Clive standing next to Austin's bike, holding Michele's Filofax.

After an excellent lunch at Mom's Kitchen we pushed on through Post Orford and saw "Battle Rak" scene of a famous siege by some Indians!

The fog set in in the late afternoon and this provided the excuse to repair to the cinema in Brookings. We got two films developed and whilst leafing through the prints made a few friends in the Tavern (which is <u>not</u> allowed to sell spirits, only wine and beer. Hmm... strange by-law).

The mist and fog was well established now and hence at 10pm we found the local park, drove down a path and slept between the swings and the see-saw.

USA

Day 158
Tuesday 12 September
Mondo Miles today: 474
Mondo Mileage: 17346

A pretty big day ahead, the plan being to get to Reno (more than 400 miles away) and to hook up with Rita. She had been one of our hostesses at the motor show in Almaty and now, 3 months and 12,000 miles later she was on a year's exchange at Reno University in Nevada.

At 367 miles and 7pm we arrived in Greenville where we called Rita to let her know we were 2 hours/100 miles away. Light rapidly faded away as we slipped into endurance mode homaging the distance king Gerald, the mile cruncher.

The temperature continued to drop and the stars were shining brightly by now. We came across a superb view of Reno from the mountains. The shining lights, the array of casino colours were all fantastic. We stopped to take a couple of snaps.

We found Nye Hall and the University of Nevada very easily – it was on the main drag where all the casinos were situated. This was excellent for Mondo Enduro as we had decided to put $1000 on the Black at a roulette table.

Rita was not around when we arrived, but Lina (her American friend) greeted us and took us back to her room where we met her roommate Candy, who was very cute. At last Rita arrived and immediately we noticed her western changes. She was dressed totally in denim with a skimpy top and a new haircut. It had been a while since we had met her at ITE in Alma Ata. She had now settled easily into this capitalist city. We headed to the nearest casino, put our $1000 money on the black-and won! $1000 richer we got out of the casino fast and went to the nearest bar and began to spend, spend, spend... How easy gambling is! We returned to Rita's flat about 1.30am to meet the gorgeous roommate Dano, to crash out (no blending) and reflect on our 474 miles today, a personal best, not a yard of it on motorway and $1000 richer. Bueno...

USA

Day 159
Wednesday 13 September
Mondo Miles today: 240
Mondo Mileage: 17586

We awoke in the air-conditioned yet asphyxiating unpleasantness of the Nye Hall of Residence. Amazingly, Rita and her catholic roommate, Dano, had resisted the temptation to climb out of their beds and test our sleeping bags' ability to take two.

A swift set of goodbyes and a photo with Rita and it was back on the road for us. The bright sunlight and crystal blue skies made for a superb start to the ride and we fondly imagined we were bounty hunters leaving town after turning in our quarry the night before. With a fat bank-roll in our pockets we headed west along inter-state 80. The sky was blemished only by the word "PEPSI", smoked into position by a small sky-writing airplane. The font was perfectly even. This *is* America.

Clive's float bowl was playing up but nothing that smashing it with rock didn't seem to alleviate. The gas station just outside Reno wanted cash up front – memories of the USSR. Also, it was attached to a minor casino which even at 0900 hrs was teeming with an unbelievable cup-carrying breed of American glaze-eyed gambling automaton.

The route took us out through the predictably beautiful Lake Tahoe National Forest. The Truckee river valley that we followed had two railways snaking alongside us in a most impressive way. Strange parallels continued with a huge wooden flume that plaited itself over, under and between the road and railway. It was carrying water down from the mountains to the town but rather than being set into the rock was permanently raised upon wooden trestles that made it look quite like a fairground log ride flume thing. It was leaking from between almost every pair of railway sleepers that it was constructed from.

As we descended from the pass at 5000ft we left Nevada and returned to California, passing unchecked through the state fruit and vegetable checkpoint. The scenery changed strongly to the characteristic yellow grass/hay dotted with randomly positioned deciduous trees. It looked so much like the valleys that have been used as the locations for so many countless US TV and film shoots. The temperature shot up too.

We had brunch at Denny's and then set off on the ride to the bay area, which was quite interminable and as boring and unpleasant as we could remember.

We approached San Francisco from the North along the State Route 101. We didn't get a very good view of the city until we emerged from a tunnel about one mile north from the Golden Gate. Suddenly we were presented with the world famous vista of San Francisco. The bridge, Alcatraz, the quayside all fought for our attention, each basking in the afternoon sunshine. It was definitely a Mondo Moment and Clive and Austin, riding alongside each other in the slow lane peeped their horns, punched the air and shouted the chant of "USA! USA!!" We couldn't believe the intensity of the moment, it was like being in a film and for about 90 seconds we felt pretty special.

The ride over the bridge and through the city was terrific fun and had a sudden air of it being an objective achieved, even though San Francisco held no special status for Mondo Enduro.

We arrived at Clayton Street and were stunned to find that our hostess, Heather McCullock, lived right on that epicentre of hippy culture, Haight Street. We spotted Mark's bike (who had been here a full two weeks in advance of us), parked up adjacent a tidy Triumph Daytona (Hinkley, not Meriden) and unloaded up to the flat. Record purchasing was done but the elusive "*Heartache*" by The Flirtations was not secured. Pride of purchase were Sergio Mendes, Nuggets (vinyl but the French re-issue) and a 'DJ only' promo copy of the "*On any Sunday*" soundtrack.

Evening time and Clive, Austin and Mark went out for a meal with beautiful Heather and her equally tall friend Christina Lynn. Our obvious attraction to these delicious women is shameful. We just look like motorcycle tramps. The streets are teeming with runaways and beggars, each and every one of whom demanded or requested a contribution to their budget. One chap had a sign laid out before him reading: "Why lie? I want to buy a beer".

A Syrian restaurant, red wine and then a few yards down the street took us to an Art Deco bar offering an acoustic guitar/piano boogie-woogie combo. Much Vodka. Clive met Amy but he still went home with Austin – aw shucks. Phone calls to Louis Bloom in South Africa, Whitaker Malem and Josh Collins in London. Where is Chas?

USA

Day 160
Thursday 14 September
Mondo Miles today: 130
Mondo Mileage: 17716

Mark woke alone in the front room, dreaming of what might have been, when he was struck by the revelation that he was back on the plot with Clive and Austin. They were crashed in Alex's bed, unfortunately for them without the lovely Alex. A storming run down Route 1 saw them outside the Hog's Breath Inn (Carmel) at 8pm. We indulged ourselves with beers, chips and onion rings in the Hog's Breath – alas there was no Leone memorabilia or evidence of the Mayor of Carmel.

We saw a police car in the street and told the officers our Michele de Sando story and produced all her effects as evidence. Amongst the recovered documents is the paperwork reserving her room in a hall of residence. We deduced that she was supposed to move in on Tuesday (two days ago). Austin rang the hall to find out if she has booked in and she hasn't. We now fear the worst, she has been abducted or murdered and the perpetrator dumped her stuff, fully expecting the next tide to wash it all away. However, he hadn't banked on the chance intervention of the Mondo Crime Scene Team. Anyway, we explained all this to the fuzz and they said that if she had neither been reported missing nor a body found then there was nothing they could do. We suggested that we *were* reporting her missing but they just seemed to think we were a bit mental. It was a great shame, they were totally uninterested so they shrugged their shoulders and returned to their burgers. Fingers crossed; let's hope nothing has happened to her. We got a jiffy bag and mailed all the stuff to the hall of residence, it seemed better than just throwing it away.

We found an excellent campsite just outside town on land that we are sure backs onto Clint Eastwood's garden. Sleeping with the stars...

USA

Day 161
Friday 15 September
Mondo Miles today: 244
Mondo Mileage: 17960

Today we pushed south down the world famous Pacific Coast Highway. A super beautiful road trip classic which we shared with hundreds of other tourists. It was probably going to be the definitive section of 'easy road' on our whole trip so we were thrilled. We were heading for a blend Mark had set up for us with a girl in Los Angeles but until then we would simply enjoy ourselves. On we rode and 60 miles later, after the most spectacular sections of route 1 we found ourselves at the Sebastian Store, an old trading post from the mid 18th century.

During this short journey there were many photo stops (Bixby Bridge etc) and during one of them the mirror fell out of the camera (unknown to us) and so that was the end of the photos in California.

Once at San Simeon we embarked on the Hearst Castle tour. An obvious tourist attraction but for once, rightly so. The first part of the visit was the five mile drive from the reception centre down on the highway up to the actual houses.   There was an informative but antiseptic pre-recorded commentary all the way to the summit that, amongst other things, urged us not to chew gum.

The outdoor pool, with its classical colonnades and stunning backdrops, was absolutely unreal. There was also a great Art Deco indoor pool that was 100% mosaic, even the inside of the pool. The roof of this pool was 2 tennis courts. The finale and highlight of the tour (with our guide Judy) around the main building of Hearst Castle was a film showing in the huge private cinema. The seats were luscious, spacious, leg-room rich, armchairs. We watched a selection of clips filmed by amateurs in the 1930's. Charlie Chaplin was just one of the amazing galaxy of luminaries who had partied hard at San Simeon and lived this fairy tale existence in reality.

The tour bus took us back down from the summit (past the former cages and dens of Hearst's private zoo!!) down to the reception centre. Here, whilst remounting the bikes we met two Harley riders parked adjacent to us. They were a couple and *she* was tiny. We couldn't believe she could control her 'hog' but she sported a Wehrmacht tin helmet *with* the HD logo emblazoned on it to show that she meant business.

We decided to blast to Santa Barbara and treated ourselves to a night in a hotel and a boogie in Disco McDisco. Once again, the Vodka monster struck us down...

USA

Day 162
Saturday 16 September
Mondo Miles today: 93
Mondo Mileage: 18053

Our single night of luxury staying a night in a motel to catch up on much needed sleep was shattered by the incessant Amtrak trains trundling by throughout the night, blowing their incredibly loud horns to warn pedestrians and motorists alike of their arrival. We now understood why the motel was so cheap. Most certainly no-one would stay here for more than one night or come back again; they obviously could survive on passing travellers like ourselves to fill their noise chambers.

We headed off a mere 800m down the road to the nearest diner for more R & R and Admin. How weak we have become in North America. Lo and behold what the Mexicans will think of us when the Mondo Pansies turn up with their bulging bellies.

We eventually got moving around 3pm for LA. We saw the Californian coastline bubbling with activity as the surfers and boogie boarders rock those perfect waves. Clive constantly reminisced of his time surfing and swimming in South Africa every time he saw waves breaking on a beach. Well, with about 10,000 miles to go before South Africa he'll have a lot of time for reflection on that matter.

A one-hour photo stop in Ventura County gave the weary travellers more time to loaf and indulge. The thrift shop was a must and we purchased bogus shades and a fantastic monster mask from an old lady of 72 who used to live in Kilburn. She looked absolutely vibrant for her last 30 years in the US away from the grime of NW6!

We pulled off the freeway at the outskirts of LA for a map of town. Austin was delighted as this was the very junction that he hitched from on his way out of LA the last time he was here in 1989.

We passed the signs for Universal Studios and caught a glimpse of the HOLLYWOOD sign set up in the hills as we made our way past the lines of traffic on the freeway. We were heading to the 'Downtown' of LA to stay with Tracy, who was a struggling actress, writer, director here in tinseltown. She didn't know any of us, however, when we finally arrived at 423½ Wall Street (the door is sandwiched twixt 423 and 424), she was waiting with open arms to take Mondo Enduro under her wing for their stay in LA. What a goddess. We suddenly discovered a Los Angeles that was not as well known as Beverly Hills or Venice Beach. This is Downtown L.A. and above all else, that meant inner city squalor on a scale we hadn't seen since leaving England. The streets surrounding Tracy's block were strewn with tons of litter. Almost every street corner sported a soup kitchen. Every alley, recess overhang or nook seemed to have somebody living in the international shanty materials of cardboard and plastic tarpaulins. The sidewalks were bustling with the hapless souls who have gravitated here. Loads of people push shopping trolleys over-spilling with the billions of morsels of rubbish they've collected that might one day prove useful. Some of them wheeled entire trains of carts filled up with old aluminium cans en route to the recycling depot where they exchange them for cash money. As soon as we pulled over in front of the block we were beset by requests for help, financial or otherwise. The stories and biogs of five or six hobos came pouring out as we unloaded our luggage and we were put on the spot. By the time we were pressing the doorbell we had learned that Buck was in the 82nd Air Cavalry at Khe Sahn whilst Miguel was a former marine who had proudly served Uncle Sam in Grenada. It was insane, we were drenched in guilt and desperately needed someone to show us the way, should we give them all cash, or what. It was like that bit in Jesus Christ Superstar where Ted Neeley is overwhelmed by the lepers. Just then, the door swung open and the delicious Tracy stood there eliciting instant cheering and whistles from the hobos crowded round her front door. "Sorry guys, maybe later" she confidently chirped and ushered us all inside. She was the hottest chick any of us had seen in months.

Her flat was one of many on three floors. It was nothing like anything we had seen before. It seemed to be like a small commune, everything was open plan and the residents are free to walk through each other's spaces. We edged down the hall past the bedrooms and the kitchen to find Joe McManus working in his bicycle shop at the end of the hallway. Joe leases the whole of the block and rents it out to the likes of Tracey and Sean Kamano (the famous DJ) and in the meantime he would spend his time working on bikes in his impressive workshop. He kindly donated us two tubes of a custard-like wonder sludge sold under the name of Puncture Buster. This slime is supposed to clog and harden in the hole if you ever get a puncture so it doesn't really Bust the Puncture, it seals it. Let's put it to a field trial on the road to Argentina.

Meanwhile, our induction into boho chic and loft living continued whilst Mark and Tracy prepared supper consisting of fish in a delicious sun dried tomato, garlic and onion sauce accompanied with runner beans and asparagus. Austin took it well as almost everything on the menu was on his top ten of hated foods. We drank beers on their rooftop which had a spectacular panoramic view of the whole of the downtown area. Clive, Mark and Tracy went to a local cheesy bar for a couple of beers before returning around 1am.

Los Angeles

Day 163-179
Sunday 17 September – 02 October
Mondo Miles In this period: 40
Mondo Mileage: 18093

The two weeks in Los Angeles were spent on restocking our panniers with essential clobber, resting and desperately trying to scrounge discounted parts from sundry pertinent sources. They are three fold; White Brothers, the kings of accessory supply to the American motocross and off-road fraternity. AFAM, admittedly, not a household name but the makers and suppliers of high end chains and sprockets and finally, Suzuki USA. Suzuki's natural place was at the forefront of our psyche. In an unprecedented spurt of forward thinking (back in Anchorage) Austin had edited together a ridiculous 3 minute video 'trailer' of us in Siberia. This truly crap promo was copied three times and a tape sent to each of the aforementioned commercial organisations. Accompanying each VHS was a weedy letter explaining how Mondo Enduro was going to re-write the adventure motorcycling rule-book and that we would not forget those that helped us when we were famous across Middlesex and Dorset and a by-word for poorly thought through bungling. So here we were, like so many struggling hopefuls in Los Angeles, trying to impress people when of course, we were desperately ordinary. The dividends though, were (in our opinion) extremely successful.

We visited White Brothers HQ in Yorba Linda, a suburb in the north of LA and realised when we arrived that theirs was a world brutally overcrowded. Their normal clientele were adrenalin junkie moto-cross gods who as well as being lethally fearless and technically skilful were all as dishy as Keanu Reeves with the easy going confidence and charm of John, Paul, George and Ringo.

We couldn't locate the bloke we'd sent the video to and no-one knew anything about us. The visit to Yorba Linda brought into sharp focus that White Brothers would have to be drowning in a full-on recession before they, for a second, needed any publicity from a clutch of English nobodies on holiday for a year. We bought a Motion-Pro chain breaker and two air filter sponges before quietly leaving.

This loosely unsuccessful debut performance was reversed at AFAM on Huntington Beach. The AFAM HQ was not the chrome clad monolith of White Brothers but was instead a humble unit on a light industrial estate. We met Steve Godoski (one of the three employees) and he remembered receiving the tape a few weeks ago but had thought it was some kind of joke. Although surprised when we turned up in person he was gracious and charming and though not in a position to give us cash if we used his product, he immediately volunteered a massive discount. After the sprocket trauma of Siberia we were like kids in a candy store that we went round his neat showroom loading up with two full sets of transmission each. Steve became our new best friend when he totted up the retail value of our booty at $130 and asked if $30 was ok? We were really thrilled, forget all other makes of transmission, if you haven't got **AFAM** chains and sprockets, you are a loser.

And finally, the nail biting visit to Suzuki USA at Brea. It was like asking the hottest girl in class to the prom we were that nervous. Heaven knows what the scale of their operation is but we must have been the most microscopic of blips on their radar right then. We piled round and were told that no-one from sales or press wanted to speak to us, we presumed, because we were zeroes. However, press elf Kathy McNaughton suggested we write a 'wants' list of parts and they would see what they could do. As a symbol of bridging goodwill she hustled backstage and re-emerged with three Suzuki baseball caps which we graciously received. We are riven with catholic guilt since we threw them away as soon as we had left. Sadly, not every man can be bought so easily and on Mondo we would rather cancel the trip and go back to London than wear baseball caps. Result. It took two days to distil our list but it must have been $600 worth of bits. We sheepishly submitted it and 24hrs later were summoned to collect our booty. Suzuki USA gave us everything we asked for and wanted nothing in return. Amongst the parts was the circlip required to hold the front sprocket onto Austin's driveshaft. It was only now, that the piece of Trans-Siberian railway wire fitted 4000 miles ago was finally removed.

Before we left England, Suzuki UK wouldn't even come to the phone to speak to us. About now we became infused with a burning new Mondo mantra: If you are American, ride **Suzuki, they rock!** If you are British, don't ride Suzuki, they suck. Perhaps we should have perceptively noted the fact that not so much as a still photo was required to earn this latest haul, only a polite suggestion that now we had the parts, maybe we should get going...

Photo Session:

Tony was a pro photographer and lived in one of the spaces in the legendary 423½ Wall Street. He had seen the bikes and suggested we do a photo shoot because he said we looked pretty cool. Overjoyed at his spectacularly poor eye for the 'hip' we reported to the location, the pavement outside the block. Tony had not only an 'assistant' but a chunky camera the size of a shoe box that instantly gave to suggest that he really did do this for a living. He had us preen and pose and after 76 years of anonymity between us we were only too pleased to pretend to be models. Tony soon realised that we should play to our strengths and he urged us to *act like dorks...*" and the satisfying results are framed below. Tony said he would go to the offices of Vogue with the prints and a précis of our story. What a result. We pulled our trousers up and naturally, never heard from Tony again.

Venice Beach:

Our first day in Venice Beach and in many respects a chance to appreciate what all the fuss has been about.

The actual beach is a vast 150m playground that stretches from the Prom (which despite being Tarmac is known as the Boardwalk) down to the water's edge. The Boardwalk is well known locally as the permanent residence of an inordinate amount of Hobos and Itinerants. What makes *these* homeless people unusual is the fact that they are all compulsive collectors of any rubbish and knick-knacks that they happen to find. These West Coast Wombles then accumulate all their effects in a rickety convoy of old buggies and shopping trolleys which they, ant-like, gruellingly drag up and down the length of the Boardwalk whilst searching for further rubbish with which to swell their portfolios. One heavily dread-locked collector was harnessed to a caravan akin to the ones classically inhabited by Romany Gypsies. Herculean.

Señor Frogs:

Nora and Jennifer are two of Austin's cousins who, despite looking normal, are in fact extremely wild. This may stand them in poor stead with parents, employers, drill sergeants etc but for three itinerant motorcyclists they had immaculate credentials. They hooked up with us in Torrance and took us down to a nightclub in Redondo Beach called Señor Frogs. Because we have no other clothes we were all in leathers but this was taken as a statement of our fashion sense rather than tiny paniers. A night unfolded of truly frantic proportions with unashamed amounts of Vodka ingestion and the first time in our lives where beautiful women came up to *us*. Why this happened we'll never understand but it really did. We suddenly knew what it was like to be dishy. The night at Señor Frogs was unbelievable, we didn't have to try. Stunning girls offered to buy us drinks, dragged us out on the dance floor and hung on our every word. Cousins Nora and Jennifer acted as our agents and bigged us up as if on commission. Austin, still new to boozing, was puking his guts up all over the dance floor by 10pm but amazingly wasn't thrown out. As we prepared to leave, a Julie Christie look-a-like approached us, introduced herself as Sandy. She was the hottest girl we'd met all night and explained that she was a professional photographer and could she meet up with us later in the week and take some pictures. We honestly thought it was a wind-up and assured her that she must have confused us with someone else, we weren't cool or good looking or anything, she must have the wrong guys. But no, she persisted, she thought we looked great and would love to 'shoot' us. No Sandy, we implored, you must raise your standards, we're not models. "OK, forget it" and she was gone. Readers; never, ever, ever look a gift horse in the mouth.

This night seemed to sum up our experience in America; somehow, and we'll never know why, for two weeks, we were cool. And yes, the 163 days and 18093 miles that brought us here were worth it 1000 times over. It was totally obvious to Austin, Mark and Clive that we would never live like this again...

Leaving for Las Vegas

Day 178
Sunday 01 Oct
Miles today: 250
Mondo Miles: 18343

This morning was supposed to see us making a quick getaway; especially since our plans to leave last night fell so easily into pieces. Austin started the day at 0700 changing over the rear sprockets from 43 teeth down to 41. This move is calculated to give us 12% more power or alternatively, allows us to cruise at higher road speeds for a given engine rpm. In fact we now can do 60mph at 5000rpm or 70mph at 6000rpm. For Mondo Enduro this is a big deal.

The pack up took three hours, just to each fill two small panniers. The Mondo Enduro slow reaction force finally began to clock miles at 12.30 and headed Southeast down highway 404 bound for Orange County Suzuki in Costa Mesa. Here we re-acquainted ourselves with Tarik Saba (of Palestinian extraction) and parts guru George Sissons, who looked like Ron Mael, unnerving organ player from art-glam combo 'Sparks'. We produced several control levers and side-stands that were for the DR650 and exchanged them for oil, a new o-ring chain (worth $90) and other goodies. We faxed Kathleen McNaughton at HQ Suzuki with our finalised wants list and left Austin's MasterCard details with Tarik ready for the days in the future when he would send us parts down to South America. In a rare pique of forward planning we stocked up on $50 worth of rear axle bearings and seals.

Finally we were on our way, save buying a chain breaker from a huge flab monster in Santa Ana's Cycle City. Amazing to think we left home without one, relying up till now on the double act of centre punch and club hammer. North East up highway 15 takes us en route to Las Vegas via the parched misery of the Mojave Desert. Big news, Mark is going back to England. A great shame for us but we will not be alone as Chas Penty rejoins us tomorrow in Vegas. Result.

The Mojave looked exactly like large parts of the desert around Almeria in Spain. A cocoa stop at Denny's in Baker and then a star spangled sky as we slept our first night on the rattlesnake rich US sand.

USA

Day 179
Monday 2 October
Mondo Miles today: 190
Mondo Mileage: 18995

Greetings, loyal readers, I (Chas Penty) am back on the plot after a lengthy period visiting relatives in absentia in North West Canada. The day began early for Chas, looking forward to his eventual reunion with Clive and Austin after a separation of some five weeks and well over 3,000 miles.

And what better setting to toast this auspicious meeting than Las Vegas, temple of tackiness and shrine to dubious taste? As Chas hove into view along the famous 'Strip', he espied Clive's motorcycle parked outside the indescribably bogus Luxor Pyramid gambling casino. At first it was difficult to say with certainty which was more suspect – the leering grin of the ersatz Sphinx or the dubious sheen of Clive's new blonde barnet.

The charms of Vegas soon faded for the newly-reunited trio however. When you have seen one monstrosity you have seen them all. All the fake legionnaires or gladiators in Caesar's Palace also start to look the same after a while, so they decided to make good their escape into the high desert of Arizona after a mere couple of hours in this temple of glitz where all standards of taste and propriety seem to be in a state of perpetual freefall.

It was but a few minutes drive out of Vegas and into the neighbouring state via the Hoover Dam. The stunning construction constraining the eager water of the Colorado River has long been the stuff of legend in the civil engineering community and did not disappoint with its massive masonry.

And so the journey continued for the triplet of tourists who made their way in the fading light to a ribbon development community on the old Route 66 known as Seligman. There they availed themselves of a Budweiser two-for-the-price-of-one promotion and unsuccessfully attempted to blend with three sturdy-thighed maidens bound for the Grand Canyon and its labyrinthine hiking trails.

And so, to bed, as the bard was want to say. But as so often is the case in Mondo Enduro's experience, the divan in question was an open field by a railway track heavily populated with sundry critters including perhaps even the lethal black widow and tarantula spiders and the dreaded rattlesnake. At least the sky was as clear as a nun's conscience, even if the night was a trifle chilly.

Still, there was time to reflect, amidst the heavy shunting of freight trains, of our fellow travellers back in England and Canada and wondering what was in store for us three as we headed into Mexico and the long drive south to Argentina.

USA

Day 180
Tuesday 3 October
Mondo Miles today: 350
Mondo Mileage: 19345

As the sun rose on that frosty morn, the Mondo trio reminisced on what seemed like an eternity of sleeping by the Trans-Siberian and were quickly reminded of those days gone by with the shunting of Amtrack cargo trains throughout the night. It was no surprise that we were quickly on our way to the nearest diner after this incessant thundering railway racket. Several coffees and hours later we reluctantly hit the road after question time from some Dutch tourists. The first news that morning was of little surprise to the duo or the world for that fact: OJ's verdict of Not Guilty had just been delivered!

By 3pm we had arrived at Grand Canyon village to collect the tourist freebies and find out which view point was the best. The line-up (queue) as it is known in North America was quite significant and the entrance fee of $10 for cars and $4 for bikes obviously was not enough and there were a multitude of tourists around even though this is the off-peak season.

The anti-climax soon arrived as the trio squeezed their way through the crowds to get a glimpse of the scenic canyon in all its glory. The second and preferred viewpoint had slightly less onlookers and no safety fence, hooray! The camera and kit was soon off the bike and Clive and Chas took turns in shooting the link shot from the Canyon of Kazahkstan.

The tourist bit was now complete and we were swiftly back on the road bound for Paradise Valley in the suburbs of Phoenix to meet Chas's Uncle Terrence and Auntie Joan. As we descended from Flagstaff we noticed the temperature rising even though the sun was rapidly sinking away. We rode down from 8046 feet to less than a thousand feet to the city of Phoenix. The scenery rapidly changed too and for the first time on Mondo Enduro we saw cacti in abundance in this arid land.

We found our way to 58th Place fairly rapidly and quite easily despite the darkness and roadworks.

However, we failed to notice the "Welcome Charles" sign sprawled over Uncle Terrence's garage on arrival but fortunately Chas recognised his uncle's figure in the shadows of his British Shrine. We were soon ushered inside to admire the family's US cars with "Kernow" proudly showing on the front of the BMW, Cornish for Cornwall. They also had several Union Jacks all over the cars too to reinforce their patriotic pride. It was very civilised and refreshing at the same time as we sat down to a cup of Typhoo tea followed by cottage pie and two veg. The team was extremely tired after their long ride and were soon bedded down in the guest room in their own beds – the crispness of cotton a welcome luxury for Mondo Enduro.

USA

Day 181-184
Wednesday to Saturday 4 - 7 October
Mondo Miles today: 0
Mondo Mileage: 19345

Our stay at the family Shelbourne was a time of ordered peace amidst the storm of trans-global motorcycle travel. Uncle Terrence and Aunty Joan proved to be splendid hosts who did their utmost to keep us all in high spirits and more than sufficient victuals.

The days were spent according to a routine so fixed that it appeared to have been prescribed by some Old Testament prophet. Terrence and Joan were up and about so early that the crack of dawn was but a minuscule fissure. Sadly the persistent barking of one of their four mutts meant Clive was also awake 'ere sparrowfart.

Breakfast would consist of assorted cereals; carefully mix n'matched from day to day, followed by toasted muffins with Aunty J's home-made grapefruit marmalade and the inevitable Typhoo tea. Fortified by this hearty repast, the first day was spent down at Apache Racing to seek the advice of the motorcycle medicine man for Chas's ailing bike. At first the news was not good when Jimmy the mechanic diagnosed a possible cracked valve. Imagine the scenes of unrestrained revelry; therefore, when it transpired that the blameless culprit was the carburettor, much defiled by rust and debris during our long journey.

On the subject of motorcycle maintenance, it is only fitting to record an episode of high farce relating to Clive's float valve seating barrel. During a day of bumbling repairs in extreme heat, Clive disassembled his carburettor only to put it back together sans FVSB. A forage to the Sony Video Shop (of which more later) was aborted when petrol started gushing from his engine and onto the pristine asphalt of Paradise Valley, apparently one of Phoenix's most salubrious neighbourhoods. The elusive part was found the next morning by Chas after just two minutes of gentle raking amidst the gravel of Uncle T's yard while Clive was disassembling his carburettor. The two events were not in any way connected, honestly...

Still, with some carb cleaner loaned by Uncle T, Clive's bike was soon up and running and ready to rock. Chas's DR, also, despite a deteriorating clutch, was now humming like a Santa Pod dragster. The front fork oil change was a great improvement also. It seems that we are constantly shackled to the orb of 'maintainance'. Although none of us has much of an idea of what we are doing there seems to be a miasma of good karma that surrounds our group tightenings, adjustments and lubrications. Fingers crossed, not too much has gone wrong so far, apart from Chas' oil-free camshaft meltdown in Canada!!

Clive's 'blending' skills had, meanwhile, been given the ultimate test during his visit to the Sony shop in Phoenix. He returned to 58th Place somewhat shamefaced having weaved the equivalent of an entire box of Kleenex tissues of lies to the sons of Sony. His conscience was easily shriven, however, with the knowledge that he had secured one AC adapter/charger and a full service for the Hi-8 camera all *gratis* (financial equivalent circa $350). Anybody reading this should be advised that aside from Fujica and Nikon, Mondo Enduro only use Sony cameras.

Anyway Phoenix was a lot of fun, even if it wasn't of the high-octane variety. There were many lazy hours spent in bed, by the pool and in the dining room and Uncle T's photo collection was an historical and social delight. His 1952 Brittany trip on board an Italian 150cc scooter was a reminder of the innocent hey-day of international two-wheeled travel.

It was nice to meet the old folks and Chas's cousins, were great fun. We will miss the strict regime of food, punctuality, Uncle T's technical know-how garnered during his long career building engine parts for F-15 fighters, and the four beautiful dogs. We will not, however, miss their pet cat who was clearly a corporal in the Viet Cong in a former life. Tomorrow we're back on the road.

Mexico

Day 185
Sunday 8 October
Mondo Miles today: 370
Mondo Mileage: 19715

Interstate 10 took us to the McDonalds at Nogales for our last meal in the US before embarking for Mexico and beyond. Fortified with quarter pounders with cheese, we went through US Customs without stopping-just to be received by the Mexican Customs who asked Chas if he had any *pistoleros* or *drogas*. Clive and Austin nodded in agreement with Chas as their Spanish was picked up watching spaghetti westerns and therefore was not quite up to scratch.

Fifteen miles further South the official border loomed on the horizon where vehicle permits were purchased and silver stickers were given to H6 , B2 and K5 in return for $11.

Day 0. Full of anticipation and with petrol pouring from the ill fitting balance pipes of our new tanks.

Day 18. The dirt roads over the mountains of eastern Turkey were an unexpected treat, Georgia here we come!

Day 78. Irkutsk and down to four riders, clueless as to the misery that awaited.

Day 43. The bulk of our research pre-departure focussed on Central Asia. Whilst in Buchara, Chas swots up on Samarkand...

Day 63. The nightly camp-fire was a crucial time for deconstructing the previous day and endlessly discussing the road ahead.

Day 85. The pattern establishing itself for the Zilov gap. Why aren't we on the grassy bit?

Day 86. Chas' gloom comes not from the mud but from the not knowing what tomorrow will be like.

Day 90. The paradox of the Zilov Gap; An excellent, easy track leading to a testing 70m river crossing. This ford can only be attempted if it hasn't rained in 2 days.

Day 103. On board barge M-27. Notice the width of the river and unrelenting birch tree backdrop.

Day 194. About to be stung but the little Mexican boy steals the show..

Day 250. Our quarter millennium and our first photographed milestone.
We had driven over the equator on day 221 without realising.

Day 339. Second crossing of the equator showing the lone trials tyre that was the knobbliest rubber between all of us.

Day 342. Loading Louis' sparkless S8 onto a passing lorry. Although technically 'full', the truck's roof was a bus for a further twelve people.

Day 357. By now we had ditched all traces of tents instead using the two poncho/three bike arrangement that sleeps four.

Day 357. Our billionth puncture, the only advantage being that by now we had our repairs done in record time.

Day 360. Ethiopia was a world away from the jungle wilds of sub-saharan Africa. The quiet dignity and graceful independence of these Amharic people was strongly felt by all of us.

Day 402. Two years in the planning, over a year in the execution but suddenly, Mondo Enduro was all over.

It was a great relief to be out of the United States, out of the English speaking world and back to full on rough camping and adventure. It has been strange to go through such huge tracts of the USA that are such horrible prickly deserts. Yet as with the Canadians and the Alaskans, they just get on with making the best of it and don't let the geography get them down. We passed a road sign bearing the warning: "State Prison nearby – don't pick up hitchhikers".

The freeway was unusually fabulous. We're sure you couldn't make tarmac any smoother. A few passing cars tooted and waved, we are not sure if this has anything to do with the Union Jack that is flown from the rear of the bikes. We were filled with excitement about finally leaving the English speaking heaven that had suckled us since we landed at Anchorage 64 days ago. In fact, it was more apprehension as to whether we could cut it South of the Border or maybe we'd gone soft. By dusk this apprehension was festering into fear, and with this fear came irrational behaviour. Americans had been regaling us with horror stories about Mexican police corruption since we touched down in Anchorage. The suggestion was that we would be far more at risk to out and out robbery at gun-point than ever before. This was, of course, the official, sagely (and wrong) advice that had almost stopped us transiting Georgia and Azerbaijan 4 months ago; doom merchants, the enemy of travel.

After crossing the frontier at Nogales we were 30 miles inside Mexico when we were flagged down by some men in jeans and black T-shirts. They looked like roadies not policemen and here we were out in the desert, far from prying eyes. Crumbs, the Americans were fact-mongering not scare-mongering. Fearing the worst and expecting *Bandidos* we gunned the bikes and raced through their improvised roadblock. This certainly generated an arm-waving reaction from the men who, as we screamed past them (at 55mph), we realised had the words '*Policia Drogas*' screen-printed on the backs of their T-shirts. Crikey, they certainly were pretty informally dressed for law enforcement types. Anyway, our collective common sense was in a bit of a jumble, either way, we reckoned that staying on this road was inviting attention down the road apiece. Literally trembling with fright and cursing our inexplicable stupidity we pulled over ¾ mile later. We revved the bikes off into the scrub and down into a sandy *arroyo* which we doubled back down until we were all concealed in the culvert that took it under the road. Austin assured the team that we were now invisible to even a helicopter search but this news was of little comfort to his sweating co-riders. It was only 6pm and we were shaking too much to do anything. Austin revealed that he was totally homesick and missed the security of having Gerald around. Manly Clive calmed him and reminded us all how lucky we were to even be in this situation.

It was so very hot and we were all sweating like the Rojos at the end of 'A Fistful of Dollars'. The flies and insects sought us out and so the mosquito net went up and we cowered inside it. The insects had already made some preliminary bites, and so, swatting, scratching and sweating we faded into a dream packed sleep.

Austin's dream: He's sure his mind has never boiled as it did on this night. He was on a limb high up on an old Oak or Elm tree in his garden in Harrow Weald. His dad was urging him to climb down since he knew from prior experience that Austin wouldn't make it to the top. As Austin reached out for a spindly twig to haul himself up, the whole tree turned to a marshmallow type material which gave way beneath his flailing limbs. If only he had listened....

Mexico

Day 186
Monday 9 October
Mondo Miles today: 365
Mondo Mileage: 20080

We awoke from a fitful sleep disturbed by the bright glare of the waxing moon and the baying of wild dogs. Luckily no probing torchbeams of rigorous drug police search parties. We were out of the sandy creek bed in no time (thank heaven's for our trail bikes). We were still north of Hermosillo so we knew there was still distance to do but after 20 miles we pulled over at the first PEMEX petrol station for a spot of scrambled eggs and tortillas plus two foaming beakers of caffe con leche. They had a rough shower here which we relished and then a 3-tiered lorry load of pigs arrived. They were squealing like mad and the lorry driver hosed them down with water to make their cramped rumbling prison just a little more bearable. We were uncomfortable, but thanked our lucky stars that at the end of a long hard ride we were not electrocuted and served up in someone's breakfast burrito.

The day got hotter and hotter. Austin's cylinder head oil leak got more and more gushing and soon, after switching to shorts, his left shin was soaked in oil which in turn became caked in dust and dead flies. This veneer of filth at least would predicate against sunburn. The group grape flavoured chap-stik acted as the oral equivalent of his left leg and the on-going task of using a gloved digit to prise out the entrapped bugs soon became very boring.

We encountered several drug check-points this afternoon (which we stopped at!) and no residual steward's enquiry from last night. Phew. Getting in the *Mondo Enduro* (a phrase which seems to make partial sense in Spanish) story early in the encounter seems to help enormously. One official asked Chas if his wife was paying for this trip. As a window into the male Mexican psyche it was revealing indeed.

About 100 miles down the road, and in mounting desert heat, the trio pulled over. Chas and Austin to buy Coca Cola and Clive to wish his Mum many happy returns for her birthday (by telephone). There, amidst a bout of foolish banter with the barman, they espied a Kawasaki KLR passing by at high speed. It's rider nearly crashed at the shock of clocking our bikes and pulled over. And so we met James Wise, an Oregonian Latin American Studies student on route to Bogata, Columbia, where he was due to study law and history. We agreed to ride together for a few days and continued onwards through multiple toll booths and unremarkable desert wasteland.

We had the coastal town of Topolobampo as our ensuing objective, with the fanciful scene of a cool Fanta Fresa on a waterside balcony as reward for a sweaty day's endurance riding (NB the heat is far worse than Turkmenistan and virtually unbearable – no, totally unbearable).

Through Los Mochis and down to the town. The flies, mosquitoes and heat even in the dark, by the sea at 8pm, were absolute purgatory. We parked up at a quayside Discoteca and a self-confessed Jack Nicholson look-a-like offered to watch the bikes while we got be-tacoed. Our strict self-catering ethos has unravelled in the Americas. We must try and do something about that.

Twelve tacos and seven cokes later (30 Pesos) we had been bored by a German marathon cyclist we'd encountered. He had ridden down the Baja peninsula and just come across the Gulf of Cortez to the mainland. We were riven with recently absorbed Catholic guilt because we couldn't wait to get away from him. We failed to find a cool spot to camp so opted for the cemetery 3 miles out of town. The incessant crackling of the overhead HT wires, combined with the sweating made for a basically unpleasant experience. New friend James didn't seem to mind but seemed surprised that we had been doing this for six months and would be continuing to do so for the foreseeable future.

And so to bed in a spider, fly and mosquito blown patch of forgotten Mexico – not for the first time.

Mexico

Day 187
Tuesday 10 October
Mondo Miles today: 471
Mondo Mileage: 20551

6 o'clock on the dot the sun was up and so was Mondo Enduro + 1 (James Wise on his KLR).

We had camped just off Highway 1 which ended up being the most expensive toll so far with 56 pesos to get on and 56 pesos to get off.

We soon heard of the earthquake in the Colimar region and heard there were tremors in Puerto Vallarte. We were only slightly concerned as we knew Mondo Enduro had a long way to go– so we rested easy.

The day's ride was certainly a hard one with breaks only after 100 miles, instead of the standard 50. We rode into Puerto Vallarte having seen a devastating crash involving a white VW Beetle and a Datsun pick-up truck. Unfortunately there was a dead body in the driver's seat and a crowd surrounding the incident – we were waved on through by the local Policia. We headed to town and rather appropriately to "*La Playa Des Muertos*" – where we could sleep undisturbed!

Mexico

Day 188
Wednesday 11 October
Mondo Miles today: 38
Mondo Mileage: 20589

GRANOLA NOCHE

All awoke after a night's sleep on the beach which had so nearly been the scene of a bizarre death. A coconut weighing the same as a hefty rock had crashed to earth during the night narrowly missing James's bonce. Another day, another potential hazard avoided.

The morning was spent in the air-conditioned haven of McDonald's writing thank you postcards to AFAM and Suzuki USA and supping numerous coffee refills. The bikes parked up outside attracted huge attention from sundry trippers mostly of the American ilk. One invited us to stay at the holiday paradise close by where he was head chef but we politely refused thereby proving that beggars CAN be choosers.

A quick plunge in the tepid waters of the Pacific refreshed us briefly before we hit the road. Near to a village called El Tuito we overtook a VW caravette with British Columbia plates labouring up a hill. It was immediately suggested that we should camp together that night and so we met the Granola couple Shane and Katie. They were heading down to Panama City and were certainly of the tree-hugging persuasion but none the worse for that. Indeed Shane proved a dab hand in the kitchenette, knocking up an avocado and potato salad which was wolfed down ravenously by the usually carnivorous motorcyclists. Naturally our Oz friends made excellent company during a beautiful evening under the stars, spoiled only by the arrival of the local farmer who informed us that his land was the home of a large green insect whose bite could cause severe breathing problems. Ooo er... cough, splutter....

Mexico

Day 189
Thursday 12 October
Mondo Miles today: 325
Mondo Mileage: 20914

It was pretty grim last night as the full moon drove us crazy, the heat made us sweat, the strange and as yet unidentified bugs feasted on us (Clive got the first teeth marks from a Mexican tick) and our equipment became progressively more soaked from the remorseless condensation. Clammy as clammy could be. Yuck.

We made our farewells to the granola Australians and set off on yet another beautiful Mexican morning. Although past 10am it becomes totally unbearably hot out here, the period up until then is a lovely time to ride and often we are riding into the sun which makes for dramatic lighting.

At an early morning gasoline stop we purchased yoghurts with Granola oat flakes. The pretty senorita who served us from the kiosk sported a cheapo T-shirt that bereaved Mexican songstress 'Selena'. She was recently stabbed to death, allegedly by the president of her fan club, whose trial began last week in Phoenix amid a flurry of media interest carried over from the recent demise of the OJ Simpson case.

The scenery has become beautiful in the extreme with lush jungle hemming the road in on either side. The 120 miles from Manzillo became the most torturously twisty road that we could remember. Even mountain sections in Italy and Greece had not lasted for hundreds of miles and so, our rate of progress collapsed to an average of 30mph. As we rounded headlands we caught glimpses of 5 mile long sandy beaches stretched out before us. Not a single human artefact blemished the scene and in many respects it blew the Oregon and Californian coastlines into the weeds.

Supper was at a roadside tortilla shack in Caleta de Campos followed by Rum and Coke on a lovely beach campsite. At an hour into our repose James spotted a local niño nearby. We thought nothing of it and fell back to our Bacardi induced dreams.

Mexico

Day 190
Friday 13 October
Mondo Miles today: 265
Mondo Mileage: 21179

A great night's sleep was had all round, except for the little light handed visitors during the night which awoke James first and then Austin and Chas. Clive slept through the whole incident and only realised something was up when he discovered the mosquito net was full of mosquitoes and their little friends and there was a gaping hole at the foot end of the net.

Austin's shorts had been rummaged through and his wallet had been removed. We soon found it only yards away from our campsite peso-free and dollarless. Fortunately, the little *bandititos* had left all his plastic behind. The next surprise then came as a little boy made his way to our camp and informed us James's passport and money had been found and for him to come and fetch it. James was jubilant and set off immediately taking the little boy with him on his bike.

We then split up the group kit and broke camp around 10am. We stopped for fuel and a swim in Playa Azul and discovered from the Guatemalan Embassy in Mexico that we did not need a visa - but we shall wait and see.

We parted company with James soon after, as he headed to Cuernavaca to attend college for a month to improve his Spanish before he headed South again to Columbia. What an excellent sense of purpose. It hadn't occurred to any of us idiots to spend even a day on a Spanish course.

It was great fun having someone ride along with us and more importantly someone who effortlessly slipped into the rough at the edges Mondo Enduro modus operandii. We then rode for the remainder of the day except for a quick film stop of the Acapulco road sign. Clive and Austin rode ahead and were the first to arrive in the chaos of Acapulco.

The sun had set as we made our way through the Acapulcanian rush hour. The odds were far riskier than in London though, as there were numerous pot holes, sand splattered everywhere, and locals jaywalking; the latter were certainly not expecting determined motorcyclists to come tearing through the gaps in the traffic. Of course for Mondo Enduro it was tremendous fun. After battling with traffic for several miles the road met the main beachfront strip and we saw the spectacular *USS Kitty Hawk* anchored up in the bay looking more like a Christmas tree than an 88,000 tonne CV63 aircraft carrier.

Our room for the night was found by one of the friendly tourist police whose objective was to find us a room for 100 pesos with secured parking. And so it was *bienvenidos al* "Suites Diana".

Clive and Chas went out for some fun to a few local bars. Our chum Andy Bell would have been in his element here as our first bar was located in probably the seediest part of town – the road of which was the worst we had seen in the whole of Mexico. The bar had no door but a huge red curtain draped over the entrance. We were escorted in to our seats. The bar was entirely Mexican and so was the band. We stayed for one cerveza and got a

VW beetle taxi back to the main strip to the Club Tropicana at which a new experience was discovered of which Chas would like to describe:

George Michael and Andrew Ridgeley were not wrong when they observed that drinks were free in Club Tropicana. They were. And so were the favours of some dancing ladies whose charms had attracted the gaze of our two *muchachos*. Upon arrival we were ushered to our bar seats by an unctuous bartender who seemed desperate to ensure that our stay in his establishment would be a comfortable one. Two Tucumcari beers were swiftly ordered and arrived while a further pair were chilled in a miniature ice bucket. Our request for tequila was immediately met and several more free rounds appeared 'ere the conclusion of the evening's bizarre events.

As *cerveza* followed *cerveza* in a line of succession as uninterrupted as a Pharoaoric Dynasty, eyes began to roam in the gloaming of the sparsely populated bar. Clive, well versed in the occult arts of flirtation, clocked the two dancers who were stepping out and crooning to a series of bumptious Latin tunes. The ladies in question made up in youthful zest for what they lacked in the classical graces but could at least be credited with some imagination. One, a bogus blonde with a lithe physique underwent several costume changes before her ultimate metamorphosis as a sex kitten in the guise of Madonna circa 'Like a Virgin'. The other, whose inspiration came from the grand tradition of flamenco and the vulnerable Latin chartreuse, sported some tight corsetry and a fluffy black boa for a succession of excruciating ballads.

As the disco cranked itself up again after a floorshow which could not be called either competent or graceful, the dancers parked themselves in the adjacent table along with their somewhat ropey friend. Clive, ever the prime mover in such matters, made his blending intentions clear by fondling the crucifix suspended somewhere adjacent to Carla's navel. Chas, meanwhile, was embarking upon an earnest voyage of discovery into the dark vortex of pain, confusion and poor dress sense which was the soul of Gabriella.

The developing scenario was being viewed with some amusement by our escorts' friend, the bartender and a chocolate-skinned waitress who could have passed for Whitney Houston in the crepuscular light of the saloon bar. The reason for such hilarity, albeit restrained, was yet to reveal itself but as long as the Tucumcaris flowed in a seemingly endless torrent, the lads were past caring.

It was during a discussion about the nature of truth and journalistic ethics that Gabriella dropped a bombshell with an explosive load roughly equivalent to a Thousand Bomber Raid. Truth will out, as Shakespeare said, and the truth about Gaby was that she was a man.

Once this technical difficulty had been assessed, processed and put to one side, conversation flowed freely. Gabrielle talked openly about the hardships of the trans-sexual lifestyle in Mexico and invited Chas for a slow dance (accepted) while Clive encouraged him to place his sweating palm on her thigh (refused).

The theme of heterosexual men having the hots for vamped-up trannies has of course been recently explored in Neil Jordan's film *The Crying Game*. The fact is though, that Gaby was actually pretty tasty to the extent that Clive offered to swap her for Carla whose exquisite form was somewhat offset by heavy equine features. And there's more.

Gabrielle had bound Chas to secrecy about her true nature at least until the evening's end, and so he was unable to inform Clive as to her uncertain gender. Poor Clive. He was in a state of sorry confusion about the whole affair. Unhappy Chas, he was bound by a solemn oath not to spill these, even by Mexican standards, quite spicy beans.

And neither was Carla's sexual identity an entirely clear-cut issue. Gaby informed Chas that Carla was *una lesbiana* who lived with her. At the time of writing, the precise nature of their relationship is not entirely clear and is perhaps best left for analysis in the pages of some learned Kinseyesque academic journal.

And so the evening drew fitfully to a close leaving a load of intriguing memories. Gaby gave Clive a mischievous snog by way of farewell, and she bade Chas *adios* in a voice as husky as Fred Trueman's.

Austin had been sleeping throughout the entire evening and dreaming that we had had a puncture. We had of course been blown out in a more spectacular and memorable fashion. But, hey, this *is* Acapulco....

Mexico

Day 191
Saturday 14 October
Mondo Miles today: 26
Mondo Mileage: 21205

The day after the night before began late for Chas and Clive as they snoozed off heavy hangovers. Austin, however, was bright as a button after his customary ten hours' shut-eye and keen to hit a roadside *barranco* for the obligatory breakfast burrito.

His ambition was temporarily frustrated by the fact that his luggage was strewn all over the floor, requiring much gathering-up. While he performed these household tasks, Chas and Clive supped on milk from coconuts expertly hacked in the hotel yard.

It was alongside the burrito barrow that disaster struck in the guise of a flat back tyre. Repairs began in this most public of workshops, whilst the world and his wife, not to mention the kids and family pets too, looked on.

It was while the task in hand was already well advanced that Frederick, an aviation fuel technician from the *USS Kitty Hawk*, put in an appearance. He waited patiently for about two hours under the hot sun while Chas and

Austin toiled away before inviting us to tour the floating airbase which had been his home of two years.

This was too good a photo-opportunity to let pass and the hombres prepared for an hour-long round trip to visit this amazing Man' o' war parked ostentatiously in the centre of Acapulco Bay.

But luck had run out for Mondo Enduro on this occasion. The sheer weight of numbers of visiting Mexicans had forced the Navy Brass to suspend the tours. At least Austin got a clip of a towering black seaman the very incarnation of the YMCA 'cabin boy' fantasy.

The road out of town was the usual whacky races experience past Disco Beach and up into the bizarre shanty towns of Las Cruces. In fading light, and with forked lightning crashing into the hills ahead, Mondo Enduro brushed the dust off our 'cold call' technique and knocked on a farmer's door, requesting shelter under the corrugated steel of his front awning. The reader should rest assured that we were merely trying to get under this rain shadow lean-to, rather than blagging an actual entry to the farmhouse.

After hiding his coconut machete and consulting his miniscule wife, Francisco (for that was his name) was happy to oblige. After a dinner of beef n'bean soup, washed down with *refrescos*, at a nearby inn, the travellers turned in at the scandalously late hour of 9pm. Clive and Austin tucked up under the Mozzy net while Chas stretched out on the porch hammock – unnaturally comfortable actually. A brief tropical downpour disturbed their repose but all slept soundly.

Mexico

Day 192
Sunday 15 October
Mondo Miles today: 239
Mondo Mileage: 21444

We awoke to what seemed like an army of cockerels all keen to impress farmer Francisco by being the first to actually call out. Hence, as we rubbed our eyes clear of Acapulco road dust, bugs and smog particles, we realised that it was not in fact dawn, but several hours beforehand. However, seeing as we had bedded down at 21.00 last night we all lay half awake awaiting the 'real' dawn rather than this bogus chorus.

Chas, cheeky as ever, had bucked convention and slept in Francisco's hammock. Although his body had been conformed to a bendy arc, he claimed complete comfort and was therefore in accord with Clive and Austin who had slept on the hard packed dirt but each slept soundly. As Francisco emerged at 0600 to release the multi-coloured piglets from their pen we realised this was our cue to motivate and strike camp.

Francisco struck the pose (whilst seated) of a rural Generalissimo when he had his picture taken and during a spot of Hi-8 video filming he was unable to take his eyes off the camera despite Austin's exhortations to ignore it. So once more we were onto the ribbon of black top that stretches, snakes then stretches some more through the sea of green that seems to be this largely uncultivated jungle vastness of Mexico.

A word on the *pueblos* that we pass through. Often without warning the road turns to gravel and becomes heavily pot-holed. *Topes* (speed bumps) and *vibradores* (vibrators!) slow down the speeding through traffic if the craters don't and small *niños* weave across the way causing much sudden braking. The dust kicked up by the profusion of local vehicles batters our gringo faces and cakes our Nivea primed skin leaving us truly protected from the dreaded UV rays by a veneer of terra firma. Clive has likened many of the towns to those that he and Matt Farrell passed through in Central Africa. In many respects they are just like almost every Russian town we ever passed through save for the glaring difference of the amount of small time trade and commerce that these little Mexicans seem to get up to.

After a few more miles we rounded a rural bend and came across a non-Mexican struggling up a gradient with his heavily overloaded mountain bike. Nicholas Ruellan turned out to be French (from Nr Grenoble) and he knocked Mondo Enduro into a cocked hat having done France, Europe, Turkey, Middle East to Yemen. Then Bombay to China to Hong Kong. Then San Francisco southwards, destination Panama. He was offered a contact by way of the legendarily resourceful Dave Greenhough since Nicolas hoped to spend a week on bicycle admin in London at Christmas time prior to doing Dakarr back to Paris. Our encounter with him was very sobering and helped us to contextualise our possible delusions of being terrific trans-global adventurers.

We had lunch in another Wild West style town amid a dining area bedecked with ceramic fruit, garlands of glazed red peppers but most reminiscent of Svetlana's Alma-Ata flat; 3 porcelain swans (full sized), yellow, green and light blue. We were stiffed for 60 pesos for this meal.

We were 220 miles under our belt and only 18 miles from Puerto Escondido when the skies darkened and the suggestion was made that heavy rainfall was inevitable. We leathered up for the first time in 10 days. Austin, minus leather jacket long since lost in Northern Mexico, proudly donned our sponsor's apparel, the Suzuki Teflon tracksuit top.

The monsoon hit us for six within 4 or 5 minutes the roads were flooded, visibility was down to a few yards and our clothes were 100% saturated! Fortunately a PEMEX gasoline station loomed and its warm neon signs beckoned us to dryness and fuelness. A few miles later we made the first of several unethical hotel enquiries. We ultimately got room 107 for $90 and all fell asleep at 20.30 watching a late 60's Latino film, which seemed to co-star Mexicans and Pakistanis in equal measure.

Mexico

Day 193
Monday 16 October
Mondo Miles today: 170
Mondo Mileage: 21614

The weary Endurists awoke after an 11 hour deep sleep that deprived them of the previous evening's supper. They therefore justified the expense of the hotel by not eating.

Chas went off hunting for nuts and bolts whilst Clive and Austin headed for a post office and telephone bureau respectively.

Chas returned not with fastenings but with an Irishman by the name of Roderick Pearce on a Honda XL 650 dirt bike, who had been living in the port for 5 years after many years of travelling around the world. He was a builder by trade and had kindly offered Chas and the team the privilege of rummaging through his nut and bolt collection.

His plot, with two semi-finished large houses, was only 2 kilometres off the main drag along some dirt tracks but situated right next to the beach. One house was constructed of wood and the other of bricks and mortar. They were both huge and he had personally brought in and connected a mains electricity supply. The water for the plot was fed from a nearby well and he had fitted all the plumbing too.

He was single and in his early thirties and seemed to have done well with himself somewhere along the line between his extensive travelling. His motto of : "A set of traffic lights and I'm gone" (which we don't understand) would soon be tested as the port had a one-way system already and was set to become the next Acapulco. Roderick was a good egg and we hope he finds a soul mate out here.

By early afternoon we were on our way again ever southwards after a quick stills and Hi-8 shoot by Roderick of the Mondo Trio. We are constantly recruiting third party's to film us so that all of us can be in the shot.

The first fifty miles took us along mainly straight sections of reasonable tarmac to just before Huatulco on a bendy section of road in the hills. Whilst sitting peacefully in the shade of some trees by the roadside of this hilly section, the tranquillity was shattered by the screeching of brakes and tyres on the sweltering black top. Out jumped two Mexicans from a battered white Ford Taurus. The first was wielding a Kalashnikov assault rifle whilst his partner in crime was sporting a pair of extra dark Raybans and held a hand gun which he casually slipped into his waistband on his approach to Chas.

Meanwhile, the driver had placed a clapped out blue 'fuzz lamp' (á la Starsky and Hutch) on to the roof of the Ford and reversed up next to our bikes, hemming us in.

The three scruffy individuals claimed they were police and the one carrying the Klashnikov asked Austin for his passport to which Austin replied "Where's your ID first" whilst fingering his mace spray nervously. The subject was soon changed and we were questioned on whether we possessed drugs or firearms. Chas at this time had his Givi panniers open, whilst the darkest of the Mexicans wearing the Raybans searched aimlessly through his belongings.

The driver, who was the shortest and fattest of the bunch, eventually came over but kept himself to himself and just listened to the charade that was being acted out in front of him. In the meantime, our gun-ho Kalashnikov wielding adversary left Clive and Austin and went to flag down a passing charabanc. He jumped aboard forcing all the passengers off and shouting at the driver to open up the luggage holds. It's hard to say but if these guys really were undercover *Drogas Policias* they seemed to have not only a fairly haphazard style about them but a truly crap motor. The whole scene was a bit scary.

We then went for the official angle and pulled out our Suzuki tops from our bags to demonstrate that we were a Suzuki sponsored expedition riding around the world (which of course, we are not). They ignored us and feasted instead on the hapless bus passengers. We quickly gathered our effects and scarpered. As we pulled away Chas spotted a tin of our processed cheese left on the bonnet of the Taurus. It seemed best to hit the road and the cheese was ceded to The Man.

This was the first scenario of this kind to take place on Mondo Enduro and certainly won't be the last as we head further into Central and South America, but we were surprised that it could happen in Mexico. After this pulse raising experience we headed on towards Salina Cruz where the roads got wigglier and the scenery became more interesting. We decided a cold call was in order; as the light was fading rapidly and we preferred the security of someone's front yard to being out in the wild.

Supper in a cheap roadside restaurant was unusually mediocre and consisted of reheated barbecued chicken with a dollop of tinned spaghetti in tomato sauce with tacos and salsa. Our self catering ethos has withered away, so necessary in the restaurant free wildernesses of Russia but here, we are surrounded by handy roadside eateries. Dessert was marginally better; being cold rice pudding with grapes and cinnamon. After postcard and log writing we kicked our bikes into action for our humble sob story for the evening.

A mile down the road we saw an ideal target, a welcoming looking bungalow with a car parked in front with walls all round. The unsuspecting family was headed by Rudolfo at the arrival of our bikes by his front gates. He immediately offered his hand to us in greeting as Austin began explaining our needs and once his Spanish vocabulary was exhausted Chas picked up the story. He primarily recommended Alcoholics Anonymous next door as he had no spare beds. Austin then explained we just wanted to camp outside. A swift word to his wife of our venture and the gates were swung open to allow us inside.

Coffee was immediately served and we were shown to our hammocks to put our heads down for another Mondo blend snuggled down in Rudolfo's front garden. Viva Mexico!!!

Mexico

Day 194
Tuesday 17 October
Mondo Miles today: 190
Mondo Mileage: 21804

As is usual in such circumstances, the day began early for Chas and Clive in their hammocks and Austin on his fold-away table. But today there was no pig or cockerel to disturb their repose, only the rumble of passing trucks and Señor Rudolfo off to work at the boat engine mechanics' shop at the unconsciously early hour of 6am.

The *Jefe's* early departure deprived the team of an excellent video interview opportunity but perhaps more importantly – meant that he could not be thanked as fulsomely as he deserved for offering us the freedom of his front yard.

Fortunately, his primary school teacher wife Maria was still around to offer us Mexican hospitality at its most gushing. First coffee was served on the verandah followed by an invitation to use the family's spotless *baños*. As we prepared to leave, she detained us further by serving up an enormous breakfast of fried red snapper. Amid pledges of undying amity and the issuing of Mondo badges we finally made our getaway from this wonderful family which had shown us nothing but kindness. Thank you Maria and Rudolfo!

The road out of Selina Cruz rapidly disintegrated in places into a mass of crumbling tarmac and deep potholes. The rain clouds over the mountains of the Isthmus brooded ominously without ever breaking into a full-on sulk and the day actually became extremely warm, belying the early chill which had prompted a rare display of leatherwear.

The endless abrasion of the dodgy roads finally took its toll on Austin's front wheel at about 1pm. A horrific grinding noise and enormous friction soon revealed a set of shattered bearings just over the border from Oaxaca into Chiapas. Just when Lady Luck seemed to have hidden her alluring features behind a dark veil, salvation appeared in the guise of a Honda 175 motorcycle driven by Jorge and his *amigo sin nombre.*

As Austin removed one bearing with a rusty metal drift miraculously secured by our friend from a nearby smallholding, the scale of the task became clear. We would need not one, but six, new parts to ensure untrammelled motorcycling for one and all into Central America and beyond.

Chas and the two Mexicans set off for the nearby town of Arriaga and its wealth of Ferreterias and Refaccionadas. There, after an electrifying orange drink at Jorge's house, they headed straight for a surprisingly well stocked auto-parts store which carried precisely the required number of bearings. Oil also was purchased before a further expedition to the nearby cycle repair shop which happened to stock two 'Made in Thailand' 18 inch rear inner tubes (which are standard gauge not heavy duty).

After a brief return chez Jorge to collect some iced drinks, he and Chas made ready to return with their booty. At this stage Austin and Clive were carrying out necessary maintenance (new brake pads etc.) without realising that they were about to become the unwitting victim of a cruel jape orchestrated by Jorge.

Chas and he returned to the breakdown scene, pretending to be empty-handed. The hapless hombres looked on in despair contemplating a possible diversion to Oaxaca and South Mexico's sole Suzuki shop before the truth was revealed and scenes of unbridled joy and barely-restrained ecstasy.

Now, gentle reader, Chas, Austin and Clive are not metaphysicians eager to believe in a 'higher hand' or some such other mystic agency. That said, it has become abundantly clear we have a guardian spirit, a 'heaven's angel', if you will, who looks after our interests in times of difficulty. Consider the evidence: If the timely arrival of Jorge was not enough, Austin managed to drive nigh on 60 miles without suffering severe damage after forgetting to tighten up his rear wheel axle bolt. Then Clive dropped his Tupperware admin box only for Austin to collect its contents, including major credit cards and his electronic "brain", from *la carretera.* And if that wasn't enough, there was no-one working at the toll road booths at Tonala so we rode through for free, *muy misterioso...*

But the clincher for the sceptical trio was the evening's accommodation – none other than a Nestlé powdered milk powdering plant close to Pijijapan, whose benign Jefé Carlos welcomed us with promises of plentiful *cafe con leche* (we presumed powdered). He allowed us to pitch our mosquito net under the awning of the loading bay adjacent to the glistening stainless steel of the pasteurising equipment. Many of the tubs and vessels were adorned with a heavy sprinkling of a mutant strain of giant Latino cockroach. They seemed to be attracted by the overpowering stench of sour milk which hangs in the clammy air like a Mexican miasma. Jefé Carlos ushered us to a primitive shower which we gladly availed ourselves of. During Austin's ablution a chunkster Tarantula was discovered clambering along the shower head and the cubicle was duly abandoned at speed. After tapas and blackcurrant Fanta in a wayside taverna, the travellers consulted maps and guidebooks to find out exactly what will await us in Guatemala. Mexico has been great. Endless beautiful beaches, great food, alluring women and kindly people. But another day, another visa stamp, let's make sure the mossie net is tucked *well* under the groundsheet...

Mexico / Guatemala

Day 195
Wednesday 18 October
Mondo Miles today: 195
Mondo Mileage: 21999

Who could have imagined, as we fought off the billions of sub-mosquito-net-aperture-sized midges, which the end of this day's motoring would take us to the brink of our 22,000 mile climax. The mileage so notable since from the day Austin and Clive bothered to get out Dave Greenhough's schoolboy atlas and work out how far we'd notionally have to drive on Mondo Enduro, 44,000 miles was always the agreed estimate. So today saw us close to *Medio Enduro*.

Anyway, the smell from the partially cleaned milk pasteurisation equipment at the recently dubbed 'Hotel Nestlé' didn't really affect our sleep, in fact all of the team woke at dawn well rested (despite the heat, sweat and bugs) and ready for the day's task of (a) making it to the Mex/Guat border and (b) crossing it without undue expense or aggro. For the reader too bored to make it to the end of this entry it can be logged that (a) was successful while (b) was not.

We were surprised, after yesterday riding on the worst roads thus far in Mexico, that the 100 miles into Tapachula was gorgeous dual carriageway and toll-free to boot. We blasted along and by 10.30 were at the less frequented border crossing near the village of Talisman.

A long sweeping curve descending a valley side took us down to the river that served as the frontier. Our blazing headlamps make us quite visible and so it was un-surprised that we witnessed about 10 youths sprinting out from a café as we approached. They looked for the entire world like they had been naughty and were being chased out by the irate proprietor. However, this being border country, they were racing out so as to apprehend us before any of the other improvised money changers that loitered around the border post could do so. It was quite ridiculous. Even before we had stopped, we were thoroughly beset by kids offering "me watch" and Mexicans and Guatemalans brandishing drug baronesque wads of Guatemalan *Quetzales*! The 'running' chaps got there last and didn't have a hope. Even while we sat astride our bikes, clearly showing no sign of alighting, small boys continued to offer to guard the bikes. Their persistence eventually gave us to imagine that there was a spectre looming, needing much vigilance that we as yet were blissfully unaware of.

We spent the last of our Mexican Pesos on a tepid bowl of shrimps, noodles and rice and a pineapple soft drink that is worth mentioning as it was so tasty.

We hooked up with a Chinese looking chap who we engaged as our 'fixer' and later learned he was named Michael and was Guatemalan. We should have suspected something was amiss from his yellow rinsed 'rock washed' jeans he so proudly sported. Even this far away from the nearest copy of Esquire, Mondo Enduro would normally have no truck with such a fashion sin.

The first bad news was that since we were *not* planning to bring the motorcycles back into Mexico we had to have our custom's dockets cancelled in a particular way. Naturally enough, not here at the border but at a place called Viva Mexico 15 miles back the way we had come. This illogical siting of the custom's booth was our first wrinkle with Mexican bureaucracy which in fairness had proved quite specifically very efficient over the last two weeks. Michael, our new red tape dissolver, knew where the exact location was so we about turned and drove back. To ensure no geographical embarrassment Austin left his panniers with an old crone selling border tacos and Michael rode pillion to point out the route. To ensure Mondo Enduro received his fullest co-operation he was treated to a high speed cornering and over-taking display with an option on driving down the hard shoulder to steal in front of HGV's. On our return, all stamped and cancelled (no charge) Michael alighted and jelly-kneed sighed to his friend about the joys of motorcycling.

A swift Mexican exit stamp later and it was over the toll bridge to the Guatemalan formalities. The toll was US $1 per person but we ended up paying US $5 each instead. This discrepancy did not come to light until later and it was our new *amigo* Michael who had pocketed the $12 difference.

We parked in a yard off the main drag and then Austin went with Michael to the officials' grotto to get all the passports stamped etc. The prices for the duties/entry permits were not posted anywhere and it soon became clear from Michael's fraternising with the *Migracion* dons that they were negotiating *uno tarifo especial* for Mondo Enduro. This wasn't a discount of course, but a special bump up for these easily led two-wheeled gringos. It is shameful to record that we ultimately paid US $30 each for the privilege of entering Guatemala. The perks for this whopping expenditure included Chas being formally entered as an Irish citizen, in *several* places on his Immigration docket and Austin cheesily being re-named Austin Vice. The only consolation from this highway robbery was that the *i*'s were dotted and the *t*'s crossed on our paperwork and it was all done really very quickly.

As we prepared to leave, Michael approached us and politely asked for his fee, the $5 we had agreed earlier on. He was left with only the whiff of our exhausts as we kicked over and headed off along highway GA2 Eastwards. Rest assured that it was still Mondo Enduro that was left with the bitter after taste (add to this whole experience the $3 parking fee we got lumbered with in the yard – *locked* in until we paid up – we couldn't believe we'd been on the road a full 195 days – saps!).

The weather was turning bad and our first yards into Guatemala were accompanied by as many drops of rain. We pulled over and water-proofed all the kit but more sadly we just bitched and griped about being fleeced at the border. Morale was low.

Within 30 miles of conspicuously poorer roadside communities we were dealing with Chas's second puncture in a short while. In went a new tube as we worked swiftly under the awning of the 'Guardroom' of a large banana plantation that we took repair-refuge in. The huge-jawed farm manager was our first encounter with the race of people down here who are clearly of Iberian as opposed to Mayan extraction. Such a racial class divide amongst people that all consider themselves the same nationality is quite disconcerting. This jaw man chap gave us some travel advice, but despite our blatant hints about camping out in the bush, he didn't offer us a place in the garage as we might have hoped. At 5pm we set off again not prepared for what lay ahead.

The weather closed in, the rains came, but worst of all the entire road deteriorated. Huge trenches and craters riddled the roadway for many miles at a time. Mud from rain wash turned what tarmac remaining into a greasy slime that was more treacherous than usual as we dodged and weaved between the erratically dodging and weaving trucks, cars and buses. The relentless rain sapped morale and at a gas station we photographed our sodden selves.

We were right royally pissed off but just when we were in danger of feeling sorry for ourselves the weather cleared and we took steps to secure a 'front garden blend' for the night.

One address that seemed very suitable turned out only to have a small girl in residence who came to within 5yds of her locked gate to inspect us, but ventured no further.

Next door a one storey building with a large front yard seemed highly suitable. We parked up on the highway verge and ventured down a dirt ramp to encounter the householders and make our introductions. We were greeted by Sandra (who looked like Lorretta Vince, one of Austin's sisters) and Irene, her toothless and trouser wearing grandma.

These two, with no male presence evident (the "lying in the hammock" shift must have just been changed) gave us far more of a vetting procedure than we were used to. We explained that we sought no entry to their house and only wanted a patch of earth to lie on, but they kept up their questioning. Through our broken Spanish they also made it clear that they expected to be allowed to stay with us when they came to England. Austin asked if the whole family would travel (we were by now surrounded by an extended dynasty of about 10 people) but they didn't detect any of the British irony that had been offered to them.

Grandma Irene then tugged our sleeves, lead us all back up to the highway and along the verge to a rude shack reminiscent of a Russian candy-booth. An awful scene then developed whereby she made it clear that she wanted us to buy about $24 worth of Coca-Cola in lieu of a night's rent. Chas was faced with the delicate task of suggesting that we weren't prepared to do this. She charmlessly acquiesced and settled for 6 cans worth 4 dollars.

Sandra then became a most congenial hostess but alarmed Mondo Enduro with her poker-faced tales of US citizens travelling the highway nearby just to steal Guatemalan babies and take them back to the States for sale. She also told of Red Cross crews collecting blood so fervently that the donors were "drained" and soon died of blood loss!! We fell asleep at about

9pm but not without first concealing Sandra's smallest son in one of the panniers.

Guatemala

Day 196
Thursday 19 October
Mondo Miles today: 129
Mondo Mileage: 22128

We awoke to both trucks trundling by only yards away and the chorus of farmyard animals squawking at the unearthly hour of 5.30am.

It had been a bug free night and therefore a cherished sleep was had by all: which also meant plenty of dreaming by all. From Clive being bitten by a rattlesnake and lashing out at the table Austin was sleeping under, to Austin crashing a Mill Hill School Minibus somewhere in Mexico that was under James Shekleton's (old school-mate) supervision.

Sandra's husband saw us in the flesh for the first time and fortunately had not minded that we had slept the night under his veranda. Grandma Irene was topless washing her hair and the rest of the family was milling around in the morning dew.

Before we set off, we got the family together to have a group photo. Little daughter Sonya was dressed up to the nines in a cute red dress outshining her other sisters in their dirty shabby frocks. We don't know if Sandra has arranged this especially or if this particular daughter has an unusually well developed sense of grooming. Breakfast of bananas, cakes and natural home made hot chocolate (delicious) was handed out to us before we finally scrambled up their driveway back on to the main drag. Thank you Sandra!

The first fifty seemed like an eternity with the awful roads and numerous road works taking place. Stopping for a banana and a slug of water and we headed off again.

Clive and Austin had lost sight of Chas soon after the first break abut were having great fun undertaking and overtaking the huge lines of stationary and then slowly moving traffic. We were weaving in and out of the traffic, dodging potholes and oncoming vehicles and sped our way to the second 50 in no time at all... no sign of Chas though.

Clive and Austin waited an hour until 10 in case he had been caught up in the roadworks or had minor maintenance to carry out. Still no sign.

Austin headed off for the final 30 to check in at the British Embassy in the capital, Guatemala City. He hoped to get the low down on the rest of Central America. Meanwhile, Clive was to slowly retrace his tracks to find Chas and help him out of his misdemeanour if there was one. RV's were made of 2, 4 and 8pm outside the British Embassy and if not phone messages were to be left back at base camp Bournemouth.

Clive found Chas 17 miles back with his back wheel off and the bike being supported by his Givi panier. It was the dreaded puncture that plagued Chas three times in the last 48 hours. The tyre was damaged and already had 2 repairs on it so it was the end of the road and into the bushes for this Avon Gripster. The spare that was to go on had been purchased two days earlier for $5 from Jorge in Mexico. It was an old off-road tyre but would more than suffice for Chas' needs till he got a new tyre in Guatemala City.

The old tyre was changed over and the repair effected in reasonable time. Thanks are due to these chaps working in the nearby field who downed tools and rushed to Chas' aid.

Meanwhile, Austin had arrived at the embassy and was doing his best to get tuned in. Quite what we think we are doing by reporting to these British missions is rather vague. Maybe the unbelievable explosion of hospitality afforded us back on day 46 at the UK Embassy in Tashkent has given us a skewed sense of why the Foreign and Commonwealth office exists. Could it *really* be to help us facilitate our holiday?

The air conditioned foyer of the embassy was a treat. Austin was trying to market himself as a harmless and rosy cheeked boy scout but then he glimpsed himself in a mirror and saw only a sweating fiend. The early exit from the tarantula shower three days ago meant that he was still filthy but hadn't realised. The vice-consul, David Harvey, was extremely courteous and thankfully didn't send Austin away. Far from it, Austin was backstage in no time and being introduced to Colonel David Farrant. Austin resisted the temptation to address this man as *el Colonel* a situation side-stepped by *el Colonel* insisting he be known by his first name.

In a bid to ingratiate himself Austin quickly revealed that he was a former army officer but didn't extend his briefing to include the fact that he hated the military with every breath in his body and the 06000 he'd spent buying himself out was small price indeed. Nay, all this was left at the door but in fairness *el Colonel* was far more civil and approachable than any staff officer Austin had served under while in the Green Machine and indeed, when Mondo Enduro were invited to crash at the Colonel's gaff *este noche* Austin enthusiastically agreed on behalf of his co-riders. Hurrah for the old school tie!!

Chas and Clive turned up and David Farrant took us back to his lovely house in a luxurious gulley named La Canada. This was clearly part of the swanky end of the city and was a world away from the humble jungle community that had hosted us last night.

After the vital ablutions David explained that he was the defence attaché, which for a Central American republic was extremely unusual. He is the only European D.A. in the city. The rough idea was that Uncle Sam had been sticking his nose in a little more vigorously than was helpful over the last fifty years. The eighties, and Reagan in particular, had been a time of unfettered interference in Guatemalan affairs, most of which seemed to be in the form of guns'n'ammo rather than tried and tested missionary schools and agriculture programs. Colonel Farrant's brief from Whitehall was to help democratise the Guatemalan military. There was a suggestion that the still, small (but definitely British), voice of calm in the Latin shell-like could be more useful in achieving the aim than the noisy clanging gong of American imperialism. They were a group, or *junta*, who were unused to the idea of a politically neutral armed forces and *el colonel* was here to suggest that if their elected politicians were crap, that was cool. Because a society cowering under the spectre of endless military intervention was uncool. Mondo immediately concurred and raised a toast of chilled beer to our host's softly-softly hearts and minds campaign.

An amazing spag bol supper and more brews with Vice-Consul David Harvey at a bar called *el establo*. David put us all to bed in the rooms normally designated for his children. They weren't really children since two of his daughters were fully developed adult females. Pictures of them adorned the bedside tables and they were beautiful. The family photos saw us sobbing into our pillows as we were reminded of the class of A-list English rose that was out of our league.

El Colonel Farrant wrote these words in this log;

I met Austin Vince at the British Embassy in Guatemala City when he first called in. I thought that underneath the oil stubble and general grime I could detect someone who would clean up reasonably well – and so it was! I am delighted to have been able to feed and shower and give beds to the 3 remaining Mondo Enduro members and wish them all lots of luck.

David Farrant (British Defence Attaché)
2.10.95
La Canada
Guatemala City

Guatemala / El Salvador

Day 197
Friday 20 October
Mondo Miles today: 120
Mondo Mileage: 22248

Fate is a strange bug-eyed monster and the *hombres* had time to reflect upon this fact as they awoke in Hugo Farrant's well-appointed bedroom.

In the cupboard was a Fender bass guitar; the bedside table was well-stocked with Sega megadrive and teen magazines. All the paraphernalia of a fifteen year old public schoolboy seeking to make his mark on the world. The contrast with our kindly but ever-so-slightly grasping and definitely Americano phobic hosts of the previous evening could not have been more stark.

Breakfast was served in the dining room by saintly Maria the maid: freshly squeezed orange juice, filter coffee, assorted cereals and Brown *Bimbo* toast. A revolving wooden tray meant that the condiments – an impressive array of Anglo-American preserves, marmalades and the invincible Marmite – could be passed with ultimate indolence.

If there was a cloud on our collective consciousness that fair morning, it was of the gastric variety and would probably, under scientific analysis, have been found to contain large concentrations of methane. We were all suffering to a greater or lesser extent from *Guate Squate* – that uncomfortable dysfunction of the gastro-enteric tract probably brought on in our case by Jorge's ancient shrimps or unusual jungle bacteria dormant in Sandra's hot chocolate.

Even carefully synchronised dashes to one of David's three luxurious bathrooms could not exhaust the sense of wonderment and relief we felt in this little corner of England, where the grass, watered by the tropical rains, actually *was* greener. Signed photos of Charles and Diana, happy snaps of beautiful daughters and antique maps and paintings all depicted a life of material plenitude and spiritual good order. As if the horn of plenty was not already overflowing, David handed out free cans of 10W-40 racing oil, NATO issue insect repellent and endless plastic bags.

And so we left David's gaffe. An Englishman's home is his castle and, in his case, this really was true. Metal gates, a two-way radio, armed guards and video cameras meant that his personal Eden could only flourish in an atmosphere of high profile security. Still, we were willing prisoners who found it hard to leave an exquisitely padded cell. Thank you David Farrant!

On the road out of Guatemala City we stopped to gas up at a Texaco station, before heading apace for the border. Guatemalan border formalities were complicated, involving several visits to various offices for apparently pointless stamps all of which cost hard cash (150 quetzales or 30$US). As we crossed the bridge into El Salvador, we carried with us some graceless thoughts about Guatemala and the apparently bottomless well of petty corruption and silly bureaucracy.

El Salvador had been depicted by Vice-Consul David Harvey as a country where the *bandidos* shoot first then rifle wallets afterwards. In fact the border procedures although long-winded were quite simple and made more so by José, a 14-year old fixer who handsomely deserved his $3 tip. He had a completely new disposition; as if he were a distant relative pleased to help rather than a wily trickster in cahoots with the Carabinieri. The aura of the winds of integrity continued with frontier officials beaming an honest smile and a sign (in English) extolling: "*Please do not offer me a tip, I will do my job properly without it.*" Armed with 60 day vehicle permits, and a 30 day visa, we were on our way into a new country with change from US $7 plus tips.

After about 50 miles, it became clear that the bad press written about El Salvador was without basis in truth. We saw a country of breathtaking beauty and full of life. On every horizon were the dramatic peaks of extinct volcanoes.

In the fading light we headed off the impressive Pan-American highway for the Lago Coatepeque – a wide clear-blue lake filling a huge seismic bowl in a necklace of volcanoes. It was one of those 'Mondo Moments' when each rider just had to drop gears, pull over and gaze in wonderment....

The lakeside itself was a bizarre mix of flash, top-security dwellings and bogus, slightly unhygienic hovels. It was beneath a fortuitous lamp-post that Chas pulled over having felt the dreaded back wheel wobble which is the sure harbinger of a flat tyre.

Watched by several curious Salvadorians, one of whom happily had a flashlight, the bogus Chinese knobbly bought from Jorge was swapped for a spanking new Yokohama cat's paw trail tyre purchased in Guatemala City. A large Salvadorian nail had been the culprit, and the gash in the tube was equally gigantic. With the second new Mexican (but made in Thailand) inner in his new tyre, Chas was ready for some serious off road action.

Bed was a parking lot next to the police station where a Mariachi party seemed to be in a state of perpetual progress. Our fragile stomachs filled by a meal of mashed beans, cheese and cream plus hefty tortillas, we drifted away into dreamland with the waters of the lake lapping the shore just a few yards away.

Joke for the day:

Q: What do you get if you cross a drum kit with the Mondo diary?
A: A Logarhythm

El Salvador / Honduras

Day 198
Saturday 21 October
Mondo Miles today: 175
Mondo Mileage: 22423

Austin dreamed last night that he was walking through Washington DC with a pretty girl (of unknown origin) whilst the rehearsals for this year's Nuremburg rally took place. It transpired that she knew two of our friends, Andy Bell and Chris Turner who both lived in an old Georgian building somewhere in London. At the end of the dream Liam Watson arrived in his new Mini bearing the Kaiser's third LP. It was pressed onto crystallized sugar, like seaside "rock" and was cellophane wrapped with free button badges enclosed, each of which featured a face of the 7 Kaisers.

So we struck camp at 0630 but not before shelling out a dollar to a small boy for us sleeping on his Dad's patch of earth. We visited the lake intruded upon by so many four star private jetties. Here we saw two boys preparing their harpoon guns, either to go fishing or to re-enact their fave moments from 'Thunderball'.

As we exited along the dirt track that runs along the periphery of the volcano's lake, the weird delineation between rich and poor on either side of the track struck us all the more, now that there was daylight.

We did a spot of filming on the approach out of the crater and took advantage of the fact that much of what yesterday evening was in shadow, due to the sunset, was now bathed in light.

A few miles later and we were out onto the most superb road since Mexico. We were riding along CA1, the actual Pan American Highway. Needless to say, this highway is only an idea/sentiment, not a cohesive and complete work of Civil Engineering. We would find in El Salvador the best roads so far, including this four-laned section, beautifully asphalted and conspicuously well signposted.

We rode almost directly into the rising sun and while the latter was low, our spirits were high after an induction into tiny El Salvador that has after only one evening left us with a fabulously warm impression. The bitterness and envy that seemed to flavour things in Guatemala appeared to have vanished. However, some things, as viewed from our fur covered seats, remained quite definitely the same.

The old US school buses that form the bulk of the privately run bus services, are as evident here as in Guatemala and Mexico. They are richly painted, often with airbrushes yet laden with detailed pictures of life down here in Central America. They are totally packed, with the aisle holding as many jammed in vertically as are seated. With the front door open a youth hangs on and acts as both conductor, traffic controller and enthusiastically screaming the intended destinations, also as human advertisement for the coach line. The rear windows of these buses often mount A3 sized day-glo transfers of either Jesus Christ or the Blessed Virgin. The blue-green sun visor is regularly embossed with Christian slogans such as "Jesus loves you" or "God knows everything" to keep the driver morally correct as well as undazzled.

It was only 7.40am when we turned off the pan-Am and took a little diversion up a side road. We were acting on a tip off from the El Salvadorian Tourist Official about a recently discovered set of Mayan ruins. What made these unusual is that this particular site had been buried in lava from one of the many mini-volcanoes that dominate the scenery in Guatemala and El Salvador. Hence, the find was being described as the Pompeii of Central America.

Up the side road we encountered huge lava beds that looked weirdly like Sci-Fi industrial waste deposits. Incongruously, opposite these beds was what passed for the San Salvador Grand Prix circuit. There was a main entrance and a little further along, a special slip road clearly marked as being only for the drivers and pit crews. However, this elitist ingress was only a muddy and ash soaked track that seemed to meander lazily through the bushes and hardly seemed to lead anywhere.

Slightly adjacent to the San Andres ruins was a huge rolling lawn about the size of a hockey field. A small sign demanded that no baseball or football was to be played on it. It was amusing therefore, to see a local family, arriving as we were departing, unloading from their car *several* footballs and baseball bats.

We reconvened as motorcyclists and headed off towards the suburbs of the capital, San Salvador. A brief stop at a huge Esso gas station saw us encountering no less than 3 pump action shot gun tooled up security guards. These guys reminded us of the chaos that was Georgia and the notion that only a few years ago El Salvador was the showcase of Central American meltdown. Nationwide, there is a palpable air of optimistic reconstruction. Let's hope they make it.

Our loose objective was to get over the El Salvador/Honduras Border before the end of business today. It was only 160 miles away and so even given time for the stamp-fest we'd doubtless suffer, it was still quite feasible.

In the cauldron of the capital's traffic system the well signposted Pan American just petered out and the *placas* we now saw were not for places but for Wendy's, Burger King and a fast food chain simply called 'BIGGEST'. With the chaos and congestion on the roads it wasn't long before we didn't really know where we were and Chas had got separated from Austin and Clive. Fortunately we came across each other on the east side of town and so continued the ducking and diving procedures that constitute beating the traffic out here. Austin's panniers were hit during a collision with the front of a bus at the climax of a particularly ill thought through undertaking manoeuvre. The panniers were partially ripped open making it their second flesh wound since the old woman was impacted in Northern Turkey (day 34).

The miles ran away and by 4pm we were meandering between the parked HGVs on the El Salvador/Honduras border. The last mile of the Pan American disintegrated into a huge slop of mud, rubble and undrained water. On our approach run the first of the bureaucracy fixers bolted out from a shack and with his tooth-rotten smile introduced himself (via his Honduran ID) as "Denys Ramon".

We slid through the thankfully honest El Salvador departure formalities with ease, but not without the help of another young administration elfkin who danced an intricate quickstep from desk to desk in the 1950's run Customs Office.

Things turned sour once we had bade farewell to the Salvadorian officials and cruised over the bridge that marks the frontier. A surly Honduras policeman barked at us to hand over our driving licences. He lectured to us about road safety and said he was going to write us a ticket for not wearing our crash helmets as we approached his country. Chas actually had been wearing his but this didn't seem to affect the overall bad impression that Mondo Enduro had made on him so far. He marched off with our pre-war style international driving licences and Denys Ramon urgently beckoned us to follow him.

There now ensued a veritable gauntlet of bent officials; the difference between each of them being only how casually they displayed their wholly corrupt approach to Gringo Transit. We ultimately were robbed of $50 each for the privilege of our 100 mile drive across this little inland isthmus of Honduras. We kicked and screamed but as Gerald Vince would say "It did no good".

We emerged from the Honduran formalities at 6.45pm. It was dark and a rainstorm came and went. We camped down a track but were too tired to erect a shelter. It began to pour about 2 hours after we went to sleep. We whacked up a double poncho but us and our gear were soaked before the erection was complete. We drifted into tomorrow plugging leaks in the nylon and talking about Austin's time at Sandhurst...

We had a multiple stamped chit, issued in addition to our actual customs documentation. We need to produce one of these slips *each* to actually get out of the border compound. Most frustratingly after paying <u>so</u> many bribes to the Honduran officials, the plod on the exit barrier had gone home by the time we left!

Honduras / Nicaragua

Day 199
Sunday 22 October
Mondo Miles today: 245
Mondo Mileage: 22678

We were up early due to our sleeping gear being wet from last night. The trusty poncho is a fickle friend and clearly doesn't lend itself to being used as a tent if poorly erected.

Mattock totin' Hondurans ambled down the track en route to another day of back-breaking *trabajo*. They seemed sullen and depressed. Is that because it's 0730hrs on a Sunday morning or is it an expression of national angst that comes from life in the tropics. We bade them "buenas dias" but they shot back a steely stare that made it clear that as far as they were concerned the dia wasn't that bueno.

Under leaden skies we rolled up at the border town of El Espino. We feared that it might even be closed on the Sabbath but at 0800hrs we weren't disappointed. Only a handful of 'fixers' were in attendance and Sebastien was recruited almost immediately because of his resemblance to Franco Nero. He led us on the customs waltz and within no time we were being stung by repeated charges from every official we encountered. This blizzard of petty theft was climaxed with a $30 'charge' coming from the inspectorino type guy.

At this point, Chas, with his ever improving Spanish, snapped. He actually started arguing with the Don and superbly, in a foreign language, made a representation that this process was doing untold damage to the reputation of Honduras in general, and its uniformed agents in particular. Chas managed to expand on this idea to bring in the notion that wearing said uniform made the migracion officials elevated guardians of their nation's integrity and that any abuse of their position had substantial ramifications for the very notion of the civilised society. Viz, if you can't trust los federales then who can you trust? The charge was lowered to $2 and the wonky barrier rose. Little Sebastien was punching the air when we emerged from the customs shack and we gave him $10 in our jubilance. It was a high point of Mondo Enduro.

We are now in Nicaragua and heading for an unusual blend. Here is the preamble; Austin has a colleague at Mill Hill called Trevor Chilton, a biology teacher and indeed celebrated author of A-level textbooks. Trevor has two claims to fame in our eyes; attending a gig by fledgling psychedelic freak-beat combo The Pink Floyd in his college bar in 1967 and having a Nicaraguan wife. Recently graduated, Trevor was sent out here in the early seventies on an Oxford University sponsored survey of coniferous trees. Quite simply because the Pinus Oocapa indigenous to this area is a hardy strain regarded as the Burt Reynolds of pine trees. Trevor's year long placement was spent mostly collecting and studying pine cones alongside Julio Moya, Nicaragua's foremost arbrologist. Every day Trevor would collect Mr Moya from his home and they would soon be scrambling through the woods, tape measures and notebooks at the ready. These daily visits were no chore for young Trevor since they afforded a chance to glimpse Mr Moya's daughter Marcia, a bundle of smouldering Latin temptation. In no time Trevor had fallen in love and they were married soon after. Marcia took the plunge and went to live in Mill Hill with her new beau. However, she never forgot her roots and strong links were forged between the young Trevor and his in-laws in the capital city Managua.

So right now we are heading towards the Managua home of Marcia Chilton's mother and father Lila and Julio Moya (retired) and her brother René. Result!

Nicaragua

Day 200
Monday 23 October
Mondo Miles today: 0
Mondo Mileage: 22678

Our two hundredth day began early as usual amidst the shrieking of small children the frolicking of 'Black', the Moya's charming and predictably coloured puppy. The sounds of a Latin easy-listening cassette which would play for most of the day, cranked slowly into life.

The soulful melodies of the Nicaraguan pop music, sung in rich tenor voices, would provide the soundtrack for a day of lazy endeavour. After a breakfast of eggs sunny side up served with bread and a curious smoked cheese, we lazily faced the rigours of a humid morning.

For Clive, the task in hand was a major tyre overhaul. The bogus rear 'Sport Flite', purchased second-hand in Portland, Oregon, finally stripped out to reveal bare canvas and demanded replacement. Both it and the front end Gripster, a trusty friend since England, were swapped for the new tyres provided by Orange County Suzuki. A spoke check, plus a double squirt of magic 'puncture-buster' goo, and Clive could claim, with total justification, to be back on the plot in mechanical terms.

Austin pottered around Managua whilst Chas did little all day except visit the market with René and get his Caterpillar boots and leather trousers repaired. The bazaar in question was a self-contained explosion of Latin-American life in all its multifarious forms. Stalls selling "*Selena – Un Homenage*" tee-shirts, American shampoos and leather products groaned under the weight of merchandise. Various broths and compotes bubbled away in large metal vats.

The scale of Chas' inactivity can be judged by the fact that he read 300 pages of an American pulp fiction book called 'The Hot Zone' detailing the emergence of certain haemorrhagic viruses which turn human flesh into a putrid soup. This apocalyptic novel is clearly the basis of the recent movie called 'Outbreak'. Could it be a total coincidence that the front page of "La Barricada" told of an '*Apocalyptica Peste*' – or outbreak of Dengue in the city of Leon which had struck down 190 people and killed four? Clive nervously examined the contents of our medical kit by way of an insurance policy.

A long, hot and sultry afternoon was enlivened by the arrival of Julio, René's elder brother, and his *amigo sin nombre*. Julio was a man of suppressed anger and high intelligence who ran the Martin Luther King Association in the nearby barrio de San Judas. He had crystal clear pale blue eyes that burned with a sense of purpose gleaned from living through two long decades of CIA fuelled national turmoil. For us pasty Brits he was the very embodiment of every pain suffered by the Nicaraguans in the seemingly endless friction of the boiling tropical cauldron of Central American politics. He had written a report outlining the need for a community action centre, underwritten by a Dutch charity, in a suburb where all social structures seem to be in a state of rapid disintegration. Child prostitution and crime is rife, along with an unemployment rate of over 70%. Heavily armed *campaninos* have been arriving from the North, where renegade Contra groupings are still active, substantially increasing the danger quotient.

By way of a theatrical gesture designed to highlight the depths of the crisis, he revealed two war wounds sustained during service in the Sandinista army.

Dinner was kidney beans and rice, salad and small meat burgers, sluiced down with Coca Cola bought from a nearby store. It is a fantastic privilege to be here in Managua where the Moya family has made us welcome in such spectacular fashion. It is extremely sad that we have to contemplate a premature departure on the morrow to make up time lost in a tripartite Panamanian bank holiday next week.

Nicaragua

Day 201
Tuesday 24 October
Mondo Miles today: 96
Mondo Mileage: 22774

The pages of this log and its predecessors have been full of recordings of the unusual noises, sights and experiences that have awoken Mondo Enduro in various campsites and bed spaces around the world. We thought that yesterday a.m.'s Latin-a-go-go soundtrack could not be surpassed for sheer irritability blended with genuine Central American flavour. As usual, we pre-conceived incorrectly and at 0500 came the first of what in this part of the world, with its turbulent political history, must be the relatively familiar sound of rifle shots ringing out from next door's garden.

Convinced it was initially a firework we all started but re-booked for another hour at the Motel Therma-a-rest. Over the subsequent half an hour it began to sound like we had woken up in the middle of the storming of the Führer Bunker. The unmistakable crack of the gun-play seemed to fluctuate in origin from the street in front of the house to the neighbours nearby. It eventually desisted at about 0630 by which time the man next door was playing a really quite listenable Hammond organ driven salsa which was being destroyed at source by the sound system being cranked to 11 and a set of speakers being employed that would probably best service a personal stereo.

Last night's shock discovery by some fine combing through the guidebook has revealed that our plans to sojourn in Managua chez René Moya for about five days will certainly be dashed. We must be in Panama City this Friday or expect *not* to leave said City until well into the first week of November. Hence it was with a sad sense of up-rooting that we found ourselves repeating, for the zillionth time, the 3 hour procedure of placing our meagre kit list into our panniers.

A visit to René's PO Box yielded a real crop of mail sent by friends and family in the UK and the USA. This was our first poste restante since Vancouver. Irony and sadness combined in Clive's visit to DHL where he collected his birthday package from Pinner only to find it torn open and most of his private envelopes ripped open (thank you DHL). A cheap(ish) but much relished watch had been stolen and so this spoiled our moment of contact with those back home. Dave Greenhough's home-made card was hysterically funny and although during its design he was not to know, it did much to cheer us all up.

The most recent batch of developed photos was collected and in the same visit and therefore reported in the same sentence, a 'mud' plate was welded on the base of Clive's yesterday fitted new side-stand. The chap who did this normally made children's garden swings and climbing frames from scratch and charged $2.

Geoff Vince called up from Bournemouth, hence completing the trinity of next-of-kin that check in with their Managuan wards. This was followed by a superbly purple natural fruit drink supplied by Grandma Moya and then René was spotted literally skulking in the shadows of his own backyard. We noticed that he was brandishing the machine that Donovan claimed "kills" – a guitar. As soon as we had clocked him, he sprang like the moustachioed pixie that he is and burst, with a Sabata-esque roar of laughter, into "Bamboleo"- played with feeling and sparkle it may be noted.

René was quickly able to change the chorus line from Bamboleo into "Mondo Enduro" and he was soon the subject of our video camera in what will surely become the best footage from our time in Central America.

Saddled up and engines running at 13.30 (only an hour and a half behind our notional schedule) we had our photos taken several more times and soared(ish) off. The most touching moment in the farewell proceedings, especially given that we weren't old friends or family, came when Grandma asked us to sign a copy of Trevor's A-Level Biology textbook which the Author *himself* had monickered with a heartfelt Spanish dedication to his Mother-in-law. In Spanish she said of Mondo Enduro's inscription something like: "I can't read this but it will always remind me of you".

A tank of gas paid for by MasterCard (always a great feeling out here) and two bottles of cherry flavoured *rojita* and we were dragging slowly up the hill out of Managua, destination: Peñas Blancas-the frontier with Costa Rica. Strangeness was noticed many miles out of town; we drove past a lone building, highly fenced and much fortified. It was revealed by a front gate plaque as the Italian Embassy! We couldn't help but sympathise with any young Roman backpacker who had to schlep all the way out here to report a missing passport. How busy is the Ambassador? What a skive.

The road heading southeast treated us to a surreal adjunct to our morning mail feast from Blighty. For geological and botanical reasons not fully understood by Mondo Enduro, there came a brief five mile period where the scenery was authentically transformed into the Devonian heaven that is

Dartmoor. Gone were the palm trees and rain forest, replaced by lush pasture, tors and rolling moorland the like of which we really haven't seen since we left England. However, at 50mph, such bursts of nostalgia can't last for long and we were soon smashing our rims into the Central American pot hole system – as yet unmapped by the Nicaraguan Ordnance Survey.

The trip to the frontier was a humble 88 miles and the weather was with us. The route skirted the southern shoreline of 'Nicaragua Lake' in the middle of which emerges the *Volcano de Concepcion*. The lake is huge and as we looked left to the North we could see no far bank. We wondered if any Conquistador, having tramped the 20 miles inland from the nearby Pacific coast, had once upon a time thought that they were gazing at the Atlantic. Further natural phenomena were literally blown the way of Austin, Clive and Chas when they drove into a full on blizzard of whitefly. They swarmed in clouds over the highway and such was their density and the adhesive qualities of their organs that a paste of them had to be cleansed from our goggles and visors. Although we can be accused of too frequently writing in superlatives – this really was one of the weirdest and totally unpleasant encounters with Mother Nature thus far. Shortly after 1600hrs we hit the border and the kids hit us. Clive made the selection as to which diminutive under-age bureaucrat to engage. He ultimately chose a coffee (con leche) coloured 14 yr old Tom Jones look-a-like simply because the witful youth sported a Biro. Harsh judge Clive said it's not unusual to use this as a barometer of an applicant's preparedness.

One and a half hours later we were given the green light to leave the Nicaraguan formalities. The reader should be aware that none of this period was spent queuing or dithering. Every minute was religiously absorbed by filling in forms, securing stamps and hand written entries into the waiting Limey passports. Whatever anti-revolutionary counter insurgency plans the government has are well matched by a national fever of counter-signatories.

Onwards through 4 miles of no-man's land and we arrived at the beautifully honest, cheap and let's not deny it, civilised Costa Rican Border control. We were all charmed by an English speaking Honduran woman travelling south with her three sons. She didn't want three more by the looks of things. We holed up for the night on the veranda of a primary school 5 miles into Costa Rica. It will rain tonight and we'll be dry.

Costa Rica

Day 202
Wednesday 25 October
Mondo Miles today: 176
Mondo Mileage: 22950

After a sound sleep under the awning of an *escuela* on a tiled floor, the only disturbance through the night was a torrential downpour of rain. As a result, Mondo Enduro were feeling particularly smug at their fantastic dry covered campsite.

When the weather had passed over, it was time to rock!

Breakfast at a roadside café in Las Conas close to the Rio Congo came after 100 miles all before 9am... what superb progress as Mondo Enduro get further and further ahead of schedule. Christmas in Sun City (with Clive's old school friend Louis Bloom) looks more and more hopeful and the Mondo miles are swept by on the smooth red tarmac of Costa Rica.

After brekkie, the paranoid trio discovered a clinic and endeavoured to get a shot of anti-malarial vaccine gratis. Chas headed the way cheekily as ever and managed to get us all booked in for a blood test. As we write, Clive is slightly nervous as he has malaria from his travels near the Zambesi back in Easter '93. Will he show positive anyway? We shall wait and see.

They went in one by one and left the Costa Rica medics some Gringo blood to examine for malaria. Unfortunately, for Clive the medic taking the blood went straight through his vein and caused internal bleeding and a nice blood clot under the skin. The test results will not be ready until next Tuesday when Mondo Enduro will hopefully be in Columbia.

Back on the road and we hit rain 40 miles before San Jose and it rained the whole way in and for the rest of the afternoon. Before long we were totally saturated and headed straight for the nearest roadside café to dry out.

We decided to stay in a hotel for a night in order to get our kit dry. We shopped around and found the cheapest deal with secured parking to be "The Royal Dutch"; whose concierge was also the first gay Central American we had met. Although that was not the deciding factor in getting a room. Once checked in, we watched some TV – The Costa Rican equivalent of MTV. It was refreshing to hear these Costa Rican/Spanish bands out here.

Our treat for the night was going to the pictures; Stallone and Banderas shooting it out side by side and then against each other in *Assassineos*. We crashed after this and chatted for an hour or so about girls before sleeping.

Costa Rica

Day 203
Thursday 26 October
Mondo Miles today: 148
Mondo Mileage: 23098

It was an auspicious setting for a vainglorious comment.

In the Costa Rican ristaurante, the *caffes con leche* had warmed hearts' cockles and pineapple juices had cooled fevered brows, omelettes and chicken dishes had filled the cavities of hungry stomachs. Pineapple rice pudding, jelly and fruit salad and vanilla blancmange gilded the lily of a perfect repast.

And then Austin spoke: "Amazing that I haven't had a back tyre puncture since Tashkent", he said in a voice cocksure enough to incite one of the mischievous spirits who direct human fortunes to take spiteful revenge. Ten miles down the road, an enormous pot hole swallowed his bike in its maw, splitting both the rear tyre and inner tube. Mankind, the inventors of Puncture Buster prophylactic donated in LA, once more had reason to despair at the fickle workings of fate.

And the day, in the comfort of The Royal Dutch Hotel's crispy linen, had started so well. The *hombres* were away by about 8.30am having despatched a fax to the British Embassy in Panama warning them of our imminent arrival. Clive did not lie much. He changed the date on the fax letter to yesterday because Third Secretary Simon Hart had been awaiting our call yesterday to inquire about Colombian ferry timetables.

The sense of purpose shared by the travellers was such that they passed by two roadside *tavernas* without stopping. Soon they were climbing steeply out of San José and into a dramatic mountain pass complete with massive pot holes, chilly temperatures and freezing fog.

Then came the aforementioned lunch and Austin's puncture. On the horizon, dark clouds frothed and bubbled as if waiting for us to make our next move. Repairs went slowly as a Michelin inner tube, carefully repaired by Chas in Fort Simpson, North West Territories (Canada), had developed a terminal case of rubber Ebola. Air spewed from its gut while the lining of the valve sloughed itself making any cure a futile impossibility. And so the search began, not for the first time on Mondo Enduro, for the friendly neighbourhood vulcanizer who mended our two Ebola – negative tubes and flogged us a new Korean one for about $6. Meanwhile a comedy of errors was unfolding as Austin parked himself in a nearby mechanics shop while Chas and Clive sent out fruitless search parties for him in the driving rain. Very much a case of the left hand not knowing what the right was doing.

At last the party coalesced amidst somewhat sour relations at the tyre repair shop. The vulcanizer was not the first earthling to learn the hard way that Clive drives a hard bargain when it comes to dollar exchange.

The day wore on at a speedier rate than miles eaten up by the six tyres of Mondo Enduro. After a spot of filming by a beautiful waterfall, the lads made only minimal progress before the Ebola curse struck again, having replicated itself in its new 'host' – Austin's replacement rear inner tube.

Fortunately this latest setback took place directly outside a completely built, but apparently unused, restaurant whose only customers appeared to be a colony of bats plus the occasional firefly. In the fading light, Austin changed his Dunlop, which had carried him from the Zilov gap, for his brand new Bridgestone provided by Orange County Suzuki. In complete darkness save for Clive's pen torch, he confidently juggled levers, teased in rubber and seated beads with the speed and assured confidence of a self taught craftsman. Imagine our surprise to find the tyre wouldn't hold any air. A laborious strip down revealed that Austin's clumsy, rushed and incompetent inner tube fitting had pinched two substantial holes in a tube which until he got his hands on it was brand new and intact. The holes were patched and with less bravado and more measured calm the inner tube was thumbed gingerly into the new Bridgestone. This log has recorded the many punctures that have befallen us across the world but the reader should know that they are almost always rooted in one of our bungled repairs from earlier on.

Dinner was chicken with rice all round plus beer, cherry fanta and cheese wotsits. Clive is now deep into "The Hot Zone" by Richard Preston and well on his way to becoming another authority on Ebola.

As we lock the metal doors of our new home tonight, we know the combination padlock we have affixed will be scant protection against this dreaded virus. We also hope that our Bat room-mates are not rabid vampires who apparently like to suck the blood from human toes. Ooh er...

Costa Rica

Day 204
Friday 27 October
Mondo Miles today: 245
Mondo Mileage: 23343

Mondo Enduro, for all its members always meant something different. One recurring experience though, forced home ceaselessly since we left London is that of vacation. It has oft been said "that if it had to end <u>now</u> it would still have been the most fun etc, etc". The spiritual 'feel-good' factor though, evaporated this morning when Clive, half man, half shift-worker, roused the snugly cheeky Chas and Austin from their (separate) sleeping bags. It was 0430, still pitch dark as well as pitch black and we had to clear up and saddle up so that we had engines running by 0500 when the natural light from the dawn made progress feasible. Hence, Clive was chagrined when Chas withdrew further into his bedding, Austin squeezed Plymouth a little closer and they both played their "it's not sensible to get up yet" trump cards.

Clive coped with this set-back as well as he did when he discovered he'd dyed his hair orange not blonde. He left the babes for 20 mins and then, stuka-esque dived in and released the valves on his slothful cohorts' air mattrii.

The rear tyre on Austin's basically trusty mount, B2, was still inflated and so, with the last of the insanely pot-holed road behind them, it was Ebola free asphalt all the way to the frontier. There only remained to juice up as soon as possible and of course to stop and repair Austin's rear tyre after a mystery deflation 40 miles into the day's riding. It transpired that the hard currency bargaining that Clive had enforced with yesterday's vulcanizer had precipitated some kind of bad (Ebola) karma from the proprietor of that most lastik of outlets. As we sighed and gazed at Austin's painfully useless *new* tyre, we imagined the Costa Rican Voodoo Gurus peeling the bogus patches from their miniature Caribbean inner tube talismen. The tyre removal showed that sure enough, yesterday's patches had crumbled and fallen away from the holes they were so relied on to seal, as easily as if we'd blu-tacked a Ritz cracker over each rip and hoped for the best.

A trip to a *new* vulcanizer , more repairs to the Russian super heavy thickness inner tube (threw away two heavily repaired old friends and purchased two brand new flimsy Korean inner tubes) and back on our way – only 20 miles to the Costa Rican : Panamanian border.

For the Central American travel fact collector, this border crossing should be given a five star rating. It was a case in point for those corrupt bastards at Club Guatemala and Hotel Honduras. Slick, efficient, free and cheerful. May an irate traveller stab the dollar gorged officials we have left in our wake!

Within a few miles Panama was clearly evident as the most Americanised of all these already highly Americanised Central Republics. It was a beautiful concrete road (our first since the USA) that 10 miles in saw Austin pull over for afternoon tyre repairs. In went one of the new inner tubes and out came the Russian one, the patch applied only 2 hours earlier flaked away like a little rubber cry-baby. (Technical Note: we fear too much washing up liquid has been poured onto the tyre trim in the bid to aid seating. The squeezy liquid does the latter but once mobile, coagulates into a form of Copydex that accelerates patch–tyre friction and ultimate removal by abrasion).

As has been standard for many days now, the skyline was a richly mottled spectrum of white – black cloud formations. Clive and Austin re-enrolled at Club Ridiculous and swathed themselves in their US Army Ponchos in preparation for the inevitable thrice daily issue of monsoon precipitation.

We drove off and were soaked through, despite wet-proofs. At least the road wasn't dangerously pot-holed, a poignant factor since basically none of the team could see what they were driving through. Clive met a lorry full of 'intrepid' overlanders battling their way from Panama City to Guatemala. Their lorry had the word 'Dragoman' emblazoned on its flank. We stopped for a chat but sadly realised that these were the kind of people we were glad to be away from in the first place. Clive deduced perceptively that there was something inherently pointless about risk-free adventure travel.

Onwards through the dusk and into nightfall, ultimately suppering in a USA style diner that gave us free pizza. We purposefully have no tent but if he did we would have missed out when the night found us in the lounge of a Mondo Classic – a partially completed building.

Panama

Day 205
Saturday 28 October
Mondo Miles today: 160
Mondo Mileage: 23503

Although a great rough campsite, it was probably the noisiest bed-space so far, getting close to the site only 15 metres away from the AMTRAK railway line near the Grand Canyon. The source of this din was the pumping bass of a club 100 metres away that blasted out Latin American Reggae all night long, until just before dawn when Mondo Enduro finally fell asleep.

Clive did not have his shift-worker hat on this morning, as it was almost 7am in bright sunshine when builder Miguel and his sidekick turned up to finish this partially built holiday home to find some gringos nestling on their concrete floor. Fortunately for *los Inglés*, Miguel and Co. took kindly to the Gringo chaps and offered them some water to wash and/or drink. We pulled the camouflage off our bikes and got moving on the smooth black top, bidding farewell to the builders as they tuned into *Radio Panama Exotico Numero Uno*!

The roads in Panama are absolutely fantastic. They are far superior to those of Mexico and the rest of Central America. The only flaw is that they are heavily policed as we soon found out.

We jumped one police check point but were stopped by the next one and Austin was questioned as to why he ran the last roadblock. He acted ignorant and actually *was* ignorant for it was only Clive who saw and heard the police whistling but kept going anyway. They let us off. The next brush with The Man was only 30 miles further when Clive and Chas were stopped for overtaking on a double yellow line in the centre of the carriageway. Verily, we are outlaws.

The *carabinieri* was about to give us a ticket when Clive managed to use his feeble Spanish to explain that we were on an official expedition and were ignorant of the traffic laws in Panama despite the fact that they were exactly the same in Europe and that we were very sorry. It worked as he screwed up the ticket and sent us on our way. Hurrah for Panama!

Just after 11am we were at Panama City. After shopping, admin and laundry it was time for another Mondo blend attempt. This time recommended by the Guide Book. It was the Road Knights Motorcycle Club at Allbrook US Airforce base just by the Bridge of the Americas that goes over the Panama Canal.

It was 7pm and dark, we turned up at the gate where two armed soldiers were standing by on guard. We mentioned "Road Knights" and the fact we were English on a motorcycle trip meant they were quick to wave us on through. Umm, so much for security on this base, we were certain that British soldiers facing the same scenario would not give our US counterparts the same red carpet treatment.

Austin was the first to find the club, which was an old petrol/service station on the base. It was in fact formed in 1972 and there are entries in the visitor's book to prove it. The Road Knights are internationally famous and the reason is simple; The Darien Gap. This is the name given to a 200 mile stretch of heavy tangled jungle that straddles the Panama: Colombia frontera. It is also an upland area riven with steep sided valleys flushed through with frothing white water rapids. For the surveyor it presents a challenge but one that is far from insurmountable. So why no road? The Darien jungles are populated by some pretty independent tribes of Indians and there is a thought that they have made things difficult for the odd teams of theodolite packin' engineers that have come through in the past. Obviously, it would be a pretty expensive project and one which traditionally, in this part of the world, might elicit some philanthropic dollar aid from the USA. After all, this is the only fissure in the entire overland journey from Alaska to Tierra del Fuego. The gap sits as an obvious challenge to all forward thinking Americans to rise up, grasp the nettle and connect the two halves of this mighty continent, currently separated in a manner deeply redolent of Michelangelo's 'The Creation Of Man' .

The Darien Gap though, performs one role in which it is exquisitely successful; an impermeable coffer dam of green impounding the endless reservoir of Colombian cocaine. The DEA knows where 90% of the class A that went up Mötley Crüe's noses came from and financing a road that would help it to arrive by the lorry load rather than the plane load would possibly seem a retrograde move. Anyway, here is the gap and the last metropolis before you get to it is Panama City and if you want to get a motorcycle across it and over to Colombia then you might need some friendly advice and that's where the Road Knights come in. At least, that's what it was like in the 1970s. Since then the word has got out that the Knights clubhouse, safe within the perimeter of a USAF base, was an excellent place from which to launch one's personal attempt on crossing the gap and consequently they have been overwhelmed. There has been a steady stream of overlanders doing this standard cape to cape pan-American route and without fail they have *all* called in at Allbrook, sought refuge and that's what we were trying to do.

We were met by Miguel, a Panamanian biker who had a souped up moped since his Harley had got a bit much for him in his old age. He did in fact sleep in the clubhouse on a hammock set up between two pillars in one of the bays and informed us that he was not officially allowed here and didn't like to venture outside the main gate too often, in case they asked him for official ID when he tried to get back in. In our experience, as a form of strangely self-imposed house arrest, this has no equal.

Anyway, he needed authority for us to crash so he tried Bill Collier but to no avail. Miguel did eventually get through to Rick, the incumbent club president and passed him over to cheeky as ever Chas. Rick originally began suggesting cheap hotels, but Chas charmed him into allowing us to stay, especially since we had already got through the gate and were currently sitting on the club sofa. It was luxury for us; loads of space for bikes and luggage, TV and video, large table, fridge full of sodas and beers, toilet basin and shower, tape recorder and security courtesy of the M-16 packing perimeter patrols... Excellent Mondo blend!

So pizza was ordered from the on-base PX pizza parlour and as we munched we went meticulously through the visitor's book reading entries and checking for some of those great bikers gone by. We screamed with a Hiram Bingham rush of 'discovery'. There in the visitors' book was the name **Ed Culberson.**

He is an official Mondo hero since after retiring from the USAF in the mid-seventies he had made it his personal mission to motorcycle across the Darien Gap. His *four* attempts to do this are chronicled in his aptly titled '*Obsessions Die Hard*'. Naturally, only the fourth one was successful and he barely rode the bike a yard. Instead, he spent months alone in the jungle, winching his weighty BMW up the greasy muddy slopes with block and tackle then lowering back down the other side. Countless negotiations with the Indians for safe passage and frequent improvised ferry crossings in their dugout canoes. Compared to Culberson's achievement our experiences in the Zilov Gap have all the out-there kudos of a school trip to Chessington World of Adventure. We salute him!

Panama

Day 206
Sunday 29 October
Mondo Miles today: 0
Mondo Mileage: 23503

And so it was that Mondo Enduro awoke to find themselves, not for the first time, in bizarre sleeping quarters and extraordinary circumstances. The weird has become so much a part of commonplace experience for us over the last seven months that if we had all contracted Ebola overnight we would not have been surprised in the slightest.

As it was we awoke in good health, despite the stench of urine from the vicinity of Miguel's hammock. His pins are not as good as they once were and he clearly finds it hard to walk the 10 yards to the nearby latrine, choosing instead to relieve himself in a drain. We knew at once that we were among friends.

As has been our want in recent weeks, given the prompt arrival of nightfall in the tropics, we were up early filling the hours after dawn with a frenzy of minor administrative tasks. There are a few close friends and acquaintances back home who care passionately about our voyage and its progress. The even greater multitude couldn't care less – but we chose to bombard them all regardless with the postal equivalent of a hot virus. A total of 50 cards were written in all to sundry well-wishers, friends, folks and the all-important future 'spongees' who even now lie asleep in their beds blissfully ignorant of the role assigned to them in providing victuals, accommodation and spiritual succour to Mondo Enduro at an as-yet-unfixed date.

As is standard, girls featured strongly on our mailing lists and even now there are several who can expect communiqués couched in the childish and slightly lewd terms which we foolishly imagine they find charming or funny. We dream that Emma Hewitt and Lucy from the BBC will be checking their in-trays with more than usual vigour over the next few days and weeks.

Other members of a ruthlessly selective mail-drop were the great Dick Baker plus our former and much missed motorcycling colleagues Bill Penty and Nick Stubley. Kathy McNaughton from Suzuki America plus the bloke who bought Chas a coffee in Fort Nelson were included in it – as was Alex (plus regards from us all to the delicious Heather) in San Francisco.

It is a happy coincidence that Will Shakespeare did not suffer from writer's block to the same extent as Clive – otherwise the world would have been deprived of some immortal works of literature. It took him a slice of pizza, an orange muffin and four cups of coffee at the Allbrook servicemen's canteen before he could contemplate writing to Candice in terms not too grim but also emotionally endearing. Dr Ebola-Bell got a brief summary of the Acapulco transvestite encounter because we all felt that he, as a man of science, should be the first to know.

Clive and Chas spent several hours in the staff mess availing themselves of that most magnificent American invention – the bottomless cup of coffee. Austin meanwhile was being an eager beaver, paying a return call to various stores visited yesterday and collecting the laundry from downtown. Upon his return he excoriated his two partners for their unforgivable laziness before revealing details of a Mondo blend several days ride away. Austin's old patrol leader in the Scouts (11th Harrow) had contacted Geoff Vince at Mondo control in Bournemouth and invited us all to stay with his sister in Peru. Result!

Anyway Austin's return set the scene for a day of maintenance tasks in the cool shade of the Road Knight's yard. All did an oil change before realising that our new filters donated by Suzuki were in fact for the 650 model (we have the 350 variant) and didn't go in properly. Both Chas and

Clive stamped on the oversize filters, compressing the frail paper construct and hey presto, they fit!! Much surprisingly-effective lubing of sundry cables was also achieved using the widget purchased in Arizona. Oh yes, and Chas changed his brake pads (front).

After a day's work hard enough to make a Canal coolie break into a light sweat, it was time for refreshment down at the nearby McDonalds (where else?) But not before 'Telephone Colonel' Bill Collier had lectured us on eugenics and the racial inferiority of Central Americans relative to Kentucky rednecks with a weakness for tasteless Harley Davidson tee-shirts. He explained that the cultures that evolved in colder climates were by necessity, far more industrious and inventive than those from warmer climes. He sincerely believed this.

Actually, apart from Bill and his arrogant demeanour borne of a long and moderately successful military career, we really enjoyed our stay at the Road Knights who have been very kind to us. We will leave with fond memories of this little Latin Motorcycling Camelot and its good-natured Knights of the Brake Cable.

Panama

Day 207
Monday 30 October
Mondo Miles today: 75
Mondo Mileage: 23578

We awoke to the ultra loud whirring of the air conditioner, staring upwards at the 1940's concrete rotunda that capped the Knights of the Road club room. It was just like being in a miniature Hanger Lane tube station. However, Greenford and Park Royal were as far away as was the peak hour chaos of the gyratory system.

This morning Clive <u>did</u> have his shift-worker ethos reinstated and as the others slumbered he was dutifully getting up-to-date on entries to this log. As a group, we'd made a poor job of organising ourselves the night before so by 0830, 2½ hours after rising we were only *just* getting ready to pull out.

We said our goodbyes to Michael Angelo – rather, we shouted them at him and he gave us not only his gold capped cheery smile but also 2½ hot dog rolls and 3 slices of Salami. If this uncalled for generosity continues, then Colombia could well be where Mondo Enduro acquires a collective cocaine habit, gratis.

We had a host of early morning tasks to perform, the first of which was to locate the British Embassy. This involved considerable riding down the pavements of one way streets but soon this UK haven was found... where else, but on the 7th floor of the Swiss Bank Tower. Panama City is wild and seems to us to be the New York of Central America. There is tons happening here, a sliver of land with an international crossroads delicately connecting the two mightiest oceans on the planet whilst joining two of its most bustling land masses!!

The cashpoint machine was approached, and for the third consecutive day a healthy wad of crisp dollar bills was spat into Austin's genuinely greasy palm. The reader may not appreciate that US dollars are actually the legal currency in Panama, so Mondo Enduro stocked up with Dead Presidents once more.

The tickets for the Colon-Cartagena ferry were pre-purchased at the plush and civilised offices of "Crucero Express" a recently opened fresh routing flicking across the Darien Gulf. This ferry is truly one of the most crucial lucky breaks for Mondo Enduro since the only two options for getting the bikes into Colombia up until now have been air freighting (expensive) or containerising by sea (very expensive and an administrative torpor drenched minefield that has no Central or South American customs paper fever equal).

So, later than intended, after a spot of filming over the Bridge of the Americas, we were grinding past the colourful local buses (some of which were dedicated in their art-work to the likes of Van Damme, Arnie, Leon(?) and assorted local soccer icons) and heading towards the conduit that would eject us out of this continent – Colon.

The road was narrow and twisty, not normally noteworthy (though asphalt conditions have formed much of the more detailed entries of these diaries) but as we curved our way across the isthmus we thought of the thousands of poor coolies hacking and scooping the path of the Panama Canal. Even with turn of the century plant, the climate and vegetation must have almost broken them.

We weakly stopped at an out of town cafe and were startled to find ourselves being meeted and greeted by the same truncheoned Pistolero security guard that had watched over our initial admin drive last Saturday lunchtime in a downtown eatery.

He smiled at us like old friends and for possibly the first time since the trip began, we worried about the impression that we would leave this young custodian of corporate rations. He must surely believe that gringos can only survive on snack food.

Colon is a chaotic Caribbean shanty town, no more, no less. The wrong turn, or lack of a right turn, that took us down the 'High Street' was really quite disconcerting as all the locals just hanging around eyeballed us menacingly. This was the most unwelcome 'strangers in town' sensation of the trip so far. Once back on course and ensconced in the calm and order of the Crucero Express terminal we got the documentation underway. The building was an old Panama Canal company warehouse built in 1919 out of reinforced concrete (very advanced). The design of the hangar was very tasteful and reminded us that concrete can be used to great aesthetic effect.

The bikes were spray-washed by order, and it was the first time any of them had ever been cleaned. There was a chemical trough last thing before we drove onto the ferry, but that was only flooded with sea water rather than providing a sluice of some Columbian de-contaminant.

The ship was superb and the ex-Royal Marine who ran the security, made us feel at home since we were the only gringos. Austin won $50 at roulette and then went to bed to sleep on his profits. This left Clive and Charles free to get to work blending with the girls from the on board Russian dance troupe! The drinking session had started when the Russian dancers did their various enactments. They were 6 girls and 3 guys all from St Petersburg. The girls were typical of their nation: absolutely stunning!

After a few G & T's Clive and Chas decided to approach the girls after the show to practice their rusty Ruskie! The girls showed interest for a while and then, as ever on Mondo Enduro, the lads found themselves sitting on their own.

Next up, was some rum with the ship's crew and band. The band was from Cartagena and it was their last night on board the Crucera, so they were going out with a splash. The party ended shortly after 2am when Security turned up and ordered the crew and the band to leave the disco lounge area. So unfortunately, Clive and Chas had no more drinking partners and staggered back to their cabin.

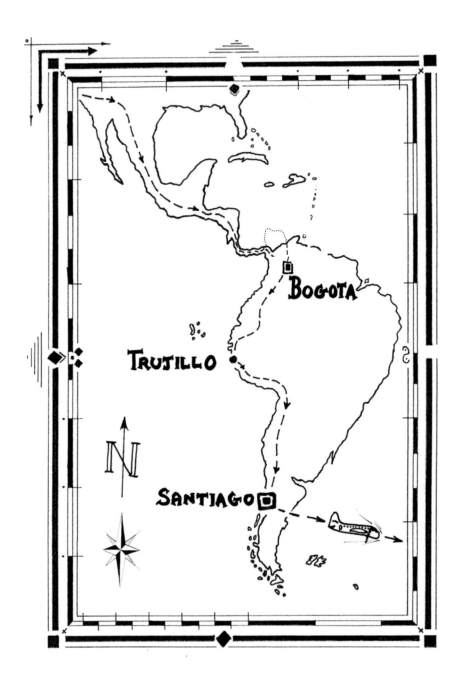

Panama / Colombia

Day 208
Tuesday 31 October
Mondo Miles today: 122
Mondo Mileage: 23700

We awoke in darkness somewhere in the Caribbean Sea. There were no portholes so we had no idea of the time.

Clive stumbled into the bathroom and for a minute had a mild panic attack. He stared at his reflection to discover his eyes were red and that he had a thumping headache. These are the first signs of the dreaded hot virus 'Ebola' and after all we were in the depths of the tropics. His panic was soon put to rest by Chas, when he explained that we had been involved in a heavy drinking session and that there was really nothing to worry about. Back to bed then, after the relief of being Ebola Free!

At 1115 hrs we docked at Cartegena and sailed through Customs as swiftly as our complimentary iced coffees went down our parched throats. Despite the Embassy's travel advice, Columbia had set off on an excellent foot for Mondo Enduro. We had received Red Carpet treatment throughout our Custom's routine. Well, here we were finally in South America and it was fantastic.

Our first section saw us ride 120 miles on reasonable tarmac and pretty much flat roads. We had one giant river crossing where Austin attempted to remove his rear disc with a stud extractor, as the allen bolts have been glued in securely at the moment of manufacture. Unfortunately, the bits that were screwed in just sheared off under the sheer torsional force that was applied by Clive! So there we have it, a free rear disc from Orange County Suzuki and all five nuts holding the existing one in place are rounded off and irremovable. The rear wheel was disassembled and reassembled in the time it took the ferry 'Caribe' to take us to the other side.

Once on the other side God flicked the switch back on labelled: "Rain on Mondo Enduro"; now becoming a daily event in this part of the world. It was therefore not long before we pulled in at a farmhouse as soon as dusk arrived and asked permission to sleep on their front porch which the owner thankfully agreed to.

Colombia

Day 209
Wednesday 1 November
Mondo Miles today: 370
Mondo Mileage: 24070

The day dawned, as is by now completely commonplace, in a bivouac which to many of the folks back home would seem absurd in the extreme. Think on, Giles Whittell, and count the number of times in your so-called 'travels' that you door-knocked a Columbian peasant and made it clear in terms at once measured but firm that you fully intended to bed-down on his roofed patio, whether he liked it or not.

After a moment's brief reflection you will concur that you are an inveterate denizen of hotels and therefore beneath our contempt. Actually Pedro did not seem in the slightest non-plussed either by our arrival or departure and marked both offhandedly ordering his petite wife to serve us with cafe tintos. It seems that chivalry is not dead even in this country where guerrilla warfare is as normal as tending an allotment and political assassination as commonplace as a fish supper.

And so we set off on a road at once flat and somewhat featureless apart from the usual chronic case of bitumen acne caused by a virus distantly related to the Road Ebola witnessed in Guatemala and parts of Siberia. Actually we do a disservice to the Colombian transport authorities who are in the process of constructing a road which will be a credit to their communication infrastructure once they remove the often lethal piles of rubble from the right hand lanes.

In all, it was a day devoid of any marked detail apart from the searing sun which beat down on us from a sky largely clear of the clouds which have made driving conditions so miserable since Southern Mexico. At least we were cheered by the fact that the road tolls in this country are free for motorcycles. So is the military protection afforded by the Government along the whole stretch of the road through Noste Santander – a haven for guerrillas apparently.

As it to provide a touch of drama to a day totally devoid of action, Chas's engine started playing up in fits and turns. It would backfire and stall before belching large clouds of blue smoke. The symptoms were clear – an engine gasping for breath and "hunting" for that elusive blend of fuel and air which makes for efficient motorcycling. It took Clive in his guise as motor doctor to diagnose fuel starvation. A full tank soon put matters right.

A moment of unwelcome tension when Clive was almost killed by a speeding truck. The dynamics of this near calamity are rather complicated and would best be explained with a flip chart and many small models being moved around a diorama. Suffice to say that the collision was averted with a blood-curdling skid which in itself was terrifying to behold. Austin witnessed the whole thing and could only imagine, for a brief second, the phone call back to Clive's mum in Pinner explaining how her son had been smashed to pieces on a remote jungle byway. If Clive had a joker to play, he used it up today.

In the dying light we pulled over, not for the first time, into a half-built restaurant peopled by a lad called Alberto and his mates who were keeping watch for its owner, Banana Farmer Palmer, who lived in the Hacienda on the Hill. We put the mozzy net up between the bikes in the dining salon and bid goodnight to our beguiled room-mates. The night was hot, the mozzies frustrated but we basked in that Mondo staple, the partially completed building. A night for fevered dreams if ever there was one.

Colombia

Day 210
Thursday 2 November
Mondo Miles today: 199
Mondo Mileage: 24269

Last night we roasted, and out here, when you roast you sweat. Even lying on top of our sleeping bags we had unpleasantly moistened them with our tropical secretion.

Our campsite of the unfinished roadside restaurant was superb, the icing on the cake being a waste trough nearby. Ever image conscious, Mondo Enduro wielded its collective Gillettes (one of the truly indispensable pieces of equipment) and smartened themselves up for the next move in "The Embassy Game". Bogota and the warm Scottish lilts of Jane Hannah and Johnny Welsh were still 200 miles away. It was 0630 when we hit the constantly improving black top of this new Colombian road and gunned a swift ton down to the mystically named *urbano* of La Dorada!

We had no local currency and were surprised that individuals and banks were not keen to *cambio* U.S. dollars with us on the streets. Plastic was not as widely accepted in the gas stations as in Central America and so El Dorada was somewhat make or break as we only had about 40 miles of gas left on board.

The hugest Mobil station so far encountered was approached by junior linguist Clive, wielding his impressive double-barrelled combo of VISA and MASTERCARD. It did no good. Maybe it was the whiff of the Ebola virus as we approached but despite the clatter of HGVs passing by, these petrol Colombians would have no truck with us. Instead, they advised we visit the

Centro Urbano where the claim was made that we would achieve satisfaction. Little did we anticipate the warm, beaming welcome (and petrol) that the sturdy high octane matron at Mobil-Centro would afford us.

As well as having the bikes filled while we sipped at "Real Colombian Coffee" this nameless angel effervesced at our every move and for some reason, the nucleus of pretty girls surrounding us multiplied. Mobil-girl allowed us to call Bogota on the office phone, it would appear for free, and rounded off our short visit to this Petropolis with a group photo. Lovely people these Colombians.

Thirty miles later were transited that Spanish homage to a rival Japanese marque, the town of Honda. We crossed a quite impressive suspension bridge which spanned a mini-gorge that frothed and boiled with a cauldron of a river that looked as if it was discharging chocolate Nesquik downstream. Other, less silty rivers we have seen, often appeared not to flow at all, rather just to evolve and metamorphose in a general direction. Mini whirlpools and inexplicable eddies of water make many of these channels really quite sinister in appearance.

Crossing the bridge at Honda was the end, in fact, of 600 miles of relatively straight road and the start of 110 miles of tortuously twisty mountain driving. Two things hampered our mission to arrive at the British Embassy in Bogota ASAP; the lorries and the torrential rain. The initial teen-rush of dangerously overtaking the former was mercilessly dampened and almost literally crashed by the amazing fall of rain that caught us half way up the mountain. 'Us' may not be the right word since Chas and Austin, not needing a weatherman to see which way the wind blows, had 'smelt' rain and holed up in a superbly fortunately located roadside coffee hut. However, not without first sending Clive off, seconds before the deluge, with a pip-pip-cheerio and "see you in thirty". The irony and guilt that drenched Chas and Austin alternately was diluted when Clive was discovered only a few miles later writing the log at a roadside fruit stall that donated us three fun sized bananas each. They were stiff little things that hardly tasted of banana, it must be the altitude.

The journey through the mountains and up to the 2000m plateau on which Bogota is sprawled was basically the most exciting riding thus far. Clive looked superb in old shorts and US Poncho swathed over him.

We arrived at the British Embassy after a hair-raising baptism of urban moto-cross in the suburbs of Bogota. Clive and Austin took a few wrong turns and found themselves at the mercy of the traffic flow systems which do not allow for any left, right or about turns once one has embarked on a given thoroughfare. At one stage, they found themselves traversing a building site; the main railway and sundry verdant central reservations were bumped over. The fantastic epitaph to this dangerous but adrenalised riding was that unbeknown to Mondo Enduro, a top local politician was being assassinated at that very moment. Unhelpfully, the assailants were making good their escape, helmeted and masked up, on two dirt bikes! Never before had we driven so wildly and looked so suspicious or subversive; we'll never understand how it was that not one of the 1000's of police, militia and gendarmes never flagged us down even once! We passed a stadium surrounded by thousands of teens and as many jumpy looking police and soldiers. We subsequently discovered that it was a Bon Jovi concert that the authorities had summarily cancelled (because of the assassination) only minutes ago just as New Jersey's finest hairspray rockers were about to take the stage.

Johnny Welsh (Scottish) at the Embassy was very convivial and immediately offered to liaise on our behalf in the miserable task that lay ahead; pleading with the Ecuador Embassy to supply us with a Pasaje *de Transito* in lieu of the hated carnet. The guidebook is ambiguous so we are once again terrified we'll schlep the 700 miles to the border only to be told we cannot get into Ecuador without some kind of convoluted customs exemption for the bikes. Whilst waiting in the lobby a security door type thing electronically clicked open and out leaked four blonde-haired, blue-eyed beef-cakes. They wafted past us clearly trying not to be noticed and heading for the lift. It was ridiculous since their rock hard chiselled features-combined with the awkwardness with which they wore beige cords and blazers-marked them out as 'military in civilian cloth' at a thousand paces. Chas reckons they are all SAS men (the regiment not the airline) en route to rescue a British Oil Executive recently kidnapped, negotiations reached a stalemate, helicopter insertion followed by 20 mile yomp, snatch raid etc etc.

Despite the most laughable hint-dropping that we never stayed in hotels and that we were accustomed, nay, chuffed to traditionally sleep on our Therma-rests in someone's backyard, we failed to elicit the dreamed for blend. Austin dropped off his heavily stamped passport (the new one will feature a photo of a mystery blondoid trying hard to conceal a burgeoning hair colour not dissimilar from grey) and we tried not interact with Jane Hannah (Third Secretary and Vice Consul) who we by now felt really disliked us. We set off empty-handed and unblended, destination the Union Jack Pub just a few short blocks away and thee Brit Pub in downtown Bogota. We saw the neon flag of the union in the distance and drew up outside a building that looked more like a Mexican Hacienda than an Englishman's castle. Three men inside welcomed us, all Brummies, save the youngest, 18 yr old Elton who had an English father but a Colombian mother and had grown up here.

We also met and chatted with Derek, marvelling at his phenomenal bigotry and view of Britain through pie 'n' mash tinted pupils. "I'M ENGLISH, AND I WANT TO BE KNOWN AS SUCH!!" he bellowed. Only an hour before, we had been waiting in the embassy reception thumbing politically correct leaflets promulgating the enviable diversity of the new multicultural UK. Somehow we reconciled ourselves to the fact that indeed, one of the minorities composing the rich tapestry of British society was the bug-eyed racist.

Concurrent to this we met Keith, a Waltham Cross ex-pat over here with his US diplomat fiancé. We did our best to appear friendly and harmless and soon he was calling home to his better half to confirm that it was OK to come back with three soiled men he'd just met in a bar. Result!! We repaired to their penthouse suite in a heavily guarded and luxurious condo and realised that we might have imposed once too far. The apartment was a jewel encrusted palace of never before seen luxury bedecked with a deep pile cream carpet. We tried desperately not to touch anything since all our luggage and clothes is coated with the road grime of three continents. We swiftly stripped off down to Y-fronts and T-shirts, our filthy leathers quarantined in the scullery. Just then Keith's fiancé returned from the shops (having gone out especially to get us breakfast) and we tried to explain ourselves....

Colombia

Day 211
Friday 3 November
Mondo Miles today: 0
Mondo Mileage: 24269

Unfortunately, we had a rendezvous with Johnny Welsh at 8am to go and speak to the local radio station. We were encouraged to scoff the last of Keith and Jonie's fodder left in their fridge as they were leaving town for ten days for *their* wedding in Andover, Massachsetts. Their honeymoon (with Keith's mates from London in a couple of cars) was going to be a road trip to Washington so Keith could get his US Citizenship. Certainly not the most romantic of honeymoons, Keith didn't seem too bothered, but I'm sure Joni will have few words to say after being squashed up with the London lager lads for 72 hours in a Chevy.

We left their luxury pad in the Mayfair of Bogota extremely sad and were saddened further to hear the radio station had blown us out. So our chances of blending were running out with blowouts from the Grimmer Jane and the radio station. There was nothing for it but to go to the DR's heart; the Suzuki dealership downtown.

We tracked them down swiftly and had soon negotiated a letter writing spree on their ancient manual typewriter and a couple of gratis faxes. Austin had meanwhile got some assistance in removing his reluctant rear disc. The insanity is that the five allen headed bolts that fix the disc to the hub must have been glued in with Loctite at the moment of assembly back in Japan. Hence, the restraining force of the glue is far greater than the torsional strength of the metal of the allen socket. End result, when you try to undo them, is that the socket walls are mercilessly rounded off. The mechanic had to drop weld on to the bolt to form a nodule so as to create something big enough to grip onto with the mole grips. It was a complete success. We left Suzuki for an RV of 1pm at the Embassy with a TV crew. Surprise surprise, they hadn't turned up. It had in the meantime started throwing it down outside with deafening thunder and lightning striking down only yards away, setting off car alarms all down the nearby street.

The TV crew presenter turned up at just after 2pm to explain they could not film in this weather and arranged with Austin to film on Sunday morning at 10am.

We then sat in a donut shop for a couple of hours whilst writing faxes, letters and captions on photographs before besetting upon the Britannia Inn only a block away from the Union Jack pub at 5.30pm. We were pleasantly surprised by the atmosphere present in this pub as we got chatting to the friendly middle-aged English couple Brian and Patricia who started up the pub. They had been running it with the help of some attractive local Colombian girls for the last three years. Brian had come out to Brasil in the '70s whilst in the Royal Navy. He was a chief engineering type guy on a brace of nuclear subs the MOD had flogged to the Brasilian Navy. As part of the service and warranty package the Brasilians got Brian as a trouble shooter two years after the purchase. He loved South America and he hadn't been back home since.

The pub slowly filled up as the evening wore on. The entire staff of the British Embassy seemed to be present including the Ambassador, his wife and their bodyguards, Colombian police personally trained by Martin Pickford – Chief of Security (RMP).

Bogota, Colombia 04 Nov 95.

To the three men who gave me the picture in McDonalds. Something in the three of you drew me to come ask you for a picture. Me and my friend Andrea were amazed by your looks and wonder if you'll call us if you have any free time in Bogota. 42985XXX-Andrea. Thank you for the picture. Bernardita. PS Good luck on your trip.

Unbelievable, a stunning Columbian female just wrote these words. She is obviously no more than fourteen. Aggro.

Back to the log:
We were offered plenty of goodies by Martin, who thankfully took a bit of a liking to Mondo Enduro and invited us to dinner and a few crates of beer at his place this Sunday. We joyously accepted and he in turn arranged with Brian that we kip the night upstairs in their spare room all for only a brandy and coke. Hurrah for Martin Pickford!

So things had started to map themselves out. We then had a beer bought for us by the British Ambassador himself (whose name eludes us) followed shortly by a Canadian who we had not even met. What luck for Mondo Enduro.

Next up, we met Michael Flynn, raised in Baltimore who was working here for the American Embassy but who sometimes stayed with his diplomat dad down in Santiago, Chile. Mike was part of an all American squad of contractors who worked only on US Embassies around the world. He immediately invited us to stay with him in Santiago and not long after offered us to stay in his serviced *apartamento* at a hotel for the rest of our time here in Bogota. We then met his buddies and were bought several drinks all kindly provided by Uncle Sam. Once again, the weirdness of arriving in a foreign city as dirty strangers but being adopted by kind-hearted souls who will never realise the magnitude of the favours they do us. We could never afford to stay in even the cheapest hotels on a trip of this length, thank you Michael Flynn.

We were also introduced to a new hard liquor named '*Aguadiente*' which is clearly the Colombian version of Sambuca. It certainly hit the spot as we were legless shortly after. We crashed upstairs sometime between midnight and 1am. Cheeky Chas got the bed, Clive the sofa and Austin on the floor.

Colombia

Day 212
Saturday 4 November
Mondo Miles today: 0
Mondo Mileage: 24269

There are days when you wake up, throw open the curtains and look at the ship which came in yesterday. And this is Bogota – 500 miles or so from the nearest coastline.

We awoke in the considerable comfort of Brian and Tricia's spare bedroom in the Britannia Inn. Soon, after the customary ablutions, we had repaired to McDonalds in the Andino Centre for a hearty breakfast of huevo McMuffins and Coca Cola. It was this far flung outpost of the world's greatest eating empire, where no allowance is made for anything out of the ordinary which might disturb the remorseless consumption of fast-food. It was there, amidst a confusion of scattered photographs and paper coffee cups, that a miracle happened. Two beautiful girls approached our table asked for a photograph and left the message on the previous page.

Soon the three travellers were decamping from the aforementioned hostelry to meet their new American friends who were to escort them back to the apartment block of La Fontana Hotel, close to the Unicentre shopping mall and surely one of Bogota's most exclusive residencies. Thank you Michael Flynn!

Dwight and Mike soon made us welcome in their tastefully themed rooms replete with every creature comfort. In no time the CD player was out, the Blues Traveller album and an impromptu party was in progress fuelled by copious amounts of *Aguadiente* and Colombian beer. A quick foray to the Unicentre for beer and pizzas and we were ready for an evening out at La Zona Rosa, open air pleasure dome and haunt of Bogota's beautiful people.

At a bar called Bulldog, we sat outside and listened with great merriment to Mike's astonishing total recall of the scripts of Spinal Tap and Wayne's World. Austin's enormous consumption of Aguadiente prior to coming out meant that he was soon *hors de combat* and sent home in a taxi. He did have enough strength, however, to boogie to Shampoo's bubblegum smash; "Uh Oh we're in Trouble" not heard since Metsovo (day 14)! The others, however, continued their odyssey into the night, arriving ultimately at a reggae club.

Feeling groovy they supped exotic cocktails and listened to the competent vibes of a band who nevertheless should dismiss their keyboard player at the earliest opportunity. His heavily accented and deeply clichéd exhortations to "*Give Jah tanks 'n praise*" and "*Praise to deh most high, Jah Rastafari*" had the Anglophone members of the audience weeping into their Long Island Ice Teas.

Still, not even the babbling of a wannabe Colombian rasta could dispel the universal sense of bonhomie. Soon Clive was deep in conversation with Magnolia, a glamorous lady of mature years and indulging in some deeply suggestive Latin dancing. It transpired that she was the boss of a large perfume and toiletries concession and had once been kidnapped by guerrillas with her two sons

A drunken drive home in Magnolia's spanking new Mitsubishi car so nearly ended in death on several occasions. On the morrow a date with stardom as we meet the film crew of *En Vivo*, Columbia's salacious breakfast TV channel. Can it possibly be better than today – one of Mondo Enduro's best ever. Thanks to Mike and Dwight (they are not a couple).

Colombia

Day 213
Sunday 5 November
Mondo Miles today: 0
Mondo Mileage: 24269

After the various excess and success of our Saturday night in security city we were excited and primed for our RV with the TV crew. Not prepared to let us just slip out unhosted, Dwight and Mike toiled until a full size authentic English breakfast had been prepared and served to the eager beaks of Mondo Enduro. Mike noted that his was his first cooked breakfast in many months in Bogota.

We saddled up the bikes and headed to the British Embassy where we met Harvey (Director), Freddy (Camera Man) and two nameless chaps who did the driving and the sound. The shoot had been brokered by one of the Columbian ladies at the British Embassy, she came along as a translator and brought along one of her cousins, the truly stunning Clarissa.

After some close ups of the bikes we were filmed driving around the Zona Rosa and then ascended the large hill that overlooks the city. Some more close ups and a chance to dodge some of the billions of sports cyclists who go someway to making pedalling a national recreation alongside revenge killings and uncoiling barbed wire.

Further into town we came across a huge street market where we were filmed dealing with the beggars, buying giant sized pork scratchings and explaining the route so far to the bemused locals, who weren't quite sure if they should know who we are. The tour of Bogota we had been treated to left us in no doubt that this was a full on European-style capital city and infinitely more 'together' than any city in the former Soviet Union. How Colombia has got itself into such a turbulent froth of instability is by no means obvious to us. The people here seem alert, interested and keen to build a better future; far from resigned to wearing the yoke put upon them by the *narcos* and those that feel their society is well served by endless political murders. Let this log record that we think Bogota rocks and it is not a fraction as obviously dangerous as Dalston or parts of Harlesden.

After an interview in a local park Clive found that he could no longer deny the pressure in his colon and had to empty out behind a prickly bush.

By now it was 3.30pm. We collected some photos taken earlier on and met Martin Pickford from the Embassy at 4pm. He is the Security Chief for the British mission here and seeing as *abduçtion del extraneros* is a substantial dollar earner for certain of the locals he takes his role very seriously. We repaired to his huge and well defended flat and met his lovely wife Jo and their two sons; normal sized Jack and giant sized Geoffrey.

Because of a breakdown in communications between our host and hostess, the evening meal was cooking for literally four hours. The in-meal entertainment consisted of a sparkler display in Geoffrey's chicken and a candid showcase of *laissez-faire* parenting. Martin realised that we yearned to self-cater and as a transitional aid he ceded us armfuls of army compo rations. They come as boil in the bag ready-meals; each one vacuum-packed in a neat silver foil sachet. Once we'd piled up our haul it looked for all the world like about two million dollars worth of shrunk wrapped class A Colombian marching powder. We are relaxed though since any subsequent raised eyebrow at a *frontera* down the line will be calmed when the innocuous 'bangers'n'beans' contents are revealed.

Mrs Jo Pickford chipped without any goodnights, we left after a night cap and all agreed that if we'd given them 50,000 pesos it would probably have been OK.

Colombia

Day 214
Monday 6 November
Mondo Miles today: 0
Mondo Mileage: 24269

National bank holiday today so most of the town was shut down and therefore no admin just R & R.

Austin and Chas had a day of tourism taking in a lagoon (*muy profundo!*), old church etc. with the British Embassy interpreter and her tasty cousin Clarissa.

Meanwhile, Clive stayed in the apartment watching TV (Wayne's World) and listening to the radio. The slackness and boredom stopped suddenly when the intercom buzzed loudly and Clive answered to be addressed by an Englishman by the name of David Parkinson. He had also ridden around the world and had just spotted our land and weather beaten bikes in the basement car park.

Clive instantly invited him up to the apartment to see what news/info he could have in store for us.

He was an ex-Royal Marine who had retired after 21 years service at the rank of Major. He had found himself struggling to find the right job, as so many do after they have spent their lives in the force, and had come to the conclusion he would go around the world alone on a BMW R80GS (1985) wearing a white boiler suit.

His journey was around 100,000 miles in five years taking a similar route to Ted Simon: London –> Cape Town –> South America –> Central America –> US/Canada –> Australia –> SE Asia –> Oman –> Europe.

His tales were impressive and he was equally intrigued by Clive's account of Mondo Enduro so far and in particular Russia. They exchanged information and stories the rest of the afternoon and he insisted he treat us to dinner. Result.

Clive gladly accepted on Mondo Enduro's behalf and the lads were thrilled to bits about the ever increasing hospitality. We dined at the Uniclub in the nearby Mall and David explained that he was in Bogota on business, that business being 'Hostage Negotiation'. He brought home to us that Colombia is indeed a tropical paradise awash with excellent coffee, until you get kidnapped, and if you are a European national working on a gas pipeline in the jungle etc then the possibilities of your abduction are about a zillion times more real than you may initially appreciate. It was with a pulse of humility that David gently revealed that the British are regarded as world leaders in this field and that many a pair of jungle handcuffs had been unlocked with a uniquely British blend of polite firmness and understated charm.

Colombia

Day 215
Tuesday 7 November
Mondo Miles today: 215
Mondo Mileage: 24269

As Hugh Grant said in 'Four Weddings And A Funeral', it's funny when it finally happens. This was the day love came tumbling down for one member of Mondo Enduro. We also possibly offended, perhaps irreconcilably, a hostage release negotiator and trans-global motorcyclist. All in a day's work.

The day began with an expedition *en masse* to the British Embassy to await our security briefing on the road South. As we waited for Martin Pickford to arrive, we flicked through old copies of British newspapers including The Observer which carried a story about KGB operatives watching James Bond films for inspiration about spying gadgets. Austin wearily pointed out some of the factual errors.

At last Martin arrived, having collected his handgun, seized by the Colombian police at a routine roadblock last Sunday. Even more positively, so did Gloria bearing the news that we only needed a passport, international driving licence and US dollars to transit Ecuador. We will believe it when we see it but at least we have the name of the Ecuadorian consul to vouchsafe our passage.

As Chas and Clive waited for David Parkinson to complete his morning's hostage release negotiations, they repaired briefly to the well-equipped gymnasium and sauna. Clive's request for a massage was politely rebuffed by the stunning hairdresser. Meanwhile letters were written to Suzuki South Africa and Colin Patterson and "The Story so Far" of Mondo Enduro updated on David Parkinson's laptop.

The rest of the afternoon was spent completing minor packing and administrative tasks including the Trans global mailshot to be sent by David and Dwight in their infinite generosity. David in fact was expecting another evening of traveller's tales and Swahili pronunciation exercises but was to be frustrated. While Clive stayed home to write letters and console our friend, Chas and Austin headed out with Gloria and Clarissa for what became a memorable evening.

To cut a long story short, whose details are etched for evermore on Chas's brain, a litre and a half of Aguadiente was consumed for the price of just one hundred centilitres due to a special promotion. Suffice it to say that the Latin grooves, the dim lighting, and the smell of Clarissa's hair, freshly-washed and black as a Raven's wing, coupled with her all-round beauty and grooviness, left Chas a happy but broken man. Austin, meanwhile, got on famously with Clara during an evening which was all but endless in its conviviality.

Colombia

Day 216
Wednesday 8 November
Mondo Miles today: 191
Mondo Mileage: 24460

Mondo Enduro was up again at 0625 after a heavy night but our curiosity to see ourselves on BDC (Buenos Dias Colombia!) had to be slaked. It did no good. After the Argentinian veto from yesterday we were ousted by some suspect beard-face frying mince in the studio. In fairness, the pretty female hostess seemed to love it!!?

We cleared up from Mike's flat and said our goodbyes, looking forward to seeing him again in Santiago, Chile at his father's house. We searched for David Parkinson downstairs. It did no good. Chas wrote the most impassioned apology to him about not beering with him last night. We feared it wouldn't heal the poison tipped darts he was doubtless preparing to fire at us from one of the weapons in his negotiator's gadget sack. We were heading now for a town to the southwest called Armenia. Austin has a cousin who did his year abroad there as part of a Spanish degree at Newcastle university. He established a firm friendship with a young lady called Liliana Hernandez with whom we had set a rendezvous for tonight. A blend in advance is not to be sniffed at out here and the next chance we have to be hosted is in Trujillo (Peru) 1500 miles to the south.

We bomb-burst to perform more sundry admin tasks. Austin was robbed at beard-point in the Lavenderia where underpants were being cleaned at the insane charge of $1 per skid. Anyway we had the last laugh because we weren't planning to have our washing done there again, ha-ho!

We all arranged to rendezvous at a bar and with unusual empathy Clive and Austin arrived at the same moment but unfortunately 2½ hours earlier than cheeky Charlie.

Eventually Chas arrived with the crap news that he hadn't been able to secure our video tapes back, with bulletin attached, that we had left with Harvey from the *En Vivo* TV shoot. A rough plan was made for Austin and Clive to get ahead to Liliana Hernandez's place, 180 miles away in Armenia. Chas would do the decent thing and spend the night with Clarissa, collecting the tapes and joining the others tomorrow morning. We quickly went to phone Liliana and ask her approval for our plan. It did no good. The phones were temporarily out of action. Eventually we got through and it was set.

By now it was 1400, it was a five-hour drive to Armenia and as we left the underground car park of the Andino shopping centre it began to monsoon down. Our exit from this subterranean haven was scotched by Clive having lost his parking ticket and the Robin Hood look-a-like *attendantas* refusing us exit. An amusing but frustrating scenario developed as we were incarcerated by an acrylic uniformed and shotgun totin' security guard, while Clive walked from pillar to post with the *Jefe*. The misunderstanding that under-pinned this incident was that Clive didn't realise you had to pay anything to park, Austin did realise, didn't realise Clive didn't realise and also, having paid at the kiosk, didn't realise that the girl had only 'taken' for one bike while he thought it was for both. Lost in translation...

Once it was finally resolved with an 80¢ fee, the safety catch was eased to the 'off' position and the Englishmen powered out into the torrential downpour.

The ill drained plateau in which Bogota sits caused the streets to flood almost immediately with a thick brown sludge. Austin got hit by a delivery van whilst using the pavement to 'get ahead'.

The dual carriageway south out of Bogota was reminiscent of the Great West Road around Hounslow and Hatton Cross. Gas stations taking credit cards were not found and so petrol was pumped in by a man with an unusually shaped head who sported the slowest discharging pump in the Andes. After what seemed like an age of gasoline dribbling in to our tanks, we togged up for the inevitable repeat of the Bogota downpour and pulled out.

The degree to which a motorcyclist's vision, road-holding etc, is diminished by the pouring rain is the same degree to which the Colombian lorry and coach drivers decide to increase their already endemic recklessness. The road was superb and one section, recently widened and re-tarmaced that went down the side of a huge gorge was incredible. The weather fluctuated extremely from baking near equatorial sun to further thunderstorms. By the time we reached Ibague it was only 36 miles to go but the worst lay ahead. It was raining as hard as ever and in the dark we noticed ponchoed conscripts lining all the main streets of the town at 100m intervals. We never discovered if there had been some recent unrest to precipitate this overt presence. It was like the pre-titles sequence of Kelly's Heroes; when the lightning bolts flashed we caught a momentary glimpse of the scale of this military roadside guard. Then it was back to peering through blurred goggles at the anonymous but standardised helmet/poncho outline. The streets flowed like rivers and the wacky one way system took us in what felt like every direction of the compass, a sentry every 100m.

The 36 miles to Armenia necessitated climbing up and over a huge mountain range. The road became as tortuously wriggly as any we'd experienced and the lack of white lines/cat's eyes and the driving rain gave us an average speed of 15mph. After an hour we stopped for a short leg stretch and encountered a local mental case with gummy smile and ripped poncho. It was well worth the journey just to experience the way he appeared to have been waiting just for us.

Colombia

Day 217
Thursday 9 November
Mondo Miles today: 0
Mondo Mileage: 24460

Clive and Austin awoke together in Liliana's sofa bed. They eventually got up when Liliana headed off to her work at the bank as a teller.

Before we knew it Liliana had returned from work at 12 o'clock and we had achieved nothing in her absence apart from rest. She informed us that Carlos (Chas) had phoned her and that he had left Bogota at 9am which made for an ETA of 3pm. Excellent news.

Around 1.30pm we received a further call from Chas – he had come across a 10 mile tail back caused by a collapsed bridge. He later found it was just being repaired and that they were holding the traffic whilst the workmen toiled. It soon transpired that the HGV drivers had had more than they could take and began hurling abuse at the workers. It did no good! Well it did eventually, as they started letting them through again shortly after.

Meanwhile, back in Armenia, Liliana and her 11 yr old nephew Daniel had got hold of some tickets to take us to a coffee theme park. The exhibits were all different species of coffee plant. At the end of the tour we were treated to a complimentary cup but it wasn't clear if it was a local speciality though. It seemed to taste like normal coffee. We felt terribly unsophisticated and guilty for not appreciating it properly. The ride home saw us soaked (it's rained torrentially every day in Colombia, how can the jungle-based rebels not go out of their minds?).

Supper consisting of toasted ham and cheese sandwiches and Liliana was pretty free and easy with the Rum and coke, result.

Colombia

Day 218
Friday 10 November
Mondo Miles today: 259
Mondo Mileage: 24719

Chas's late arrival after a perilous journey through the mountains was an excuse for an impromptu party chez Liliana. Mondo Enduro was back as a threesome once again after one of those separations which seem almost intolerable. The previous evening had developed an almost *film noir* intensity in the teeming rain and dense mist not to mention the shadow cast over his soul by his enforced departure from Clarissa's embrace.

And so the reunion at Liliana's was the cause for much merriment especially as Chas had arrived bearing a copy of the '*En Vivo*' footage from Bogota. The pop star image, sixties soundtrack and ace graphics made us look so much cooler than we really are. The real answer to why Mondo Enduro? Is surely that it allows us to wear fancy dress with a valid excuse. Friday morning started early after the previous evening's conviviality featuring Rum and cokes, victuals and ablutions. Despite our best intentions to start early, we were detained by the sound of Liliana's maid preparing breakfast, caffe con leche, scrambled eggs and Kellogg's cornflakes served AFTER the main course. Liliana herself looked great in a sailor's blouse and dark skirt which went some way to salving the lovesickness, which all Mondo members are experiencing to a greater or lesser extent.

Soon we were on the road after a brief call at the Avianca office to deposit mail. The road to Cali was straight and fast though a flat river valley surmounted on both sides by towering hills. The low altitude meant that most of the rain clouds spilled themselves on the lofty peaks sparing us from fresh inundations until well after Popagan. The road through what everyone (from Martin Pickford, Embassy close protection expert, to David Parkinson, hostage negotiator and Trans-global biker) had warned was alive with guerrilla activity passed without incident. *HOWEVER*, if we *do* get captured David's address is; 9 Ringwood Gardens, SW15 3QY. Chas cannot speak for the others but ransom negotiations should begin with the £50 on deposit in the Uttoxeter branch of the TSB.

And so the road, surprisingly well-graded and even-cambered, wore on through scenery which is becoming evermore dramatic. As the evening drew in, Clive and Austin prepared a meal of chopped onions and army compo ration's mixed vegetable soup. The result, a delicious broth, was later washed down with Vodka in a real mud hut, which served as our overnight accommodation.

As yet more rains came, depositing itself on the three travellers as they tried to achieve slumber, Austin, who had consumed a medium-sized Vodka tot, counselled Chas in a raised voice on how to win Clarissa's hand in marriage (for the record: lots of postcards from every country around the world then an air ticket to London to show her a groovy time. Then see what happens). Clive meanwhile dreamt of Candice and his 26th year which starts tomorrow. Standard.

Colombia

Day 219
Saturday 11 November
Mondo Miles today: 195
Mondo Mileage: 24914

Armistice Day and Clive's 26th birthday. It was a classic Mondo birthday in the field as so many before, i.e. waking up in an abandoned shed only now being charmed by the scent of stale urine.

It rained sporadically for the 100 miles to our *café con leche* stop. The journey then took us in and out of cloud; weaving in and out of debris from landslides and up into some fantastic mountain roads. We are coming into the Andes.

The coffee stop saw us move in and take over the patron's restaurant. Austin had his sodden Rab draped over their brick built dome oven, Clive had pulled out all his personal admin (including birthday cards) and Chas had the map and the moistened log out. All of these strewn over a couple of the restaurant tables in a desperate attempt to dry everything. This has been the form for the last three weeks, it rains so frequently and heavily our boots have never properly dried out. However, it is rarely cold.

Two coffees, army ration biscuits and some of their local cheese down us and an hour and a half later we were ready to leave for the final forty miles to the Colombian/Ecuador border.

Clive and Austin once processed, headed back into town to buy some more gas and Clive phoned home. The phone call took thirty two minutes and Clive managed to speak to most of his uncles and aunts who happened to be at Chestnut Cottage drinking the night away in his absence. Meanwhile, Chas changed over his screeching brakes for genuine Suzuki pads compliments of the gorgeous Kathleen McNaughton.

Shortly after 5pm we crossed a bridge welcoming us to Ecuador and began to worry slightly in case the officials were still persistent about carnets despite our intelligence from Bogota. Over the border without incident, result.

Daylight was now rapidly fading away so thirty miles later and it was time to seek out a campsite in darkness. We turned down a track attracted by a faintly glowing bulb dangling outside a distant farmhouse. As we pulled into the yard about 15 people emerged and Chas made our representation and respectfully asked if we could sleep in a barn or under the lean to. Within a second of finishing his stumbling faltered Spanish an old woman shook her head with a vehement "*no es possible*" and motioned for us to leave. Our first failed blending on Mondo Enduro. We walked away thanking them, rather embarrassed at the imposition we seem to have made. We ventured to some cowsheds 800 yards away and discovered the local herder whose *mi casa es su casa* was gratefully acknowledged with six Marlboro' Reds. We bedded down end to end in the long cement troughs that the cows feed out of – so we didn't fail really – *fantastico!*

Ecuador

Day 220
Sunday 12 November
Mondo Miles today: 255
Mondo Mileage: 25169

Morning didn't break on day 220, because we were raised while it was still definitely night-time, by a representative of Ecuador's version of 'Eden Vale' dairy products. Although given our cue to leave by this horse drawn *hombre*, the reader should know that we were very much awake as of about 0330 hrs. This was due to the three dogs that had gorgeously cuddled up with us (literally on our sleeping bags). It was snuggly but they later chose what was for humans, the middle of the night, to commence their intra-farmyard barking contest. To our road-dust clogged ears, it was the dogs in *our* cowshed that won this morning's heat. Doubtless the quarter finals will kick off at a similar time tomorrow morning.

As we sleepily arose, stumbling in the black of night, the collective Mondo Enduro adrenalin glands squirted urgency to our dulled brains. Moving relentlessly up the track, which was our only route out, there was approaching, a fog of Friesian cows, udders heavy and keen for some dairy relief in the very location that we had parked our bikes!

It was a ridiculous scene as these three toughened travellers flustered and fumbled as they tried to 'bug out' in quick time. Sure enough, the whole herd had hemmed us in, to say nothing of a multi-aged gang of farm-hands who had arrived concurrently to 'squeeze "n" pull'. Our weedy *Buenos dias* (even though it was still *noches*) did nothing to creak a single member of the milk detail's face into a smile. Our embarrassment could probably only have been averted by us producing from our panniers a complete battery of the latest EEC mechanised milking equipment. Half a mile of manure later we were back on the Carretera Pan Americana and loosely heading south.

By now, dawn had started to creak into life, but the mist and rain here at 8000 feet helped to extinguish the few rays of light that could have gone some way towards illuminating the route. What are we doing? It seems like we've been on the road forever and it's impossible to imagine the journey yet to come up through Africa. Hurrah! We're young, free and riding dirt bikes across the Andes!! Our lives will never be this good again!

As we wound our way through the few people that chose to be up at 0500 we were already cold and wet just 20 minutes into the day. How could we ever comprehend the hardship and physical misery that these lonely ponchoed souls, which tramp the verge, daily endure. The plain ½ blanket type poncho is king of outdoor gear in Ecuador. Male or female, young or old, almost everybody sports a trilby and undersize poncho. The latter looks quite useless as it seems rarely big enough to keep any heat in, nor could it sensibly be used as a blanket however, it looks pretty groovy.

Fifty miles in and the weather cleared (i.e. it stopped raining) we got a bamboo fire going and Austin changed his oil. Austin's oil filter was thickly encrusted with substantial glittery metal flakes and the oil was dark grey and opaque. These were more 'flyback to London now' omens. The congealed wad of metal flakes is clearly the remains of a part of the engine that is gradually grinding itself to death. However, we are clueless and were this a comic strip, a giant **?** would be printed over each of our heads. The new oil, decanted from the pink plastic fake wine flagon, bunged with the core of a corncob, was quickly poured in, along with a few cornflake sized foreign items. It's for sure these chickens will eventually come home to roost with that most hated sound of metal against metal, but when?

We rode onwards through further ranges of hills, all of a sudden denuded of the brilliant green vegetation that was the norm in Colombia. Instead, we found ourselves in scenery specifically reminiscent of Arizona and the area around the Hoover Dam. The road also lost much of the Colombian switchbacks and ridiculously tight bends and became a gloriously smooth hill bound racetrack. For several miles at a time the road was strewn with huge boulders, mud and rubble. Much of this debris was compacted by days old truck tyres and gave an indication of how the maintenance of this arterial route was basically zero.

In places, we could see the remains of the 'old' road's black top. This helped to illustrate how even these "B" and "C" class roads by British standards were huge undertakings of civil engineering. What really characterises the work are the vast cuttings and embankments that go some way to levelling the route. The Italian 'tunnel into viaduct' approach to thwarting this deeply incised valley terrain is clearly too expensive or technically advanced for the South American surveyors. Possibly because it was easier to have an army of labourers toiling on old skool 'cut and fill' tasks rather than the specialist and space constrictive alternatives of concrete work.

A minor confusion at an unlabelled T-junction caused Chas to become separated from Austin and Clive. The team wasted 4 hours getting re-coagulated just outside Tambillo (30m south of Quito, which we by-passed).

South of Quito the road widened to a huge dual carriageway. However, with no central reservation or road markings it was like driving along an airstrip. Our fellow Ecuadorian motorists kept things spicy by engaging in a 30 mile long linear version of dodgems which when combined with the torrential rain made for hair-raising near misses with the mobile disco-buses.

South of Ambato we pulled in at an oasis of Alpine hospitality. On the snow capped peak to our west rose Mount Chimborazo, we were soaking, freezing cold and we'd just crossed the Equator. Suddenly, around 7pm there loomed out of the drizzle a chance to get coffee handed in what seemed to be an authentic Austrian Gasthof! It looked just like the Swiss Cottage pub (which we acknowledge is neither Swiss nor Austrian). After the hot chocolate we weakened, looked guiltily at each other and booked in for the night. Er...happy birthday Clive!

Ecuador

Day 221
Monday 13 November
Mondo Miles today: 195
Mondo Mileage: 25364

We awoke disorientated amidst the comfort of crisp cotton sheets in our cavernous room in the Hoteleria Andaluza. A glimpse out of the window revealed the kind of leaden skies associated forever in our minds with Yorkshire or the Leek Army training grounds. To our knowledge, however, neither Hebden Bridge nor Macclesfield are surrounded by snow-capped volcanoes.

Anticipating a deluge similar to yester-evening's, which forced us like lambs into the warm shelter of the hotel, we togged up wearily in multiple roll-necks and layered long johns, not glimpsed since Alaska's sub-arctic climes. After a breakfast of luke-warm coffee and tasteless cheese, we set off on the dramatic ride to Bucay.

The road climbed steeply over ever-ascending terrain and past lonely road construction gangs, trilby-and poncho clad *campesiños* and the occasional goat. The highway afforded vista-vision views over an eccentrically stunning landscape which is in itself a testament to the unvanquished flame of the human spirit. It is not everyone who would happily tend an allotment 10,000 feet up and cut from the side of a volcano. Not even a Yorkshire man.

The road to Bucay was so beautiful that we just had to stop in the fold of a valley so Welsh that we felt vaguely let down having come all this way. We wonder if Ecuadorian tourists to the Brecon Beacons feel a similar sense of belonging. There we tarried awhile eating compo puddings and capturing the definitive Mondo meal imprint destined for Martin Pickford's mantelpiece.

Beyond Bucay the mountains suddenly split asunder to reveal a dramatic gorge. It was too photogenic a moment to let pass and Austin filmed remorselessly as Clive and Chas rode repeatedly across the bridge. Soon afterwards the road descended suddenly into the landscape of the Ecuadorian Oriente marked by an abundance of banana plantations. The contrast between craggy Andean and tropical coastal terrains could not have been more marked. The aforementioned warm clothing peeled away at a rate relative to the osculation of temperature.

Before Naranja, it became clear that Chas's clutch, diagnosed as dodgy in Whitehorse, was at last nearing the end of its much-abused life. Stuck fast in between fifth and sixth gear, only repeated kicking from manly Clive could free it from its torpor.

And so the last few miles of the Andes and indeed Ecuador sped away from us past a landscape owned almost entirely, it seemed, by the Dole banana empire. Austin raced ahead to begin border formalities and unfortunately was buzzed by a roadside dog. Many a rural motorcyclist will tell the tale of approaching a farmyard and suddenly being tracked by a screaming, galloping hound intent on shooing you off his 'manor'. Unusually, this particular canine was determined to make an impression and literally bounded into and under Austin's spinning 21" front wheel. It was a terrible mess, Austin almost crashed and such were the dog's injuries, *Pedro el pero* was dead within a minute. This event has saddened us all.

We arrived at the Peruvian border just after 6pm as the flag was being lowered and the chains being lashed across *el Puente internacionale* that marks *la frontera*. After lengthy negotiations and a $5 bribe we were allowed ingress into the chaotic township of Agnas Blancas whose *migracion* office was notionally closed until the morrow. The mood eventually warmed and the officials all oozed onto the pavement to check out the bikes. They were joined by the inevitable throng of money changers, snack vendors and no man's land freebooters that these places are home to and then *el Capitano* noticed Austin; he drew the crowd together and began some kind of high speed but brief Spanish exposition about Austin's face and hair. The onlookers were captivated by the customs chief but Austin was clearly bewildered. "*No entiendo señor Capitano*" he bemused. The Chief put his hand up to Austin's chin and gently rotated his head, offering the audience both of his English profiles. Once the inspection was complete he smiled at his beaming crowd and proclaimed: "Baldan!" With this, the hotch-potch of Ecuadorians erupted in hoots of laughter and were literally holding their sides as they wept tears of mirth. If the reader can explain what occurred here then they should contact Mondo Enduro forthwith.

Less frivolously, Austin's motorbike had given up the ghost literally on the Ecuadorian/Peruvian cusp leaving us stranded in this seedy barren town. It's rather serious, Austin went to kick his bike over as we finally were encouraged away from the Ecuador exit formalities and it locked solid, seized and unable to be turned over. Only delicate negotiations with the Customs headquarters staff, some 3 kms out of town, allowed us the comparative calm of a disused inspection hall in which to slumber.

And so, after Clive had towed Austin through the swarms of moto-taxis, the bikes were parked up in their latest garage much strewn with turds. We chose to sleep outside in the cool desert air swarming with mosquitoes hungry for Gringo flesh.

Peru

Day 222
Tuesday 14 November
Mondo Miles today: 200
Mondo Mileage: 25564

The morning spent at the Customs building – not only never used but also a makeshift public toilet – was highly pleasant. Chas's Canadian stove saved the day and created civilised brews which when combined with the rolls Clive had acquired set us up nicely for the tasks ahead.

Which were:
Have all our documentation squared away for our entry into Peru,
Get Austin's bike onto a lorry which could go all or part of the way towards Trujillo.

Deliverance was just around the corner when Clive met Van, a Californian who had driven his pick-up down from the States and was en route (in his own time) to the Southern tip of Chile. He was very interested in our trip and was keen to help, result. Sadly, when it became clear that the only way he could offer Austin + bike a lift south was by ejecting his two recently acquired female hitchhikers (Canadian) he made his apologies and left.

Although not worth its own paragraph one of the women in *migracion* was a surly cow.

A few negotiations later, the smallest but stockiest man in Peru – showing off a nose and forehead that proved he was a direct Inca descendant – struck a deal with us to take the bike as far as Chiclayo. This town is 120 miles North of Trujillo.

Over much huffing and puffing the bike was heaved onto the back of the lorry and wedged in alongside 7 billion *frijoles* <u>and</u> the tiny insects that resided amongst them. Clive and Chas set off and an RV was made for some time tomorrow at a petrol station on the North side of Chiclayo.

The Big Peruvian melted away and Austin discovered that the actual owner of the vehicle was Augusto, a limping 45 yr old sex maniac who drove the slowest and ropiest 1969 Volvo in the South. Augusto is second from the right of this photo and can be brought to life if one simply imagines such a thing as an Aztec Bernard Manning.

The bean mobile eventually set off at 7pm and crawled its way South down this recently re-paved section of the Pan American. Yesterday was torrential rain and jungle yet now we are surrounded by golden sand as far as the eye can see. Austin slept on the beans; the others did 200 miles and slept in the desert.

Peru

Day 223
Wednesday 15 November
Mondo Miles today: 150
Mondo Mileage: 25714

Clive and Chas awoke in the desert about 10 miles South of Piura bright and early. Clive discovered his whole body was covered in an extremely itchy rash which he calls 'suss skin'. None of us know what causes this alarming condition. The ruddy swellings seem to afflict any part of the body and do not appear to be the result of the bitings of any small midge, gnat or mosquito. Austin has been suffering for a while but Chas has escaped for the time being.

They had 150 miles to cover to meet Austin at the Nord Oriente gas station at Chiclayo. Eventually they arrived at the huge gas station cum bus depot cum truck stop at around 8.45am. There was no sign of Austin. He had either already found a lift to Trujillo or maybe he hadn't arrived yet.

Our suspicions were put to rest when a sprightly lad of European descent came over to Clive and Chas and introduced himself. This was Hernancito the 17 yr old son of Barbara Pasco (our future blend 150 miles South of here in Trujillo). What a teen God!

He had, in a panic subsequent to Chas's phone call the night before, taken a night bus from Trujillo to Chiclayo and had arrived there at 2am to stay with his Grand Aunt who lived nearby. He told us he had been there since 8am and Austin had not arrived. He was here to help us get to a mechanic or get the bike on another truck to Trujillo. What a teen God! So after a tasty lunch of chicken and veg at his Grand Aunt's we found a truck to take B2 with Clive and Ernancito too for 50 soles.

Austin on H6 and Chas followed the truck for the remaining strip of the Pan American to Trujillo. It got really cold and to minimise the wind chill Austin hunched in behind the lorry's slipstream. The only place where the biting desert gusts were minimised was about one metre from the tailgate. At 50mph this was as dangerous an exploit as we have seen on this trip.

10 miles North of Trujillo the truck decided he would have supper, so we all took a coffee break. It was now around 7.30pm and was dark. The truck dropped us off less than a mile from the Pasco Connor residence for a further 20 soles. We pushed Austin's bike the last mile.

We walked into Barbara's home at 8.30pm to meet her other son Carlitos (13 yrs old) who were there but her two daughters Christina (15) and Barberito (19) and husband Dr Pasco were elsewhere.

Barbara greeted us like old friends. There was much talk of Harrow where she came from and where her Mum and Dad still lived. She regaled us with altruistic tales of coming out here in 1971, recently qualified, bright-eyed and determined to nurse Peru into the future. We had a gorgeous supper and shortly after wobbled out on the floor of her dining room.

Peru (Trujillo)

Day 223 - 245
Thursday16 November – Thursday 7 December
Mondo Miles today: 0
Mondo Mileage: 25851

Chez Pasco-Connor

The Pasco residence was an oasis of quaint chaos amidst the order and sophistication of "*Urbanizacion El Golf*", one of Trujillo's more salubrious neighbourhoods. We found ourselves in a modern house, bought by Barbara with a modest family inheritance, which she and her charming family had conspired to wreck within the space of just a few years. In many respects, 479 Cocoteros, Casa No 17, was a time capsule from 1972, the year Barbara came to Peru to work as a nurse for a Catholic charity. The bookshelves were lined with an impressive array of sixties crime novels, whodunits and original James Bond paperbacks some of which included Ian Fleming's autograph.

One of the notable features of the *casa Cocoteros* was a bathroom that was in a state of DIY flux. Barbara warned us that on the electrical wiring front there were literally, some loose ends. Part of the guest briefing was not to touch the cold tap whilst the hot was warming up etc. Only Chas attended the bathroom briefing and when he relayed the key points to Clive and Austin not all the facts came across. Hence, it was with considerable surprise that Austin sustained a substantial jolt of 210 volts simply by adjusting the angle of the shower-head. It transpired that once the immersion heater switch was in the 'on' position then all the plumbing was 'live'.

A collection of National Geographic magazines dating back to the mid 1950's meant that we would never be short of reading matter. Two particular articles, one relating the exploits of an American academic on a 1958 jaunt to Russia, the other describing the Apollo moon mission prompted many animated discussions. Whilst here Barbara became our surrogate mother and we will always be indebted to her for such unconditional generosity to four people she had never met before.

A rapid strip-down of Austin's bike on the day after our arrival quickly revealed the cause of his seizure – a worn-out over-stretched camchain. It had jumped the teeth of the camchain sprocket, jammed and frozen the crankshaft. Hence the impression being one of engine lock up which thankfully it wasn't (hail seizure!!). A cursory examination of Chas's clutch revealed a serious problem but, with regard to the endless bounty of K McNaughton and Suzuki USA, we thought we might as well order a complete set of friction plates and springs. And so all that careful grooming of Miss McNaughton as our premier 'spongee' paid off with dividends again as she offered to provide the parts gratis. Thanks too to Tariq Saba at Orange County Suzuki for his help in packaging and despatching the array of gaskets and gadgets which will see us back on the road.

We met a couple of local girls in the town square, the tastiest of whom was Sandra. They became very attached to us but preferred not to blend us in. We filmed Sandra leading a political demo with the mayor and then she arranged for us to be the guests of honour at the opening of a small supermarket. Everyday that we saw them they insisted we take their pictures. We must have about fifty so far.

The parts were sent by DHL and two weeks later hadn't arrived. We reported to the local DHL agent every day until he knew us like old friends. He rang through every day to the 'hub' at Lima to chase up our crucial bundle. Always the same reply; "*possiblemente mañya*". Eventually we called the Lima office ourselves and the bloke said: "Sure, I've got it right here, you were meant to come down and collect this ten days ago." Verily, we spent *three weeks* sorting out this cam chain farce and that was the time we were meant to be noodling around Cusco and Machu Piccu. When we finally got going we were on a mission to be in South Africa by Christmas which was 17 days away. We gunned it south across the desert, heading for Chile.

Peru

Day 246
Friday 8 December
Mondo Miles today: 304
Mondo Mileage: 26155

Although sleeping within 20 yds of the highway, we may as well have been in the remotest niche of the Sahara. This Peruvian desert is quite definitely the most desolate, grassless, dusty wasteland that any of us have been to. It looks a lot like many of the more, impressive locations that were employed in 'Lawrence of Arabia'. The desert out here is superb. Clean, quiet, bug-free and devoid of Jacksons who well meaningly torture us in their quest for conversation.

The first irksome task of the day was to unload K5, Chas's steed, and push it up the sandy bank back to the road. The engine on this bike is fine but the splined fittings, male and female, on the gear change lever have been ground away, thus disallowing Chas from ever selecting humble first.

As Chas affected a repair on the early morning kerb, the exclusively HGV traffic honked, sirened and waved at us without fail. It was reassuring; after our first night in the field after an embarrassing 21 night absence, to be reminded that there really is some kind of ridiculous kinmanship between all those people whose lives see them permanently on the road.

Chas's gear lever bodge held out for 20 miles, by which time we discovered a steel yard complete with whopping great lathe and sundry other steel working knick-knackery. We also needed our 2nd dose of aluminium welding since Chas's rear Givi rack fractured during last night's sand pushing PT. The latter repair will have to wait, but with the gear lever permanently welded in place we were off once more.

The desert continued ad infinitum and the coast that we were hugging began to look more and more like California's. However, this is the first place we have seen thus far where there seem to be no coastal towns or fishing villages. The desert stretches all the way down to the actual shore – just blending in without any delineation. Every now and then we'd see a lone figure walking across the dunes, not a building in site, not a starting or finishing point in evidence for these David Carradine types. *Muy mysterioso!*

Austin slowed down proceedings by virtue of his spark plug working loose and causing the engine to cut out. The noble Clive returned to save him with a 40 mile detour. Austin in fact went onto reserve and then ran dry just as we reached the first town in a long while. This is the first recorded running out of petrol on Mondo Enduro. Much embarrassment and after only 233 miles – such is the headwind we battle against all day.

Lima gradually approached and we were soon sucked into the ultra-dangerous minibus stock car race in the suburbs – several requests to pay for gas with our VISA card were met with "*No Internationale*". Bah! We should make an advert for Visa showing us motorcycling all over South America getting our credit cards declined. A detour in downtown Lima saw us riding along the pavement once more. The mud-brick shacks and hovels plastered all over the hills make for a depressing sight. The poverty we have seen across the rest of Peru is worse here, and on a far larger scale. The main river that flows through the centre of town is a black rubbish strewn sewer – matched only by the excellent examples of open sewerage to be found in Morocco.

75 miles past Lima, the dual carriageway passed by some lovely beaches and coves. Three dirt bike riders, returning from a day on the hills, waved at us as we rode south. A burning sunset over the Pacific cued us off the Pan Am and into the desert. An old quarry and a cup of soup saw us as happy as ever – back on the road at last.

Peru

Day 247
Saturday 9 December
Mondo Miles today: 380
Mondo Mileage: 26355

We were woken in our first disused quarry on Mondo Enduro, by stones tumbling down around us throughout the night. We were constantly under the belief it was going to be Jacksons. However, it was only mini-avalanches and we slept soundly in a dry, mild, quiet and bug free area.

We set off a little while after dawn back on that beautiful black ribbon of tarmac of the Peruvian Pan American Highway. This highway has been as good as any section of road in the US or UK for that matter. It is even better though as it has practically no traffic lights or roundabouts, and the scenery alongside has been absolutely breathtaking.

We stopped for a brew and breakfast after 100 miles in a field which had fresh clear water running along one edge of it probably for irrigation. Full tummies for the Mondo Men were provided by rolled oats mixed with the new found scrumptious Cerevita (a Peruvian version of Ready-Brek), that we lived on at the Pasco's in Trujillo.

Once again the wind was blowing strongly against our dirt ridden faces and ageing DRs. So it was no surprise to find our fuel consumption blown right out of the window achieving just over 200 miles before switching onto reserve. This was made worse for the budget boys as Peru has the most expensive petrol since way back in those days of Italy at $2 a gallon: however, with our recent self catering splurge it isn't so bad as all that.

We arrived at the world famous Nasca Lines at midday. The sky was blue and it was damned hot as we scaled the *mirador* look out tower to admire these ancient scrawlings in the dust. They were hard to appreciate but apparently a lot better from the air (by plane). We confused the tree for the monkey and vice versa. It was all a bit of a mess if the truth be known. But as they were less than 10 metres off the Pan American we had to pay them a call!

The wind became progressively worse and we battled against it trying our best to make ourselves as aerodynamic as possible and protecting our faces from the blasting with sand at the same time. We rode through some stunning lunar landscapes again and couldn't help comparing this to Azerbaijan and Turkmenistan. One particular section where the road ran parallel to the ocean roughly 20m from the beach saw the worst winds yet and even the sea was turning green with envy at our progress. The sand and wind jointly almost blew us off the Pan American and into the bordering desert dunes. This setting was almost identical to day 37 when we negotiated the blustery road into Baku.

However, we then climbed into the hills and the wind died down. The remaining hours of daylight were superb as we weaved into and out of some slinky bends on the stunning mountainous coastline. It was here that Chas found a magnificent campsite in a hidden valley perpendicular to this spectacular sea front. Soup, bread and Vodka and we merrily drifted into the land of nod under another stunning star lit night.

Chile

Day 248
Sunday 10 December
Mondo Miles today: 382
Mondo Mileage: 26737

Chas owes Austin £100.

The day began, like so many before, with the sound of Clifford Greenhough exhorting us to rise and shine. The night had been long and peaceful and had left us feeling perky after approximately nine hours of repose.

The road which had afforded such stunning views the previous evening continued for some miles along this ruggedly beautiful desert coastline. After just 11 miles, and a spot of filming, the day's first technical drama struck in the guise of a warped front brake disc which had caused Chas's front pads, installed in Panama City, to decay at an alarming rate. A new set, the last of the Los Angeles hamper, was quickly installed and we shall have to have our sponging technique at its most polished if we are to secure the lengthening list of necessary genuine Suzuki parts from Mr Swanepoel of Suzuki South Africa.

An initial blast of 70 miles saw an arrival in Camana, a bustling town on the cusp of a major inland switchback of the Panamericana. Austin changed money and fulfilled stores lad duties, purchasing bread, bananas, rum, coke and a delicious variety of fudge brownie. Austin, meanwhile, rang Sandra in Trujillo in the teeth of fierce opposition from his fellow travellers.

And so the road continued through alternately stunning and boring landscapes of lofty cliffs and featureless desert. The miles slipped by almost effortlessly in stages of 70 miles as we made rapid progress down the superb Panamericana.

Lunch was some dried fruit or nut of uncertain identity shared with a Peruvian hitchhiker outside a tunnel where we did some filming. He gave us Coca-Cola and showed us his rosary beads by way of saying thank you.

Perhaps it should also be mentioned that Austin "Rotting Man" Vince was today sporting a new lesion to go with the long-standing Suss Skin condition and yesterday's globulous eye. Today it was the sub-cutaneous blackhead spilling its puss through the heaving pores of his nose. Asked why it should be he, and not any other Enduriste, who appears to be suffering from a progressive wasting disease, he replied that it was because of his recent electrocution. We await his total physical disintegration with eager anticipation! (Austin's ear sported a super-large yellow head tomorrow).

Anyway, ever onwards to the town of Tacna which is just 40 kilometres from the Chilean border. We arrived at 4.40pm and decided to make a dash for the border. There, under the beady eye of a Peruvian Customs official, we consumed pineapple which apparently is deemed a cholera risk in Chile. We also met Tara, a British teacher of English in Lima, who was slipping over the border to have her visa extended.

Customs formalities on the Chilean side were somewhat extensive with various stamps to obtain from the state fruit monitor and a decidedly unhealthy looking *Ministerio de Salud* official. By now Chile's clocks had advanced two hours and its nightfall was long gone. We pulled off the road just yards from the border close to a gaping river gorge and surmounted by a throng of military bunkers and OPs. We've done 353 miles a day for the last three days. No dramas, let's hope we can keep this up. There again, we've never been able to so far.

Chile

Day 249
Monday 11 December
Mondo Miles today: 402
Mondo Mileage: 27137

When anybody reads these pages, a few days either side of this particular entry, we should point out that the week from 7-14 December 95 represents the Mondo Enduro 'dash' for Santiago, capital of this slender nation. It's incredible to think that with notionally 18 months set aside for this 44,000 mile journey, we should ever have to punish ourselves with a minimum of 350 miles a day for a minimum of 7 days. In all the hard riding that we have achieved to date, we feel that these 2500 miles from Lima to Santiago are the most unpleasant to date. One word will perfectly capture what this time has been characterised by: "DESERT".

The heat during the afternoon is unrelenting. However, more serious than the temperature is the intensity of the sunlight. We have all been burned whilst in Trujillo, but here on the road our lips and noses are suffering like never before. Barbara Pasco supplied us with a 1950's looking brown ointment for mouth ulcers whose remit we have expanded to include the scabby yellow sores on our lips. Puritanical healing doctrine is satisfied, since when this bilious juice is applied, it not only stains the lips brown in a most unsightly manner, but it also elicits a scream of pain that curtails much jaw holding and hopping about the hard shoulder.

Chile is expensive. The gas here is costing us over $2 a gallon and apples cost $1 a kilo. The scarcity of settlements here in the Atacama Desert means that we can never afford to pass through a town (i.e. one per day) without stocking up on the necessities for our life (bread, fruit, petrol, rum).

So today continued, ploughing across the endless sand and hoping that the wind direction will favour us. If it doesn't, it makes the progress very hard work and annihilates our mpg. Virtually the only other traffic we see are Volvo 'executive' coaches hammering between the towns, and of course HGVs. Although irrelevant, we noticed the transition from Peru into Chile by many different barometers, one of which is that the coach drivers clearly wear a uniform peculiar to their coachline.

At one of the afternoon rest ups we saw a shimmering haze approaching over the horizon. The tell-tale shape of a large motorcycle loomed upon us and soon we were swapping stories with a German couple on a short 7 week tour on their 750cc Africa Twin. They had paid $2000 to ship it out and back from *Deutschland* to Buenos Aires with Air France. We never even asked their names.

We broke 400 miles at sundown and drifted off into the desert and enjoyed another starlit night. This is definitely the most striking part of the world any of us have been to. A railway sleeper fire warmed our hearts and bodies as we drifted off.

Chile

Day 250
Tuesday 12 December
Mondo Miles today: 380
Mondo Mileage: 26355

Once again Clive was up bright and early just before dawn, this time though to rekindle the fire. There was no timber so he leathered up as it was freezing cold and headed off on the scrounge for wood. It must be said, a difficult task in the desert but essential as our stove from Canada is being a bit temperamental in these arid, dusty conditions and with that ghastly leaded fuel.

Warm Orange, a cup of coffee with oxtail soup residue (last night's supper) and a third of a banana each was the power meal to get Mondo Enduro going on this chilly morning.

A quick negotiation again of some deepish sand and tricky terrain and we were back on the tarmac destination Antofagasta (45 miles). We crossed the Tropic of Capricorn on the way and stopped for a quick photo.

Twenty minutes later we descended through a twisty valley down into the Port of Antofagasta to replenish food, petrol and cash.

It was a major success as Shell actually accepted our credit card and allowed us to recharge our video batteries (from their mains) whilst we went about our tasks around town. Our twelve volt battery charger thing is smashed; it couldn't sustain the rough and tumble of life outside a flight case. We were still in desert after our brief encounter of the shoreline in Antofagasta and had been for many days now and we were hoping it would end soon.

We discovered at our next fill up that the desert continued for a further 500 kilometres. Oh No!! We were gutted. Another day, of sand lined up for tomorrow too. Oh well it can't be hot and dry all the time! Mondo Enduro beginning to yearn for cooler weather, even a touch of rain would not be frowned upon now.

Our prayers were answered soon after and there were clouds on the horizon. The air cooled down and the wind stayed the same – blowing as hard as ever and occasionally with us too. We had reached the coast again and now it was totally overcast and threatening to rain.

We then met George the German on his heavily laden push bike. He was cycling from the Northern tip of Chile to Santiago or thereabouts for a 5 week holiday. Maybe he didn't realise this part of Chile was all desert. For he was covered head to toe with peeling skin. This was the second day we had met a German in Chile and we also saw one in Northern Peru. They seem to be the only race doing extraordinary journeys in far away places. He had hoped we would camp the night with him after his struggle and self-imposed boredom of crawling through the desert. Unfortunately for him we were only 310 miles for the day at 7.10pm and there was 1 hour of daylight left. So sorry old chap you should have brought a friend as Mondo Enduro are on a mission. We've got at least 50 miles to do in this last hour and bade him farewell.

Our abode for the night was on a cliff top near the 900km post. It was flat and occasionally rocky but mainly covered in millions of ancient shells in their sedimentary layers.

Austin made the fire with the scrap wood we had collected during the day. It's a never ending chore but the treeless wilderness of the Atacama offers no fuel for the rough camper. Hence, there is an ongoing league table that is topped by which of us has accrued the greatest mass of twigs, old pallets and smashed up crates by day's end. As we pool our hauls each evening it makes quite an unusual sight.

The choice of the day was mushroom and beef stock soup followed by chicken and beef stock soup with our still fresh bread rolls purchased from Antofagasta. Dessert was apples and oranges followed by *Ron sin Coke* to help us sleep.

Chile

Day 251
Wednesday 13 December
Mondo Miles today: 400
Mondo Mileage: 27891

The overcast skies had provided an extra blanket for us last night, for which fact we were grateful given the desert chill of the previous evening. We awoke to the same glum clouds which seemed to have moved not one inch during the relatively balmy hours of darkness.

The battleship grey of the new dawn gave us the perfect opportunity to check out the fossil landscape of our sleeping quarters. Millions of shellfish had been petrified into the living rock creating a strange Jurassic Pond full of crustacean life forms.

After coffee and the remainder of the Antafagastan apple teacake, we were soon on the way southwards along the interminable Pan-Am asphalt. The weather by now was playing strange tricks on us – huge blankets of sea mist would billow in from the coast prompting involuntary wearings of cold weather clothing not glimpsed since Ecuador. Then just as suddenly the fog would lift to reveal more empty blue skies.

By Vallarmar, we needed a fuel stop and pulled into a Copec gas station within minutes of an impromptu fashion mag style shoot in front of a giant Suzuki poster. With this image in our folio we are sure to be provided with free bikes for life by this eternally grateful company. Chas, ever safety conscious, had secured the Golden Globe for the two cm ride to the fuel pumps, but Clifford and Austin had failed to take similar precautions. A vigilant *carabineri* clearly welcomed the opportunity to indulge his officious nature and nicked them both for a *no casco infracion*. A lengthy two-hour delay ensued whilst they were whisked away to the cop-shop for payment of requisite $12 penalties.

And so the journey continued through terrain which was at last becoming ever-less desertified. The appearance of a few goats and the increasingly barbed-wire fence enclosed landscape was heralding our arrival in the Chilean heartland. We have done 2040 miles across unbroken desert in the six days since we left Trujillo. None of us realised that outside of the Sahara there was a place on our planet like the Atacama.

As the evening hastened on we pulled into the verge exactly on the dot of 400 miles. We selected a campsite close by the river populated by herds of wild horses, the occasional gaucho and the odd mosquito. Soon the billy was boiling on a fire of pre-collected wood and the usual soup mixtures plus Tabasco sauce and bread rolls was being served to the hungry travellers. Much of the dregs of the Peruvian rum was consumed before sleep softened our senses and although Austin's alcoholically amplified ramblings delayed our collective shuteye. Remember the Greek half-built house; the Ecuadorian mud-hut...

Chile

Day 252
Thursday 14 December
Mondo Miles today: 157
Mondo Mileage: 28048

It took postman Cliff to raise Chas and Austin from their shared groundsheet. It was still dark and we estimated the hour was before 0530. Last night's impulse purchase of a carton of peach 'nectar' was gratefully necked, and the *al fresco* refrigeration afforded from it laying out in the cool desert night made it taste that much sweeter.

We ploughed (literally) back across the soft sand and made it to the safe haven of route 5 – Pan Americana Sur and twisted open the throttles.

Austin even wore his poncho to keep the unexpected desert chill at bay. We'd waited a long time for the chance to creak off the bikes for a rest and lament; "Phew, this is Chile", and no-one was gonna stop us!

We pulled in at a Mobil station and called the British Embassy at Santiago to warn them off. The petrol station sported a mini-market and diner. We'd been really impressed by the pump-side 'Visa' card sweep at a gas station in La Serena last night and the sensation that routines were becoming more European with every mile southwards.

As the infrastructure firmed up, so calmed the vegetation. We were intrigued to see how the broad elements of the area's geography changes with latitude, because we're interested in that, and a few more specks and flecks of green manifested themselves to challenge the oppressing monotony of the desert. Man's impact was noticed by the fencing that flanked the highway which shortly before had never existed.

It stayed overcast for a while but as the traffic congealed on the outskirts of Santiago, we witnessed the sun pouring through. A meaty car crash on our southbound carriageway caused a tidy snarl up which we short cut by some judicious hard shoulder riding.

We eventually arrived in Santiago and it was time to locate our host. Clive had duplicated, in his own hand, Mike Flynn's excellent sketch map leading us to his Dad's house. All three Mondo men were map handed and hence loosely independent. We located Mike and Dan Flynn's palatial embassy residence with ease but Mike was at the shops. We surprised him with our new short dark haired appearance and he didn't recognise us. Austin has dyed his hair black and shaved it to be homogenous with his chunkster sideburns. He now looks like an idiotic version of Emperor Ming.

We teamed up and went downtown on vital errands. We went to the British Embassy first where a tough and unhelpful Chilean beauty refused to allow us into the inner sanctum. Fortunately, our luck changed when Ray Dalton emerged from the lift. Former RAF man turned FCO security watchdog – Ray ushered us in and introduced us to Judy Cairns and her Chilean (gorgeous) assistant.

In no time these two ladies had us hooked up with local TV and newspapers plus a gratis coffee thrown in. Ray let each of us call UK on his phone and Judy invited us to a production of Cinderella for tomorrow night. Faxes were sent and mail posted (for free), things were looking blendful.

The remainder of the afternoon was spent with the superbly affable and jovial Mike Flynn guiding us around town as we visited HiFi shops, Air Malaysia (beautiful sales assistant), B/W film developing and of course our much deserved first visit to a restaurant in a while.

The evening was spent with the hospitable Dan and Mike toiling over the Weber BBQ, joking about Austin's desire to own an "above ground pool" and theories espoused that South Africa's organisational status was born of the Germanic influence therein.

Much MTV, the "Menswear" video (weak) and a night followed sandwiched between crisp cotton sheets. Thank you Mike Flynn...

Chile

Day 253
15-21 December
Mondo Miles: 0
Mondo Mileage: 28048

It has turned out that Santiago was to be our last port of call in the Americas, by bike anyway. The dream was always to ride the length of the continent down to Tierra del Fuego but our self imposed desire to spend Christmas in South Africa with Louis Bloom has moved things on a bit.

We have been forced to fly from here (Santiago) rather than Buenos Aires since the Argies were going to charge us $700 even though it's closer to Africa. So although cutting our journey short we did the neccessary thing and flew from Chile; thus depriving Argentina of our precious dollars and instead reserving them for good times and essentials in South Africa.

Our time in Santiago has been principally taken up in arranging to get the bikes and ourselves on to the African continent. They are being flown by Lufthansa from here to Johannesburg (via Frankfurt) for about $500 each. Pretty cool, it means they'll be there the day after us! We're flying with Al Italia.

We have stayed as guests at the homes of Dan Flynn (US Embassy) and Ray and Mary Dalton (British Embassy). It has been a superb time staying in comfortable, clean and ritzy homes with all the mod cons and pools. Our experience on Mondo Enduro would have been completely different if instead of being blended in by our hosts we were reduced to being normal people and getting a hotel. It is quite surprising to us that this rhythm of hospitality has established itself, it was never considered when we plotted this adventure in the Pizza Hut in Nottingham.

Once again, we find ourselves leaving another vast continent by plane. A continent that has brought us great roads, wonderful and beautiful people, the most magnificent scenery so far on Mondo Enduro and with of course fantastic banking facilities, credit card outlets and sound communications.

Suddenly, after the numbing delay in Trujillo followed by this 2000 mile desert dash across the Atacama, we can gather our thoughts. Except that we can't because it's kick, bollock, scramble to get across the South Atlantic before the world shuts down for Christmas. With Eurasia, the Americas and 28,000 miles behind us it's suddenly dawning on us that we are definitely two thirds of the way round. Psychologically we are starting to feel that we just might pull this off whereas up until now it was impossible to even contemplate the distances *yet* to be covered. We are finally confident with our machines, we're ready for any border aggro, our admin on the road is excellent and our credit cards haven't yet been recalled. So now for the most exciting part of our journey so far, Africa…

MONDO ENDURO

PART 3

SOUTH AFRICA BACK TO LONDON

South Africa

Day 261
23 Dec
Miles today: 0
Mondo Miles: 28047

We arrived at Johannesburg airport and immediately contacted Louis Bloom at Sun City who arranged transport for us in a little minibus. Accompanying us in the vehicle were two charming English people, Nick and Irene Holmes who invited us to dinner with them that evening up at the Palace Hotel. What a result, a blend on our first night!! Nick was a marketing guy for booze giants Interbrew and entertained us with vignettes from the cut and thrust of pub makeovers.

They drive on the left here which took us all by surprise. The 100-mile journey to Sun City through heavy bush drew to a memorable close when Louis came to greet us at The Cascades hotel on board the head chef's "VOS.XOD" Soviet hair-dryer motorcycle. Cliff and Louis soon introduced us to the delights of the Staff Bar and a memorable Mondo Christmas party was enjoyed by all, complete with turkey, mince pies and most of Louis's collection of classic South African wines.

Day 262
26 Dec, Boxing Day
Miles today: 0
Mondo miles: 28047

As promised our bikes had arrived via Lufthansa's peerless air freight service from Frankfurt and were awaiting collection at the airport. However, the following day almost spelt disaster for us when we were confronted by a pair of terrifyingly Teutonic Customs Officials demanding to see our tryptieks – or carnets de passage, a costly document which we have spent our entire journey trying to circumvent. The carnet (or tryptiek) is a travel document of such spectacular incomprehension to a European that we should explain: It is an official booklet that pages are stamped onto and ripped out of as one crosses a frontier with a car or motorcycle. It can only be acquired through the motoring organisation of the parent country of the vehicle's registration (in our case the AA) and it is expensive. Well no actually, carnets for our bikes would only cost about £85 per bike but to secure them one has to lodge two and a half times the bike's new value with the AA. So for us, that would be about £7000 each!! The basic idea being that if you illegally sell your vehicle whilst abroad, when you try to leave the country you sold it in you won't get the carnet booklet properly stamped. No stamp, no refund of the £7000, simple.

It seems that since the borders of every single country in Europe, the former USSR and the Americas manage to survive without their use that means that there's one place on the Earth that feels the need to embrace them: Africa.

So here we were, in the customs equivalent of hand-to-hand combat with two blonde haired, blue eyed, square jawed tryptiek fascists. Naturally, they knew we were British yet could clearly detect that both Austin and Chas has attended anti-apartheid rallies back in the eighties so guess what fellas, it's payback time. The officials were resolute that the bikes couldn't be released from customs without a tryptiek and in fact as they spelled this out to us they looked pretty bloody pleased with themselves. Clive both bit his lip and held his tongue, instead, launching an unexpected charm counter-attack. It was smoothly suggested to the intransigent customs Nazis that what made the New South Africa a beacon of hope in the southern hemisphere was reconciliation and that reconciliation's ever present bed-fellow was compromise. Clive brought our bikes' jailers around to the idea that pedantry surrounding the paperwork was not only unnecessary, it was un-South African.

Within 45 mins they were unloaded from the Lufthansa pallet and two hours later we were riding them through the welcoming gates of the Sun City entertainment complex. Result.

South Africa (Sun City)

27 December – 13 February

These dates reveal an unscheduled seven week hiatus for Mondo and the reason for that is best captured in two words: Louis Bloom.

Louis was in the year below Clive at Mill Hill School and they had been firm friends ever since. Louis had always been our first line blendee for South Africa but within a few hours of our arrival we began to notice the change in him. It was clear that if offered to join the trip for the remaining leg back to London then he would surely accept. Louis had neither bike licence nor motorcycle but he did have something far more important: zeal. Louis is as likeable a bundle of effervescing A.D.D. energy as you are ever likely to meet and for we three slightly flagging *Enduristas* he was a welcome shot in the arm. We weren't road weary but we were certainly extremely accustomed to getting up in the morning, jumping on the little 350s and doing whatever we damn well pleased. This phenomenal freedom was beginning to be taken for granted and it was Louis, when he became the fourth member of the team, who reminded us just how lucky we were.

So there we have it: Louis resigned within a few days of our arrival but of course he had to work another month before actually going. Hence, we settled in to spending the January summer in Sun City whilst Louis served his notice and the rest of us found him a bike and made it expedition-ready for him.

Sun City

One of the many advantages of staying in a complex geared purely around entertainment is that it is very easy to be entertained. With Louis Bloom (Head Concierge) as our host, it was more importantly, very easy to be entertained for free, whilst those seated alongside us had paid top dollar.

Hence we found ourselves as guests of the irrepressible Ibrahim, the beautiful Jo, the diminutive Andy and occasionally, the strangely proportioned Michelle, all dancers in the Sun City nightly dance feast known as "The Extravaganza". Much partying was done with the aforementioned and with a month to kill there began a period of unrestrained hedonism that was the closest we ever got to truly fulfilling the emancipation that comes from having no job. Through these dancers we made the acquaintance of the two blonde lady trapeze artistes, one of whom was a moto-cross rider of phenomenal natural skill (and sadly for Mondo Enduro – totally married). We

333

all agree that the South African accent, so clipped on men is a delight when spoken by the ladies.

Hartebeestport Dam

We had only been in South Africa a few days before Louis had appointed himself our PR Svengali and was jacking up press exposure for us. We were of course hungry for coverage as it would mean more ammo when we went scrounging spark plugs and brake pads from Suzuki South Africa. Within a week we were on the news and then the SABC called us back for a ten minute slot on *Good Morning South Africa*.   Austin was interviewed on the radio and we were on the front page of *The Johannesburg Times*. This lead to a phone call from 'Redline', South Africa's only real 'biker' magazine.   They wanted to hook up for an interview and photo-shoot and suggested the local beauty spot that is the reservoir impounded by the Hartebeestport dam.

We naturally jumped at the chance and a rendezvous was made with the editor for Sunday lunchtime.

It was great fun being interviewed if only because back in England we are ordinary people and no one ever asks any of us for our 'story', and then prints it! The editor guy was a cross between a full on Back Street Hero and an unreconstructed old skool *boer*. Fiercely independent and determined not to have his spirit ground to a paste on the merciless cogs of 'the system'. He rocked!

After the interview proper we went up to the actual dam wall to lunch at a burger van that the editor recommended. We were stuffing our faces with a scrumptious Transvaal hot dog when the police arrived. Out they sprang from a little panda car and immediately the stewards began:

"Whose are these bikes?"   Delivered in the most authoritarian clipped Afrikaans accent.

"Excuse me officer they belong to us."

"Well you must get them off the road, immediately. They cannot be ridden on the public highway." Now more impatient, nay, irritated.

"Crikey officer, what is wrong with them?"

"They must have South African registration plates and look, they haven't even any flickers! (indicators)" These are the most officious police we have ever encountered.

"But officer, we are British tourists who brought these bikes here by plane and will be riding them back to London in a few weeks, there hasn't been a problem with any of the 34 countries that we have driven across so far. We don't live here, we're in transit."

"It doesn't matter, all vehicles on the public road must be registered with the department of motor registration, and you must have flickers!!"

By now a knot of people had gathered around and the roadside court was becoming a public hearing. A portly man then piped up: "Hey, you're the guys who were on TV last week aren't you?" That was the crack in the dyke we needed as it transpired that almost everyone present knew about these Englishmen that had just arrived from Russia and the Americas. Things took a turn for the better when several of the crowd began remonstrating with the coppers and basically encouraged them to get back in the car and catch some 'real' criminals. This they did but not without the predictable:

"OK, we'll let it go for now, but make sure you get some flickers!"

The hairdresser and the article

In early January two spools were uncoiling; one of them was that Louis was brokering an interview for us with a South African adventure travel publication called 'Out There'. We humbly supposed that our low budget ethos would qualify us for their pages, and what pages they were. 'Out There' was a recently launched perfect bound newsstand glossy with real publishing muscle behind it. If anything, we could see that our expedition might just be rather *too* vagabondo and not enough wholesome *voortrekker* but we were super excited all the same, none us had ever been in anything apart from the Mill Hill School magazine. Many phone calls with the features editor, and the magazine sent a photographer to meet us in downtown Johannesburg to pick up some shots of us for possible use on the cover!

Meanwhile, we had become the objects of attention for two of the hairdressers that worked in the luxury beauty parlour that was attached to the Sun City resort. Leonard and Ibrahim were extremely plucky, colourful characters and stood out from their normal rugby and barbecue fixated countrymen by being black and extremely homosexual. Ibrahim in particular would pester us for lifts on the back of our bikes and once on board would squeal and shriek whilst 'holding on' with an unnecessarily firm grip. Leonard was the chief stylist at the salon and insisted that he treat us to a four-headed hair-dying session so that we could set off back to London looking as chic as possible. Since the offer was free of charge we accepted immediately and were soon clamped into the salon's reclining chairs with burning goo and plastic bags on our heads. We were surprised to find that the active ingredient in the hair dye needed three hours of cranial incubation for it to fully take effect. Eventually though, Leonard sashayed into the parlour, gave us each a needlessly thorough scalp massage and announced with a flourish that the master's work was complete. We looked ridiculous but at least we would sport our electric blonde hair-dos with equal shame.

The next day was the 'Out there' photo session and we hooked up with Karl a budding photo-journalist. We insisted Louis be in the shoot since he was now an official team member. We whizzed around the streets on the bikes and Karl snapped us as we pursued his car. Then he took us up to a weirdly derelict hillock that commanded the city, which in turn was looked down upon by a circular concrete tower block crowned with a giant 'Coca-Cola' advert. This struck us as possibly the least African location we could imagine; in fact when gazing upon this backdrop the one word that sprang to mind was 'Birmingham'. We goofed about in our ponchos and soon Karl declared it a 'wrap'. We got his card and he promised to be in touch about the piece.

Days turned to weeks but nothing more was heard. We took turns pestering their switchboard but it did no good. A few days before we finally hit the road north we got a call from Karl. Aha!!! In the nick of time. He would surely have news of when our feature was hitting the stands.

"Owsit, er... sorry 'bout not getting back sooner fellas, it's all been a bit mad at the office. Er... I'm afraid the editor doesn't want to do the story he thinks you all look far too gay. Er... I'll mail you the shots and maybe you'll see where he's coming from, er... sorry.... and good luck for the rest of your trip."

Aggro.

SafeSeal

After the Good Morning South Africa appearance we were contacted by a local entrepreneur who thought he had something we should know about. George de Pontes was a 45 year old inventor who looked like Salvador Dali and had developed a product he called SafeSeal. As the name rather cleverly suggests this was a puncture preventer goo just like the yellow stuff Joe McManus had donated us back in Los Angeles. In fact, that stuff didn't seem too amazing so we didn't hold up much hope for this southern hemispherical version. Mr de Pontes ardently explained that he had developed it at the request of the South African Army. Back in this country's 'sinister white past' the army patrols into Soweto and other townships would come under gun fire and their tyres would duly be punctured. There wasn't enough money to refit all the vehicles with solid rubber wheels so enter the de Pontes wonder goo.

George de Pontes met us in Johannesburg and he struggled out of his car with a 30 litre canister weighty with his miracle product which had the consistency of curds and whey. As he pumped the requisite portion into our waiting inner tubes he explained the ultimate SafeSeal test: an armoured car tyre was loaded up with the milky paste and then a machine gun emptied into the waiting rubber. On inspection there were 27 bullet entry points yet the tyre remained inflated. As Mr de Pontes reached the climax of his test report he could see that we were impressed. Our expedition is plagued by unrequested deflation and we gladly adorned the bikes with the SafeSeal stickers that he proffered. We have undertaken to feedback to him the results of our four bike 10,000 mile field trial. Thank you George de Pontes!

Springs

Springs is a small town to the northeast of Johannesburg and has the same relationship to it as Brentwood does to London. It was here, nestled in a quiet backstreet, that we found the low key command bunker of Suzuki South Africa. Our silly postcards had been raining down on Steve Swanepoel the boss man, at regular intervals over the last six months and now it was time to meet him.

Louis had booked us in and in his brief phone conversation with Steve he had described Mondo Enduro with language so overstated and exaggerated as to suggest we had motorcycled to the moon and back. Hence it was with a foreboding sense of guilt that we were ushered into the great man's office. He looked like the road manager to a hugely successful rock band c.1974 with the easy sophisticated confidence normally reserved for the very worldly. Steve thanked us for our cards and press clippings but was chagrined to inform us that since the DR350 was a model that wasn't sold in Africa he wasn't sure what he could do for us. We were quick to enquire as to whether he could get us the parts we needed and with a warm smile he said that this, he *could* do for us.

The ripples of Steve Swanepoel's generosity began to emanate out from his office and soon we were officially given the run of the company workshops on the ground floor. The chief mechanic was a bounteous font of advice, tools and kindly smiles. He deduced in a thrice that the oil that continued to gush from the end of Austin's camshaft would be deftly stemmed by the replacement of a humble fibre washer. We spun spanners and wrenched ratchets in a three day maintenance binge that set the bikes up for the next 10,000 miles. We were allowed to use the office fax machine and requests were made for certain kit and supplies from England. Hence we now all have ponchos, no tent and Nick Stubley sent over his bespoke Mondo petrol tank for Louis to mount when he got a bike. A further bonus of us being at the Suzuki workshop was the giant dustbin round the back. We discovered on a routine visit to deposit some garbage that it was full of part worn motorcycle tyres. Clive dived in and we salvaged six tyres that we are sure will get us most of the way home.

Meanwhile, Steve Swanepoel had one last trick up his sleeve for which we were eternally grateful. Through his network of contacts he put the word out that we were in the market for a DR350 for Louis. He got a call a few days later and incredibly, it was a dealer in Springs who had just inherited a grey import 1993 DR350. We walked around there and several fistfuls of Rand later Louis was on board the eighth bike to be inducted into the stable and within a few minutes he was sticking his callsign onto the front mudguard: S8.

Carnets:

Despite having blagged our way past South African customs without carnets the intelligence we were gathering was bringing into crisp focus a picture of sealed borders and huge bribes all the way through the rest of the Dark Continent if we *didn't* get them. We had a bit of a tight spot developing but were plucked from the jaws of calamity by the helping hand of Geoffrey Vince (Austin and Gerald's Dad) back in Bournemouth. He liquidated some of his assets and put the money up for the *AA* carnet bond. Not content with this amazing lifeline he gathered our vehicle details and drove his camper van up to the *AA* head office in Basingstoke and spent the whole day there filling in forms. He resolutely refused to leave until he had the carnets in his hands. This was a considerable achievement since the application normally takes weeks to get processed and the Basingstoke office doesn't have a 'counter service' facility. Quite what they made of this persistent 71 year old we'll never know but let this journal record that yet again our year long holiday would have ground to a halt without the relentless efforts provided by 20 Maxwell Rd, Bournemouth.

South Africa (leaving Sun City)

Day 311
Tuesday 13 February
Mondo Miles today: 137
Mondo Mileage: 28185

This morning the apartment gradually came to life around 0800. We had set ourselves an optimistic departure time of 12 noon and our last minute debacle of a departure on 11 April 95 had taught us how eleventh hour tasks and duties just materialise from nowhere.

Maps were 'fabloned', further foodstuffs purchased and trivial inessential bolt sorting was indulged in. The four hours flew by and by noon we were ready, but in our wake we had left a bombsite so awful and chaotic that we may as well have done an oil change in the lounge. Our part-time Mondo helper Kelly Jane Farrell kindly agreed/suffered the chance to clear up our mess but were still all smiles at 12.30 when Jo, elfin Andy and Rick (Jo's boyfriend) showed up for the farewell. Clive produced a *real* monkey's skull to be affixed alongside H6's plastic novelty artefact purchased in Mexico on day 187. We hoped to visit Sundown Ranch, 6 miles distant, to play with the lions (cubs up to adults). This was something we had failed to do over the last seven weeks. We finally got packed, kicked over the engines and at last we were to be free of the thrills and shackles of Sun City.

Torrential rain was followed by driving rain which heralded further 'spitting' and a heaviness in the air which discouraged the thought of even leaving at all. The grey-gaffer-patched US Army ponchos were to hand and we prayed to our respective Gods that a window of brightness could be provided for our filming exploits.

Harrington, the don of Sundown Ranch Lion Park was a former Louis Bloom and Clive neighbour and welcomed us like old friends. The years that Louis has spent being pleasant to the residents of this part of the world paid off royally for Mondo Enduro as we all wallowed in the warmth of spirit and generosity that Louis elicits from those that have got to know him

Harrington hosted us exclusively and spoiled us all with the chance to take pictures of the sweetest little lion cubs. However, they are not a fraction as fluffy as most domestic pussy cats and their underbelly was all wrinkly pink skin and wiry hair. Louis was allowed into the pride proper and held his cool as the humungous tigers and lady-tigers and lions mauled his feeble 21" front wheel.

After the fun and filming was over, we had to make a hasty departure as it was 1400 and we were expected in Springs for a meeting/goodbye session with our kindly benefactors Ian Bradshaw (parts manager) and Steve Swanepoel.

We were probably going to be an hour late for our promised 1600 RV... Ooops! We opened up the throttles, our emotional final farewells behind us and thrashed it out onto the highway only to stop 400m down the way. Clive had left the camera tripod back with the lions.

After this false start we bathed in the first sunshine Bophuthatswana has seen for many days and pushed off across the *veld* for Johannesburg.

The bikes lapped up the miles, but a cheeky puncture on Chas' K5 gave 'the Pumphouse' (our new 12V electric air compressor) it's first role in a war scenario. We phoned Suzuki and admitted lateness but Bradshaw bounced back and invited us (after we'd asked if we could stay) back to his home. Clive felt ill, we were all dirty, it had started to rain again but more relevantly, "When Bradshaw drinks, we all drink...".

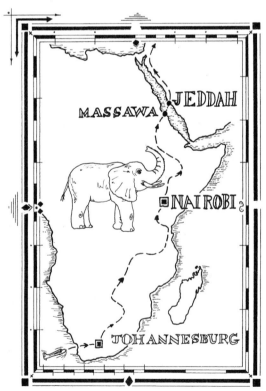

South Africa

Day 312
Wednesday 14 February
Mondo Miles today: 38
Mondo Mileage: 28223

Valentine's Day dawned like many other mornings of late – in the lap of comparative luxury. Today, on the feast of love, Clifford, Chas and Louis all found themselves asleep on soft bedding of some description in bedrooms in Ian Bradshaw's imposing mansion. Only Austin, as is his want, went native, having stretched out his Thermarest on the thick pile carpet.

But then again, perhaps Mondo Enduro needs to break slowly into the swing of trans global motorcycling after six weeks of wine, women and song – not to mention the odd man as well – at South Africa's premier pleasure-dome. The previous evening we had more or less eschewed endless offers of drink in the Bradshaw Arms and so Mondo Enduro awoke – for the first time in a month - with moderately clear heads after a good night of 10 hours shuteye.

Who knows what dreams troubled our repose during the dark hours as all the Enduristes have reason to mourn their passing from Sun City? The sultry Mena, the gorgeous Nicole, the elusive Kelly and the babelicious Jo probably all figure prominently in our night-time ruminations.

Clifford was the first awake, nursing the livid red welt on his arm caused by the mystery insect bite of the previous evening. His first task of the day was to act as Postman Pat to deliver a surprise Valentine's Day card from Kelly Farrell to "the cheekiest Charlie in the whole wide world".

After a breakfast of tea, scrambled eggs and toast, and a viewing of our hosts's "Bike Wars" video, we were outside and engaged in a frenzy of tasks – an oil change, air filter clean and pannier painting job for Louis, a new back tyre for Austin and a permanently affixed blue haired troll for Chas. Louis also attached his Winnie the Pooh to his brake fluid box making the beloved children's cartoon character appear for the entire world to be having sex or defecating.

At about 5pm, Mondo Enduro was finally ready to chip from Springs and after bidding fond farewells to Ian – our genuine benefactor – we were on the road to Zimbabwe – or sort of. After about 20 miles we pulled over on to a disused road to pitch camp. While Chas and Austin set up a textbook basha, Clifford and Louis got busy in the Mondo field kitchen cooking a tasty tuna 'n' pasta all-in.

It seems so strange to be back on the road but the experience is entirely welcome. Sun City continues to exert its strange gravitational pull but soon we will be well and truly out of its orbit, Zimbabwe beckons. Perhaps this is where Mondo Enduro really begins? If only Ibrahim and Leonard were here to see it.

South Africa

Day 313
Thursday 15 February
Mondo Miles today: 204
Mondo Mileage: 28427

Mondo Enduro awoke on this dull grey morning to the light pitter-patter of rain on their superbly erected double-poncho. Despite the clear starry night that shone before them as they dozed off, they knew only too well how miserable and grim it can be to wake up out of deep slumber with a dripping wet Rab and Thermarest.

The team were not fooled by these temperamental South African skies and a relatively solid nine hrs kip was had by all. Even Louis after five years of living and working in the five star hotel industry was like a fish to water on his first night in the field on Mondo Enduro: a noteworthy, environmentally sound fire and an undisturbed sleep on the old Bapsfontein road.

A lie-in was in order as the rain ceased to stop for the four bottle blondes. The next hour, waiting for a break in the weather was spent reminiscing on our conquests and adventures in Sun City of the past 6 weeks.

We were on the plot and mobile just before 8 o'clock and covered our first fifty miles by 9am on the road to Groblersdal.

Our leg stretch at fifty doubled up as a photo shoot with a burnt-out BMW. The abandoned roadside wreck was just what we needed for a photo shoot with a real live fire. We jumped in the petrol dowsed car whilst the camera timer ticked away and Clive sparked the bomb for another great Mondo Moment. It was clear that we should have used more petrol.

Onwards from Groblersdal armed with cotton sleeping bag liners, fabricated minutes earlier by the rep from the Singer sewing machine store and a whole host of goodies from the supermarket, we set off towards Pietersburg in a brief spell of sunshine.

The next hundred miles breezed by in almost complete dryness and everything was going fine when suddenly gremlins reared their ugly heads in Clive's SafeSealed front tyre. The outcome; a total front wheel blow out causing bike and rider to lose control and go sliding down the road in unison. Afterwards Cheeky Chas said it was an amazing crash – straight out of a Bike Wars video! He should know, he was right behind Clive reporting for 'eye witness' news.

Clive came out with a graze on his hip and bruising to the same plus his elbow. Thank heavens for leathers or it really would have been tears all round. An hour later, Clive's bike was roadworthy and Louis' clutch cable was rerouted whilst Chas brewed up with the ultimo windbreak – three 18" tyres.

A mile down the road and with nightfall approaching we knocked on the door of a *boreplaas* (farmhouse) to seek shelter for the evening. Despite our protestations that a barn would be a fabulous treat he showed us to his snooker room where we camped on the floor. Our host was an old school *boer* called Michael Greylens and this was indeed an ostrich farm! Michael was the very incarnation of Afrikaaner hospitality. In no time the snooker table was strewn with wet documents (i.e. photos, carnets, licences – etc) that Austin had lain out after our over-flooded road crossing a few hours ago. Michael returned once we had settled in and brought us tea and biscuits for the perfect end to the first day of our journey back to London.

South Africa

Day 314
Friday 16 February
Mondo Miles today: 205
Mondo Mileage: 28632

Well hello there readers! Louis Bloom here finally getting his chance to add more scribble to the already famous Mondo Enduro Diary. I must begin by saying that as a late participant to the Expedition and a member of the Mondo Enduro Family, I would not like to be anywhere now or with anyone else other than with my Fellow Mondo Endurians!

The day began with Austin the insomniac telling Louis and Clive how much shouting took place in their sleep, (obviously due to lost loves). The hospitality shown to us by Mr and Mrs Greyling of the ostrich farm was overwhelming (Mrs Greyling even made us sandwiches and prepared a pot of tea to see us off – charming people). We all hit the road at about 0830hrs for our journey north to Zimbabwe; our objective for the day being Bulawayo.

On arriving at Beit Bridge (the border crossing to Zimbabwe), we discovered the most organised petrol station in South Africa (and of course it had to be the last one!). So with our tanks full we sped to the South African/Zim border and then a delay of four hrs. We were a spit from Beit Bridge and immobile due to Red Tape. When we finally made it out of Zim Customs Louis led the ride forward to Bulawayo, only to be caught in a speed trap 500 yards from where he started!!

"I want $50 (Zim) from each of you as a fine for speeding; if you don't pay, you go to court on Monday!" said the 1950s dressed policeman.

"You must be joking, forget it! We don't have that kind of money, we'll go to court" said Austin.

"How much money <u>DO</u> you have?" said The Man.

Hence, we escaped jail and a rather heavy fine; Louis did however, have to sign an admission of guilt for his naughty deed.

From the first mile into Zimbabwe if was obvious we were no longer in South Africa; but 314 days on the road had done little to hone the keen blade of Austin's luggage carrying skills. His leather trousers were found lying on the road, accompanied by a number plate half a mile further on. His expensive tailored leather jacket 'fell off' his bike in Mexico and so if Clive hadn't discovered these strides then that would have been the complete suit gone, all thanks to Austin's bumbling bungee bungles.

While Austin set up the sleeping chamber, (which even Earls Court Ideal Home Exhibition would be proud to have), Chas and Clive prepared supper. Tonight we are out in the bush and we dine again under the Seven Sisters, with our squawking neighbours watching over the new species introduced into their park.

Zimbabwe

Day 315
Saturday 17 February
Mondo Miles today: 425
Mondo Mileage: 29237

Mondo Enduro had an excellent night's sleep despite the interrupted rain showers that always precipitate furrowed brows, as the integrity of the double-poncho is chewed over. Although physiologically undisturbed, the tot (or multiples thereof) of rum that we had sedated ourselves with the night before took its effect and drilled our bush-brains with wild and inexplicable dreams: Louis found himself as a VIP guest on a guided tour of an ostrich abattoir. He was treated to sundry stories from the meat workers who both sickened and amused him with tales of ostrich gore et al. Clive, meanwhile, had been given the task in his dream, of joining a hastily recruited execution squad. He was shaky on the details but clearly remembered that the work was not done until he and his team had tamped down the last patty of earth that concealed the mass grave that was required to consume their handiwork. Austin continued his self-punishment and dreamed of former girlfriends who had dumped him, were now married and appeared in his imagination, having left their husbands and begged him to have them back.

These random visions were not the product of life on the road but more likely spawned of the Tabasco used so liberally to add a hi-octane element to last night's stew.

The elfin drainage channels hewn last night in the red-brown clay that floors this country, served Mondo Enduro well. Water ingress was precluded and with the ponchos properly poppered together provided total refuge from a night of virtually non-stop precipitation. Hurrah for the double poncho!

We struck camp at 0630 and were grateful that it happened not to be raining. The normal procedure upon leaving a rough campsite is for us to reconvene once back on tarmac just in case someone didn't make it. As we have become more confident of late we dispensed with this precaution and Austin encouraged Clive and Chas to get going. Louis and Austin were ready 90 seconds later, Austin waved Louis on and a pledge made that he would catch up. Austin, smug and jubilant that his bike had fired up first kick was soon eating humble pie when he realised that the huge ex-dustbin rear tyre so gleefully inflated at Springs was now totally flat and he was alone.

Austin dashed from the bike up to the road and hollered at Louis 400m down the road but he was gone.

Austin pushed his bike through the bush and he found himself marooned and sweating in a muddy gulch about 12 tantalisingly close metres away from the perfectly smooth wearing surface of Zimbabwe's A6 Bulawayo highway.

As a showcase of good team riding, the speed with which Clive, Chas and Louis all independently realised that we were not a foursome was quite excellent. The simple rule of convoy work is that most of the time you should be able to see someone behind you. If every rider ascribes to this dictum then all is well. It slows things down in the short term but will always save time in the long run. Hence, it was within a few miles that Louis knew that something had happened because Austin wasn't behind him. A more selfish or less team-spirited rider would have gone for an hour, pulled over and after fifteen minutes later wondered where the fourth guy was.

Eventually Louis back tracked and came to Austin's rescue and with some 'Missing in Action' type gallantry and much sweating, Louis towed Austin up to the road and back to what had quickly become Mondo Enduro's roadside shanty town. Cheeky Charlie, the galloping Penty, had soon about-turned and already had a brew afoot to boost morale and line the stomachs of his *compañeros*, hitherto wrestling the goodness from a solitary bogus biscuit issued by biscuit burgermeister bugle boy Greenhough.

Despite being charged with a piston full of SafeSeal puncture exclusion juice, Mr De Pontes' wonder-glue had singularly failed to meet the challenge posed by a humble pin prick to the side wall of the mighty Russian triple-thickness linoleum inner tube.

Ahah!! A chance to perform a repair with the outrageously expensive Tip-Top West German tyre/rubber solvent. Purchased in Sun City at great financial cripplement because as Mondo Enduro knew, on occasions such as this, only the best will do!!

There was much snide commentary directed at the Master race as the basically useless, lumpy sputum was ladled from the container. A repair would clearly be impossible and so the long lasting Russian tube was folded up and stowed away, making the void inside the invincible Cheng Shin tyre available for one of the Michelin Enduro inner tubes. Despite Mondo Enduro's unwritten boycott of French goods and services, an expedient concession has been made in the respect of these overpriced slices of so-called trouble free protection.

The pumphouse and the Vaseline played their part and the need for a smaller than usual spoon was mooted. So the day began on the hard shoulder, the brooding clouds thinning, allowing the first glimpses of blue sky for a few days. We were finally mobile at 0930, destination Bulawayo and with the finest road imaginable beneath our spinning wheels.

We whizzed through the hoped for metropolis of Wes Nicholson but found only an overgrown single track railway, a 'general dealer' (the name given to most shops out here) and large crowds of people just hanging around the edge of the road. There are no asphalted streets in these towns. Once you stray from the highway it's packed earth all around.

On the outskirts of Bulawayo the road broadened to an impressive dual carriageway and we were ushered into a smaller version of what parts of Johannesburg had been like. A spacious verdant 1950's new town. It is strange to see the optimistic pre-independence architecture and we think of how the population must have wondered what their lot was to be, so much of it being plotted and planned in the Colonial office somewhere in London, SW1.

Louis failed to see the traffic lights at one major urban intersection and so he consequently didn't notice that they were red. The rest of the team winced as he skidded to a halt, traffic flowing all around him, irate and confused. Only eight lives left Louis, and you'll need them all in Ebola country.

The attractive green road signs and their quaint post-war white typeface proclaimed that Victoria Falls was still a healthy 270 miles away and it was 1300 hours already. Austin was sceptical that we'd make it but Louis, Clive and Chas persuaded him that with our new standard cruising speed of 63mph at 5000rpm we could thrust it by dusk.

The superb quality of the road continued as did the quite surprisingly low density of population. The roadside is virtually permanently fenced by a six-string barbed wire construction (the strands diverging the higher up the fence post). This apparently keeps the wildlife off the road but doesn't prevent Simians from sundry traversements. We don't know the appropriate collective noun for a group of baboons so we'll coin one. Hence, it was Austin and Louis who had to slow down and halt while an entire customs hall of bare bottomed monkeys pegged it across the A6. There must have been almost 40 of them, the mums cradling those too small to run at the required speed. They were all shrieking and screaming. Dr Doolittle would doubtless have translated their mutual exhortations as: "Come on everyone, quickly cross the road before the motorbikes get here!"

We passed by hundreds of small circular mud huts, thatched roofs and mothers outside, babies slung over their backs – very sweet. As with so many parts of the world, everyone waved at us, we returning their salutation, Louis, with the most bravado and enthusiasm. He doubtless shouted his catch-phrase "Believe!" at the smiling children, and they probably did.

We pushed blobs of 70 miles at a time, the 350 engines singing, Chas throwing good oil after bad but neither us nor our steeds over-heating. We passed by the quarrying town of Hwange and saw Russian style pollution for the first time in many months. We crossed loads of muddy, silty rivers, all in spate and hence invariably inundating the single track concrete bridges that provided the crossing point on the 'old' road that ran parallel to the A6.

With perfect timing we flicked past Victoria Falls (International) Airport as the sun was waning. We were booked into the municipal campsite in no time and were soon erecting an unusually ridiculous looking harem cum basha arrangement. We were nestled in on the same plot as Marcus, the predictable German (travelling with Chris on two Yamaha XT 600s). Soon, the Daily Mail Camping and Outdoor exhibition effect was complete as we scanned our surrounding campers and observed that there was one of every type of decent sensible tent available, staked out all around us. We were confronted once again with so many co-travellers who had not yet ascribed to the philosophy that turning your clothes into a house was actually the way ahead. It's unusual for us to stay in a proper campground but there is wisdom in our madness. We hope to pick up some valuable intelligence from other overlanders who have come from the north and can comment on the viability of crossing the Congo basin or the Sudan.

We are struck by how much in common we have with all of these white, male, European Landrover types, and also by how little. We collectively composed an ode in an attempt to describe them.

OVERLANDERS:

Hair plaited
Sleeping matted
Goretex booted
Third world ethnic art t-shirt suited –
Blond and tanning
Journey planning
Thrills from sex and humping
Or bungee jumping
Travelled so far
With their MSR
Sandal wearing
Environmentally caring
Keen for culture adoption
With money no option
Saying: "Zambezi boiling pot jaws of death canoe rush, if we go will you go?"

Zimbabwe

Day 316
Sunday 18 February
Mondo Miles today: 0
Mondo Mileage: 29237

A day (which will not be unremarked upon when the final Mondo reckoning comes) dawned with the by now usual dark clouds mottling the horizon. But actually, as events turned out, it would prove to be 24 hours of hi-NRG thrills and spills and dark prognostications about our route northwards through Africa. Clive and Louis also beat all comers to the Down Time disco pool table which ended the day on a note of wild optimism.

The high point of the day both physically and metaphysically undoubtedly came with Louis's decision to leap 137 metres off the Zambezi Bridge attached to little more than an outsized elastic band. We all legged it to the Zambian border to watch this feat of daring do from a video-friendly vantage point. A short rain storm delayed proceedings for about half an hour and as tension mounted on the Bungee parapet, Chas took up smoking for the first time. Finally all the straps were lashed and the buckles fixed and Louis was ready to plunge into the frothing gorge. As Clive and Austin watched proceedings through the Hi-8 viewfinder, Louis perched himself on the brink muttering a stream of gibberish to himself in which the phrases "mental", "radio rental" and "believe" surfaced frequently like pieces of verbal flotsam.

As the bungee countdown began, Louis' Big Heart began beating visibly faster through his official tee-shirt. Then, with a roar of "Let's go, Mondo Enduro", he plunged into the abyss with all the easy grace of a dislodged boulder. As he hung suspended above the seething morass of the mighty Zambezi, many male observers felt a strange twitch in the groin region, the cause of which only became clear when Louis's breathless form was hauled bodily back up to the bungee platform.

In the tension of the moment, the pain of an overtight harness snagged around Louis's left testicle had been felt empathetically by the Bungee Brotherhood as the levels of adrenalin and hormonal imbalance reached critical proportions.

We returned immediately to our campsite to find our German friends still guarding our bikes and chatting to a chunkster Eric who had clearly intended to audition for the Camel Trophy advert but turned up either too early or late. Not easily downhearted, he had even gone to the considerable lengths of purchasing a long wheel-base Land Rover and picking up a suitably photogenic Erica with whom to live out the overlander fantasy. It was with some mirth, therefore, that Mondo Enduro watched his dream fall apart before their very eyes when his mysteriously miffed girlfriend packed her Karrimor and legged it out of the municipal campsite and into a new life "*Ohne seine mann*". To make matters worse his MSR stove also started to mysteriously dysfunction as if the entire pantheon of Teutonic gods had decided spontaneously to piss on his own personal victory parade of preposterous male vanity...

Austin got chatting to a family of German overlanders who had travelled in what looked like an armoured car all the way from Morocco via the Central African Republic and Zaire. The news is not all rosy – appalling roads and fuel available only from Christian missions – but at least they made it after only 11 months! We have decided to peg it straight to Nairobi.

The afternoon was spent in a froth of literary activity penning a record 60 postcards to our nearest and dearest and various Mondo benefactors around the world. George da Pontes and his much-maligned SafeSeal puncture prophylactic came in for a well-aimed dart from Clifford's acid biro and will no doubt spontaneously liquidate like an old repair in contact with his worthless product as a result. Amongst a few of the other Mondo correspondees were GJ Vince (running base camp Bournemouth), Barbara Hay (UK ambassadress to Uzbekistan), fragrant as a sprig of Highland heather and Suzuki Genuine Part Ian Bradshaw. Even the chillingly sinister master of hostage negotiation, David Parkinson received a card; such was Mondo Enduro's spirit of almost limitless bonhomie.

Dinner was a spicy meatball 'n' chilli casserole served up by Louis after an hour of selfless toil at the campside hearth. Soon we were all sweating less with the piquant flavour of his stew than at the prospect of a gin and tonic fuelled evening at the Explorers' Bar which we assumed, rightly as it turned out, would be heavily populated with Abba-fixated citizens of various Scandinavian kingdoms.

It would be nice to report some noteworthy adventures from a night of relentless socialising but Mondo Enduro left the club, not for the first time, alone and wanting to know "What's the Name of the Game." Not to be outdone, three of the four resorted to the Down Time Disco for a spot of pool.

Zambia

Day 317
Monday 19 February
Mondo Miles today: 47
Mondo Mileage: 29284

And rocking was the notion for today. Our new found news of it being difficult but possible to get through Central Africa has given us newfound hope. The only constraining factor being the start of the rainy season in Zaire in April. So there must be no delay in getting to that part of the world.

Christopher and Marcus bade farewell to us this morning with a small chance that we may meet again before Europe. In fact, there is a distinct possibility that we could meet them in Nairobi whilst we await new visas for our journey home.

Final tasks before we left the army of backpackers and semi-overlanders was to stock up on food and petrol for our journey through Zambia. Clive and Chas went off to do this whilst Austin and Louis finished off packing their kit.

The shoppers returned fully laden with enough food and goodies to last 7 days which will definitely see us to Dar es Salaam.

We did a spot of filming of us crossing over the Zambezi with the Victoria Falls in the background. Zambian Customs and Immigration formalities were a breeze. In fact, the easiest after Canada and the good old USA.

At the Custom's post itself were a huge family of baboons making themselves at home. A couple of them were licking sugar off the road that had been recently discarded by prospective traders heaving their produce over the border to Zambia. While we were getting processed Clive got the tools out to make some minor adjustments but had to go into the hall to sign a vehicle permit. As he was walking over a baboon pegged it to the glittering shiny tools, grabbed our tyre pressure gauge and was gone in a thrice. We were deflated.

We all had a feeling that we were now entering real Africa. The carnets seem to have already, on their first use, have been worth their weight in gold. They made our path (as far as the bikes were concerned) exceptionally easy.

We set off for Livingstone and beyond along a pretty reasonable section of black top. The weather at this time was fantastic. Austin and Louis were wearing shorts and all of Mondo Enduro were just wearing tee-shirts.

As we cruised along watching the sun going down we were constantly waved at by the locals walking or standing by the roadside. The faces were very smiley and it lifted Mondo Enduro's spirits to an even higher level.

We pulled over to camp 45 minutes before sunset. We literally just drove 200 yds into the bush to a clearing and set to erecting a camp.

Austin began constructing the ultimate basha and Chas and Louis prepared supper whilst Cliff made the fire and began writing the log. The meal was a potato based stew with runner beans, onions, sweetcorn and cabbage.

We exchanged stories about Mill Hill and its teachers around the fire with a few dashes of rum. A classic Mondo evening with all the bugs. Incidentally, we saw a 10 legged spider / cockroach hybrid come crawling into our sights. None of us have ever seen anything like it before, even on TV. Austin studied it for a while and then carried it back to the bush. Meanwhile, the stars came out and Mondo Enduro enjoyed one of the best starlit nights ever seen. It probably wasn't, but a feature of this trip is that we keep thinking in superlatives.

Zambia

Day 318
Tuesday 20 February
Mondo Miles today: 358
Mondo Mileage: 29642

Heavy dew and jungle smells greeted Mondo as we awoke from yet another exhibition style slumber nest. We were on the road and moving by 0740 wasting no time to seek adventure and clock up the miles. More dreams rose themselves in the head of Little Vince last night, making him believe he was beating back bullies at boarding school with the porcelain slab from the top of a toilet cistern.

After about 100 miles we pulled into Choma (a small Zambian town). Fortunately water was not hard to come by today – Austin filled water bottles at the petrol station whilst Louis filled up at a café which played country music.

On returning to the petrol station Louis discovered Austin having an enlightening conversation with a man with no tongue! Meanwhile at the bank Chas was being given the full VIP treatment – (it's a good thing the rest of Mondo didn't follow him in there!). Outside the bank watching our rides

Clive was collecting tangerines for our journey from three elfin children. Onward we went on progressively worse roads, weaving our way along and almost avoiding all potholes except those made by bombs. At one point a half-starved dog pulled away from his long grass shelter and straight into the path of an oncoming Austin; brakes were applied, but the frail little creature seemed to want to end it all and use Austin's bike as it's executioner – don't worry readers, the dog will live to see another day.

After about another 100 miles we encountered a pub called The Ploughmans Inn. It was clearly the project of a homesick ex-pat since it was a welcoming country pub down to the last detail. Here, surrounded by steaming verdant jungle and patronised only by Zambians it was incongruous indeed! Mondo came to a halt and went in for a few standard beers. Inside this mock Tudor hostelry Clifton and Chas got their beers on the house whilst Austin did some necessary filming and Lou played with the pub dog (a Jack Russell – Believe!).

Once we were back on the road again we looked for somewhere to rest our weary heads, and then first signs of rain all day began to be felt by the fatigued four. We decided on the Mondo Blendo option and Chas came back with news of a large house up the road owned by a Mr Jones; so we piled up at his door and discovered he was local, but had Welsh roots. Fortunately he took pity on us (and us on him) and thus shelter was found. Austin mistakenly burnt Clive with the stove and was sent to Coventry.

Maths teacher Austin has complied the current Mondo fuel economy league table (4.54ltrs = 1 gallon)

Bike	Reading	Litres	Galls	MPG (1dp)	(229 mile run)
Austin	47.7	13.4	2.96	77.4	1st
Clive	14.5	14.5	3.20	71.6	2nd
Louis	32.0	15.7	3.46	66.2	3rd
Chas	61.1 77.6	16.6	3.66	62.6	4th

Siga-Siga
Mr Mumbi Chileshe
Serenje Filling Station
Box 650161
Serense, Zambia.

Zambia

Day 319
Wednesday 21 February
Mondo Miles today: 308
Mondo Mileage: 29950

Although details of the previous night's sleeping may make for a diary of limited interest, the truth will <u>not</u> remain hidden! In the old storeroom provided by the Jones family, we all slept better than we have in many nights. Nobody was bitten (cf Louis' buttocks and Chas' shoulder blades 24 hrs previously) thanks to the insanely expensive mosquito net gaffer taped over the open doorway.

We rose at 06.15 and noble Chas pumped the stove into life and soon the tell-tale rush of petrol vapour through tiny apertures foretold of the inevitability of coffee. However, the inevitability of Mr Jones' hospitality had <u>not</u> been taken foretold and just as the boiling water had been added to the appropriate portions of our valuable instant coffee, milk and sugar, out from the farmhouse appeared one of the servants bearing a silver tray bedecked with coffee apparatus. Uhoh! Dilemma the reader might muse to himself. Not so, in a scene reminiscent of the Bird's instant coffee advertisements of the late 1970's, we covertly threw our self made blend into the gutter and suckled at the nipple of the Zambian-Welsh coffee-bean.

The morning mist cleared and after some visits to our hosts' up until then unblemished, toilet bowl, we pushed on up the highway.

The endless bush seemed endless, almost *without* end if you will. The local population as ever, appeared to be on the verge, walking along. Though these locals always seem to be in the middle of nowhere, neither apparently approaching nor departing from anywhere in particular, they all walk with a great sense of purpose as if they were just about to arrive.

We drove a full 100 miles without alighting and then finally, on the verge, paused for our daily chain grease up and ritual oil check. Clive and Louis took the opportunity to don their PT instructor's hats and after ensuring that their pupil's prayer mat cum blanket ponchos were laid out (on the tarmac, safety first) the exercises began.

It must have totally baffled the two lorry drivers that swerved to avoid our pumping bodies as these bare-chested honkies, counting the time and simultaneously wheezing "up" and "down", partially blocked the highway. Louis in particular is determined to tone up before we get back to London. He pledges subsequent gymnastic displays between Zambia and London.

A decision was made to change some tyres over at the next petrol stop. This would decrease the sheer mass of rubber that we are carrying and by removing Louis' moto-cross front tyre, preserve it for the tough and slippery conditions ahead that we regretfully anticipate should we have to go through Zaire and the Congo.

The reader should be made aware that our initial planned route, north of Nairobi, was to traverse Ethiopia, the Sudan and roughly follow the course of the Nile northwards through Egypt. From Cairo, Gaddafi permitting, we would like to swing west and follow the North African coast of the Med all the way across Libya, Tunisia, Algeria and Morocco, finally disembarking at Tangiers or Ceuta, for Andalusia in Southern Spain.

Even in its embryonic stages, this proposal, in the Sudan department, has been not so much put on the back-burner, rather machine-gunned out of existence. For reasons best known to their respective foreign offices, the Sudanese and the Egyptians have sealed their mutual border, hence slamming the door shut on Mondo Enduro. Southern Sudan is a permanent rebel convention aimed full time at anything that might possibly represent the agencies of the government. Hence the possible route out of the Sudan into Libya is also forbidden by Khartoum. A last chance of a boat from Port Sudan, flicking over the Red Sea to Jeddah, has been postulated but initial reports suggest that the Saudis are more likely to allow the import of Star of David shaped ham patties than to issue Mondo Enduro, circumcised to a man, with Transit Visas.

So finally, the route out of Kenya may force us to go West across Uganda and then into Zaire, the nation in whose language there is no word for tarmac. From here into the Central African Republic, Cameroon, Nigeria and continuing West to Mauritania following the Atlantic coast up to Morocco. Phew! Only tens of hours of fruitless footwork in Nairobi will help to confirm what course we four motorcyclists will eventually steer.

Anyway, the tyres were changed, the last two syringes of liquid De Pontes magic SafeSeal were forced into inner tubes, and an attempt was made to bend Louis' side stand so that it leans at a more user friendly angle. Austin took a few photographs of local children, but soon regretted the waste of film. A petrol pump attendant, with a tie that reached virtually to his knees, posed with us for a relatively comical photo, but only after much pleading from Austin and both a written and verbal oath that a copy would duly make its way back to the BP station. Thus, their address is inscribed 3 pages prior to this one, underneath this morning's 'mpg' computations.

Charlie got busy in the forecourt, wielding loaves and knives in a blur of movement that would leave Jackie Chan politely clapping. Chris Donald would have dubbed the end result; Chas' cheese and bread snack. Suitably gorged, Mondo Enduro creaked back into life after what finally proved to be a two hour petrol collection, not though, without Louis roaring off, testosterone levels overflowing, in a semi-rage that his exhaust was slowly burning a hole in one of his panniers, in completely the wrong direction. Fortunately, Mondo sheepdog Greenhough affected an about turn from Louis with a chirpy "peep" from what is this expedition's solitary working horn.

The afternoon rolled on (it was 2pm by the time we got away from BP) and soon the spectacular darkening of the skies ahead us turned to an opening of the skies above us. We were pathetically caught short by a sheet of rain so spectacularly well defined that Clive, Chas and Louis on one side of the road were being soaked whilst Austin, only metres away on the other side was still dry.

The storm that followed was punishing and somehow defeated the ponchos. Just after we made it out of it, after about an hour, Louis heard a screaming from his engine and looked back to see his virtually brand new chain lying on the road behind him. Clive and Chas were 20 miles ahead and waiting for Austin and Louis. So it was like a gypsy caravan that the forward party witnessed Austin towing Louis up to the mark.

This tow was Mondo Enduro's longest, at 20 miles and indeed fastest with a top speed of 50mph being achieved. It was with particular surprise that this high speed coupling overtook several convoys of trucks and brought many a stare and dropped jaw from the villages they bisected.

After a full chain repair using the tool we'd bought in Los Angeles; it was nigh on dusk and we were near Mpika. The top blend-broker, Cheeky Charlie, was sent on a mission to locate some shelter. He failed not, and these words are being written on the steps outside the hair salon attached to a grain wholesalers called "KAZABI" – staffed exclusively, it would seem, by born again Christians, all named after Christ's disciples. The one exception to this is Anset who leaves a message and his address below:

Anset Smwanza
Pentecost Assemblies of God
PO Box Private BA9 29
Mpika
Zambia

"I love you all in Jesus name. May God Bless you. Please write me one. I will be very happy".

And so to bed with the thought that tomorrow will see us achieve our 30,000th mile since leaving home.

Zambia

Day 320
Thursday 22 February
Mondo Miles today: 262
Mondo Mileage: 30212

The heavy splash of dew drops cascading through cracks in the corrugated iron roof of the Kazabi vehicle shed served us better than an alarm clock today and we are up with the larks at 5.45am. Our repose had been disturbed not by the usual mosquito and other mercantile activity but by the truly deranged bleating of a farmyard animal which we took to be a goat. Surely all the horrors of Bedlam could not have been worse than the suffering of this poor creature whose blood-curdling death rattle was the cause of much restlessness within the Mondo *kraal*.

The new morn brought bright sunshine, however, and also the promise of spiritual salvation in the sprightly form of Anset. As well as urging us to surrender our souls to the Holy Lamb of God, he also handed out a biblical tract describing the evils of immodest apparel. We took this to be a subtle hint to dress more fashionably and wash more often. Cleanliness is next to godliness after all...

And so after a morale-boosting cup of coffee brewed on the Coleman stove, Mondo Enduro was up and about and ready to face the rigours of the new day. We left the Zambian Billy Graham, aged 22, to continue with his rather extended schooling. The night-time had not been without its fevered visions - notably Chas' dream about being forced to mend Louis's broken chain with a strip of Biltong beef jerky. The theme of foodstuffs being put to a practical technical use has of course already been well-established by Mondo Enduro. In Irkutsk we had the chocolate winter sprocket, whilst work

356

is already continuing apace on the cheese fuselaged Hawker Stilton bomber currently being prototyped in Mill Hill School's design and technology department (following the award of a generous development grant from the Ministry of Defence and United Dairies plc).

Soon we were eating up the miles with all the voracity of a herd of wildebeest.

Following last night's chain problems, the Tanzanian border was still a mighty 230 miles distant, so much hard riding had to be done to keep Mondo Enduro on schedule. But after the excesses of Sun City and the Explorers Bar, a new mood of healthy if not clean living has overtaken the Endurists who, as they had bravely resolved yesterday, stopped after 100 miles for a spot of physical training with our very own Instructor Louis Bloom barking out commands. After 100 sit-ups and as many press-ups, the riders rewarded themselves with a swig of banana and peach juice. Surely the sight of four dishevelled motorcyclists putting themselves through their physical paces would be taken back home as a telling vindication of private education?

Feeling fit and trim after the Bloom aerobathon, the Endurists set sail along a long and winding road to a town called Isoka and its gleaming set of Total pumps. Mondo Enduro, for the first time in many leagues, had almost come a cropper fuel-wise when Chas and Clive's litres went onto reserve well in advance of the petrol oasis. Fortunately the decidedly scruffy little town's sole service station was up and running and situated across the road from a bank where dollars were changed (twice) to effect the transaction. Earlier Clive's SafeSealed tube had suffered a veritable geyser of a puncture which spurted the worthless goo out through his spoke apertures. He and Austin affected a roadside repair, inserting the mighty Michelin tube into the rear tyre seated yesterday and bracing himself for miles of ebola-free motorcycling.

Attempts to call Sun City for latest news on the gorgeous Little Jo scenario foundered on the reef of Zambia's collect call disagreement with the new South Africa. And so we set off along a dramatically deteriorating road towards Tanzania some 117 km distant, dodging potholes and rain clouds along the way. At the border, Louis and Clive attended to the lengthy but reasonably smooth administrative technicalities while Chas and Austin did an impromptu cash call. The much-feared $60 insurance scam levied by Tanzanian Customs did not materialise, although Clive had prepared an elaborate falsehood in anticipation. His Euro Assistance medical insurance card was to have been produced as evidence of our worldwide motorcycle cover should push have come to shove and Tanzanian shillings demanded from our coffers. Fortunately, no cash was asked for and so Cliff can sleep with a pure conscience knowing that his soul will find eternal peace with God. Thou shalt not bear false witness.

At last, after much tarrying at the border security barrier, poised like thoroughbreds waiting for starter's orders at the Grand National, we were off into the Tanzanian Hinterland. Unfortunately, we had not ridden more than a few fences when Chas suffered a rear puncture. Examination of the Guatemala City Yokohama revealed it had been stripped to the canvas, ripping the chubster Michelin Enduro tube therein.

Louis manfully attempted a patch repair but ebola is a tenacious virus once it has replicated itself inside a new host. In fading light and in the company of a throng of intrigued Jacksons, Austin, Louis and Chas inserted a Costa Rican tube while Clifford went in search of a blend.

As storm clouds gathered ominously with lightning crashing into the hills, Clive knocked on the door of a nearby secondary school and secured a memorable night's shelter thanks to the saintly headmaster Mr Mbeya. The day's events took one final burst when the Coleman stove spluttered and died before as much as a single onion had been completely sliced.

As if by magic, Louis produced some baps from the ongoing food hamper and Clifford got busy preparing a tuna, onion and tomato mix. What with side orders of cheese triangles and cold baked beans and pudding of army compo pears in chocolate sauce, butterscotch sauce 'n' dumplings and peach 'n' syrup (carried all the way from Bogota) , this was a feast fit not exactly for a king but a banquet indeed for tired and hungry Enduristes.

Tanzania

Day 321
Friday 23 February
Mondo Miles today: 186
Mondo Mileage: 30400

It may have been raining but the chaps were still snug snoozing away in the Land of Rab. The Cheekiest Chas in the gang insisted we rested a bit longer and so Mondo Enduro did. It was not until we heard the movement of activity outside, that we remembered Tanzania was 1 hour ahead and that school was about to start.

Our shelter for the night was in a new but undecorated and unfinished building of the secondary school where Mr Mbeya, its kind Headmaster, had permitted us to rest for the night. It was roll call for the smartly turned out co-ed school and there was a humdrum of activity happening outside whilst we packed our kit ready for departure. The boys were dressed in white shirts and beige slacks whilst the girls sported white blouses with green skirts. The overall impression was of extreme smartness and pride in their uniform. They showed up the populations of many a British secondary school. They were all assembling in the yard next to the building we had slept in and there was much discussion going on amongst them as they observed our scruffy and grubby bodies to-ing and fro-ing from the building to our bikes.

Clive in particular was trying to keep a low profile with the shiner that he had inherited the day before from a wasp's lethal blow. We were not certain if the blue mirrored shades he wore to conceal his wound brought more attention to himself than the actual black eye, as the pupils all stared at him incredulously.

Mr Mbeya soon turned up and asked us to come to his study for an 'interview'. We four of Mondo Enduro had overnight all become 'teachers' in an attempt to blag the night's shelter in the school and understandably the Head wanted to know what we all taught.

Louis had become a Hotel Management teacher, Clive the Business Studies and Economics teacher and Charlie an English teacher – all at different schools though.

We chatted about teachers unions and their merits/demerits, as well as talking about Mill Hill School and the British Educational system. Mr Mbeya spoke apologetically about what he called the school's 'micro library'. When he showed us, the bookcase was as small as he described it which was incredible considering there were 35 teachers and 300 pupils. On our departure we promised we would send him books from Mill Hill's overflowing coffers. He was delighted and took us for a mini tour of the school and introduced us to some of his staff on our way round.

We left after a badge presentation and a photo and headed northeast towards Dar es Salaam.

We arrived in Mbyea forty five miles later to buy some provisions and make two phone calls. Not much to ask the reader might wonder. This relatively simple task in a first world country like our own would take less than an hour. This was a gargantuous task in Mbeya Tanzania taking a little more than half a day of non-stop effort.

Chas and Clifford sat it out in the rain at a public phone office for an hour or so to no avail. They were then recommended to try the Hotel Livingston. Chas got through to Nairobi eventually to warn off his mate Greg Barrow that Mondo Enduro were set to arrive on Monday evening. As a result we had one night secured in Nairobi. Meanwhile, Chas headed off to let Louis and Austin know of our escapades. Clive then called London direct for a staggering 18,000 Tanzanian shillings (US$33) for 3 minutes so a message could be passed on. He managed to get Simon, his 10 year old brother. So he repeated the hotel phone number to him and asked him to call back. He waited and waited and eventually decided to leave a message with hotel receptionist of our progress and our route intentions as little Simon could not get through.

Just as Clive was going out of the door to join the others on the outskirts of town, the hotel phone rang and it was Gemma Greenhough (his mum) calling from London.

Cliff then began to depart and was greeted by Chas on his way out. They headed off together to the market to buy further provisions and then meet up with a tired and bored Austin and Louis who had been waiting patiently at least three hours for them.

Back on the plot the Enduristes endured the rest of the afternoon in incessant rain right up to the moment when they stopped for the evening. In fact one hundred and thirty miles in over three hours of solid rain.

So the tired, sodden and hungry four little puppies found a semi-built church which looked inviting and proceeded to park up next to it and to see if anyone would mind us sheltering the night here.

The first man that came along was Mr Ndomo who we mistook at first to be the minister of the newly built church. He told us it was too dangerous to sleep in the church buildings but instead we should join him and his family at their house.

His home was 400 yards from the church up on a slope above the main road. The house had a thatched roof and was made of mud coloured bricks or perhaps even mud bricks with a floor of packed earth. It had only two rooms and almost no contents. We met all the family (five beaming children) and were brought inside the dark building to find a pot full of hot embers warming up the room. Just what the doctor ordered to dry out the dripping wet Mondo men.

A paraffin lamp was brought in and soon followed by mint chais (which was truly delicious and really warmed us up). Incidentally, we all introduced ourselves as Christians, even Louis. Mr Ndomo said prayers before supper which consisted of the tastiest potatoes we had ever eaten followed by *ugali* (a maize dish) with a side bowl of spinach. We were soon all totally full and had more mint chai to wash it all down with.

By now we had two pots of embers burning and were drying out rapidly as well as becoming more and more tired.

At Mr Ndomo's invitation Austin and Louis read aloud extracts of the 'famous' Great Controversy, a Christian tome given to Mr Ndomo by an American evangelist now living in Yemen. He was now giving it to us and asked that we read it to one another every night until we got home. We agreed with our host but knew that we were sufficiently Godless to renege on this verbal contract. However, steadfastly refusing to accept this evangelical paperback struck us as rather un-Christian and so we took it to our collective spiritual bosom.

Soon after we were bedded down in the warm, dry and very snug building and Mr Ndomo's youngest got bedded down with Plymouth (Austin's teddy bear). We were all very tired and content and if we were cats, would have purred endlessly.

Tanzania

Day 321
Saturday 24 February
Mondo Miles today: 329
Mondo Mileage: 30729

Our sleep chez Ndomo dwelling was one our deepest since we left South Africa. The warmth of the burning embers surrounded by six damp smelly socks and eight boots along with four well fed Endurians snugged-up together brought for a night of rare bliss.

Mr Ndomo gave Mondo a wake-up call at 0600 and offered to feed us all again before we left; before we could even answer more spuds were placed on the table along with the magnificent mint tea, (both grown in the smallholding at the back).

Chas had a dream about having the word 'Mondo' tattooed on his belly, and Austin having the same tattoo except that his tattooist was dyslexic. Clive presented Mr Ndomo with our baseball cap from 'Redline' (the South African biker magazine), while Louis gave him his watch compass. We awkwardly proffered some cash but our host was clearly offended. Suffice to say the Ndomo family treated us as their own. They are without doubt the poorest people we have ever stayed with, their lives being pure subsistence.

Yet their kindness and hospitality was endless. Let us hope that there *is* a God so that this decency is rewarded more properly when the family Ndomo finally stands before the Great Heavenly Throne of Judgement.

So after photographing his children sitting on a bike we hit the road, stuffed with potatoes and humbled.

The petrol fill up came early today and so we decided to change money at the bank at the same time. The day had started so well and we were ready to do the 'Big Four Hundred'. The roads were good and the scenery beautiful and then our luck ran out! It all began after we passed three overturned lorries, which had only recently been involved in a horrific accident. Austin was the first to stop to deal with an extremely loose back wheel axle and a lost R-clip. Chas was reporting under performance and visibly burning oil; as was Clive. As for Louis, his front wheel had locked (fortunately at low speed) and put him immobile in the middle of the road. The road was narrow and only twenty yards up was a bend; traffic (being lorries and buses), were moving at around 70mph which would not give him much time to clear the road and would mean Mondo down to three bikes. Just as an enormous lorry pulled round the bend at speed, 'Super Chas' appeared from behind and literally dragged Louis' bike from the path of the oncoming vehicles. Apart from a few lost nuts and bolts and worn tyres we all began once again.

The road eastwards towards Dar es Salaam was truly magnificent, with bends at every hundred yards. We had to gun it to make up for lost time.

Cold in the morning and hot in the afternoon as we approached the humidity of the North. After playing "Musical Ponchos", where Clifford tangled himself in his rear wheel, we set up camp in a secluded part of the woods. Austin made the fire and cooked the meal in the rain while Chas and Clive carefully positioned the bikes, poppered two ponchos together and deftly suspended them between the handle bars of the two machines. This is the means by which we do not need to carry tent-poles.

We are only four hundred miles from the Kenyan border – morale high. Tomorrow we tackle Kilimanjaro!

Tanzania

Day 322
Sunday 25 February
Mondo Miles today: 443
Mondo Mileage: 31172

Last night was notable for what in Mondo Enduro legend will become known as: "The Great Sweat". Even though we were all heavily overheating in the Tanzanian dusk, Louis had gone to bed under the poncho and climbed fully into his South African Army sleeping bag. The remainder of the team was gasping for oxygen just lying on top of our multi-coloured single ply calico sheet sacks. How Louis could bear to swathe himself in so much insulation baffled the others, but he claimed it was "good for you to sweat heavily after a large meal". And sweat he did, for somebody who didn't have a fever, the quantity of fluid excreted from the Bloom pores was very alarming. The smell of this natural coolant though, once incubated and matured by the pressure and temperature of Louis's body, made for a repugnant caustic vapour that would best be used to scatter crowds of Anti-Mondo Enduro protestors. Naturally enough, there was no agit-prop demo on hand on which to test this deadly new Hendon-based virus, but Austin, Louis's poncho partner found himself the sole participant in the field trials of this doubtless-to-be-banned-by-the-Geneva-convention crowd suppressant.

At 0600, Louis and Austin struck up a conversation and shouted a combination of abuse and calls to arms to Chas and Clive who, out of nasal range, had slept soundly without any burning of the nostrils or watering of the eyes.

Fortunately, despite dampness all round it hadn't rained during the night, though our slumber had been disturbed by the ritual and rhythmic percussive action of a nearby village's banging on its logs and drums.

We sprang up with the quick reactions of a loaf of bread and began the miserable miracle of non-achievement that is the hour and a half it takes us to get dressed, strike the poncho and roll up (or wring out) our sleeping bags.

0730 on the road, and with engines running all and sundry have that sixth sense, so finely honed in AA and RAC men, that something mechanical was quite definitely amiss. Hence, with a certain amount of stage fright, we ventured forth onto the strip of tarmac that 500 miles away would deliver us into Nairobi.

Tanzania passed us by for mile after mile. We had been introduced to the mud hut once we'd entered Zimbabwe, but here we are flanked left and right by the mud village. A monochrome red-brown earth brick comprises the sole constructional unit in these parts. The mud in between the hovels is packed down but a similar colour. These poor folks live their lives in stifling heat or merciless thunderstorms that turn their alleyways to slop and erode their humble dwellings one stage closer to the horizontal.

Alongside the road there are countless small plots overlooked by a simple thatched roofed shack. The crop is invariably corn and the lack of any variety is quite strange. We're sure David Parkinson (Bogota hostage negotiator) would have something to say about that. However, after our potato binge at Joseph Ndomo's the night before last, it may be that the Tanzanian interpretation of paradise would be a supermarket stocked with shelf after shelf of identical products.

Other features of the road were:

Dead dogs left in the road, not out in the bush but right in the middle of a town.

Old women waiting until you are right on top of them before creaking out, quite purposely without looking, right into the road. Many near misses this way.

Chas swerved to miss a goose waddling across.

Mis-spelled trading signs e.g. "MORDEN ELECTRICAL REPAIRS" – Hmmm, toaster repairs in Colliers Wood.

Waving, waving, waving.

Lorry crashes a-plenty; in fact as many as there are varieties of vitamin pill in Louis Bloom's supplementary health action pack.

And finally, even more waving.

We oil changed and lunched a hundred miles south of Arusha. We feasted on Mrs Adkins chutney and some peanut butter sandwiches. Also, we purchased oranges (which were green) from some wayside waifs but they were so bitter we all elected to sniff a whiff from Louis's still soaking sleeping bag.

We'd had rain storms this morning but now we were baked by a burst of sunshine the like of which we hadn't wallowed in for a while. We soon reached Moshi, after driving along a strange road that was largely in a cutting. Every now and then it dipped down to cross one of the heavily eroded streams that are gradually transporting this part of Tanzania to Dar es Salaam and the African Ocean. These bridges were subject to a heavily rutted surface and sometimes a speed hump/ramp effect. We soon got the measure of these and began to make attempts to "take some air". Whilst thrashing over a section of this tarmac undulation, a bungee on Austin's bike broke free allowing his £150 leather trousers to jump loose out onto the road. Austin didn't actually realise his loss though, until many miles later. Being tail rider, he caused much delay up ahead by about-turning and retracing his steps. He almost gave up hope since he found nothing as he back-tracked. Luckily though, an honest local had found them and he enthusiastically used them as a flag to wave down Austin who was by then resigned to spending the next 2 months in shorts. This act of lost and found earned Austin's trouser saviour a cash reward of US$20.

We experienced more terrific thunderstorms around Arusha, and a keen eye would notice plans and posters heralding the construction of the Arusha International Conference Centre. Good luck with that one fellas...

At 1700 we swung north, in sight of the mighty Kilimanjaro (whose personal weather system had so recently soaked us) and with the Kenyan: Tanzania frontier within striking distance.

We rose up out of Arusha and onto the lush rolling Masai Steppe. This was truly stupendous and with the Masai herdsmen (toga, spear and earrings) tending their flocks, really worth recording in this journal as a

Mondo Moment. The further we penetrated the bush, the more Masai appeared to melt out of the undergrowth onto the verge. They seem to be powerful walkers and should therefore be looked at as a potential source of entrants for sponsored walking events. The bright colours of their robes were striking indeed, yet the elfin herdsmen, still in spear-holding apprenticeship seemed only to warrant drab khaki robes. Perhaps once a certain quantity of livestock has been grazed in their "pastoral" care, they are eligible to graduate up to an orange or scarlet tunic.

We arrived at the Kenyan: Tanzania border at 5.30pm and were full of gung-ho about gunning it to Nairobi for tonight. This Paul Reveresque dash relied on us contacting Greg Barrow, Chas' old varsity chum (and East Africa correspondent for the BBC), and confirming we could crash with him tonight. Ultimately, the lack of telephonic communication twixt the border and Nairobi meant that Greg never knew we were coming, and we never got there due to a puncture on Clive's front wheel. Exhausted by today's 443 miles we enjoyed our first night in the Kenyan bush, 40 miles into the country – thorns, Masai, starry, starry night.

Kenya

Day 323
Monday 26 February
Mondo Miles today: 60
Mondo Mileage: 31232

The drooping lobes of a Masai herdsman were among the first sights we saw on this beautiful dry morn after a night devoid of mercantile activity. Imagine our horror, therefore, when we inspected our tyres and found them variously lanced with the dreaded fruit of the toothpick tree.

Fortunately Clive's puncture of yester-eve was the only deflation we faced as that beautiful day dawned on the Masai Steppe. Soon the ponchos were down and Clifford's tube up and we were back on the road to Nairobi.

But not before our extended lobed friend had shown us his army ID card which also detailed his service as a captain with the United Nations in the Balkans. The mind boggles at the thought of how the Serb militia reacted to these tartan-robed, Reebok-trainer shod denizens of the African bush and his collection of bead jewellery.

After a few miles of untrammelled motoring we were soon in a small but decidedly tidy township where adverts for Sunlight Soap and Cadbury's Chocolate belied its colonial heritage. Soon, on the advice of an automatic rifle toting copper, we were ensconced in a small café slurping draughts of thin but strangely delicious maize porridge. The double egg omelettes with sliced bread and margarine and coffee made from hot milk followed and comprised an utterly satisfactory repast.

The road to Nairobi was smooth and trouble-free but interrupted occasionally by police checkpoints and their grisly looking nail beds to deter speeding motorists. Imagine their utter horror and dismay when Mondo Enduro flicked round the obstacle emitting bursts of oil fumes from our shot pistons in the universally recognised motorcyclist's gesture of contempt for the talmudic prescription of international traffic regulations.

Enola Highway was not (as we imagined), the title of a Jamaican road movie, but the main thoroughfare into Kenya's capital city and we soon found the workplace of Gregory Barrow and Jane Standley, our hosts for the immediate future. Greg escorted us to his well-appointed home where our dishevelled appearance visibly shocked Beatrice the buxom but very friendly maid. Soon after defiling Jane's exquisite collection of ethnic African drapes, we were on our way to the British Embassy and an assignment with Gillian Wilson, HM Information Officer.

Clearly intrigued by our mysterious blond barnets, Gillian listened intently to the tawdry blend of half-truths, exaggerations and bona fide exploits which is the chronicle of our round-the-world motorcycle attempts. We, however, were even more fascinated by the gorgeous translucence of her bright green eyes which fixed us with all the splendour of a field of blooming heather. Austin made an outrageous pass at her, quizzing her about her fave nightspots with the clear implication that her next after dark excursion should be in the company of Mondo Enduro. She responded with the emphatic crossing of the arms and limbs which in prehistoric times was a signal to sabre toothed tigers and other primordial predators to retire to their lairs and cease their bothersome meddling in the affairs of humans with their mighty gift of fire...

Anyway, in spite of these attentions, Gillian was very kind and even set up an interview with GTN, the 'independent' Kenyan television station in which Prime Minister Daniel Arap-Moi is the exclusive shareholder. Soon we were being ushered into the offices of this media organ, whose basement, Greg later informed us, is one of Africa's most gruesomely efficient torture chambers.

A truly bizarre film session ensued in which Mondo Enduro was requested to drive round a car park while a home video cam whirred pathetically in the middle distance. After bidding a warm farewell to the fragrant Gillian, we soon arrived back at the Barrow gaffe to find Greg tapping half-heartedly at his keyboard and clearly anxious to visit his refrigerator where several bottles of Tusker ale were chilling in anticipation. We chatted awhile with him and Jane about possible routes out of the dark continent and back to our safe European home. The Goma region of Zaire is apparently in the grips of a brutal ethnic conflict in which the belligerents adorn themselves with necklaces, bracelets and watchstraps made of human hands, ears and other body parts. Along with tales of villages where the ebola virus lurks like a Zimbabwean speed trap, the Central African option is - according to the Beeb in Nairobi - very much a last resort.

An attempt by Clive and Louis to find their old Mill Hill School chum Arthur Oyugi ended in spectacular triumph when they flukily encountered him at a gas station where they were pumping up a flat front tyre. Great Joy!

His huge mansion is at the command of Mondo Enduro and its South African Bureau Chief Kelly Farrell who flies in from Johannesburg on the morrow. Little Jo has meanwhile decided to go to Botswana with her boyfriend Rick, a decision we all obviously respect.

Soon we were adorning ourselves with the rags and leathers which pass for our party attire in these compact luggage times. After 15 minutes walk we were down at the Norfolk Hotel, Nairobi's oldest, and whose restaurant harks back to the golden age of the Berni Inn. There was munched various right-on ethnic foods like curry, pizza and steak and kidney pudding which we washed down with frothing goblets of Tusker Ale. Afterwards we retired to the bar to watch ourselves on telly as living rooms across Kenya resounded to our "Let's Go!" motto.

After some bourbon whisky, gin and other spirits, we retired to our beds contented to be here in Nairobi, the 18th capital city we have reached so far.

Kenya (Nairobi)

Day 324 - 338
Tuesday 27 Feb – Tuesday 12 Mar
Mondo Miles today: 0
Mondo Mileage: 31232

Nairobi for Mondo Enduro was essentially an admin stop. With respect to the profusion of government missions it is the Vienna of Africa. We collected visas for Ethiopia, Eritrea and Saudi Arabia here with a significant and essential bit of help from SNP Hemans the High Commissioner of the British High Commission and some of his staff; in particular Gillian Wilson, the Press Information Officer. She did an excellent job of liaising between the Saudi Embassy, our High Commissioner and us. She even sent back letters and some of our precious Hi-8 footage for us too.

The Saudi Visa was a particularly tricky quarry since the Saudis do not issue such a thing as a 'tourist' visa. They deem that the only two reasons for attempting to visit their great nation are to work or on pilgrimage. Because we were clearly doing neither our initial application was rejected. Hence we had to trouble the big boss Mr Hemans to write (or at least sign) a formal request that we be granted this unprecedented break from the routine. The shilly-shallying that accompanied the securing of the Saudi transit visa was what most of the two weeks in Nairobi was spent doing. The Ethiopian and Eritrean visas were simple overnighters.

Almost every single white person we met was involved in some avenue of the 'aid industry'. Naturally all the big players had an office here; Freedom From Hunger, Oxfam, UNICEF, WHO, War On Want, Christian Aid, The Peace Corps, VSO and the lesser known but equally worthy; Project Sweetwater and Africa Food Action. Not only was Nairobi the East African hub for all these agencies but it was usefully close to The Sudan, Ethiopia, Djibouti and Somalia all of which have been ravaged by their own local but lethal admixtures of Civil War and drought. The overall impression to us was of huge amounts of not only cash but more obviously time and effort that was being offered to these nations. The unsavoury and bitter converse to this western do-gooding was experienced while out on the bikes one day. We arrived at the head of a queue of traffic but our way was blocked by one of the 1950s dressed policeman. It soon became clear that the cause of the delay was the clearing of the streets for the President, Daniel Arup Moi. His motorcade came screaming along and it was like being at a level crossing waiting for a goods train. We counted 32 Mercedes in the convoy. Austin had seen the Queen drive past when he'd been a dispatch rider and reflected that she got two bikes and a Range Rover as her escort. The clash of the President's extravagance agin' his countrymen's subsistence lifestyle was indeed unpleasant to bear witness to.

By far our kindest benefactor was Arthur Oyugi. Arthur an Old Millhillian (88-92) and was in the same boarding house as Louis and Clive with Clive's brother David Greenhough. Once again, we are in debt to Dave for providing us with this great friend of his as a contact. Arthur took us under his wing even though we showed up without notice. He even provided us with a whole house in his late father's mini estate just for us. We also, under Arthur's instruction, were given a cooked breakfast everyday.

We stayed with him for two weeks and in that time went to visit his Mum in Kisumu on Douglas (Arthur's elder brother's) plane. Austin was ill and vomited so violently that he almost passed out. An attempt to jettison his bag of sick was unsuccessful with the high air speed outside the Cesna causing most of the problems. On that visit, we had lunch on a deserted island on Lake Victoria prepared by an Indian hotelier who had built a couple of huts on this island. Arthur explained that the people who lived in this region were 'Loor' and they were *his* people. He spoke in chilling terms about the friction between the Loor and other tribes and suddenly the reason this great continent is tearing itself apart made complete sense...

Kenya

Day 339
Wednesday 13 March
Mondo Miles today: 221
Mondo Mileage: 31453

Well intentioned – up with the larks – admin administered to – disaster at dusk. Read on...

Arthur's 3 mansion complex played out its last 12 hours of hospitality and so at 0800 Mondo Enduro bade farewell to the permanently smiling Tom and the faithful servants who had tended to us so fully over the last 2 weeks.

The road to Moyale on the Kenyan: Ethiopia border beckoned but our hearts were heavy for having to leave this East African paradise. However, after our recent Visa successes we can almost smell London and so the desire to clock on even more miles is being fanned to a white heat.

After some back street jiggery pokery that took us through the suburbs of Nairobi, we passed the Saudi Embassy and struck out on the beautiful dual carriageway that is the A2. The clouds hung heavy over us but we didn't anticipate that by the end of the day, rain would be the very least of our worries.

We'd stocked up on biscuits and fruit juice from an Esso Station at the Westlands shopping centre. Although the major world oil producers are well represented in Kenya this Esso station was the first we had found that sported the full range of candy, booze, cookies and of course all washed down by Visa and MasterCard.

We plugged out the miles, the dual carriageway became single, and the outskirts of the capital gave way to the rolling hills and bush that we have hardly seen over the past fortnight. The roadside waving is not as ardent as it once was but the ability of HGVs to belch rich black unfiltered exhaust into the air remains unabashed.

A lunchtime break of a Snickers bar (comes up peanuts slice after slice) distracted us from hunger as we reached Zero degrees North, aka the Equator.

Lying deserted adjacent the formal "EQUATOR" sign were two jugs and bowls. Clearly this apparatus was for the demonstration whereby a northern hemisphere vortex (in H_2O) descends clockwise whilst the opposite is true in the southern hemisphere. Some of the locals, who worked at the handful of nearby Equator souvenir emporiums, asked us if we needed 'The Professor' to effect a demonstration of this North: South phenomenon. We declined the offer and our very own Dr Greenhough performed the test for himself.

The theories were proved and after some dusty filming, leaving behind some disappointed vendors, we pushed on north. Mt Kenya was to our right (east). We knew this - not because the stunning peak was there to behold - nay, but because the map doth never lie, and there it revealed that behind the cloud would be this nation's volcanic namesake.

However, the map can be deceiving if left unattended. Sadly, a right of way misunderstanding saw the brotherhood of Mondo heading 15 miles due East, and out of our way, en route to Maru, a bustling market town and physical and spiritual home to the unmarked speed ramp.

After an about-turn and 30 'dead' miles we were descending from the plateau that had been our home and down we cruised onto the plain, arid indeed and physically stunning. Shortly we reached tarmac's end, at the small town of Isiolo. The unmade road stretched out into the desert before us and as mpg would have it, it was here that we disgorged the contents of our jerry cans (one of which has gone from 10L down to 8.5L after being crushed when a bike fell on it) and re-charged the tanks. At this time we were beset by children, some offering small plastic bags of fruit while the others, obviously attempting to short circuit the traditional 'small business' money making system, simply demanded "GIVE ME MONEY!" Austin was ungenerous, only offering to 'give money' in return for clothing or services. Disenchanted with this self-help approach to aid for the developing world, the elves melted back into the dust; leaving behind only the young girls offering micro-mangoes, fun sized bananas, and two men.

We tooled up with goggles, face masks and all the other anti-dust measures we could muster and set off north along the dirt road. The next objective is the mid-desert oasis of Marsabit. The riding style on the dusty (volcanic rock) road is to be roughly 100m apart. This means that the dust of the previous rider doesn't affect his successor.

The afternoon wore on, but not before Chas ploughed into a sand drift at 45mph. He was heavily spilled and utterly covered in the fine white dust that was kicked up as he impacted. At least the sand broke his fall.

This little disruption was the beginning of our drama. Austin's re-installation of a cam chain in Nairobi had necessitated the removal and refitting of the rocker cover. The captive threads within the cylinder block, into which the rocker cover bolts engage, are notoriously weak. Only a slight over-tightening will shear them out and sure enough, this is what Austin did. The problem developed into an oil leak since the cylinder through which the bolt passes is also a conduit for the oil feed to the rockers. The pressurised oil made short work of the partial seal afforded by the 'unstrained' bolt and over a few miles, oil began literally gushing out from the rocker box like a scene from "Giant".

Austin's right leg and boots were utterly soaked in oil. We about-turned and Austin was lamely towed back to what we thought would be our salvation. Five miles back we had passed the Kenyan Army School of Combat Engineering. This was Austin's former unit when he was in the British Army, so we reported to the Guardroom and asked the duty sergeant if we could be allowed to use any workshop area for our repairs. The answer was a firm "No" and we felt a definite twang of revenge at the recently imposed Visa requirements for Kenyans that our government has introduced.

It was 6pm by now, and the sun was setting over the rocky mountainous horizon.

A three point turn, which is hard to pull off whilst remaining cool with the bulk of the Junior Ranks mess looking on, and we creaked back onto the dirt road which previously we regarded so cockily. Little did we know that it was to be our home for several days more than we would care.

Two hundred yards into the bush and the team bomburst for the tasks which by now are carried out so efficiently it would have a time and motion man dabbing the corner of his eye with naked respect. Clive created a cooking fire, Cheeky Charlie sliced, diced and conjured a truly stupendous meal from the humblest of ingredients, Austin began the pain of *another* engine strip down whilst Louis unloaded from our front racks and jacked up our 'bedroom'. Louis should be singled out for praise as his thorough job saw us all adjacent but comfortable, everybody's pillow etc perfectly placed and puffed up and even little Plymouth tucked up ready for Austin's cuddling.

Louis has hi-jacked the diary and candidly writes:

I've spent the last three years in Africa but I've never seen anything of the place. We've camped in the bush in Northern Kenya, under a fabulous starry sky, and this thing is totally mental. I know I did the right thing to pack in my job. Austin has got some aggravation with his bike that he is having to fix it by torchlight. Chas cooked one of his delicious mixtures which we've just finished. I've written a whole load of letters, loads to all the folks in Sun City and also to everyone back in England including some people who I didn't even notify that I was going to pack in the job. One thing I'm very annoyed about is that I managed to leave behind my trusty Swiss Army penknife and I've already had to borrow Chas's one about eight times and although he's too nice to say anything about it I can tell it's getting on his nerves. In fact, even if I had remembered to bring it I probably would have managed to lose it during my bungee jump at Victoria Falls as I usually just keep it in my pocket.

There are some strange noises coming from the bush so a party of us are going to set off with a trusty torch to investigate. So long for now, dear Diary!

Kenya

Day 340
Thursday 14 March
Mondo Miles today: 67
Mondo Mileage: 31520

The day began earlier than usual for the slumbering riders when Louis, woken by the troublesome mosquito, alerted us all to the presence of a troupe of nearby warthogs. Their snuffling and snorting amidst the bush might have been the cause of some annoyance had it not been for the incomparable semi-desert setting yielding cool clear air and a stunning canopy of stars.

Daybreak was, if anything, still more magnificent and numerous colour photos and some video footage were taken as we lazily broke camp. After a breakfast of chocolate, orange juice and coffee brewed up by Clive, Austin got down to the serious business of repairing his stripped out head bolt and the oil gushing there from.

This was achieved with surprisingly little ado after we fabricated a makeshift washer from a rubber tank seating ring. As Cliff and Louis went into the hamlet of Archer's Camp to seek water, Austin and Chas followed behind – or at least that was the idea.

Chas had made it only a few hundred yards from the road when he noticed that his carelessly slung Golden Bulb was chafing against the back wheel. More seriously still, the purple Smith goggles which had revolutionised his vision, especially in rainy weather, were nowhere to be seen despite a lengthy reconnaissance mission back to our campsite.

It was with a mixture of confusion and relief therefore that on driving back down the road he spotted a fully-extended lobed, heavily beaded and spear-carrying Masai herdsman proudly wearing the afore-mentioned eye-wear as he shepherded his flock of billy goats down towards the School of Combat Engineering. After brief negotiations and a hearty handshake, the goggles were reunited with their thankful owner.

Just the other side of Arthur's Camp a right turn from the main road gave way to a 60-mile length of track. This was marked on our Michelin map as a White route which cut perhaps 40 kilometres off our journey. The road and the promise of some serious scrambling was too good an opportunity to let pass and soon we were slipping and sliding along the sandy carriageway which, in its early sections at least, proved a stern test for bikes whose wheels were imperfectly shod for this type of terrain. Chas and Louis both slid off, although none was injured by their falls in the soft sand. Another more serious accident was only narrowly averted when Louis ploughed into Austin's stationary bike as Austin replaced his spare chain which had worked free from the back plate where it had been temporarily stowed. Austin's bike suffered only minor damage, including a slightly bent rear end but Louis's bell-end may well have suffered more serious trauma following its impact, shortly followed by that of both gonads with his 20-litre fuel tank. Let's hope that his own power unit can still operate at full capacity following this latest of motorcycling mishaps.

And so onwards, after much compass consulting to a dry river crossing where Clifton suffered a front wheel puncture – miraculously our first in this thorn-strewn adventure playground; where earlier in the day he and Chas had spotted a giant ostrich and a menacing hyena lurking in the bush. A gang of amazingly-technicoloured Masai teens immediately appeared from the undergrowth carrying spears and sporting a magnificent array of beads, buttons, headscarves, ear and body piercings. One, however, was clearly ill with yellow jaundiced eyes and a pain in the right abdomen which he and his colleagues seemed to think was malaria. Austin gave him a Lariam pill by way of medication.

Soon we were joined in this most remote of spots by a Land Rover full of Masai and two gun-toting policeman one of whom claimed to be an inspector and asked to see Chas' passport. After chiding us for taking short cuts and warning of the bandits (what bandits?), he and his friends disappeared up the road, carrying the malarial Masai with them.

A few miles down the road and the puncture gremlins struck again in Cliff's front tyre – this time after an impromptu stop for some filming in an acacia copse. While Louis and Austin helped Clive effect a repair, Chas seated himself in the shade of a tree to start writing the day's log entry. Was it his imagination or did he see a lioness prowling in the far distance? Maybe, but it was certainly a large cat.

After some black and white stills photography we were surprised to find ourselves on the main road again so quickly. Within a few yards was a snack bar, heavily populated by Masai and our two aforementioned friends from the Kenyan Constabulary. We swiftly ordered cokes, Fanta and a bottle of "Stones" ginger ale which tasted delicious despite being far from chilled.

Still, it was a rare moment of luxury on a day which had been full of sweat and toil and there would also be tears to come before bedtime. A matter of 10 miles or so outside town we stopped for a spot of luggage adjustment and Louis's bike for one did not start again. A mysterious ignition fault had manifested itself and despite the best leather shod aggravation by several Mondo members, resolutely refused to fire up.

Austin drew the short straw and drove back the five miles or so to tow Louis back, determined as he did so, to ride like the wind at 55mph. It was with some trepidation, therefore, that Cliff and Chas were alerted first by a Msunga-filled Land Rover that all was not well with the winching operation. Back they were labouring on heavily laden motorbikes when a lorry hove into view, all the while flashing its headlamps.

As the confused Enduristes pulled over, the familiar moustached features of D'Artagnan Bloomingdale popped up from beneath the truck's awning. Inside was all his luggage and his motorbike while Austin was stranded down the road on his own dysfunctional DR350.

After much puffing and panting Louis, Chas and a platoon of dark helpers lowered the bike from the truck which smelt strongly of ganja and perhaps other illicit herbs. Cliff meanwhile had headed back down the track to winch Austin to our enforced roadside camp. While Louis purchased some tomatoes, brief negotiations ensued over the possible purchase of water from the truck drive "We do not sell water", he said, but did accept three Peter Stuyvesant fags by way of recompense. We are in his debt and will be from this day forth.

And so the sun set on a day which has seen its fair share of tribulations. The road to Moyale, has despite its desiccated and heavily rutted state, become something of a vale of tears for Mondo Enduro who, it also transpires, cannot rely on a fuel refill in Marsabit. Suddenly the Catholic mission, where we had fondly imagined we might have a couple of beers, seems a long way away.

But at least we have a Mondo meal to look forward to, prepared by Louis and Cliff, and a comfy night's repose thanks to Austin's meticulous arrangements of the sleeping bag and mozzie net combos. And if we run short of water we can always squeeze out Louis's sleeping bag which was still drenched from last night's perspirations.

Is this where Mondo Enduro really begins? If only Leonard, Ibrahim and little Andy could see us now. Or perhaps not.

Kenya

Day 341
Friday 15 March
Mondo Miles today: 0
Mondo Mileage: 31520

The day began at 6.25am when Austin began filming and taking photos of the sun rising in our camp.

We were still 100 miles from Marsabit and the friendly Catholic mission with half of Mondo Enduro fully off the plot. Austin with a shagged thread in his cylinder head and Louis with the mysterious electrical fault whereby he cannot get a spark.

The day began with a carton of peach juice saved from our shopping in Nairobi, followed by the remnants of last night's Mondo meal which was delicious once warmed up in the embers of the fire.

Cliff had managed to get a flat in his back wheel overnight and Louis's slow puncture in his front tyre had gone that way too. So their first task was to carry out their respective repairs.

Meanwhile, the air temperature began to soar as early as 7 o'clock in the morning. Austin's frustration also soared after he discovered his battery and the $300 cash he keeps hidden behind it had gone. We believe it may have disappeared when he rode back unladen to assist Louis the day before.

Clive went off on Chas' K5 (the only bike mobile at this time) to look for the battery and cash whilst Louis and Austin went to work on their machines.

An hour later and Clive returned empty handed. There was no sign of them anywhere. All that remained on this inhospitable road was the odd strip of tyre or rubber left long behind by its previous owner to swelter in the unforgiving heat.

The day wore on and Mondo Enduro continued to toil, battling against bike gremlins in the unbearable heat. We set up a poncho and awarded ourselves a shady siesta.

By now it was 10am and we were down to our last half litre (of water) and at least 20 kilometres from the nearest town. But 20 kilometres is about an hour's ride each way on this bumpy and dusty road. However, as luck would have it a truck came trundling along and was soon flagged down by Clive wearing only his boxers. The truck stopped and the driver and passengers were more than happy to fill our water containers. Naturally, they were all awarded a Mondo Enduro badge for this charitable deed. They seemed bemused but pinned them on all the same.

The multimeter was also doing a mentionable job of testing the numerous sections of wiring on the DR but unfortunately to no avail. The Clymer manual gives a list of tests to perform and what readings to expect. However, in the crushing heat we got into a bit of a jumble remembering which tests we had and had not done. Louis' magneto cover was removed after damage was spotted on part of it. Further testing in comparison to another bike found Austin's bike with electrical problems of its own and so not a great comparison for Louis's electrical diagnosis cul-de-sac.

On a lighter note the radiator seal putty that Austin plugged up his cylinder head with seemed to have held and hardened after a few hours in the African sun. Austin then went off on an official test ride and secondary search of his cash to come back empty handed though with a fragile but running trail bike.

Water ran low in the afternoon and we flagged down another truck for more *Agua sin gas*. We learnt from the driver that Monelli, the next town from here, had more trucks departing to Marsabit and Moyale (towns to the north) than where we were currently holed up. So we decided to tow Louis's bike to Monelli tomorrow.

So, a day of nicht Mondo miles for the lads as we began preparing for supper. For the record Lou made his mildest dish so far and a damn tasty one at that. His co-travellers are hoping that he will be able to calm his gushing torrents of Tabasco without which he feels a meal is too bland to ingest.

We need an early start tomorrow so we'll try and bed down even earlier tonight with the help of the sedative effects of the Kenyan rum.

Kenya

Day 342
Saturday 16 March
Mondo Miles today: 91
Mondo Mileage: 31611

We had broken camp and were on the bumpy corrugated road by 0700hrs. We towed Louis for an hour and that got us pretty much to the small town of Monelli. Once we had the towing rhythm established we tried some towed bump-starts. Louis held it together (this can be pretty fraught) but the engine just turned over repeatedly without so much as the hint of it even possibly firing.

Once at Monelli Austin found a big yellow lorry and arranged a lift north for Louis and the non-sparky S8. Lucas the lorry driver was spectacularly aware that we were in a bit of a pickle and he climbed into the cab with a crisp US$50 folded into his breast pocket. They don't drive in the dark out here so Lucas said he was only going as far as Marsabit today. Louis would have to sleep there tonight (on the lorry) and continue on to the Ethiopian frontier tomorrow. The lifting of the 130kg of DR350 onto the top of the pre-existing goods was like a deleted scene from Gulliver's Travels. We didn't have to recruit the help of the townspeople, instead the lorry was spontaneously over-run with locals pushing and toiling swarming like ants around the stricken Suzuki. We were hugely grateful that we weren't attempting this with a chunky Africa twin or one of those 900cc BMW adventure things.

Whilst waiting for the lorry to leave we began to get a better look at this Samburu Oasis. Graceful Masai glided across the ochre dust. It is evidently normal for them to be carrying a spear at all times; indeed, they appear refreshingly unaffected by the twentieth century. Their aloof independence is a clear indication of how these people never needed European influence in their lives, they're very cool.

Off rumbled Louis atop the lorry escorted by the three healthy bikes. He made friends with Jantu and Nkola two herdsmen who were heading north to try to get work at the bustling border town of Moyale. Louis' easy going charm and three years working in Africa meant they were all friends in no time. Nkola had worked in South Africa and was impressed by Louis' command of the *Tswana* dialect.

Meanwhile, after passing through Solombi, Loisamis, Logologo, Kakaram and Ulan Ulan the out-riders had a surprise when they met Derek Price a few miles ahead. Derek was another of that ultra-hardy breed of long distance cyclists. He had pedalled away from Redland in Bristol six months ago and had got this far on his journey south. Crucially, he had hot and recent intelligence from the Red Sea where he had got a boat south from Suez to Masawa in Eritrea. This news is vital to us since we don't yet know by what route we'll be able to leave Ethiopia.

The relentless rattling of the corrugations continued all afternoon and the progress was slow but admittedly sure. The whole day had been set aside for getting the dud bike on a lorry and driving north and by late afternoon we'd accumulated 91 miles to our name. As the wheezing bikes coughed into the little town of Marsabit we naturally split asunder. Clive and Chas to scrounge shelter at the Catholic Mission whilst Austin waited on the outskirts of town for Louis' orange lorry to turn up. It took ages but at dusk its distinctive silhouette hove into view on the dusty horizon. Louis was kept company by Austin as Lucas let them sleep atop the cargo.

Just then, a VW camper van trundled up crammed with a collective of South African Granolae. We chatted briefly and were immediately impressed by their determination to get to Egypt *without* a carnet. Well done them, they'd got this far. They also repaired to the Catholic Mission and so the day ended with half of us on the lorry whilst Chas and Clive lay with the lamb of God. Austin and Louis slept well snuggled upon the roof of the prodigal truck. Once safely located, they bedded down between the prostrate awkwardness of S8 and an elfin Kenyan lorry lacky who slipped into a metallic crevice that both of the Enduristes had decreed was too small to sleep in. It was another spectacular starscape that prompted Louis to exclaim: "This is just like the Planetarium!" Oh mercy...

Kenya

Day 345
Sunday 17 March
Mondo Miles today: 155
Mondo Mileage: 31766

Sadness greeted us in the morning with the discovery that meanwhile, back at Father James' Catholic Mission, somebody had stolen Clive's spare rear tyre. The beautiful Cheng-Shin Trials. Sob, sob.

Our Granola South Africans had silently struck camp in an almost ninja-esque wordless display of cohesive teamwork that (on awakening) left Clive and Chas with huge Tintin style question marks over their heads.

After *finally* eating the last of the compo quick rolled oats bequeathed to us by Martin Pickford at the Bogota Army Surplus Centre, we said our goodbyes and at about 0800 rolled out of Marsabit under an uncharacteristically overcast and cloudy sky.

The rough aim was for Austin, Clive and Chas to catch up with the yellow lorry carrying Louis and his bike at 10mph (max) Northwards to Moyale. The lorry had almost a 2 hour head start on the 3 bikes, increased and compounded by Clive's recently repaired (last night) front inner tube mysteriously deflating overnight. It was repaired first thing, then deflated again at the 11th minute, just as we were wheeling out of the Mission yard. Bah and humbug but a chance to be surrounded by another crowd.

The landscape north of Marsabit degenerated from the thorny tree-ed semi-arid bush that prevailed south of town, into a fully arid, lava sprinkled lunar landscape. We saw a humungous crater the size of a town and easily 100 yds deep. Truly an extra terrestrial impact must have sent the locals scurrying for their reed huts when it once smashed into the desert out here.

The road was initially of the 'improved' variety, a sub-base of granular material making for a steady 45mph and a dramatic cloud of dust behind each bike. As we took turns up the front of our trio, the sight over one's shoulder of two headlights, a moving black speck and a plume of haze in the wake of each bike, was quite striking.

By 10.30 Louis and his lorry were apprehended, refreshingly caught fixing *their* second puncture. Just prior to this rendezvous Clive had filmed a 4 beast camel train (an express!) known in these awful parts as a *dani*. The camel train engineer or driver had been particularly unhappy as his brain cogs realised that his soul was being stolen by the sinister Sony VX-1. Not content with the usual stick waving, which urged Clive on to record all the more, he began throwing stones at our tenacious/disrespectful cameraman. Austin tried to defuse the situation with the offer of a slug of rum and a ham sandwich, but this being a Muslim desert, it did no good. Finally, in a scene straight from "Roger Cook amongst the Masai" our diminutive herdsman closed in on the lens and smothered it with a lens cap of his own, namely his calloused and bony hand.

As the seemingly interminable 150 miles to Moyale rolled by, often at no more than 20mph, the road quality reverted to the sharp boulder and rock strewn chaos that had made yesterday such hard work (not the Beatles' hit, rather, the day before this one). Fortunately, the burning heat which us English have such a propensity for going 'out' in, remained numbed and dulled by the homogenous blanket of cloud that stretched as infinitely above us as this miserable volcanic wasteland did beneath us.

The remaining miles to Moyale were ploughed through, not withstanding two more punctures for Clive and Cheeky Charlie's first in his second hand (fitted in Tanzania) rear end. Added to this, the butt weld that had been holding K5's gear change in place since Peru (see day 263 of this journal) finally failed and so Chas was finding it increasingly difficult to change gear. This ailment lead to some spectacularly daring riding as rather than attempt to slow up and change down, Chas would throttle it through some of the more challenging sections of dirt road.

We finally arrived at Moyale close to 1700hrs. Clive and Chas went in search of *this* town's Catholic Mission, seeking sanctuary and a place to really get to grips on Louis's electrically lacking bike. The latter had not yet arrived in their ten ton eight wheeled slug and so Austin parked up in the 'suburbs' to await their arrival. In no time he was mobbed by the requisite platoon of small children, many of whom sported mobile shoe shine apparatus.

These children were genuinely fascinated and charmed by the long-suffering purple haired troll, unflinchingly vigilant as it stood glued to the lid of the front brake fluid reservoir. However, the spell was broken as they were all shooed away by a gangly root-chewing man in his twenties. A woman on the far side of the road warned Austin: "Beware, this one is totally insane!"

Fortunately the truck then arrived and after a carnivalesque drive through the rutted streets of Moyale, Louis' bike was lowered back down to terra firma. Clive and Chas showed up on cue and as S8 was towed to the sanctuary afforded by the Mission, literally 150 small children ran after us up the street, cheering and whooping like it was the end of Ramadan. A fine meal from our chefs in the pastor's kitchen and we were in bed by 8.20pm.

Kenya

Day 346
Monday 18 March
Mondo Miles today: 0
Mondo Mileage: 31766

A shower in the night had all sleepers scurrying for the Mission's workshop whose corrugated iron roof provided shelter from the light overnight rain. Apparently Kenya and Southern Ethiopia are bracing themselves for the 'long rains' which last from March to mid-May. Mercifully these particular rains, of only 10 minutes duration, were especially short and did not severely disrupt our night-time's repose.

Still, the Muezzin were up well before us, calling the 95% Muslim population of Moyale to prayer at 5am with a variety of ululating vocal disharmonies. What could be more disheartening for Father Alex and his small troupe of Catholic brothers and sisters than a variety of loud speakers intoning the "Allah Aqbar" litany at this unearthly hour of the morning?

In fact, the Catholic father, perhaps piqued by the ascendance of Islam in Northern Kenya, had departed early in the morning on an unknown quest which would take him away from the Mission for most of the day. Only Joseph the Mexican lay brother joined us for our breakfast of coffee and biscuits before quizzing us on camera aperture adjustments and procedures for swapping the fork seals on his Yamaha DT125.

Soon the Mission compound had turned into the quintessential Mondo workshop with a variety of tools littering a ground already heavily soiled by the taint of bogue oil. The big task of the day was to find what buggery was up with Louis's firing system, with lesser problems; including Chas's stripped out gear shift shaft, also to be attended to. The morning passed in a whirl of technical activity, including a rear brake pad change for K5 and much testing of the continuity of Louis' electrical loom, all lubricated by two steaming brews from Clive's field kitchen.

Work on the wiring system was not going well until the timely arrival of the South African granolae for a spot of late breakfast in the Mission compound. Tim, the semi-albino muesli-guzzler, showed himself to be a dab hand in the motorcycle mechanics department by wiring up Austin's magneto to Louis's bike; the result was a pulse of current which gave Louis perhaps the most perversely pleasurable electric shock ever to course through pores still sweating at the prospect of prolonged technical breakdown. The spark generated from Austin's alternator also soon had Louis' bike coughing and spluttering into life like a body mistakenly presumed to be lying dead on the mortuary slab.

Any reader bored by the prospect of technical details should skip this next paragraph.

Diagnosis: These bikes have an electronic ignition, i.e. no points. The symptom on Louis' bike was no spark at the plug. We had changed and checked literally everything that was in anyway connected with the production of the spark and all the components were healthy. What South African Granola Tim knew that we didn't was that there is a secret pea sized blob in the alternator housing. This little guy is connected up to the CDI and it electronically monitors the rpm of the crankshaft sending a pulse of current up to the CDI on each turn. This info is the electronic version of the points and it means that the frequency of the pulses of voltage that cause the sparks are of course linked to the engine speed. Anyway, this little solid state doo-dah has packed up and that's why we had no spark. We are pretty resourceful but if saviour Tim hadn't specifically brought this to our attention heaven knows how we would have got to the bottom of this torpor. Naturally, exactly why this crucial nodule is now non-functioning is part of the broader malaise of solid-state circuitry. No one will ever know the reason.

Chas' gear shift welding had meanwhile gone swimmingly for the not unreasonable fee of 2$ (100 shillings) although he did have to queue behind a

Moslem cleric who had come to have the mosque's crescent moon weather vane repaired. Close examination revealed that it appeared to have been fired at by some kind of heavy bore rifle. Perhaps this explained Father Alex's mysterious disappearance – not wishing to be caught with the smoking gun as it were. Anyway the granolae soon pottered off in their Volkswagen Combi towards Ethiopia and, who knows, perhaps another Mondo encounter. Actually they were great company and Tim especially was well worth his Mondo badge earned for distinguished service in the auto-electrician's department. We wish them luck on their self-imposed mission was to get to the north of Africa *without* a Carnet using only charm and guile instead. Fair play to them, they'd got this far.

Lunch was some mushroom and garlic soup stuffed down with bread and orange juice while Father Alex's maid looked on in horror. Meanwhile Austin went down to the post office to book a phone call to GJ the DJ (naturally, 71 year old Geoffrey Vince is *not* a DJ) and order the requisite magneto podule for Louis's bike. The plan is for Louis and Austin to swap electrics so that Louis' bike is healed and Austin's becomes the casualty. Austin will then try and hitch (plus bike) onto a truck north to the capital. The rationale being that Louis is only on Mondo for a short time so we should maximise his time in the saddle. Meanwhile, Clive and Chas made use of Father Alex's refreshing 'holy water' shower facilities.

It was while Chas was performing these ablutions that a roar of a large motorcycle was heard on the Mission driveway. It was none other then Geoff Brotherton-Ratcliffe, our biking colleague from Nairobi who had driven the 500 miles here in an extremely impressive two days. He looked well despite a nasty wipe-out on the Marsabit road which had cracked a fuel can and the radiator reservoir and smashed his headlamp. It was great to see him. *Los quatro mosqueteros tienen otro companero!*

As the evening drew on, we began to make tentative moves toward a departure but were frustrated by a gushing petrol leak from Louis's carburettor. Frustrations mounted as we struggled to remove a recalcitrant screw but we are British and therefore triumphed in the end.

Chas went to Ethiopia twice to check out the trucking situation with regard to transportation of Austin's bike to Addis Ababa. The scheme is to get the sickly bike onto a truck and to Ethiopia's mighty capital whereupon DHL will take receipt of the crucial new parts dispatched from Frank at Crescent Motorcycles Bournemouth. On Chas' second journey he met three Californians of indeterminate age and sexuality "*in East Africa to research the beliefs of the Boron people*" who apparently have x-ray vision. Interesting to think what they make of the shadowy image of Austin's ancient underwear phosphorescing dimly in its radioactive afterglow.

Beer was purchased at a nearby bar and the quintet settled down to enjoy an evening meal prepared by Clive. Father Alex, it has to be said, did not look entirely happy to welcome us into his humble compound and cut

Clive short when he tried to blend him in. Hopefully we will not be the first Englishmen to feel the wrath of the Holy Roman Church.

Ethiopia

Day 347
Tuesday 19 March
Mondo Miles today: 170
Mondo Mileage: 31936

Up and at 'em for matins but Louis' bike had further problems with a misbehaving carburettor that permanently gushed out petrol from the overflow tube: one that needed addressing immediately. So this was the first task of the day before packing and breaking camp from Father Alex's Catholic Mission amongst the Muslims. We fear he tires of overland spongers like us but we made a substantial contribution to the collection box so as not to over tax his near-saintly patience. Lou pulled the carb apart and Aust adjusted the float valve mechanism so it would regulate the petrol flow effectively. By 9 o'clock we were at the border and managed to get stamped out of Kenya and into Ethiopia within 2 hours (bikes and all).

In the meantime, Austin managed to blend a lift to Addis Ababa with his bike for $50 on the back of a double truck carrying steel reinforcing bars. However, the lift was not going to leave until the following morning. So Clive, Chas and Louis headed north towards Addis and kindly Geoff kept Austin company until he leaves tomorrow.

The Mondo trio made their way zig zagging and riding past innumerable roadside children for the first 30 kilometres away from the border.

The road then began to improve and so Chas, who was leading at this time, began gunning it. Whilst looking down at the map to check the route forward, he ploughed straight into a huge mound of gravel in the centre of the road. Ethiopian roadworks are yet to have any warning signs. His co-riders only saw a cloud of dust and then a bemused Chas staggered onto his feet wondering where the hell had this huge gravel mound come from.

Damage report: Chas grazed his nose, K5 has tail-light broken off, totally smashed up front rack, another dent on the petrol tank and just a general shake up.

All the nearby road workers flew to Charlie's rescue even though Cliff and Louis had the situation under control. Ten minutes later after we had repacked Chas' kit and cleaned his graze we were back on the plot. We all had noticed since crossing the border the drop in temperature, the increased cloud cover and the change in relief. The light rains that we had heard about loomed on the horizon. However, the sky looked very dark and menacing for just light rains. The next thing we all knew, we were riding through a torrential downpour.

By now Mondo Enduro's vision was negligible and it was with great shock and horror that we found ourselves riding through a river and no longer on a road. This was our first 'flash flood'. The river that gushed across and along the road was fast and deep in places and with an extremely strong current; in fact it almost washed Chas and bike clean away. Clive battled through the water to Chas' aid and the two of them, supporting each other struggled inch by inch through the cascades to dry land. The current was *so* strong that if Chas had lifted his leg to kick-start his stalled bike then he would have been bowled over completely.

The saturated and shivering trio mounted their bikes and rode off in search of warmth and comfort to dry themselves out. It was only three days ago that we were baking in as inhospitable a desert as we've ever seen! Anyway, we found instead a police checkpoint who wished to see our identity cards.

We managed to get a free glass of chai inside a mud hut compliments of the policeman at the checkpoint. We did in fact try to change money with him and the mud hut coffee boy but at a useless rate so we abstained and were satisfied with a hot drink *gratis*.

It was now 5.15, so we did another 40 miles and found a camp site.

Cliff erected a den whilst Lou perfected his pyrotechnics and Chas prepared supper; with our only ingredients tomato puree, onions and pasta. The surprisingly strong tomato heavy dish did its job and filled the three weary lads; they were all tucked up in bed by a little after 8pm. Austin plus his bike is somewhere on a truck in southern Ethiopia.

Ethiopia

Day 348
Wednesday 20 March
Mondo Miles today: 237
Mondo Mileage: 32173

No lie in for the rest of Mondo this morning as was expected. The fire was still hot from the previous night so Chas made a welcoming pot of coffee at 0700; and thus we were up and away by 0800. However, before we actually hit the road 'Magic Legs Greenhough' was required to start an extremely stubborn K5. Louis led the way north and our priority was changing money to purchase petrol. Louis went into the bank whilst Clive and Chas were left to deal with the thousands outside. Once we had local currency it was then necessary for Chas to call his contact in Addis for our blend. So off to the telecommunications house we sped. Clive waited outside and Louis went off in search of fruit, coke, and some tuna fish, (obviously Austin would not be joining us for dinner tonight!).

Once we had gassed-up it was time to clock-on the miles! No rain, no wind, good roads and smiling faces greeted us for miles and miles. It was then mutually agreed upon that a few standard beers be consumed at any promising spot. A welcome retreat was thus found and Mondo parked off with some tasty Ethiopian beer. By the time another round was ordered by Louis in respect of the absence of Austin, a large crowd had gathered outside the pub where we had pulled over.

Only one man in the crowd spoke English and sat with us to converse. His name was Mahmood and he introduced us to some of the local customs; so once we had eaten enough herbs and sugar, back on our wheels we got and north we went!

A further 60 miles was reached until we decided to set up base. People to the left of us, huts to the right of us, and nowhere secluded for us to camp. The sun was going down so off-road we went in our usual fashion. An Acacia tree in the middle of a potato farm provided an ideal spot so Chas laid bedding whilst Clive made fire and prepared food, both of which they did in record time! Our tummies full we laid to rest. Out of all the African countries we have visited so far, Ethiopia is the most appealing. Perhaps this is so because this enchanted country has never been colonised; or because it has been at war for years and now at peace its people want only to live in harmony. Whatever the reason it is not something that we have met before.

Ethiopia

Day 349
Thursday 21 March
Mondo Miles today: 82
Mondo Mileage: 32255

The sound of Clive shuffling the coffee pots was the first noise we heard on this beautiful Ethiopian spring day. He was up before the larks to film a dramatic sunrise and the arrival of several locals who had turned up to watch our breakfast. The slender but graceful Ethiopians are perpetually curious and we feel rather acutely our role as ambassadors for Europe in general, but Britain in particular.

We broke camp relatively quickly after a warming cup of coffee and bread roll with marmite. Soon we were on the rapidly improving road to Addis, after we had stopped at a service station to perform our ablutions (before some extremely bemused washerwomen).

Addis Ababa was reached without further ado and we soon negotiated our way through the chaotic streets to the calm oasis of the British Embassy. We had heard that Our Man In Addis lived in sumptuous surroundings and so he did – all 87 acres of them donated by the Ethiopian Emperor Mahmoud in 1896 after the Italian defeat at the Battle of Adua. Apparently it has one of the finest collections of native trees in the country and was also the birthplace of the British explorer William Thesiger, but such fine historical details were lost on the three weary travellers who were merely grateful for some welcome shelter.

After changing into the requisite Mondo tee-shirts in a futile attempt to look 'smart', we were met on the Embassy steps by the Information Officer, Jeremy Astle-Brown and the Big Shilton himself, Robin Christopher. With his fluffy hairstyle, he really did look a bit like the hero of an AA Milne novel. Jeremy had already been primed over our arrival, by both Jane Standley and Gillian Wilson in Nairobi and ourselves in a phone call from the town of Dilla, and was extremely welcoming, even offering to arrange accommodation for us at the local Anglican Church. He was, however, forestalled by Winnie the Pooh himself who more or less demanded that he accommodate us in his own home.

And so we retired to Jeremy's well appointed gaff where he fixed us toast, marmalade, peanut butter and our first genuine cup of Ethiopian coffee which was every bit as delicious as we had been led to believe. Soon Jeremy's wife Marisa had also returned home and we were feasting on a sumptuous meal of vegetables, bacon, scrambled eggs and fried potatoes. To enjoy this exquisite a cocktail of kindness and generosity from complete strangers, merely because we share citizenship, is humbling indeed. Our 32,000 miles so far, especially those in Africa, have taught us that we must all be kinder to strangers when we get home. During the afternoon we met Colin Sanguay, Jeremy's houseguest and a York University student working for the 'Farm Africa' charity. After arrangements were made for us to split up and stay with two other Embassy staff, Second Secretary Mike Stead and Technical Officer Dave Mills, we went with Colin to the Hilton Hotel for a quick haircut and a beer in the bar.

On our return we were blended in with our respective hosts, before heading out to the Armenian Community Club (not sure why it's called this) with our new found circle of diplomatic friends. We had a fantastic meal there – cheese and potato pasties, kebabs and chips and honeyed doughnuts – and all paid for by Mondo Enduro (plus drinks) with change from £20.

And so home and to bed after another remarkable day on our round-the-world adventure. Chas would like to record the fact that he had two of the green cans of draught Guinness bitter specially ordered by Dave from the British Army Naafi in Nairobi and surely the most wonderful liquid to pass his lips since the Georgian sherry consumed under the Siberian railway bridge (day 84).

As we fell into a deep sleep in comfortable duvet-covered beds, only two thoughts troubled the deep blue oceans of our sleepy consciousness. The first was where on earth were Austin and Geoff on their own odyssey from Moyale to Addis? The second was; when on earth *is* our own good fortune and the bounty of HM Diplomatic Service going to end?

Ethiopia

Day 350 - 353
Friday 22 March
Mondo Miles today: 0
Mondo Mileage: 32255

Today started with Clive, Louis and Chas snuggled up in the 240V AC mains driven Embassy compound cum National park, temporary co-rider Geoff Brotherton-Ratcliffe (on a notional K9) still heading North and with Austin crammed into the rear of the lorry cab, parked at 0530 outside a downtown 'building materials' emporium.

Whilst unloading of Austin's Volvo began to creak to life, Austin set off on foot in search of the British Embassy. A local do-gooder and zealous English language conversationalist escorted Austin to a minibus which took him all the way to the door.

Louis fired up S8 and took Austin back to the lorry and his waiting bike. One tow later and they were moving into the circular mud hut construction of David Mills, Embassy Admin man. Faxes were sent to confirm the alternator status. Chas and Clive felt unwell and went to St Gabriel's Hospital. Evening spent in the 'Embassy Club', and all to bed earlyish.

The following days were spent doing essential tasks in Admin Ababa.

Ethiopia

Day 354
Tuesday 26 March
Mondo Miles today: 8
Mondo Mileage: 32263

The remainder of the afternoon saw us pack and make our final adjustment to the kit and machines. During the humdrum of activity Austin managed to mace his four comrades *and* himself, causing coughing, sneezing, Clifford's nose to bleed and tears all round. It is a bitter irony that this illegal pepper spray, purchased covertly by Austin whilst shepherding some schoolboys across Paris last year, has yet to be used in anger but has caused endless bouts of retching and acid throat due to Austin's clumsiness in its handling.

After our farewells to Dave Mills, Mike and Her Majesty's Embassy Security Team we slid through the Embassy huge steel gate at 5.30pm.

Rush hour in Addis was more chaotic than most cities; with suicidal pedestrians, useless drivers and mindless animals to manoeuvre around on our way north. We were soon out of the traffic and heading into the wooded hills after only 8 miles from the Embassy and were already totally exhausted and ready for bed. Light was rapidly fading as we scrambled into an idyllic spot in the woods.

Austin set up our ponchos, Geoff his tent, Chas on the grub and Lou entertaining the local teenage lasses. We celebrated Geoff's first night in the field as an honorary member of Mondo Enduro. We feasted on British army compo soup, kindly donated to us 28 weeks ago by the military attaché at the embassy in Bogota! This M.O.D. treat was washed down with a bottle of Ethiopian red wine whose squiggly Amharic label we singularly failed to decipher.

Ethiopia

Day 355
Wednesday 27 March
Mondo Miles today: 148
Mondo Mileage: 32531

03:00 hrs – "Oh crikey! The poncho is leaking" said Austin
"Let's just snuggle up to Clive on the dry side" said Louis.

It rained all night and all morning and only Geoff and Chas remained dry in the safety of the tent. Austin, Clive and Louis were all under the poncho bivouac of which Austin is such an ardent fan. The mud and our lack of knobbly tyres made the simple exit from the campsite a mud and sweat bath and it took about an hour to get all the bikes onto the tarmac.

We had a late start and only 73 miles before a lunch break. Chas and Geoff made some soup, Austin took some stills while Louis and Clive continued their latest craze; roadside body building. They lurched into 3 sets of 10 knuckle push-ups and 20 sit-ups. Standing bar-bell raises and 'Z' bar curls then took place with the aid of rocks and it wasn't long before Chas did some necessary sit-ups. Some local kids discovered us and were so confused it almost scared them.

We soon reached the Blue Nile Gorge and it can only be described as something out of a fairy tale. This was a Mondo Moment *in extremis*. We approached a precipice and gazed across the biggest canyon any of us had ever seen. Despite clear skies we could barely make out the other side. There in the lowest groove of nature, snaked the upper reaches of the mighty Blue Nile. They say that the river is a vertical mile beneath you here. There is nothing like this in Europe (we reckon). We chose this as the location for our official picture of us with new member Geoff Brotherton-Ratcliffe (standing).

After 10 mins of awe and wonder we started our descent. The road north takes us right down to the bottom, crosses the river and then back up the other side. Louis suggested a bravery contest and so it was engines off and coasting then took place down the winding road. The use of brakes was temporarily forbidden and we all quickly accelerated towards the hairpins. Within about 7 seconds of 'casting off' we had all dabbed the anchors and it was agreed that we collectively lacked the courage for such antics.

We cruised all the way down to within sight of the Blue Nile Bridge where we met a Swedish couple in a V8 Land Rover. We had the standard euro-chat then halfway through our conversation, two gun shots were heard and soil fell from the cliff side just above our heads. Austin was adamant he had heard the 'crack' and 'thump' that he assures us is the tell tale sign that you are coming under fire.

Louis encouraged the concerned Helga back into her car and with a look of absolute fear from the noise she took his advice. We didn't really know what to do so grasped the nettle and headed for the Bridge. Upon arrival we were accosted by the dick-head that had shot at us "Camera, where is your camera?" said dick-head waving his AK-47 "You're a bandit not a soldier you arse, where's your ID then?" (Louis' words). There were two shabbily dressed men with guns and what Austin describes as a stomach churning display of 'mixed dress', most hated of military fashion crimes. All five bikers were at this point lined up next to each other and revving; the scene was enough for the soldiers to hesitate and we were quickly over the bridge, all except Chas that is. He stalled but thankfully got it on the second kick. We have replayed and recounted this shooting incident to each other over the camp-fire and we cannot deduce what exactly was happening. Anyway, if one of the rounds had hit us that would have been a shame.

Some stones were thrown at us by children on the side of the road and Austin was caught in the crossfire. Louis noticed Austin travelling back up the road chasing two girls scared out of their wits. The guilty girls scrambled up the side of a cliff chased by a dismounted Austin. Lou assisted with a few grenades thrown up into the cliff, but was no match for the madman in front of him. Bullets, rocks?? What is going on?

We stopped in a little town for water, and once Austin returned with H2O Louis and Geoff went back into town looking for gasoline. Geoff negotiated hard for fuel and finally returned with 5 litres. With the sun going down rapidly (but admittedly, probably no faster than last night) we yet again set off-road covertly and found solitude in an open field. Clive and Austin set bedding while Chas and Geoff made a killer meal using only cabbage potatoes and onions.

Rain, Rain, Stay-Away, come again another day...

Ethiopia

Day 356
Thursday 28 March
Mondo Miles today: 100
Mondo Mileage: 32631

As this journal traditionally runs from midnight to midnight, it shall be entered that bright eyed and muddy tailed Mondo Enduro's day began at 0020 not even half an hour into Thursday.

PREAMBLE TO MUD FEAST:
After the debacle of our sundry attempts to leave yesterday morning's campsite we were 'mud-wary' and couldn't consider a campsite that required the ascent of a gradient. Bearing this in mind, last night we drove 200 yds off the road across a piece of Ethiopian prairie. The land is semi-cultivated in a patchwork of roughly ploughed plots, undisturbed straw stubble and some areas that are a blend of the two. We anticipated that our easy traversement of this open ground was due to a day's dry weather. Clive pointed out that if it rained in the night, our route out would quickly metamorphose to sticky clay gruel and that we would be trapped once more. Thus the contingency was hatched that we would sleep without tents/ponchos and if it started to

rain in the night we would instantly de-camp to the verge of the road to pre-clude the need for an awful trans-ploughed-field slog in the morning.

MIDNIGHT MUD FEAST:

So it was, that at twenty past midnight the rains came; the beautiful starry nightscape that had prompted Chas's recollection of the northern lights as seen from a Canadian log cabin, were a dim memory as all the moonlight was snuffed out by a blanket of nimbus McNimbus cloud that was like a huge ashen blob of misery.

Clive's foresight from only hours previous had been dulled by the un-named Ethiopian wine we had sedated ourselves with. Once the first droplets were felt and we woke up, Clive suggested that instead of striking camp promptly as per the contingency plan, we merely pull the plastic tarpaulin over ourselves and hope that the weather changes. Amazingly, this is what we did; he is most persuasive! The rain intensified, we huddled further underneath our vinyl cocoon but an anxious Geoff Brotherton-Ratcliffe exhorted us to arise and get going. For several crucial minutes we failed to heed his call to arms.

"A lazy man takes the most trouble" (Gerald Vince). By the time we *did* kick into action, the simple task of packing away the sleeping kit became a huge mission. All the thermarests were soaked and the sleeping bags were heavily wet even before we'd got going.

Geoff set off into the darkness first, retracing our route in from last night. This was a bad idea since it was longer than necessary but more woefully, took us back over some really quite muddy sections which would present more of an obstacle to our progress than a concertina barbed wire fence.

By now, the rain was torrential, Chas and Louis couldn't get their bikes started and everything was getting wetter by the second. Austin left last since he was lucky enough to be riding on a tread rich Malaysian 'Golden Boy' trail tyre. Of the ten wheels on our collective wagon, this is the only one that could ever claim to have a whiff of usefulness in the dirt. However, its well intentioned but useless tread pattern was clogged with Rift Valley clay within a few yards. Austin took a shorter route back to the road, which as Geoff had predicted after an earlier recce, was mostly stubble and basically unploughed. Hence, he was at the road first after about 2 mins of slithering, only to look back and see all the remainder of Mondo Enduro trapped in the mud, only 50 yds from where we'd been sleeping.

MUD MISERY:

This was where Mondo Enduro really began. It was a nightmarish flashback to the back breaking pushing and shoving of the Zilov Gap in Siberia. The reader should now go and don a pair of industrial sized tar spreader's boots, and gaffer tape a 4kg clay patty to each foot. Then oil their bathroom floor and attempt to adhere this newly weighty footwear to this infinitely slippery tiled surface!

Such was the scene as we drenched ourselves, internally with the sweat of exertion and externally as the relentless rain found ingress through the cracks in our clothes and under the ponchos as they flapped in the wind and either bashed us in the face or threatened to get trapped in the spinning rear wheel of whichever bike we were struggling behind at that instant.

After an hour and a half we made a wretched sight. Huge clods of clay adhered magically to the soles of our boots creating comedy 'mud' snow shoes. Clive's size 10½ plates meant that naturally he was cursed more than the rest of the team. We were totally bush-whacked and had only succeeded in getting Clive's bike to the road whilst the remaining 3 were only half way from the original campsite.

We decided to call it a day and Geoff's tent was erected at the very spot where the marooned bikes had 'fallen'. Chas, Louis and Geoff climbed in but suffered a soul breaking night – devoid of sleep, rife with flatulence borne of onion over consumption, and with mud coating every surface that one might want to lay a weary cheek upon. Clive and Austin wheeled their bikes into a ditch, positioned them the requisite 10ft apart and with their luggage as anchors and the camera tripod (topped by helmet) as a centre pole; a prize winning poncho-basha was up in no time. It was 0220 and still raining.

DAWN CHORUS:

A few early morning lorries brought Clive and Austin to stir. They were super dry under the poncho. By 0630 the skies were as heavy as a Honda TransAlp 600 but mercifully it had stopped pouring at about 0400. There is a God! And it was this deity that allowed Chas' K5 to be ridden free at first attempt. Louis, swearing and sweating, nursed his bike out of the swamp, despite a looming clutch problem and that left Geoff's lumbering beast, recently dubbed K9 in these pages.

After some/much portage, K9 was unloaded and Geoff had coaxed his two wheeled car up to the road. All of Mondo Enduro were in their Old MillHillian rugby shirts and the large crowd that had by now gathered (despite us being literally miles from the nearest building) was genuinely intrigued and baffled by these mud caked white men all in matching outfits. Geoff took a photo to commemorate this morning of pushing and shoving.

SET OFF:

The single lane road that is this part of Ethiopia's sole carriageway is strangely routed, almost as if the prototype had been a series of Scalextric segments. Long straight sections are followed by an abrupt 90-degree turn. This phenomenon is also evident on the crests of hills making for dangerous driving. Our local co-motorists are most civil and thankfully infrequent. We have seemed to strike the same rapport with the truck drivers which ply *this* route as those with whom we brushed mud flaps on the Pan-American Highway. Waves, smiles and hoots at every meeting.

The scenery is quite like Northern Ecuador, but very like the Yorkshire Dales. One thing for sure is that the forests and pastures which we are driving through give this whole country the feeling of being a land of plenty, not the Trini Lopez song, rather an abundance of harvestable knick-knacks. None of us can understand how this lush and verdant land has become a by-word for famine and malnutrition.

There is a town/village about every five miles. These always seem to be a one street affair where the entire population is out <u>on</u> that street. As usual, small children sprint from the 'porches' to wave and dance at us, teenagers merely wave, throw stones or ask for a lift, old people stumble out into our path, looking neither left nor right as they approach and absolutely everybody combines these actions with the rhythmic appeal of "You, You, You, You, You..." The requests for pens, stickers, trolls, goggles and above all cash, continue unabated every time we stop.

Geoff observed that there was malice evident in some of the local shouting that marked it out as different from that which we've experienced in other countries further south. However, watching a youngster help scrape the mud off K5 for Chas this morning, reminded us that the Ethiopians are superbly warm and merely curious of us, that's all.

The tarmac ended after the relatively swinging town of Debre Marcos (it had a Bank), but a first class dirt road awaited us. Ironically this was wider than its tarmac predecessor and so made passing oncoming (or is it incoming) lorries less of an ageing experience.

Forty miles later Geoff had a puncture. This wasn't immediately obvious to the four Mondo Enduristes that pre-ceded him since they were wobbed out under the shade of a tree. Cheeky 'search party' Penty volunteered to back track and search for the unarrived Geoff. This caused us to cut short our grand plans for the marketing of Mondo Enduro after our return. Who knows, it could all be brought to a horrible demise tomorrow (in fact, we know its not because tomorrow we were doing OK, these words being written at the roadside whilst Louis and Clive repair an H6 front blow out, with at least 20 members of a village huddled around Austin, watching with awe as he writes this strange non-Amharic script).

Geoff's puncture was soon repaired thanks to the reassuring whirring of the Pumphouse, the affectionate moniker bestowed upon our Taiwanese 12 volt electric tyre inflator. However, Geoff reported that our Posse's latest edition, his interestingly frame numbered K9, was suffering its second rather serious clutch malaise since leaving home.

The five of us brainstormed under our tree and thrashed out all the options. None of them really saw Geoff and K9 remaining part of the line-up and so a truck bound escape seemed to coalesce the more we chatted.

Time marched on, it was 4.30 and Austin suggested that a nearby coniferous forest could be, for this part of the world, a possible source of firewood that had not already been viciously depleted. We have seen many squads of early morning wood children and pensioners whose lot in life seems to be to creak along the hard shoulder bent double under the weight of their most recent collection of twigs and kindling.

Duly, we repaired to this idiosyncratic arboretum and set about fire construction. Before flint had been added to our possibly lethal environmental hazard cocktail of twigs plus loads of petrol, local AK-47 toting forest wardens arrived urging us to change our plans. We placated them with an impressive combination of mime and monosyllabic English words and in no time a standard Mondo meal was afoot. In fact, this wasn't exactly a standard Mondo meal since it was cooked in two sittings and hence a huge amount of cooked food was mistakenly generated.

With our forest warder overseers as our dinner guests we scoffed 50% of the food, left the remainder in our trusty enamel billy and swiftly packed away. It was 5.30pm and off we went in search of a campsite. Ten miles down the road we came across an unusually clear stream; most of the surface water in Ethiopia is usually thick red-brown silt. We were denuded of water and so much to the intrigue of the residents of a few nearby mud huts we filled up the water bottles. During this operation Austin's bike fell over and the Tupperware box he calls 'The House of Pasta' was shattered by the impact.

Watered up, we backtracked to a campsite that Clive had recce'd. We wanted to wait till dusk so that we could effect a 'covert insertion' and sure enough the gradient allowed us to roll across an English style pasture down to a superb wooded hollow.

We scored some lovely sunset shots on the video camera. We set up a top class double basha which saw Mondo Enduro fully snug and protected from the elements. Thankfully, here in Ethiopia there are few mosquitoes (too high) and hardly any small crawling creatures. It was to be our last night with tempo Mondo man Geoff Brotherton-Ratcliffe. He slumbered solo in his blue tent, reading the section on Addis Ababa we had ripped out of our guidebook for him.

Ethiopia

Day 357
Friday 29 March
Mondo Miles today: 162
Mondo Mileage: 32793

Few sights have more favoured our eyes than the vision of the beautiful mountain valley which adorns our gaze even as this log entry is being written. It has been an eventful and successful day in which good fortune, as well as the Ethiopian sunshine, has shined brightly on us.

The day began in our shallow depression which despite being the significant topographical feature of our night time's refuge was a wholly inaccurate description of our state of minds. We had slept extraordinarily well after the energy expended at the Mud Feast and even Austin's appalling flatulence failed to taint our spirit of general well being.

The one cloud on our figurative horizon was our imminent leave-taking of Geoff, K9 and Mondo Enduro season-ticket holder, who had joined us for our ride out of Moyale. Reader, you will judge whether there was any causative link between his brief liaison with us and his suffering a sequence of strokes of quite dastardly ill fortune. First there was the bacillary dysentery, then a trace of awe-inspiringly ill-chosen campsites. Next was a set of toasted clutch springs and plates and a back wheel puncture and if that wasn't bad enough, he had the bad luck to have found four new friends who scrounged his Rothmans and injected him with opiates when he was barely able to protest. Still, he seemed genuinely sorry to see us go and we reciprocated the emotion, wishing him well for the long haul back to Addis and hoping to catch up with him again in the UK and blend free holidays at his pad in the South of France, obviously.

Our departure from the Mild Depression was videoed by Geoff on our behalf and will represent yet another great cinematographic recollection in the years to come.

After about 30 miles we pulled over by a wooded copse for a spot of breakfast comprising of last night's veg and pasta which Chas reheated and spiced up with some Peri-Peri flavouring and a black pepper garnish. Cliff got a fire going, and while Austin got cracking on the diarist's equivalent of a running marathon or some such other endurance feat, Chas ventured forth to collect kindling. Or rather, six charming elfin gentlemen, draped in blanket cloaks and sporting Ethiopian crucifixes, ventured forth with their Dad to collect kindling while Chas marshalled them from a comfortable distance. As the miniature negrito porters returned to the hearth heavily laden with assorted timber, Chas, who bore a single twig, bore the brunt of some well-merited abuse from his fellow Enduristes.

Anyway, breakfast was delicious and after a bout of washing up, we were back on the road again bound for Bahir Dar and Northern Ethiopia's mountain vastnesses. A back wheel puncture, probably about the 32nd to befall us on this round-the-world adventure, slowed us down briefly on the way to this bustling settlement on the banks of the extremely scenic Lake Tana.

The scenery by now had transmogrified into a gently undulating plain quilted with a patchwork of ploughed fields. The road too had improved greatly allowing for speedy motoring along its flatter sections which were only occasionally caked in asphalt. As usual, the man-made scenery was the strangest and frequently we would come across a ruined piece of Soviet Bloc heavy armour jettisoned by cavalry and armoured infantry units fighting the Ethiopian Civil War.

One such armoured vehicle, a motorised anti-aircraft weapon with four mounted cannon, served as an impromptu prop for the long-awaited Mondo Enduro Movie! As we parked the bikes up alongside the vehicle, the ubiquitous bystanders must have imagined that they were being caught up once again in a distant battle from a forgotten war. A dose of petrol, the whoomf of petroleum ignition, the brisk flight of helmeted occupants from the blazing tank and another memorable moment was freeze-framed forever within the Mondo Film Archive Can. Austin tells us that such a shot has no place in the narrative but will instead be placed in the short trailer that he will send to British broadcasters on our return. They will then hopefully commission a Mondo Enduro TV show and will end up paying to edit our holiday film for us.

Then, to ensure the eternal attention of all of posterity, the shot was repeated for the stills camera.

Bahir Dar was a happening place by the civically-challenged standards of Ethiopia complete with asphalt, a palm-lined boulevard, banks and several quite appealing hotels. A mysterious dysfunction at the local soft drinks factory meant that sodas were hard to come by. So, after changing Louis's traveller's cheques at the Commercial Bank of Ethiopia, we retired to a nearby hostelry to partake of chilled bottled mineral water mixed with orange squash.

On the way Austin had picked up a young violinist who surely in Western societies would have been hailed as a child prodigy and invited to appear on the Barrymore show. Instead of studying in the Paris Conservatoire, or making a mint in vaudeville, this small musician was reduced to scraping his bow across the single string of his timber fiddle whilst intoning a truly remarkable ditty characterised by little yelps and ululations in each final phrase and tapping his tiny feet.

We filmed him while the chunky but really rather beautiful landlady of the establishment clapped along in perfect rhythm. A round of coffee was ordered, with the help of George our street-wise Angel and francophone toy tour guide, and after a welcome spruce-up in the hotel sink we were back on the Gonder road whose asphalt ran out after precisely half-a-mile.

Still, the road northwards was well-made and beautiful, affording stunning views of the monastery infested Lake Tana whose crystal waters had yielded the tinned fish consumed only a few days earlier. It was going a little bit too well, however, and Cliff suffered another front wheel puncture repaired by him and Louis in surely record time while a crowd of Ethiopians looked on.

Special mention should be made of the little girl with the punk hairstyle and four silver crucifixes who with her elfin school chums made this an especially visual puncture repair.

So, on we pressed up into a dramatic mountain pass and past a huge dildo-shaped outcrop. Our campsite was a well-chosen clearing off the road where we consumed a tasty tatties 'n' veg all-in prepared by Louis and Clive with no less than seven peppers to give it extra bollocks.

As the night was starry and the locals for once were marked by their absence we decided to lay out sleeping gear and ponchos and risk a night at the mercy of the elements. As we discussed our favourite Sergio Leone films we watched scores of little fires twinkling in the gloaming of this glorious evening in our stunning mountain valley. Ethiopia was going to sleep and so were we, dosed by over consumption of local gin bought in Bahir Dar. Tomorrow, we descend to the northern second-city metropolis of Gonder, the Birmingham of Ethiopia.

Ethiopia

Day 358
Saturday 30 March
Mondo Miles today: 65
Mondo Mileage: 32631

Just before dawn Mondo Enduro were disturbed and awoken by the chattering of 3 very bemused locals who wondered why they had found 4 foreigners sleeping by the road with various bits of foliage all over them and their kit. They decided to just observe them and were lucky enough to witness Austin getting up and dashing for the bushes to have a movement three times in the space of twenty minutes.

We headed off shortly after dawn through the village of Addis Zenen and then stopped for a video and stills shot of us riding along the dusty road.

Before long we were on the city limits of Gonder and ready to load on two more day's food and fill up with petrol. We had this completed in record time and reconvened just on the North side of Gonder once our tasks were carried out. We have a rhythm and there is a real momentum afoot.

Rolling again and Cliff took the lead on the dusty and stony roads. It all happened 30 km North of Gonder just after the first breathtaking view of the road North and the spectacular Simar mountains.

Cliff was riding 'point' at about 30 km/h around a right hand bend when from the opposite direction and on the same side of the road (i.e. the *wrong* side of the road) came a large orange 4 x 4 Toyota pick-up not doing less than 40 kilometres an hour-and bearing down on him (this was witnessed by Chas who was riding no.2).

The outcome was inevitable; there was no room to go to the right of the truck as it would mean suicide over the cliff edge. So Clive veered to the left but the Toyota driver must have been thinking the same thing and he followed suit. That was it, thinking time over, the truck smashed into Clive and he just went straight down under it's greedy radiator. This all happened so fast that the truck was still motoring along when it hit Clive and over the pick up went, front and rear wheels over Clive's rib cage and then his lower back. H6 (his bike) which was next to him had the other wheels to contend with and suffered bent handle bars, split tank and a totalled front rack. His kit fared well with only one destroyed water bottle to report on the casualty list. Sleeping kit, givi and the tin shed (our improvised larder) all survived.

So Clive lay on the dusty gravel next to his bike unable to move. Blood seeped from his nose and into his mouth. The pick up stopped and the rest of Mondo Enduro were soon to follow to see their comrade fallen but not knowing what had happened. Austin had a particular shock since he was riding at the rear. He was too far behind to see the impact but arrived to find Clive prostrate with Ethiopians alighting from the truck and Europeans from their bikes. Austin, at 5 years Clive's senior had pledged to Clive's over-concerned mum (8 months ago) that he would 'look after' her precious son. With Clive utterly motionless, silent and with blood all over his face and mouth there was ten seconds of Austin's approach when he fair well thought Clive was dead or dying.

Chas was first over and heard Cliff gasp "They rode over me with both wheels – my ribs are caved". Great, he could speak. The lads helped Clive to his feet and put him in the cab of the pick-up. His vital signs were all there and despite him being in tons of pain he was clearly going to live. The pick-up driver and crew were guilty as sin and agreed readily to take Cliff and ride to the nearest hospital (which it turned out was back in Gonder).

Clive meanwhile needed relief from the pain of his suspected fractured ribs and Austin was soon by his side with an ampoule of Nubain ready to inject. Louis was standing by with the Hi-8 to document the occasion. This was only the second ever injection that Austin had ever administered, the first being his 'practice shot' six days ago to a delirious Geoff Brotherton-Ratcliffe. He wasn't really sure of the dosage but we all assumed that the glass phial could surely not contain what amounted to an overdose. We didn't know much about these opiate based pain killers when we 'found' them but a Doctor friend said they were like morphine.

The Hospital in Gonder was more of a clinic really but was about as depressing a place as a sick person could imagine. There were skeletal patients aplenty and it seemed just like that bit in 'A Bridge Too Far 'when the mental asylum gets bombed and all the patients just wander about the countryside groaning. Everything was white, absolutely everything.

Surely our trip has taken a sour note with one man so close to death? It was with a great surprise and relief that he received the all clear (no fractures on x-ray!) from the Doc. This was a result because the X-rays seemed to have been done on the most primitive of machines (no doubt a gift from a tractor collective in Magnitogorsk). We studied the prints and they just seemed to be a light grey mush. How on earth you could tell if there was a fracture we couldn't say. It just looked like Clive had one giant rib; there was almost no delineation between that which was bone and that which was soft tissue. Oh well, Doctor knows best but Clive is our hard man and if he cannot walk, breath or swallow then we are sure he is actually seriously injured and are slightly loathe to just assume he'll 'get better'.

So after Clive had thrown up twice in the hospital grounds after hearing the results the guilty pick-up party moved us up to a hotel nearby. It is a bit muddled but we tried to impress upon them that they should pay for us. Their culpability was not something that we were just going to laugh off. On reflection, and as our chief witness. Chas says he cannot understand why Clive isn't dead; such was the ferocity of the collision. Our combined risk appraisal skills put his survival down to his wearing of leathers, the gravel road (as opposed to tarmac) and the reduced tyre pressures on the pick-up.

Clive is extremely poorly and was put to bed. Anything he tried to drink or eat came straight up and with great agony. The skin on his flanks and thighs was deeply ripped and needed cleaning and dressing. He was in 100% pain, whatever position we tried to manoeuvre him into.

By dusk Clive had managed to drink some water and had taken some painkillers but was still in a very poor state, unable to move without the assistance of his fellow team members. We have become concerned that his weakened condition will worsen if he cannot eat or drink. We used to have two saline drips which would have got whacked in about now but we sold them to an army surplus store in Johannesburg.

The hotel room has no running water and is fairly squalid. There are two beds, one for Cliff and the other to be the rotational bed for his Mondo Nurse. We have done some thinking and it would be amazing if he could ride on these Ethiopian dirt roads again for another week or ten days. He has a regular check in phone call to his mum so we have resolved that Austin should call her tomorrow with a fabrication as to why he cannot come to the phone. Hopefully she will forgive this deception in the fullness of time.

Mondo Enduro once again stopped in its tracks but this time in the most unfortunate way and tomorrow is April fool's day.

Days 359-363
Monday 01 April – Thursday 04 April
Miles: 0

This week spent nursing Clive in the Fogera Hotel Gonder. Not much to report save an unusual find in town. We discovered an old cinema and went to explore. It was functional but had now been eclipsed by technology. Instead of films being projected they were put in a VHS player which was duly crowded around. The amazing thing was not in the auditorium, it was in the foyer. There, high on the wall was a huge four folio (8ft X 4ft) poster for a film called 'The Boyfriend'. The poster clearly revealed that the star of the picture was none other than Neasden's finest daughter,

Twiggy. Meanwhile, Austin revealed that this movie was made in 1971 and was the only musical directed by Ken Russell. There were no other posters up in the foyer and we mused as to what the story was behind its still being here. Quite possibly the most unusual thing we have seen in Ethiopia.

Ethiopia

Day 364
Friday 5 April
Mondo Miles today: 174
Mondo Mileage: 33032

Not even another Spag-Bol could prevent us from finally leaving the Fogera Hotel. We left at 0545 with a taxi, as arranged and so Clive made his way to the Bus Station followed by Louis towing Austin. With Austin's bike B2 having a possible cam-shaft problem and Austin already having fixed H6, it was agreed that Austin's bike sit-out the journey to Asmara on the roof of the bus and Austin himself would ride Clive's mended beast.

The bus station was surprisingly organised with people queuing silently next to their respective bus with tickets in hand. However, disruption was only round the corner – Mondo Enduro arrived on the scene! It had been agreed the day before with the Don of the bus depot that we put one bike on the roof of whatever bus Clive was inside. However, upon first sight of Austin's bike B2 the assistant bus boss reneged on the deal. Aust and Louis kept calm and tried to negotiate while Clive waited patiently in pain on the pavement.

And so after consulting with the Don and with more money changing hands Austin was given the all clear to mount the wagon. He climbed on top of the bus, and with the ropes attached, he directed the lift. With a final push from Louis the injured 350 was strapped in and laid to rest. Clive made his way into the bus with the five thousand (sleeping bag and pillow in hand). So once he had found a comfortable seated spot amongst the dense mass of bodies we said farewell to him and it was back to the Fogera to get Chas.

Within 5 minutes we were back on the road, (time 0730). Austin did some filming at 'Death Bend' and a few moments were savoured in thought at what could have happened. A minor Mondo theological fracas erupted when Louis suggested that God had indeed been watching over Clive on that fateful day and our man was lucky to be alive. Austin disagreed, suggesting that if you had an arrangement with someone to 'watch over you' and they let the only truck for a hundred miles run you over, then you had every right to feel totally let down.

The road did not get any better and we started to drop altitude rapidly. With the sun getting hotter and hotter the smell revealing itself from underneath our leathers gave way for a whole new scent; a bath was more than a dream away when suddenly Austin discovered running water underneath a bridge. An old dilapidated Russian tank used in the Ethio-Eritrean War had embedded itself into the hillside going down to the river and had become part of the landscape. Upon further discovery a lagoon was spotted under the bridge so Lou grabbed a small sachet of shampoo and headed straight for it. It was only after he had got all his kit off and removed his pants that he found no easy way of entering the lagoon. Austin was soon on the scene with his bar of soap and with the help of another tank turned upside under the bridge we entered our bath by employing the broken tracks of the tank as a step ladder.

It was a scene from the 'Blue Lagoon' except not a Brooke Shields in sight. Some of the locals gathered at the top of the bridge to watch the spectacle and must have discovered two of the whitest bottoms they had ever seen; Lou struggled to get out from the lagoon scaling the hot rock face wearing only his leather necklace and performing moves that would even put Spiderman to shame. Chas bathed in a shallow stream of water treading carefully over the slippery stones underneath with his under-crackers pulled down below his knees!

With the three of us squeaky clean it was time to catch up with Clive and his bus boys. After a long hard ride we finally caught up with the bus just before Shiri, but not before we passed through some of the most impressive terrain that Mondo has ever seen.

Upon arrival at Shiri, Louis and Chas stayed with the bus while Austin went out of town to recce a campsite. With an enormous crowd gathering around the bus it was not going to be easy to remove B2 and place her on top of another bus that was going to Asmara. However, with Clive finally off the bus and settling down after a cramped and bumpy ride, Louis met up with Daniel. He was an Ethiopian that had spent much time in the USA, who helped him negotiate a price to put B2 on a bus to Asmara. Austin was soon back at the bus station and the poorly bike was lowered to the ground with just four pairs of hands. This sounds impressive but it was another bungle, during the lowering the bike became a 140kg pendulum bob and smashed into the rear window of the coach. As well as clearing up all the broken glass it took a fat wad of cash to smooth the bus driver's ruffled feathers. The bike was then lifted onto another bus, but not before long discussion and argument by the locals as to how this should be done, (we could not get a word in!).

Despite the Italian occupation of Ethiopia only lasting from 1936 – 41 their influence on the national palette has been profound. Even the humblest roadside eatery will serve some kind of pasta dish. So it was that a dish developed in Bologna was the suggestion made for dinner and so Daniel took the lads to a restaurant that was known to serve such treats. Upon sight of the *Injera* and *wat* (Ethiopian delicacies) that was served to Daniel there was a hesitation at the pasta jump. Louis had eaten *injera* a few days before and ebolafied himself as a consequence. Never one to shirk from a colonic challenge Louis ordered it again. Chas and Louis subsequently devoured the dish in Vince fashion while Clive managed to take in a Spag-bol along side Austin's three.

After saying farewell and thanks to Daniel, we went off into the darkness while Cliff was destined for a night in the bus. They don't drive the buses at night it seems, so he can rest on it until dawn when it will pull away.

Chas, Louis and Austin rolled their bikes off the road into the woods and set camp. After Louis had stepped on a turd (sadly, human...) and Austin had drunk the gin it was nighty-night for Mondo Enduro!

Ethiopia

Day 360
Saturday 6 April
Mondo Miles today: 150
Mondo Mileage: 32182

The moonscape last night was truly terrific and is best likened to the melodramatic full moon and passing cloud ensembles so favoured by the makers of horror films. Its also worth noting that all of Mondo Enduro had never before witnessed a moon of such inexplicable luminosity. The effect as we watched it pass overhead (this effect was obviously 'apparent' since Mondo Enduro is aware that it was the earth that was moving, not the moon) was most eerie as we awoke occasionally during the night to see it beaming down at us through the shimmering of the Eucalyptus. These skinny trees appear to have been the salvation of Ethiopia since they are relatively recent botanical import from Australia. The indigenous tree population has been victim to the national obsession with pruning – a form of arbricide if you will.

Clive had been left to sleep in the coach upon whose roof the troubled B2 convalesced and within whose hot house interior Clive would today be ushered over the frontier into Eritrea. He and his 750 co-passengers were scheduled to haul out around 0545. The remainder of Mondo Enduro, camped 2 miles outside of town, were anxious to be sure that they were in front of this bus so that they could hook up with Clive at the border and save our wounded (and bandaged) hero the trauma of a full steward's enquiry from the doubtless under-worked and under-amused border officials.

With perfect Mondo timing, Chas, Louis and Austin emerged from their plantation *pensione* to focus on a cloud of dust heading towards them- preceded by the green and white bus (opped with the awkward horizontal silhouette of a DR350 stricken with valve-mortis.

So it was, the soon to be scorching African sun not yet over the memorable craggy horizon, but the 3 bike 1 bus convoy was en route and the time wasn't yet 0600.

The route towards Axum heads virtually due East and as the sun rose it literally blinded us – riding as we were straight into its harshness. It was Easter Saturday, and the majority of the rural population was 'on the road' totally ant-like, marching towards Axum where they would congregate for sundry Christian celebrations. Hence, with our temporary blindness, the predictably rubble strewn dirt road, and the Monaco Grand prix style twisty mountain roads – progress was slow and in parts dangerous. All the riders had close calls with pedestrians and livestock who all across this mighty country have a *really* frightening propensity for diving straight in front of your spinning 21" front tyre in their bids to cross the highway. The road safety campaign over here has probably got an Amharic slogan or catchphrase that translates to: "Go on, have a go, you'll probably make it..."

On a serious note folks, Austin missed a two year old toddler, left free to totter and roam on the only road for 200 miles in any direction, by only an inch. This tiny would-be infant mortality statistic was unaware that his playground was *the* road north. His parents clearly *did* realise, but thought Austin was over-reacting as he screeched to a halt and went berserk on them for their negligence.

Just after Axum, and consistent with the predictions of the Michelin road map, the wearing surface upgraded from billiard ball style rubble to an evenly rolled and pressed fine grit on a sub-base of packed sandstone. The scenery dried out even more and it was like being back in Mexico or Arizona. We rounded a bend and were greeted with this view of the rugged Ethiopian rock-scape that has so confounded the attempts by foreign armies to transit this wonderful land.

Ethiopian immigration was beautifully civilised albeit our last chance to be mobbed by the people of this nation. An attempt to video record the crowd that emanated from us was met by the polite but firm rebuttal: "That is not necessary".

It was with pulses racing *à la Midnight Express* that we approached the piece of wire stretched across the way. This sinew represented the Ethiopian customs machine now challenged to pick up the fact that we had only paid lip service to their currency declaration bureaucracy. In fact, there was hardly a member of staff at the Fogera hotel back in Gonder with whom we had *not* changed money illegally.

The Chief Cashier stepped towards us, pad and carbon papers in hand. He demanded of Chas: "Do you have dollars?" It was then we realised, like most guilty schoolboys, that we hadn't really confirmed between ourselves what our story was to be. Chas sent a searching look over to Mondo banker Louis Rothschild to detect what answer to concoct. He was hurried along by the official who rather too pertinently remarked "I am asking **you** not them – how much?" Things looked bleak, our cocky playing of the black market – carefree two wheeled Gordon Gekkos – no deal too inside for us to contemplate – was about to backfire on us. Chas side-stepped the "dollars" starter-for-ten by mumbling: "I only have Ethiopian Birr". This seemed to slake his desire for rigour and there was an Oxbridge sigh of relief when pad-man stepped on to Austin and quipped back to very cheeky Charlie "Then you are finished".

This routine was repeated twice more, and strangely our wire-marshall seemed unhappy with the exit stamp, still wet in our passports bearing today's date. He mysteriously pointed to it, shook his head and tut-tutted. Maybe one of those cultural oddities Desmond Morris knows so much about, whereby this sombre reaction in fact means "everything in order".

Across the barren no man's land, five miles later, back on tarmac, we encountered the Eritrean piece of wire that indicates *"you must now cut your engine and prepare for five hours of time wasting and bureaucratic posturing whilst we locate any trivia concerning your visa and turn minutiae into mountains and mountains of drama."*

Chas, admin broker on this occasion, summed up the desperate situation in the sparse immigration inner sanctum by emerging to report to his co-riders, sighing and uttering the single word: "Stewards". Thus it came to pass O Reader! Our Eritrean visa, secured at a cost of $27 per hombre way back in Nairobi, should have been 'used' by the close of play yesterday, the fifth of April. We were 12 hours late. Why? Because one of our number had been a victim to the Ethiopian malaise which as well as confusing 1996 with 1988, juxtaposes left with right and saw unlucky Clive being used to trial Toyota's latest independent suspension designs. However, Clive's truly pathetic and heart rending performance at the police shed met with a stony hearted response, the immigration officials would *not* cut us any slack. They suggested we drive 200 miles back down into Ethiopia to get the visa renewed and as with so many times before, Mondo Enduro ground to an unequivocal halt.

Compromise: light was dimly perceived at the end of the 55km metaphorical tunnel that led to Mafara, a town inland of Eritrea where apparently an immigration bigwig lay in wait, capable of dealing with international decisions of this sort. A deal was struck; the healthy element of Mondo was to tread water at the coke and Fanta-less border post. Clive was to continue on the bus to Mafara, escorted by a minor customs minion who took *all* the Mondo passports off with him.

Clive reported later that a runaway youth who had been successfully 'border busting' emerged from the bush to rejoin the coach-from which he had jumped ship in no man's land. Imagine the acid in his stomach as the youth cheerily climbed aboard his mobile salvation only to end up right in the lap of this uncompromising customs hot-shot. Mr Customs Man stopped a passing truck and sent our great escaper right back where he'd come from.

Five hours passed, Clive's drama workshop did the trick, the customs *hombre* returned and it was "Let's go, Mondo Enduro" once more. We're in, Africa's youngest country and hopefully our springboard out of this continent.

The asphalt beneath our tyres hummed a welcome monotonal refrain. We rose up a steep escarpment onto the lush quasi-evergreen Eritrean plateau. The late coming Chas, Austin and Louis hooked up with Clive at the £2.50/night cheesy Aberates Kharsi Hotel. Austin was not to know it but tonight he was to contract scabies from his bed in the Kharsi. Another huge bowl of Macaroni and at 11pm we finally realised we'd conquered Asmara.

Eritrea

Day 361-362
Sunday 7 April
Mondo Miles today: 0
Mondo Mileage: 33182

"La Dolce Vita" was the title of a classic Fellini film but might as well describe the adventures of Mondo Enduro in this beautiful and atmospheric Eritrean capital city.

Chas and Louis awoke in the sparse splendour of the Diana pension in whose colonial precincts we had spent the previous night in comfortable but slightly uneven beds. It was not the sweet symphony of neo-Italian urban life which stirred them, however, but the rhythmic rat-a-tat-tat of Austin knocking on the bedroom door with Clive following closely in the unwashed slipstream of his rank body odour. They had bugged out early from the Aberates Kharsi Hotel and made their way by taxi to the Diana whose meticulously scrubbed corridors soon reeked of the filth of a World War One trench.

Communal ablutions seemed the order of the day as Austin for one had not bathed since Addis Ababa and was grievously in need of both facial and body soaps. The ancient plumbing of the pension, however, failed to produce anything more substantial that a dribble of tepid water which made the shower experience something akin to being spat on with a stream of warm sputum. Still, after a few minutes of careful application of foaming suds, we were presentable and ready to greet Asmara, the gleaming jewel in the distinctly lop-sided crown of *Il Duce's* Abyssinian dominions.

But first a quick word about the Diana. Its walls are papered with Alitalia posters and a tourist advert for Ethiopia; featuring the same smiling DC Lee look-a-like but with the offending moniker carefully obscured by sticky tape. The don is a strange character with an unnerving squint and a predilection for garish shell suits which would seem quite remarkable anywhere outside Merseyside. Mondo Enduro would incur his wrath, and offend Eritrean principles regarding multiple room and same sex bed occupancy before the day was out but more of that later, reader. Erm, that's all we have to say about the Diana at this stage.

Soon, while Clive reclined on the double bed and Louis logged the previous day's events in his almost indecipherable ahmarical cypher, Chas and Austin ventured forth into the acacia and bougainvillea lined boulevards of Asmara, the loveliest city seen by Mondo Enduro on its pan-African travels. Chas, answering some mystical questing in his soul ventured into the red brick Catholic cathedral where the Easter Mass (Latin rite) was being intoned in mellifluous tones by the Italian bishop. It just so happened that he bumbled in just as the aforementioned prelate was enjoining his flock to give each other the Christian sign of peace, and he was snogged on the cheek by a very tasty Italian girl with dark hair cascading down her smooth shoulders in dark ringlets. Peace be upon you...

Eritrea

Day 363
Tuesday 9 April
Mondo Miles today: 0
Mondo Mileage: 33182

Due to the fact that two men are not allowed to share the same bed in any of the hotels in Eritrea, Mondo had to split up last night. Louis thus left the comforts of sleeping next to Clive and checked into Room 12.

Chas also checked into a room of his own and when the sun eventually rose he and Lou went looking for a new "Inn" to infiltrate. Austin got to work on his valves at a breakers' yard.

A nice little gaff with a courtyard was found just around the corner and so it was "Let's Move" Mondo Enduro. Aust had fought the bike gremlin all morning but it wouldn't release its evil grip on B2's valves; and so after a telephone discussion with Geoff Vince it was agreed to DHL Austin's cylinder head (including valves) back to Crescent Suzuki in Bournemouth; 3½ kgs but only £88.

Meanwhile, back at the ranch Chas and Louis had made the acquaintance of Faizal (a Sudanese Legal Consultant living in Eritrea for the past 11 years), and Sadik (also Sudanese and had previously worked as a Customs Official in Jeddah). These two gentlemen gave Mondo invaluable information about our move forward. This included names and numbers of Captains at the port of Massawa. It would appear that there are no scheduled boat services out of Massawa. However, the *ad hoc* services are surprisingly frequent and the thought from Faizal and Sadik is that once we turn up at the quayside we'll eventually get a passage to somewhere!

The 'Inn' was chock a block with overlanders, Aussies, Kiwis, Brits, South AF's and Yanks; most of which had arrived in an old "Boots" delivery truck; and so after many shared stories of border crossings and insurance papers, Austin and Louis got to work on Clive's bike H6. It was roadworthy again in no time but not before useful instruction from Austin and absence of Mr Rachet and Mr Screwdriver. With our bellies empty we hit town in search of grub. The St Georges' restaurant proved to be a suitable spot and Cliff, Lou and Chas resigned themselves to watch the Human Dustbin do his stuff.

Austin made it clear that he was the 'Carbo King' and the waiters watched in utter disbelief as bowl after bowl after bowl, disappeared under a shower of splattering bolognaise.

With our stomachs full (and three of the four still managing to walk in a straight line) we headed back to our beds. Unable to sleep, Aust and Lou spoke for hours about Spaghetti Westerns.

Eritrea

Day 364
Wednesday 10 April
Mondo Miles today: 70
Mondo Mileage: 33252

Dear Diary

It has been a highly exhausting day, the eve of Mondo Enduro's first birthday and much rising of the ambient temperature as we descended from the breezy altitude of Asmara to the Arabesque dusty hell of Massawa down on the Red Sea coast.

The day began in our twin rooms of the overlander exchange that our pension had become. The ageing but superbly friendly Sudanese guests who had previously advised us were flicking around, and Louis and Austin's room adjoining the toilet/bathroom complex rattled with the clatter of ablutions.

Clive's H6 was finally made roadworthy and Louis had a piece of garden hose taped around his front brake hose which sufficiently stiffened it and prevents it from being rubbed against by the front wheel. Hmm... Abrasion, Mondo Enduro's sworn enemy.

Another trip to our local breakfast emporium, the cathedral-facing Cathedral Café saw us order our standard cappuccinos but "sin leche" (we have no command of Italian so we have commandeered Spanish as a surrogate).

By 0900 we were all at the public bus station, negotiating a passage for the cylinder headless motorbike, B2 and the 90% healthy human, Clive Greenhough.

After much haggling, ropes were being affixed, the wounded bike was painstakingly hoisted aloft and the left hand indicator on the bus roof was smashed by the unstoppable upward ascent of the motorcycle.

Austin, Chas and Louis returned to the pension, packed up the gear (including Clive's) and whilst Louis and Chas pursued Chas' missing laundry, Austin back-tracked to rendezvous with Clive's bus and to escort it downhill to Massawa.

The stunning descent from Asmara was truly a Mondo moment. The old Italian built single line railway wove its way alongside the road. It was a stunning display of the surveyor's and civil engineer's tenacity. No valley remained unbridged and the line featured over 35 tunnels in a short 20 mile stretch of track.

Austin took a short cut via the old route that the railway followed. This was a terrible error as Austin (riding Clive's H6) almost lost the bike over two separate cliff edges and gauged the folly of his ways by having to drop his trousers four times in 40 minutes for an emergency hillside delivery.

Passing by the Eritrean labour gangs, increasing the radius of curvature of the mountain road, we saw further evidence of this elfin country trying to make good the damage from so much civil turmoil. The perpetual descent was incredible; Asmara sits on a plateau as flat as Suffolk but more than a mile above the sea! The mountains finally gave way to desert and in the heat haze the port of Massawa appeared on the horizon.

Austin was first in town, having overtaken Clive's slowly creeping bus *en route*. He discovered a virtually deserted conurbation whose only souls seemed to be a French film crew. They were shooting an action-adventure feature film and Massawa was doubling for Djibouti. They explained that real Djibouti, only 300 miles down the coast was too dangerous and unpredictable to film in. Massawa looks like an Arab ghost town and almost every building is hugely pock marked with bullet holes. The air of desolation and desert wind dried decay gives the impression that the civil war only ended about 15 minutes ago. This place has been smashed to pieces and stands in stark contrast to the charmingly unique Afro-Italo aesthetic of Asmara.

The bus, escorted by laundry laden Louis and Chas finally crawled in at 1700. The 70 mile journey had taken 7 hours. The bike was unloaded from the roof and a chance comment from a local revealed that the boat currently loading at the quayside was Saudi bound within the hour!!

We dashed to the port, sweating profusely but amazingly got processed by Customs and Immigration. We were in a bit of a tizz but a deck hand called Masood kindly took a picture of us on the loading ramp discussing the route from Egypt onwards. We sailed away at 8pm destination Jeddah – goodbye Africa – Saudi Arabia here we come.

Crossing The Red Sea

Day 365
Thursday 11 April
Mondo Miles today: 0
Mondo Mileage: 33252

Perhaps it was entirely fitting that Mondo Enduro's first birthday should have been spent in a mood of great disquiet over the state of our finances. We had boarded the ship as poor men and will leave it almost destitute after being stung for a mighty $100 for the privilege of stowing our motorcycles on an entirely empty car deck.

Along with the $80 fare for our personal passage, our drained resources meant we had to pinch every penny on our visits to the air-conditioned ship's canteen to assuage our growing hunger with plates of vegetable and lamb stew and rice and our raging thirst with goblets of Pepsi and Mirinda. Fortunately Louis had stowed £60 sterling on his bike in a secure place so secret that even he had trouble remembering where it was. But it was entirely due to this foresight that Mondo Enduro rolls into the world's richest nation state solvent but with a combined wealth of about 20 Eritrean Birr.

Still the day had dawned bright and lovely and although we had been awakened early by the call to prayer over the ship's tannoy at 5am, we were all refreshed from a night's sleep on deck.

There wasn't much to do on board the *Al Rasheed* which was not especially well-equipped to cater to its passengers' needs in the light entertainment department. It is true that the Sudanese pilgrims flocking to the 'prayer pen' for a spot of religious instruction provided some momentary light relief but even this soon palled as the minutes turned into hours during our long maritime sojourn. In the absence of deck quoits, ping pong, a cocktail bar bedecked with scantily-dressed ladies of the night or even a cinema; we had no choice but to pass the time by resorting to the last refuge of the bored traveller – a Vince general knowledge quiz.

This test of our general knowledge was different from previous ones not least in its exotic location in the middle of the Red Sea in which the occasional dolphin splashed happily. What also made it remarkable was the presence of three new contestants – Bet and Steve from Sussex, and Buck from Minnesota, to provide a fresh admixture of brainpower.

Amongst the choices of category was one testing our knowledge on the subject of 'Furniture' and suggested by Bet, a carpenter from Uckfield. Quizmaster Vince rose magnificently to the challenge, setting a series of unanswerable conundrums pertaining to the chippy's art. Anyway after teasing our brains with a series of well-chosen questions it was time for some serious snoozing on deck.

A word on our fellow travellers, a motley crew of Sudanese and Eritrean pilgrims bound for Mecca and The Prophet's birthplace. Many slept in the mosquelet on the lower deck for maximum praying efficiency at the Mullah's bidding.

Most were self-catering and served themselves unwholesome looking millet gruel washed down with water contained in old oil bottles. The female corps of passengers, all of whom were heavily veiled, were meanwhile sequestered in the lower deck cabin accommodation and were barely sighted during the entire voyage.

And so a year has passed since that bright spring evening when we quit Mill Hill and embarked on a journey which would afford us saddle sores and high jinx in about equal measure. A time to raise a glass of our soon-to-be-contraband gin to all the people who have helped us on our way – Rita, Natasha, Nora, Dima, Craig, Roger, Neil, Uncle T, David Farrant, Barbara P, Mike F, Dave F, Joseph, Greg and Arthur and the Addis Embassy gang. Thank you folks...

Saudi Arabia

Day 366
Friday 12 April
Mondo Miles today: 5
Mondo Mileage: 33257

The good ship *Al Rasheed* decided to take a breather at around 2am as it had made such excellent progress ploughing through the relatively calm Red Sea in the previous 24 hours.

We moved on again a tad before the final dawn call to prayer at sea for our Muslim co-travellers. From the crow's nest Austin announced "Land Ahoy" for the Mondo wake-up call at around 7am. We all took a quick glance squinting in the intense sunlight to survey the dusty horizon to see Jeddah's impressive docks and 21st century skyline. A world away from the former battlefield that is Massawa.

Austin chatted up one of the ship's company who translated the squiggly Arabic biro that had been written alongside our Saudi visas. He pointed out that the stamp was definitely a 'transit' visa that was only good for the port of Jeddah. It states clearly (if you can read Arabic) that we are only allowed in Jeddah for as long as it takes for us to get anther boat up to Suez in Egypt. Austin had done this very journey back in 1984 when he was 18 and remembered these stringent rules were in force even back then. In other words, we cannot drive across Saudi Arabia up to Jordan, we must leave by sea. Aggro.

The sea became very choppy the closer we got to Jeddah. We then stopped and began to go back in the direction of Eritrea and Africa when a message boomed over the tannoy that none of us could understand, even though it was in English. We soon realised it was the announcement that the pilot ship was on its way to direct us back the way we should have been going to dock at Jeddah.

We eventually docked in at around 8.45am. We could see the flurry of activity on the bow of the *Rasheed* by the Philippine immigrant workers whilst their filthy rich employers looked up at them for a change from the ground.

The two Arabs in question were wearing Raybans and the standard red criss-cross pattern head shawl on their heads and a long white jilabah to set the whole outfit off nicely.

We waited a couple of hours whilst immigration dealt with the passengers of a ship that had arrived a short while before us. In the meantime, two Saudi doctors embarked and injected everyone on board. Mondo Enduro were jabbed up for meningitis and force fed a couple of pills.

Eventually, we were allowed off the ship and were pointed in the right direction by a Scottish port official wearing shades and carrying a radio. He worked for the harbour authority and when we asked about the transit visa allowing us to drive up to Jordan he said; "Forget it, you won't even be allowed out of the port".

We then climbed aboard a port bus bound for the immigration halls and had to leave our bikes behind. Apparently, some Sri Lankan lads were going to bring them over for us. We would wait and see.

Meanwhile, back at the ranch a full on sandstorm was taking place and we were relieved to get inside the newly built, air conditioned, space age immigration hall.

We handed our passports in and Louis began to sweat immediately – we waited roughly 2 hours until they came back with an entry stamp on them. We shared two candy bars and coffee to pass the time with the handful of Riyals that we possessed and were then ushered into the next hall – the checking zone – everyone and all their belongings were checked without exception.

Before they could check us, there was prayer time and by 2pm we had cleared immigration.

Next up for fun and games was Customs. Meanwhile, we were off the quayside now but our bikes were still by the ship.

Much form filling took place and discussion about our still absent bikes. Since we had cleared immigration the customs officials said we were free to leave the precincts of the port. We didn't chance our luck by asking them to repeat that. So Louis headed into town in search of an ATM to pay the $10 (35Riyal) customs fee for each bike. He came back with loads of cash and tons of fried chicken, chips and drinks. Hoorah!

We devoured the food and fell asleep. We were awoken an hour later to find our bikes arriving.

Then the search began. For the record, this was our most thorough search to date on Mondo Enduro. They even looked in the air filters, watched our videos (checking for porn) and quizzed Chas on the purpose of his survival knife. Incidentally, some Pakistani stevedores who were moving our bikes from the ship to Customs tried to kick start the lame bike that had no cylinder head. Austin intervened as the cam chain was about to snag on the bungee that was supporting it, otherwise it was an amusing spectacle!

We sat around remaining very calm and laid back. Africa had taught us this and eventually, as in all good endings, everything came right and we were allowed to go around 5.45pm. Yes, an entire day being processed – I think that beats Turkmenistan!

So Louis towed Austin down the service road, through the gates (no guards or barriers) and out onto the wonderful Saudi road network. We were free!!! We began to head north, snaking our way with Austin in tow through the Jeddah rush hour. The rope snapped a couple of times and tactically right near McDonalds at around 6.20pm. It's a sign.

We darted into McD's – our first since Santiago and ordered plenty of 'food'. During our feast the Philipino manager of the restaurant was fined by the religious police for being open during prayer time and serving food to non-Islamics. Nothing better to do obviously. Cliff found a campsite nearby on a building site behind a mound of sand. Lights out 10.30pm. Roger!

Saudi Arabia

Day 367
Saturday 13 April
Mondo Miles today: 150
Mondo Mileage: 32182

Clive and Louis had a terrible night's sleep constantly being woken up by the building site residents – Mr Mosquito and Mr Flea; Meanwhile, Chas and

Austin slept like babies. Cheeky Chas knocked over the mosi repellent bottle in his sleep and literally swamped himself with 'Deet', which obviously aided his slumber!

Austin and Louis went back into Jeddah to visit the British Consulate. Hazel behind the counter was most helpful and even prepared coffee and biscuits for the two dirty and scruffy individuals sat in front of her glass window. There was a stash of *poste restante* and we were able to collect the Mondo credit cards that Geoffrey Vince had kindly sent.

With the peanut butter and cheese sarnies in their tummies, Austin and Louis made good progress. The detour they took along the coastline (on their way to the Consulate) was a pleasant one. They decided first to visit the Post Office to dispose of the 'Postman Pat Mondo Satchel' and then to shop. Two pairs of bogus cotton trousers were purchased, a washing line to use as a tow rope and a small calculator for the Mondo Bank. It must also be mentioned at this point that the ATM that Austin withdrew cash from was the same bank that he was nearly arrested outside on his previous visit to Saudi Arabia eleven years ago (Oh yes, the crime was taking a picture of a woman in the street!).

After drinking just coffee and starving ourselves, we decided it was best to get moving. Louis towed Austin and Clive is finally riding his bike again for the first time in nine days, though it is still too painful for him to kick-start it. We feared we would be stopped at a check-point at the city limits of Jeddah but none materialised, we just kept going. We are at large in Saudi Arabia. Result!

We stopped at dusk to drive under a bridge to make fire and bed. The wind was almost unbearable and so an abandoned truck tyre made for a good windbreak for the Mondo fire, which was until the tyre caught fire. We fought against the blaze and it would have made for a fine audition for 'London's Burning' – but we were not successful in putting it out! With the heat becoming more intense and the fear of somebody noticing the flames we made a getaway with empty bellies. The scene was quite ridiculous as Austin was hitched up to Louis' tractor bike. Trying to pull away on the soft sand was extremely difficult but Louis discovered that it was just possible with sufficient swearing. We rode into the darkness and over our shoulders caught sight of the lorry tyre now fully ablaze and a beacon to our campfire bungling. This must have been how Lot felt. A few miles later we made camp just off the road. Clifford wasted no time and wobbed out almost immediately after his cheese sarnie; while Chas, Louis and Austin snuggled in their sleeping bags and attempted to answer the musical conundrum; 'Beatles or Stones?'

Saudi Arabia

Day 368
Sunday 14 April
Mondo Miles today: 187
Mondo Mileage: 33498

The night was filled with the non-stop roar of HGV traffic that thundered constantly alongside. We slept *incredibly* close to the road.

The reason for this was that the wind had turned to a force 5 on the Beaufort scale, to venture into the desert for peace and solitude would have netted misery as our gear and bodies would have been infiltrated with the fine Arabian dust that whips like an airborne chainsaw.

We had no breakfast, but within five miles we had our first checkpoint since leaving Jeddah and the predictable steward's inquiry ensued. We completely confused the tan uniformed Saddam Hussein look-a-like who spotted the Arabic script on our visas which clearly stated "*In transit by sea to Suez*". They needed a superior authority than ours to allow us to continue our journey and hence the white suited governor was summoned from the shed, he took one look at the passports and immediately waved us on. Be advised reader, that in the world epicentre of police states that this country is, the fact that "by sea to Suez" could be liberally re-interpreted as "by land to Jordan" has left Mondo Enduro totally confused but nevertheless thoroughly elated. This interest and checking by the police, followed by a 'green light' was to set the scene for the remainder of our time in Saudi.

We pulled in for a breakfast of coffee and doughy pancake only a few hundred yards upstream of the checkpoint. We were in a roadside truck-stop conurbation that was definitely out of step with our Jeddah experience. This whole area was more like Morocco or Turkey especially with the proliferation of 'Vulcanizers' and oil/lubricants emporiums on every corner.

Our hearts fluttered when whilst finishing off our coffees, a police car pulled up alongside the bikes "This is it" we thought, "we're rumbled!" He was merely driving past and paid us no mind, another hugely paranoid sigh of relief oozed from our table.

The decision was made, thanks to Louis's generous disposition and relatively healthy bike, for Louis to continue the towing of the cylinder headless B2. This was in preference to the bike being bought a passage on one of the billions of northbound lorries whose drivers seemed to have been weaned on a TV diet of Spielberg's "Duel" and "Whacky Races".

The road was of a superb quality and although only a single yellow strip on the Michelin maps it outclassed everything we had driven on since we left South Africa. This, combined with the straight and hill-less terrain meant that Louis ultimately towed Austin a staggering 180 miles today, including 9000 police checks and two oil changes.

We were surrounded to our right by desert and a distant mountain range; whilst several miles to our left (west) was the occasional glimpse of the Red Sea upon whose shores were an impressive array of petro-chemical, cement and de-salination plants.

Another police check in the town of Yaban gave us a further chance to sample the stunning spontaneity of Arab hospitality. A traditionally dressed gentleman approached us and proclaimed "Welcome". We smiled and shook his hand to which he added part (b) of his salutation which was; "Welcome.... Cafeteria?" He then took his Arab hospitality to 'the next level' by blandly enquiring "Welcome to my country, do you need some extra money?" Unfortunately time was getting on and our progress was not overly fantastic so we had to decline his kind offer.

As the heat of the Saudi afternoon wore on and wore in, the desert continued unabated as the solitary form of scenery in this part of the world. At a swift oil change location, firewood was collected but the oil bottle that had come with us from Sun City, courtesy of Jim Davis, blew away.

The ill wind that carried off this trusty vessel intensified in its ferocity over the late afternoon and by 1700 we were booked into a class one sandstorm. The wind and razor-edged granular barrage came at us full on and penetrated goggles and nostrils with ease. This torment reduced Louis and Austin's progress to a painful 15mph. At a nearby gas station and truck stop we holed up and made several beseechments of 'pick up' drivers to let the sick bike be loaded aboard one of them and be carried northwards.

Most applicees were not going our way or failed to understand our mime. Then we struck gold and a poacher offered Austin a lift. Fabulous, we heaved and puffed and hoinked the bike into the back of Yusuf's pick-up truck. A cheer and then our mini convoy powered off across the desert. Unluckster, this benevolent soul had broken down within 6 miles of accepting us within his bosom. Much huffing and puffing as we unloaded the bike from Yusuf's tail-gate and Louis towed it away. Hence, 7 miles down the road, Mondo Enduro was reunited and camped in a ruined building.

Saudi Arabia

Day 369
Monday 15 April
Mondo Miles today: 265
Mondo Mileage: 33763

We awoke to a bright morning which seemed immediately to banish the spectres lingering from last night's ghost story-telling session. Any remaining mental cobwebs were also swiftly dispelled by Austin who got busy brewing up a coffee on the embers of last night's fire. The steaming beverage was served up in our Ronald McDonald beakers – their first and last application in the field, but thanks anyway, Philipino friends!

The first 60 miles vanished in a blur of passing scenery and pristine asphalt gliding beneath our wheels. The sandstorm which had so curtailed our progress of yester-eve had completely abated to make way for a cool, clear morn which proved an ideal setting for Enduristes to practice their art. Soon we were in Um Lajj and over the fold of the Michelin map which now reveals the Mediterranean twinkling in the far north of our cartographical horizon. As if in celebration, Chas and Clive, who were leading the pack, surged past a posse of sleeping traffic cops and into the town itself where they were immediately seated at a roadside hotel and served with sugared chai and mineral water.

Austin and Louis were not far behind and soon we made a merry foursome chomping away on the unleavened bread and chickpea 'foul' which was to comprise a very welcome breakfast. We were clearly the most unusual travellers to pass through Um Lajj since the first disciples of The Prophet unleashed the mighty Koran on its Bedouin populace; and a large crowd of teacloth wearing gentlemen swiftly gathered round to discuss this latest revolution in spiritual and moral values. To ensure that Mondo Enduro did not get completely out of hand, no less than two Nissan patrol cars full of coppers watched us with a hilarious mixture of befuddlement and nervousness as we polished off our nosh. This in fact been paid for by an anonymous Arab benefactor whose fee for this generosity was for us to take his picture.

By this time, a large queue had assembled by the public telephone, whose members were obviously anxious to call distant relatives and inform them of our unexpected arrival. All seemed lost in terms of making prompt calls; firstly to the British Consul in Jeddah to apologise for having mysteriously disappeared and to enquire whether the Israeli-Jordan border was open, and secondly to Geoff Vince in Bournemouth to tell him to hold fire on sending Austin's repaired cylinder head to Talut and despatch it instead to Tel Aviv. Good news from the Brits – the Allenby Bridge is open – but we suppose we shall believe it when we see it given Israel's inconsiderate and, from our point of view, ill-timed decision to invade the Lebanon.

Louis also hooked into the global system of telecommunications even though it does appear to be short-circuited in terms of verbal intercourse between Jews and Saudi Arabs. His efforts to ring his great friend and soon-to-be Mondo blendee in Tel Aviv, Jo, was met with a 'barred call' signal from the operator. It's warming to know that in this *fin de siècle* era of glasnost with the Berlin Wall in ruins and apartheid a thing of the past in the New South Africa, any chance of telephone *détente* between Jew and Muslim is blocked at the very highest level.

And so we glided northwards along a Red Sea coast which looked lovely for a swim. Unfortunately miles had to be eaten; indeed they were as inexorably as a bar of Snickers in Austin's pannier. After Al Wajj things went slightly wrong when Chas, whose myopia is nearly as far-advanced as Mr Magoo's, failed to spot Clive pulling off the road into a gas station. Confusion reigned as he ploughed onwards, not knowing what had befallen his comrades until possible fuel starvation forced him to pull over in a gas station some 75 kilometres distant.

After about two hours, the team was back on the road and bashing out another 50 kilometres to our latest billet – a half-built breeze block hut of indeterminate purpose. And so Louis hauled Austin and bike through its tatty portals to end the second full day of his mammoth towing operation which must surely be setting some kind of mobile recovery record. Their two-bike-coupling cruises at a steady 55mph, which Austin has admitted is on occasion harrowing.

It has been a good day. The transmission gremlins, who had behaved so mischievously yesterday on Chas' bike were less in evidence today and the going was fairly smooth. Israel and the promise of various vices outlawed by Islam but licensed by the Judean-Christian tradition beckons only 400 odd miles away. Mondo Enduro, however (and not for the first time), finds itself a puppet in the hands of our political masters in the Middle East.

Saudi Arabia

Day 370
Tuesday 16 April
Mondo Miles today: 221
Mondo Mileage: 33984

Today's objective to cross over into Jordan was started on the right foot for Mondo Enduro: the restless Austin and Louis were standing to and ready to roll in semi-darkness at the early-bird hour of 6am to catch that Jordanian worm.

Meanwhile back in slumber, Cliff and Chas dozed dreamily away. They lay in Rab land for a further three quarters of an hour and then set to the task of decamping as fast as possible to catch up with their comrades.

Another cloudless blue sky above as Mondo Enduro in their separate parties headed north.

The landscape was turning from a flat desert to a semi-lunar mountainous landscape. In fact Clive mentioned that this was the identical terrain to the Sinai Peninsula which was not that far away – with a few short hops across the Gulf of Aqaba.

Clive and Chas caught up with Louis and Austin 160 miles from their campsite of the night before. The towing couple were jubilant to see Clive and Chas as they had just gone to reserve and had no idea where the next gas might be.

With wheels rolling again, we found a petrol station 20 kilometres down the road to fill Louis' bike up and ourselves up with soda and snacks.

Our final stop in Saudi was once again a gas station where we filled up everything (including the bike being towed, Austin's B2) with this incredibly cheap gas at 80 cents a gallon. A final bit of provision buying in the gas station followed and we headed for Saudi Immigration and Customs.

Even as we are leaving Arabia, we are shown kindness all the way to the door; with a couple of glasses of chai to take the heat out of the day and the small amount of bureaucracy that might be present. A most pleasant departure was had by all.

We were then back on the bikes but Louis' refused to start. "Had towing B2 finally taken its toll on Louis' young and sprightly bike?" we hear the reader ask. A push down the hill and she fired up with a bump-start to reassure Mondo Enduro that she was AOK.

Jordan's Customs and Immigration were only a kilometre or two down the road, and a nice windy road at that, which hugged the Red Sea on its way down to Jordan's border.

There were alarm bells ringing in the Mondo Enduro camp after reading Jordan's Custom's regulations clearly posted in English and Arabic on the Custom's building wall in black and white.

Our alarm bells rang because it listed tools, camera and video cameras as being compulsory to declare and register. "Ooooh not more money" we thought to ourselves. The bizarre restriction on entering Jordan from Saudi was the allowance of one litre of alcohol. At the end of the day they let us off with that and there was no mention of the "C" word – yes "No carnet required folks". Hoorah! (wait a minute, we've *got* carnets).

So it was a hop, skip and a jump with no searching of the bikes and we rode the 13 miles to Aqaba and its impressive coastline and hotel chain.

We went on the hunt for a bar and a telephone, preferably one that accepted credit cards. After a few enquiries we found the Coral Hotel with two Austrian overlander bikes – a 600 Trans Alp and 750 Africa Twin, standard, with pristine kit – obviously they had just hit the road or indeed knew how to take care or their gear so it wasn't ruined within a few weeks.

Some Amstels and coffees, then Louis and Austin called London to find out information about the road ahead which included DHL diversion details (Austin's cylinder head) info. on ferries to Cyprus from Israel and 'could Jo Kaye blend us in Tel Aviv?' Nail biting stuff hey reader – well wait a little while and we will tell you the answers.

The report from England was this: Austin's cylinder head is *still* in Bournemouth after Crescent Suzuki failed to remove valve guides. There is a solution to the problem: fortunately, the men in Bournemouth just happened to have a cylinder head lying around spare in the parts department. So we were on standby for its immediate despatch to the town of Mondo Enduro's choice. Hurrah! We then high tailed back towards the border to camp just near the sea behind the piles of rubbish in an old quarry and right next to a Radio tower.

It was late for the Mondo Enduros at 9.30pm but as ever on Mondo Enduro the lads pulled together and a mega Mondo meal was on its way. Ahh! Another starlit night, another country conquered by the two wheeled amigos!

And what a treat for tomorrow; we have the wonders of Petra to look forward to – how will we ever sleep?

Jordan

Day 371
Wednesday 17 April
Mondo Miles today: 0
Mondo Mileage: 33984

Clive spent some of the night sleeping on top of a turd, sadly human again! Unlucky! The four Jordanian truck drivers we met on the hard shoulder were great company and had a well developed slapstick comedy routine. By 0830 Mondo had adjourned to the beach with them sipping strong Turkish coffee and furthering Anglo-Arab relations. Chas perused their paper at length though unable to read a word of it.

Louis and Clive heated up the previous night's meal (that babyish Austin didn't eat because Louis had spiked it with fish!). It was very kind of the drivers to let us use their gas stove and there was enough leftovers for Clive to offer a portion to every driver. Mondo also made it into the Gulf of Aqaba where we rinsed our soiled undercrackers whilst dodging jelly fish. Our fellow long distance drivers also made for a dip, but more obviously they were not long distance swimmers. After tiring from teaching one of their number how to swim, they played a game of 'throw the jelly fish' at each other. The lorry driver learning to swim (right hand side, white pants) managed to cut his foot on a sea urchin, but after a Mondo Medical his foot was as good as new; this included removing part of the sea urchin from his foot with a pin that Austin had carried with him since Russia!

And so after saying farewell to our new friends we headed for a café to sit down and write. We scribbled all afternoon banging out letters and thank you postcards left, right and centre to countries and continents far and wide. A new ratchet was needed and a tool shop beckoned. Only Arabic was spoken so Clive mimed the ratcheting action with appropriate sound affect. It wasn't in the least bit comical but the wizened old man behind the counter wept with laughter as he did it. Clive also wanted a three-eighths to quarter inch adaptor for our sockets but now explained himself with a simple sketch instead of a performance.

Late in the afternoon our stomachs started to rumble (as they do on the road), and so it was off to feed. We needed to entertain ourselves before the much awaited 2000hrs Geoff Vince call; and that we did with conversations on stunt women, bike trips to Spain with no kit, twins, amusement parks, the Isle of Man, Gerald in the 70's, 16mm and super 8 film, Josh Collins, Steve McQueen and Dick Baker.

The information from Bournemouth revealed that it is no trouble to enter Turkey from Greek side of Cyprus – except we have to entertain the fact that we get a ferry from Israel to Cyprus; ferry from Cyprus to Rhodes and then a ferry to Turkey! Israel and Cyprus would have been a lot of fun, but Mondo is about roads and small money!! So Thank you GJ our course is set, Syria here we come.

Jordan

Day 372
Thursday 18 April
Mondo Miles today: 130
Mondo Mileage: 34204

We awoke after a blustery night that saw Clive's plastic skull rattling against the side of his pannier as a constant audible reminder of the weather. It rained lightly in the night but not enough for us to need to do anything.

Our campsite was a quaint ornamental garden adjacent to the promenade 6 miles south of the town and literally *on* the Gulf of Aqaba. For once we had no harsh riding routine to hook into and so we appreciated the lie in. Our going to bed at 11pm last night was uncharacteristically late and so it was 0800 before any of us moved. Austin brewed up but the trip to the fireplace over the road was too far for bleary-eyed Mondo Enduro.

A hose wielding gardener moved us on and so Louis and Clive decamped to the beach, 10 yards away, whilst Austin and Chas went back into Aqaba for shopping, posting our latest bumper mail-out and a chance glimpse of the 4 strong gang of Swedish 20 yr olds who had excited us so much after blonde-free Africa and Saudi Arabia (they *were* girls).

The morning unwound with us all reunited for a cheese, peanut butter and Coke breakfast. Aqaba's shops and markets bulged with quality fresh and canned produce and this bade well for the rest of our time in Jordan. Aqaba reminds us of Trabzon, Black Sea Turkish flesh pot, port and action-town that seems strangely out of context in these dusty surroundings, and so close to fun-starved 'virtue'-rich Saudi. There are a considerable volume of tourists here, many of which appear to be German or Austrian. We never quite discovered its popularity with these Teutonic sun-seekers.

It's worth recording the stunning view from our deserted beach base camp. Across the 3 mile wide Gulf of Aqaba we have the fierce heaving sedimentary cliffs that mark Egypt's eastern seaboard of the Sinai peninsular. The almost monochrome brown that this impressive rock escarpment was presenting made it smack of an old 1920's B/W print; one hand-tinted in a Soho basement by someone who'd read that all the Middle East was sandy but had never actually been there.

Looking half right north of the Egyptian shore you are immediately struck by the dominant feature of this gulf – Eliat.

This Israeli Las Vegas has gate-crashed its way onto a coastline that doubtless piques its Arab neighbour's sense of territorial sensibility even more than the existence of the Jewish state itself! To rub a pillar of salt into the wound, Eliat looks as if its just been unwrapped from a box marked "Super resort for the year 2000", the best recommendation it can have is that from a range of five miles it looked absolutely irresistible, somewhere that Aqaba should be transited through en route to. At night, the sodium lamp pleasure-glow that it radiated sent a quiver of itinerary changing temptation down both the spiritual and geographical Mondo Enduro compass.

By lunch time though we'd had our lunch, we realised it was time to 'wagons roll' and for us to go some way towards achieving today's destination – the spectacular rose-red city of stone at Petra.

Louis performed his final tow and dragged Austin and bike over the mountains that encircle Aqaba to a dusty truck registration stop 10 miles outside town. *Every* truck leaving the pulsating container port at Aqaba has to book in with the Jordanian police (who look a lot like Metropolitan Police cadets with respect to their uniform).

Within 10 minutes Mondo Enduro had met Jacob – heading north, beyond Amman, with 20,000 kg of hair oil. Louis, as usual, was the first to introduce himself and in seconds we four had loaded the headless B2 into a space at the rear of Jacob's container. So for the nth time, Mondo Enduro was divided as Austin rode shotgun with Jacob whilst Clive, Chas and Louis made their way to Petra.

Austin and Jacob soon settled into a tea drinking marathon that alternated with the 20 mile stretches that Jacob's slug-like lorry could knock out before collapsing into a lay by.

Jordan

Day 373
Friday 19 April
Mondo Miles today: 80
Mondo Mileage: 34284

This was another of those heartbreaking days when the team was split asunder; with its component parts splayed across the girth of an entire nation state dawned amidst bright sunshine.

At one end of Jordan lay Austin, asleep in the soft bed of the hotel in which he had been deposited by Jacob the angelic truck driver who listed culinary talents alongside his skills in the road haulage sphere. Louis, Chas and Clive, meanwhile, were waking from a slightly chilly but nevertheless comfy night's slumber in the £2-a-night roof top dormitory of Petra's Ali-Mussah Hotel.

Actually, the previous evening had passed quite convivially in front of the Hotel TV set watching Indiana Jones and Last Crusade, filmed at Petra, and supping cans of Castlemaine XXXX, served by Johnny of the Exodus overland tour truck parked outside. Still slightly sizzled from an unaccustomed over indulgence, we stirred bleary-eyed but still elated at the prospect of a visit to one of the world's great archaeological sites.

Entrance to the Rose-Red city of Petra cost a mighty £20 a head but Mondo Enduro, true to form succeeded admirably in securing a considerable discount when a group of French granolae offloaded the second part of their two-day pass for a very reasonable 12JD each. Soon we were making our way down the Siq gorge, the legendary portal to the lost city of the Nabateans.

We had all read about the visionary aspect of the Great Treasury looming into view through the slash in the sandstone which marks the Siq's final exit. In fact it was every bit as magnificent a sight as we had been led to believe.

Soon we were making our way up a steep incline to the High Place of Sacrifice – an imposing altar hewn from the rocks of a dramatic escarpment overlooking the valleys of the Petran megatropolis. Perhaps even more impressive, however, was the awesome superstructure of an American *touriste* studying in Jerusalem who had caught the eye of both Clive *and* Louis through the camcorder viewfinder.

A spot of impromptu archaeological commentary by Louis Magnus Magnusson Bloom erroneously credited this awesome work of ancient masonry to the Nabatineans – a blunder corrected on camera by Chas to the enormous amusement of all parties. Moments later Louis dropped the camera accidentally but the damage did not seem too extensive.

We retired to a cheapo café after the long slog back up the Siq to feast on humus and chicken livers and ponder the loveliness of this magnificent troglodyte metropolis (whose splendour was not dimmed by hordes of German, French and Dutch coach parties). Soon, we were on our way back to the Desert Highway to Amman and hopefully a rendezvous on the morrow with Austin.

The arrival of seriously bollock-freezing weather each day at around 4pm has been a worrying feature of the last two days' travels and so we settled into a roadside café for coffee to warm us up before the onset of evening. Cliff especially was nursing a mild fever and was anxious to wrap up warm in our customarily squalid desert campsite. From Palace in Wonderland to turd-strewn hovel – all in a day's ride. Result.

Jordan

Day 374
Saturday 20 April
Mondo Miles today: 30
Mondo Mileage: 34314

Three quarters of Mondo Enduro were awoken by the dazzling morning sun at about 7am. Clive was feeling better after his high temperature and fever at bedtime, but all thanks to a couple of Disprin and also being wrapped up good and proper.

A quick breakfast consisting of unleavened bread and *La Vache Qui Rit* and Mondo was on its way leaving another rubble strewn campsite in its dust.

Amman, Jordan's capital was only 50 miles away and it was motorway all the way. A very boring but fast road and once again we were subjected to an alternating strong side and head winds. Once in the town, we pulled up in the forecourt of the largest hotel in sight to enquire about the location of the British Embassy.

Twenty minutes later, after a few lefts and rights and the odd double back on ourselves, we arrived at our little bit of Britain. No sooner had we pulled up and cut engines than Austin peeked his head from around the anti-truck, tank-ramming gate to greet his fellow biker buddies.

The Embassy was closed and so we exchanged stories of our last respective 48 hours since parting company just outside Aqaba. Whilst twiddling our thumbs on the grass verge opposite the Embassy, a Pajero 4 x 4 pulled up with two Brits inside. The driver who looked and sounded remarkably like Will Carling and also like Howling Wilf the blues singer from London, approached us and asked the question, "Are you Mondo Enduro?"

Martin was in the Political and Economic Section of the Embassy, born and bred in North London and was schooled in Enfield. Martin and his buddy Simon Collis who was the Deputy Head of Mission had received our fax from Aqaba. They had tried to fax us back at the bureau we had sent it from but obviously we had moved on. We received some super important additional information. Austin's new cylinder head arrived and found its way from DHL to the British Embassy – Hoorah! Also, we were all very amused by Gerald's letter from Canada that Clive read out.

Martin's first suggestion to us was, "Do you fancy going round to Simon's and we'll have a couple of beers". In a thrice our engines were kicked over and we eagerly followed him off to Simon's palatial residence for some cold refreshment.

Simon was in fact married with two children – a girl of sixteen and a boy of twenty. In fact, he looked far too young to be a father of children that age. He had split up from his first wife and his second lady was in Scotland having just applied for redundancy in her current employment to come and join Simon. They met in India and they co-habited in Morocco on Simon's previous posting. What a life these Foreign office types lead! So we enjoyed a few beers, a delicious buffet lunch and discussions ranging from Desert Storm to diplomatic relations with Jordan and Syria to even Andy McNab's tales of misfortune.

We moved inside for tea and biccies and were lucky enough to hear a sample of Simon's 60's and 70's music collection with Dylan and The Troggs featuring prominently. We hear hardly any popular music on the road.

A little after 8pm and Simon had to shoot off for dinner with a diplomat from the Spanish Embassy whilst we headed for the delights of the nearby

Irish bar. An initial falter on arrival as a sign clearly stated 'couples only', so Mondo Enduro quickly held hands and walked briskly towards the door.

Fortunately, the doorman had been tipped off about us and let us in to the bar which was located in the basement of the grand "Dove Hotel" and adjacent to the heavily guarded Egyptian Embassy.

Martin was at the bar making polite conversation with Douglas – whose name he had forgotten by the time we had come in, so he wasn't able to introduce us. In fact, Douglas had a shady story of being a freelance Education Consultant from Glasgow working for the Americans to help westernise Jordan's curriculum. Considering he was helping the Jordanians he would do well to get his geography of the Middle East up to scratch, as he suggested that we cross from Israel directly to Syria at that well known border crossing. Chas politely pointed out the Lebanon was in the way and that may pose a problem. Nothing more was said on the subject after that.

Martin bought us a round on arrival and left money behind the bar for us to have another one after he had left. What a top bloke – sheer decency!! One senses a Mondo Enduro badge coming his way.

At £4 for a can of Guinness and only shrapnel in the Mondo wallet – Mondo Enduro's time in the Irish bar was running short. After two drinks and a couple of handfuls of peanuts it was time to bid farewell to Douglas and the overpriced Irish bar and head for the Embassy to pick up Austin's sleeping kit.

Martin had headed off for dinner and was hoping we might stay in the bar until he got back. However, we were shattered so 'no blendo' for the tired *compañeros*.

We bedded down on some waste ground a stone's throw from the Embassy. Once comfortable and ready to wob out – it began to rain, so poncho and plastic sheet was pulled over the tired lads. Austin slept in dryness by opting to sleep under a truck and the others just slept through it. This may be the most ridiculous camp-spot of the trip.

Jordan

Day 375
Sunday 21 April
Mondo Miles today: 0
Mondo Mileage: 34314

"Life at the British Embassy."

Austin was up early, anxious to get to the British Embassy where his cylinder head was waiting to be attached to his bike. Chas, Louis and Clive soon made it to the Embassy after clearing the damp campsite. With Austin working on a re-assembly, Louis connecting a new de-compression cable and Cheeks tackling an oil leak, Clifford went into the Embassy and got to work on getting our Syrian Visas. Austin's B2 was assembled in no time and after testing left all of us bewildered – Knock, Knock, Knock went the valves on the rockers. Austin was disheartened, but not defeated.

The Chief Security officer on site, Tony Cross, came outside to greet us with Clive also returning with Syrian visa Application Forms. Tony offered us the use of the Embassy Garage Facility – and thus B2 was stripped down *again.* Clive had organised breakfast with Hassan, (The Chief Driver), which was sent for and delivered to us with the compliments of the Embassy. We stuffed ourselves with Humus, Pitta bread, Tahina and Falafels and it was lovely! And so after our morning feast it was back to the garage for Aust while the rest of Mondo stayed in the Drivers' Office next door to write more postcards and letters.

Only a few postcards had been written when an enormous smiling face appeared from behind the office door "Eureka!" said an elated Vince; and so he had done, the main problem on his bike had *nothing to do with the cylinder head*!!!! All that DHL malarkey had been a waste of time and money. The problem was that the cam-chain tensioner wasn't tensioning the cam chain, the timing was thrown out and the slack in the chain had been causing this strange valve sticking clicking noise. After much trial and error using H6's chain-tensioner, Austin refined his diagnosis and B2 appeared to be fixable so Mondo could breathe again.

The Embassy drivers were all characters and wonderful people and made us feel extremely welcome. Lou went off to the Sony dealer to collect the Hi8 and battery charger, both of which had been fixed. Late in the afternoon Tony Cross had delivered five enormous pizzas, *gratis*! What's more he said we could sleep in the office under cover rather than on the waste ground outside the front gate. Please remember reader, this is part of the official compound and in this age of the jobsworth it was great to have Tony show some flexibility when the rules were quite clear that tourists may *not* camp within the confines of any British embassy. Hurrah for Tony Cross!

That night we went off for *the* Mondo treat; the movies. We broadened our cultural horizons with the De Niro robbery flick; *Heat*. The audience stood ramrod straight during the playing of the Jordanian national anthem.

Jordan

Day 376
Monday 22 April
Mondo Miles today: 0
Mondo Mileage: 34314

Today saw us treated to another breakfast that celebrated the chick pea and of course the bear-like George, Embassy driver and lion wrestler who starts the day by saluting Mondo Enduro and punching many of his colleagues.

As usual, for our time in Amman, Austin was trying to make progress with the diagnosis of the beleaguered B2 and the heartrending cacophony of metal against metal sounds that come from its top end and timing chain. The screeching and clanking seemed to repeat to chant the dirge "you're flying home – you're flying home".

By mid morning, our Syrian visas were imprinted and an Embassy driver was sent round to the austere Syrian mission to collect our passports. Result!

We were able to do some more vital shopping in town, including a visit to the finest tool shop we had seen since we were in the USA. Maybe even of *all* time! We purchased a hard to find 'expander' for our collection of sockets and made a selection from the stunning "Loctite" array of products. Some bogus Egyptian grease (£1 worth) was added to our lubrication stockpile; it was more like dried dung and quite unlike any other grease we've seen before (apart from the Russian stuff).

Amman is a fantastic place and as, has been said before, full of incredibly friendly people. People would come up to us in the street offering us food, asking if we liked the country etc. Almost every shop has someone to hand who speaks English and proprietors will happily show you to another premises if they feel they cannot satisfy you. The VAT avoidance culture of 1970's Britain is also evident as storekeepers ask if you want a ball (meaning a bill) and when you decline they breathe a sigh of relief, look shiftily around, raise their eyebrows and enquire: "Discount?"

Amman is built not like Rome, on 7 hills but on what seems to be 700 hills. Steep sided valleys criss-cross the town almost randomly, this is unhelpful for navigation and also means you can't see any more of the town. Sandstone is the predominant building material, and is used tastefully either structurally or for cladding concrete buildings.

The evening was spent in the Irish bar where Mondo Enduro reached a dead end dealing with the Shannon based morality of a gang of Aer Lingus stewardesses who were in town for the night. They didn't appreciate it when we said we were just here for the *craic*.

Jordan

Day 377
Tuesday 23 April
Mondo Miles today: 0
Mondo Mileage: 34314

A day which will not be remembered for the splendour of its achievements dawned at the over-early hour of 7am for the three members of Mondo Enduro who had over-indulged in the Irish bar.

"How can you say you've been round the world when you haven't been to Cork?" had been the question levelled at them by the Irish Jordanian Airlines stewardess in the drinking hole beneath the Dove Hotel. Perhaps it was the restless hours spent considering this conundrum, or the heavy consumption of lager and peanuts, or possibly both which led to a general sense of exhaustion and nausea after only three hours sleep.

Austin, meanwhile, was up sprite and early to start work on his still poorly steed which is suffering from a number of as yet wholly undiagnosed problems to its top end and cam system. The driver's depot kettle, as hazardous to health as a rebel Ethiopian tank driver, spluttered into life to deliver another round of chai and coffee.

The morning was spent in torpor of non-achievement as Austin slaved fruitlessly over his top end and Louis hibernated behind the fridge freezer. Chas disappeared into town where he gorged himself on two bananas and milk dishes in a downtown street stand. On leaving, he espied Clive propped, apparently dead, against a streetlamp having expired before his time due to the intense energy expended on finding the post office. The two then repaired for a regenerative cup of chai in an upstairs cafe where elderly Arabs were playing chequers and slurping numerous cups of thick and treacly coffee.

Some words about downtown Amman: a living testament to the spirit of free enterprise and the undiminished power of market forces greets the traveller to this apogee of the street-hawkers art. It seems you can buy almost anything in the numerous stalls, booths and boutiques which line the boulevards in a crazy jumble. Shops selling second-clothes, quality hardware, pots, pans, sheepskins, shoes, candle wax, car parts and bubble-pipes all vie with each other for the custom of the passer-by. Jordan is such a friendly place that shopping here is not the ordeal that it is in certain African nations we could mention but choose not to in a spirit of post-colonial benevolence.

Austin's still ill motorcycle forced him to shave off the moustache which had defiled both his features and the image of the Englishman abroad for too long now. With a new Michael Caine hairstyle and the heir in a long unbroken dynasty of dreadful sunglasses, he went with the proverbial helmet in hand to Tony to request leave to blagg another night's free shelter. As if to prove that his sense of decency knew no frontiers of fashion, he immediately consented and ordered us yet more lunch of Humus, Tahini and Pitta bread it would appear, at the expense of the Foreign Office. Another empty evening loomed ahead of us and Cliff and Chas nursing heavy hangovers, decided that slumber was the better course. Austin and Louis, meanwhile, repaired to the Philadelphia cinema to watch a truly pathetic 1983 film called "Dogs" starring a bearded David McCallum, and an unknown Dallas starlet Linda

Grey being mauled to death by a rottweiller. Louis meanwhile was forced to sleep by the door by order of the Royal Health and Safety Executive.

Jordan

Day 378
Wednesday 24 April
Mondo Miles today: 20
Mondo Mileage: 34334

Louis woke first at 5am shivering uncontrollably as his cruel so-called mates had moved his bedding closer to the door because of his foul smelling body odours. The door was left 4 inches ajar and the biting Jordanian night froze him in his sleep.

Action in the morning (as usual) started as soon as we heard the first voices of the drivers turning up for work, then a flurry of activity would take place as we put our respective "yards" (yards being underwear) on and opened the door wide to decontaminate the drivers' room from predominately Louis's unfortunate body odours.

Austin set to taking the clutch cover off his bike, with Louis, to unearth the gremlins that lay within, whilst Cliff scribbled away writing to the rest of Mondo Enduro to summon them up for the Mondo reunion and the Slide feast. He also wrote to Noyan Nihat (OM) whose Mum and Dad are going to hopefully put us up in Istanbul. There was a card to Ray Dalton who put us up for a night in Santiago and who is hopefully going to put us up again in his new post at Sofia, Bulgaria.

The mechanic duo soon found the source of Austin's problem. It had a cracked lower camshaft sprocket and its woodruff key that locked it on the crankshaft had come lose causing play in the cam chain. To the reader – this is quite a bad mechanical situation.

So on the phone to the demi-god Geoffrey Vince to explain the latest predicament and to order more parts that would be despatched to Southern Turkey.

We had chosen Adana – the largest town in the South of Turkey as we had got a reasonable repair made with a Chromium welding rod. As a big Muslim holiday was coming up, this was a sensible bit of planning ahead.

We did some final bits of tinkering and adjustments to bikes and kit and we were ready to leave the Embassy just before 5pm. We headed out of town on the road north with the Syrian border only 60 miles away.

The road north was a dual carriageway that was *fantastico* and the four amigos cruised happily along it. They were especially happy as Mondo Enduro were riding as a four and that had not officially happened since

Gonder. So now there are eight wheels rolling northwards and homeward bound.

Nineteen miles up the road we had to stop as Austin's dipstick is showing no oil and Lou's clutch is giving grief and is under performing. Austin went to recce a campsite up a hillside – he beckoned us up and found a Jackson who sent us down. So off he went again in search of somewhere else. One mile later Cliff spotted a track going down into a dip right next to the road. It turned out to be perfect as it was on rough ground and had a dry 4ft x 6ft x 50m concrete storm drain right next to the camping area in case it happened to rain on us during the night.

Our spirits are high, the tarmac smooth and we hit a new country in the morn, Syria.

Jordan

Day 379
Thursday 25 April
Mondo Miles today: 100
Mondo Mileage: 34434

Cliff, Lou and Aust opted to sleep under the cover of the storm drain while Chas slept outside, deterred by the sight of human turds that Clive probably slept over. When morning came Chas and his maggot were inevitably covered in dew – Unlucky! Louis offered that next time Chas sleep next to him in the comfort and warmth of his maggot of which Cheeky replied: "I'd rather sleep in a river!" So be it.

After Austin helped Louis adjust his clutch and Chas had finished throwing lifeboat matches on to the fire, Mondo were back on the road. We were soon at the Jordanian/Syrian border and after coffee, sarnies and a smooth admin exit by Clive we crossed Syrian lines and YES more admin. Austin touched base with DHL in Damascus by phone for any news of arrival of the cam chain tensioner. Clive had been gone a long time dealing with the Syrians and returned with the look of defeat.

"We're getting fleeced for the bikes, $40 each and they want it in dollars!". We had $21 and practically no other money. We pleaded with the Chief Customs Official who wins the prize for being "The biggest arse" Mondo has met. Our plastic friends were all we had, but we needed hard cash. There were Visa machines back in Amman, but we had already left Jordan and would thus have to pay to get back in. Austin therefore opted to go north to Damascus, (over 100km away) and draw the necessary from an

ATM. After more pleading and the arse of arses taking literally every penny we had, Austin was stamped through and off he went.

Chas, Louis and Clive, waited, stuck between two borders, immobile and helpless. To make matters worse Cliff and Chas then heard from one of the locals that Visa/MasterCard do not operate in Damascus as Syria is not a free market. A frustrated Austin returned 4 hours and 120 miles later with the news that Visa/MasterCard are not accepted anywhere in Syria because it is not a free market.

Mondo was tired and frustrated (not more than Aust), and ready to burn the whole place down when Austin insisted that he go back to Amman in Jordan where there was a cashpoint machine that we *knew* accepted our plastic. The reader should know that due to poor admin our combined assets were zero local currency and US$7! So after blending with the Jordanian border officials, that's exactly what he did, rode the 50 miles back to Amman (a civilised country). The rest of us ate the leftover pasta-man from the day before and entertained ourselves with a "Clive Quiz".

Another four hours later Austin returned with the money we needed for the bikes to cross the border. Unfortunately, what we didn't have was any extra money to purchase food and petrol and get our Turkish Visas. Austin had done more than enough riding for a day and so after a pow-wow we decided that Louis should re-enter Jordan, ride back south to Amman and go to the cash-point again. Why he had singularly failed to extract sufficient funds to do anything more than pay for the entry stamps is quite beyond all of us, especially Austin.

This is what happened to Louis:

"I left Austin, Clive & Chas in no man's land to go back over the Jordanian border. The problem was they thought I was entering for the third time! Because we all looked the same with our bleached blonde hair and identical motorcycles and Austin had already crossed over both borders before me; they quizzed me as they thought I was peddling something across the border into the two countries: "Why you go then come back?"

Before leaving I spoke to some people crossing the Syrian border from Jordan and asked if there were any ATM machines that were located close to the frontier. That would save me having to go all the way back to the city of Amman (which was a 3 hour journey). They told me that once I crossed over the Jordanian border I should make a right turn and head east whence I would come to a small town, (I forget it's name) and there I will find cash machines. So, thinking I would save loads of time not having to go back to Amman, I headed for this town which unfortunately took about 2 hours to find. I think I left the Syrian border at around 5pm, it took another hour to get past the border officials and I was in the small town with cash machines by 8pm. It was getting dark and to my utter dismay every cash machine I went to refused to accept my Visa card and I was in Jordan!! Other credit cards yes, but not Visa. So, I spent a good hour going around all the cash machines.

Aggro, I would have to go all the way back to Amman (which by now I wish I'd done in the first place). I knew I had to get back on the main road which by memory would take me to the capital city. It was dark, the roads were not lit. I made it back to the main road and proceeded on my journey. I was by now bursting to take a piss. There was absolutely nobody around, so I stopped the bike and just as I was about to dismount I could hear in the distance the spine chilling sound of wild barking rabid dogs descending rapidly from the hillside in my direction, and the sound just got louder and louder! Hence, no pee, I just kick started the bike and sped off!! I had been on the road for about 3 hours and should have been in Amman or at least seen it in the distance. There was not a soul around to ask, it was now around midnight. In the distance I could see an enormous road sign displayed directly above the road, just like a motorway sign you would see above the M1. And when I got to below the sign I stopped. In big bold letters it read: 'IRAQ BORDER 500 Km' I remember looking at the sign but behind me was another one stating 'AMMAN 160Km'. I had been going in completely in the wrong direction! At least now I knew exactly where I was going and which bloody road I should have taken. So, I made a U-turn and headed back east to get back on another road to head south to Amman. Amazingly, the route was deemed to be so straightforward that I had left without the team map!

A few hours later I could see in the distance the shimmering lights of the capital city, finally, now I knew all would be well. The first cash machine I found, (which incidentally was the last one we used before leaving Amman) I was able to use. The necessary money was withdrawn for Mondo to carry on its journey through Syria and beyond. I was then back on S8 and heading for the Syrian border. On the ride back I remember being overwhelmed with worry about the others. I had been gone for over 8 hours on a mission that Austin had just completed in three! How were all of you doing at the border? You must have been thinking where the hell is he? I was willing my way back to you. I must have been an hour's ride from the Syrian border when my bike's fuel ran low, so, with S8 starting to cough a little I reached down to turn the fuel switch to reserve only to discover to my utter horror that she was ALREADY ON RESERVE!!!! S8 stopped and therefore so did I. About half a mile up the road I could see a small structure of some kind with the light on, (the only light I could see, it was now around 3am). I could also hear the sound of a barking dog.

When I got there I thought my prayers had been answered as the structure turned out to be a small petrol station (in the middle of nowhere) however, it was being guarded by a large rabid dog. I walked back to my bike and wheeled her up to the petrol station. Once there I took out my spray can of mace and approached the dog. The animal was now snarling, white froth hanging from it's mouth. I needed fuel, I had to get back to the boys, and nothing was going to get in the way of me and the petrol pump. The hound from hell began to close in, I released the safety switch from my mace, when it was just 10 feet away from me I shouted at it to "LOSE ITSELF" and to my amazement it ran away. The dog literally pegged it up the hillside. I was just thankful I didn't have to mace it. I wheeled S8 right up to the pump, there was no attendant around, I needed the fuel. With nozzle in the tank I squeezed the pump, nothing. I squeezed again, nothing. The fuel pump was controlled from inside the station. Gutted. I walked over to it. It was locked. I saw some loose bricks on the floor and picked one up. There was a window to the side of the structure. I was desperate, the boys needed me; with the brick in my hand I leaned back to get a powerful throw. Just before I leaned forward to release I could see scrunched up in the corner directly in front of the window I was about to break, the body of a sleeping man. He was wearing the same Jordanian head scarf as me.

At this point, (I think from utter exhaustion), I slid down and with my knees up and with my back against the wall I went into a mode of composing myself and just rested my mind for a few minutes. When I opened my eyes again there were two men banging on the window shouting at the man inside. It wasn't dark anymore the sun was coming up, I'd been asleep there for 2 hours! The petrol guy opened the pump, the other two were still shouting at him, they spoke to me, I just nodded, and they too were also wearing the same colored head dress as me. With S8 now fueled up, it was off to the Syrian border to be re-united with my comrades. However, leaving Jordan again was another conversation but it was all worth it, the re-union of Mondo was euphoric. It was now 6am and I had been separated from Austin, Clive & Chas for 13 hours, it felt like a life time. Never have I been so happy to see anyone as much as I was that morning."

Syria

Day 380
Friday 26 April
Mondo Miles today: 85
Mondo Mileage: 34519

So Mondo Enduro was reunited at 0830 in the garbage strewn back yard of the Syrian Customs hall. Austin, Chas and Clive had slept well throughout (possibly) the coldest night we had endured for many months; In the background was the sound of a gazillion Arabs having their worldly goods ripped to pieces by the unfeasibly zealous customs goons, desperate to find that piece of evidence of a previous trip to Israel, ahem, we mean 'occupied' Palestine.

Austin though, dreamed a grisly episode that saw one of the trash haven rats curled up on his head. He awoke with a start to find Rodney the Rat staring into his hooded tracksuit top, sitting cheekily on his head. It must have been the warmth! A quick flick of the neck and our rodent squatter was lobbed into a nearby mash of old polystyrene and the inevitable chickpeas.

Anyway, Louis cruised into sight at 0830 and the largest *ever* sigh of Mondo relief was exhaled. The 'stay behind' party was really flapping. Remember reader, Louis had been fully briefed by Austin, hence no time wasting antics at either border. So how could Louis have taken thirteen hours to do what Austin had done in five? We feared the worst: a horrible crash on the Amman autopista, detention in the Jordanian border post, an unlucky breakdown – so be advised, when Louis was spotted it was a reunion as emotional as any that this trip has seen.

Aside from getting out of this no man's land, our job for the day was to get to DHL Damascus and secure the cam chain tensioner for Austin's bike B2. It had been rapidly despatched by Mondo prophet and admin icon – Geoff Vince. Hence, with Austin already processed and paid for (from yesterday), he burned off to the oldest continually inhabited city in the world in search of the DHL office. A rendezvous was booked for Chas, Louis and Clive on the Aleppo road, a spot Austin had noticed on his futile initial trip to Damascus yesterday.

So, we motored through the Syrian border town of Da'ra and past the grisly Soviet inspired anti-aircraft battery that marked the start of the Autoroute headed North.

For the travel blurred English eyes of Mondo Enduro, a few observations that distinguish Syria from its Middle Eastern neighbours might be too difficult. As usual the people are generous, friendly and benevolently curious as in Saudi and Jordan. Its worth noting that the interest here in Mondo Arabia is definitely more positive and warm than the wide eyed "give me one banana" attention that characterised much of Africa. The pages of this journal could easily be filled with merely a list of the people who, upon noticing us, grab our forearms and insist that we take tea with them. It would require several more volumes if we recorded all the people who, beaming and bright faced, approach us hand outstretched, eliciting the standard Islamic greeting of *Asalaam Aleikum* and closing with "welcome to Syria/Jordan/Saudi Arabia".

However, if Islam is more than a religion out here, than the Heads of State are more than just political leaders. Sage-like King Hussein smiled at us benignly from every bank note and public building in Jordan. He needs to know that the multiplicity of versions of his likeness are mere bagatelle in comparison to the blizzard like inundation of walls, hoardings, car windows and lapel badges upon which President Assan of Syria crooked headedly looks out over his people. He is joined, more often than not, by a photo/image of Gerry Adams, who we discovered is his late son. Killed before he could have corrective surgery to remove his sunglasses in a tragic car 'accident' on the road out to the airport.

To a Westerner, photos, tea towels, you name it, it's got President Assan on it, and memorabilia of the personality cult is hard for us to swallow.

However, this double act of life president and flakey pimpoid paratrooper pretensioned ponce off-spring is far more than sinister.

Although irrelevant, it is funny to see the hand painted versions of this father and son; most are quite accomplished, but those that are out of perspective or with hands or torsos that are to a different scale as the head are a combination of grotesque, comical and frankly, pathetic, and certainly very demeaning to the subject. Anyway, these two guys are absolutely everywhere.

Austin's visit to the DHL office in the oldest continuously inhabited city in the world yielded an encounter with a Syrian Eli Wallach look-a-like who was basically the skeleton crew, this being Friday the Muslim day of rest or 'less' work depending on your occupation. Eli Wallach could just about manage a few words of English but after logging in our DHL airway bill no. he confirmed that thankfully the chain-tensioner, sent from England 3 days ago was fortunately still in Bahrain. It seemed there was a chance that it might arrive at the airport that afternoon and so Austin suggested that a call be made to Mr DHL at the cargo office and then he could intercept the shipment. Sure enough a Mr Anees Mohammed was raised on the other end of the 1970's phone and Austin headed out to collect his *compadres* and stake out the airport.

The remainder of Mondo Enduro was all tasked when Austin located them on the Aleppo Road. Louis was basted in Baby Oil, Clive was buying lunch and Chas was engaging an unshaven bike cop (Big Honda Four) in a bit of Mondo Enduro hearts and minds.

After Clive's lunch we crawled through the pedestrian laden Bazaar of the old town. Surely, only in Damascus would the civic authorities, as a result of major roadworks, re-route a primary road through a full-scale street market.

So it was, we avoided hubbly-bubbly salesmen, sheepskin peddlers and of course the 30,000 policemen that are sprinkled every few yards across this, the oldest continually inhabited city in the world, as we crawled out of town to cover the mystery 15 mile drive over pancake-flat scenery to reach Damascus international airport.

The one-time 'park' in front of the terminal was awash with hundreds of people asleep and picnicking. It was like a visit to Arabstock.

We parked off in the inexplicably over-priced café and treated ourselves to a drink. On the table next to us were a gang of Russians and it was strange to hear the language again.

Austin did a foot recce of the airport in a bid to find the cargo hangar and thus Anees Mohammed, the DHL contact. He eventually found the 'king' of cargo who cordially hosted him but assured him that nobody called Anees Mohammed worked at this airport.

At 4pm Austin returned to the café, found his *compadres* asleep on the table, roused them and we all repaired to a bush we had spotted just outside the airport terminal compound.

A gun wielding youth in civilian clothes guided us off the road and in no time we were all crashed out under the shade of a strip of eucalyptus. Within 5 minutes another security don turned up and said we'd have to go soon.

So go we did, a mile further down the road, into another patch of woodland that acted as a screen between the road and the airport perimeter fence.

We bedded down and by 8pm half a bottle of Vodka had disappeared, we didn't make a meal because we weren't hungry.

Syria

Day 381
Saturday 27 April
Mondo Miles today: 0
Mondo Mileage: 34519

A day of doing absolutely *nicht* loomed ahead of us as we contemplated another 24 hours in the field – this time quite literally in our campsite within range of Damascus Airport. The major task facing Austin was to try to track down his errant cam chain tensioner caught somewhere in the lines of international communication between Bahrain and Syria. The major task facing the other three Enduristes was to avoid the occasional security patrol which buzzed us along the airport perimeter fence and to think of ever more complex strategies to elude boredom.

Austin's preliminary foray to DHL revealed their progress in the parts procurement department. Apparently today it was the turn of two quite lovely birds to inform him of the mysterious disappearance of his part which was at least an improvement on the Eli Wallach look-a-like of yesterday. But the news remained negative and he had nothing to report on his return to base camp which would ensure our early departure.

He did however, arrive bearing goods and victuals in the form of envelopes, some writing paper with a hearts and doves watermark, a Middle East road map, cheese, bread, fruit and possibly the best orange cordial ever consumed on our trans global travels. A word of praise also for the biscuits which were definitely of the posh variety – rare in this recession hit land.

Clive made a brief foray to the airport in a bid to do some of the slightly suspect foreign exchange dealing of which he is the undisputed impresario. He returned with a crisp 1993 50$ bill swapped with a Turkish traveller for our Syrian pounds at a rate 42:1 – a considerable achievement in this country where the monetary sophistication of the free market is nowt but will o'the wisp.

It was shortly prior to his return that Chas and Lou were bussed by one of the clapped-out Subaru jeeps made at the suitably-named WAZ automobile factory in the Ural mountains. It would have been easier to take this fuzz seriously if he had not had GEG13 printed on his spare wheel cover in some hilarious mockery of the jeep marque. Later in the day we were also paid a visit by a Hitler look-a-like driving a white Merc, but he was cool.

Anyway, Austin returned from his second visit to DHL of the day with ill tidings. The part has been well and truly mislaid on its far Arabian travels from Bahrain and is the subject of a major steward's inquiry at the hands of the Damascus' office's Pommie Don. It will, on receipt, be despatched to Istanbul for collection by Mondo Enduro on its last disco pit stop prior to Europe's more familiar fleshpots.

While he was absent, Chas made his way to the airport to collect water from the gents to the immense amusement of the 38,000 security guards, one of whom asked the purpose of his errand. 'Radiator', he replied pointing to the bash plate of his air-cooled machine "Otrag, welcome" answered the guard.

Meanwhile, Clive and Louis were making a forest fire to prepare the meal of meals made from a cornucopia of choice vegetables, including leeks, courgettes, egg plants and no less than two chicken stock cubes – one experimentally blended into the pasta juice. We then retired to bed where Austin drank almost 250cl of anis liquor and started shouting very loudly.

Syria / Turkey

Day 382
Sunday 28 April
Mondo Miles today: 290
Mondo Mileage: 34809

Austin began the day as he went to bed the previous evening – shouting loudly. Yes readers, he was still drunk and it was dawn. He was hollering to wake up the rest of his colleagues as it was a brand new day with miles to be made.

All of Mondo Enduro were soon by the roadside after negotiating the multitude of earth furrows and dodging the branches and trees of the mini forest, that was specifically grown to conceal the airport and runway from prying eyes driving by.

So off we rode doing lefts and rights through small towns on the outskirts of Damascus surprising many a local as our four Suzuki's raced through these sleepy conurbations.

After a stop for gas, we proceeded a little further down the road to the town of Homs to take a chai and kebab on board for breakfast. With 109 miles down and just before 8.00; things were going well for the Enduristes with this tremendous progress. Another 50 miles of riding through this flat and relatively green land and we stopped on a rocky hillside for a break and a photo shoot.

If only our sponsors "SafeSeal", "Seal Line", McDonalds and even Suzuki could have seen the needy Mondo Enduro posing just for them they would have been impressed. Just as we were ready to hit the road, after helping locals take their punctured rear wheel off their moped, Austin then discovered his front wheel was as flat as the surrounding land.

The temperature was rising rapidly and the sky was a bright blue as Mondo stripped down to their shorts to sun their out of condition, pale bodies and Austin set to work on repairing his 21" SafeSealed tube.

Incidentally, we have all made our prediction for Mondo mileage and the day we return to Mill Hill with dates of arrival spanning from 16-22 May and from 37,900 – 38,015 miles respectively. The sweepstake is £5 per head. So one Mondo member will have his first night out paid for on the epic return of us round the world goons.

Back on the black top through this very French looking land and we began to see signs for the Turkish border Hurrah!

We reached the border and consulted the map – it was all a bit strange! Had the Turks taken 60 miles of Syrian land – surely not ref. In fact further

447

investigation showed the map makers had made a rather large 'boo boo' and rather than scrap the whole map – they let Turkey have a bit extra on paper.

Chas smoothly took us through Immigration and Customs with only a $10 bribe proposition by a plucky Customs official. Anyway, he swiftly sidestepped the official by asking if we could see his Chief to which he hushed up and blended into the background never to be seen again. We are certainly more bullish than ever at these borders.

Meanwhile back on the ranch, Cliff put his 'wheeler dealer' cap on and went on the immigration floor to trade with a shady banker.

He did remarkably well getting rid of the remainder of the Syrian pounds and Jordanian Dinar and came out victorious holding US$127 and about $7 in Turkish Lira which he changed with the Immigration Officer.

The team moved swiftly on round a couple of bends in a small valley to arrive at the Turkish side of things. Once again, Charlie blended us through officialdom and at long last we reached civilisation. Proper prices for visas and superb efficiency – it's all here in Turkey. £10 for a multiple entry visa that lasts for three months. Hurrah!

Austin put a call into Bournemouth to ask them to send his parts to Istanbul and he bought some much needed duty free. After one of the slackest Custom's checks in history where the official said "I must come and search your baggage – Ahh motorcycle – OK, off you go" and so we did – what a breeze.

The journey on the smooth ribbon of tarmac from the border weaved its way through prim and proper cultivated green lands with the occasional trees dotted here and there.

A quick gas-up and semi heart attack when we discover petrol is 45p a litre and were back on the perfectly made tarmac waving to the numerous bikers going by on their 125's and Jawa 350S with girl or family on the back. It was a real life morale booster – spirits soared in the Mondo camp as we sing to ourselves and thought that England was almost around the next bend. Still 3,000 miles to go!

It has been exactly 365 days since Mondo Enduro as a 7 went through this friendly and picturesque country and it's good to be back for the final push.

It's the first time for Louis Bloom in Turkey and he seems to be over the moon – especially at leaving the Middle Eastern Arab countries and now at last he can be back to his good old Hebrew self; *Muzzletoff!*

So we were now in Adena and eventually Istanbul bound as the road began to climb in a well-planned fashion with good safety features. We noted a two foot high concrete crash/safety barrier all around the bends on the mountain road. All other countries especially Ethiopia and nearby Greece take note!

Over the mountains and we spotted the Mediterranean Sea. The road wound nicely down to the coast and we noticed the increase in temperature as we descended. We drove through Iskenderum and stopped briefly to collect firewood. On again as the sun began to set sinking into the Med, and it was time for Mondo to camp.

Austin spotted a great site on a rock promontory which went down to the sea. It had what appeared to be a Pill box but that actually was a canteen or someone's house overlooking the sea. The only catch was we had to cross a set of railway tracks.

This was no problem for our trail bikes. Fully laden we all got over – Louis' bike was unstable with an extra 10 kg of petrol on one side and that sent him on to the tracks but not for long. There was an army base above us – troops walked by but no-one seemed to be bothered by our arrival.

This was a great Mondo moment for us as another knockout meal is prepared and we sup on our Danish beers in a new and civilised country. We suddenly feel like we're finally on our way home.

Turkey

Day 383
Monday 29 April
Mondo Miles today: 240
Mondo Mileage: 35049

A night of Vodka and talking Meriden Triumphs made for a deep Mondo sleep. By 0530 we were up with nature calling Louis under the full watchful eye of the Turkish soldier on sentry duty across the road. Just as we were about to hit the road on our way to Adana we realized the map had chipped the night before, a victim of the strong sea breeze; in Africa this might have posed a problem, Turkey however, has signposts.

After a few hours on the road Austin found the only open café in Adana, with its food and beverages laid out all over the gaff and its owner wobbed out on his bunk bed. For the life of us we couldn't raise him. We resigned ourselves to biscuits and pressed on. Louis was able to nurse his lip after hitting a nasty bug at 60mph and pulling out it's sting from underneath his tash. At a town called Mersin we stopped to make a call home to the UK. Aust spoke to Mrs Vince and ordered the necessary parts while Clive tried to bump-up his paleness in the sun. The bank was not flooded enough to pay for the call and it was lucky that Austin discovered a Turk Angel who not only paid for our call but managed to find us a map of Turkey – a delightful chap.

On our way out of town, Louis got stewards by a local copper for not wearing his helmet. After a fuel up, we hit more coastal roads passing many hotel resorts with their own bays to swim in. The temptation was too much and water baby Clive was first in, followed by an odd looking Aust then Chas then Louis; and all (we're proud to say) wearing their pants!

Back on the bikes we climbed into the hills. At one stage Louis passed a snake crossing the road; it's length was half the width of the road and his African background told him it was a Black Mamba. Mondo stopped not far from the sighting on a historic site. We camp tonight next to caves made by the Troggs, (not in the 60's but in about 600 AD, we are in Capadocia); and so after yet another culinary explosion and we sleep as a foursome next to old bones and mamba Men.

Turkey

Day 384
Tuesday 30 April
Mondo Miles today: 270
Mondo Mileage: 35319

It was a crystal clear starry night that the four peas in a pod slept through. The spirits of these former cave dwellings calmed our brains and gave for snugness on our patch of black polythene that will forever be England. The spirits from the bottle of Finlandia Vodka also played their part in ensuring the integrity of our slumber. We fell asleep last night marvelling at our gorgeous surroundings, free, beautiful and as far as we could tell a piece of land devoted to us.

Dawn brought more silly photographs of our "formation sleeping" display and Louis mumbling from the end of the line of four adjacent Enduristes. Louis was laughing and exclaiming "I can't clothe my mouth". We all looked up to discover that the bee sting in Louis's top lip had swollen to the size of a bicycle inner tube and that frankly, our endlessly effervescent Hotel worker co-traveller now looked quite grotesque. We administered Louis some of the anti-inflammatory wonder drug "Piriton" but not without first laughing at him and taking close up photographs.

We rode off at 0730, really quite cold and climbing up to a pass at 1650m. The road to Konya was superb and the stunning mountain scenery was strongly reminiscent of Northern California.

Clive was stopped by a lovely police car who was unhappy about his lack of number plate. Austin stopped 200 yards short of this roadside inquiry, whipped out his telephoto lens and as he twisted to focus, observed in close up the police car pulling away and hence destroying the shot.

The road and countryside had levelled out on to a huge featureless plateau that stretched out before us like a desert. Sycamores lined the route and the Turkish tradition of a petrol station every 2 miles continued unabated. Over to the west, huge mountains loomed, their snow capped peaks confirming that the easy world of the Mediterranean Coast was off to our south and that things were a little rougher at the edges here in the hinterland.

The road lanced across this Turkish steppe as straight as an arrow and finally brought us to the metropolis of Konya. We worshipped and praised Turkey once more, since without moving more than 100 yards from the centre of town we found a cashpoint, a cafeteria and a petrol station that took credit cards. These are the things we need to survive.

The streets were awash with off-duty soldiers, all looking vaguely communist in their ultra-minimalist olive green uniforms. We were surrounded by men, there not being so many women on the street now that we're away from the coast, and fielded the usual questions about our route. A chap pulled up on a scooter and soon revealed that he had a girlfriend who lived in Finchley. Hurrah!

The municipal clock/thermometer revealed that it was 11.30 and 26 degrees and so the seemingly endless swamp of high rise that constitute Konya's suburbs passed us by as we ground off towards Afyon.

This part of Turkey does not remind us very much of the Turkey that by weird Mondo coincidence, we entered exactly a year ago yesterday. Instead, the rolling plains and clay tile roofed farmhouses bring to mind central Spain or parts of France. It's only the skinny minarets of the millions of mosques that tell us where we are.

The prairie here is lush and fertile; meltwater running off from the nearby mountains is efficiently channelled into neat and ordered agricultural plots. Every river is flowing, something which after the Middle East is somewhat of a rarity. Portly middle-aged women, head-dress up to remove temptation, toil in the fields, their ballooning voluminous trousers, gusset at ankle height, giving them complete freedom of movement for whatever task their husbands set them.

A roadside ditch made for a short PT and biscuit break 65 miles from Konya. We grabbed rocks for trunk curls, employed the gradient of the land to make press-ups and sits more tiresome, and then all fell asleep in the shade of the bikes. Several passing cars of youths tooted at us and all of us agreed for the nth time that we were thoroughly pleased to be in Turkey.

It was boiling hot by 2pm but refreshingly cool as we continued towards Afyon. We pulled over for a short filming opportunity but Clive never turned up. A half hour passed as we anxiously debated where he could be. Smiling broadly, he rolled into view, it transpired that he'd gone back to look for Chas a few miles back, not realising that Cheeky Charlie was in fact in front of him. Louis took the chance to barrack Clive, the latter's noble intentions not being considered circumstances of sufficient mitigation for abuse hungry

Louis Bloom. A group of Turkish youngsters who had gathered were quite bemused by the non-stop shouting and name calling that seemed to divide what in all other respects looked like quite a homogenous team...

We rolled on into the late afternoon, the warmth of the sun and the immaculate road making for ideal riding conditions. Clive and Austin are now riding sitting on their partially inflated Thermarest mattresses. This alleviates much of the ardour of long distance work and it should be formally noted that both these team members have buttocks much scarred, pimpled and blemished from countless hours incarcerated under heat and pressure in their baking leather strides.

Twenty miles outside Afyon we encountered, walking south, an old man pushing a pram. He was a 'walking a prayer for the world' all the way from Sweden to Cape Town. His route was almost identical to Mondo Enduro's except of course in reverse. We chatted for a while and gathered that he believed that money was the root of all evil. We argued the contrary, in fact going further and postulating that pram-pushing was the scourge of mankind. We parted amicably but grateful that we were aided on our mission by 350cc's of power derived from the Otto cycle and not by the steely eyed sense of evangelical purpose that fired this perambulating pensioner.

We cruised into Afyon, passing evermore of the agricultural buggies so popular in this particular area of Turkey. The engine is exposed up front; the back is of a 'tipper-truck' and loaded with all the living relations of the driver. The women shrouded, children all over the place and the whole thing chugging along at a maximum of 15mph, its unsilenced exhaust announcing its arrival.

On the outskirts of Afyon we passed a military airbase. It was predictably encircled by a barbed wire fence, with the traditional gloomy faced conscriptees standing by to repel an invasion of Turkey's "Greenham Peace movement". On one outpost, the lonely sentry has as support, a miniature version of the Rapier anti aircraft missile system, so effectively used by the Royal Artillery in the Falklands campaign. The laughable thing was that these elfin rockets looked for the entire world like flashy fireworks, or a scaled down harmless plastic schoolboy model of the real thing. Maybe there were big rubber bands in the back to send them skyward silently.

As we reached the outskirts of town the unusual but unmistakable outline of expedition laden BMW's loomed into view. Needless to say, Mondo Enduro knew it was about to encounter those masters of long distance motorcycling: Germans....

These four chaps, of similar age to us, were a fairly humourless bunch that had just driven up from Izmir today. They had ferried it over from Venice (a notoriously expensive route) and were en route to Syria and Jordan. Mental eh reader? The second co-travellers we've met today doing our route in reverse.

We gunned off out of town, the sausage eaters genuinely bewildered at our raggedy appearance, they, so immaculately turned out in parade ground leathers. They probably thought we'd made up the '75,000 km' story since compared to them, we didn't look as if we'd be able to make it around a roundabout yet alone the world.

Five miles out of town, the sun setting, we hauled over to collect scraps of wood for our evening cooking. We needn't have worried, a class one campsite hit us square between the eyes a mile later. Grassy fields, woods, a lovely river and a railway adjacent our spot – ideal for soothing Austin's karma and reminding us of the spirit of missing Mondo man Gerald Vince. A phenomenal meal was enjoyed and with Istanbul only a day away Mondo Enduro is once again.... unstoppable!

Turkey

Day 385
Wednesday 1 May
Mondo Miles today: 230
Mondo Mileage: 35549

The tart pong of ammonia billowing from a deserted chemical factory filled our nostrils as we prepared to pitch camp this evening in an adjacent orchard. It has been quite a day full of sunshine, strenuous physical exercise, partial nudity and further progress to our immediate goal of Byzantium.

This morning started not with the call of the larks but with the chirrup of a somewhat lazier bird as the travellers arose at the unfashionably late hour of 8am. Give credit where credit is due, however, and today the accolades pile at Austin's feet after he selflessly washed the cooking pots and prepared coffee for his companions who dosed all the while in their dew-moistened sleeping bags.

We were on the road by 8.45am and after a mere 40 miles or so in the saddle found ourselves in a township where we repaired to a shady arboretum for several cups of coffee and chai. Chas, meanwhile, ventured downtown in search of a bank in which to cash his under-employed plastic but to no avail. When the Moslems slaughter their fatted calves, they do so with a gusto which perhaps can no longer be matched in the secular West and we assume it is complete kebab overload which forbids businesses from opening for a whole five days.

Anyway, after Clive left the waiter smarting from a few well-chosen phrases in cockney slang when he tried to cheat us of 50 pence in a bill surcharge scam, the lads were back on the road. We stopped only to buy petrol, a yoghurt dessert and also bread; the seller was the most hirsute woman this side of the Himalayan lair of the abominable snow-woman. The road in its earlier sections was smooth but soon gave way to some hilly sections with surfaces rocky enough to raise memories of some parts of Eastern Turkey travelled through almost exactly a year ago. Such impressions, are however, only fleeting and we continue to marvel that *this* Turkey, with its liberated women, ubiquitous petrol stations taking credit cards and low-profile *Jandarma*, could possibly be the same country.

Lunch was taken in a daisy-strewn meadow by a stream frothing with chilly snowmelt. Despite the cold temperature of the churning waters, all of the travellers immersed themselves to a greater or lesser extent with some, notably Clive and Austin opting for almost total washes.

After our ablutions, we then performed some actually quite rigorous physical exercises including sit ups, press ups, curls with a few rocks and presses with a large boulder. The lure of Istanbul's nightspots, our imminent homecoming, has made us vain, and so we try vainly to render more pert muscles emaciated by under-employment and arses and bellies made flabby by a year of almost no physical exercise and massive abuse of candy.

Lunch, for the record, consisted of cheese portions and bread which was consumed under the gaze of many schoolchildren who seemed transfixed both by us and their new game – chuck a football into a raging torrent and then risk the lives of yourself and your comrades by attempting to retrieve it with a large stick. This, though, was beautiful spot, as apparently is the whole of Turkey in Springtime, and we made sure we saw all of it by trotting round its boundary in a hideous parody of the athletic achievements of Britain's finest middle distance runners.

The road stretched ever onwards past a stunning inland lake reached only after Clive had risked permanent goosement by negotiating a sharp, roughish slope with *nicht* brakes. Shortly beforehand we had stopped to make a phone call and imbibe cola in a chalet.

On passing the lake, and after Cliff's latest near death experience, we followed a pick-up truck brimming with toothless grannies with head shawls and teenage girls so winsome they could have been extras from 'The Darling Kebabs of May'.

The highway switched at a T-junction to become a dual carriageway which led ever onward to the waterway with the name which launched a million Turkish restaurants – the Sea of Mamara.

After supping apple juice, coffee and rice puddings in the Shell garage across the road, we repaired to a meadow behind a factory where, having been splashed earlier in the day by a few rain droplets, we erected an excellent poncho with the 90 pence plastic sheeting we had purchased in Jordan. We all went to sleep, talking about girls, hair dye, pop music, brawling baboons, chocolate sprockets, cheese bombers, drunken rebel tank-drivers and everything else we had encountered over these last 385 days.

Turkey

Day 386
Thursday 2 May
Mondo Miles today: 60
Mondo Mileage: 35609

We awoke in our factory campsite to find there had been no rain or dewishness upon us during the night. It was 7.30 and the sun was fully up – time to chip!

So we headed off to Yolova where we hoped we could catch a boat directly to Istanbul and then film the only city that spreads over two continents, but it did no good! The boat used to run but did no more. So we repaired to Topucula to catch a boat to the other side just so we could satisfy our water crossing needs and save 60 miles of riding. The ferry was a small drive on-dive off one that went at tremendous speed. We had time for a civilised toasted sarnie, fruit juice and coffee before disembarking 40 miles east of Istanbul.

The ferry cost 200,000 TL = £1.80 and was a worthwhile experience. Cliff did some filming on the boat and Austin shot the others riding off the ferry with cars and coaches all making a dash for land with Mondo Enduro stuck in the middle.

The forty mile drive into Istanbul was the only section of road on Mondo Enduro that we have actually ridden on twice. The first time on our way to

Ankara and beyond exactly a year ago and now on the road home. So is Mondo Enduro really over now?

There's partying to be done in this liveliest of cities divided between Europe and Asia with a grand total of 15 million people in it. Half of which should be female – "Hurrah for the Hols" the four Enduristes shouted in unison.

A trip to the British Embassy to seek out Shane Campbell who greeted us exactly a year ago in order to attain various bits of info. No blending afoot here, Shane gave us a rather frosty reception. We did however cold call them and without the Mondo fax in advance that generally seems to tune us in.

A trip to the Bulgarian Embassy was in vain for Austin, as he stood outside the Embassy walls for the remainder of its opening hours with a crowd of desperate individuals all trying to barge their way through to the Bulgarian compound. We had hoped to get Bulgarian Visas in advance to save being fleeced at the border. However, after a failed attempt to attain a visa and with the Mondo clock ticking furiously away – we would take on corrupt officialdom instead.

Meanwhile, cheeky Charlie was not having much luck tracking down Sally Campbell (our blend here a year ago) with numerous phone calls and visits to her flat however, to no avail. She was either genuinely away for her holidays or she was either becoming a recluse to avoid Mondo Enduro. The latter we conclude!

We then swiftly cut along to the Golden Arches of Istanbul for a light snack and to make a base to nail some admin.

Accommodation was looking dire as Louis reported his contact was 900Ks from where we sat munching on our Big Macs and double cheeseburgers. Oh dear. So it was a hostel/cheap hotel recce for Chas and Louis whilst Clive got logging and Austin tucked into another ice cream sundae.

Before long Louis and Chas returned bringing news of a room for four with one on the floor. So off we went to pay two night's rent. Tonight was a special treat for the lads as we had finally reached Europe after 38,000 miles and 380 odd days. So the evening began with local *Effes* beer and G & T's in our room before we headed off into town about 10.30pm.

Off we went in search of the bars and clubs we frequented with Sally Campbell on our first visit. The night began in a classic student bar with a clientele of many long hairs, cheap liquor, 60's music, and The Doors film being projected on one of the walls. Austin was first to crash and collapse at 1.30pm on the landing outside our room having failed to open the door with the key. Lou, Cliff and Chas found a great club with live rock and returned at 4am to find Austin unconscious in the hallway.

Turkey

Day 387
Friday 3 May
Mondo Miles today: 0
Mondo Mileage: 35609

Clive snidely left the phone next to Louis' head for the 0600 wake-up call
– but he didn't hear it! Nor did the rest of Mondo! The craving for food and
fluid encouraged us to be seated at the breakfast table with the conversation
at a minimum. Louis was still shivering after a night of no sheet and no
blanket, due to Clive wrapping himself up in all the bed linen on their double
bed; and so after brekkie we went off to DHL while Chas slaved behind a
Turkish typewriter banging out our latest and possibly final press release.

The three that went off to DHL literally jumped for joy when they received
their package over the counter. They huddled next to each other on a couch
next to the shop window and with Austin seated in the middle, carefully
peeled open the fragile package Geoffrey Vince had yet again performed a
miracle – Mondo can keep moving! Upon their return to the hotel they found
Chas still typing and so Louis and Clive went to work on Clive's front brake
installation whilst Austin made some necessary calls. Tim Dingle the deputy
head back at Mill Hill School has agreed to host a formal 'homecoming' at the
school for Saturday 18th of May. So that's it, we're committed to being back
on a certain date.   With all our work done for the day and Chas finally
leaving the grip of the typster we decided to reward ourselves with a trip to
the movies. 'Copycat' seemed to be the best on offer and so after seeing this
class movie we devoured a few kebabs, downed some beers and had a mellow
night in the comfort of Hotel Aruba. We spectacularly failed to blend with a
troupe of Russian go-go dancers also billeted in the hotel. Their uninterested
stance in our London-Magadan leg was resolute indeed.

Turkey

Day 388
Saturday 4 May
Mondo Miles today: 50
Mondo Mileage: 35659

The hotel room was in a terrible state when we awoke and we had many
tasks to perform. The latest and last ever press release back to the UK was
brewing and so Chas drafted a whopping four sider and patiently single

digitally tapped it out on the Turkish typewriter that Kamal, the landlord, had kindly provided.

The cash point machines were mercilessly emptied as we loaded up with Turkish Lira which was immediately changed into crisp US dollars. £300 worth ought to get us to Hungary, next land of the ATM; we couldn't possibly spend £300 on the few days journey across Bulgaria and Serbia, could we?

We collected the laundry and our hearts sank when we realised that the idiot laundry boy had thrown in a red garment with the whites and our OM rugby shirts and Mondo Enduro T-shirts were now all a bright pink. We were furious and Clive immediately took the stained garments back with a demand for some form of remedial action.

We still had our filming to do; so, after slowly, slowly packing the bikes, we helmeted up on this blazing Turkish day and headed for the St Sophia mosque over on the other side of the Golden Horn. We met an Australian tourist who was reading a recently up-dated and re-packaged version of *Desert Biking* written by our friend Chris Scott. We were highly thrilled since this edition wasn't out when we left. We were very proud to have met him and that at last he is getting some proper sales.

We met some Turks from Tottenham and feigned interest in a carpet purchase so as to be allowed to film inside the Bazaar.

We finally finished our round Istanbul film tour and after changing the last of our lira into dollars we headed west for Edirne, the frontier town.

We clicked out 50 miles and the sun set on us eating an expensive meal in a roadside *lokantia* (café) - £2 a head. 5 miles further on and a ploughed field behind a copse was our hotel this night.

Turkey / Bulgaria

Day 389
Sunday 5 May
Mondo Miles today: 200
Mondo Mileage: 35859

Today we headed for Eastern Europe leaving the charming Turkish men and sadly their adorable females behind.

Yes, we were heading for the Eastern block, communism, badly dyed hair and gold or rather brass teeth... fond memories of mother Russia come quickly to mind as we arrived at the border on this beautiful sunny afternoon.

Dark clouds began to loom on the Bulgarian horizon as we discovered it was a whopping $90 for a transit visa and the last of the Mondo cash was handed over to the smug Slavic Immigration Official. "Do you realise this is the most expensive visa in the world Doris" Clive declared to the woman-like person behind the glass screen. She just crossed her arms and looked to the next vehicle and passengers ignoring the frustrated and broke world travellers.

Customs just waved us through without any questioning or searching. It was then that Chas realised he was not wearing his glasses nor did he know where they were. He searched through his kit but to no avail. He then explained to the Bulgarian officials in broken Russian and a touch of theatre workshop that he had left his glasses back in Turkey. They agreed to let him go, only on foot though.

There was no sign of them anywhere. However, on the second visit accompanied by Austin, Turkish Customs had found them and gladly handed them over to our Chas. So then Mondo Enduro was back on the plot and there was still some daylight left.

We banged out 80 miles in one go along a lovely section of road that was well signposted to the capital of Sofia. With half an hour of light left, Austin discovered a location for our campsite in between a public rubbish dump and a dam – it was very nice and we scoffed a grand broth! However, the unending bungling had a new face tonight and it was that of Louis Bloom. He was changing his oil filter, a task we've all done several times before, no big shakes. What Louis didn't know was that the new oil filter he was inserting was the last of the batch of 'wrong sized' filters that we'd been mistakenly given back in Los Angeles. They were the correct diameter but 2mm too high. Our unsuspecting mechanic was routinely tightening down the three bolts of the metal oil filter cap and met with some resistance as the cap came to bear on the proud bit of the oversized filter. He of course just kept on tightening. It was with a loud swear word that the other three became aware that Louis had just fractured the oil filter cap in two. Aggro. It's 130 miles to Sofia so we will have to tow Louis there and try to find an alloy welder when we arrive.

Bulgaria

Day 390
Monday 6 May (The day after Phyllis Vince's birthday)
Mondo Miles today: 130
Mondo Mileage: 35989

We awoke in our bivouac beside the dam to find the sun shining brightly – but not for long. In the distance, although not yet visible, clouds frowned on us with all the malign intent of a Zimbabwean speed cop or a Honduran Customs official. Still, after towing Louis across the field, we were on the quite impressive stretch of hard top which leads to Sofia and hopefully the welcoming precincts of Mr and Mrs Raymond Dalton Esq. (they had tuned us in way back in Santiago and had since been posted here, to Sofia).

The route into Sofia was a slightly depressing journey back in time both to the days of Soviet Central planning and our own experience in the former Communist block. Huge, drab apartment blocks rose carbuncle-like at the fringes of this depressing city which looked utterly at home in its mantle of mist and freezing rain. Clive and Chas were soon surging ahead of the towing party and had arrived at *Boulevard Vasil Levsky* to find the hideous red-brick structure of the UK Embassy-closed for a UK Bank Holiday would you believe. The lure of a summer picking strawberries in the English shires was apparently strong enough, however, to entice a posse of students to sit outside waiting its opening on the morrow. A chat with a toffee-nosed but once-tasty ambassador's wife revealed Ray Dalton's phone number which was repeatedly tried on several occasions but to no avail. Could it be that Ray and Mary on learning of our arrival had fled to join the Chechen rebels or more plausibly, retired to their oft-mentioned holiday flat in Cyprus?

But no! The screech of Land Rover Discovery wheels marked their appearance outside the Embassy. After much cheek-pecking we were introduced to the Deputy head of Mission Janet Gunn, and the charming Scots engineer Derek Hynd and his wife Mandy. Then we were whisked into town for a spot of what we do best – hard currency exchange. With dollars accumulated for what amounted to a 17% commission, we were back on the road to Ray's plush 2-bedroomed apartment. On the way he apologised for his three-door vehicle "Don't worry, *we* don't have *any*!" came the waggish reply.

We arrived to find Mary slaving over a lunch of pork medallions, peas and rice and soon we were drowning in a sea of warm hospitality which extended to the use of Ray's razor and Mary's facial <u>and</u> body soaps. The Dalton's largesse seemed to know no bounds, which is thoroughly in tune with their generous-spirited world view: "There are no pockets in a shroud," as Ray sagely pointed out. Hurrah for the Daltons!

After an afternoon getting stewed, talking football and discussing racial issues, Derek and Mandy turned up to whisk Austin and Loius away for yet more revelry of the Caledonian ilk and a bed for the night. Chas and Clive were already asleep in beds dreaming of the green fields of England far away.

Bulgaria

Day 391
Tuesday 7 May
Mondo Miles today: 45
Mondo Mileage: 36034

Austin and Louis woke to the welcoming aroma of an English fried breakfast. Mandy (Derek's wife), had laid out all the best stuff with Kellogg's Start and Frosties to begin our morning meal; and so Louis and Austin were at the Embassy bright and early expecting to see their co-riders:

"I let the lads lie in this morning." Said Ray Dalton.

Louis then went with Ray in his 4 x 4 and went to collect the other two. Fortunately, Chas and Cliff were nearly ready to leave for the Embassy when Ray and Lou arrived. They could hardly even walk after a killer breakfast made for them by Mary (Ray's wife). Derek had a look at Louis' broken oil filter cap and spoke to one of the Embassy mechanics who took him around town to get a result. Clive persuaded Janet (boss in foreign affairs) to write a letter to the border officials at the Bulgaria border as his and Chas' visas had already expired (transit visas are only valid for 72hours). Louis returned with a fixed fragile cap and Cliff then went off to the Serbian Embassy with Mondo passports to obtain visas.

We moved our bikes around to the embassy garage and laid our kit down. Chas got to work on his rear brake light, Clive fixed his front wheel and he and Louis finally attached their number plates. Austin went off to DHL and returned empty handed; and after many calls to Geoffrey Vince it was discovered that DHL Damascus had sent the package back to Heathrow instead of sending it to Sofia! Our Serbian visas were ready for us late in the afternoon and with no time to spare we packed up and got ready to move on.

Steve, (Derek's son) got a ride with Clive on H6 and Derek kindly donated waterproofing for Austin and Louis. Derek and his family also waited for us to go so that they could see us off and direct us, in convoy, to the right road out of town. The hospitality shown to Mondo in Sofia was unforgettable. Your taxes well spent!

Yugoslavia

Day 392
Wednesday 8 May
Mondo Miles today: 138
Mondo Mileage: 36172

So, our first day's riding in the former Yugoslavia, apparently, still known as Yugoslavia. Our night's sleep was unusually calm and despite the clear sky we weren't too cold in our partially used farm shed cum barn building. The beautiful blossoms on the orchard that surrounded us made for a scenic start and the piles of perfectly sized firewood placed all around us had us thanking farmer Slobodan and his twig detail.

Chas and Louis, under the weather, started the day with a Lemsip and as any around the world expedition would – we munched on macaroons.

To leave our campsite we didn't need to re-cross the railway tracks since a dirt road led down to the nearby town. We re-assembled there and did a little filming alongside a road sign plastered with household names like Sofia, Belgrade and Sarajevo.

A police car/Lada rolled up and stewardsed Clive about the camera. He asked what we were doing here and Clive said "Expedition". "Ahh... but what kind of expedition?" asked the Kommisar. "An Expedition, Expedition" replied Cliff. By now, the policeman's co-pilot was urging them to continue their journey to the police station, and it was then noticed by us that there were two crooks in the back of the Lada who were obviously helping the police with their enquiries. We also read two of Clive's recently acquired editions of 'The Economist'. These were very absorbing and are hoped to provide a much desired step up for Clive's PGCE interview this summer.

It wasn't all filming and economics though; Louis was struggling with his throttle cables and was getting quite exasperated as the power on the usually indefatigable S8 had been lacking recently. We watched crowds of kids en route to school, it was only 0730 after all. They don't wear a uniform, which may explain why the policemen are so chuffed with theirs when they finally get them. A crowd of labourers gathered close to us. A few examined the bikes but we were too tired and/or engrossed in World affairs to entertain them.

Because of the ludicrous road tolls that Serbia has seen fit to levy, we elected to take a parallel 'back' route up to Belgrade. We were laden down with cheap Bulgarian petrol, squeezed into every Fanta bottle and old oil container we could muster. We hope this will allow us to pop out of the far side of Serbia without having to buy any petrol in this country.

Yup, they have mosquitoes in Serbia.

The scenery was coloured much as it had been in Turkey. Field upon field of grasses and wheats, trees everywhere and neat and tidy plots being meticulously cultivated by the locals. It seems to be only old men and women working on the land. Invariably by hand, they tread barefoot across the ruts and furrows, hand pumping chemicals from a canister on their back. Huge oxen walk stupefyingly slowly along the little roads. Creaking behind them is an ancient cart with a couple of old dudes sitting cross-legged with all the time in the world. "What a load of bullocks" we hear you say. The old women usually seem to have a black headscarf. In mourning possibly? Yes, but they wear them in the evening as well. We are not waved at and smiled at as before on Mondo Enduro. We suppose we're not very unusual out here. The girls though, are substantially plainer, nay, uglier than the eye-watering stunners that we left behind in Sofia. We sense that there is many a village out here twinned with an opposite number in Syria.

At 10am we pulled over at a beautiful meadow fully equipped with crystal clear stream, swathed with luscious grass and bordered by an orchard *so* picturesque it looked as if it could only be for 'demonstration' purposes. Strangely, by our own standards, we had only done 32 miles but were already contemplating a brew break and possibly some upper body exercises. In no time, a fire roared and so did Louis as his throttle cable gremlins vexed him further. The baby oil was decanted on to waiting pale flesh and soon 2 hours had been wasted with drinking coffee and sun bathing. We filmed ourselves being pummelled under a nearby waterfall and Louis began to vent his mechanical frustration on Charles, alternating between the two old chestnuts of age and hairline. Chas refused to rise to the bait, instead kicking and punching Louis as and when the whim took him. We capped our stay at this Serbian idyll with the quite peerless treat of high speed fording.

Eventually, common sense and that incredible attraction that has been dragging us back to England eventually came into play. Clive Greenhough filmed his co-travellers driving through this beautiful but thankfully typical Serbian vale. Sadly, despite months of practice Mondo Enduro still hasn't worked out that the riders need to be close together, equidistant and moving at speed or else the shot just doesn't quite hang together.

Through the Serbian towns and on towards Petrovac. The roads varied between twisty mountain and straightish mountain thoroughfares. The sunshine was fast fading away and after descending down a dirt road from a spectacular mountain summit we feared that a major thunderstorm could be brewing up for us ahead.

We decided to hole up under a road bridge that spanned a small stream. On the bank under the protective canopy of concrete there was room enough for slicing, dicing and spicing as another truly splendid Mondo Enduro casserole came into being.

We supped an expensive but mouth watering tropical cordial and, while chatting after dinner, our parked motorcycles attracted the attention of some passing policemen. They beckoned us out, like little leathery trolls, from under the bridge and predictably asked to see our passports. They left us after five minutes and as dusk turned to night we chatted on the parapet, reading aloud to each other the closing sections of the last volume of the Mondo Diary. The Turkish Raki bottle passed from hand to hand and our powerful DEET insect repellent caused the ink on the label to melt and smear into a modernist work of art.

An abandoned barn type shed thingy with a quaint red tile roof lay waiting for us only 150 yds down the road. Under cover of darkness, with an efficiency and silence that comes partly from experience and partly from team-work, we moved into the 'forecourt' of the shed.

Once again, we slipped into a deep sleep thanks to the alcohol and the weariness of another day in the saddle. Austin began his psychological profile of Mondo blendee to be, Matthew Medcalf. Matthew was a childhood friend of his and he described him as thoroughly as could be to his co-riders. A history of expert scouting skills, lead smelting in a Harrow garden and commercial stamp sorting lies behind our soon to be Budapest host. He and Austin started their lead smelting partnership in 1976 when they were ten. Their first project was the lead they 'recovered' from the stained glass windows of the United Reform church in Station Road Harrow during its demolition. The lead was melted down in Matthew's garden and then poured into the frogs of bricks to make the final ingots. These were then bicycled to a real scrap yard in Wealdstone where an Irish gentleman bought them for cash money. Austin assures us that as a child entrepreneur Matthew Medcalf had no equal.

Yugoslavia

Day 393
Thursday 9May
Mondo Miles today: 240
Mondo Mileage: 36412

The dew laid heavy on our furry seats this fair morn which dawned bright and beautiful over our Yugoslavian hovel. We were a little late away, however, as we stayed overlong in our sleeping bags slurping *Cappy* cherry juice and recounting tales of the conquest of Canada. Cliff, meanwhile, took the intellectual high ground, continuing to read the Economist out by the roadside.

The first section of our journey today was not especially memorable, weaving as it did through quite pretty but not stunning mountain scenery. Soon, however, we found ourselves alarmed witnesses to another Clive accident who had hit a diesel slick at low speed as he entered a sharp bend. Fortunately damage to both rider and machine was less than minimal and both were able to continue immediately.

The road led inexorably to yet another hovel which offered the perfect setting for a roadside brew. On this occasion, however, our humble cups of tea or coffee were upstaged by seething beakers of steaming broth concocted by Clive and Louis from our Turkish powdered soup sachets, potatoes, salami and a few other vegetable ingredients. With two loaves of bread, purchased earlier for the not unreasonable price of 1$US, we also consumed two portions of Turkish cheese to make this more of a full-on meal than mere elevenses.

The highlight of our short break was, however, the long-anticipated "exploding vegetables" film shot. Loosely, reader, the plot goes like this: Chas and Louis discuss the contents of a hypothetical meal liberally laced with spices. Austin, a satisfied customer, comments on the excellent taste of the food and its piquant taste just seconds before a giant Chinese firecracker, purchased in Johannesburg, exploded, sending burning wadding and potato chunks in all directions. Suffice it to say that the filming, done in two takes, was an enormous success despite a puncture to Austin's Thermarest (it was blasted by buckshot) and the severe flash burns to Chas's back. Louis's McDonald's tee-shirt likewise suffered an entry wound right in the centre of its wearer's torso.

And so the road continued ever onwards through little towns which with their large alpine style houses and satellite dishes, looked almost German in nature – it is clear now that Europe is getting more western as we travel northwards, if that is not too idiotic an observation. The Cyrillic lettering on every signpost, which was almost ubiquitous close to the Hungarian border, was now making way for Roman script which made navigation an easier exercise.

Cliff, meanwhile, as map-reader-in-chief was doing an excellent job negotiating the highways and byways which made up the Serbian 'back passage' for travellers like us not blessed with huge wads of Yugo dinars. Only once did we take a wrong turn, on the road to NoviSad, and the error was swiftly corrected by Austin who nevertheless managed to get hit by a reversing bus.

For the second time this day, a Mondo member rose from the dust to tell the tale of another tankslapper. This one was not at all serious, however, and soon we found ourselves in Blovny, which we negotiated with some slight difficulty before being flushed out on the other side of its erratic traffic system. There we pulled over outside a rather plush restaurant next to a petrol station whose patron quickly became non-plussed at our slovenly appearance. Rescue was at hand, however, the chunky form of Dejan Beric, a vendor of Italian clothes and owner of a gleaming Kawasaki 22R 1100 parked nearby.

He insisted on buying us a drink – coffees for Louis and Austin, beers for Chas and Clive – and setting us straight on the road to Budapest.

A heavy rain cloud, briefly threatened to drench us before we entered NoviSad. There underneath a bridge we were pulled by the local Militsia, one of whom spoke excellent English. Only a tollbooth and about 100km now stood between us and the border with Hungary at Jubokca. Fortunately a $10 bribe, negotiated with standard ease by Clive, blended us through and we were quickly on surely the worst paid-for road in all of Europe.

The Militsia, who have flattered us by the keen interest in Mondo Enduro throughout our stay in Serbia, could not resist hurling one final brickbat at the departing Enduristes. With all the cunning of their counterparts in Zimbabwe, the cops had set a radar trap just a few hundred yards from the border and Austin was caught in its snare having clocked an outrageous 76 km/h through a built up area. More serious than the 10 DN, paid only in Kraut cash or local currency, however, was the need to exchange 10$ to pay it while the copper kept Austin's passport. The Enduristes were then left with 25 Dinars in a currency so bogus that not even the Duty Free shops would accept it in payment for candy or vodka.

Border formalities were exactly that – although Louis nearly caused an international incident by slicing garlic in a bonded customs area. With money changed and a call to Matthew Medcalf logged in, we were ready for anything. Hungry for Hungary if you will.

Bed was a copse just over the border and reached by a muddy track from the road. Cliff was on poncho detail while Louis and Austin performed the culinary tasks. It looks like the dark days of Honduras, Jordan, Syria and Bulgaria are behind us now and we can look forward to some cheepo border crossings on our way home to England.

Hungary

Day 394
Friday 10 May
Mondo Miles today: 100
Mondo Mileage: 36512

Our first night in real Europe for Mondo Enduro went by peacefully. We all slept well except Austin, who despite several swigs of vodka throughout the night, and a call for nature, failed to enter the land of nod for more than an hour.

A gust of wind in the middle of the night blew half the Sub-Earls Court Standard poncho away into the rainy darkness. Suddenly, the Enduristes were victims of a midnight cold shower. Cliff as the bivouac builder jumped up in guilt to amend his hodge bodge and sealed the flaw to secure a full night's sleep.

Hungary is an hour behind that of Yugoslavia and hence the sun seemed to rise earlier for us.

Austin was first awake at 4.52am – the rest of us, except Lou, came to at 6.52am. He woke up just as were packing up around 8ish... lazy dog! So we left our wooded den and hightailed in the direction of Budapest.

The sky was overcast and it was quite chilly as we cruised along the fantastic Hungarian roads with clear and proper markings. We stopped roughly half way on our journey to the Hungarian capital for a brew 'n' break. This bar/café had a very dishy waitress working there. We therefore decided to stay for two coffees instead of one – so we could gaze at this beauty just a little longer.

Off he went again for the last forty miles to Budapest and the 'Rain man' began to splatter on us and our kit. The spray from the lorries and cars soon clouded up our respective glasses and goggles and slowed our pace right down.

On our arrival in the centre of town, we managed to get split up: Clive and Louis in front headed for Alpad bridge where our new host Matthew Medcalf (Old Millhillian and ex 11th Harrow Scout) was set to meet us and lead us back to his pad!

Cheeky Charlie had no idea where he was heading for-except he knew it was a bridge for a rendezvous; so that's where he began looking for the lads when Austin ran into him. In the meantime, Austin had phoned Mondo HQ to report us lost. However, we were only split up for about an hour before we all were together under Alpad bridge.

We awaited the arrival of the one and only Matthew "Mudguard" Medcalf, Chief Garden Lead Smelter and top Boy Scout. He was our main man here in Budapest and was ready to take Mondo Enduro under his wing for the next 48 hours. A very cool and laid back chap, as he let us take over his office situated on the first floor of a Hungarian council estate for our stay here. It was, in effect, the first brick in MJM (Matthew John Medcalf) Enterprises that was borne all those years ago whilst at Quainton Hall with Austin and their lucrative lead smelting partnership. Apparently Austin informed us he was a wheeler dealer from the word "go". Back in Harrow in 1978, if you needed anything MJM Enterprises could get it for you.

And now here we are in Hungary being blended by this very man.

So after a couple of beers to get us in the mood he took us in hand to "Beckets" – the Irish pub here in Budapest. It was quite a large establishment with a small restaurant, 2 bars and a small stage. The night began at around with 7.30pm, plenty of beer, wine, women and song for Mondo Enduro including Dutch, American, Canadian and local talent to entertain and tempt us.

The lads stuck firmly together being strong in mind and heart and crawled home at 5am with no more than a peck on the cheek.

Hungary

Day 395-396
Sunday 12 May
Mondo Miles today: 0
Mondo Mileage: 36512

We awoke at 0100. What had happened? Last night was Saturday night – Mondo partying was afoot yet here we were in the small hours snuggled up in Matthew Medcalf's office, nestled between the blank betacam cassettes.

Our giant meal from last night was finished off at 9pm. We had swilled it down with a bottle of local wine so cheap that it was virtually free and the combination of alcohol and full stomachs made us as drowsy as a dormouse. Hence, we all passed out spread all over the 'office'!

At 0800 we were up, chatting and exchanging the pitifully immature small talk that makes Mondo Enduro the most tragic of around the world motorcycle expeditions. The coffee was made with milk from a bladder (but previously from a cow probably) and predictably morale soared.

We planned to indulge in another of our formal filming sessions around and about beautiful Budapest. Matthew and two of his friends Chris and Ian volunteered to be the film crew and Chris's Land Rover was to be the mobile film platform.

We whizzed around, past the Parliament building (highly Gothic), up to the old mid 19th century fortress known as 'The Citadella'. We saw a huge Aspencade motorcycle pull up with a ridiculous looking couple on board. They had all the touring clobber but then there was a sharp intake of Mondo Enduro breath as the pillion passenger took off her helmet and revealed that she was totally beautiful. They were Austrian and the physical perfection was too much. The filming over, we picked up Matthew's wife, Edith, and tiny Laura, their daughter.

Off we all went, dodging trams and drawing curious looks as we rode as a four man blob to a suburban restaurant. A parking misunderstanding with a local almost spiralled into a fight until he backed off. Edith informed us that he owned several strip joints in town and that he had strong mafia connections.

Hungary

Day 397
Monday 13 May
Mondo Miles today: 100
Mondo Mileage: 36612

The most pressing task facing *Los Enduristos* on this fine East European morn was the need to discharge our responsibilities with regard to domestic hygiene. Matthew our supremely laid-back host was due in work at 9am and his office resembled nothing so much as a municipal landfill site.

Still we were up and about at an early hour, sweeping, swabbing and stashing away household items. Actually, Mathew was in much earlier than usual and surprised us as we laboured at our domestic chores. Still the office was presentable enough at the witching hour for Matthew to embark upon his daily business: which seems to consist of selling on average one video tape per day and talking a lot on his mobile phone.

Anyway, Austin was quickly engaged in conquering our most telling challenge – to track down our DHL package amongst the labyrinthine morass of Magyar Customs formalities. Louis meanwhile, was out and about to the Xerox Office and Clive and Chas went shopping for victuals and hair dye.

After the third paint job in as many weeks, Chas' hair is still blazing auburn or minging ginger depending on your perspective of the fashion world.

The lull in proceedings which coincided with Austin's absence afforded the ideal opportunity for Chas to contact North Sea Ferries and attempt a bare-faced confidence trick by requesting free ship passage to the United Kingdom. A brief phone call and follow-up fax to John Pylons, Deputy Head of PR, yielded about £400 of blend: This was in the shape of free stowage of motorcycles and a token £17.50 fee per head for a 12 hour crossing complete with dinner and brekkie and an on-board cinema and disco.

The scheme does have drawbacks, however. Apart from our first destination being Hull, which despite being the birthplace of the poet Andrew Morrell and the slave emancipator William Wilberforce, and being able to log a realistic claim to being the town where the English Civil War started, is still somewhat bogus as a port of re-entry.

Anyway an already bright morning was made even lovelier by the arrival of Christina, Edith's cousin, and Matthew's employee and partner in almost total inactivity. Her sole task in an utterly empty morning was to collect the cash for a bulk order of two video tapes and Clive, ever the gallant musketeer, offered to ferry her on his motorcycle. The prize of Christina's favours was hotly contested by Louis such that Matthew eventually had to separate the warring knaves, while Chas wisely (given his unseemly hair colouring) maintained an ironic silence on the fringes of the romantic fray.

After some time spent haggling with DHL and Customs Officials up at the airport, Austin returned bearing gifts in the shape of push and push throttle cables and recompression cables for Chas and an oil filter cap for Louis von Blomberg. The cable looping was effected with reasonable efficiency and the result is that Chas' bike K5 is performing as it did in the days before the Anchorage partial piston seizure.

By about 4pm we were finally all ready to depart, which we did amidst hearty shaking of Matthew's hand and emotional leave taking of Cristina: who blew kisses from the apartment balcony. Only later did Clive reveal that he has secured her business card with a view to blending her in at a future date.

The Slovak Republic was but 130 kms away now and we strove to cross the border before nightfall. This we did with some ease before finding an excellent campsite situated in deep woods. This was reached only with considerable difficulty along a muddy track which claimed both Louis and Austin within its mire-filled maw. In the gathering nightfall we had time to consider our route on the morrow when Prague beckons and we work into the Trans-Euro Autobahn system. Could this be where Mondo Enduro really begins to end?

Slovak/Czech Republics

Day 398
Tuesday 14 May
Mondo Miles today: 240
Mondo Mileage: 36852

Today was a plentiful day; plenty of miles, great roads, rain, wind, sunshine and some gloom thrown in too. It all began in the early hours at around five o'clock, as we rose blearily eyed and decamped from another perfect campsite in a forest.

We were dressed to the nines, to the hilt if you will, wearing every last item in the ever shrinking Mondo Enduro wardrobe on our shivering pale bodies.

Cliff recce'd a route out of the forest to save us from the fun and games of the Siberianesque, kilometre waterlogged mud track that we had taken the night before.

There was a way and it was the other way. It led along this overgrown track but there were a couple of obstacles on the way to tackle, including a huge fallen tree lying across the leaf strewn path, as well as several tree stumps dotted around and a head height wire fence to duck under on exit from the dense undergrowth.

We were destination Prague and it was 360 kms away at a quarter to nine. So time was on our side as we set off again all wearing ponchos to protect us from the blustery showers and incessant road spray.

The road was smooth but not without incident. Austin and Chas were ahead when Clive and Louis suddenly had to weave around some obstacles in their path. Both Clive and Louis through their road-spray-smothered goggles seemed to partially recognise these objects. Yes, it was our kitchen box and a bag of Mondo food. Cliff and Lou did an emergency brake and floored it back along the hard shoulder to save them from the wheels of the ever increasing fleet of HGVs heading to the Fatherland.

Everything was reasonably intact, including the video camera battery that had been on charge on K5. They had taken a nasty fall but fortunately had not been run over yet. So the day was saved.

Reunited at the Slovenska/Czech border and a quick change of money was in order. Soon to be followed by a definite no-no on buying the Czech road tax for a year at a tenner a shot just so we could ride these highways. We didn't have enough cash – so we would chance it claiming ignorance.

We arrived in Prague just before 2pm and found ourselves at the biggest and flashiest Hilton that any of us had ever seen before. We pulled up outside and a quick fire of "bagsy not go inside" found Chas walking past a nervous group of porters to the concierge to get a map of town. We hate these moments since we at best get stared at or at worst are denied entry due to scruffiness, bah.

He was victorious and we left the flash mirrored building in search of the St Charles Bridge in the very heart of this beautiful fairy tale city.

We soon found it after a near death experience for Chas. The second tram incident for him on Mondo Enduro. He tried to do a U-turn on a busy street when an oncoming tram sounded off its siren and stopped just inches away from his original British number plate.

Along some cobbled streets and under a huge stone archway and we saw the old and magnificent St Charles Bridge to our right. It looked like Tower Bridge would look like, if it was to be left unmaintained for a decade or two.

We found a couple of bars nearby and stationed ourselves there for an hour or two, whilst we set about a few administrative tasks including shopping and a cash advance.

Outside the bar but on the pavement, Clive changed his 18" Bridgestone tyre which had done practically all the way from LA to Chile and from South Africa to Prague. The canvas had just begun to show through and we understood that Germans are very hot on vehicle standards, much more so than the UK apparently.

Around five o'clock after a few beers and some pasta it was time to leave this quaint city and head for the border. We were all momentarily tempted to rest a night here to explore Prague's nightlife, but soon reminded ourselves that we still had a hefty distance to cover to catch the Thursday overnight ferry to Hull.

We did a spot of filming on our way out of town and headed out on a smooth stretch of black top towards Karlovy Vary. About half way the four reconvened and parted with a cheery "see you at the border". Austin and Clive raced off leaving Chas and the ever slowing Louis to bring up the rear.

Louis' clutch at this time was seriously playing up and affecting the drive of the bike. Hills were a serious problem for the sickly bike. Louis' selfless 720 mile tow of Austin across Saudi Arabia must have gone a long way to explaining why the clutch was so frazzled.

Chas had been waiting for Louis but finally in Karlovy Vary Louis could drive no more. The clutch had given up.

Meanwhile, Austin and Cliff had already arrived at the border and although keen to get back into the EU they waited for their pals. Chas arrived 10 minutes later explaining Louis was 50 kms back and that we would be going no further tonight. Infuriating. Whilst getting of his bike at the border Chas slipped on some petrol and his head (helmet) smashed on the floor. Thank God for the Golden Globe.

So it was hated 'dead miles' as the three rode back through the night to the lay by where a depressed Louis awaited.

Daylight had disappeared by the time we had all met up with Louis and the temperature had dropped. Lou had found an ideal rough campsite behind a disused building on some waste ground. Louis and Austin took the clutch cover off S8, Louis' bike. The diagnosis was inconclusive. Lights out around 1am. With spirits not specifically that high.

Germany

Day 399
Wednesday 15 May
Mondo Miles today: 217
Mondo Mileage: 37069

It was in the early hours of this morning when Dr Bloom finished surgery on Austin's left eye. Last night Austin had been working in darkness underneath S8 and unfortunately collected plenty of grit in his eye (something else to scratch). The itching and discomfort was impossible to sleep through and so at 0330hrs Austin was driven to wake Louis and equip him with a torch and a fine twig with which to attempt to hook out the offending amalgam of grit and globular puss.

Clive was our wake-up call this morning with Austin and Louis springing into action and attending to their bikes. The sickness of S8 was soon diagnosed, once her clutch assembly had been dismantled. She had extremely worn clutch plates, and so after a Cheeky brew and discussion with Austin, Lou did some fiddling around with the plates and re-assembled them. Amazingly, we had kept 3 of our old friction plates from South Africa so Louis ditched his worst three and replaced them. Rather dispiritingly, the 'new' ones he was putting in, looked to have no greater a covering of friction material on them than the ones he was throwing away. Oh well. Austin tightened the clutch nut and Lou then put the splined lock washer firmly into place and so it was all down to God's Will. Louis cheered in triumph when the engine kicked in. However, there was nothing wrong with the engine in the first place. He gingerly engaged first, eased the clutch lever out, she bit and Mondo was back on the road. Result!

We recognised that the situation was not healthy and so cooked up an action plan; Louis would set off immediately for the Czech/German frontier with Clive as his rescue bike if needs be. Austin and Chas stayed in Karlovy Vary and resolved to get into a phonebox and not to get out of it until they had somehow located some new clutch-plates on the road ahead in Germany, France or Belgium.

However, 100 km of recovery later it appeared the battle with the bike gremlins had been won, but not the war. Louis was once again immobile. At least he did make it into Germany and onto the Autobahn. Clive was soon in the picture and performing a tow. Well, what goes around comes around. Clive and Lou rolled in to the nearest town (Bamberg) and stopped off at a corner café to wait for the lads. Austin and Chas arrived soon after and

Austin then went straight off to follow-up on the information he had been given earlier in the day about Suzuki stores. This morning he had called his mate Julian Grant (who is fluent in German and was sat at a desk in Bristol) asking if he could access a German yellow pages and find a Suzuki dealer in Frankfurt. Frankfurt was the nearest *big* city 160 miles away. We had carried a printout of the bike microfiche all the way around the world and so were able to furnish Julian with the exact part number that we needed. Fingers crossed, we have to be back in London at 1pm this Saturday (72 hours from now) so our usual 'wait here until the parts arrive' credo won't work this time.

Mondo *übermensch* Julian Grant had neglected his role in the world of corporate leasing and had been phone bashing whilst we'd been riding from this morning's camp-site. Julian had totally come through. He gave Austin a dealer's name and address in Frankfurt and Julian had already called them up and spoken *auf Deutsch*. Austin returned to the group with news that the Suzuki man in Frankfurt had the clutch plates *in stock*. Julian had explained that we were trying to beat the clock and so the owner said that if we didn't get there in time (close at 6pm) he would take them home with him. Moreover he was prepared for us to collect them from his gaff this evening – a promising result ahead for Mondo. Chas went off to the train station for the back-up plan. Louis waterproofed his Mum's pressie and Clive calculated the distance home and sipped coffee. An aside, but here in Bamberg there are American soldiers in uniform all over the place.

It was time for the second 'action-plan' of the day; Austin would go ahead solo, locate the dealership (Hölger's Zwei Rad Shop) and collect the clutch plates. Clive and Chas would take turns and tow Louis westwards for the next 180 miles. A rendezvous was convened in time honoured Mondo fashion, at the eastern 'city limits' sign of a small town just west of Frankfurt called Babenhausen. Our map showed only a single inauspicious B-road leading there so we reckoned that this location would be unambiguous and easy for all even though none of us had ever been there. The rendezvous was for 9pm and on the half hour thereafter. It was 1pm now. Any drama, call Geoffrey Vince at base-camp Bournemouth. It seemed that we had snatched victory from the jaws of defeat.

Although we were on the back foot, we were rather elated and it was in high spirits that we were rend asunder in the ratio 1:3. Austin left first and the mission was underway. Clive, Chas and Louis were a little slower getting going, their departure scotched by the multiple sightings of some German traffic cops who we were quietly confident would, on sighting our potential towing configuration, be caused to shout: "*Halt! Das ist verboten Englander!!!*" They melted away eventually and it was Mondo a-go-go once more.

About 7 minutes later they were just getting out through the light industrial estates that blight so many a euro-community: only to find Austin flagging them down, brandishing a four inch nail that he'd just withdrawn from his rear tyre. It was a minor setback but once again we were pleased because, for all our bungling, we were pretty strict on our policy that our puncture repair kit must be carried in the rear most bike. Twenty minutes later and we were all off again, but it was now 2pm and Austin still had 155 miles to go. And of course had to actually locate the dealer in a strange sausage-like city.

Two and a half hours later Austin was pulling into a pretty substantial Esso gas station on the outskirts of Frankfurt and like so many dispatch riders before him was hoping to consult one of the A-Zs for sale without actually having to buy it. To soften the blow he filled up and went in to pay. Needless to say, the man on the till was *ein gastarbeiter* but he had a kindly face. His plastic name badge revealed that he was called Mahmoud. Austin found the 'library' section of the travel-shop, extracted the notes taken from Julian Grant's info and nervously thumbed the index. Gadzooks, there must be some kind of mistake, the street name wasn't listed. Austin tried to focus and remember all his time at Courier Systems. It must be mis-spelled, or maybe it's a confounded kraut abbreviation. The problem was compounded by the annoying Teuton habit of adjoining about six different words and then using the first letter of each as an abbreviation. Add to this, Austin was starting to touch cloth and Mahmoud kept looking over at him disapprovingly. Brainwave!! Call the dealership and confirm the address, simplicity itself! Austin put the road atlas back carefully and searched for change. *Teufel!!, nicht Deutschmarken haben mein!!* Back to the bike and amazingly a stash of notes waited, sensibly proffered by Oxbridge Chas in a "you might need this" moment back in Bamberg.

After buying a Nutkin shokalade bar Austin had enough shrapnel to use the payphone. First attempt didn't work; try using the area code, maybe not actually in the greater Frankfurt *bundesteil*. Second attempt, it's ringing, result, crumbs, fax machine, check the number, it's 5:30pm. Third attempt, use the second number that Julian had sourced, ringing again, answer phone. That's not fair, they're supposed to be open. Maybe the shop's overwhelmed and they can't get to the phone. Ooh er, touching cloth more than ever. Run inside and re-establish a *détente* with Mahmoud. There is no public loo. With a combination of poor schoolboy German and toilet-mime Mahmoud weakened and let Austin use the staff facilities. Phew. Fourth attempt, still answer phone, bah, it's 5:44pm. Fifth attempt, call Holger (the owner) on his home number, no answer but leave a voice-mail message saying that Austin is on his way. Please wait for him if possible. Off the payphone and back to the A-Z liberty taking, this time to suss out where Holger lived. Austin prided himself on his map-memorising skills but this was no time to be cocky. A rough sketch map and plenty of detail in the area close to Holger's homestead. It took Austin a while to work out where the gas station actually was and the route to Holger's seemed to cross about 8 different pages, aggro. It was 6.10pm when he bade Mahmoud farewell with the only Turkish phrase known to him, a cheery "*Güle Güle!!*" (bye bye).

Despite Austin's dispatch riding credentials, he had been faffing about at the petrol station for 50 mins, not exactly 'rider of the month'.

Sure enough, Holger's place was miles away on the other side of Frankfurt but the efficient German sign-posting meant that Austin was ringing Holger's doorbell by 7pm. There was no answer. Surely he'd be home by now? Suddenly the door opened and there was a *fraulein mit kinder*. This turned out to Holger's wife but she seemed pretty nervous and despite Austin's answerphone message didn't seem to know what was going on. Austin was politely requested to wait outside on the pavement until Holger came home. This didn't happen for another half an hour but when he turned up Austin greeted him like a prodigal son. Holger looked a bit confused as he stepped out of his 3series BMW. In perfect English he asked: "Why didn't you come to the shop, I was waiting there for you until seven?" Yoinks, some kind of crossed wire. Further dashing of plans when Holger revealed (with some irk) that he had left the clutch plates at the shop and er, no, he had *never* said that he would bring them home. Slightly exasperated with this British buffoon Holger excused himself and walked up the garden path to the remainder of his domestic bliss. A slighty weary exchange between them and Holger disappeared inside. Austin didn't know what was happening but thankfully Holger re-emerged putting his jacket back on striding towards a sheepish Austin with an end-of-the-tetherish "Come on, we can to the shop in my car now go."

Austin rode shotgun and as the journey unfolded he tried to build bridges with his new hopefully bike-friendly driver. It worked a bit but he didn't want to distract Holger from driving though he seemed unperturbed doing 190kph on the ring road. The Zwei Rad Shop was miles away and although going faster than Austin had *ever* been in a car the journey still took 45 minutes. By now, Austin was desperate to urinate but felt it could wait until they got into the shop. Holger parked outside but as they strode up to the door there was a bit of pocket patting and Holger announced: "The keys, I have them left at home". There was not so much a groan as a blow torch of red hot embarrassment on Austin's face. Mondo Enduro did not want to impinge on this man's private life but there was nothing for it, it was back to the house. It was 8.15pm and the others would be staking out the road sign *treffpunkt* pretty soon. Unbelievably, we had set a super generous 8 hours for this task and Austin was still going to be ages.

Back in the car and a rather more frosty ride home. The exchange between Holger and his wife was conducted behind closed doors but it was obviously painful judging from the dirty look Frau Holger gave Austin. One imagines that she is always playing second fiddle to a) the bike business and b) Holger's endless cohorts of spongers, freeloaders and friendless souls that gravitate to the dealership. Austin imagined the serious conversations where Holger insisted that once the baby was born it would all be different. He loved her and he would change, just wait and see...

At 9.30pm we had the clutch plates (but no clutch cover gasket), it was dark but as Holger re-set the alarm Austin could see that our German saviour was smiling to himself as he reflected on the madness of it all. He seemed particularly interested by the notion that the other members of the team were presently waiting by a road sign some 20 miles away. Farewell to Holger, a Mondo badge and the heartiest handshake Austin could muster. Then it started to rain.

Meanwhile, the Babenhausen roadsign *did* exist and Chas and Clive *had* successfully towed Louis' bike all 180 miles of the way to it. They had arrived at 8pm and within a mile of it had found a rich belt of prime German coniferous forest to make camp in. Towing Louis down the tracks was slightly testing but in no time the three bikes were inserted into a dense thicket and whilst Chas set up the tarpaulin Clive pre-prepared an incredible vegetable risotto. It wasn't put on to cook though, that was selflessly delayed until we were a four again. At five to nine Louis went out to his sentry post and awaited Austin's return. The rain soon came and Louis put on his poncho and huddled under a piece of old lino that he found by the sign. At ten o'clock he saw a lone headlamp in the distance and rose up to greet what he hoped would indeed be his co-rider laden with spares. From Austin's viewpoint it seemed through the drizzle that there was *no-one* at the sign. He was sure this was the right place, what could have gone wrong? Just then, it seemed that a whole pile of rubbish adjacent the sign 'came alive' and the dripping amorphous poncho silhouette revealed itself as Louis. There was some considerable back-slapping and whooping and for all the world it looked as if these two had been separated since birth. They rode back to the campsite, more jubilation and Clive put the match to his petrol-drenched camp fire kitchenette. Louis got straight on with accessing and dismantling his clutch, pausing only when Clive had forced him to take a plate of food.

Louis worked like a man possessed by the firelight and as that dimmed he stuffed his pocket Maglite into the folded hem of the woolly hat that he wore. It kept falling out so he got the electrical insulating tape from Chas' tool box and wrapped it around his crown and under his jaw, fastening the slender torch behind his ear rather like a carpenter would his pencil. The 'jaw strap' meant that Louis couldn't really speak properly without dislodging the tape and encouraging the torch to work loose. His diction reduced to grunts and guttural utterances, rain streaming down his face, he seemed like a forest primate running amok with a socket set. It was one o'clock in the morning when we bedded down, Louis still working on the clutch.

Germany / Belgium

Day 400
Thursday 16 May
Mondo Miles today: 198
Mondo Mileage: 37267

It had been raining when we went to sleep last night. Except that it was only three of us going to sleep. We had nodded off under our home-made polythene poncho with Louis still grafting on the clutch re-build. He had insisted that the rest of us get some sleep and he would carry on alone. His selfless display of team spirit and determination was a high point of Mondo Enduro.

As we awoke to a sunny dawn, we expected to see Louis' clutch still in pieces, the rain, darkness and lack of a manual conspiring to scotch this ill thought through forest rebuild. But nay, it was all done and Louis was up first getting the fire going and preparing the coffee. This seems like a strange Germanic Rumplestiltskin moment since we don't know how Louis pulled it off (to say nothing of deftly preserving the delicate clutch cover gasket for the refit).

Today is intended to be our second last day in Europe. After 400 days on the road we are suddenly on a promise. We had left all those months ago from Mill Hill School in NW London, where Louis, Clive and Austin had all been pupils and now we have pledged to Tim Dingle, the deputy head, that we will roll back onto the playground at exactly 1pm this Saturday. Tim Dingle has in return, allowed us to invite all our friends and family to the school for this appointed time and so that's it, about 48hrs from now Mondo Enduro will be over.

Meanwhile, Louis kicked up his bike and went for a trial crash around the forest. We were fairly well embedded in the bush so he was almost bounced off by sundry roots and trailing branches. He covered about 40yds on a circuit of the woods and returned with a diagnosis. An adjustment on the cable tension thingy and it was all perfect, incredible.

We stripped out the campsite and loaded up the bikes, our movements and routines being automatic. Everything has its place and our hands manipulated straps and buckles with the ease that comes from having lived on and next to our luggage for so long. We even know our way around each other's panniers and the sensation of 'personal' possessions is giving way to the notion that everything in this foresty glade is a group asset. Clive in particular has thinned out the ephemera of travel to the nth degree and has ridden since Johannesburg with no personal kit except the leathers that he stands in. We now have a communal wash kit that contains one razor blade, a bar of soap, nail brush, toothpaste and four cut down toothbrushes. There is one small Cascade Designs 'pac-towel' between us and that's plenty.

The engines were gunned up around 9am and we tottered out onto a rough trail. We went along here for about 20yds then hit a more substantial forestry track that would lead us back to the tarmac. No sooner had we shaken out onto this track when we encountered a platoon of American soldiers patrolling through the woods on exercise. We felt terribly guilty at spoiling whatever their C.O.'s 'scenario' was. As we drove through their arrowhead formation we all bade them "good-day", desperate not to shatter that special Anglo-American relationship that so many NATO staff courses had sought to foster since 1948.

With the sun shining morale was sky high and with a euphoria normally reserved for westward rolling Wehrmacht armoured columns, we pointed our front wheels at Belgium and bade farewell to the Fatherland.

A coffee stop was enjoyed a little earlier than we deserved but it gave us a chance to bash the phone-box and call a few more mates and ask them if they could be at Mill Hill for this Saturday. We are like nervous teens who have just had our offer of a ticket to the high school hop accepted by the prom queen. We cannot believe that we just might pull this off. Fingers crossed.

The crossing into Belgium was just past Aachen and of course, it was the first 'paperless' border in a long while; thanks to the civilising effect that the EU has on the stamp-happy border guard mentality. Clive mused that any kind of work-exchange between a Guatemalan and a European frontiersman would surely exasperate each of them to equal degrees.

The good weather had given way to sombre nimbusness and as we approached Brussels we realised that we didn't know if we were heading into this city or if we intended to avoid it. We pulled off the Bruxellian version of the Periphique and found ourselves outside a faintly bogus looking bar. However, it was clearly 100% *authentique* since the second we set foot inside it the two old men therein gave us the evil eye. Thankfully, Clive, the very antithesis of our collective cowardice purposefully strode up to the bar and ordered four Stellas. Austin doesn't like beer (or lager) and so sipped his slowly but the rounds of toasts along the lines of "we've almost made it" saw his chalice emptied soon enough.

It was approaching dusk and Louis sensibly suggested that we finish on a high note with a slice of our speciality 'urban' rough-camping. We were all up for a secret night in a *pension* but we knew Louis was right. There'll be time enough for 'showers'n'towels' back in England. Back on the bikes and a rather weird cruising of central Brussels looking for those staples of the Mondo *pied à terre*; the half-finished building and the fly-tipped brownfield site. Austin saw it first, that giant atom-molecule structure type thing that was always used on British rail posters to encourage one to indulge in an 'awaybreak' to Brussels. It seemed to be surrounded by a patchwork of parkland and light industrial units (with the hoped for Shangri-la of a covered loading bay). We headed down a service road and split up to recce for our secret slot.

Once reconvened, it was Clive who had the best result. Atop a large grassy knoll was a billowing umbrella of a weeping willow tree. Clive leading the way, thrashing the 350 up the slope and crashing into the curtain of weeping willowery branches that drooped all the way down to the ground. Amazing, as soon as he'd punctured that leafy curtain, he was completely invisible to the rest of us at the base of the knoll. It was like that bit in Hannibal Brooks when Oliver Reed hides behind the waterfall with his elephant.

The other three hit the freqs and in no time the four of us were concealed within the canopy of the tree. We were so confident of the effectiveness of our camouflage that we left the bikes unattended (we have no locks anymore) and soon found ourselves in a nearby multiplex cinema complex. As we joined the queues of silver screened Belgians we strove to shake off the mantle of motorcycle tramps and reassimilated ourselves back into that most welcoming of social blobs, the general public.

We were back at the willow tree by 11.30pm, had the giant poncho set up within 10 mins and after a swig of medicine, were sleeping our last night away from home. It was strange; we four will never live like this again.

Belgium / Kent

Day 401
Friday 17 May
Mondo Miles today: 172
Mondo Mileage: 37439

We had an excellent night's sleep with only light showers to disturb us. Everyone was snug and bone dry. It was overcast when we awoke and for the rest of the day things didn't really brighten up.

We'd picked up a carton of pineapple juice last night at a gas station and so that became the teamly breakfast. In the daylight we could see how immersed in central Brussels civilisation we actually were and so a fire was vetoed in favour of getting going. We packed up our sleeping kit and rolled up our Therm-a-rests for what we realised could be the last time. This morningly ritual of squeezing the reluctant air from our foamy camping mattresses is a truly ridiculous sight. Although it was a process that we all conducted on reflex, the required scrunching, pushing and shoving associated with it meant that we always started each day looking red-faced, clumsy and oafish.

We emerged rather suddenly from under the willow and clearly alarmed a few passing pedestrians. In a thrice we were back on the *Periphique* and heading clockwise then west to Ghent. Most of us had traversed this hinterland of the channel ports on previous trips so although tingling with excitement, the bland scenery and cloudy skies negated any excited tingling we might have felt.

Our plan was to get across the channel this afternoon and get up to south west of London tonight. Although a romantic night of rough camping in the grounds of Leeds castle was mooted, this was over-voted by the possible blendees that are Maria and Tony Shaw. They are Austin's cousins and they live in the leafy suburb of Chislehurst. If we can get to them tonight they have suggested that we can crash there prior to the final push back to Mill Hill tomorrow morning.

We bucked off the *autoroute* after Ghent and followed a load of minor roads across the fen-like Pas de Calais *department*. Louis' clutch was holding up, we hadn't had a puncture since Germany and we were going to make it to a ferry. At last, something going according to plan. We rolled onto the apron at Calais and as Chas took care of the ticket purchase our eyes smarted at the strange familiarity of the UK car licence plates that blossomed around us. After loading into the hold of 'The Pride of Dover' and ascending to the lounge decks, we realised this was the largest density of Brits that we had been surrounded by since we'd left home. The seemingly mundane became absurdly exotic and we stocked up on familiar brands of candy bar just because they were 'there'. Clive and Chas were absorbed by the range of newspapers and anyone following us would surely have thought that we had just got out of prison.

We disembarked at 5pm and by now the skies had cleared to reveal a glorious early summer sunset. There was a spring in our step, but because we were on motorbikes it wasn't really evident and we emerged out of the ship's hold for our first miles back in England. There was no flamboyant kissing of the ground malarkey, just a rough plan about the route up the M2 or should we stay off the motorway. It was getting rather chilly so we elected to gun it up to the Shaws in Chislehurst as fast as we could. We set off in fine spirits and headed into the sun that was slowly setting behind Tunbridge Wells.

It was about now that we began to realise that we were blithely riding what may have been the four nailiest bikes in the south east of England. We were expecting a clean section through customs and immigration but had completely forgotten about the stringent road safety criteria that any pending traffic policeman would expect our British registered bikes to meet. All of the bikes had licence plates that were home-made and indeed Austin's was just a piece of red plastic unscrewed from inside a Givi pannier upon which he'd written H876 LEL with a white felt tip. Naturally, none of us had either tax, insurance or M.O.T. and Louis had rather gamely joined us in South Africa without ever having even *taken* a motorcycle test, yet alone passed one. All the tyres were bald and Austin's rear 18" was riven with deep cracks through which the canvas cheekily peeked (interestingly enough, this was a bogus budget ChengShin sports bike 'racing tyre' which we had rescued from a skip at the rear of the Suzuki workshop back in Johannesburg. It had been fitted shortly after, cracks and all, yet has neither ruptured nor blown out as we always presumed it would).

The going was good and of course event free, save for the fact that Clive and Austin got separated from Louis and Chas somewhere near Chatham. We had all pulled into, and then out of, a petrol station but there was some adjusting of waterproofs so Chas and Louis waved the other two on ahead. Within a few miles there was no sign of the late-leavers so Clive and Austin pulled into a lay-by to wait for them. After 20 mins they hadn't showed up so not for the first time on Mondo Enduro, an about turn (at the next Junction) was affected and back-tracking commenced. Fortunately, and with dusk unravelling into darkness, the Dover bound search party soon spotted the, for us, distinctive on-coming shapes of Chas and Louis. Unfortunately, *they* didn't spot Clive and Austin on the opposite carriageway and failed to pull over. So there we were, still separated but with Chas and Louis thinking they were the 'rear two' when in fact they were the 'front two'. Inevitably, they were racing as fast as their 350s would allow them, wondering why Clive and Austin hadn't pulled over to wait for them!

Our joint adventure motorcycling genius meant that *only* Austin had the directions to the Chislehurst blend and so Chas and Louis didn't know where to go. Clive and Austin persevered up the M2 and upon reaching the Chislehurst turn off were hoping to find the others waiting in that vicinity. However, they were nowhere to be seen. A quick pow-wow and they decided to get to their hosts and to call Geoffrey Vince at base-camp Bournemouth with news of the separation. This was a standard response after these all too common mondo-convoy-bungles.

The Shaws greeted Clive and Austin with Tea and crumpets (with lemon curd!) and the phone call revealed that Chas and Louis had had a vague drama of their own:

With light fading Chas had noticed that his headlight was intermittently flicking on and off. The wiring seemed to have a mind of its own and no amount of jiggling could convince the beam to stay on. The sidelight had blown long ago so he was without any front light. Whilst attending to this electrical torpor on the hard shoulder a Police 'traffic' Range Rover had pulled over and the scene was set for an almighty stewards' inquiry. Amazingly, the *Federales* were rather impressed with the Mondo Enduro back story and rather than citing tomes of Road Traffic Act infractions they escorted Louis and Chas to the next service area and wished them well. This act of sheer decency was surely the jewel in the Kent Constabulary's public relations crown!!! Let this humble log record that verily, no note was made of these kindly officers particulars but we pray that an angel of good fortune smiles down upon their every moment in the hereafter.

We think that it was whilst in this service area that Clive and Austin had rolled past, London bound, consequently 'missing' Chas and Louis for the second time that evening.

So, our last night on the road and Mondo Enduro finds itself in a game of two halves. Clive and Austin snuggled up in suburban swaddling whilst Chas and Louis are wobbed out under a poncho on some waste ground behind a north Kent Little Chef.

Kent / London

Day 402
Saturday 18 May
Mondo Miles today: 57
Mondo Mileage: 37496

Crumbs, the last day, so sad. The weather was grey and drizzly. Not the mayday sunshine festival we had hoped would bless our homecoming. Chas and Louis treated themselves to the 'Farmer's Breakfast' from the plastic-coated Little Chief menu whilst Austin and Clive gorged on cereal with the Shaws. Austin knew of their hosts' exciting past and duly, Maria and Anthony Shaw were forced to regale the motorcyclists with tales garnered from both having worked in top London casinos in the 1970s. Mucho bendico exotica-a-go-go!!!

The separation drama of last night was replaced by calm since we had scheduled a rendezvous at noon adjacent to the roundabout known as 'Kelly's Corner' near Mill Hill East tube station. More specifically, we intended to meet on the pavement outside our favourite eatery there, which was a humble greasy spoon known as Peter's Café. It was owned and run by a giant Italian Friar Tuck-a-like chap called Peter! He knew us all personally and had been our nourisher of choice in the last few days before we had left Mill Hill

13 months earlier. He had taken our collective claims of trans-global expeditionitude with a healthy pinch of catering salt and so we had been sending him postcards from around the world so as to prove that we just might pull it off. More unhealthily, we darkly hoped that if we made it back to *his* hostelry and reported in before even seeing our own families he would be so flattered as to treat us to one of his Lombardi mega-breakfasts, gratis.

We thusly spent the morning making our ways from Kent to Kelly's Corner. Clive and Austin going by south circular and the excitement and spectacle of the Woolwich ferry whilst Chas and Louis pushed on up onto the Rochester relief road through Eltham then through the wonder-duct of the Blackwall tunnel (western bore).

For all of us, the sensation of being on our familiar loaded 'expedition' bikes on these familiar London roads was most strange. Unconsciously we had come to associate these raggedy trail bikes with places far and wide but which were klept alike in that none of them was *home*. The dirt, the damage, the scuffing, the stickers, the inordinate amount of cable-ties, wire, string and in Austin's case, rags, that were holding these bikes together meant that they had aged ten years in just one. When we had left Mill Hill 402 days ago they were all pretty clean and everything on them 'worked'. The luggage in particular was neat and ordered. Not so now. Their super-weathered cosmetic neglectitude only served to highlight how disjointed it felt to be riding through Finchley when we looked like we were meant to be in some kind of two-wheeled hobo freakshow.

All's well that ends well and the four of us were reunited outside the café on time and on target (a little roundabout joke). Heartaches, shame and misery!! The word 'Peter' had been removed from the above glass hoarding and we found that we were now standing before '*Glenn's* Café'!!! We shuffled in and were met with genuine looks of disdain by a seemingly new breed of clientele who all would have down well to answer Central Casting's next call for '*Sun reading white van man*'. They clearly thought we were outsiders but no, this was *our* café! The man at the counter waiting to take our order filled in the gaps; he was 'Glenn' and he'd bought the café from Peter three months ago. Peter had gone back to Royston (it's true, he used to drive from Royston to Mill Hill every morning and be open by 0630) and thence retired to Tuscany. Glenn was keen to process our order but naturally could never have imagined that these scraggly dirty bikers were hoping for a complimentary slap up feed. We ordered, paid and took in Glenn's superficial changes to the café's previously legendary interior décor. Gone was Peter's electric waterfall painting (with rippling river effect) only to be replaced by sundry photos of professional soccer teams. Alone and in a corner was a black and white publicity photo of some stranger with a squiggly signature. Clive studied it and deduced that it was a picture of a man known as 'Bonehead' who apparently is the bass player for Oasis. Glenn told us that 'Bonehead' has recently bought a mansion in the Mill Hill area but by partaking of Glenn's bacon rolls has demonstrated that he hasn't lost his common touch. We were crestfallen. It's only a café for heaven's sake but although we were desperate to be home, *this* wasn't what England meant to us.

We got our timings talked through and paced our way through our respective fry-ups. At ten to one we went to leave and attempted to catch Glenn's eye as we exited, expecting to offer the standard "thank you that was great" valediction as we left. He didn't notice us going. Peter would have.

We rode up the hill as a tight foursome and just shy of the school Chas checked his watch; it was the only one we had between us. It said 1259 so this was it. We were expecting our family and friends and maybe a few teachers that knew Austin but we weren't ready for what lay in store.

We rounded a bend on the little school path that lead back to Wills Grove and approached our last 70 yards of Mondo. As we cleared the hedgeline a roar rose up for ahead of us there seemed to be a crowd of about 200 people. We had about 4 seconds of riding left but never had we imagined this. It was a terrible mistake; there was clapping, cheering and shouting and the crowd surged forward to meet us as if we were heroes. Didn't these people realise we'd just been on holiday for a year??? They were held at bay by a string of school prefects all linking arms and a channel was proffered for us to drive along to a huge banner suspended overhead that proclaimed 'Mill Hill School-FINISH'. Concurrent to this intense experience our old friend Dr Andrew Bell was running around spraying us with the spumante gushing out from a champagne bottle that he was all at once vigorously shaking whilst trying to aim.

Those first few seconds back were like a dream, a collage of smiling beaming nearest and dearest, there was Bill Penty, Mark Friend, Josh Collins (shooting it all not on a handycam, but with a Bolex 16mm film camera), Geoffrey Vince, Onion, Paddy and Keir, Dick Baker, Gemma Greenhough (Clive's mum). It was like the end credits from Kelly's Heroes where, one by one, all the characters freeze-frame alongside the shot of the lorry driving off with the Nazi gold. We were reeling, intoxicated with the good cheer and sky-high on a heady brew of back slapping and hand shaking. It's an awful thing to say but this surprise ending could very possibly be the best moment on Mondo Enduro. *Everybody* gets their 15 mins of fame and by jove, this was ours! Mercy!

Eventually the euphoria died down and the school children went off to their Lunch. However, the Headmaster, Mr Winfield, had a treat up his academic gown for us! We, and all the well wishers were rounded up and taken over to the staff room. We imagined that this was because the weather was still vaguely inclement and that shelter was being offered before the next inevitable downpour. Not so, the spacious staff room had been converted into a mighty Mondo hospitality suite. Every surface was bedecked with food and the school's generosity extended to members of the catering staff patrolling with drinks for all and sundry. It was unbelievable, we were looking pretty dishevelled but here we were being treated like kings. It brought home the notion that we had learned on the road that it's the warm embrace of one's kith and kin that we couldn't do without.

Suddenly there was a scream for Austin's mum! She sounded like she was having a coronary but she was surprised into speechlessness for another reason: standing there before us was the founding father of Mondo Enduro, Gerald Vince. He was supposed to be in Canada!! It transpired that one of Austin's sisters had 'smuggled' him back to England and spirited him up to Mill Hill for our return. This merely added fuel to the fire and the embers of Mondo togetherness were fanned to a white heat. Oh what a day!!!

The Head master called us to order and made a very touching "welcome home chaps" address. A reply was made from the collective ranks of us four and the words "thank you" uttered incessantly. Within another half an hour or so the farewells were made and the cluster of folk began to dissipate. Clive went back to his Mum and Dad's in Pinner. Chas went to stay with a friend in Islington, Austin crashed with deputy head Dingle and Louis went home to the welcoming arms of Harold and Tina Bloom. As we went to sleep that night it was truly weird to be thinking that at last, come tomorrow, we wouldn't have to leave.

ACKNOWLEDGEMENTS

Mondo Enduro wish to thank:

Chris Scott, Kevin and Roberta, Ray and Gemma Greenhough, Sun City International, Berinda Banks, the woman who massaged Clive's back in Gonder, Trevor Chilton, Tim Dingle, Barbara Pasco-Connor, The family Markert, Ed Strachan, Whitaker Malem, Josh Collins, Neil James, Kathy Goodyer and all at NOMAD, Tina and Harold, Clarita Bermudez, Frank Hayden and Paul Denning at Crescent Suzuki, Clarrissa, Uncle John Wezelman , John Sayre, Aunt Elizabeth, Russ Malkin, David Fielden (for the fax machine), Jim and Marilyn Hill, Chaintec, ScottOiler, Cascade Designs, Katadyn water filters, Rab sleeping bags but most of all to our endlessly giving 72 year old admin guru back at base camp Bournemouth, Geoffrey Vince.

Ripping Yarns.com wish to thank:

Austin Vince for taking a year of his spare time to bring this book together; Richard Robinson (Cordee) for distributing this travel epic; Matt Hill for the cover art; Jean Goodier for typing up the handwritten "Mondo Logs" (including those soaked in a Siberian river!); Sian Harrison, Kim Harrison, Krystina Lotoczko and Laura Booth for proofreading.

And finally – a big thanks to all the guys from Mondo Enduro, for showing us that you don't need Ewan McGregor-style sponsorship to go and have a real travel adventure.

Other Austin Vince Adventures...

If you enjoyed the *Mondo Enduro* book, you may also enjoy...

Mondo Enduro DVD

The DVD of the TV series, plus extras footage.

Terra Circa DVD

The follow-up expedition to Mondo Enduro. Austin and Gerald set off around the world again – with the objective of conquering the infamous "Zilov Gap" on two wheels.

Terra Circa Book

To be available from Ripping Yarns.com – watch our website!

Roadside USA DVD

Austin and Clive's mammoth hitch-a-thon round the USA, from gun-toting Texas to spaced-out-California. "No crew, no money, no change of clothes..."

Links

www.RippingYarns.com	For other classic adventure books.
www.Aimimage.com	The Austin Vince DVDs
www.Cordee.co.uk	Distributors of Ripping Yarns.com books to the book trade